John H. Hann, historical sites specialist for the Bureau of Archaeological Research, Florida Department of State, is based at the San Luis Archaeological and Historical Site in Tallahassee. His book *Apalachee: The Land Between the Rivers* won the 1988 Rembert W. Patrick Memorial Book Prize for best book on Florida history. William H. Marquardt is associate curator in archaeology and director of the Southwest Florida Project at the Florida Museum of Natural History on the University of Florida campus. He also directs "The Year of the Indian," an archaeology/education project that includes volunteer-assisted excavations at archaeological sites in southwest Florida.

MISSIONS TO THE CALUSA

Ripley P. Bullen Series
Jerald T. Milanich, general editor

Tacachale: Essays on the Indians of Florida and Southeastern Georgia during the Historic Period, edited by Jerald T. Milanich and Samuel Proctor (1978).

Aboriginal Subsistence Technology on the Southeastern Coastal Plain during the Late Prehistoric Period, by Lewis H. Larson (1980).

Cemochechobee: Archaeology of a Mississippian Ceremonial Center on the Chattahoochee River, by Frank T. Schnell, Vernon J. Knight, Jr., and Gail S. Schnell (1981).

Fort Center: An Archaeological Site in the Lake Okeechobee Basin, by William H. Sears, with contributions by Elsie O'R. Sears and Karl T. Steinen (1982).

Perspectives on Gulf Coast Prehistory, edited by Dave D. Davis (1984).

Archaeology of Aboriginal Culture Change in the Interior Southeast: Depopulation during the Early Historic Period, by Marvin T. Smith (1987).

Apalachee: The Land between the Rivers, by John H. Hann (1988).

Key Marco's Buried Treasure: Archaeology and Adventure in the Nineteenth Century, by Marion Spjut Gilliland (1989).

First Encounters: Spanish Explorations in the Caribbean and the United States, 1492-1570, edited by Jerald T. Milanich and Susan Milbrath (1989).

Edited and Translated by John H. Hann

Missions
TO THE Calusa

Introduction by William H. Marquardt

The Ripley P. Bullen Series
University of Florida Press/Gainesville
Florida Museum of Natural History

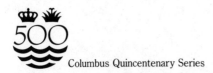

Columbus Quincentenary Series

Copyright 1991 by the Board of Regents
of the State of Florida
Printed in the U.S.A. on acid-free paper ∞

Library of Congress Cataloging-in-Publication Data

The University of Florida Press is a member of the University Presses of Florida, the scholarly publishing agency of the State University System of Florida. Books are selected for publication by faculty editorial committees at each of Florida's nine public universities: Florida A&M University (Tallahassee), Florida Atlantic University (Boca Raton), Florida International University (Miami), Florida State University (Tallahassee), University of Central Florida (Orlando), University of Florida (Gainesville), University of North Florida (Jacksonville), University of South Florida (Tampa), and University of West Florida (Pensacola).

Orders for books published by all member presses should be addressed to University Presses of Florida, 15 Northwest 15th St., Gainesville, FL 32611.

Library of Congress Cataloging-in-Publication Data

Missions to the Calusa / edited and translated by John H. Hann, with introduction by William H. Marquardt.
    p.   cm. — (The Ripley P. Bullen series)
    Translations from Spanish.
    Includes bibliographical references and index.
    ISBN 0-8130-1075-6
    1. Calusa Indians—History—Sources. 2. Calusa Indians—Missions. I. Series.
E99.C18M57   1991   91–1849
975.9′004973—dc20   CIP

Cover illustration by Herman Trappman

CONTENTS

Acknowledgments   ix
Translator's Preface by John H. Hann   xiii
Introduction by William H. Marquardt   xv

Part I. Calusa in the Late Seventeenth Century

Introduction   3
The Documents   49
  1. The Initial Move, 1680–1682   49
      Autos *of Don Juan Garcia de Palacios, Bishop of Santiago de*
        Cuba, August–December, 1682   50
      Bishop Garcia de Palacios to the King, January 20, 1682   66
  2. The Council's Decision, 1683   71
      Notes by the Council of the Indies, January 28, 1683   72
  3. The Calusa Mission Idea Resurrected, 1687   73
      Correspondence Concerning the Royal Decree of September 30,
        1687   74
      Diego Ebelino de Compostela, Bishop of Santiago de Cuba, to the
        King, February 20, 1689   75
      Diego de Peñalver and Others to the King, February 15, 1689   77
  4. Calusa Visit to Apalachee, 1688   78
      Governor Diego de Quiroga y Losada to the King, April 1, 1688   79
  5. Fray Feliciano López and Andrés Ransom, the Pirate, 1688   83
      Fray Julian Chumillas to Antonio Ortiz de Otalore, September
        12, 1688   83

6. The Calusa Head Chief's Visit to Cuba, 1689   85
  Don Diego Ebelino de Compostela, Bishop of Santiago de Cuba,
    to the Dean and Chapter of Holy Cathedral Church of Santiago
    de Cuba, January 2, 1690   85
7. The Mission Is Given to the Franciscans, 1690   92
  The King to the Father Provincial of the Province of Santa
    Elena of Florida, September 8, 1690   92
8. The Bishop's Final Ploy: The Fray Romero Episode, 1692   95
  Diego, Bishop of Santiago de Cuba, to the King, July 3, 1692   96
  Petitions of Fray Francisco Romero, n.d.   100
  Episcopal Decree of Don Diego Ebelino de Compostela, Bishop of
    Santiago de Cuba, July 3, 1692   103
  Testimony of Fray Francisco Romero, 1693(?)   104
9. Mayaca and Jororo, 1693   110
  Fray Juan de Carmenatri(?) and Others to the King, December 5,
    1693   110
10. Fray López' Petition, 1695   116
  Petition by Fray Feliciano López, October 1695, and Comments
    by the Council, November 1695   116
11. Reflections and Summation by the Council of the Indies,
    1695, Spurred by Fray López' Arrival in Spain   123
  First Extract of Dispatches Relating to the Proposed Calusa
    Mission, 1695   123
  Second Extract of Dispatches Relating to the Proposed Calusa
    Mission, 1695   133
12. The Florida Governor's Report on the Revolt of the
    Mayaca-Jororo Missions, February 1697   142
  Governor Laureano de Torres y Ayala to the King,
    February 3, 1697   143
13. The Florida Governor's Report on the Distribution of Fray
    López' Mission Band, 1697   155
  Thomás Menéndez Marques to the King, August 8, 1697   156
14. The Friars' Arrival at Calusa, September 1697   157
  Fray Feliciano López to Fray Pedro Taybo, 1697   158
15. Testimony about the Calusa Mission's Failure, 1698   161
  Testimony of Friars Relating to the Calusa Mission, February–
    March 1698   162
  Testimony of Lay Witnesses Relating to the Calusa Mission,
    February–March 1698   181

Fray Francisco de Contreras to the King, March 5, 1698, Cover Letter for His Inquiry   205

16. The Council's Comments on the Calusa Mission Debacle, 1698   206
    Notes by the Council of the Indies, August 8, 1698   206
17. Governor of Florida's Reports on the Calusa and Mayaca-Jororo
    Missions, September 1699   211
    Governor Laureano de Torres y Ayala to the King, September 19,
    1699   211
    Governor Laureano de Torres y Ayala to the King, September 16,
    1699   213

Part II. Calusa in the Late Sixteenth Century

Introduction   219
The Documents   230

1. Calusa in the 1560s   230
   Father Juan Rogel to Father Jerónimo Ruiz del Portillo, April
   25, 1568   230
2. Rogel's First Contact with Florida's Natives, 1566–1567   278
   Father Juan Rogel to Father Didacus Avellaneda, November
   1566 to January 1567   279
3. The Florida Missions, 1607–1611   285
   Report on the Florida Missions by Father Juan Rogel, Written
   Between the Years 1607 and 1611   286
4. Two Letters of Pedro Menéndez de Avilés, October 20, 1566   298
   Pedro Menéndez de Avilés to the King, October 20, 1566   299
   Pedro Menéndez de Avilés to the King, October 20, 1566   302
5. Flour, Biscuit, Wine, and Meat, 1566–1567   303
   A Listing of Provisions Sent to the Forts at Carlos, Tequesta,
   and Tocobaga, 1566–1567   305
6. Juan López de Velasco on the Geography and Customs of
   Florida, 1575   308
   Part 1. Excerpts from Geografía y Descripción Universal de
   las Indias   308
   Part 2. Brief Memorials and Notes, 1569(?)   315
7. Rumor of Enemy Settlement on the Gulf Coast   319
   Pedro de Valdés to the King, July 11, 1604   320

Part III. Calusa in the Early Eighteenth Century

Introduction   325
The Documents   334
   1. South Florida Natives' Flight to Cuba,   334
     Bishop Gerónimo Valdés to the King, December 9, 1711   335
   2. Tocobaga in Apalachee, 1677–1718   347
     Excerpts from Domingo de Leturiondo's Inspection of the
      Provinces of Apalachee and Timucua, January 9 and 16,
      1678   349
     Excerpt from Joaquín de Florencia's Inspection of the Provinces
      of Apalachee and Timucua, December 3, 1694   354
     Joseph Primo de Rivera to Governor Juan de Ayala y Escobar,
      April 28 to August 3, 1718   355
     Joseph Primo de Rivera to Governor Juan de Ayala y Escobar,
      August 3, 1718   356
   3. Governor Benavides' Report on Natives Baptized Between
     1718 and Early 1723   357
     Notes by the Council of the Indies, September 17, 1723   361
     Register Composed by Fray Joseph del Castillo,
      February 25, 1723
   4. Governor Benavides' Visitation of 1726   363
     Governor Antonio de Benavides' Visitation of Settlements near
      St. Augustine and San Marcos de Apalachee, December 1-11,
      1726   363
   5. Fray Bullones' 1728 Report on the Missions   368
     Fray Joseph de Bullones to the King, October 5, 1728   371
   6. Cuba's Governor on the Fate of the 270 Indians Brought to
     Havana in 1711 and on Renewed Efforts in 1732 to Bring
     Natives to Havana   380
     Governor Dionisio Martínes de la Vega to the King, July 7, 1732   382
   7. Background of the 1743 Alaña-Monaco Report   399
     Governor Juan Francisco de Güemes y Horcasitas to the King,
      July 26, 1743   400
     Governor Juan Francisco de Güemes y Horcasitas to the King,
      September 28, 1743   408
   8. The 1760 Version of the Alaña-Monaco Report   418
     Report on the Indians of Southern Florida and Its Keys by
      Joseph María Monaco and Joseph Javier Alaña Presented to
      Governor Juan Francisco de Güemes y Horcasitas, 1760   419
References   433
Index   445

ACKNOWLEDGMENTS

The events that led to this book began in February 1986, when Michael Hansinger and William Marquardt conversed about the need for archival research on south Florida materials to supplement ongoing archaeological excavations. Dr. Hansinger was planning a trip to Spain in March and kindly offered to go to the Archivo General de Indias (AGI) in Seville at his own expense to try to find someone who might do a preliminary search of the records for us.

Dr. Hansinger first contacted Michael Gannon to ask what archival work had been done by the University of Florida in the AGI. Dr. Gannon advised that Eugene Lyon was then near Madrid transcribing the Menéndez family archives. Dr. Gannon provided phone numbers, and Dr. Hansinger was able to reach Dr. Lyon in Spain. Dr. Lyon highly recommended Victoria Stapells-Johnson as a person possessing the specialized skills and experience needed for the work we had in mind.

Ms. Stapells-Johnson agreed to make a preliminary search through the records. The Wentworth Foundation (William Goza, president) provided a grant of $500 for the initial expenses of historical research and microfilm copying, and by the end of April Ms. Stapells-Johnson had located a number of promising documents relevant to south Florida.

The Southwest Florida Project's Calusa Constituency supported the expenses of transcription and additional microfilming. A duplicate set of the microfilmed documents was donated to the P.K. Yonge Library of Florida History. Ms. Stapells-Johnson continued to look for additional documents pertaining to south Florida as she did other historical research, and in this way we obtained several additional documents through her kindness.

By mid-1987 we had begun to form plans for reporting our archaeological findings, and it seemed desirable to include translations of some of the documents. William Marquardt called Gary Shapiro, then director of the San Luis Archaeological and Historical Site in Tallahassee, to ask his advice on finding a historian who could translate our documents. Dr. Shapiro suggested John Hann. Dr. Hann had just finished a major research effort on a number of Apalachee documents. Dr. Shapiro suggested that Dr. Hann be asked to work on the Calusa documents as time permitted. With the approval of James Miller, director of the Bureau of Archaeological Research, Dr. Hann began work on the documents in October 1987, and they were completed by February 1988.

In the meantime, other documents previously translated but not published were suggested by Dr. Hann for inclusion, and further research in the P.K. Yonge Library of Florida History revealed such interesting information as mention of the so-called Rinconada of Carlos and the background of Fray López' intercession in the case of the pirate Andrés Ransom. We began to realize that with the documents from the Yonge Library's Stetson Collection and the documents located by Ms. Stapells-Johnson we had the most thoroughly documented of all the Florida missions. Not only did we know the dates, principals, actions, and results of the 1697 mission, but we had background information on the genesis of the mission effort and the testimony that followed it. This information was enough for more than a chapter in a monograph; it warranted a book of its own.

The final step was to add sections on the late-sixteenth-century documents and those of the early eighteenth century. With these sources and the seventeenth-century mission story together in one place, students of south Florida's history will have a useful volume to complement those of Fontaneda, Solís de Merás, and Dickinson. In the fall of 1988 Claudine Payne organized and collated the book and made many useful editorial suggestions. Early in 1989 John Hann added introductions to the various documents and wrote a general introduction to the seventeenth-century mission. William Marquardt did the final editing and wrote an introduction to the volume in the summer and submitted the volume to Jerald T. Milanich to be considered for the Bullen Series in August 1989.

We express our gratitude to Bill Goza and the Wentworth Foundation and to the Calusa Constituency for funding and to Michael Hansinger for acting as our agent in Spain in 1986. We also thank the P.K. Yonge Library of Florida History at the University of Florida and the

Florida Collection of the Strozier Library at Florida State University for providing excellent resources for historical research. James Miller and the late Gary Shapiro of the Bureau of Archaeological Research made it possible for John Hann to complete the book, and Kathleen Deagan, chair of the Department of Anthropology, Florida Museum of Natural History, made available the funds to hire Ms. Payne. Victoria Stapells-Johnson's research skills and Claudine Payne's editorial insights are much appreciated, as is the assistance of Jerald Milanich in seeing the book through the publication process.

The author wishes to thank the Jesuit Historical Institute, Rome, for permission to use translations of documents from *Monumenta Antiquae Floridae* by Felix Zubillaga, S.J.

John H. Hann
William H. Marquardt

TRANSLATOR'S PREFACE

The Spanish documents translated in this volume, and especially those presented in Part I, contain many abbreviations and departures from modern rules for the use of upper and lower cases. In many instances letters were made in such a way that they seem to be midway between those two categories. Many of the Spanish abbreviations do not lend themselves to an intelligible abbreviation in English. Consequently, in translating the documents I have written out the abbreviations except for those that appear in signatures at the end of documents and for the familiar H.M. for "His Majesty." Similarly, I have followed modern English usage for upper and lower cases.

In my rendition of the Spanish text I have tried to be as literal as possible while maintaining intelligibility. On the few occasions when I have altered word order or sentence structure substantially to achieve a modicum of intelligibility for a passage too muddily worded in Spanish to be intelligible in a literal translation, such tampering with the text has been noted in footnotes. Passages for which my rendition is tentative have been similarly noted. In the rendition of native names, I have followed the spelling that appears in the document rather than adopting a uniform spelling. Where I have found a passage particularly difficult to decipher, I have included the Spanish text. In situations in which I felt that anthropologists and archaeologists or historians like myself would like to know what Spanish word lies behind my English translation, I have included the Spanish word in parentheses.

John H. Hann

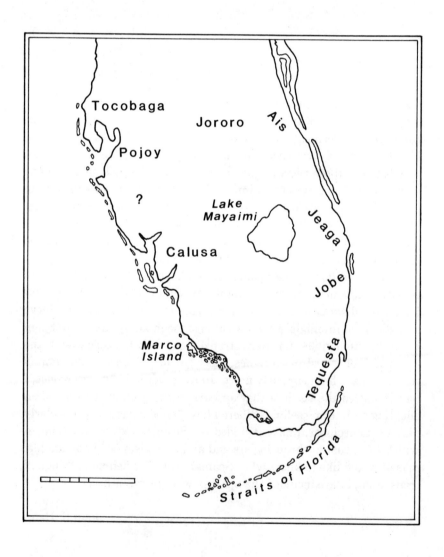

Tocobaga

Jororo

Ais

Pojoy

?

Lake
Mayaimi

Jeaga

Calusa

Jobe

Marco
Island

Tequesta

Straits of Florida

INTRODUCTION

The Calusa constitute one of the great enigmas of anthropology. When Europeans arrived in southwest Florida in the early sixteenth century, they found a complex and powerful society. The Calusa were divided into nobles and commoners, supported an elite military force, and demanded tribute from towns hundreds of kilometers away. They possessed a complex belief system that encompassed daily offerings to their ancestors and a notion of afterlife. Their elaborate rituals included processions of masked priests and synchronized singing by hundreds of young women. They painted, carved, and engraved. Inside their great temple, the walls were covered by carved and painted wooden masks. The head chief's house was said to be able to hold 2,000 people without being crowded (Fontaneda 1944; Solís de Merás 1964).

What is the enigma? It is simply that almost all the known people who achieve the measure of complexity described above are agriculturalists; they depend on one or more staple crops for their subsistence and are thus able to produce and distribute a surplus. The Calusa were a complex, tributary, fisher-gatherer-hunter society. So far as we can tell from our study of both historical and archaeological data, the Calusa and their south Florida neighbors raised no crops whatsoever.

One part of an explanation for the Calusa enigma can be found in the extremely high productivity of the estuarine marine meadows on the southwest Florida coast. Some scholars have concluded that the rich inshore food resources were entirely sufficient to fulfill the role usually played by agriculture (Goggin and Sturtevant 1964: 207). A sophisticated model for Calusa development has been proposed recently by Randolph Widmer, who believes that the complexity of Calusa political organization was a result of efforts to provide for the subsistence needs of a growing population (Widmer 1988: 262–263). Widmer thinks that the period between 500 B.C. and A.D. 800 saw constantly increasing populations, until by about A.D. 800 the bounteous environment had finally reached its capacity. This led to the establishment of a centralized political power structure in order to resolve disagreements and to distribute food and other materials effectively. Widmer believes that this situation remained essentially unchanged until the European era (Widmer 1988: 261–276).

Alternatively, one could argue that the Calusa complexity noted by sixteenth-century Spaniards was not the result of a slow and steady process of cultural evolution. Instead, it was a sudden and recent development, stimulated by European presence in the region that we know today as the southeastern United States and the circum-Caribbean. I suggest elsewhere (Marquardt 1988: 176–179) that south Florida natives were in both direct and indirect contact with Europeans as early as the first few years of the sixteenth century.

It is plausible that significant changes in Calusa social and political organization occurred as a result of the south Florida natives' being swept into the broader European-dominated mercantile/imperial economy. When European goods found their way into traditional exchange networks, they were accorded high value by the natives. As these goods came increasingly into the hands of those on the periphery of the Calusa sphere of influence, there might well have been a tendency toward decentralization of authority, the response to which triggered an imposition of new power and tributary relations (Marquardt 1987: 103–110).

Suppose that the traditional currency of chiefly authority was not the possession of or ability to distribute resources and products. Instead, it was the possession and manipulation of esoteric knowledge and control of a limited number of *sacra*—representational art objects, artifacts, and icons charged with supernatural meaning, used in the context of ritual activity and/or display (Turner 1969). Suppose further that although priests and captains of war had responsibilities for conducting fertility, purification, and warfare rituals, political and spiritual authority were mediated in the person of the paramount chief. He and he alone was the one Calusa mortal privileged to comprehend the origin of the universe, the one human capable of using certain powerful sacra wisely for the benefit of all. Although speculative, this scenario has ample ethnographic precedent.

Knight has suggested a similar institutional organization for Mississippian culture (ca. A.D. 1000–1500) in the Greater Southeast, except that in Knight's model it is the priestly cult (controlling temple statuary sacra) that mediates between a communal cult (emphasizing fertility and purification) and a chiefly cult (manipulating a warfare/cosmogony complex and controlling certain ritual objects made of exotic and costly materials) (Knight 1986: 675–682).

If a system of mediated spiritual and political authority did characterize the protohistoric Calusa, the sudden availability of metal swords, cotton cloth, exotic foods, and inebriating drink—not to mention the competing icons and images of the Roman Catholic church—would have had a dramatic impact. Local chiefs on the peripheries of the Calusa domain could have attempted to increase their own authority by serving as intermediaries between their constituents and the new symbolic and political order represented by the Spanish. Such a process would have presented a serious challenge to the authority of the paramount chief and an imperative for him to reassert control (Marquardt 1988: 187–188). Such a reassertion, if successful, would have required a demonstration of the paramount's capacity not only to handle the compelling European sacra with equanimity but also to amass the resources necessary to support an army and to distribute largesse to local and regional supporters. Only then could he enforce his claims against regional pretenders. In short, it is possible that in the first half of the sixteenth century the Calusa social formation shifted from a chiefdom to what Gailey and Patterson call a weak tribute-based state (1988: 79).

Did the surprising level of Calusa complexity result from a gradual process of cultural evolution, or was it something that happened suddenly in the first half of the sixteenth century? It was this question that first led me to initiate a search of the archives for new information on the historic Calusa. I reasoned that historical data on Calusa politics, ideology, and daily life, in combination with both archaeological and environmental information, were needed if we were to shed light on the central issue of how and when the Calusa attained such remarkable complexity. Although there is much work left to be done, the gathering of basic background information, both archaeological and historical, is now finished. A volume reporting the archaeological and paleoenvironmental findings (Marquardt 1991) is in preparation. *Mis-*

sions to the Calusa is a compilation of documents concerning the Calusa and their neighbors in the sixteenth, seventeenth, and eighteenth centuries.

The central focus of *Missions to the Calusa* is an ill-fated Franciscan attempt to convert the Calusa to Christianity late in 1697. The documents in Part I furnish a wealth of information on the Calusa heretofore unavailable. Coincidentally, the missionaries were among the Calusa only a few months after the Englishman Jonathan Dickinson and his shipwrecked party made their way northward along the eastern coast of the Florida peninsula. Dickinson gives a detailed eyewitness account of the native populations along the eastern coast of Florida, from Jupiter Inlet to St. Augustine and points north (Dickinson 1985). Thus, with the availability of John Hann's translation of the 1697 Calusa materials, students of southern Florida's Native Americans can now study two detailed and reasonably contemporaneous accounts.

Those who have read *Apalachee: The Land Between the Rivers,* which appeared in 1988 in the Bullen Series, are already aware of John Hann's stature as a historian. In *Missions to the Calusa* he continues his work in seventeenth-century Florida history, this time focusing on south Florida. In addition to translating the eyewitness testimony of both priests and laypersons about the Calusa mission effort, he includes a number of documents that provide insight into broader-scale political dynamics—soldiers and priests, governors and bishops, provincial officials and the king. A general introduction sets the mission effort within the broader framework of the Spanish colonial system, and each document is introduced by a brief commentary that places the piece in context.

Also in this volume are several important documents from the sixteenth and eighteenth centuries (Parts II and III, respectively). Some have never been published and others have appeared only in Spanish. Among the documents in Part II, the reader will find the eyewitness accounts of Juan Rogel, previously available only in Spanish (with Latin notes) in the compilation of Zubillaga (1946) and in English in the hard-to-find Jesuit historical studies of Vargas Ugarte (1935). Rogel's articulate and detailed letters bring to life the wrenching experience of a native society in drastic and irreversible transition. Also included are letters by Pedro Menéndez de Avilés and excerpts from López de Velasco's *Geografía y Descripción Universal de las Indias.*

Part III documents the final half-century of Calusa existence as a culture. Here are poignant accounts of warfare, slavery, staggering population losses, and failed migrations, as the once-dominant Calusa find themselves literally pushed into the Caribbean Sea by Native Americans acting as agents of European opportunists. In Part III is the complete text of the 1760 version of the Alaña-Monaco report, the 1743 version of which was one of William Sturtevant's sources for his 1978 article "The Last of the South Florida Aborigines" (Sturtevant 1978). The Alaña-Monaco document is a detailed account of yet another unsuccessful mission effort. Like their seventeenth-century Franciscan counterparts, the eighteenth-century Jesuits found that native south Floridians were willing to talk about becoming Christians only when the missionaries distributed European goods. The document provides fascinating insights into the tenacity of the south Florida belief system. Reduced to a precarious existence and an uncertain future, stripped of their power and influence, the natives still clung stubbornly to their spiritual beliefs, and commoners still procured food for the nobles.

It is a pleasure to have been able to join with the Bureau of Archaeological Research in making these new sources available to a wider audience. The documents contained in *Missions to the Calusa* probably do not exhaust the ethnohistoric sources relating to south Florida, although the point of diminishing returns is probably being reached in the Archivo General de Indias (AGI) in Seville. I hope that the publication of these documents will stimulate further research in AGI and in other archives where documents relating to south Florida may be found.

William H. Marquardt

PART I

Calusa

in the Late Seventeenth Century

INTRODUCTION

Despite only brief and episodic contacts between Spaniards and the Calusa natives of southwest Florida, in some respects the Calusa are among the best known of Florida's natives during the first two centuries after contact. Concerning the Calusa's religious beliefs and practices and their persistent faith in their own view of the cosmos, our knowledge is particularly rich in comparison to what we know of the beliefs of other Florida peoples of this era. Archaeologists' discovery of a substantial iconography associated with Calusa religious ritual further enhances our knowledge derived from documents.

One of the fruitful episodic contacts between Spaniard and Calusa stemmed from a short-lived 1697 mission effort by five Franciscan friars who came to Calusa territory from Cuba. This mission effort, from its conception in the mind of Florida's outgoing governor in 1679 to the postmortems into the causes for the mission's failure, is far and away the best documented of Florida's mission efforts.

The documentation from the 1697 effort is one of three such assemblages that portray the Calusa, which might be likened to the panels of an altar triptych. Documentation from French and Spanish sources of the 1560s comprise the major central panel, limning the Calusa world still probably more or less as it was at first contact. The documentation from the 1697 mission effort, which is presented here, is the first of the side panels. That panel portrays a diminished but still relatively strong and vital Calusa society. The documentation from a 1743 Jesuit expedition from Cuba through the Keys to the region of present-day Miami is the other side panel. It portrays a beleaguered remnant of the

3

Calusa in amalgamation with remnants of the natives of the Keys and of the Tequesta, facing dissolution as a result of thirty years of relentless attacks by natives identified as Uchise who would later become known as Seminole and of several migrations to Cuba during which the population was decimated by disease.

This work focuses on the first of the side panels, presenting documentation from the 1697 mission effort. But images from the earlier central panel are reflected in Marquardt's introductory essay on the Calusa as seen from an archaeological and anthropological perspective and in presentation, in Part II, of a few early descriptions of the Calusa and their neighbors. Part III presents documents from the eighteenth century in which the Calusa are mentioned, as well as a later version of the report on the 1743 expedition. This new version is superior to my translation of the original 1743 version published by Arva Moore Parks (1985) in volume 2 of John W. Griffin et al., *Archaeology and History of the Granada Site* and to the transcription published in *Tacachale* by William C. Sturtevant under the title "The Last of the South Florida Aborigines" (1978).

Although the Calusa were one of the first Florida peoples with whom Spaniards established communication, official contact was very intermittent from the time of Ponce de León early in the sixteenth century to the disappearance of the Calusa as a distinct people in the second half of the eighteenth. Throughout those two and one-half centuries the Calusa were remarkably consistent in remaining totally impervious to the several missionization efforts directed at them, even when the mission efforts were launched, supposedly, at the request of the Calusa themselves. The Calusa are notable as well for the survival of their faith in their own belief system, which lay behind their disinterest in the new religion brought by the Spaniards.

The Calusa are unique among Florida's natives in that such contact as they maintained with Spaniards between the era of Pedro Menéndez de Avilés and the year 1763 was largely with the authorities in Cuba rather than with those at St. Augustine. During those two centuries no Calusa leader seems ever to have visited St. Augustine, while the Calusa, or at least the Keys Indians who were tributary to them, seem to have thought nothing of a voyage to Havana with Spanish fishermen from Cuba who frequented Florida's southwestern coast to exploit its mullet fisheries. It is conceivable that Calusa or Keys Indians made such voyages in their own dugout canoes, although I have seen no clear documentary evidence for such trips. The Indians' awareness of the Tortugas during Ponce de León's 1513 visit indicates that native craft ventured considerable distances from land (Herrera 1720: 248).

Such visits to Cuba may well have been a continuation of an intercourse that had prehistoric roots. Julian Granberry has recently postulated such maritime intercourse with Florida's natives by Florida's neighbors, but on an even grander scale. Granberry sees signs in the Timucua language's vocabulary and grammar indicating that it originated in the interior of northern South America (1987: 43–50). "All evidence, in short," he suggests, "points to the development of the Timucuan language in the Vaupés-Caqueta region of Northwestern Amazonia at a time level between 3500 and 1800–1500 B.C." and that some trading people who spoke a language of that region that was ancestral to Timucua came to Florida directly from the mouth of the Orinoco between 2000–1500 B.C. at about the time of the appearance of fiber-tempered Stallings Island and Orange wares in late Archaic period sites (1987:50).

Fontaneda recorded a migration to Florida from Cuba early in the sixteenth century, noting that "many Indians landed formerly (*Antiguamente*) in the province of Carlos" and that "the father of King Carlos, who was called Senquene, took them and formed a village of them." Those Cuban Indians' descendants, Fontaneda maintained, were still to be found among the Calusa during the time Fontaneda was a captive among the Calusa (1944: 68–69). Henry Dobyns interpreted Fontaneda's remarks as evidence that the Cuban Indians' migrations to Florida in search of miraculous waters were a response to the deadly new diseases introduced by the first Europeans (1983: 256–258). In 1513 on Florida's southwest coast Ponce de León encountered a native who understood Spanish. Herrera noted of this native that "it was believed he must have been from Española or from another island among those inhabited by Castillians" (1720: 248).

Even more recently Barbara Purdy has gone beyond Dobyns to maintain that "early historic documents provide some evidence that Indians from the West Indies traveled regularly to Florida before the invasion of Cuba by the Spanish in 1511" (1988: 641). But a strong argument against such migrations in early historic or late prehistoric times is the absence of any evidence of the Florida aborigines' use of Antillean staples such as manioc or *yuca,* yams, and sweet potatoes or *zamia,* which one would expect to find if such intercourse were common. And Sturtevant, in his *Significance of Ethnological Similarities Between*

Southeastern North America and the Antilles, concluded that "the ethnological evidence thought by various writers to point to Antillean influences throughout the Southeast does not in fact run counter to the archaeological indications that such influence did not take place" (1960: 45).

But whatever may be the truth about such migrations in prehistoric or early historic times, the 1697 mission to the Calusa, reflecting the existence of this path of communication somewhat later, was launched from Cuba under the aegis of Cuba's governor and bishop rather than by political and ecclesiastical authorities at St. Augustine, although initial impetus for the mission in 1680 came from Florida's governor, Pablo de Hita Salazar. The 1743 attempt was similarly a Cuban-based operation. By and large the same may be said for the initial effort under Menéndez de Avilés.

Appearance of a place named *rinconada* de Carlos on a 1726 census of fourteen native settlements near St. Augustine might suggest that Calusa were drawn eventually to that Spanish capital for Florida. Belief that the *rinconada* had a relation to the Calusa apparently led the researcher in Spain who located many of the documents presented in the body of the book to include the 1726 census among her documents pertaining to the Calusa. That all thirty-eight of the *rinconada*'s inhabitants were non-Christian is compatible with Calusa tradition, but the *rinconada*'s inhabitants were identified as belonging to the Piaxa nation. Piaxa or Piaja is probably a variant of Aypaja. During the 1696–1697 revolt in the Mayaca-Jororo mission territory, a young cacique who was native to Aypaja was killed by rebels at Jororo's Atoyquime along with Fray Luis Sánchez and his sacristan. In reporting the incident, the governor identified Aypaja as one of the places of Jororo Province, noting that its people had not joined in the rebellion and that in the rebellion's wake they had moved to San Antonio Anacapi (Torres y Ayala 1697). The term *rinconada* appears to have been used loosely at times to describe all the interior of south-central Florida between Mayaca and Carlos as well as to denote specific portions of that territory such as the *rinconada* de Carlos or the *rinconada* de Macapiros. Thus the *rinconada* de Carlos was in Jororo territory rather than in Calusa.

Literally *rinconada* means "corner." *Rincon,* from which it derives, means "inside corner," "angle," "nook," "remote place," "private or lurking place." Among gauchos *rincon* or *rincão* has the sense of "a very sheltered place surrounded by woods or river or a box canyon that would serve for penning in cattle." In Spanish Florida *rinconada* seems to have had one or more of these senses. In 1702 Florida's governor applied the term to all of peninsular Florida: "La Rinconada, as they call it, is a stretch of land (*estendido de tierra*) in the shape of a horseshoe, which in the two extremities [has], in the one, the Presidio [St. Augustine], and in the other, the port of San Luis de Apalachee, which are seventy or eighty leagues distant from one another" (Zúñiga y Zerda 1702). Twenty-one years earlier another governor, alluding to the natives' retreat from Guale "because of the fear of the English enemy and of the heathen Chichimecos Indians [the Westo] who roam the woods," noted that these refugee Indians "being aware of the support that they have in the present Governor and defense and guarantee that they have in that presidio, have been coming out and incorporating themselves with the peoples (*pueblos*) that they call of Carlos, forty leagues distant from this presidio" (Marques Cabrera 1681). Although the governor did not indicate whether his *rinconada* de Carlos was north or south of St. Augustine, circumstantial evidence and later usage suggest that it was to the south.

In orders to the leader of an expedition sent by Florida's governor in 1701 to persuade San Salvador de Mayaca's fugitive inhabitants to return to their mission village, he instructed that leader that after he had completed preparations for the march at San Francisco Potano, "he will continue his march to the *Rinconada* by way of the region that he will have determined to be most appropriate, keeping in mind that the principal motive for this order and this trip is to go to search for and bring back to their village the Indians from Mayaca. . . . And from there he will go on penetrating all the *rinconada* to the extent that may be possible, getting along amicably with all the nations that he may run across." Here the governor seems to have used *rinconada* in its broad sense. Later in that order the governor remarked, "and he will penetrate into the land as far as may be possible, down to the lake of Maymi [Lake Okeechobee] and the borders of the lands of the cacique Carlos" (Zúñiga y Zerda 1701). The forty leagues separating St. Augustine and the *rinconada* de Carlos of 1681 is compatible with the Mayaca-Jororo territory. The documented presence of Yamasee at the Mayaca mission of San Salvador also points in that direction, as Yamasee would have been likely fugitives from the English and Westo attacks.

After Menéndez de Avilés' visits to Carlos in the 1560s and the unsuccessful Jesuit missions at Carlos and Tequesta that Menéndez de

Avilés sponsored, there was a very long hiatus before Spaniards renewed formal contact with the Calusa. This hiatus resulted undoubtedly from the tensions and violence that marked the Spanish presence
among the Calusa in Menéndez de Avilés' time. The Spanish commander deposed and executed a number of Calusa leaders whom he
found intractible for Spanish purposes. Two successive head chiefs
were among those executed. After the execution of the second chief,
the Calusa burned their head village and fled. Thereafter crews of ships
that came to grief on that coast could expect death at the hands of the
natives, if they survived the shipwreck itself. In 1574, for example,
Captain Alonso de Lobera and four of his men were killed and many
others wounded as their ship approached Tequesta, a settlement tributary to the Calusa ruler (Connor 1925, 1: 105; Guttiérrez de Miranda
1578).

To solve this problem for shipwreck survivors, when abandonment
of St. Augustine was under consideration in 1600, a royal official suggested that there was need for a fort at the head of the Martyrs [the
Keys] (Alas 1600). The official noted that

> in order that the land that lies from this part of the South to the
> head of the Martyrs might be brought under control, it would be
> important to put a fort at the aforementioned head with up to 100
> men. This head is at 24½ degrees at the said south coast, 70 leagues
> from St. Augustine presidio, which is at the aforesaid 30 degrees.
> And from this presidio of St. Augustine to the aforesaid head of the
> Martyrs is all low and swampy land and the Indians there do not
> plant anything, but live from fish and roots of some fruits of the
> earth. And the Indians are few and do not have established villages
> but wander, rather, from place to place, building huts wherever the
> fish and fruit are present. . . . From this spot that is called the
> head of the Martyrs, which is at the entrance to the Bahama
> Channel, which is at 25 degrees, where all the ships going to Spain
> from the Indies come out and where many are lost every year. And
> the shipwrecked people who survive are killed by the Indians with
> terrible torments. And it is said even that they eat human
> flesh. . . . From the said fort of the Martyrs it is sixty leagues to
> the Bay of Carlos at 30 degrees, and twenty-eight leagues from
> there to the Bay of Tocobaga. And the latter is at 28 degrees.[1]

1. This is an obvious error. The Bay of Tocobaga is north of the Bay of
Carlos.

Seven years later Governor Pedro de Ibarra repeated the suggestion that Spain build a fort at the head of the Keys (Parks 1985: 43).

The Calusa's hostility appears to have persisted through the first decade of the seventeenth century. But the Calusa chief responded to a 1612 message from the governor by stating that the Indians no longer wanted war with the Christians. To confirm that report Governor Fernández de Olivera sent Juan Rodríguez de Cortaya with twenty soldiers to journey across Florida by river and then down the Gulf coast to Pojoy. Swanton locates Pojoy on the south side of Tampa Bay (1946: 173). The governor already had a launch and canoes on the river from an expedition sent earlier to punish the leaders of Pojoy and Tocobaga for attacks they had made on recently Christianized Potano (Ibarra 1608). From Pojoy, Cortaya was to proceed southward along the coast to the land of Chief Carlos.

The first thoughts in the seventeenth century about a renewed mission effort among the Calusa date to that 1612 expedition. To the king, the governor reported thus on the fruits of the Cortaya expedition.

> Similarly, Your Majesty ordered me to inform him of what I know about the trail and river that was discovered for going to the coast of Apalachee and bay (*ensenada*)[2] of Carlos, which I wrote I would have reconnoitered this summer with the launch and canoes that I caused to be built on the said river for the punishment of the caciques of Pooy and Tocopaca.[3] When I had [everything] prepared for it, I sent word to the heirs of the said caciques that from that time forward they should not harm the Christian settlements. For that, punishment was inflicted because of what their predecessors had done. I sent them some gifts also, offering them peace and friendship on the part of Your Majesty. As a result of this and of the fear from what had happened [earlier], they reciprocated fully. And by this path I sent the same message to the cacique of Carlos, who is the most powerful one on that entire coast, sending him some gifts as well. He replied that he wanted war with the Christians no longer and that he was desirous of peace and friendship with them.

2. This might be rendered also as "inlet of Carlos."

3. Pooy is a variant spelling of Pojoy or Pojoi as it is written at times. In the seventeenth century Spaniards often used the name Tocopaca for the people whom we know as Tocobaga, who lived from Tampa Bay northward to Apalachee. By the 1670s at least there was a Tocobaga settlement in Apalachee itself. The settlement was located on the Wacissa River near Ivitachuco.

And in order to confirm it, the said launch was sent to his land. And with this favorable opportunity, I ordered it to go and it left from the said river in mid-June and in it the ensign, Juan Rodriguez de Cortaya, a person fitted for such enterprises, with twenty soldiers and a pilot, so that he might go about reconnoitering all of it. And [having] arrived at a large bay (*bahia*), which is that of the cacique of Pooy, where he lives at the latitude of twenty-seven and one-third degrees.[4] They confirmed the friendships and they gave him additional gifts that they were carrying for that purpose. As a result he became content and assured. Then they set out toward Carlos and entered into a large river that they call Tampa at the latitude of twenty-six degrees and a sixth (*un sesmo*).[5] There and along the entire coast there were large settlements of Indians subject to Carlos. And because of the order that he had given them, they came out to receive the launch, presenting the soldiers with fish and other things. And [having] arrived at the village of Carlos itself, which is within a large river and bar (*barra*), which is in the latitude of twenty-six degrees, as soon as they saw it [the launch], more than sixty canoes came out with a great number of unarmed Indians, bringing many women with them. Among this people this is the greatest sign of friendship. And after giving the welcome to the said ensign on the part of their chief, he sent word to him with the interpreter that he brought with him that, in order to confirm the friendships that he was coming to discuss, he should come to the launch. To this he replied two or three times that he had never gone aboard [a boat] (*que el no se auia enbarcado jamas*); that he should come on land [instead], where they would see one another. And the ensign, on excusing himself in consideration of the few people and the order that he was carrying, obliged the said cacique to embark in a large canoe with more than forty Indians and many other canoes [filled] with people. And after [having] reached the said

4. Swanton said "this is Tampa Bay or that part of it known as Hillsborough Bay" and identified Pooy with de Soto's Ocita (1922: 328; 1946: 173).

5. Cassell defines *sesmo* as "division, administrative unit of territory." The word does not appear at all in Larousse. In his reproduction of a translation of this document, Quinn rendered this as "a sixth" (1979, 5: 138). It seems that I have seen it used elsewhere in that sense or as "a bit." All the latitude readings appear to be understated. Weddle places the original Tampa in the vicinity of Charlotte Harbor (1985: 52). The Tampa River is possibly the Peace River. If so, the village of Carlos would be on the Caloosahatchee.

launch, he embraced the said ensign, saying that he gave him that in my name and as a sign of the friendships that he wished to have with the Spaniards from that time forward; that he, for his part, would do nothing else. He and his people, after showing great signs of rejoicing, had two golden *chagualas*[6] brought out [that were] as big as the palm of one's hand and smaller ones that would weigh about two ounces, that they are accustomed to place on their forehead. He gave these to the ensign, saying that he gave them to me as a sign of the friendship that they were discussing. And he also gave him a Negro from Havana that he had, who had been blown off course in a canoe in a storm and who had landed on that coast, saying that if he had had other Christian people, he would hand them over just as readily and that from that time forward anywhatsoever Spanish people or ship that should be thrown upon that coast by misfortune would have a good passage. And if it should be necessary, he would set them on the right road to this presidio with great security because this cacique is so feared by all the rest that those near here even pay tribute to him. The ensign, after thanking him profusely, gave him assurances of the same friendly intention and gave him some gifts that he brought with him for that [purpose]. And he did the same to the other caciques and Indians who were with him. As a consequence they became very content. And I am [equally] so with its happy outcome. And I trust to God that within a short time religious can be placed there with safety, who should have a very rich harvest [of souls] because this cacique has more than sixty villages (*pueblos*) of his own, not to mention the other very great quantity that pay tribute to him, that I spoke of.

All this coast [in the] district of Pooy and Carlos, from near the river where the launch is, in the latitude of twenty-eight degrees, down to 25, which is the head of the Martyrs [the Keys], the said ensign and pilot assure me, is the best and clearest (*mas limpia*) that one could desire and so easy to traverse (*tan endable*) that in all of it one may go close to the land in large ships. And that there are bars

---

6. *Chagualas* does not appear in modern dictionaries but appears frequently in sixteenth- and early seventeenth-century records to denote ornaments worn by the natives of the Georgia and Carolina hinterlands. In New World Spanish, one of its meanings is the gold rings that natives such as the Cuna of Panama wear in their noses.

and rivers such that one can enter within, in particular the bay
(*bahia*) of Pooy, which, the Indians say, is where the adelantado
Hernando de Soto landed. And such is its capacity that an armada
and armadas can enter within it. As the weather did not permit it,
they were not able to take soundings and see [it], but it will be done
at the first opportunity and I shall send a collection of pilot books
(*derrotero*) for the entire coast. And should it appear to Your Majesty
that it would be appropriate that some point in it be occupied,
suitable both for the support of the ships and fleets and for the
support of the religious who may be stationed there [in Carlos] and
in Apalachee, where a warehouse (*almazen*) could be maintained and
from whence food could be brought to them with greater ease than
by land, because that is very difficult from here, I shall go to see
and reconnoiter all this in person.[7] And this would also have a great
effect in closing that region as a refuge for pirate ships and this
could be done by having a small fort in which forty or fifty men
would be stationed. (Fernández de Olivera 1612)

Governor Fernández de Olivera did not live long enough to realize
his desire to send friars to Carlos or to hear from the Crown on the
various suggestions that he made in the above letter, written on October 13, 1612. He died about five weeks after writing this letter (Arrazola and Olivera 1613). His successor is unlikely to have had such
thoughts vis-à-vis an expansion of the mission effort, as he called for a
reduction in the number of friars and an end to their being paid as if
they were soldiers. In a 1617 letter to the king, the leaders among the
Florida Franciscans arraigned the new governor for his failure to support the work of evangelization, charging that the governor's interest
in the amber trade was the reason for nothing having been done about
the missionization of Carlos.

In view of the important ethnographic content of the friars' joint letter, the entire letter will be reproduced below rather than simply ex-
tracting the sections alluding to Calusa.

7. I have rearranged the word order somewhat in this extremely lengthy
and convoluted sentence. The clause "I shall go to see and reconnoiter all this
in person" appears, in the Spanish text, following the closing words below,
"would be stationed." In the interest of readability, I have made a separate
sentence of what follows.

Sire

After the lengthy forbearance and hope that we the religious and chaplains of Your Majesty in these provinces of Florida have had for going on four years, believing that with it [this procedure] we would oblige him to help us for the fulfillment of Your Majesty's holy intentions looking toward the conversion of these souls and the great desires for their welfare that we brought with us to this land, disillusioned from so prolonged an experience and mistrustful of any remedy for it, if we do not encounter it in Your Majesty's most Christian breast, we, the provincial and definitors of this province, resolved to turn our attention to it to avoid problems with the person who is governing and the loss of so many souls as have perished for lack of help.

Beginning by giving an account to Your Majesty of the state of affairs that prevails at present, after having first made a diligent and truthful examination, we find that from four years ago down to the present half of the Indians have died because of the great plagues and contagious diseases (*por las grandes pestes y contagiosas enfermidades*) that they have suffered. Your Majesty has had a very great share of merit in this, which will be given to him in Glory. Thus, with the help of the twenty-two religious that Your Majesty ordered sent to these regions five years ago, a very great harvest of souls for heaven has been made in these mortalities. More than eight thousand Christians remain alive, at the least; more rather than fewer.

Many are the heathens that remain, for up to now *doctrinas* have never been placed in the Province of Apalachee, nor in that of Tama, nor in that of Santa Helena, nor in that of the coast of Carlos. And in the latter because of the greed for the amber that is found on this coast, as it appeared to the governors that their interests would suffer by this path [being followed], setting more value on the corruptible and the vain than on the incomparable treasure of so many souls as have been lost and will be lost with these [steps]. But instead, with these [moves], he would protect many Christians who are cast ashore upon that coast along with their ships. Because the Indians are not Christians or even true friends of the Spaniards, they can do them great harm. And the Indians at least will protect all those who land on the coast along with those refugees from the sea who are wont to find greater affliction on land in the rest of the provinces mentioned. Even though the religious have become enthused about and are enthused about making *entradas,* they have not given us consent for this or given permission to enter on a formal basis (*de assiento*) on the grounds that there is no order from Your Majesty for this. But rather they always urge us to pull back toward the presidio as if Your Majesty had sent us in order to protect it and to be worldly soldiers (*soldados materiales*). Nonetheless, the good spirit and zeal of the religious have not suffered them to be idle, but rather, the aforesaid have carried out many and very important *entradas* into the heathen provinces. As a consequence of them, all the Indians are peaceful and quiet in the service of and in obedience to Your Majesty because of the exhortations of the religious. And that the standard of the Holy Cross is raised among these heathens and that they have houses and churches built, waiting for ministers of God to be given to them who may help them in the salvation of their souls. With great fatigue, those heathens come from very great distances to beg the governor who is [installed] in this presidio by Your Majesty, and they return home disconsolate. This is the disposition that these provinces have and the effects that the hurried *entradas* of the religious have wrought with divine favor. Only to the Province of Carlos have they not gone, even passingly, because no one is permitted even to dream of entering there because of the amber. Were a religious to enter there, the effect would be the same as in the rest.

But what we do not cease to lament (*llorar*) is that when the *entradas* of the religious have had such pious effects in the barbarous breasts of the Indians, it has not been the same in those of the Spaniards, who, full of joy for the welfare of souls and for the spread and exaltation of our Holy Catholic faith and of the royal estates of Your Majesty, had the obligation to make them great and Christian. But instead they have unjustly made this an occasion for calumniating us, discouraging the spirit and fervor of the good religious, and saying that we did wrong and that the entry was effected in a warlike manner, because some Indians who went with the religious brought along some harquebuses, the Indians' very own, which some of them use in order to shoot such deer or bear for food as appear along the trail. And saying that a banner that they carried there with them to instruct the heathens reverently about the Holy Cross that was emblazoned on it had been a battle standard (*vandera*), and other such things, all without foundation. We are reporting this because it will be very possible that they have given an account of it to Your Majesty along with other matters as being the most certain of truths. Great are the oppressions and grievances that we suffer and that the most Christian intentions of Your Majesty suffer [in that] they make them [*the entradas*] a subject for charges and blame. And more deplorable is the exceedingly great multitude of souls that have been lost and are being lost among these heathens because this conversion is not being supported as Your Majesty commands.

The affliction and grief would not be so great, if the evils and harm that exist here were solely the above-mentioned ones, but it is not only among the heathens that they prevent us from producing results, but also in that conquest [of souls] achieved over a long period of time at the cost of great expenditures and efforts on the part of Your Majesty and of labors on our part. In the alluded to short space of four years [the conquest] has been diminished notably because of the great liberty that the Indians have taken, occasioned by what the natives hear and see among the Spaniards sent from this presidio. For even though the public orders are above criticism, the other secret ones that they give them are very abhorrent to Christendom, as is well known and as the Indians say out loud and publicly. And even though all the governors state publicly that they are shocked, saying that they send out orders that we religious are to be respected, we do not know why they now order the opposite. The soldiers state publicly and say to the Indians that the purpose for which Your Majesty has sent the religious is nothing more than to pray and to say Mass and thus for this [reason] the religious cannot take steps to remedy the offenses to our Lord that exist among the natives.[8] But rather, with the liberty and protection that are given to them, everything stands so shattered and they so lacking in the fear of God or of the religious and so lost is the respect that they used to have for the ministers of God that the religious of the Province of Guale have passed many days in great fear that they would take their lives, as they did some years ago to five religious and to royal officials of Your Majesty. This should

8. The authors here refer to the friars' penchant for inflicting corporal punishment, such as whipping neophytes who returned to native practices in conflict with Christian mores.

suffice for not giving them undue freedom, for once they have lost respect for the religious who keep them at peace, the following day they will lose it for Your Majesty, taking advantage of the opportunity as [do] people unaccustomed to the liberty that is given to them. The frequent contact with Spaniards also does them much harm. Where they used to go among them only from time to time, now they go among them constantly and every day. From this flows many offenses to our Lord and unrest among the Indians.[9] On their seeing what the soldiers do, not those of worth, they lose their respect for the religious and speak to them without reverence.[10] And also because of the great deal of labor and ill-treatment imposed without any sort of need or benefit to the presidio or service to Your Majesty, the Indians wander through the woods as fugitives. All of this is an occasion for them to die there as barbarians.

The support that should be given to us so that, [with] the fear of God assisted by the human element, the natives would become good Christians, is so scant or nonexistent, it has come to pass that when we sent him the most reprobate Indian and one who has apostatized repeatedly from the faith with the result that, on bringing him among Christians, he soon returned to the company of heathens. And believing that there was now no remedy for it other than that the government should put the fear of God into him, it sent him [to it], without its paying any attention to the matter as if it were something of no importance.[11] And in order not to bore Your Majesty with specific cases, I will say that in general the government attaches little importance to matters of conversion. And [now] they do not even give it the mere support of lip service as [was

9. Here the friars are probably alluding in part to sexual liaisons between the soldiers and native women. Many of the same issues reappear in the friars' complaints during the 1650s.

10. My rendition of this tortuous and elliptical passage is tentative. The Spanish here is "Viendo ellos que soldados y no de los de consideracion pierden el respeto a los Religiossos y les hablan sin miramiento."

11. My rendition of this passage is equally tentative. The Spanish here is "El favor que se nos devia dar para que aiudado el temor Divino del humano fuesen buenos Christianos los naturales es tan poco o ninguno que ha sucedido remitirle indio perdidissimo y muchas vezes apostata de la fee que en trayendole entre Christianos se bolvia luego entre infieles y desconfiados de que ya avria remedio sino es que el govierno le espantasse le envio tan sin hacer casso dello como si no importaua nada."

done] formerly. Ever since Your Majesty sent this new government here, it does not say it [merely] in secret, but shouts it out loud in the public square that the conversion of the Indians is a chimera, that neither for the present nor for the future can anything be expected from it, [and] that it is all a hoax. And thus, in the matter of conversion, after [the present government] took over here, it has behaved as it would have if Your Majesty had sent it orders to undermine everything achieved at the cost of such great toil and of the blood of the religious [and] cost and effort on the part of Your Majesty, which have been made for so many years now. With such great lack of support and lack of prudence that, if he wished in order not to scandalize us and to scandalize whoever might hear him, he has not even been willing to utter good words.[12] We would very much have wished not to tire Your Majesty with such matters. And we have waited four years [to do so]. That from the first day on which he set foot here, he made it so clear, that we could have done this [then], but we waited to see if he would reform. And thus, afflicted over the state of affairs that has prevailed, as well as fearful lest the souls that should be lost be placed to our account because we did not warn Your Majesty, it has become necessary to do so.

The ill treatment that we are subjected to by way of words and writing, the terms so foreign, not only to chaplains of Your Majesty and to priests of the most high God, but also [terms] that would be [strange] even for very ordinary people and for those of low estate. It is what we take notice of the least because we know that God will hold him to an accounting, although we mention it in passing to Your Majesty in this [report]. It is given because the ministers of the gospel will be held in low esteem in these regions to the extent it is neglected.

However, because we are speaking in general and without distinction, we are not including in the blame, under the name of government, those who bear no blame. We mean to say that it is not our intention to place blame on the royal officials whom Your

12. My rendition of this passage is equally tentative. The following is the Spanish text: "despuses que aqui entro a echo lo pudiera si V Mag^d le huviera inviado a desfaborecer quanto con tantos travajos y sangre de Religiossos costa y dilgencia de V Mag^d aque sea hecho tantos anos a con tanto disfabor y falta de recato que se quiera por no escandalicarnos y escandalizar a quien le oye no a querido siquiera dar buenas palabras."

Majesty maintains here. That this would be an injustice, because
Your Majesty has very Christian officials here. The treasurer in
particular, whose name is Juan Menéndez Marques, is a very good
Christian [who has] long been a servant of your Majesty. We and
this entire presidio clamor for him for this government because we
know that there would be no one better than he to provide a remedy
for so many public wrongs as there are to be seen here, both the
oppression of the poor and notable losses for the royal treasury of
Your Majesty, the poverty and great affliction in which this presidio
exists, and the great fears that we all have of many evils and
disturbances because of the tight situation in which this port exists,
which could not be worse, and for the welfare and conversion of
these souls. The factor whom Your Majesty sent now is also a very
satisfactory man and a very Christian one and one who has been a
great consolation to the presidio besides the remedying of matters.
That an account has been given to Your Majesty here. We beg for
others relative both to the conversion as well as for the consolation
of the chaplains that Your Majesty has here. For these [purposes]
we are sending a memorial to him that is going along with this,
most confident of a remedy for everything. May Our Lord protect
Your Majesty. City of St. Augustine of Florida, seventeenth of
January of the year one thousand six hundred and seventeen.

    Chaplains of Your Majesty, whose royal hands we kiss. Fray
Francisco Pareja, definitor provincial   Fray Lorenço
Martínez   Fray Pedro Rruiz   Fray Alonso Desquera
Fray Juan de la Cruz   Fray Francisco Moreno de
Jesus   Fray Bartolomé Romero

One expects that the Spaniards' salvage of shipwrecks such as that of
the plate fleet in which the Nuestra Señora de Atocha went down in
the Keys in 1622 might have led to contacts with the Calusa, but if
such contact occurred it does not seem to have left much trace in the
records. Eugene Lyon observed that the salvage records for the 1622
shipwrecks reveal that the salvors gave gifts to the Indians of the Keys
to maintain good relations and to employ the natives as divers. But,
Lyon noted, such allusions contain no ethnographic information and
do not mention the Calusa to whom the Keys Indians seem to have
been generally tributary (Eugene Lyon, personal communication, 1988).

    Early in 1623 Florida's governor made the following report on that
plate-fleet shipwreck.

About the month of September some remains of ships were found
on this coast that indicated shipwreck and the loss of some. And
soon thereafter I had word from the Indians of the coast of Jega and
Santa Lucia[13] that many others had come to grief on their [coast].
This caused me notable concern and grief because of its being time
for the Galleons and Fleet to be coming through the Channel.

I sent the sergeant-major, Gabira, to the point[14] with forty
soldiers so that he might search along those [coasts] and collect
whatever he might find on them. And as it appeared to me
appropriate that I should make this investigation in person as well, I
did so. . . . I reached as far as Santa Lucia, which is the farthest I
was able to go, hunting over all of them without finding anything of
importance or anything else other than broken chests (*petacas*) of
rotting tobacco and three shallops (*chalupas*).[15] And I dispatched a
frigate at the same time so that it might run along the keys of the
head of the Martyrs and the bay (*ensenada*) of Carlos, but on the
voyage it developed a leak that the pumps could not keep up with
and this obliged him to return to this port. And on the first of this
[month of January], another one arrived, sent by the Marquis de
Cadereyta, with news of the loss of three galleons and five dispatch-
boats (*pataches*) at the head of the Martyrs, requesting that I make
the investigations that were [already] made many days earlier. And,
on considering that some people, artillery, and boxes with some gold
and silver could have come ashore on the Keys of Matacumbe,
Tachista, Muspa, Tampa, and the bay of Carlos, I dispatched this
frigate again without any delay, so that it might search along those
areas, equipping it with provisions for fifty days and with people
and munitions and some trade goods, all of which were in short
supply. This is all that I have been able to do. May it please God
that some good may come of it. And, when a frigate of Your Majesty
comes out of the careening that it is receiving, I shall dispatch it to
the isles of Vahama, because it is my understanding that many
things are to be found on them. (Salinas 1623).

Governor Juan de Salinas went on to remark on the poor reception
that the survivors of such shipwrecks usually met from the Indians of
the coasts of Jega and Santa Lucia, noting that the Indians usually

13. Indians of the lower southeast Florida coast.
14. "The point" is probably an allusion to Cape Canaveral.
15. *Chalupas* might be rendered also as "launches" or "canoes."

killed them all. The governor also repeated the suggestion already noted as having been made in 1600 (and repeated by Governor Pedro de Ibarra in 1608) about the advisability of putting a fort with 100 soldiers in the area in order to check such depredations. Governor Salinas observed that he had done what he was able to "in order to punish these Indians, running along the coasts many times, but that it had not been enough, because once the soldiery was withdrawn, they returned to their posts" (Salinas 1623). But only five years later another governor, Luis Rojas y Borja, reported that such a fort would not be necessary.

To deal with the problems posed by English and Dutch trade with the natives of Florida's southern coast, the latter governor succeeded in establishing friendly relations with these natives. Although he did not identify the specific peoples involved, they undoubtedly included the Jega and the Santa Lucia. Rojas y Borja noted only that, in response to the experienced envoys he had sent to speak with them,

> the most prestigious and powerful caciques of all that coast had come to this city, and I had them here many days, entertaining them as much as possible, from which they became satisfied and great friends of this presidio. And they have gone on continuing this friendship until the present. And later the same caciques have returned here and very many others. And all have been entertained to preserve these good relations. And they are such friends that, many times I send two or three soldiers all along the coast and they go very secure. And the caciques and the rest of the Indians entertain them, giving them food to eat, from what they have. And from that time, on the occasions when English and Dutch ships have arrived on the coast of these Indians, they have not admitted them or traded with them. And they have come to give me news that there are enemy ships on the coast. And on two occasions when they landed to obtain water, they abandoned their places and withdrew to the woods and others came to give the report and to ask for help. (Rojas y Borja 1628)

It is likely that this governor's contacts were confined to natives of the Atlantic-facing coast.

A friar's brief comments toward the end of 1634 indicate that contact with the Calusa resulted from salvage operations for the ships lost in 1622. After commenting on the start of the evangelization of

Apalachee's alleged 34,000 souls, this friar went on, "and the Province of Carlos, Posoy, and Matacumbe, where the Marquis de Cadereita took refuge (*se retiró*) to gather together the people from his ships, who were lost on that coast, are waiting for religious. And they did the same after the soldiers and sailors whom Governor Melian[16] sent to search for and extract the silver from the galleons of the Fleet of the aforesaid Marquis de Cadereita." On this point the friar concluded, "And he considers it certain, because of having been in the said provinces and because it was patent to the aforesaid marquis, and is well known to those who sail those coasts, that they would receive evangelical preachers with great pleasure" (Jesus [1634]).

There seems to be no further seventeenth-century mention of the Calusa prior to that made by Bishop Gabriel Días Vara Calderón in 1675. This allusion to Carlos is most brief. In discussing the features and peoples of Florida's southern regions, Días Vara Calderón wrote, on mentioning the head of the Martyrs,

and through the latter a large river disembogues, which enters into the large lake (*laguna*) of Maymî, where, according to tradition, there is a treasure on one of its islets from a galleon that was lost[17] on that coast. From this inlet (*boca*) one goes by sandbanks (*placeres*) and keys inhabited by savage Indians to the bay (*ensenada*) called of Carlos. And from it to the Bay (*Vâya*) of the Holy Spirit the coast is northwest to southeast. And the Port of Tampa is four leagues further. At six from the beach (*playa*) of Pusâle, the river of Pojoy; at twelve, that of Tocopâcas. Twenty to Majuro and another twenty to Guaza. And three to the Port of St. Martin [the Suwannee] and at twenty that of St. Marks, province of Apalachee. From there one goes by a small bay (*ensenada*) eighteen leagues to Matacojo, where, they say, Fernando de Soto built brigs (*vergantines*) in order to sail it. And at three leagues from it the River Agna [the Ochlockonee] disembogues. And, rounding the point of the cape, which they call of Apalachee, and others, of Hibinieza, one comes to the small Bay

16. In Lowery's copy the name was written as Meleon and there is a marginal note, "so it appears." In the Connor copy the name "de Salinas" was written in pencil above "Melian."
17. The Spanish here is *se pedió*, but probably it should be *se perdió*, which is how I have translated it.

(*ensenada*) of Taxaquachile,[18] where the great river of Apalachocoli flows out.

On all this coast, from the aforementioned Bar of Mosquitos, which they call of Surruquê, to the river of the Tocopacas, both on the islets that they call (keys) (*sic*) (*cayos*) and on the mainland dwell thirteen nations of savage heathen Caribs in groups of huts (*rancherias*) without having a permanent settlement (*lugar fixo*), sustaining themselves solely on fish and roots of trees. They are Surruquêses, Aŷses, Santalûces, Jegas, Jobêses, Viscaynos, Matacumbêses, Baya Jondos, Cuchiagâros, Pojoyes, Pineros, Tocopâcas, and those of Carlos, who are great fishermen and divers. (Días Vara Calderón 1675)

The most valuable feature of this passage is the bishop's listing of all those people by name. Beyond that, except for the scant information he provides on those natives' food sources and settlement pattern, his account's utility is limited, being lessened by the generality of much of the data and uncertainty about the identity of some of the features and places mentioned, such as the beaches of Pusâle and Guaza. It is obvious that the bishop's "Port of Tampa" and the "River of Tampa" at 26½ degrees of the 1612 account are not the modern Tampa Bay. The large Bay of Pooy of the 1612 account is obviously the present Tampa Bay and the bishop's River of Pojoy is apparently the Manatee or the Alafia. The Majuro, rendered elsewhere as Amajuro, is Withlacoochee River.

If one excludes the ill-defined contacts resulting from the 1622 shipwreck salvaging operations, after the Cortaya expedition of 1612 Spanish authorities made no formal effort to reestablish contact with the Calusa for more than half a century. But if the friars' charges about the amber trade are valid, informal contact may have continued. Governor Diego de Rebolledo purchased amber in the latter half of 1654, but on that occasion the natives who supplied the amber lived "on the seashore close to the Bahama Channel" (Rebolledo 1657: 131). Once the Apalachee missions and the Port of St. Marks had been established in Apalachee, it is possible that ships making the run between that

18. A name with some resemblance to this, Claraquachine, appears as the name of a river flowing into what seems to be the present Ochlockonee Bay in the 1693 journal of Francisco Milán Tapia, describing the coast from St. Marks to Pensacola Bay: "This river is called Claraquachine in the Apalachina tongue." Leonard identified the river as the Ochlockonee (1939: 283, 304).

port and St. Augustine and Havana made occasional calls at Carlos, if its ruler was amenable to such contacts, or at some of the other Gulf coast settlements tributary to Carlos's ruler to trade for amber and precious metals from shipwrecks. The Calusa leader is known to have collected such items as tribute from a number of non-Calusa settlements. A ship that English pirates captured at St. Marks in 1677 had a small amount of amber on board (Leturiondo 1678: 584). However, documentation from a 1679–1680 attempt by Florida's governor to establish formal contact with the Calusa ruler suggests that Calusa maintained a "closed door" policy and that Spanish authorities, at least, were completely ignorant of developments in Calusa territory proper.

In 1679 Governor Pablo de Hita Salazar heard from Don Thomás de Medina, cacique of Timucua's Santa Fé, that through that cacique's native contacts on the Gulf coast the cacique had learned that captive Spaniards were being held as slaves at the Port of Carlos. The Potano leader allegedly offered his services for an attempt to ransom the reputed captive Europeans. The governor accepted the offer, dispatching a small Spanish force on a mission to Calusa with Medina and a troop of his warriors. Although the expedition proved to be unsuccessful, turning back before it reached the heart of Calusa territory, this episode appears to have been the catalyst for a chain of events that led eighteen years later to the dispatch of the 1697 ecclesiastical mission to the Calusa after several abortive attempts dating back to 1680.

Available documents tell us nothing explicitly about the identity of Cacique Medina's Gulf coast informants. It is probable, however, that the informants were Tocobaga from the Tampa Bay region who had been living in Apalachee for some time. These Tocobaga handled the shipment of produce from Apalachee and Yustaga to St. Augustine by a coastal and fluvial route that carried the produce to a point on the Suwannee or Santa Fé rivers. That enterprise provided ample opportunity for contact between the Tocobaga and Cacique Medina. Just a year or so prior to 1679 both the Tocobaga and Medina had contracted to carry the material possessions of migrant Yustaga whom Spanish authorities had persuaded to move to a place called Ivitanayo, where a new village was to be established to serve as a way station for travelers on the royal road going westward from the St. Johns River crossing point at San Diego de Salamototo to San Francisco Potano. The Tocobaga were to place the Yustaga's goods at a landing place on the Santa Fé River. Cacique Medina was to provide packhorses to move the goods the rest of the way to the new settlement of Santa Rosa de Ivitanayo (Hann 1988: 153; Leturiondo 1678: 596, 598–599).

The three documents that follow illustrate the phases of this 1679–1680 expedition that was to lay the groundwork for a renewed effort to missionize the Calusa and other natives of South Florida among whom no such effort had been made since the 1560s. The expedition was to descend the Santa Fé and Suwannee rivers to the coast and then head southward toward Calusa. Juan Bautista de la Cruz, a soldier who was an interpreter of the Timucuan tongue, led a small party of soldiers. At Santa Fé Medina and a group of his Indians joined the expedition. The first of the following documents is an *auto* formed by the governor to detail the genesis of this episode. The second document contains Cruz's account of his trip, given to the governor under oath upon his return to St. Augustine on February 20, 1680. The third document is the governor's letter to the king of March 6, 1680, to acquaint him with the incident and to forward the statement by Cruz.

> *Auto.* In the City of St. Augustine, provinces of Florida, on the 20th of the month of February of 1680. The señor Sergeant-major don Pablo de Hita Salazar, governor and captain general of this said city and of its provinces by the king our lord, stated that, inasmuch as don Thomás de Medina, cacique of the village of Sancta Fée of the province of Timuqua, during the past year of 1679, had given his honor an account of how, through some Indians of the coast of the sea of the bay (*ensenada*) of Apalachee, he had reports that in the port of Carlos, one of those of the said bay (*ensenada*)[19] in the settlement of heathens that there is in it, there were some Spaniards, captives of the said heathens, whom they treated as slaves. And that if his honor were to grant permission and were to give him Juan Bautista de la Cruz, a soldier of this presidio and interpreter for his language, he would go to the said port of Carlos, because of having communication with its Indians and he would ransom the said Spaniards. And after the offer of the said cacique was seen by his honor, the said señor governor, moved by compassion for saving the said Spaniards from captivity, as well as by the chance of obtaining reports about the said settlement of Carlos and about the rest of the provinces of the said coast, granted

19. The governor appears to be using the term "*ensenada* of Apalachee" to encompass the waters of the entire west coast of peninsular Florida.

permission to the said Cacique don Thomás de Medina and to the said Juan Bautista de la Cruz so that they might go and ransom the said Spaniards; and, inasmuch as today, the said day, the said Juan Bautista de la Cruz has arrived at this presidio and informed his honor of some things that are appropriate for relation to his majesty, his honor orders that he be put under oath and that, under it, he declare what he saw and learned in the course of the said trip and in what settlements he was and how many people they have; and that he be questioned in accord with the tenor of this *auto* and that the appropriate copy or copies be made of it and of the said statement and that they be delivered to his honor. And I so provide, order, and sign. Pablo de Hita Salazar Before me, Alonsso Solano, notary for the public and for the government

Declaration. In the City of St. Augustine of Florida on the said 20th day of February of the said year of 1680, the señor Sergeant-major don Pablo de Hita Salazar, governor and captain general of this said city and of its provinces by the king our lord, in fulfillment of the *auto* of the preceding page provided by his honor, ordered Juan Bautista de la Cruz to appear before him, [who is] a soldier of this presidio and interpreter for the Timucuan language. The oath by God and a sign of the cross was received from the latter in the form of the law before me, the notary. During which, and under the burden of it, he promised to tell the truth. And after the said *auto* was read to him, in accord with its tenor, he declared and stated the following. That he departed from this presidio in the company of the cacique of the village of Sancta Fée, don Thomás de Medina and [that] as soon as he reached the aforesaid village, he provided himself with what was necessary to go on a trip. And that they all embarked in canoes with some Indians from his place and descended by way of the River of St. Martin until they reached the sea at the bay (*ensenada*) of Apalachee. And they went along toward the port of Carlos, skirting the coast until they arrived at a place of heathen Indians, which is called Alcola,[20] that would have up to 300 persons. They remained in this place for three days and at the end of them

20. Swanton gave Chosa as an alternate form of the name (1922: 331). He identified it as a Calusa town. But it is not among those mentioned by Fontaneda.

they went by land to another settlement, which is named Pojoi.[21]
There they were received in a very friendly fashion. This village had
up to 300 people. As they were about to leave to continue their trip,
the chief of the said village knelt down, heathen though he was, and
begged us not to go forward because they would have to kill them.
That the Cacique of Carlos, who was the most powerful of all of
them, had ordered it because he did not want them to come to where
he had his settlement and that they were putting him in a bad
situation because he had communication with the Indians of the
Province of Apalachee.[22] And that, if the said Cacique of Carlos
learned that he had consented to let them pass on, he would order
him to be killed. And they went forward despite this and reached the
place of Elafay, which had up to forty people.[23] And they said the
same thing to them also. And without paying any attention, they
passed on to another place, Apojola Negra, which had up to twenty
people. And they told them the same also. And without paying any
heed, they moved forward again until they reached a settlement of
about 300 people named Tiquijagua.[24] Here they were much more
insistent that they should turn back. And as they were about to go on
forward, the aforesaid Indians, whom the aforesaid Cacique don
Thomás de Medina had brought from his village, fled. Finding
themselves alone after this, they decided to turn back. And they did
so without going forward any farther. And that everything that he
has stated and declared is the truth . . . and that he is about

21. Events at Pojoy support that Calusa's suzerainty reached farther north
than it had in the sixteenth century.

22. This suggests that Pojoy may have been the ultimate source of Medina's intelligence about the Spanish captives either directly or indirectly. Early
in the century when Potano was beginning to be Christianized, Pojoy was a
close enough neighbor to make war on the Potano in conjunction with the Tocobaga. And the presence of Tocobaga in Apalachee also made them a likely indirect conduit for such intelligence.

23. Swanton identified both Pojoy and Elafay as Calusa towns, based on
their appearance in this account (1922: 328, 332). But in view of their earlier alliance with the Tocobaga, it is more likely that they were not Calusa, but
rather people who had become tributary to the Calusa. Elafay is doubtless the
Alafay of later accounts (see section 3 of Part III). In 1735 Alafay was alluded to
as a distinct nation thus, "Don Antonio Pojoy, head as I am of the Alafaia Costas Nation."

24. Fontaneda mentioned a Calusa town named Yagua.

forty-five years of age more or less. And he did not sign as he does not know how.

Lord

Even though the seraphic Order of the Señor St. Francis is working at the instruction and teaching of the holy Gospel among those [natives] in these provinces that are reduced to it, with the mission band that arrived with Father Fray Alonso del Moral, I promised myself that they would move forward with the conversion of the neighboring heathens. That these provinces are surrounded by them. Some from the region of the coast of Havana [i.e., facing Havana] (*de la Havana*), others to the mainland (*a la tierra firme*), where the religious will go by way of that region, and to that of the coast, the difficult one because of that one's having been neglected and because of not having introduced any other effort with reference to it than in a place to which a religious was sent a short time ago and works there with the successful result that is desired.[25] And if they went on entering by way of two or three areas (*partes*), I do not doubt that this will be successful because of the docility of the natives, as is established by the statement of an interpreter, whom I sent with other subjects to explore and reconnoiter the land of the Cacique of Carlos in the region of the coast of the Mexican Gulf (*ensenada Mexicana*);[26] that I am stating what is evident from the copy [of his statement] which I am placing at the feet of Your Majesty and that makes me believe that there are many people in that region both on the Mexican [-facing] coast (*en la costa Mexicana*) and on the one [facing] Havana (*en la de la Havana*) and these provinces;[27] and in the center [the interior of the

25. It is difficult to decipher what the governor had in mind when he wrote some of these expressions, such as his reference to the mainland. It refers, probably, to the area from Miami north, as opposed to the Keys. The only new mission that he could be referring to that I am aware of would be the resurrection of the old missions of San Antonio Anacapi and San Salvador de Mayaca in 1679.

26. This seems to allude to the peoples of Alcola, Pojoy, etc., but no mission was ever attempted in that region, seemingly, unless one interprets Swanton's remark about Jororo to mean that he believed Jororo was located on the west coast (1946: 195).

27. Again it is unclear what the governor means by "these provinces" and by "*en el centro*," which follows.

peninsula?] a quantity of Indians camping together (*aranchados*) in various regions and all very docile except for those of Carlos, who dominate all of these, oppressing them and making them pay tribute to their great cacique, as they call him. I have not wanted to neglect giving your Majesty an account from the reports that the licentiate, Sebastian Pérez de la Cerda, curé vicar of this holy church, has given to me (that there are some clergy in the City of Cuba [Santiago de Cuba] who wish to cross over to this conversion), if Your Majesty should grant them permission for this. He has also given me to understand that he will go along, accompanying these caretakers who are of a monastic group (*a estos celadores que son de una profesion*).[28] I would leave this government post content with having left this [enterprise] started, from which I am able to promise myself its success because of the docility of the natives, who, with these priests and the fortification of the fort (*fortificación del fuerte*) in Apalachee[29] should be a restraint on those of Carlos who oppress that region. Its location and its district can be learned from the map that I am sending to the feet of Your Majesty in duplicate on this occasion. That after having seen it, he will command what pleases him. Whose Catholic and royal person may God preserve for many years, as Christendom requires. Florida, March of 1680.

Pablo de Hita Salazar[30]

In view of the failure of the governor's expedition to reach its intended target, the port of Carlos, one is left to wonder what made the governor so sanguine about the prospects of the missions that he was recommending to the crown and especially why missions were not attempted among some of those supposedly docile peoples, which would seem to be what the governor had in mind, rather than among the admittedly difficult Calusa. Governor Hita Salazar was not an inexpe-

28. It is not clear what the governor meant by *celadores*. Its usual meanings are "guard," "warden," "monitor," "curator," "attendant." Perhaps he meant to say "zealous one" (*celosos*). "Who are of a monastic group" could be an allusion to members of the Oratory of St. Philip Neri.

29. This is a reference to the short-lived fort that the governor had had constructed to protect the port of St. Marks. It was destroyed only two years later by pirates.

30. In Connor's copy of this letter, it is followed by this note: "For the absence of this map see Torres Lanzas' 'Planos Mexico y Florida' vol. 1, p. 13."

rienced neophyte in the mission-promotion field. He was aware of the problems to be encountered. The founding and the demise of the Chacato missions of the Marianna region and the Savacola mission on the Apalachicola River in present-day Chattahoochee, Florida, occurred early in his watch. In 1679 he had sent two friars up into the Chattahoochee River Valley to reestablish contact with the few Savacola who had been Christianized. Those friars were forced out after only three days by the hostility of the head cacique of Caveta (Hann 1988: 48). One would expect the Calusa chief to react similarly to any intrusion of the friars among people who were his tributaries. In 1675 Governor Hita Salazar, stressing the need for a fort on the Apalachee coast, had described the Pojoy and Calusa thus: "Heathens of Pojoy and Carlos, these are the worst." He noted that they had never given obedience to the king and that they were accustomed to kill the survivors of shipwrecks as well as neighboring Indians who were the king's vassals (Hita Salazar 1675). That does not always seem to have been the case, however. In 1668 another governor reported that a storm had forced the grounding close to Carlos of a maize ship from the port of Apalachee, noting that "with a great deal of difficulty the people had escaped" from the grounded ship, presumably (Guerra y de la Vega 1668).

The Council of the Indies was appreciative of the problem represented by Carlos. In approving of the new missions on December 3, 1680, the council cautioned, "and that in relation to the Cacique Carlos, let him strive by every good path and friendly means that may be possible to reduce him to friendship, so that with this the reductions to our holy faith may be achieved without this causing a rupture or hostility" (Council of the Indies 1680).

In relation to the missions recommended by Hita Salazar among the supposedly docile peoples, it is conceivable that attempts were made among some of those peoples and that knowledge of those attempts has not yet come to light. There is the governor's enigmatic reference about a friar who had been working with success for a short time in one of those nebulous new regions of which the governor spoke (see note 25 above). It is possible that missions that were established shortly thereafter at Jororo, Atoyquime, and Atissimi represent ventures inspired by Governor Hita Salazar's zeal. Although there is ample documentation on the Mayaca-Jororo missions of the 1680s and 1690s, no one has exploited that material to date. Evidence as to the location of the Jororo missions is equivocal. Those new missions' links with the better-known Mayaca mission of San Salvador of the upper St. Johns River Valley suggests that they were not very far to the south or west of it. A 1697 mission list placed Jororo sixteen leagues from Mayaca, Atissimi at nine leagues from Jororo, and Atoyquime at nine leagues from Atissimi (Torres y Ayala et al. 1697).[31] Jonathan Dickinson's comment on the killing of the friar at Atoyquime suggests that the Jororo missions were near Cape Canaveral. He describes the Jororo as "Cape Indians" and the town where the friar was killed as "northward of where we were cast away, but it lay within the sound" (1981: 60). But other evidence points strongly to an inland location in the lakes district from Lake George south to Lake Apopka. The Indians of Atoyquime, after killing their friar, sought refuge from Spanish retaliation by flight to the vicinity of a coastal village named Yuamajiro. A reference to the Jororo as living on islands and very large lakes also indicates the above-mentioned lake region (Solana 1697). Thus the Jororo proved far from docile. They killed a soldier and some Christian natives as well as a friar just prior to the launching of the short-lived Calusa mission of 1697. Swanton notes that some time after 1726 Indians known as Macapiras were associated with "the Pohoy in a town called Jororo" (1946: 195). In a 1726 census of the native villages around St. Augustine, the Macapiras (or Macapexos) were identified as Indians of la rinconada, a name associated with Jororo territory as has been noted earlier (Benavides 1726).

Whatever were Governor Hita Salazar's intentions and expectations, his March 1680 letter to the crown reproduced above precipitated a chain of events that led seventeen years later to the dispatch of the 1697 mission to the Calusa after several abortive attempts, the first of which dated from the latter half of 1681. The first consequences of the governor's letter can be traced in the following comments from the Council of the Indies. The first of these pieces reflects the council's action upon receiving the governor's letter and its enclosures and its fiscal's assessment of their content.

Council
On October 21, 1680.   That the señor fiscal see it.
    The fiscal, in view of this letter from the Governor of Florida and the copy that accompanies it, in which the statement comes that an

31. This 1697 list placed the San Salvador mission at twenty-six leagues from St. Augustine, ten beyond Anacapi, but the 1655 mission list placed Mayaca at thirty-six leagues distance from that center. Other documents from the 1690s dealing specifically with the Mayaca mission place Mayaca in the range of that thirty-six league figure.

interpreter made whom he sent to reconnoiter the regions of those provinces, states that keeping in mind the advances that the new conversions have achieved with the arrival of the Franciscan religious that Fray Alonso del Moral brought over, but that it will experience difficulty in being able to handle an operation in the region of the coast of Havana because of having abandoned (*dexado*) the said region and that if they were to send *doctrineros* by way of two or three regions (*partes*), it would be possible to achieve the conversion of the said coast because of the natives being docile except for those of Carlos, to whom they are subject.[32] For this purpose he also proposes that it would be appropriate to send some clergy from the city of Cuba who desire to cross over to the said conversion and the licentiate, Sebastian Pérez, curé vicar of the holy church of Florida, has offered to work in it and dedicate himself to it. From this and from the rest that is contained in the report from this letter and from the statement of the interpreter who reconnoitered the said regions, it appears appropriate that every concern be devoted to the said conversion and that the council should deign to take the measures that are most suitable for its good success with the means that this governor proposes, to whose judgment the fiscal leaves it. Madrid, December 2, 1680.
Within the decree

Council   Florida

At the time of going to interpret in the secretariat the dispatches that flow from the enclosed letter from the Governor of Florida of March 6, 1680, about the clerics from the bishopric of Cuba who say they wish to cross over to the new conversions of those provinces, the following observations have suggested themselves:

1. that the Council order that the Governor of Cuba be written to so that he may see to it so that the priests may cross over to Florida whom the governor of the said provinces alludes to. And with respect to the possibility of points of jurisdiction concerning this [operation] arising between the governor and the bishop with each one maintaining that the clerics are to cross over with his permission alone, it appears appropriate that the bishop be written

32. This seems to indicate that the council interpreted the governor's "*por la parte de la costa de la Habana*," which I rendered earlier as "the Havana-facing coast," as the west coast of the peninsula from Tampa Bay southward.

to as well, charging him with responsibility for it so that he may encourage it and assist it for his part and that he choose (*dija*)[33] the clerics who are most suitable and most to his satisfaction for the said conversions, giving a hand along with the governor for this [purpose] and that they should cross over with the license and permission of both.

2. Likewise the council orders that the clerics who cross over be given the necessary assistance from the royal treasury for that, as is done with the missionary religious. With reference to this, it is proposed that, as this assistance must be drawn from the royal coffers of Cuba, it is necessary to consult His Majesty about it because one cannot withdraw or spend anything at all from the royal coffers without His Majesty permitting it and deciding on it, consulting with him on it first. And that this assistance it appears would have to be whatever might be necessary, both for their sustenance and clothing and for their mounts until they reach the city of Havana; and that they stay there waiting for the arrival of the ship that the governor and royal officials of Florida send to Havana each year for flour, provisions, and other things that the soldiery needs, in order that they may be transported [there] in it, also giving them what is necessary for the embarcation, for there is no passage by sea or by land from [Santiago de][34] Cuba to Florida. And with respect to there not being any proprietary royal officials in [Santiago de] Cuba, as they are deputies (*thenientes*) of those of Havana, it will be necessary to command these that they should order those of [Santiago de] Cuba that they should make the expenditures that may be necessary with the said clerics until they arrive in Havana, and to the royal officials of Havana that they should assist them from the day that they reach it until the one on which they sail for Florida, with the portion that the council should indicate for each day for their sustenance or that it be left to the judgment of the Governor of Havana and of the bishop of Cuba (who ordinarily resides in Havana) so that they may indicate what may be necessary and indispensable. And to the royal officials of Havana that they should provide what may be necessary for the navigation from there to Florida, consulting His Majesty about all this.

33. The context here seems to call for *elija* or "choose." In modern Spanish there is no form such as *dija* for the verb *decir*, "to say."

34. "Santiago de Cuba" is written in brackets above the line in the Connor copy of this document.

3. It will also be necessary that the council indicate the number of clerics who are to cross over from Cuba to Florida because the governor did not allude to it. And that the council should keep in mind that there are no more funds of His Majesty in the royal coffers of Florida than the *situado* that is brought over from that of Mexico for the sustenance of the soldiery of that presidio [and that] is given and granted to each one of the seventy religious who are employed in the *doctrinas* of the Indians of Florida, with the salary of a soldier's position, which is 115 ducats of silver per year for their sustenance and clothing, as the Indians do not pay any tribute at all to His Majesty, nor have there ever been any entrusted to private individuals.[35] And if clerics from Cuba are to cross over to Florida, it will be necessary to order the viceroy of New Spain to increase the *situado* by as many soldier's salaries as there are clerics. And it is not known whether the clerics will be able to sustain themselves in Florida among barbarous Indians with what a religious sustains himself, because the clothing and manner of living of the friars is very different from that of the clerics. And this increase in the number of positions is also a point for consultation.

The council, after having seen everything, will order what is to be carried out so that it may take effect.

Council on the 10th of December 1680.

That it is to be written to the bishop, that the clerics are to be those who wish to cross over voluntarily; the assistance and provisions, as is proposed by the secretariat; and the stipend, once they arrive in Florida, the same as is given to each religious.

As a consequence of these recommendations by the council, the king sent orders to the governor at Havana and to the bishop of Santiago de Cuba for the establishment of missions in south Florida with resources

35. The last clause alludes to *encomienda,* which was not introduced in Florida. Encomienda was an assignment of tributes and services from an Indian community to favored individuals or reserved to the crown itself. The system was designed practically to assure an adequate supply of foodstuffs and Indian labor for the Spanish community and theoretically to provide for the Christianization and acculturation of the natives. The *situado* is the royal subsidy for the maintenance of the Spanish presence in Florida, granted from the surplus funds of the royal treasury in Mexico because Florida's development was far from adequate for generating revenues for paying troops, officials, and religious persons supported by the crown.

and personnel from Cuba. The king instructed the bishop to appeal to his secular clergy for volunteers to work among the Ais and Calusa and he ordered the governor at Havana to outfit and supply the volunteers and provide their passage to Florida out of royal funds available in Havana and Santiago.

In response to the appeal made by Bishop Juan García de Palacios, five priests from Santiago de Cuba volunteered for the projcted new missions in August 1681. Leader of the band was a canon of Santiago's cathedral, the learned Doctor Juan de Cisneros. The canon's example inspired several of the volunteers to make that commitment. As youths they had attended classes in grammar, arts, and theology taught by the canon. Father Sebastian Pérez de la Cerda of St. Augustine's church, who had first suggested such a secular-staffed mission to Governor Hita Salazar, was also a disciple of Canon Cisneros. One of these volunteers, Thomás de Fonseca y Haze, served as assistant to the pastor at Santiago's cathedral church and chaplain for its choir. Another of the volunteers, Francisco Bejarano, served as head sacristan and master of ceremonies there.

Despite the weakness of this response and opposition to the departure of Canon Cisneros among Santiago's civic leaders, the bishop gave the appearance of forging ahead with plans to dispatch the mission, informing the governor of Havana of the response to his appeal and asking the governor to provide living expenses for the volunteers during their stay in Havana, to outfit and provision them, and to provide passage to Florida for them. To cover the cost of the volunteers' mounts and other expenses of their trip to Havana the bishop appealed to Santiago's governor, Francisco de la Guerra y de la Vega, who had served earlier as governor of Florida. Guerra y de la Vega responded that he had no funds available for that purpose but would notify the bishop should any funds become available. But even after receiving the *situado* funds for Santiago's presidio, Guerra y de la Vega refused to divert any money from the *situado* account to dispatch the clerics to Havana, even though the *situado* account owed more than 4,000 pesos to the royal coffer in Santiago for advances the treasury officials had made from royal funds to provide sustenance for the soldiers while the governor was awaiting the arrival of the *situado* funds from Mexico. The syndic, speaking for the town council, argued that Canon Cisneros could not be spared because of his educational work and his obligations as canon of the cathedral and protested to the crown, asking the bishop to delay the departure of Cisneros until the crown could be heard from on this issue. Governor Guerra y de la Vega's obdurate refusal to provide funds to send the priests to Havana led the bishop to document the steps that he had taken to carry out the king's orders and the obstacles and objections to the mission raised by the king's political authorities in Santiago and to send the documentation to the Council of the Indies for resolution by the council and the king. Guerra y de la Vega's conduct effectively stalled the bishop's first effort to launch the mission, as the five secular volunteers never left Santiago.

The strength of Bishop García de Palacios's commitment to the mission is suspect, even though he gave the appearance of being willing to forgo the services of Canon Cisneros for the benefit of the mission. A later source indicated that a mere 300 pesos would have sufficed to send the five volunteers on to Havana in 1681 (Royal Officials at Havana 1689). That seems to be a sum the bishop himself could have provided as a gift or a loan or one which he could have secured from a pious lay benefactor. Later, an itinerant Augustinian friar, who volunteered to recruit people for the mission, offered to finance the entire enterprise with support from such benefactors. But it is possible that local political opposition to the departure of Cisneros influenced the bishop's decision to refer the matter to the Council of the Indies for resolution rather than acting more decisively on his own. It is conceivable, nevertheless, that both Palacios and his successor, in their involvement with this enterprise, were merely posturing and going through the forms of complying with the orders sent from Madrid.

It is equally conceivable that all or some of the volunteers themselves did not really expect to go. Bishop García de Palacios must have been aware that the crown would look askance at the canon's absence without the canon's having giving up his benefice. That all the volunteers who held sinecures insisted on retaining the remuneration for those positions while they were absent in Florida does not seem to ring true for supposedly selfless men willing to face the rigors of life on a mission frontier.

The documentation available on actions taken by the Council of the Indies is scanty. The council began its deliberations on the matter in mid-1682 unaware whether the initial volunteers had been dispatched or not, but it considered delay of their departure a distinct possibility. By February 1683 the council resolved to tell the bishop that if the five volunteers had not yet left Santiago, Canon Cisneros was not to be allowed to leave with them. If the volunteers had already left, Cisneros was to be permitted to proceed, but the three-year leave from his obligations as canon granted him by the bishop was not to be extended.

At the instigation of Havana's governor, the bishop, despairing of attracting additional secular clergy for this mission, suggested that the mission be entrusted to the Jesuits, who were said to be interested in establishing a college in Havana, or to the Dominicans, who were established there already. The council rejected that suggestion, fearful of its potential for generating jurisdictional conflicts between the newcomers and the Franciscans, who had exclusive control of the missions elsewhere in Florida. The council chose instead to inquire of the Franciscans whether there were sufficient Franciscans in Florida to staff the new missions and, if not, whether it would be possible to increase their number to enable the Franciscans to undertake that responsibility. Nothing is known of the outcome of those inquiries except that the Franciscans seem to have made no move at this time to assume that responsibility (García de Palacios 1682).

We do not have any additional indications of the instructions sent by the crown to its authorities in Cuba down to 1687, but presumably the initial reliance on secular clergy continued to be considered a viable option. On September 30, 1687, the crown again ordered the governor and the bishop of Cuba to appeal among the secular clergy of Cuba for recruits for missions in south Florida. In April 1689 a new bishop reported that only three priests had responded to his appeal. The three were Canon Cisneros, Father Thomás de Fonseca y Haze (now a canon as well), and Francisco Bejarano of the 1681 mission band. The bishop maintained that Cisneros and Fonseca y Haze could not be spared, noted that the others who had volunteered earlier had since died, and concluded that the objectives envisioned by the king could not be achieved through reliance on the secular clergy (Charles II 1690; Ebelino de Compostela 1692). By the time the crown's new orders were acted upon and responded to, Diego de Ebelino de Compostela had replaced García de Palacios as bishop upon the death of the latter (Leturiondo 1700: 197).

In the meantime news from Florida gave new impetus to the king's determination to see the missions established. Florida's governor reported that during his visitation of Apalachee early in 1688 he had talked with "the son of the Great Cacique of the Keys of Carlos," who had been sent by his father with many of his leading men to give obedience to the crown and to inform the Spanish authorities that he and his people were ready to accept the Catholic faith (Quiroga y Losada 1688). In the wake of this development the crown seems to have suggested that the bishop should try harder to raise volunteers in Cuba for the new Florida missions. The new bishop issued a third appeal for volunteers addressed to the "Dean and chapter of our Holy Cathedral Church of the city of Santiago de Cuba, our dearest brothers, to the beneficed pastors, exemplary priests, and virtuous clergy of this our entire bishopric" to undertake the missionization of the provinces of Ais and Carlos as the Florida Franciscans did not have the personnel to establish missions there (Ebelino de Compostela 1690).

Six months after the bishop's third appeal at the start of 1690 and after having received two pessimistic letters from the bishop, written early in 1689, ruling out Cuba as a source of volunteers, the king appealed to the Franciscan provincial in Florida in September 1690 to undertake the work in south Florida, reminding him that earlier that year twenty-six new friars had sailed for Florida under the charge of Fray Rodrigo de Barrera. The king ordered the provincial to send the friars that he found to be most fitted for that task, but specified that they should be "mature men of a suitable age and skilled in the languages spoken by the Indians of those regions to which you are to send them and that they be experienced in the teaching and administration of the holy sacraments to Indians of other *doctrinas* so that the communication and management of their ministry may be easier for them in the new conversions to which you are to dedicate them" (Charles II 1690).

It is not known what pretexts the Franciscans used to ignore the king's order, but the Florida friars' probable lack of the language qualification specified by the king would have provided an excuse. But a continued shortage of friars was probably the cause. If Governor Quiroga y Losada is to be believed, many of the 1690 mission band of twenty-six new friars were soon transferred to Cuba and several troublesome friars were shipped back to Spain. A number of the existing missions of northern Florida lacked friars (Quiroga y Losada 1690). In June 1692 and September 1693 the crown repeated its orders to the Franciscans in Florida to provide friars for the new missions. In a 1693 report to the crown the Florida friars' provincial council made no mention of Calusa while noting the progress being achieved in the recently established relatively southerly missions of San Salvador de

Mayaca, San Antonio de Anacapi, and Concepción and San Joseph de Jororo (Provincial Chapter of the Province of Santa Elena of Florida 1693).

By the beginning of 1690 even more urgency had been given to the pressure for a Calusa mission by the Calusa chief's visit to Cuba late in 1689 in response to an invitation from the bishop. The bishop described the visit thus: "And on the 3rd of December, feastday of the Apostle of the Indies, St. Francis Xavier (a favorable and fortunate omen), he came through my doors bringing in his company two brothers, two sons, the captain of his arms, whom they call the great [captain], and up to twenty Indians to whom they give the titles, nobles and knights (*cavalleros*), asking for holy baptism and offering the conversion of all his vassals in circumstances in which the most high providence and mercy of the lord shines forth" (Ebelino de Compostela 1690).

Early in July of 1692 the bishop reported to the crown on his continued efforts to achieve the missionization of the Ais and Calusa. Not long after the failure of the bishop's 1690 appeal for volunteers became evident, an itinerant Augustinian friar from the Lima viceroyalty caught the bishop's eye. This friar had been working in Cuba as a revivalist, conducting parish missions and rebuilding rundown churches. The Augustinian, named Francisco Romero, acceded to the bishop's entreaties and agreed to recruit some Augustinians for the projected missions. However, Romero was unable to obtain approval from the local Augustinian prior, who refused to give his blessing to the enterprise despite the bishop's warning that the prior would bear moral responsibility for all the souls that might be lost thereby.

The bishop then sent Romero to Spain to recruit twelve priests there from his order for the missions of Ais and Calusa and gave Romero documents attesting to his virtues and asking the crown to facilitate the departure of Romero and his band for the Indies. On reaching Spain, Romero left at once for Rome, unaware allegedly that the king had ordered Romero to report to the Council of the Indies as soon as he arrived in Europe. On his return from Rome, Romero was not permitted to undertake the mission, even though he claimed to have the twelve recruits that he had sought and the requisite financial support from benefactors in Cuba, which would free the crown from all financial responsibility for the new missions.

The council was no more favorably disposed then toward the introduction of another religious order into Florida than it had been back in the early 1680s when Bishop García de Palacios had suggested recourse to Jesuits or Dominicans. In October 1693 the council's fiscal stated unequivocally that the new missions should be given to the Franciscans as Florida was their territory (Council of the Indies 1695). Fear of jurisdictional disputes with the entrenched Franciscans was doubtless a factor as well as the bad impression probably generated by Fray Romero's involvement in an imbroglio with the Spanish ambassador at Rome, not to mention the impression left by Romero's having hurried off to Rome before contacting the council. The king's 1680 decree that first ordered establishment of missions among the Calusa and Ais with secular clergy from Cuba had cautioned the bishop explicitly to "determine the regions into which they are to enter for the new conversions . . . in such a way that they do not infringe upon or interfere with the work of the religious of St. Francis and so that they will not at any time be able to manage to meddle in those [conversions] which they have established already, nor in those which they may be likely to establish in the future from those bases, so that you may strive to put special care into avoiding (as I charge that they avoid) any whatsoever problems or disputes over territories and jurisdictions, which might arise with time" (Charles II 1680). Introduction of a "loose cannon" like Fray Romero contained too much potential for such disputes.

In view of the Florida Franciscans' inattention to royal orders to provide friars for the new missions of south Florida and especially for those among the Calusa and the Ais, the crown began to intervene more directly to secure establishment of the new missions. In response to one of the king's orders to that effect, the Florida provincial sent a veteran missionary to Spain to bring back a new band of friars, some of whom were to be assigned to Carlos and Ais. When that friar approached the council for permits and money for the passage of fourteen new friars for Florida, the council insisted that four or six out of the fourteen were to be assigned definitely to the Calusa. To forestall their diversion to another mission upon arrival in St. Augustine, the council stipulated additionally that the mission band destined for Carlos was to "leave directly from the port of Havana without stopping in Florida [i.e., St. Augustine] and that the governor and the royal officials of Havana should give them the necessary supplies for their passage and the ornaments and everything necessary for their ministry and for their sustenance in advance. That stipend that belongs to them is also to be sent from Havana, deducting it from the *situado* that comes from Mexico and is assigned for the Province of Florida." The crown specified also that the remainder of those fourteen new recruits were to be assigned to the already established but relatively new conversions of Mayaca, Jororo, Anacapi, San Antonio, and San Joseph.[36] Fray Feliciano López, the friar who came to fetch the new recruits, was to be director of the mission to the Calusa (Council of the Indies 1695; López 1695).

Fray López met several of the qualifications set by the crown in 1680 and 1690 for the priests to be chosen for that mission, namely, that they be mature men with experience as pastors and capable linguists. Fray López had almost twenty years' experience working among the Indians of Florida and in 1688 was portrayed by the Franciscans' Commissary General for the Indies as "one of the best ministers, the most capable in the languages of those Indians that the province has" (Chumillas 1688). But at the time Fray López received that tribute, he was under a cloud with the council for having joined with two other friars to prevent the execution of an English pirate, Andrés Ransom. The council had ordered that the three friars be exiled to a convent on the remotest frontier of New Spain. The council acquiesced apparently to the commissary general's plea for compassion. He asked that the guilty parties be given "the regular penance within their own province" that was proportionate to their guilt as established after an investigation, noting that the "difficulties of exiling them to a place so far away are manifest because of the degree that they will be missed in the Province and the hardships that they are bound to suffer in so distant an exile" (Chumillas 1688).

It was at this time, seemingly, that the administration and supplying of the Calusa mission was transferred from St. Augustine to Havana. Back in 1680 and later, the crown had stipulated that the Cuban clerics chosen for the mission proceed to St. Augustine and that once the missions were founded, the priests in them should receive their stipend and supplies via St. Augustine. This was doubtless a reaction to the delays and problems the project had experienced since 1680 and influenced by an awareness of St. Augustine's royal officials' possible hostility toward Fray López and of the city's chronic supply problems.

On this occasion the mission band encountered no roadblocks such as that raised by Governor Guerra y de la Vega in 1681 in denying funds for the first volunteers' journey from Santiago to Havana. Fray

36. San Joseph and Jororo are one mission named San Joseph de Jororo. The crown undoubtedly meant to say either La Concepción de Atoyquine or Atissime (see Hann 1990: 91–93, 507–509).

López and the five recruits that he chose set out from Havana well supplied on September 11, 1697. On reaching the Key of Bones (Key West or Cayo de Huesos)[37] in one and one-half days, they tarried there for almost two days before continuing on to Carlos, which they reached early on September 18. Showing a healthy mistrust and fear of the Calusa, the master of the sloop anchored at a considerable distance from the Calusa's head settlement on a small key of about half a league.

A new young cacique came out to meet the friars and Fray López accompanied him to the village of sixteen houses. This new cacique was probably the "great chief's" son who had visited Apalachee in 1688, as Fray López recorded the new chief's having conversed with him soon after his arrival in a mixture of Apalachee and Timucua. Although the Calusa's initial reception of the friars was moderately friendly, the natives' attitude soon turned markedly hostile once they realized that the friars' presence would not mean a steady supply of provisions and gifts of clothing as compensation for their acceptance of baptism.

The Calusa grew steadily more hostile as the weeks passed, subjecting the friars to pummeling and other indignities and even to threats of death. The young chief and others seem to have been disposed to kill the friars, but they were restrained by the old chief, by a brother of the new young chief who was the "great captain," and by other leaders who warned that such extreme action would bring sure retaliation from the Spaniards in Cuba and from Apalachee. After about two months of this tense situation the friars acknowledged the futility of the mission effort and asked the cacique for canoes in which to leave. While pretending to carry the friars' remaining provisions, clothing, and church furnishings down to the canoes, the natives made off with everything, leaving the friars only what they themselves carried down to the landing place. Over the next several days while the friars were being ferried to the Keys, the several groups of Indians who accompanied them or Indians whom they encountered stripped them of their remaining supplies and baggage and even of the clothing that they wore except for their undershirts.

After the friars spent about a month in the Keys on the verge of starvation and to some degree in the service of the natives there, they were rescued by the same Spanish ship master who had brought them.

37. The English name *Key West* is doubtless a corruption of the Spanish name. *Huesos* is pronounced somewhat like "west." The key is believed to have been the site of a major native charnel house.

Traumatic as the experience must have been for the friars, we can be grateful that they suffered and survived those indignities. Upon their arrival in Cuba an inquiry held by the authorities into the experiences of the friars produced records that add significantly to our knowledge of Calusa ethnography and ethnohistory and that would not have been generated but for the friars' misfortune.

These documents provide details on the population of the Calusa's head village and on the Calusa population as a whole; on relations between the Calusa and the natives of the Keys; and on features of the temple in the main Calusa village and on the structure in which the chief lived. The documents reveal much about the psychology of the Calusa and their continued confidence in the superiority of their own system of beliefs over that of the intruders. A number of the Keys or the villages on them are identified by their native names. Various witnesses set the total Calusa population in 1697 at about 2,000 people. Fray López noted that upon the friars' arrival the Indians at the Key of Carlos amounted to about 400 men and he described the children as innumerable. Because the women remained at home indoors he had not seen them at the time he wrote the letter except for the twenty or so in the chief's house. During their first thirteen days at the Calusa village the friars were lodged in a part of the chief's house while they were building a structure of their own. That the large population of this head village was housed in only sixteen structures indicates that all were large communal structures like that of the chief, similar to the five structures of 1743 at the mouth of the Miami River mentioned by the Jesuits as housing "up to one hundred and eighty people" (Alaña and Monaco 1743, 1760). It is not clear whether these Calusa structures of 1697 were as impermanent as those mentioned by Bishop Días Vara Calderón in speaking of the thirteen south Florida tribes in general, but that this was the case is suggested by Fray López' remark about the roof of the cacique's house. He noted that it provided poor protection from sun and rain and that even the evening dew entered freely.

Perhaps the most fascinating account presented in the documentation for the 1697 mission is the description of the natives' temple structure. Fray López portrayed it as "a very tall and wide house" with a mound in the middle and a structure on the mound all closed in with reed mats and containing benches (*barbacoas*) around the walls. The walls were covered entirely with masks that were colored red, white, and black, "one worse than the other" as Fray López put it. The principal idol had a nose two yards in length. The masks doubtless were similar to those pictured in Marion Spjut Gilliland's *Material Culture of Key Marco, Florida* (1975).

These documents reveal the Calusa of the 1690s to have been as sophisticated or streetwise as the natives in the Miami area, who told the Jesuits in 1743 that the clothing that they expected to receive for their nominal conversion to Christianity had to be something better than burlap, which they despised as associated with blacks. The invitations to establish the missions both in the 1690s and the 1740s seem to have been issued solely with the expectation of receiving gifts from the Spanish authorities. In 1697, after allowing two children to be baptized, the young chief remarked that the friar should give him the clothing that the king had ordered him to give on such occasions, observing, "because if he was not going to give him clothing and food, it was no good to become a Christian and no one would want to become one." In this stand the chief anticipated the attitude noted by the Jesuits in 1743 that the natives' idea of conversion was that "without their doing any work, the king our lord is to support and clothe them, and not with burlap (*cañamaso*), which they despise as identified with blacks, and that he is to furnish them with rum" and that the natives were to be allowed to continue their own traditional religious practices (Alaña and Monaco 1743). It was to be a regime of "idols and altars" and not simply "idols behind altars."

In this 1697 encounter the Calusa displayed a wry sense of humor at times. The captain of the sloop that brought the friars to Calusa testified that when the Indians saw some hoes among the goods being landed, "those who were streetwise (*ladinos*) asked why they had not brought blacks who might dig with the hoes, because the Indians did not know how to hoe." And, by implication, they had no intention of learning.

Behind the Calusa's seemingly mercenary attitude toward conversion lay a firm adherence to their traditional religious system. The constancy and vigor of that belief is epitomized in several remarks made by the Indians. The earliest was a warning delivered in secret by two of the more cautious native leaders that the friars should stay indoors because all the natives "were annoyed because their God was irritated with them because they had welcomed them [the friars] and allowed them there." Fray López then noted, "And when I told them that my God was more powerful than their Holy One, they told me not to jest and that I should take care how I proceeded" (López 1697). The same strong belief is reflected in a remark by the young chief that "just as the Christians could not cease to be Chrisians and live without the rosary, neither could they abandon their law and become Christians."

The same fidelity to traditional beliefs characterized Jororo as well, if Dickinson's account of the killing of the friar at Atoyquime is reliable. Dickinson reported that the townspeople were "much incensed against the friars" for winning their chief to Christianity and "therefore would have their Casseekey renounce his faith and put the friar to death; but he would assent to neither: therefore they killed him and one friar" (1981:60).[38]

These documents also graphically reflect the ethnocentrism and lack of compromise of the friars' approach to the conversion of the natives and, particularly, their determination to begin their labors with the destruction of the natives' religious center and to challenge the natives' religious practices boldly. That determination produced several dramatic encounters between the friars and irate natives. When the friars made their first sortie to the natives' temple (of which Fray López remarked, "They say [it is] the house of Mahoma"), the natives fled, fearing perhaps that their god was about to loose a thunderbolt to chastise the imprudent intruders. The Calusa's alleged adoption of the name "house of Mohammed" for their temple may be another instance of their wry sense of humor. It certainly illustrates their familiarity with Spanish culture. Despite a warning to Fray López from the "great captain" that the Indians would kill them if they dared to return to the natives' church while the natives were engaged in their ceremonies, the friars persisted. On another night, on hearing the hubbub from the natives' temple, the friars set out to reprehend them. Donning fine red surplices and carrying lanterns and a statue of the Blessed Virgin, the friars set out to confront their competition. A short distance from the native temple Indians armed with darts and arrows met them to block their progress. When Fray López made a lunge in an effort to push forward, one of the Indians picked him up bodily and carried him back to where the other friars were. Then, one of the friars recounted, the natives "picked the others up with violence and ill usage and brought them to the house [where the friars lived]."

In the physical abuse that the Calusa inflicted on the friars, the natives showed statesmanlike restraint in stopping short of killing the

38. A Spanish source identified the murdered cacique as "a young cacique native of Aypaja" (Solana 1697).

friars, aware of the retaliation that such conduct would surely bring. In this the Calusa's behavior contrasts sharply with that of the Jororo, who only months before the launching of the Calusa mission had killed a friar working among them at Atoyquime and then shortly thereafter killed a soldier from a troop sent to apprehend the culprits, investigate the fate of the friar at Atissimi, and secure the church ornaments. The soldier who was killed had punctured a foot on the trip down from St. Augustine and was left behind to recuperate among the seemingly friendly people of the village of Jororo. When the expedition returned after having been led astray and then abandoned by guides furnished by Jororo, the soldiers found Jororo abandoned and their comrade and several Indians who worked at the church murdered and the church there desecrated. Four years later the crown was still insisting that Florida's governor take steps to apprehend and punish the perpetrators of the murders in Jororo territory. But no retaliation against the Calusa seems ever to have been contemplated. The Calusa leaders seem to have had a fine appreciation of the parameters within which they could move with impunity in ridding themselves of the friars.

These are but a few of the highlights and insights into the mind of the Calusa to be found in these documents, which give us a glimpse of the Calusa's world just before it entered the period of dissolution that followed the destruction of the Spanish missions of Apalachee and Timucua in 1704 and 1705. Removal of the barrier afforded the natives of southern Florida by the chain of missions extending across northern Florida left the rest of the peninsula, or the *rinconada* as Governor Zúñiga y Zerda called it, open to raids by the Creek and other groups allied with the Carolinians. Before long south Florida natives from Tampa Bay to the Keys would speak of Uchise and Talapuce as their inveterate enemies. Surprisingly, the first repercussions were felt as early as 1704. In that year the chief of Cayo de Huesos (Key West) migrated to Cuba along with another group of Indians (Güemes y Horcasitas 1743). By 1711 the terror had reached greater proportions, moving thousands of the natives of south Florida to request transport to Cuba.

A possible explanation for the rapid spread of this violence is that its perpetrators had already established themselves in Florida to some degree prior to the destruction of the missions in 1704. The leader of a 1701 Spanish expedition to the Mayaca-Jororo country, which assembled at San Francisco Potano, was instructed to spend some time in the woods and environs of the La Chua hacienda "to clear the land of *yndios cimarrones* (proto-Seminole?), who had been wandering in them for some years" (Zúñiga y Zerda 1701). Six years earlier a Timucua from San Pedro de Potohiriba (in present-day Madison County) out in the woods for a Sunday afternoon's hunt spoke of encountering four hostile Apalachicola as though it were a not uncommon occurrence (García 1695). The already mentioned Yamasee, reported as present in Mayaca territory with Spanish permission as early as 1680, would have been well positioned for launching or leading sweeps down to the Keys as early as 1704. In the 1670s a Tama or Yamasee band, at first believed to be Chisca, terrorized missions in Apalachee and western Timucua (Jones, Hann, and Scarry 1991: 155).

The following excerpts and notes from a 1711 letter by Cuba's bishop illustrate the dimensions of the panic that had seized south Florida's natives.

> In the past month of February of this year a ship entered this port, which came from the keys that border on the entrance to the Bahama Channel and the mainland of Florida. The heathen Indians of the chiefs, Carlos, Coleto, and others live in those keys. And some of the above-mentioned Indians who came in the aforesaid ship told me about very serious persecutions and hostilities, which they are experiencing and which they have experienced on other keys, which the Indians whom they call Yamasees have destroyed. That the Yamasees have killed some of the aforementioned Keys Indians; have made others flee; and that they have captured the greater part of the latter, whom, it is said, they carry off and sell, placing them into slavery at the port of St. George [Charleston, S.C.] of the English Nation (Valdés 1711).

The bishop informed the king that many of the surviving Indians of south Florida wanted the Spaniards to transport them to Cuba so that they might become Christians. In this letter the bishop detailed his efforts in raising funds to achieve that goal and contributing money himself to arrange the needed transportation. As a result two ships were sent, and on their arrival,

> on not encountering the above-mentioned Indians in the aforesaid Keys because they were then some distance off engaged in a savage war with their enemies, the Yamases, the aforesaid Captain Perdomo sent word of his arrival and he [the chief of Carlos] decided to come with a brother of the said chief and other Indians of the first

importance in order to discuss and arrange in this city for the best way of bringing them over and saving them because all those of that province are disposed to become reduced to our holy Catholic faith. And in fact the said captain brought about two hundred and seventy of them to this city [Havana] and stated that he would have brought more than two thousand if he had had the ships and that those who are seeking baptism amount to more than six thousand. (Valdés 1711)

On the arrival of the 270 refugees and on learning of the magnitude of the projected migration, the authorities expressed concern over the cost to the royal treasury of such an operation. But, prodded by the bishop, they met in a junta held at the bishop's palace to consider what action should be taken to bring over the rest of the Indians and to maintain them until they could be settled in Cuba. The majority decided against bringing over any more without an express authorization from the king for such an expenditure of royal funds. They remained firm even when the bishop continued to press for immediate action and offered to assume responsibility for the money if necessary (Valdés 1711).

A later governor, referring to this migration, gave the number of migrants as 280 and the year of the migration as 1710. He identified as being among the leaders of those migrants the hereditary chief of Carlos, his "great captain," the chief of Jobe, the chief of Maimi, the chief of Concha, the chief of Musepa, the chief of Rioseco, and "the principal chief who took Your Majesty's glorious name at his baptism." That governor went on to note that "when the latter died along with three other chiefs and up to two hundred Indians from the violent illnesses brought on by the weak constitution that they have manifested, the remainder split up, with some being taken into private homes and with some sixteen or eighteen returning to the Keys according to the information that has been sought diligently." The governor remarked that a similar outcome had resulted from the migration from Key West of 1704 and from other later migrations, concluding that it would be better to leave them in the Keys and to minister to them there if they were genuinely interested in becoming Christians. (Güemes y Horcasitas 1743). The result of his decision was the abortive mission effort of the two Jesuits in 1743 (see Part III). They found the attitude of the remnant of the Calusa, Tequesta, and Keys Indians to be no different than that of their forebears in 1697.

One wonders whether the outcome of the late seventeenth-century effort to Christianize the Calusa would have differed if it had been launched earlier, either in 1681 as originally contemplated by Cuba's bishop or in 1688–1689 when the Calusa chief who requested missionaries still controlled his people. But the old chief's attitude in 1697 and his people's steadfast devotion to their own religious heritage suggest that the outcome would not have been much different than it was in the 1560s and in 1743.

In addition to its ethnographic content, the documentation for the three Calusan mission efforts is particularly valuable for the insights it provides into the natives' reactions to the missionaries' efforts to introduce the Christian view of the cosmos. There is no parallel documentation for the mission efforts among either the Apalachee, Guale, or Timucua. The following documents reflect the genesis of this mission effort, highlighting its developments from the royal order for the mission late in 1680 through the launching and expulsion of the mission in the latter half of 1697 and the postmortems held in Havana early in 1698.

THE DOCUMENTS

The documentation for the late seventeenth-century mission is presented in roughly chronological order. The documents are grouped in assemblages that reflect discrete episodes through the seventeen years between the king's initial order for the mission late in December 1680 and the landing of five Franciscan friars at the Calusa's principal settlement in September 1697. In some cases the assemblages of documents that illustrate the various episodes were made by participants in the process. In other cases I have put together the documentation for individual episodes.

1. The Initial Move, 1680-1682

Juan García de Palacios, bishop of the island of Santiago de Cuba, put together the documentation included in this first assemblage. The bishop's purpose in doing so was to send evidence to the king and to his Council of the Indies of the efforts he had made to execute the king's orders and of the problems that he had encountered that required further action by king and council.

The first piece in this section is the bishop's appeal to the secular clergy of his diocese. In Santiago de Cuba, the bishop's seat, a special invitation was issued to all the clergy of the city, the secular authorities, and the populace at large to attend High Mass on August 24, 1681, to hear the bishop's appeal. The bishop's secretary read the appeal from the pulpit after the singing of the Gospel. The secretary dispatched copies of the appeal to the rest of the parishes of the island of Cuba, including those of Havana, which was then under the jurisdiction of the bishop of Santiago.

A copy of the king's decree of December 26, 1680, forms the core of the bishop's address to his clergy. The king's order indicates unequivocally that it was the letter from Governor Hita Salazar, discussed in the preceding introduction, that moved the monarch to this action. The king assured the bishop and sent orders to his lay officials that the expenses of the recruits were to be borne by the royal coffers at Santiago de Cuba and Havana and that ultimately the *situado* for Florida would be increased to provide a yearly soldier's stipend for each of the volunteers once their number was certified by the royal officials at St. Augustine. The government at Santiago de Cuba was to provide for the needs of the volunteers until they should reach Havana. Thenceforward the governor at Havana was to see to their needs and arrange for their transport to Calusa territory. The monarch cautioned in particular that the territory assigned to the missionaries be clearly defined so that there would be no opportunity for their intruding upon territories considered to belong to the Franciscans of Florida or for their meddling in the established missions.

Autos of Don Juan García de Palacios, Bishop of Santiago de Cuba, August–December, 1682

AGI, Seville, Santo Domingo 151. Photostat from the Stetson Collection of the P.K. Yonge Library of Florida History of the University of Florida. In the Stetson Collection the assemblage bears the following identification: AGI 54-3-2/3, Santiago de Cuba, January 20, 1682, 70 pp. The large bundle of photostats has two separate library covers. The first bears the following notation (in Spanish) on the bundle's contents: "Testimony from the *autos* that have been made in this city by the Illustrious sr. Dr. Don Juan García de Palacios, bishop of this Island of Santiago de Cuba, of the council of his Majesty, in order to carry out a royal decree of his Majesty in which he orders that the clergy who might wish to cross over to the new conversion in the provinces of Florida are to be outfitted from the royal treasury." The second cover bears the following brief caption (in English): "AI 54-3-2/3 1682. January 20   Cuba   6 pp. + 70 more pp. The Bishop of Cuba to the King relative to religious matters in Florida, with covering *consulta del consejo* of September 31 [*sic*], 1682." The first six pages of the Stetson photostat represent the "covering *consulta del consejo*," which is the second group of documents below, as it postdates that put together by the bishop. The bishop's assemblage begins on page 7 of the photostat.

Testimony of the *Autos* that have been made in this City of Cuba by the Illustrious sr. Don Juan García de Palacios, Bishop of the Island of Santiago de Cuba, of the council of his Majesty in order to give fulfillment to a royal decree from his Majesty in which he ordered that the clerics who wished to cross over to the new conversions of the provinces of Florida were to be outfitted from the royal funds. It is written on thirty-two pages.

We, Doctor Don Juan García de Palacios, by the grace of God and of the holy Apostolic see, bishop of this island of Santiago de Cuba, Xamayca, and provinces of Florida, of the council of the king our lord, etc. To all the priest clerics of our obedience, health and grace in our Lord Jesus Christ, who is the True Health. We are informing you how his Majesty the king our lord with his most pious and Catholic spirit, desirous of the spiritual health of his vassals and of the conversion of the heathens to the body of our holy Catholic faith, was pleased to issue his royal decree, the tenor of which is as follows.

Decree
The King. Reverend in Christ, Father Bishop of the Cathedral Church of the city of Santiago de Cuba, of my council. Don Pablo de Hita Salazar, who has just completed his term as governor and captain general of the provinces of Florida, in a letter of the sixth of March past of this year of one thousand six hundred and eighty reports that even though the Order of St. Francis serves with its *doctrinas* and posts for the teaching of the Holy Gospel to the Indians who are reduced to it in those provinces with the mission that Fray Alonso del Moral of the same order brought over, it was promised that there would be progress in the conversions of their neighboring heathens. And that the said provinces are surrounded by them, some on the side of the coast of Havana and others on the mainland, where the religious worked on that side because they made it difficult on that [side] of the coast because of having left that and because of not having made an effort except in one place to which a religious was sent a short time ago. The latter [religious]

was working there with the successful results that were desired. And that if they were to go entering by two or three regions, he [the governor] had no doubt that they would be successful because they [the Indians] are docile by nature[1] as has been proved by the statement of an interpreter that he sent along with other people to reconnoiter and explore the land of the cacique Carlos on the side of the coast of the Gulf of Mexico. Concerning this it is established further by the testimony that he sent and that he gave to understand that there were a great many people in those regions both on the Mexican-[facing] coast and on that [facing] Havana and in the provinces of Florida [i.e., the mainland] a quantity of Indians camping together on various sites in the center and all very docile. And that the licentiate Sebastian Pérez de la Cerda, curate vicar of the parochial church of the city of St. Augustine, reported to him that there were some clerics in our province of Cuba who wished to cross over for this conversion, if I would grant them permission for it. And that he gave him to understand likewise that he would go with them. And the governor said that he would leave office content if he were to leave this mission behind established [successfully], as was promised by the docility of its natives and with these priests and the building of the fort that he has established in the province of Apalachee[2] [with which] he was hoping to achieve this intention. And when this had been seen in my Royal Council of the Indies along with what my fiscal requested, and having held a consultation [on it] taking into account the great number of heathen Indians that the governor of Florida reports that there are in different parts of those provinces and especially on the Mexican-[facing] coast and on that [facing] Havana and that all of them are of a docile character and that the religious of St. Francis who are engaged in *doctrinas* of the Indians [who are] already reduced and Christian could not assist in the new conversions of the heathens, I have resolved to ask you and give you the responsibility, as I do by the present [order], that as soon as you receive this dispatch you are to publish it in all the cities and places of the district of your diocese and bishopric so that its clerics who wish voluntarily to cross over to the new conversions of Florida, the

1. The Spanish here is *naturales* or "natives" rather than *naturaleza,* which is what seems to be called for to fit the context.
2. This alludes to the fort at St. Marks in Apalachee that was viewed as being somehow a curb on any hostile action by the Calusa.

coast [facing] Mexico and that [facing] Havana may do so, congratulating you for your part in all this to the extent that it may be possible in order to facilitate their passage. And of the clerics who are inclined to go, you shall choose those who are most suitable to your satisfaction, giving them a hand for this along with my governor of the city of Santiago de Cuba (as he has been ordered to do by a decree of this same date), regaling them with your permission and leave and his. And I am giving orders similarly to the royal officials of the city of Havana that they command the deputies whom they have in my royal treasury of Cuba that they should give whatsoever maravedis and monies that there may be in it or that may enter into it to the clerics who go in this fashion for the rations and the outfitting necessary for the trip from this city of Cuba to that of Havana for both their sustenance and their clothing and for their mounts and that they may make the expenditure for this that may be necessary and that from the day that they arrive at Havana until the one in which they embark for Florida in the ship that the governor and the royal officials of those provinces dispatch to it each year for flour, supplies, and other things that the soldiery needs, they are to assist them from my royal treasury with the portion that you and my governor of Havana assign to them for each day for their room and board. By a decree of this date I make you and the said governor responsible for this and for whatever else may be necessary and unavoidable. And I command the royal officials of Havana that they are to provide them with whatever is necessary for the voyage from there to Florida, with one and the other executing all of it in the way that is provided for and that is practiced with the religious missionaries. And I charge them that they are not in any case to permit that any one of the clerics among those who dedicate themselves to the aforesaid new conversions should remain in any other area or that they should wander away to other [areas], but rather [they shall see to it] that they pass precisely to them as the religious are ordered to do [who are sent on such missions.] And in relation to there not being any more money in my royal treasury of Florida than the *situado* that comes from Mexico for the maintenance of the soldiery of that presidio, I am sending a command to my viceroy for New Spain to increase the *situado* by so many soldier's salaries (that each one receives one hundred and fifteen silver ducats per year) as there are clerics who cross over, in accord with the number that it is established by a certification from the royal officials of Florida that they constitute. And that he will make good what these salaries amount to and remit them along with the rest of the *situado* for the aforesaid presidio so that they may support them with them from the day that they arrive at the city of St. Augustine of Florida. And I am giving orders to the governor and royal officials that they execute it in the way that they do with the religious of St. Francis who are stationed in the *doctrinas* for the Indians of those provinces, so that with this they will have what is necessary for their sustenance and for their clothing. And I am charging the present governor of Florida that he should reach an agreement with you and with the governor of Cuba for the better disposition of what is contained in this dispatch. And I charge you similarly that you should strive as much as you can on your part, on joining forces for this [purpose] with the governors of Havana and Cuba, [to see to it] that the clerics whom you choose and who cross over are mature people and good living priests with good habits and all the rest of the necessary qualities to a sufficient degree, so that they can be employed in the position of pastors in the new conversions of the Indians soon after they arrive in Florida, and that they see to it that the expenditure from the royal coffers of Havana and Cuba that is made on them, both in the said cities and from the days that they depart from them and from the rest of the places belonging to both governments that comprise the diocese of your bishopric until they embark in the port of Havana in order to proceed on their voyage to Florida and what they give them for the voyage and sailing be [only] what is necessary and unavoidable with total moderation and a good accounting and without any superfluity, working out with both governors that which pertains to each one and with you having an agreement with them and in accord with them. That this is the order that was sent to the governors under the [same] date as this one. And you are to give me an account of your receipt of this dispatch and of what you may do in fulfillment of it so that I may have a report concerning it. And you shall report to the governors of Florida with full precision the number of clerics who cross over to those provinces together with their names so that it may be known who are the ones who were sent and that they are going destined for the purpose alluded to. And you will determine the regions into which they are to enter for the new conversions for the heathen Indians in such a way that they do not infringe upon or interfere

with the work of the religious of St. Francis and so that they will
not at any time be able to manage to meddle in those [conversions]
that they have already established nor in those which they might be
likely to establish in the future from those bases, so that you may
strive to put special care into avoiding (as I charge that they avoid)
any whatsoever problems or disputes over territories and
jurisdictions that might arise with time [and] that the one and the
other may be engaged in the conversion of the souls assigned to
them and that belong to them. Done in Madrid on the twenty-sixth
of December of the year of one thousand and six hundred and
eighty. I the King. By order of the king our lord. Don Joseph de
Veita Linage. [It continues:] And so that what is contained in the
royal decree may have the requisite fulfillment that the most ardent
zeal of his Majesty desires by so many and such mild methods, we
order the present edict dispatched, by the tenor of which we exhort
and most affectionately beg and charge all the priest clerics of this
city of Santiago de Cuba and of that of San Christóval de Havana
and of the rest of the places of this island and to all those of our
bishopric who are desirous of dedicating themselves to the apostolic
ministries of missions and who might wish to be employed in the
new conversion of the heathens of the provinces of Florida and in
the administration of the holy sacraments, following in this the
advice that Christ our Lord gave through St. Luke in Chapter 15
with the parable of the one who, having lost one sheep out of the
hundred, left the ninety-nine in order to set free from danger and
save the one who was lost, in it giving us to understand the great
joy that his divine Majesty and the holy angels in heaven possess in
seeing one sinner redeemed. In compliance with this counsel of the
Lord, let this be a motivator so that all of our beloved sons, the
priests, may be encouraged and may exert themselves to sacrifice
their own comforts in order to save one soul for God and to bring
him to the fellowship of his church and let those who so dedicate
themselves manifest themselves before us, those of this city, and
those of the city of Havana and the rest of the places of our
bishopric before our vicar general and their ecclesiastical judges
within eight days of the publication of this our edict so that, after
choosing the most suitable ones and the ones of proven virtue as his
Majesty commands, [we may go on] to make the rest of the efforts
that we are ordered to in the aforesaid royal decree. That they will
be given everything necessary for their provisioning and for their

sustenance in the said provinces of Florida as is expressed in the
said royal decree. That in doing this, they will do a great
service to God our Lord and to his Catholic Majesty and
particularly to our liking because of what will be achieved
in the salvation of the souls and conversion of so many
heathens as there are in the aforesaid provinces, in which there is
no doubt but that they would gain great and eminent merit before
the divine Majesty and from whose powerful hand they would
receive many temporal and spiritual rewards. And we would make
the adjustments [that are] possible in maintaining their title to
their chaplaincies that do not require personal attendance at the
altar. And so that it may come to the attention of everyone, we
order our edict published in the holy cathedral church of this city.
And by our attorney general (*Promotor fiscal*), I summon all the
priest clerics of this city and [order] that copies of this our edict be
sent to all the vicars and ecclesiastical judges of the towns and
places of Bayamo, Puerto del Principe, where there are resident
clerics until one reaches the city of Havana so that our procurator
and vicar general may order it published in it and the other vicars
and ecclesiastical judges in their places. And we are sending a copy
of it with the nomination of the clerics who are destined for so
apostolic a ministry so that we may proceed on the basis of that
knowledge to the rest of the efforts and to the outfitting of them
and the giving to them of what is necessary for their journey and to
the rest that his Majesty ordered in his royal decree. Given in our
episcopal palace of Santiago de Cuba on the twenty-third day of the
month of August of the year one thousand six hundred and eighty-
one. Juan, bishop of Santiago de Cuba. By order of the bishop my
lord. R. Juan Fernández de Vergara, secretary

The following document by the bishop's secretary, dated August 26,
1681, attests to the publication of the bishop's appeal for volunteers
and describes the manner in which publication was effected in Santiago and elsewhere on the island.

Publication
I, the B^r Juan Fernández de Vergara, priest, secretary of the
chamber and government of the Illustrious señor don Juan García
de Palacios, bishop of this island of Santiago de Cuba, Xamayca, and
provinces of Florida, of the Council of his Majesty, etc., my lord, I

certify and give witness in the manner in which I am able to, how, in accord with what was ordered by his Illustrious Lordship through his *auto* of the twenty-first of August of this present year, the convocatory of the preceding pages was dispatched with the insertion of the royal decree of his Majesty for the purpose contained in it. I read and published the latter in the pulpit of the holy cathedral church of this city of Santiago de Cuba in a loud and intelligible voice on the past Sunday which is reputed to be the twenty-fourth of the said month of August at the High Mass after the Gospel had been sung in the presence of his Illustrious Lordship the aforesaid bishop my lord and of the venerable señores dean and cabildo of the said holy church and in the presence of the clergy and the secular cabildo of this city and a great concourse of people who were present, who had been invited for that said purpose. And similarly convocatory edicts were dispatched for the purpose alluded to [and] that they were published in the parish churches of the city of San Christóbal de Havana and of the towns of San Salvador del Bayamo and Puerto del Principe. And so that it may be evident where it is appropriate, at the order of the said my lord bishop, I furnish the present in the city of Santiago de Cuba on the twenty-sixth day of the month of August of the year one thousand six hundred and eighty-one. In witness of the truth. B^r Juan Fernández de Vergara, secretary

Five priests, all from the city of Santiago, responded to the bishop's appeal. The volunteers included a canon and two other priests who held positions on the cathedral staff. From these petitions I present only excerpts that suffice to identify the volunteers, to indicate the nature of the petition, and to note the conditions under which they offered their services. A formal statement followed each of the petitions, in which the bishop's secretary, acting as an ecclesiastical notary, attested to the validity of the petition of each of the volunteers. The secretary's statements are omitted.

Petition
Illustrious señor Thomás de Fonseca y Haze, priest, chaplain of the choir and assistant to the vicar (*Theniente de Cura*) of the holy cathedral church of this city and master of ceremonies in it, I appear before your Illustrious Lordship and I state that in accord with the edict that was published in the said holy church on the

twenty-fourth of the present month and year by virtue of the royal
decree of the twenty-sixth of December of the past year of eighty in
which his Majesty was pleased to determine that some clerics from
this city and bishopric should cross over to the new conversions of
the heathen Indians of the coast of Florida [facing] Mexico and
Havana, with the favor of God our Lord I would like to cross over
for the said conversion to achieve the result that the royal piety
desires. [He goes on to ask permission to retain the income from his
chaplaincy.]
Thomas de Fonseca y Arze

Petition
Illustrious señor Francisco Bejarano, priest, head sacristan of this
city by his Majesty, appears before your Illustrious Lordship.
. . . [He asked to retain his position as head sacristan and to
continue to receive the salary that went with it as well as the
stipends from the chaplaincies that he served.]

Petition
Illustrious señor Vicente de las Heras, domiciliary priest of this
bishopric. . . .

Petition
Illustrious señor Juan Troncoso, priest, patrimonial son of this city
and general preacher of this bishopric. . . . [He goes on to describe
himself as] "finding myself unoccupied with any ecclesiastical
ministry that could interfere with his departure because of his not
having any [benefice] that demands personal residence except for
some chaplaincies. The latter do not have designated altars or a
church in which they are to be served. . . ."

Petition
Illustrious señor The Doctor Don Juan de Cisneros Estrada
Luyando, canon of the holy cathedral church of this city of Santiago
de Cuba, appears before your Illustrious Lordship in that way and
manner that is most appropriate for the service of both Majesties
and I state that having heard and understood the royal decree
inserted in your lordship's convocatory edict. . . . [He asked
permission to keep the income from his benefice in order to support

his family and to be able to assist some poor people who depended on him.]

The five petitions are followed by a formal statement by the bishop on September 3, 1681, attesting to the suitability of the candidates and stating that he would write to the governor at Havana to learn whether he would have the financial resources to support the missionaries while in Havana, to outfit them for their mission, and to provide them passage to Florida to begin their work in Calusa territory. Ascertaining this was appropriate, the bishop noted, before expending any funds from the royal coffers at Santiago to outfit the volunteers for the trip to Havana.

Auto
In the city of Santiago de Cuba on the third day of the month of September of the year one thousand six hundred and eighty-one the Illustrious señor Doctor don Juan García de Palacios, bishop of this island of Santiago de Cuba, Xamayca, and provinces of Florida, of the council of his Majesty, etc., my lord. He said that with reference to his Illustrious Lordship having issued a convocatory edict in conformity with what was ordered by his Majesty with his royal decree inserted in it, directed at all the clerics of this bishopric who might wish to cross over to the new conversions of the Indians of Florida, that they should present themselves before his Illustrious Lordship. And the aforesaid edict having been published in the holy cathedral church of this city on Sunday, the twenty-fourth of August, five suitable and adequate clerics, residents of this city, presented themselves for the said ministry, dedicating themselves to the said conversions with the desire of serving God and his Majesty. And because, in conformity with the said royal decree, he orders that they be outfitted from the city of Havana to the said provinces of Florida, it will be advantageous that they give news of this to the señor Field Master don Joseph Fernández de Cordova Ponse de León, Knight of the Order of Calatrava, governor and captain general of the said city of Havana, so that in the case that the señor governor of this plaza should outfit them [for the trip] from this city, he may arrange beforehand in that one for the sustenance of the said missionaries and their passage in conformity with the order from his Majesty in the aforesaid royal decree. And

in the latter he reported that it would be dispatched in them to the said señor governor of Havana, because if there were some problem in the said city on account of not having the wherewithal in those royal coffers, it would be a loss of money for the royal funds from the coffer of this city to outfit them without having the appropriate passage [to Florida available] in that one. I was ordering and ordered that a letter be written to the said governor and captain general of Havana. His Illustrious Lordship is ready to write this so that he may advise him whether he has the wherewithal for the outfitting of the said missionaries, so that he may take the appropriate resolution in accord with what he replies in order to give complete fulfillment to the royal will of his Majesty. And so that this may be evident, he ordered that it be placed as an *auto* that he provided and signed. Bishop of Cuba. Before me, B^r Juan Fernández de Vergara, secretary

In the document that follows, Francisco Ramos, syndic procurator general for the city of Santiago de Cuba, objected on various grounds to the departure of Canon Cisneros for the Florida mission. First and foremost, Ramos complained that Canon Cisneros's departure would leave the cathedral shorthanded, as one of the other canons was then residing in Castile. Ramos noted, apropos of this additional absence of Cisneros, that the crown had repeatedly forbidden beneficed clergy to be absent from the churches that they were appointed and paid to serve. Ramos also stressed the educational services that Canon Cisneros provided for the youth of the city. Only a few excerpts from his lengthy petition are presented here.

Petition
The Ensign Francisco Ramos, syndic procurator general of this city of Santiago de Cuba. . . . It was the will of his Majesty and has always been that beneficed clergy should not absent themselves or depart from their churches, as he has repeated in various decrees, from which it is plain that, if it were the will of his Majesty that the canons, pastors, and other ministers should leave for the said conversion, he would have said that already in the aforesaid decree [of December 26, 1680]. In addition it is well known in this city that the señor Doctor, Don Juan de Cisneros was occupied and is so presently in teaching grammar, [and] reading arts and theology with [people] having profitted from his teaching, such as the

licentiate Augustín de Castro, who today is pastor of this city; the
Doctor Don Sebastian Pérez de la Cerda, who is pastor of Florida;
Francisco Bejarano, head sacristan of this said city; Thomás de
Fonseca y Haze, assistant to the pastor; Juan Troncoso; Diego
Bezerra Gallon, *cura doctrinero* of the village of San Luis de las
Caneyes, all persons who at present hold titles of preachers general
for all the bishopric and who have benefited greatly from his
teaching. And the affliction of the students who currently are
pursuing the course of grammar will be great because of not being
able to go on to higher studies. Nor would they be able to go to the
kingdoms of New Spain to achieve it, nor to that of New Granada
[Colombia] because of the supreme poverty of their parents. For it is
certain that, were it not for the charity with which he teaches
them, they would not be able to undertake the aforesaid studies."
[Ramos goes on in this vein for another page and concludes by
asking the bishop in the name of the city that he not select Canon
Cisneros for the Florida mission until the king could be heard from
in this matter.]

The next twenty-odd folios contain documents that are not presented
here. Many deal with formalities. For the rest it will suffice to note the
nature of their contents. The first few pages deal largely with formalities. Sandwiched between those documents is a petition by Canon
Cisneros dealing with the issues raised by the syndic Ramos. The second round of formalities is followed by an *auto* that records a session
held on September 12, 1681, in which the bishop informed the five clerics formally that they would be permitted to go to Florida and that the
objections raised by the syndic to the departure of Canon Cisneros
would be ignored. The bishop assured the canon that he would receive
his salary as canon for three years, counted from his departure from
Santiago de Cuba, but subject to any modification that the king might
make to the bishop's resolution of the matter. The next document is
the bishop's appeal to the royal officials of Santiago de Cuba to provide
the funding necessary to enable the missionaries to proceed overland
from Santiago to Havana. The bishop reminded those officials of the
provision in the royal decree that the clerics who volunteered for this
mission were to be outfitted for that journey and have their other travel
expenses paid from the royal treasury at Santiago de Cuba. In that appeal the bishop also defended his right as bishop to permit the absence
of the canon for a limited time for such a good cause. The bishop indi-

cated as well that others among the city's clergy were capable of taking up the canon's teaching responsibilities. The bishop's appeal for funding is followed by more documents dealing with formalities and then by an exchange of letters between the bishop and the governor at Santiago de Cuba dealing with the issue of funding. The exchange closed with a certification by the royal officials of Santiago that there were no funds available there for sending the missionaries to Havana or with which to outfit them in any way. The officials noted that they were borrowing money to maintain the soldiers in the area to supplement the relatively few maravedis collected locally. And one official remarked that since 1671, when he assumed the office, the books did not show any assets from the *situado* as having been received in Santiago. This series closes with an exchange of letters between officers of Santiago's cabildo and the bishop, treating of the impasse created by the lack of financial means to send the missionaries on to Havana.

As a contrast to the lack of assistance to the mission and to the outright opposition to it of the civil authorities at Santiago, the bishop then introduced an *auto* containing an excerpt from a letter from the governor at Havana that highlighted his cooperation. Havana's governor had pledged that if he could not find the requisite funds in the royal coffers, then he would provide for the missionaries out of his own salary.

Auto

In the city of Santiago de Cuba on the fifteenth day of the month of December of the year one thousand six hundred and eighty-one the Illustrious señor Doctor Don Juan García de Palacios, bishop of this island of Cuba, Xamayca, and Florida, of the Council of his Majesty and my lord. After having seen the *autos* made in fulfillment of the royal decree of his Majesty in the matter of the missionaries that he orders to be placed in the provinces of St. Augustine of Florida, he said that in order that the efforts that his Lordship had made looking toward the fulfillment of the aforesaid royal decree might be evident, he was ordering and ordered that the present secretary place as part of this *auto* a copy of a paragraph of a letter written by the señor governor and captain general of Havana to his Illustrious Lordship dated in this November of this year in which he manifests the zeal that he has for cooperating in what it contains looking on his part toward making effective what was ordered by his Majesty.

And by this *auto* he so provided, ordered, and signed. Juan, bishop of Santiago de Cuba Antonio B^r Fernández de Vergara, secretary.

In accord with what was ordered by his Illustrious Lordship in the above *auto,* I the present secretary caused to be copied and copied the paragraph of the letter that the señor governor of Havana wrote to his Illustrious Lordship, that in it he was ordered to do, dated the second of November of this present year, whose tenor is as follows.

Letter
"About what Your Illustrious Lordship said to me in the [letter] of the twenty-sixth of August about the clerics who have shown enthusiasm for crossing over to the new conversions of Florida and in relation to what his Majesty orders that they be supplied from these coffers with what appears to Your Illustrious Lordship and to me sufficient for their sustenance while they are in this city and that they should be given the provisions that they would need in order to cross over to the province of Florida in his Majesty's frigate that comes to this plaza, he will give entire fulfillment even though the wherewithal does not exist in them, even if it should be necessary to furnish it from my own salary. And thus your Illustrious Lordship can send them on their way. With respect to the [new] (?) frigate of Florida (according to what they tell me), it will be here in December as a result of which there will not be much time to lose [blotted out word]. I have expounded to the precursor of your Illustrious Lordship [so that] (?) similarly *lo targa* understood for those who were to come from the places of this jurisdiction and to one that his Majesty gives the guide in his royal decree, that what is done with the religious missionaries of our father St. Francis be done with the clerics who would be going to these conversions. From that I understand that what seems proper to your Illustrious Lordship should be assigned to them daily for their sustenance. Therefore, in order to do what is best in this and in everything, I shall observe that which Your Illustrious Lordship considers to þe best."

It agrees with the paragraph of the said letter of the señor governor and captain general of the city of Havana. That for the purpose of making this copy, his Illustrious Lordship, my lord bishop gave the original to me, in whose possession that to which I refer remains. In virtue of the said mandate I give the present [certification] in the city of Santiago de Cuba on the fifteenth day of the month of December of the year one thousand six hundred and eighty-one. In witness of the truth. B^r Juan Fernández de Vergara, secretary.

Finally, there is a letter of December 18, 1681, by Bishop García de Palacios to inform the crown that an impasse had developed to prevent his moving forward with the mission. The bishop revealed that since October, when the governor had first pleaded a lack of funds, *situado* monies had arrived, but that the governor steadfastly refused to pay any money from the *situado* funds into the royal coffers to repay a 4,000-pesos debt owed to those coffers from the *situado* account.

Auto
In the city of Santiago de Cuba on the eighteenth day of the month of December of the year one thousand six hundred and eighty-one the Illustrious señor Doctor Don Juan García de Palacios, bishop of this island of Cuba, Xamayca, and Florida, of the Council of his Majesty, etc., my lord. After having seen the *autos* that have been made in order to give fulfillment to his Majesty's royal decree of the twenty-sixth of December of the past year of [one thousand] six hundred and eighty in which he was pleased to order that the clerics in this city who were destined to cross over for the new conversion of the heathens of the province of Florida were to be outfitted from whatsoever Royal possessions and maravedis that there might be in the royal treasury of his Majesty of this said city until they reach that of Havana. And having seen also the reply that the señor Don Francisco de la Guerra y de la Vega, governor and war captain of this said city gave to a written proposal (*consulta*) from his Illustrious Lordship on the ninth day of the month of October of this year in which, despite the great zeal that he has for the service of God and of his Majesty, he told him that, because of not having the wherewithal on that occasion in the royal coffer, he would not be able to outfit them; that when he had them, he would notify his Illustrious Lordship so that they might confer on what would be necessary for the outfitting of the said clerics. And his Illustrious Lordship, considering that the *situado* for this presidio has come already, given at the order of the said señor governor and

remitted by his Lordship for his Illustrious Lordship, and that it is owing more than four thousand pesos to the royal coffer of his Majesty according to what is established by the certification that Don Jacinto Osorio de Pedroso, lieutenant of the royal officials of the city, gave. From this one supposes that there are means of the Royal Treasury for outfitting the said clerics, all the more inasmuch as it is a debt that is owed to his Majesty. For this reason it should be paid in preference to any other debt whatsoever that the aforesaid *situado* owes. Therefore I was ordering and ordered that a *consulta* be dispatched to the aforesaid señor governor [with] this *auto* inserted in it, so that, with the great zeal that he has he might place in execution the mandates from his Majesty [that] he was pleased to send, as his Illustrious Lordship begs him to with complete affection. That from the said *situado* he should restore the aforesaid four thousand pesos to his Majesty or at least the quantity that would be necessary for the outfitting of the said clerics who have offered themselves with such great fervor for the aforesaid mission, for if we do not take advantage of the present opportunity, it could come to be that on another [occasion] people so ready for the aforesaid exercise will not be encountered, from whom his Illustrious Lordship is promised the result that his Catholic Majesty the King our lord intends. For with much less than the aforesaid four thousand pesos there would be plenty for the said outfitting, with respect to which the señor governor of Havana has written to his Illustrious Lordship that he will provide the supplies for them from that city to Florida even if he must supply it from his salary [because of the great(?)] desire that [word blotted out] to see the order of his Majesty carried out with full promptitude because of what it means for the service of God and for the spiritual welfare of those poor heathens and that he wants to see them in that city as soon as possible as he is expecting a vessel from Florida in it in which they can obtain their passage to it, motives on account of which his Lordship the said señor Governor Don Francisco de la Guerra y de la Vega on his part should cooperate in a work so much in the service of God and of his Majesty, ordering them outfitted as his Majesty orders and as his Illustrious Lordship expects from the great Christianity and zeal of the aforesaid señor governor. And by this *auto* I so order and sign.

Juan, Bishop of Cuba Before me, B^r Juan Fernández de Vergara, secretary.

On the eighteenth day of the month of December of the year one thousand six hundred and eighty-one a third consultative letter[3] was dispatched to the señor Governor Don Francisco de la Guerra y de la Vega with the insertion of the *auto* of this page, to whom I delivered it closed and sealed in my own hand, today, the day of the date. And I give witness to it. B[r] Juan Fernández de Vergara, secretary.

The assemblage of documents made by the bishop runs for another five pages, devoted mainly to legal formalities. The motive of the bishop was to forward all of this documentation to the Council of the Indies for a resolution to this matter by it and the king. In them the bishop also sought to demonstrate that he had done what he was able to do to carry out the order sent to him by the king to provide for the evangelization of the province of Carlos.

The packet of documents forwarded to the Council of the Indies by Cuba's bishop included the following cover letter, in which the bishop summarized the steps that he had taken to carry out the king's order of December 26, 1680, praised the cooperation proffered by the governor at Havana, and reported the lack of cooperation from the governor at Santiago that was stymieing the departure of the five volunteers. The bishop explained why he had bent the rules to accept Canon Cisneros as one of the volunteers, revealing that his example had inspired the other four and that the bishop had hoped that Cisneros's example would similarly inspire others in Havana. The bishop also expressed doubts that additional secular clergy would volunteer and suggested that to meet the anticipated need for additional priests for this Florida mission the work be entrusted to the Jesuits, giving that order permission to establish a college in Havana as a base of operations, or if that was not feasible, that the work be entrusted to the Dominicans of the Havana friary.

Bishop García de Palacios to the King, January 20, 1682
AGI, Seville, Santo Domingo 151, SC.

Sire
I put into effect at once Your Majesty's decree of the twenty-ninth

3. The term *consultivo* applied to matters that the councils and tribunals were obliged to lay before the king, accompanied by their advice.

[*sic*] of December of the past year of [16]80 which you were pleased to order me to publish in this city and bishopric so that [from] all of its clergy who might wish to dedicate themselves to the new conversion of the Indians of Florida I might choose the most suitable ones, with the governor of this plaza[4] [Santiago de Cuba] giving me a hand with it. And that the latter would outfit them with whatever might be needed until [they should reach] Havana. And that [then] the governor of that city is to give them their sustenance and the supplies for crossing over to Florida. And after publishing edicts in the holy cathedral church of this city, I sent them to the rest of the settlements of this bishopric all the way to the city of Havana. And in response to it five clerics, residents of this city, presented themselves in order to be employed in so apostolic a work as the conversion of those heathens. And after they had been recognized as being suitable for this ministry, I consulted about them with Don Francisco de la Guerra y de la Vega, governor of this plaza, so that, if it should meet his approval, he might see to it that from the royal coffer of this city they were given what was necessary for their outfitting to take them to Havana as Your Majesty orders. And the governor requested a certification from the lieutenant of the royal officials about the maravedis and royal possessions that they held in the coffer [available] for outfitting them. He gave it, saying that there was nothing at all, but noting on the other hand that the *cituación* [*situado*] for this presidio owed more than four thousand pesos to the coffer that it had furnished to him [Guerra y de la Vega] for the provisions (*socorro*) for the soldiery. And after I had conferred with the governor so that he might return the four thousand pesos to the coffer from the *situado* that was expected from New Spain, because they belong to it, so that they might outfit the missionary clerics from it and carry out the wishes and satisfy Your Majesty's most ardent zeal. Indeed much less would suffice for outfitting them. He replied to me that there was no money belonging to Your Majesty in the coffer for this purpose. And that when they should have some, he would notify me of it so that then what Your Majesty was ordering might be put into execution. And he replied once more when the *situado* arrived that he would restore

4. The right-hand edge of this page is crumbled away, eliminating part of the end word in places. Here only the P of "Plaza" remains, but the meaning is obvious. When the identity of the mutilated word is not so clear, I have put such words in brackets accompanied by a question mark.

to the coffer what the soldiers' [account] was owing to it; but that did not take place, as this all will be made evident from the testimony of the *autos,* reports, and inquiries that I have made in this matter, which I am remitting together with this [letter].

I wrote to the governor of Havana, informing him of the mandate that I had from Your Majesty so that he might make the means available on his part in that city so that when the clerics arrived they might cross over to Florida as Your Majesty orders in the decree that he said that he sent to him for that very purpose. And he replied to me that he would outfit them, even though he might have to do it from his salary. Among the clerics who have dedicated themselves to this apostolic work was the Doctor Don Juan de Cisneros, a canon of this cathedral. And although it is [stipulated] that by reason of the benefice he cannot be absent from his church, I have permitted it for the sake of these conversions and this effort, for a limited time, until such time as Your Majesty orders otherwise, because in addition to being learned and virtuous, he is a man much beloved in the city and bishopric and it was his example that motivated the others, and he was expecting that it would motivate many in Havana when they see that this person would lay aside his own calm life and its comforts solely for the conversion of those heathens. In [doing] this, I was of the opinion that it would be in accord with the pleasure and the liking of Your Majesty, who desires this conversion so much, as your piety [in this matter] is so evident in the decree and in your reminders, and because, with the experience that he has because of having been a pastor for many years in this city, he would handle the administration of the sacraments in those churches very well so that from his training of those new plants deep roots would be established.

In this business I cannot omit giving gracious thanks to Your Majesty with a full heart for such apostolic zeal for the salvation of souls as you have shown, in which you give instruction to us bishops so that we may imitate it with all the ardent desires of our soul, but as these are [still] so weak, we are left with nothing more than the desires [that it come to pass], as has happened on this occasion, although I have firm hopes that the most pious spirit of Your Majesty will provide the means for its achievement. One of the most efficacious that occurs to me from the experience that I have acquired (even though it appears like a jumping ahead of myself, for the means are so superabundant in Your Majesty's great providence), I shall not omit proposing it because of the zeal that I have to see Your Majesty's holy intention crowned with success. It is that Your Majesty entrust these conversions to the Order of the Company of Jesus, giving it permission to establish a college in the city of Havana, as that city has requested from Your Majesty and to put clergy there. And in it the religious would be received that Your Majesty should deign to send from those kingdoms [Spain] or from New Spain as missionaries, as he sent the religious of St. Francis. And they would pass over from there to the provinces of Florida. Or that they be made the responsibility of the religious of St. Dominic of the convent of that city, in which they would receive those whom Your Majesty should send, because even though five clerics are now destined for these conversions, they are few for so great a harvest, and for the future it could come to pass (it pains my heart to say it) that no other clerics will be found who will apply for this ministry, because their rule[5] and estate does not demand such great self-denial and they do not have so strict a vow of obedience as do the religious[6] that would permit their bishop to compell the ones that appear fitted for the work to devote themselves to this ministry. Indeed, for the position of pastor (*cura*) for the city of St. Augustine and chaplains of the fort there, it is necessary to beg them and to

5. The rule, or manual, that the various religious orders have spells out their obligations as members of the institute and is supposed to serve as a guide for them in their quest for perfection. Strictly speaking, secular clergy do not have any such formal rule, although bishops may have an informal code that they expect their priests to observe.

6. Here the bishop refers to another of the distinctions between the secular and the regular or ₊eligious clergy of the Catholic church. Strictly speaking, secular priests do not take vows at all, either of obedience to their bishop or of chastity, but only a promise of obedience and celibacy that is regarded as being less solemn than the formal vows of obedience to superiors and of celibacy taken by a religious priest. Under the vow of obedience a religious can be sent anywhere his superiors choose to send him, although usually the wishes of the religious are taken into consideration. Secular priests cannot be sent to serve outside of the diocese whose bishop accepted them for ordination. As Florida was part of the diocese of Santiago de Cuba, the bishop theoretically could order his priests to serve there at least for regular parish work such as that at St. Augustine or in the long-established Indian missions, but he would be on very shaky ground in ordering them to undertake the work of establishing the beachhead in a new territory. Another consideration alluded to in the bishop's remark is that secular priests do not make either a vow or promise of poverty

provide them with many special perquisites so that they will serve there. I was very greatly consoled in that those clerics dedicated themselves to these apostolic ministries, but as much as I desire the spiritual welfare of those sheep and cooperate in [my] part with Your Majesty's zeal, even though it may be in diminution of my authority, I suggest this means to the sovereign will of Your Majesty because I am of the opinion in the Lord that it is more suited for achieving that which Your Majesty orders with such outstanding piety so pleasing to God and so beneficial for the good of souls. Your Majesty will order what he finds most to his liking, which will be for the best [and] which I shall be waiting to execute with strong desire in special and submissive obedience, asking of God continually (as I do, although so badly) for Your Majesty the succession that all your vassals desire[7] and the most felicitous health, for the support of Christendom and the propagation of the Catholic faith. Cuba, January 20th of 1682.
Sire
Br & L R P rlm, the least of your chaplains
Juan, bishop of Santiago de Cuba

The remainder of the page following the letter by the bishop is blank, but in the wide margin at the left-hand side of the page in the lower half there is a note written by someone at the Council of the Indies early in 1683, when this matter apparently was being considered by the council. The piece that follows is that marginal note.

Council, 8th of February, 1683
   In order to provide better [for resolving this], let the commissary general for the Indies[8] be asked for a report and question him whether there are sufficient religious in those conversions of

---

as do religious. Although seculars, ideally, are to observe the spirit of poverty in the sense of detachment from worldly possessions, that detachment is tempered in practice by their need to provide for their own retirement and incapacitation.
   7. Charles II, the last of the Spanish Hapsburg line, is believed to have been impotent.
   8. The Commissary General for the Indies was a Franciscan who served as liaison with the crown in matters dealing with the Franciscans' work throughout the Spanish New World.

Florida and whether it would be possible to increase their number. And with reference to the canon and the clerics, let the bishop be told that if the Canon Don Juan de Cisneros has left already, allow them to go on in their avocation, but taking into account how his absence will be felt in his church, the permission that was granted to him [to be absent] for three years is not to be extended.

2. The Council's Decision, 1683

The first page of the Stetson Collection photostats from which the preceding translations were made contains a complex of notes written on the cover page for the original document by people belonging to the Council of the Indies. The principal note, which occupies the majority of the space on the first page of the photostats and all the second page, contains a summary of the contents of the bishop's letter of January 20, 1682, and the decisions reached by the council in response to the bishop's letter and the lengthy documentation that accompanied it. The council approved of the bishop's actions except for those relating to Canon Cisneros. If the five missionaries had not yet departed from Cuba when the council's orders arrived, the canon was not to be permitted to leave with the other four. If he had already departed, Cisneros was not to remain away more than three years unless he gave up his benefice. The council firmly rejected the idea of introducing Jesuits or Dominicans, affirming that if more priests were needed for the Calusa mission, then an appeal should be made to the Franciscans.

The notes on the first page of the photostats constitute something of a jigsaw puzzle as they appear in four separate columns written vertically and transversely on what appear to be two separate half-pages that face one another like the pages of an open book. The principal note begins at the top right-hand side of the right-hand half-page and continues in the right-hand column of the left-hand half-page and thence in the material written transversely in the left-hand margin of the half-page on the left. From there the continuation of the principal note is found in a five-line passage in the lower left-hand margin of the right-hand half-page, from whence it moves to the following page of the photostats. The wider column on the right-hand side of the page below represents the principal note. The briefer note that appears in the upper-left-hand margin of the half-page on the right is reproduced in the left-hand column below.

Notes by the Council of the Indies, January 28, 1683

AGI Seville, Santo Domingo 151, SC.

Cuba, 20th of January of 1682 The Bishop

Received in Galleons at the council, 31st [*sic*] of September, 1682.

The señor fiscal. And he says that as soon as the bishop received [it], charging him anew with these conversions and in the report about the Doctor and Canon don Juan de Cisneros, there is set forth the zeal with which he offered himself to go to these conversions.

To his Majesty
Having caused the decree of the 29 of December of 1680 to be published in that bishopric, five clerics of that city presented themselves to be employed in the new conversions of Florida, suitable people, and among them don Juan de Cisneros, canon of the church. And even though as such he cannot be spared from it, I permitted it and gave permission for a limited time until his Majesty does not order otherwise, because in addition to being learned, virtuous, and versed in the ministry of serving as pastor (?), he is much beloved in the city and bishopric, and the rest were moved by his example and there in Havana many will follow it.

That even though he has made repeated inquiries before the governor so that he would outfit them [for the trip] to Havana, he has not achieved it. And he wrote to the one at Havana so that he might furnish means for them to be transported to Florida when they arrive there. And he replied that he would outfit them even though he should have to do it out of his own salary. And he forwarded evidence concerning all of this. And on this occasion he proposes that the most appropriate solution would be to entrust the responsibility for these missions to religious of the Company of Jesus, giving them the permission for establishing a college in Havana that the city has begged for and should he permit having religious in it,[1] that might be sent from Spain or from New Spain as missionaries as those of St. Francis come [from Spain] and from there [Havana] to cross over to Florida, or that it be entrusted to those of St. Dominic from the convent of that city, where they would receive those who might be sent, because these five clerics are very few and it could come to pass that no others would be found in the future who would be willing to devote themselves to this ministry. The fiscal, having seen the letter of the bishop of Cuba and the evidence that accompanies it and the letter of Governor don Francisco de la Guerra of the 24th of January *of 1682* [*sic*]. That it covers all the same material. He says that he has carried out this order

1. My rendition of the poorly legible Spanish here is tentative. The Spanish appears to be *dexo* (?) *Naviendose*. A reviewer suggested *Naviendose* was meant to be *habiendose*.

that was sent to him in order that he might strive to send some secular clergy to the new conversions of Florida from the said province. Five clerics presented themselves and among them don Juan de Cisneros, a canon of this church of the aforesaid city. That it had not been possible to implement it because of not having the means with which to outfit them. And that the governor replied to him in this vein and so he reports in the letter alluded to. And the bishop reports that on this occasion the said governor suggested to them that it would be more appropriate to put the responsibility for the missions of Florida on the religious of the Company of Jesus, granting them the permission they have asked for to establish a college in Havana, or that they give the responsibility to the religious of St. Dominic from the convent of the aforesaid city. What the señor fiscal recognizes from all of this [is] that if the council should be pleased to do so, it will be able to approve of what the bishop has done, except in the case of don Juan Cisneros; and if the clerics should have crossed over [already], that they be assisted with what is necessary. That even though he granted him permission to go to the said missions for a period of three years, taking into consideration that because of being a canon he cannot be absent because he would be sorely missed in this church of so small a number [of canons]. And there being other reasons as well that were mentioned along with this one, it must be ordered that if they have not departed, then he not be permitted to absent himself. And if [his departure] is a fait accompli, the time limit for his absence is not to be extended unless he should come to give up his benefice. And that he be thanked for the zeal with which he has offered to devote himself to the said conversions. And for the future, it does not appear to be necessary to assign the responsibility either to the religious of St. Dominic or to those of the company [i.e., the Jesuits], because the religious of St. Francis, to whom they are entrusted [already], find themselves engaged in them. And all that is needed is a greater number than there are at present [and] they could be made the responsibility of the aforesaid order. Let it send the rest of the religious that would be necessary and make the adequate provisions for it by this means. And by this means adequate provision can be made, even though it may be necessary to send secular clergy, [but] not religious of other orders and the expenditures will be avoided.
Madrid, January 28th of 1683

3. The Calusa Mission Idea Resurrected, 1687

There is no documentation available to show what action was taken in Cuba or Spain in the immediate wake of the council's decision at the beginning of 1683 to veto the participation of the mission's projected leader, Canon Cisneros. Presumably the removal of Cisneros dampened the ardor of the other volunteers who were his disciples. By 1689 at least one or two had died. The death of Bishop García de Palacios sometime during this interim also probably contributed to the apparent inaction between 1683 and 1687. On September 30, 1687, the crown renewed its orders to the governor at Havana and to the bishop at Santiago to appeal to the secular clergy of Cuba for recruits for missions to the Indians of south Florida. The next two documents illustrate the renewed impetus from the crown for the launching of this mission and the response it generated in Cuba.

The first is an undated copy of a note by the governor at Havana to Santiago's new bishop, Diego Ebelino de Compostela, forwarding the renewed orders from the king relative to the Calusa mission. The second piece is a letter to the king written by Bishop Ebelino de Compostela on February 20, 1689, reporting on the action he had taken in response to the king's 1687 order and the results produced by his action. The bishop went on to suggest the need for soldiers to accompany the missionaries, whenever they should be found. The governor's note is an enclosure in the bishop's letter.

Correspondence Concerning the Royal Decree of September 30, 1687

AGI, Seville, Santo Domingo 151. Photostat from the Stetson Collection of the P.K. Yonge Library of Florida History. In the Stetson Collection this bundle no. 2782 bears the following identification: AI 54-3-2/8, February, 1689, Havana   13 pp. The Bishop of Cuba to the king relative to the conversion of Florida as ordered by the cedula of September 30, 1687.

The captain general of the artillery of the Kingdom of Sev^a, don Diego Antonio de Viana Hinojossa, Knight of the Order of Santiago, governor and captain general in this city of San Cristóbal of Havana and of the island of Cuba by his Majesty, etc.

To you the most Illustrious señor Doctor don Diego Ebelino de Compostela, most worthy bishop of this city and island, Xamaica, and Florida, of the council of his Majesty and his preacher, etc. I make known that his Majesty, whom may God protect, has deigned to send a royal decree to this (?) señor and of the *auto* and the following is the copy of its content provided.

The King. General of artillery don Diego Antonio de Viana Hinojossa, Knight of the Order of Santiago, my governor and captain general of the island of Cuba, city of San Cristóbal of

Havana or to the person or persons who are in charge of its government, on the twenty-sixth of December of the earlier year of one thousand six [hundred] and eighty, I ordered given and I gave a decree of the following tenor.

The King. Field Master don Joseph Fernández de Cordova, Knight of the Order of Calatrava, my governor and captain general of the island of Cuba and city of San Cristóbal of Havana or to the person or persons who may be in charge of its government. [This is the king's decree of December 26, 1680, which is reproduced in the first assemblage of documents. But this 1687 copy closes as follows: "Done in Madrid on the thirtieth of September of the year one thousand six hundred and eighty-seven. I the King. By order of the King our Lord. Don Antonio Ortis de Otalora."

Diego Ebelino de Compostela, Bishop of Santiago de Cuba, to the King, February 20, 1689

AGI, Seville, Santo Domingo 151, SC.

Sire

By the royal decree of the 30th of September of [1]687 that don Diego Antonio de Viana Hinojosa, governor and captain general of this plaza, informed me of by the dispatch enclosed here and by the one [directed] to the same purpose that I received, Your Majesty deigned to order the execution of the royal decrees inserted in the [dispatches] cited, to the effect that some clerics from this bishopric should cross over for the conversion of the Indians of the Gulf of Mexico and of this coast of Havana and that for that purpose they were to be assisted for their outfitting and for their departure with what was necessary. And what it occurs to me to inform Your Majesty of is that the Doctor Don Juan de Sisneros, who is the one who encouraged others to cross over to Florida for the conversion, is occupied in the precentorship of the cathedral church and don Thomás de Fonseca, who followed him in the canonry that he occupied, impediment enough for them not to be able to absent themselves, because, in addition to the serious harm from their failing to meet the obligations of their own ministry, and were this to be overlooked and the impediment not viewed as sufficient, and should they persevere in their good zeal, I have learned that there are no other clerics who might accompany them because those who voluntarily offered themselves for the making of this voyage have died.[1] And even if there were an adequate number of clerics who would resign themselves with fervor to the hardship and to occupying themselves in so exalted a ministry, and even if they were to be assisted with the support that the Catholic providence of Your Majesty deigns to order, I am convinced that it is not possible to achieve your intention, because according to the information that I have from reliable people of experience and skill, the people of the Indians are numberless who dwell on the Gulf of Mexico and on the [other] coasts and in such diverse and remote regions, some on the mainland and others on different keys, so that they are considered incapable of being counted. And on taking into account that their evil tendencies are not known from experience, inasmuch as with the religious of St. Francis as *doctrineros* and with the lay people (*seculares*)[2] they have launched some uprisings and some treacherous actions implying little fidelity because while they persevere with humility as long as they recognize benefit and subjection and it has been the experience in the presidio [St. Augustine] of Florida and in the port of Apalachee that, with respect to the soldiery, they are subject and obedient, nevertheless, in the distant *doctrinas* they have given vent to their damned wickedness. Consequently, in order to achieve success in an operation so [propitious] for the service of God and of Your Majesty, it would be most appropriate that at the same time that there are ministers who work at their conversion that they be accompanied by a garrison of soldiers who might defend them in case the Indians attempt an uprising or try to injure them, because it is very probable that it could happen as it has happened before, and this after they were reduced already and instructed in the mysteries of the faith. And this is the reason that the missionary Capuchin fathers have withdrawn, who, after having come for the reduction and conversion of the Indians of Daxiel,[3] returned to Spain because the garrison and defense for them was lacking in case of oppression,

1. This is not entirely true as it is known from other sources that at least one of the other volunteers of 1681, Father Francisco Bejarano, was still alive at this time.
2. Although the meaning here seems clearly to be "lay people" this could conceivably be rendered as meaning "secular clergy" as contrasted with "religious clergy." In these documents, *clericos* is used invariably for secular clergy.
3. I am not familiar with any district having this name. It was possibly

because they were a people commonly considered to be of little trustworthiness and treacherous on the inside and their exterior behavior of great obsequiousness and of superficially pleasing demeanor. And so that they may persevere in this manner, one must keep the military arm in sight. Above all Your Majesty will provide what contributes most to his royal service. May his Divine Majesty favor your Catholic and royal Person as Christendom needs. Havana, February 20 of 1689.

Diego, Bishop of Santiago de Cuba

The cover to the bishop's letter, which is page 3 of the Stetson Collection photostats, contains notes written in the Council of the Indies. The principal note merely summarizes the contents of the bishop's letter and its enclosure. A second note reveals that the bishop's letter was "Received with a note from Peru on the 23rd of April," presumably, of 1689.

Next is another document illustrative of the response generated in Cuba by the king's order of September 30, 1687. In it the royal officials at Havana express their readiness to make any funds possessed by the royal treasury at Havana available for the sustenance and outfitting of the mission to the Calusa. The timing of their letter to Don Jacinto de Fuentes (December 14, 1688) may indicate that it was not until that time that the king's 1687 order reached Havana.

Diego de Peñalver and Others to the King, February 15, 1689

AGI, Seville, Santo Domingo 151. Photostat from the Stetson Collection of the P.K. Yonge Library of Florida History. In the Stetson Collection this bundle no. 2781 bears the following notation: AI 54-3-2/6 February 15, 1689, Havana, 15 pp.   Royal Officials to the king acknowledging receipt of cedula of Sept. 30, 1687, re sending religious to Florida. The decree is enclosed.

Sire

In view of what Your Majesty was pleased to order us [to do] by your royal decree, dated in Madrid on the thirtieth of September of one thousand six hundred and eighty-seven directing us to strive to obtain the passage of some clerics from the city and bishopric of

---

meant to be Darien, where the Colombian coast meets the isthmus of Panama on the Gulf of Urubá.

Cuba to the new conversions of the heathens of the coasts of Florida and Mexican [Gulf] in the manner that is determined in the enclosed decree that was cited above. We wrote to don Jacinto de Fuentes and to our deputy of the accountant for the royal treasury of Cuba by a letter of the fourteenth of December of the past year of eighty-eight, that he is to give whatsoever moneys that there may be in the coffer under your charge to the clerics that may come from that city to this one in order to cross over to Florida for the purpose alluded to for the sustenance and outfitting necessary for their trip. In conformity with this we ourselves will carry out our duty [in this respect] when the occasion arises for us to do so with the means [?] corresponding to matters of such consequence, which involve the service of Our Lord and of Your Majesty, whose royal person may God preserve as Christendom requires. Havana, February 15 of 1689.

D. Diego de Peñalver [and two other undecipherable signatures]

Inasmuch as the king's decree of September 30, 1687, has already been reproduced, there is no need to reproduce the copy enclosed with this letter. The other material enclosed in this letter is also not reproduced; the one bit of information this material contains that merits attention is a remark that back in 1681 when the five secular priests were ready to leave Santiago de Cuba for Havana to prepare for the trip to Florida, a mere 300 pesos would have sufficed for their expenses from Santiago to Havana. This remark, if true, raises a question about the sincerity of Bishop García de Palacios's commitment to the mission. If the bishop's heart was in the enterprise, why was he unable to find such a sum among the diocesan revenues or in his own funds to advance as a loan, or why did he not find some lay benefactor willing to donate or loan the money that was needed to put the volunteers in Havana? After all, Fray Romero, the itinerant Augustinian of 1695, had allegedly found benefactors who were ready to finance the entire cost of the mission effort among the Calusa.

4. Calusa Visit to Apalachee, 1688

While Governor Diego de Quiroga y Losada was visiting Apalachee province soon after his installation, the son of Calusa's chief came with a retinue to render obedience in his father's name and to ask for friars.

The information appears in Governor Quiroga y Losada's report on his visit to both Apalachee and Timucua. This report also contains two letters written to the king by the chiefs of Apalachee and Timucua in their respective native tongues, along with translations of the same into Spanish. These enclosures are followed by four pages of notes written at the Council of the Indies, notes devoted largely to summarizing the contents of the governor's letter and its enclosures. Briefly, the notes reflect action taken by the council. Additional brief notes written at the council reflect developments in Cuba or in Spain as late as mid-November 1693 that relate to the Calusa mission.

Governor Diego de Quiroga y Losada to the King, April 1, 1688

AGI, Seville, Santo Domingo 839. Photostat from the Stetson Collection of the P.K. Yonge Library of Florida History. In that collection this document bears the following identification: AGI, 58-1-26, St. Augustine, April 1, 1688, letter to the king by Governor Diego de Quiroga y Losada.

The left-hand margin of the first page of the document contains an initial note very briefly summarizing the document's contents.

The Governor of Florida gives an account to Your Majesty about having made a visitation of the Province of Apalachee and Timuqua and what dispositions he left behind; and that he will go to make a visitation of the Province of Guale once he finds himself with the time to do so; he sends an attestation in the form of a letter that the caciques of Apalachee and Timuqua have written to Your Majesty showing themselves grateful that the governor had gone to visit them and other matters that are contained in it. And that if he helps them, they will build a blockhouse in Apalachee and a watchtower in the port of St. Marks because a fort cannot be built there.

Sire
In order to fulfill the obligation that I have from the office with which Your Majesty has honored me, soon after I reached these provinces, I arranged to go in person to make the customary visitation of them both because Your Majesty ordered me to and because I knew how important the consoling of these poor native Indians was for your royal service because it was so necessary. On the one hand because no governor had gone to make a visitation for

more than thirty years[1] and on the other because of seeing many of them abused and insulted from the time of my predecessor; and even entire settlements fled to the woods (*montes*), living in them like barbarians without attending to any of their obligations as Christians. That they are fewer, disappearing[2] in this fashion and becoming depopulated.[3] For this and as a remedy for it, I agreed to go together with the royal officials of this city not only to run through them, as was done, with the trade goods for provisions for the peons of the royal workshop as well as for the authority of their persons; so that the poor Indians may be comforted and become aware how much Your Majesty supports them for their preservation. And having visited the provinces of Apalachee and Timuqua, receiving their natives warmly and consoling them, I left them very content and grateful to Your Majesty to whom they give the thanks due in the enclosed letters that their caciques wrote to Your Majesty in their own language and style, [which] they gave me that I might present them in their names at your royal feet as I am doing. Of these originals and translations remaining consoled that Your Majesty would deign to see them. And Sire, not solely all the Christian chiefs offered to give due obedience and vassalage to Your Majesty, but also many remote heathens and in particular the son of the Great Cacique of the Keys of Carlos who had never before come [to render] obedience. And his father sent many of his leading Indians with him, which was of great consequence because of the pleasure with which they came to give it and to offer their submission to our holy Catholic faith and other heathens of Vasisa[4] from the sea coast and to live as Christians with villages (*pueblos*)

1. This is a reference to the visitation conducted by Governor Diego de Rebolledo in 1657 in Apalachee. However, Governor Hita Salazar in 1675 had delegated others to conduct a formal visitation of all three provinces. Governor Quiroga y Losada's predecessor, Juan Marques Cabrera, claimed to have made a visitation to Apalachee.

2. The Spanish verb here is *cavandose,* which means "digging oneself in" or "penetrating deep." It is possible it was meant to be *acavandose se,* which is the sense in which I have translated it.

3. In Apalachee a considerable number left for the Apalachicola country. Quiroga y Losada talked a number of them into returning.

4. This passage alludes to Tocobaga who settled in Apalachee at Wacissa at least as early as the mid-1670s. A mission was never established there, however.

and religious. And in order to secure this, I helped them with some trade goods and iron tools so that they might build their places. And likewise I populated those of Guacara and Vittanayo,[5] that are of Christians and that were uninhabited, assigning religious there. And under the peal of the bell I brought the rest of the places back under submission and gathered them together to their great pleasure. I composed their differences and freed these natives from the vexations and the injuries that they had received, not permitting that they should experience any now, with everyone generally becoming grateful to Your Majesty for the support that they recognized he gives them and with a strong desire to excel in your royal service. And as a demonstration of it, all of the caciques of Apalachee have offered to me that, if I help them with iron tools, they will build a wooden blockhouse (*casa fuerte*) at their own expense for the soldiery that serves there on garrison duty [and], in addition, a stone watchtower (*attalaya*) in the port of St. Marks as it is not suitable for a fort (*capaz de castillo*) and has no other defense. And I entertained everyone generally in the name of Your Majesty and from your royal account, as the royal officials will give it [i.e., the accounting], while I assisted to the extent that my resources have permitted, touched by their misery and cognizant of the loyalty and docility of these poor Indians. That because of it they deserve to be assisted by the royal protection of Your Majesty. And I was compelled to hasten my return to this plaza because of reports from the Indians of the coast that some pirate vessels were cruising along it, an occurrence that prevented me from continuing on and passing to the visitation of the Province of Guale, while keeping in mind that I must do so. As time permits I am giving Your Majesty an account of all of this, as is my obligation. For whose Catholic royal person may Our Lord reserve happy years as Christendom has need of. St. Augustine of Florida, April 1, 1688.

Diego de Quiroga y Lossada

5. Here the author refers to the mission of San Juan de Guacara on the Suwannee River where the Spanish trail crossed. Vittanayo is the village of Santa Rosa de Ivitanayo established factitiously in the late 1670s by Governor Hita Salazar when a few Yustaga were persuaded to create this stopover between the St. Johns River crossing and San Francisco Potano in Gainesville. By 1695 Ivitanayo's population had disappeared again and Guacara had been destroyed.

The first enclosure with the governor's letter is a note by Fray Marcelo de San Joseph. The note is followed by that friar's Spanish translation of the Apalachee chiefs' letter to the king. That translation is followed in turn by a translation of the letter written in Timucuan. The remaining pages contain comments and notes made at the Council of the Indies. The following is the allusion to Carlos in the council's four-page summary of the contents of the governor's letter and its enclosures.

> And with reference to the obedience given by Prince Carlos, who dominates the region that they call the keys, it is evident from more recent letters written by the bishop and governor of Havana [that] Cacique Carlos had crossed over to that city to ask for missionaries. And it is stated also in the memorial presented by Father Fray Francisco Romero of the Order of St. Augustine, to which a reply will be given separately and concerning whose particular [request?], I asked for an order from the council so that the fiscal might confer with the Father commissary general of the Indies on these reports. With his prior effort, the council will be able to make the decision that appears to it to be most appropriate.

Here are the brief concluding notes made in the council.

> This dispatch boils down to two points: the one, about the sending of missionaries to the province of the Cacique Carlos because of his having asked for baptism for himself and for his vassals: in which the señor fiscal says that he has responded to the dispatch separately, what there is about this. And the other, about the building of a wooden fortification in the port (*Puerto*) of Apalachee[6] and a great tower or watchtower (*torreón o atalaya*) in the Port of St. Marks.
>   In reference to the first point, the provincial of the Franciscans of the province of Santa Elena of Florida was charged by a dispatch of the 12th of September of 1692 to send religious to the new conversions of Indians of those coasts and especially to the Province of the said Cacique Carlos and to the other of the Cacique of Ais,

6. Here the council refers to San Luis de Talimali, which was occasionally referred to as a port despite its inland location. Streams that have since gone underground allowed canoes from the coast to approach closer to San Luis than would be possible today.

who are asking for holy baptism. And there is in addition to this, by reason of a copy of a letter from the bishop of Cuba of July 8, [1]692 that the señor fiscal, don Martín de Solís Miranda, presented, concerning the sending of missionaries to the province of the aforementioned Cacique Carlos. It has been handed over to the council. He has met with the Father commissary general, Fray Julian Chumillas, and conferred with him about the manner and measures that it would be well to avail themselves of in order to achieve the reduction of these Indians. And the Father commissary general was given the same charge so that, in view of what they both discussed, the commissary should deliberate [?] what he was to carry out.

And as to that which pertains to the second point, concerning the fortification of Apalachee, that which this governor reports, and the señor fiscal says, has been set down on a paper separately. It was seen and a decision was taken by an acuerdo of the 14th of November of 1693.

5. Fray Feliciano López and Andrés Ransom, the Pirate, 1688

This document does not deal with the Calusa per se, but it is of interest for the light it sheds on an activity of the leader of the Franciscan mission to the Calusa of 1697 prior to his assignment to that task. Because of their role in saving the life of an English pirate condemned to hang at St. Augustine, the civil authorities in Spain had ordered that Fray López and two other friars be exiled to one of the most remote missions on the frontier of New Spain.

Fray Julian Chumillas to Antonio Ortiz de Otalore, September 12, 1688

AGI, Seville, Santo Domingo 856. Photostat from the Stetson Collection of the P.K. Yonge Library of Florida History. In the Stetson Collection this bundle no. 2752 bears the following identification: AI 58-2-6/14   Sept. 12, 1688, Madrid,   2 pp.   The Commissary of the Franciscans, Fray Julian Chumillas, to Antonio Ortiz de Otalore re the three religious in St. Augustine who prevented the execution of justice on an English prisoner, Andrés Ransom.

My lord. I received your Lordship's note dated on the 9th of June last in which the council orders me to verify who the religious were who prevented the execution of justice in the city and presidio of St. Augustine on a guilty English pirate called Andrés Ransom, and that having verified [it], that I exile those involved to the convent most distant from Florida that is in the most remote of the provinces of New Spain. And having sought to obtain information from the delegates (*vocales*) who have come to the general chapter, the pro- minister and *custodio* of that province, I discovered them to be three whose names are: Fray Diego Bravo, preacher; Fray Feliciano López; and Fray Juan Perdomo, preacher. Of these Fray Diego Bravo is to be found presently in the presidio [St. Augustine] because of having come to be cured of a chronic indisposition (*achaque habitual*) that he suffered from in the village of San Juan del Puerto,[1] where he was minister; and today he is the [minister] of that of Abadalquini,[2] twenty leagues distant from the presidio, for which reason, and I say that they so inform me, he may be less culpable. Fray Feliciano López is one of the best ministers, the most capable in the languages of those Indians that the province has. Today he is in the *doctrina* of San Matheo de Tolapatofi,[3] which is seventy leagues distant from the presidio. Fray Juan Perdomo is today conventual preacher of Havana (*Abana*) and this one is the principal [culprit] because he was at the presidio then and was in a position with more authority than the two who assisted him. The difficulties of exiling them to a place so far away are manifest because of the degree that they will be missed in the province and the hardships that they are bound to suffer in so far away an exile. I find myself forced to feel pity for my subjects. Consequently I beg the council to deign [to order instead] that they be given the regular penance within the same province making it proportionate to the guilt of each one, after the verification of everything has been completed, for there is no lack of mortifications available in the order. That they could be [punishments] such as, that they may not return to the presidio of St. Augustine or that they not be given any position (*officio*) in the

1. This was a Timucuan mission on Fort George Island at the mouth of the St. Johns River.

2. The mission of San Buenaventura de Guadalquini was originally on Jekyll Island, thirty-two leagues from St. Augustine. If Quiroga's twenty leagues is correct, the mission had moved to Cumberland Island.

3. This was a Yustaga mission in present Madison County, Florida.

province without first having a special patent from this commissariat. This is what occurs to me [to be best], keeping in mind how the absence of these religious would be felt in the province. I remain ready in everything that the council may order me [to do]. May God protect your Lordship for many years as he can and I desire. San Francisco, on the 12th of September of 1688.
S. l. m I your Lordship
Your servant and chaplain
Fr. Julian Chumillas
To don Antonio Ortiz de Otalora

6. The Calusa Head Chief's Visit to Cuba, 1689

Moved by new pressures from authorities in Spain to launch the mission to the Calusa and impelled particularly by the Calusa chief's acceptance of the bishop's invitation to visit him in Cuba, Bishop Ebelino de Compostela appealed to his clergy anew for volunteers to evangelize the Calusa. The Calusa chief visited the bishop on December 3, 1689, asking for baptism and allegedly offering the conversion of all his subjects as well. The bishop renewed his appeal for volunteers on the very day of the Calusans' departure for their homes, on January 2, 1690.

Don Diego Ebelino de Compostela, Bishop of Santiago de Cuba, to the Dean and Chapter of Holy Cathedral Church of Santiago de Cuba, January 2, 1690

AGI, Seville, Santo Domingo 154. This translation was made from a microfilm copy of the document located in the Archive of the Indies at the behest of the Florida Museum of Natural History. Victoria Stapells-Johnson located the document.

Bishop Diego Ebelino de Compostela, appeal to all the clergy of his diocese, Havana, January 2, 1690.

Vos Don D.[1] Diego Ebelino de Compostela, by the grace of God and of the Apostolic Holy See, bishop of this island of Santiago de Cuba, Jamaica, and Florida, of the Council of his Royal Majesty.

---

1. This probably stands for "Doctor."

To our venerable[2] dean and the chapter of our holy cathedral church of the city of Santiago de Cuba, our dearest brothers, to the beneficed pastors, exemplary priests, and virtuous clergy of this our entire bishopric, health in our Lord Jesus Christ. We would have you know that the king our lord (whom may God protect) manifests his affliction born of the ardent zeal with which he desires the exaltation and propagation of our holy faith and occasioned by the reports that he has received that for much of the year the heathen Indians who live on some islets or keys at a distance of thirty leagues frequent this city of Havana, and that there is no one to catechize them especially as they are desirous of it and are very peaceful [and] accustomed to dealing with the Spaniards and many of them know the Castilian tongue, with many souls being lost, who at little cost could be brought within the pale of our holy faith. And similarly he says to us that, although the Order of St. Francis works at their indoctrination and teaching in the Provinces of the Timucua, Apalachee, and Guale in the thirty-two *doctrinas* that are established among them and although they are employed in preserving the Indians in the faith who are already converted who exist in them and they cannot undertake the new conversions of the heathens and especially those of the two provinces that are the closest to this port and city of Havana, which would be up to two hundred leagues in length and more than sixty in width. And one of them extends along the coasts of the Gulf of Mexico from the cape that is called "of the Martyrs" up to the Province of Apalachee and the other one corresponds to it along the coast of the north on the Bahama Channel. The former one recognizes as master and renders vassalage to a cacique whom they call the [cacique] of Carlos and they give him the title of the great chief. And the number of people in those regions is great and in the center a great quantity of Indians settled in different parts while others are gathered together in forty settlements. And five of them which are the ones that are in the vicinity of the one in which the great chief has his seat in the mouth of a very capacious bay (*Voca de una ensenada mui capas*), which they call that of Carlos, sixty leagues distant from this port to which they come regularly in three days of navigation.[3] The

2. The Spanish abbreviation here is *V^e*. I have not previously encountered this abbreviation. This is an educated guess as to what it stands for.
   3. This might also be rendered as "which one might reach regularly."

other cacique is called he of Ais, who has many fewer people and vassals. And his Majesty is convinced that if the appropriate means were to be applied and that *cupussem*[4] in the natural providence, it would be possible to achieve such a Christian enterprise. Similarly he was told that some among the canons and clergy of our cathedral church were offering to cross over to this conversion as soon as they might be granted permission to do so and they might be assisted with the means necessary for their foodstuffs, with the promotion of so holy a work becoming less difficult because of the security that is offered with a fortification that was built in the extremity of the Province of Apalachee[5] where that of the cacique Carlos begins.[6]

In view of what his Majesty determines, as soon as I received this dispatch, I am having its content published in all the churches of the cities, towns, and places of this bishopric so that its priests and clergy who might wish voluntarily to cross over to these new conversions, especially to that of the land of the Cacique Carlos, may do so and they will be permitted to on asking to do so. We for our part [will do] everything that is possible in order to facilitate their crossing, choosing those who seem to us most suited and those with more spirit such as so holy a work requires.

And that likewise we should communicate with the viceroy of New Spain and with the governors of Havana, Cuba, and St. Augustine of Florida and with their royal officials, to all of whom various decrees and orders of his Majesty have been sent so that the quantities that might be needed for this purpose both for the supplying of the missionary priests and for their sustenance and all the rest of the expenditures that they might consider necessary in order to establish, maintain, and decorate the churches from the greatest to the least, should be taken from the royal treasury and from the most available and secure assets punctually and expeditiously in everything. And it being so, that on the part of his Majesty there is no room for him to be able to manifest the burning ardor of his Catholic and fervent heart with a more vivid expression with respect to the conversion of more than ten thousand souls

4. I have not been able to find such a verb.

5. This seems to refer to the fort at San Luis, which had been talked of but not built as yet at this date, although lumber had been cut for it.

6. The bishop seems to be overlooking the Tocobaga in extending the Calusa domain thus, unless Calusan conquest of Tampa Bay was the reason for the Tocobagan move into Apalachee.

whom the Devil holds in tyranny. And the wretches live under the dark shadow of death, destined for eternal punishment. We for our part must also concur and advance as much as possible a business of such seriousness and importance. And for a start we wrote various letters to the Doctor Don Juan de Cisneros, choirmaster (*Chantre*)[7] and dignitary of our cathedral church, making known to him his Majesty's will and determination, and begging him earnestly that he might enlist to serve our Lord in so apostolic an enterprise, accepting the nomination and title of prefect[8] and commissary of this evangelical mission. And he replied to me that for his part and that of the canon, Don Thomás de Fonseca and of the licentiate, Francisco Vexarano, head sacristan, they were resolute in obeying his Majesty and unalterable in preparing for the voyage, having come to this city so that they might be able to be transported from there directly to the settlement where the said cacique of Carlos lives and that they would go with the intention of sticking it out (which we cannot omit alluding to with great fondness of heart) and of persevering while God gives them life, even though it might be necessary to resign their positions of honor and their benefices.

After having seen this, we made an effort so that a fisherman, resident in this city, left from its port headed for the bay of the said cacique with whom he said he held communication and correspondence so that he might bring to his notice these dispositions on the part of his Majesty looking to the promotion of their greater welfare, and that he was to sound out his disposition and observe the distances and the location[9] of those areas and the nature and the customs of their people and everything that might be conducive to initiating and advancing an affair from which so much honor and glory could result for his Divine Majesty. And likewise we charged him that he should greatly encourage him so that he might be willing to come to this port in his company so that we might have the occasion for entertaining him and of conferring [with him] about this matter.

7. *Chantre* is defined as "Precentor, a dignified canon of a cathedral church." He was the one who directed the singing.

8. A prefect usually held certain episcopal powers, although he was not formally consecrated as a bishop.

9. The Spanish word here, *çituacion*, could also be rendered as "state of affairs."

God's hour arrived; because he offered to him and assured him that he would come on the first occasion that he might return and on it he delivered a letter to him so that it might be read to some of the Indians who understand our language and so that he might explain it in his own. In it he promised to receive him with the fullness of love and charity in the name of his Majesty and to entertain him to the degree that it was possible. To this he had reply that he was believing very strongly and that he was certain that he would fulfill it thus, but that it was necessary for him to convoke the noblest Indians, with whom he would discuss his voyage and that he would decide on what appeared to be most appropriate.

And on Saturday the 3rd of December, feastday of the Apostle of the Indies, St. Francis Xavier (a favorable and fortunate omen), he came through my doors bringing in his company two brothers, two sons, the captain of his arms whom they call the great [captain], and up to twenty Indians, to whom they give the titles nobles and knights (*cavelleros*), asking for holy baptism and offering the conversion of all his vassals in circumstances in which the most high providence and mercy of the lord shines forth so much that there is no vestige of the curse of human nature[10] to be found. That he does not come brought by the hands of grace: for this savage having had it fixed in his mind, and the Gentiles, that the objective of converting them to our Holy Law was in order to hold them captive, and it being so that other Indians that had come to this city in other times and who have returned to that land to live, affirmed to him that they had received bad treatment in this [city] and that even the young boys persecuted them and threw stones at them. Nonetheless he overcame these difficulties and fears and trusted a poor fisherman who brought him in his vessel, assuring him that he would be received with great love and affability. And accordingly they have done what they have been able to feast him and to entertain him, and he was permitted and they saw to it that he would find himself present at divine services and at ecclesiastical and political functions, taking care so that the interpreters would explain them to him, so that after making a comparison [of them] with the orderless manner with which they govern themselves, he might recognize the good order of our Holy Law and Christian

10. This is probably an allusion to the effects of Original Sin.

Republic. And those who were with him assure me that he was approving of everything that he saw being carried out and that he characterized it as more consistent with reason.

After having lived in this city for a month, I heard that on the second day of January of this current year of one thousand six hundred and ninety he returns in the same vessel in which they brought him, giving signs of being very pleased and very happy at having made this voyage. And so that he would return well supplied, the appropriate provision was made for those foodstuffs and gifts that they hold in the highest esteem, although both in this and in all the rest the señor governor and captain general of this plaza outdid me.

From all this one can see that this new vineyard of the Lord only needs workers who may plant it and ministers who may cultivate it and I, playing the role of paterfamilias and of first agricultor, that I should grasp the hoe in my hands, I offer to ready myself as I must to give a start to so apostolic a task; but I can scarcely do so, if I find myself alone and with the first three comrades who offer [themselves] for the purpose of helping us coming from our cathedral. As two religious of the Company of Jesus also made themselves available, who came with me from Spain for this purpose with an order from the Father General,[11] that they are my right arm, truly apostolic men, for since the day that they entered this port with me, such has been their vigilance and dedication to the welfare of the souls in our charge as has been experienced in the first and second general mission[12] that one of them has conducted and he is continuing [to do so] in all the bishopric with such inexpressible results and tirelessness.

And the other one is permanently in this city, helping me with the administration and education of twelve little boys who have been gathered together in the house of St. Ambrose, living at the same time from dawn on in a confessional, one of those of the head church. The result of this has been that many souls have developed their favorable qualities, having grown very much in perfection, without this preventing him from attending also to the visitation of the sick and to helping the many who call on him to die well.

11. This is the title of the overall superior of the Jesuit order.
12. This is a reference to the "revival" type of mission.

I report all this to the venerable exemplary priests and virtuous clerics of this diocese. And your bishop and prelate, breast on the ground and prostrate at the feet of all, begs them and pleads with them with complete humility by the bowels of Jesus Christ and by his divine love that those who would be able to go should wish and resolve to, that they would have a great obstacle,[13] to sign up as comrades and to enlist for this holy conquest, making this great sacrifice from which so much glory and honor to our Lord is bound to result and such good opinion and renown for the ecclesiastical estate[14] of this diocese, and for the king our lord such great consolation and satisfaction in seeing success crown the liberality with which he offers to assist with the necessary supplies, expenses, and provisions and in having at the forefront of his royal memory this great service that is rendered to him as he will take it into account when it is the occasion for distributing rewards and advancements. And he remains strongly confident that our Lord is not going to permit the great dismay and dissatisfaction that we would experience if it came about that all or most were to excuse themselves and hold back out of cowardice and weakness of spirit and that the number of the chosen and valiant ones offering themselves [should be so small] among whom the crowns and eternal rewards will be distributed that will come to them by the hand of God. May he protect you dearest brothers and our beloved sons and comrades of this diocese for many years and preserve and reward them with his holy grace. Havana, January 2, 1690.

Venerable and most beloved brothers, most beloved comrades and sons, servant of all in Christ and slave of all the diocese.[15]
Diego, Bishop of Santiago de Cuba

13. My rendition of this convoluted passage is tentative. It is possible that the emotion with which the bishop wrote was responsible for the seeming muddiness of this passage. A reviewer has suggested that the *obstáculo* may be a reference to the personalized trials through which the Overcomers seated at the right hand of God have passed, as in *Pilgrim's Progress*.

14. Estate is used here in the medieval sense of first, second, and third estates.

15. The latter half of this salutation is in Latin rather than in Spanish: *Omnium Servus in Chro et totius Diocesis mancipium. Servus* and *mancipium* might both be translated as "slave."

7. The Mission Is Given to the Franciscans, 1690

The king ordered the Franciscan provincial in Florida to provide men suitable for staffing the contemplated new mission to the Calusa after receiving a letter of April 20, 1689, from Cuba's bishop informing him that two of the three volunteers who responded to the bishop's second appeal could not be spared from the cathedral staff and that no other volunteers were to be had among the secular clergy. The king reminded the provincial that a complement of twenty-six new friars destined for Florida had sailed from Spain on March 14, 1690, under the charge of Fray Rodrigo de la Barrera, a hardheaded veteran of the Florida missions who in 1675 had been able to dispatch a Chacato assailant after being floored by hatchet blows to head and face. A skeptical assessment of the behavior of the two bishops and the perennial volunteer Canon Cisneros, who was "essential" to the cathedral staff, suggests that they may have been insincere in their compliance with the crown's orders.

The King to the Father Provincial of the Province of Santa Elena of Florida, September 8, 1690

AGI, Seville, Lima 151. Translation made from a microfilm copy of the document located in the Archive of the Indies at the behest of the Florida Museum of Natural History. Victoria Stapells-Johnson located the document.

The King
To the B^e and devout father provincial of the order of St. Francis of the province of Santa Elena of Florida; by decree of September 30 of the past year of 1687 I charged the bishop of Cuba and I ordered the governors of Havana and Cuba[1] that they should see to it that the decrees inserted in them should be carried out with reference to the passage of some clerics from the bishopric of Cuba for the conversion of the heathen Indians of the Gulf of Mexico and coasts of Havana and those provinces of Florida in the manner that was laid out in them. And now the bishop of Cuba in a letter of the 20th of April of 1689 in compliance with the decree that was sent to him reports that the Doctor Don Juan de Cisneros, who was the person who was encouraging another to cross over to those provinces of Florida for the aforesaid conversion, was occupied in the

1. Cuba here refers to Santiago de Cuba.

precentorship of his church and Don Thomás de Fonseca in the
canonry that he held, which was enough of an impediment to not
permit his being absent because it would entail the most serious
harm for him to fail to fulfill the obligation of his own peculiar
ministry and when he agreed to serve, the nature of things was not
so pressing as to be an impediment to his absence and [such] that he
would have been most correct in resolving to go, [but since then][2] he
has learned that there are no other clergy who would accompany
him because of those having died who had promised [to go] on the
occasion that the said conversion was [first] discussed, and that
although there might be an adequate number of clerics who
conferieor[3] might be willing to occupy themselves in so exalted a
ministry, he is convinced that it is not possible to achieve my
intention for the reasons that I expressed, and [having] seen his
report in my Royal Council of the Indies together with what the
said bishop wrote to me on this matter in another letter of the 20th
of February of the same year of 1689, and [what] the royal officials
of Havana [reported] in theirs of the 15th of it and above all that
which my fiscal requested and [having] considered that these
conversions were necessary and that by the means anticipated, that
clergy from the city and bishopric of Cuba should cross over to
them, has not borne fruit, not can it produce any according to what
the bishop reports, and that it is necessary that they enter into
them [instead] by way of those provinces of Florida, where the
majority and principal portion of the Province of Santa Elena of
your order is to be found and to which in recent times a mission of
twenty-four religious priests with two lay brothers that belong to
them have journeyed under the charge of Fray Rodrigo de la
Barrera, their commissary and general procurator of that province,
with the Galleons that departed on March 14 of this year of 1690 to
sail for the Province of *Tierra firme*,[4] it has appeared appropriate to

2. My rendition of this passage and the additions that I have made to it are
tentative, as a strictly literal rendition of this sentence does not make sense.
3. This might also be read as *conferuor* were it not for the dot for the letter
"i."
4. Literally this expression means "mainland" or "solid land." It was one
of the names used for the Viceroyalty of New Granada. A portion of the fleet
that sailed for Portobello in Panama to supply the Viceroyalty of Lima peeled

charge them (as I do [charge them] by the present [order]) that as
quickly as may be possible you should send the religious of your
order that you find to be most satisfactory to the new conversions
for the heathen Indians of those coasts of Florida and of the
Mexican and Havana [coasts] and that possess the necessary
qualifications and capacity for so sacred a task, and that they be
mature men of a suitable age and skilled in the languages that the
Indians of those regions to which you are to send them speak and
that they be experienced in the teaching and administration of the
holy sacraments to the Indians of other *doctrinas,* so that the
communication and the management of their ministry may be
easier for them in the new conversions to which you are to dedicate
them. Thus by this means it will be certain not only that the
success of this effort will follow more immediately but also that
they will [not][5] experience in its postponement the damages from
not attending to the reduction of these Indians with promptitude,
presuming and hoping that by the [efforts of] the religious of this
province the fruits of this reduction will be entirely equal to those
that might have been achieved under the directions of the clerics
[from Cuba], especially as the religious are so skilled and
experienced in this type of work. From this experience and skill
there is no doubt [about their success] and accordingly there is no
reason for hesitance in entrusting this enterprise to the religious of
that province, but rather by means of them and from your direction
and caution [in choosing them] great results are expected from these
conversions. And on the receipt of this dispatch you will carry out
what is [necessary] for its fulfillment and you will arrange matters
for the objective that I desire that the heathen Indians of those
coasts of Florida and of the Mexican and Havana ones should be
converted and be instructed very quickly in the mysteries of our
holy Catholic faith. You will continue giving me an account [about
it] on every occasion [that arises] so that I may have reports about it
and about the status that these new reductions and conversions go
on assuming. For in addition to the fact that in [doing] it you and
that province will be fulfilling your obligation under your rules, it
will be very much in the service of God and in my service and to the

off to dock at Cartagena as this fleet sailed along the northern coast of South
America.

5. Although the word *not* does not appear here, its insertion seems to be
necessary in order to make sense of this statement.

welfare of the souls of those poor heathens that you devote yourself to them and that you improve their chances for progress and for the easier achievement of their salvation to which all of us need to give so much attention. Done in Madrid on the eighth of September of the year one thousand six hundred and ninety. I The King. By the order of the king our lord. Don Antonio Ortiz de Otalora and signed from the council.

8. The Bishop's Final Ploy: The Fray Romero Episode, 1692

Seemingly anxious to convince the crown of his genuine interest in the Calusa mission, in mid-1692 Bishop Ebelino de Compostela recommended Fray Francisco Romero to the crown as the man to undertake that mission and one to the Ais as well. Romero was an itinerant Augustinian friar from the Lima province of his order whose provincial, according to Romero's own words, had "begged him that he should go to Spain for spiritual and temporal restoration from the privations that he suffered." He had interrupted his trip in Cuba to conduct revivals in various towns there. Bishop Ebelino de Compostela suggested that Romero would be able to raise as many as a dozen recruits from the oratories of St. Philip Neri in Spain.[1]

The bishop's letter is followed here by a number of other pieces written by Fray Romero or by the bishop relating to Fray Romero's undertaking responsibility for the Calusa mission. These pieces include comments made by personnel of the Council of the Indies.

Although the bishop praised Romero extravagantly as an extraordinary holy man, who had done much during his stay in Cuba to restore the fabric of a number of parishes both materially and spiritually, Romero seems to have rubbed a number of influential people the wrong way. In Havana both the governor and Romero's own superior, the Augustinian prior in Havana, opposed Romero's involvement in the mission. In Europe Romero incurred the wrath of the Council of the Indies

---

1. This is an allusion to the Oratorians, members of the Congregation of the Oratory of St. Philip Neri, founded in Rome in 1575 to improve the quality of the secular clergy. The congregation consists of independent communities of secular priests, living under obedience very much as do religious priests, but without the vows taken by the members of the religious orders and congregations.

in going on to Rome as soon as he reached Spain rather than consulting with the council as soon as he arrived, as the council had instructed him. In Rome Romero became involved in an imbroglio with the Spanish ambassador there. On his return to Spain Romero's offer to bring twelve men to the south Florida missions at no expense to the crown met with a cold reception.

Diego, Bishop of Santiago de Cuba, to the King, July 3, 1692

AGI, Seville, Quito 90. This translation was made from a microfilm copy of the document located by Victoria Stapells-Johnson in the Archive of the Indies and from transcripts made by her for the Florida Museum of Natural History.

Sire

Although I reported to your majesty on various occasions the problems and the great difficulty that were involved [in the expectation] that the bishop who had charge of the spiritual government of this island would be able to take care also of the provinces of Florida and that he was considering its separation [as] an abbacy as very necessary, it being very certain that each day I recognize new grounds for the need that exists for taking such a measure.

Nevertheless, I would make known to your majesty that by every means possible I would like to promote the conversion of two of those provinces that are called that of the Cacique Carlos and that of the [Cacique] of Ais, and that are the closest to this city and coast of Havana, and that I gave an account to your majesty of how the Great Chief, as it is thus they call the one of Carlos, had come to visit me, asking me for baptism and along with it ministers so that all his vassals might receive it, to which there would be no resistance. And after having made the effort with the efficacy and intense application that this case demanded, it being so much a part of my duty and recommended by your majesty with such strong expressions, three priests only, and two of them canons of the cathedral, offered themselves voluntarily to heed me and to cross over to those provinces, and because of this number being so small and because of there being only two other canons left who would be able to hold divine services, I had to suspend the decision until God should see fit to improve the situation.

And while I found myself in this agony, the master,[2] Fray
Francisco Romero, a religious of the order of St. Augustine, an
apostolic missionary, appeared on this island. He disembarked in
Puerto Principe and conducted the mission[3] in that settlement,
achieving very considerable results. And because of his having done
the same in those of la Trinidad, Santi Spiritus, Villa Clara, and
San Juan de los Remedios, which are in the center of this island
[Cuba] and cut it in half, their four parish churches have been
newly built,[4] restored, and provided with rich furnishings and
adornments, with such very considerable sums having been
expended on this that it did not appear to be possible to us without
the intervention of a manifest miracle, and it did not [seem possible]
either that he could leave all those places united in Christian
charity and salutary peace in view of such great and deeply rooted
discords and enmities as those under which their inhabitants
labored.

And after having left behind such holy works in a very good
state, proceeding with his journey, he came to this port in order to
take passage on a galleon that was getting ready to cross to Spain.
In the meantime he occupied himself in conducting an apostolic
mission in it,[5] with such attendant circumstances that they are
easier to be marveled at than to be described. And I confess to your
majesty that after having gone to hear some of the sermons, it
seemed to me that it was the Apostle St. Paul who was in that
pulpit or St. Vincent Ferrer.[6] And having finished his holy task, he

2. *Maestro* is a title of respect or dignity in monastic orders. It might be
rendered also as "teacher" or "professor."

3. The word "mission" here is used in the sense of the Catholic equivalent
of the Protestant "revival."

4. *Edificados* could also be rendered simply as "edified" in the spiritual
sense, but in view of this priest's edifice-complex and the context, "newly built"
seems preferable.

5. It is not clear what is the antecedent of "in it" *en ella* here, as "it" is
feminine here, while both "galleon" and "port" are masculine. Possibly the
bishop was thinking "city" when he wrote this.

6. Vincent Ferrer, born in Valencia in 1350, was a member of the Order of
St. Dominic renowned as a dialectition and in later life as a preacher. He was involved in the Great Western Schism as a partisan of the Avignon papacy but
eventually denounced Benedict XIII, the Spaniard Pedro de la Luna, for his obstinate refusal to resign to permit an ending of the schism.

went on to Guanabacoa, which is a settlement two leagues distant from this city, from which [visit] there resulted the decision for the building of a new parish church in a more desirable location, the one that it occupies today, than the one that it had and that is threatening to come tumbling down. And through his persuasion and efforts they offered and collected more than three thousand pesos for this project and its inhabitants are so fervent in carrying it forward that the site is presently being cleared of trees and leveled on which they are to open the foundations for this church and to create a new settlement plan for this village in a region so delightful and possessed of such advantages that we are hopeful that it will lose its former name of Guanabacoa, as unpleasing to the ear and heathen, and that in the future it will be called Monte Alegre.

He returned to Havana and applied himself with such tenacity and vigilance to perfecting the congregation of the priests of St. Philip Neri and to persuading them that some of them should live shut away in a house as the saint commanded in his Constitutions,[7] which they not only set themselves to fulfilling with such saintly determination but also so that there would be a way through the [diligence] of this religious for purchasing the houses of almost an entire block in the center of the city with plenty of space to build living quarters on them for four priests. And at his urging and through his persistence they have ready more than six thousand pesos collected and offered for this purpose.

And I, on seeing that wonders of this sort are not achieved except by the hand of a minister greatly favored by God, proceeded to communicate to him the ardent desire with which your majesty seeks to and orders me to promote the conversion of a province of Florida named province of the Cacique Carlos, who came through my doors asking for baptism for himself, for his children, and for all his vassals and, together with it, ministers who would preserve and develop the faith and the religion that they sought to receive. For this purpose I expended as many efforts as my energies were capable of, exhorting all the priests of this diocese to that end, and only three signed up and offered to go, and two of them canons of

7. "Rules and Constitutions" is the name usually given to the book of regulations that governs the lives of the members of religious orders and congregations.

the cathedral, whom he could not accept, because inasmuch as there were no more than four of them, it was impossible to satisfy the requirements for religious services. And having assured [myself] that such was the state of affairs and having expressed my dismay to this apostolic man and having learned through circumstances easily recognizable[8] (which I shall be able to explain) that this was the will of God manifested by dint of very prudent and very Christian efforts, he came through my door one day a while ago offering himself to take up this enterprise if Fray Pedro de las Alas, prior of the convent of St. Augustine, that exists in this city, thought it was a good idea and gave it his blessing. For this purpose most assiduous efforts were made, showing him samples of the decrees of your majesty in which you order me in such strong and efficacious terms that, by whatever means may be possible, I should promote and advance this conversion for which you would consider yourself well served. And no matter how much he was begged, demanded, urged, and given satisfaction and response to the difficulties and doubts that he raised, it was not possible to reduce him to agree to it. It is clear in part from the testimony attached, for which he is going to encounter a horrible reproach before the tribunal of God and on account of the fact that because of his resistance he may be putting the salvation of fourteen thousand souls[9] at risk perhaps, who seek the faith with holy baptism. Because of his decision, so powerful an affliction took hold of my heart that I was carried away by it from the zeal that my obligation instilled in me and with my judgment obscured I left my house without taking notice that I went out without cloak or cap. And without waiting for the family to accompany me, I entered through the doors of my church, lamenting to myself in the presence of the tabernacle and asking our Lord for mercy because for my great sins I had not found help or favor in his creatures and because, without being able to remedy it, I was losing fourteen thousand souls who asked me for baptism. And if perchance this action and conduct should be characterized as imprudent, it deserves some

8. This word *reparables* could well be rendered in other ways, and to a lesser degree this entire phrase could also be rendered differently. Consequently, my rendition here is somewhat tentative, although because of what follows this rendition seems to me to be the most logical one.

9. The bishop greatly inflated Calusa's population. Friars put the population at 2,000.

consideration, because it was not entirely deliberate but rather inspired by impulse and by the great desire to carry out what your majesty has commended me [to do] by three repeated decrees, and placed at your feet, imploring your great mercy, I beg of your majesty to console me by ordering that this religious should return as minister and head of this conversion and that he should bring twelve priests with him (it being possible) of those who live shut away in the houses and oratories of St. Philip Neri, whether in the one that there is in that court, whether in the rest of the cities, as I consider it very certain that those who offer themselves are bound to be many more and that they be brought to this city where they will find secure hospitality and where in three days they can cross over to and find themselves in the land of the Cacique Carlos, carrying out all of this in the form and the manner that your majesty has laid down in the latest decree, dated the thirtieth of September of eighty-seven. For from these works results so great an extention of the greater glory and honor of God. May he protect the Catholic and royal person of your majesty for the good of Christendom. Havana, July third of the year one thousand six hundred and ninety-two.

Diego, Bishop of Santiago de Cuba

In a petition addressed to the king Fray Francisco Romero informed him that with the assistance of the Augustinian province of Castile he had found twelve Augustinian friars ready to work for the conversion of the Calusa of Florida or the Tames of Popayán[10] province and that once they had the crown's permission they were ready to leave for Florida or Popayán or both.

Petitions of Fray Francisco Romero, n.d.

Sire

Fray Francisco Romero of the order of St. Augustine says that, after

10. Popayán is a province in southern Colombia in the midportion of the intermont basin where the Rio Cauca emerges from the Cordillera Central. It was on a main communication route from the Ecuadorian highlands. The Tames, referred to as the Tunebo by Julian Steward, were eastern neighbors of Colombia's Chibcha. They spoke a language related to Chibcha and "were evidently more backward and less organized but presumably shared many specific elements of culture with the *Chibcha*. This accords with their terrain . . . into which *Chibcha* habitat graded off from the high savannah" (Steward 1946:893).

having reported to Your Majesty the desires that he has of
employing his life in the conversion of the pagan Indians of the bay
of Carlos, a region where the light of the gospel has not penetrated
and where no religious of any other order reside and of the Tames of
the Province of Popaian, he finds himself ready[11] to conduct twelve
religious of his order, ten of them priests and two of them lay
persons, in order to plant the faith in either one of the said two
provinces or in both, in conformity with the determination that
Your Majesty has manifested to the bishops to whom jurisdiction
over the said provinces belongs by the very recent decrees
concerning the reduction of the said pagans, dispatched to them in
the latest Galleons. The provincial of this Province of Castile of the
aforesaid order dispatched his letters of writ, having them
published in its most important convents in order to awaken the
spirits of the religious so that they might have zeal and enthusiasm
[to volunteer] for so holy a duty and enterprise. May Your Majesty
deign to grant them permission [to leave for the mission]. For this
purpose a duplicate of the said present letters *yf*—

After considering the aforesaid letters as presented,[12] he begs
that Your Majesty deign to grant the permission to lead the mission
of the said religious to the said two provinces or to either one of
them[13] without any burden to the royal treasury because they find
themselves ready and able to place the conveyance into execution
with brevity once they shall receive permission.
Fr. Fran^{co} Romero

The cover page for the petition bears the following note addressed
to the king made by someone at the Council of the Indies.

Council   Sire
He says that he wishes to be employed in the missions, particularly
in the conversion of the Indians of the land (*estanzia*) of Carlos, a
region where the light of the Gospel has not entered and of the

11. In Spanish this phrase and the preceding one are two long participial
phrases without a main clause that would make this a complete sentence. In
the interest of readability and intelligibility I have converted this second partici-
ple to a verb.

12. This probably refers to the two letters that follow below.

13. It is possible that one of the reasons Romero was not given clearance for
the Calusa mission is that he was sent to Popayán.

Tames of the provinces of Popayan. For this [purpose] he has readied himself to bring twelve religious at his own expense, ten of them priests and two, lay brothers. For this [purpose] the provincial[?] of there has dispatched him to bring the said mission to either one of the said two provinces without cost to the royal treasury.

Although the following piece bears no caption, its contents indicate that it was addressed to the Bishop of Cuba. It was probably a formality, written to accompany the statement by the bishop that follows it here as proof that Fray Romero had indeed volunteered. It bears no indication of its point of origin or date.

Illustrious Lord

The priest Fray Francisco Romero, religious priest of the order of our father St. Augustine, apostolic missionary, I appear before your [most] illustrious lordship, as is most appropriate, and I state that, after having arrived at this said city, as Your [most] illustrious lordship had reports and firsthand knowledge that the Indian, head chief of Carlos, and those under his jurisdiction were asking for an ecclesiastical minister for their reduction and conversion, I offered myself to your [most] illustrious lordship with the love and desire that is necessary for such occupations. And I offered myself voluntarily to go to the said conversion, conditioned on the prior consent and permission of my prelate[14] and without any charge or cost to the royal treasury. Instead your most illustrious lordship, for what might be necessary, offered to supply me promptly from his own income with everything that might be necessary. And in view of the fact that God our Lord has not deigned to permit such an employment to be achieved, so that it may always be patent, of my deliberate will, I ask and beg his illustrious lordship to deign to interpose his authority, certifying what has occurred in the matter under discussion and that he hand over the original to me. That in doing this you will receive V^a merit.

Fr. Fran^co Romero

The piece that follows, written by Bishop Ebelino de Compostela, was obviously designed to support Fray Romero's efforts to recruit volunteers in Spain for the Calusa mission and to secure the requisite permission from the crown for the volunteers to pass to Florida to

14. This is most probably an allusion to the Augustinian prior at Havana.

begin their work among the Calusa. The bishop blamed the Augustinian prior at Havana for thwarting Fray Romero's desire to begin the work at once, presumably with recruits drawn from the Augustinian community at Havana. In approving of such a plan, the bishop chose to ignore the crown's earlier strictures against the introduction of another religious order such as the Jesuits or the Dominicans, which might lead to jurisdictional disputes with the Franciscans entrenched elsewhere in Florida. The peripatetic tendencies of Fray Romero made such trouble a distinct possibility.

Episcopal Decree of Don Diego Ebelino de Compostela, Bishop of Santiago de Cuba, July 3, 1692

His illustrious lordship the bishop, my lord, having seen the petition of the illustrious Father Fray Francisco Romero, stated: that, after becoming acquainted with the ventures of his spirit and holy zeal and the degree that he looks out for and labors in the search for s^n [sanctity?] that he has experienced, results worthy of attention in this city and in the places of the island, his illustrious lordship, finding himself with an order from his Majesty for the conversion of the pagan Indians of Carlos, who live so close, suggested to the said priest whether he could assist with the said conversion for some time and perform so special a service for his Majesty, because he had not been able to achieve it in the manner that was called for in the royal orders. And he replied that because it was a deed so much in the service of our Lord and so pleasing to his Majesty, with a submissive will he would put it into execution at once, even if it should involve a risk to his life, on the condition of receiving the prior permission of his prelate. And although many serious efforts have been made by his illustrious lordship that have gone far beyond the routine, so that the proposed goal might be achieved, and such that they have included public manifestations of the great grief that was occasioned for him by the loss of so many souls, he has not been able to achieve the permission of the Father Fray Pedro de las Alas, prior of the convent of St. Augustine of this said city, because he has refused, as appears from the *autos* made in order to give an account [of it] to his Majesty. And so that this may be evident the petition and this decree is handed over to the said illustrious Father Fray Francisco Romero because he is about to embark in continuance of his voyage to Spain. So the most

illustrious señor don Diego Ebelino de Compostela, Bishop of this
island of Santiago de Cuba, Jamayca and Florida, of the council of
his Majesty and my lord, decreed. That he signed it in Havana on
the third of July of the year one thousand six hundred and
ninety-two.
Diego, Bishop of Santiago de Cuba
Before me, Juan [undecipherable] de Valle

Next is a petition by Fray Romero addressed to the crown after he
had returned to Spain from Rome. Chastened, Fray Romero summarized his experiences as he worked his way from Quito through Colombia and Cuba and then on to Spain and Rome, admitting his fault in
the misstep of the trip to Rome, but pleading that he had been unaware that he had been ordered to go first to the Council of the Indies.
Romero blamed the governor at Havana as well as the Augustinian
prior for thwarting the bishop's zeal to have the work among the Calusa begin at once.

Because the microfilming of this document halted one or more pages
before the end of the document, it is not clear whether it contains data
on its point of origin or the date of its composition. In Victoria Stapells-
Johnson's microfilm copy of this assemblage, the next shot presents
cover notes for what appears to be a different document.

Testimony of Fray Francisco Romero, 1693(?)

Fray Francisco Romero
Sire
Fray Francisco Romero of the order of St. Augustine of the Province
of Lima states that, after having gone out, on the orders of his
provincial, to conduct missions [of the revival type] in that kingdom
in the places that seemed most appropriate to him for the exercise
of the said ministry, and after having reached the borders of the
Kingdom of Quito, the provincial of that province begged him that
he should go to Spain for spiritual and temporal restoration from
the privations that he suffered. He displayed a permission for that
from the Father General, which he presents, in which he was given
the option of naming the religious whom he preferred; that finding
himself in these borders . . . , he resolved to carry on with his
missions, putting aside everything that did not involve the
conversion of the pagans. In fulfillment of this he arrived at
Popayán and passed on to Santa Fé [Bogota] and with the permits

that he was carrying and along with it the permit and the approval
of the Bishop of Popayán and the Archbishop of Santa Fé, he
engaged himself in the said ministry, about which there are reports
enough in the royal council. And having passed through Santa
Maria[15] and arrived at Havana, the bishop of the said city asked him
with insistent pleas that he engage himself in the reduction of the
heathen of the Gulf of Mexico who were calling for ministers at the
top of their voice and that he had explicit orders from Your Majesty
for that [mission], in which he would do a great service for our
Lord. And the said Fray Francisco, bowing to the appeals of the
bishop, [agreed]. The prior of St. Augustine of that city, assisted
and aided by its governor came out in opposition to this holy work
and brought the zeal of the bishop to nought, preventing the
conversion of so many souls who might have been brought under
obedience. And so with the obligation that he should go on to Spain
in virtue of the writ from the [Father] General, entirely against his
will, for his sole intention and interest is the reduction of those
heathen. With that, having arrived at Cádiz, and encountering an
opportunity to go on to Rome and put himself at the command of his
[Father] General, he followed through on that, <u>unaware of the order
of Your Majesty to come first to his Royal Council of the Indies, the
fault for which he acknowledges.</u> And similarly the making up for
it, for the moment that Your Majesty's ambassador notified him
that he should fulfill this obligation, he set about doing so with
complete submission and with brevity. And even though it is said
that from Milan he wrote a memorandum with complaints about
the said ambassador, that is malicious because the said
memorandum is the one that he is presenting with the rest of the
notes and the letters, all in support of him, without their touching
upon the said ambassador in any way; and lastly, señor, the said
Fray Francisco comes for no other thing, neither does he have any
other intention than the one alluded to of employing himself in the
conversion of the heathen as he has done until now. For this
[mission], he has a great many pledges [of supplies] that devout
people have given him so that he may engage himself in so holy a
work. And there is no need for Your Majesty to assist him with
anything at all, but rather he will put everything that he has into

15. María probably should be Marta. Santa Marta then was one of Colombia's principal ports.

your hands so that they may be distributed at your order and as you see fit, sending the missionaries that you see fit to and from any whatsoever order as well. And if it should appear [to Your Majesty] that the said Fray Francisco can be one [of those] among them, he will obey the order of Your Majesty, and if not, he will remain in any whatsoever convent of his order. And lest all the council should be hindered and so that Your Majesty may be informed with ease about the utility and the advantages of this holy work.

He asks and begs Your Majesty that he deign that a minister. . . .

In the Stapells-Johnson microfilm the reproduction of this document ends thus in midsentence at the bottom of the page of a document that was written on sealed paper. The next frame on the microfilm appears to be the cover sheet for a different document. It bears the note that follows written by someone at the Council of the Indies.

Lord	Council
Fr. Francisco Romero of the observants of Our Father St. Augustine	He says that he has begged that he be granted permission to carry a mission of twelve religious at his own expense for the conversion of the Indians of Florida and of the Province of Tames in that of Popayan and with respect to eight religious of the Province of Castile and that of Aragon, as is evident from the documents that he presents. He begs that they be approved and that they be issued the dispatches that are customary in such cases.

Sire

Fr. Francisco Romero, a religious of the order of our father St. Augustine states that, having begged that Your Majesty deign to grant him the permission to conduct a mission of religious, without burden to the royal treasury, for the conversion of the heathens of Florida and of the Province of the Tames close to the bishopric of Popaian, where there are no religious of any other order in residence, nor any clergy at all; and eight religious having offered themselves up to the present for so holy a work, five of them from this Province of Castile and two of them from that of Aragon, as can be seen from the document and letters that he presents: and hoping strongly, Our Lord, for others to raise the number up to twelve religious priests and two lay persons.

He begs Your Majesty to deign to consider the list of those who are ready as presented and to order that they be given a letter of approval and the rest of the necessary dispatches for the conveyance of the said mission in the meantime that he will receive the favor.

The microfilming of this note also ends in midsentence at the bottom of the page. The next frame contains the following note written on the cover page of another document by someone at the Council of the Indies.

Lord
Fr. Fran^{co}
Romero of the
order of St.
Augustine about
the missions
that he has
proposed

Coun[cil]
He reports that after having composed a memorandum in Havana and that on coming to these kingdoms, he was exhorted by the bishop and by the governor *Comandancia*[16] through various letters received[17] so that [undecipherable word] and go on to the coasts of Florida and land of the Cacique

Carlos for the conversion of those Indians, which he did not carry out because of finding himself without companions and without the blessing of his prelate, even though he recognized how easy they were to reduce. And for this mission he offered to bring twelve religious priests and two lay persons contained in the writ that he presents. He would convey these [people] without burden to the royal treasury, for their clothing and equipment (*adexxe*) for it; that he has applied the assistances that his benefactors and relatives gave to him *Vrau* [?] because he does not give his attention to anything other than the propagation of our holy faith. And with respect to the great desire that the Indians of the Tames in the Province of Popaian[18] as he experienced[19] when he was among them and if it is [in the interest] of the royal service, he will send half of the said religious for that purpose supplied with everything

16. My rendition of this is tentative. It appears in the Spanish text as C_m^a. A *comandancia* is a military district or province. The English equivalent would be "command."

17. The abbreviation here L^{as} R^s could also be rendered as royal letters, but that does not fit the context.

18. Above the word "Popaian" between the lines there appear the letters *tan* and $_{ban}ma^l$.

19. The Spanish here is *o extrimento*. My rendition is tentative.

necessary. And he begs that these be approved and that he grant the permission for the said mission that he has asked for and that they may give him the rest of the dispatches necessary for it.

The memorandum [?] on this subject in which he asks for the permission alluded to, he says is in the possession of the señor fiscal.

Because this note ends with a complete sentence, it is not clear whether the microfilmer omitted part of this note written at the Council of the Indies. The next frame on the Stapells-Johnson microfilm is the statement by Fray Francisco Romero that follows here. In its opening lines Fray Romero seems to contradict his earlier statement that the governor at Havana backed the Augustinian prior there in thwarting his immediate departure for the Calusa mission.

Sire

Fray Francisco Romero of the order of St. Augustine of the Province of Lima states that, after having conducted a mission[20] in the city of Havana, he came to these kingdoms. In the name of Your Majesty he was exhorted by the bishop and the governor of the aforesaid city to carry out the royal decrees,[21] one dated on August 20 of the year [16]80, another of December 26 of the same year, and another of September 30 of [16]87, so that he might go and cross over for the conversion of the heathen Indians who live on the coasts of Florida facing Mexico and Havana in the land of the Cacique Carlos; as Your Majesty is aware from the letter of the said bishop[?] dated July 3 of [16]92. This [order] was not carried out because he was lacking companions and the blessing and permission of his prelate, even though the petitioner knew how easy it would be to reduce [them] to our holy [?] faith and how innumerable [are] the people in the center [i.e., inland] and populated for the most part, as [?] is apparent from the report that don Pablo Iyta Salazar, governor of Florida, made to Your Majesty in a letter of May 6 of [16]80. Because of all these [reasons] the petitioner has offered himself to serve Your Majesty in the said mission with twelve religious priests

20. Here again "mission" is being used in the sense of the revival-type exercise that is given this name in Catholic practice.

21. My rendition of this phrase is tentative as are the rest of the words appearing subsequently in this document that are followed by a question mark. The script of this letter is faded and consequently difficult to decipher in places.

from his order and two lay persons. The latter are contained with their descriptions[22] and titles in the documents annexed [to this] and in the authorizations[?] and permission of their prelates and the signatures of the said religious, with remarks; that neither for their provisions[?] nor the fixtures for the church will they need to be a burden to Your Majesty in the royal treasury in view of the petitioner's having asked for [this] from his acquaintances[?], [several undecipherable words], and from his benefactors and those indebted to him. They gave it to him for his assistance and not having anything else in view other than the propagation of our holy faith, nor desiring any other reward than [that] of serving Your Majesty better in the royal service.

He begs and beseeches Your Majesty to consider the said religious[?] as presented and to order that [several undecipherable words] be issued and the same documents[?] that Your Majesty had issued[?] prior to this to the bishop for this mission, taking into account that they are adequate because of their having been issued [an undecipherable word] and zeal of your fiscal, as is evident from the said decrees.

Likewise the petitioner also says that he has informed Your Majesty of the great desire he has to reduce to our holy faith the heathen Indians of the provinces of the Tames who live between the bishopric of Popayán and Santa Fé [de Bogota] on account of his experience when he dealt with them; [they] even went to the point of pretending to be dying, so he would not defer their holy baptism. For this reason, if it is the royal pleasure that half of the said religious cross over to reduce them to our holy faith, he would be ready to provision them with everything necessary, because he desires solely that God Our Lord may be known and Your Majesty served in a work so strongly sought for by the bishop of Popayán because of the great need of the said heathen and that the Tames, having [an undecipherable word] in their countries being abundantly fertile for everything. However, the petitioner wants

22. When friars were embarking for the Florida mission it was customary to send the crown a list of their names that detailed their place of birth, age, and the religious province in Spain to which they belonged. Such lists at times contained physical descriptions as well noting their complexion, stature, corpulence, and distinguishing features such as a big nose or ears or a scar.

whatever is the royal pleasure in this; that thus he will receive merit. q^a

Fr. Fran^{co} Romero

The remaining page belonging to this document is blank except for a seal and four printed lines, the major part of which I was unable to decipher. The last part at least is a date, as these four lines end thus: " . . . year of one thousand six hundred and ninety-three."

9. Mayaca and Jororo, 1693

In a letter to the crown the provincial of the Florida Franciscans and his council of definitors reported on the progress of the missions in the territory of the Mayaca and Jororo. The friars briefly described the territory of central and south Florida along the fringes of which the Franciscans had begun to work by the late 1670s at least. The friars asked the crown for iron tools with which to convert these largely hunter-gatherer peoples into sedentary agriculturists and for financial support for expeditions into these territories for the purpose of establishing contact with the peoples beyond the fringes.

Fray Juan de Carmenatri(?) and Others to the King, December 5, 1693

AGI, Seville, Santo Domingo 235. This translation was made for the Florida Museum of Natural History from a microfilm copy of the document located by Victoria Stapells-Johnson in the Archive of the Indies.

Sire

Our provincial and definitors of this august province of V. N.[1] of Santa Elena of Florida in view of what we have reported on other occasions about the new conversions of San Salvador de Maiaca, San Antonia de Anacapi, and Concepción, and San Joseph de Jororo,[2] it occurs to us in this [letter] to Your Majesty giving him an account of how those conversions are increasing and of how more than four

1. This not very legible abbreviation could possibly stand for "Your Majesty." Everywhere else in this document where this was abbreviated the letters $V M^d$ were used.

2. "New" is a relative term. Mayaca and Anacape appear on the 1680 mission list as "new conversions" (see Swanton 1922: 322).

hundred people have been brought under obedience to our holy faith, with the hope of many more, because the people who are being discovered are numerous both in the region to the south and in that of the southeast and to that of the east, whose land has the form of a triangle terminating on the Cape of Cañaveral on the southeast side. And on that of the east, running along the coast of Florida to the north; and along that of the south in the Keys of the Bahama Channel and along that of the southwest[?] and west[?], to the Mexican Gulf in the inner parts (*medula*) and edges of which, that would cover more than three hundred leagues, there is an abundance of nations, some idolaters, others heathens (*gentiles*)[3] with the provinces being differentiated in accord with the languages. These [people] on the whole do not work at plantings. They are able to sustain themselves solely with the abundance of fish that they catch and some wild fruits. A great part of this land is swamp (or subject to flooding, (*añegadiza*). For this reason our people take sick because they pay heed solely to the health of the souls [they serve] and to the service of Your Majesty, from whom we beg, as our king and lord, that taking account of the supreme poverty of this people and what our people endure, so that he may substitute for the alms that Your Majesty provides for them annually hoes and other iron tools in order to induce them to take up planting and so that they may live as rational[4] beings. Let Your Majesty deign, with your nobility and customary charity, to give orders for the issuance of some alms so that they may buy iron tools and for the exploratory expeditions (*entradas de descubrimientos*)

3. Gary Shapiro found, on checking the *Jewish Encyclopedia*, that in the Middle Ages, Jews made a distinction that may be the source of this one, dividing gentiles or non-Jews into those who were idolaters and those who were simply godless, and forbidding Jews to have any dealings with those who were idolaters. In the Middle Ages there was a debate whether Christians were to be considered idolaters with respect to this prohibition and it was decided that they were not idolaters. The distinction made here by the friars between idolatrous Indians and those who were simply godless heathen or gentiles is probably the same one, with the friars considering Christians as the new People of Israel or God's Chosen People and reflecting the strong Semitic influence on Iberian culture. The friars frequently referred to Indians who were not Christian as "gentiles" much as a Jew would use the term to refer to non-Jews.

4. The Spanish here is *nacionales* rather than *racionales*, which is what the context seems to demand. The same expression recurs later with *racionales*.

because neither this province [i.e., the Franciscans] nor the
governor have the wherewithal that would enable them to supply
them; looking out solely for the welfare of these souls and in order
to facilitate their reduction, while we remain under the obligation of
beseeching the Almighty Lord for your Majesty's health that he
asks for,[5] as a happy succession requires. St. Augustine of Florida.
December 5 of the year ninety-three. Señor, Prostrate *BSa* us of
Your Lordship and Royal Majesty *q sus p Bs.*[6]

Fr. Juan de Carmenatri [?], Minister-Provincial	Fr. Jacinto [?] de Barreda, father of the province
Fr. Pedro de Luna, ex-minister-Pl[7]	Fr. Matheo Arguelles, definitor
Juan de Mercado, definitor	Fr. Salvador Bueno, definitor
	Fr. Juan Chrysostumo, definitor

The cover page for this letter and the margin of the document's first
page are crammed with commentary notes and a note summarizing
the document's contents. Some of those notes are reproduced below.
Portions of the notes are not very legible, in part because of the illegi-
bility of the handwriting, in part because of the use of abbreviations.
Words about which I had considerable doubt are followed by a question
mark in brackets. Abbreviations that I could not decipher are presented
in Spanish. Two of the notes are clearly indicated as having been made
at the Council of the Indies. The content of the rest suggests the same
source.

The first of these notes presented below fills the broad margin of
the first page of the friars' letter. This piece is of particular interest
for its listing of the carpentry tools that should be sent to the friars
"as the ones most necessary for the new expeditions for the building of
the temples and houses for the villages that they are to establish." The
mention of augers of various sizes, from "large" to "medium" to "the

5. The Spanish here is the abbreviation p^{de}, which I have presumed to be
pide.

6. This abbreviation stands for *que sus pies Besa* or "who kiss your feet."
BSa earlier in this sentence stands for the same.

7. Although the abbreviation *Pl* differs from the abbreviation *Prov* above, it
doubtless also stands for "provincial," the title of the superior of all the Franciscans of Florida's Province of Santa Elena. From other sources I know that
Fray Pedro de Luna was the Franciscan provincial as late as 1690. Definitors
were members of the provincial council or chapter, and both were chosen for
limited terms of office.

thinnest," casts light on the possible building techniques used in such enterprises.

Madrid, November 22 [?] of 1695.

And inasmuch as it is correct that in the vicinity of the conversions that exist in it [Florida], there continue to be many nations of heathens (*Gentiles*) and that these missions have progressed very little, for they are in almost the same state as at the beginning of the conquest despite the royal treasury supporting 20[8] missionaries, from which is presumed the little fervor that there was in the past in looking out for the conversion of so many souls, with the missionaries contenting themselves with peacefully enjoying those who had already been reduced by their predecessors.[9] It appears that with respect to proposing this initiative they have hopes and indications that the conversions will go forward. For the four areas that they mention, they may be sent two hundred double mattocks,[10] six large saws and six small ones, fifty *maizeses*[e] or large *hoges*[11] for cutting down, four large augers (*barrenas*), four medium ones, and four of the thinnest ones, because even though they do not specify in this letter the type of iron tools except for the hoes, these are the most necessary ones that they need for the new expeditions (*entradas*) for the building of the temples and houses for the villages that they are to establish. Let these be sent under the control of royal officials and of the governor so that, with the intervention of both they may be handed over and used precisely for the aforesaid new entradas with no possibility of their being able to be diverted for some other use. For inasmuch as these would involve such a limited expense, it is appropriate to send them at once to avoid the situation in which for the lack of those

8. This number was not very legible. I am not at all certain that I have deciphered this correctly, as twenty seems a rather large number of friars.

9. This reflects the general belief that the late seventeenth century was a time when many of the friars lacked the fervor and devotion to their work of the earlier friars, such as Francisco Pareja and Baltasar López a century earlier.

10. The Spanish word used here is definitely *azadas,* which means "hoe" or "mattock." The latter in modern times at least is often made with two edges like a pickaxe or *azadon* but the context here seems to me to call for axes (*hachas*) as well and they are not mentioned, surprisingly.

11. I have not encountered either *maizeses*[e] or *hoges,* but I suspect they are meant to be scythes or sickles. *Hoz* or "sickle" resembles *hoges.*

iron tools they should fail to go out for a . . . [some letters appear to have been cut off the edge of the page here] and new entradas.
M^d November 22 [?] of 1695
[signature with initials that appear to be] Pfo

The remainder of the notes that follow here are taken from the cover page. Some extend across the page and are quite legible. Others are crammed into a narrow column on the left- or right-hand side of the page and are not very legible in places. The first two brief notes below appear respectively in the right- and left-hand columns.

Florida   to his Majesty
Received on the 17th of February of [16]95, on the packetboat (*aviso*). The provincial and definitors of the province of Sta Elena of Florida of the order of St. Francis.

Council
With it[?], 13th of April, q s^r (señor?), with that which was known earlier about the matter indicated with respect to these alms. Let it be brought to the official.
[An illegible initialed signature]

There is no[?] other precedent than [that] each religious of St. Francis among those who are employed in the *doctrinas* and conversions of the Indians of the provinces of Florida is to be assigned 115 ducats from the *situado* which the presidio [St. Augustine] enjoys equaling[?] (guasds), the salary of a soldier for his provisions and clothing. This is brought from the coffer of Mexico with the rest of the *situado*. And each one of the seventy religious who are employed in this ministry[12] are assisted with this portion at the order of His Majesty.

The next note appears at the bottom of the cover page, written across the full width of the page.

#The fiscal, in view of this letter written by the provincial assembly [of the Franciscans] of the province of Florida, states—that its

12. This does not mean that there were actually seventy friars in Florida at this time, but merely that there were seventy slots allotted to them on the military pay roster. The number of friars was usually much less than seventy.

content boils down to the fact that, in the four new conversions that it alludes to more than 400 people have been reduced already and that there are many heathen. They border on diverse nations with different languages[13] and that they expect that they will make great progress and they conclude by asking that orders be given to release some funds in order to buy hoes and other iron tools that are necessary in the new reductions; that is to say that they should spend on them the annual stipend that is issued to them in the *situado* for that province. [This is the end of this item on the microfilm.]

The following two pieces are crowded, in the format indicated, into a column on the left-hand side of the page and they are written in different hands. I suspect that the piece on the right-hand side here, beginning with "#poverty of that people," is a continuation of the piece that precedes this one here despite the lack of continuity grammatically. Both are written in the same hand and begin with "#." Such a device is used elsewhere in the council notes to indicate how the discontinuous pieces fit together.

Reply *fy ca la^s* to Your Establish[?] first[?] *Ug s-f* what the señor fiscal says and that if[?] there is a precedent for the matter, let him expatiate[?] on this. [An illegibly scribbled initial] Done [*Ex^{do}*]

#poverty of that people and what the ministers endure in order to convert these people. The annual alms which are given to them[?] (*ques desda*) in hoes (*hazadas*) and other iron tools in order to induce them to planting and so that they may live like rational beings. That they should be given some remittance (*limosna*) for the iron tools and the exploratory expeditions, because neither that province of the Franciscans nor the governor have the wherewithal with which they would be able to supply it, looking solely toward the welfare of those souls and in order to facilitate their reduction.

13. This remark parallels that made by the Jesuit Fray Antonio Sedeño in 1570 about the Calusa domain: "for in Carlos there were twenty-four languages in the thirty chieftainships there were, as they did not understand one another" (Zubillaga 1946:425).

10. Fray López' Petition, 1695

Fray Feliciano López, Franciscan veteran from the Florida missions, arrived in Spain in the latter half of 1695 to secure transport for four-teen Franciscans whose departure for Florida had been authorized for the preceding year but not realized because of lack of means. Possibly to win quick crown support for his effort, Fray López suggested that four or six of the new friars be designated especially for the Calusa mission and that they be transported there directly from Havana, with-out the usual stopover at St. Augustine. Fray López made suggestions as well for the provisioning and equipping of the missions and proposed that the fourteen new friars be sent via a permit ship[1] from the Ca-nary Islands to expedite their departure.

On October 20, 1695, the council ordered the friar's note given to the council's fiscal so that he might prepare an answer for it and for other dispatches dealing with the same subject. The rest of this as-semblage consists of various brief pieces, presumably written by the fiscal, followed by a relatively lengthy summary, written in November 1695, reviewing a number of the vicissitudes through which the effort to establish the Calusa mission had passed, as well as related topics.

Petition by Fray Feliciano López, October 1695, and Comments by the Council, November 1695

AGI, Seville, Santo Domingo 235. Translation made at the behest of the Florida Museum of Natural History from a microfilm copy of the document located by Victoria Stapells-Johnson in the Archive of the Indies.

> Fray Feliciano López, missionary preacher in the conversion of the Province of Florida, states that on his having come over to these kingdoms on business pertaining to the progress of the said conversion and to the propagation of the holy Gospel in the aforementioned province, of which Your Majesty has already been informed, it seemed appropriate to the commissary general of the Indies, who resides in this court of Your Majesty, that the supplicant should bring fourteen religious of the mission that Your Majesty deigned to grant last year, whom he was not able to bring because of the lack of space in last year's fleet. Accordingly, the

1. A *navio de permiso* was a ship licensed to sail outside the annual con-voys, which did not sail annually in this era of Spanish Hapsburg decadence.

priest, Fray Christóbal de Molina, *Custodio*[2] of the said province, in view of this asks Your Majesty for the following things:

First, that Your Majesty should approve that the supplicant may bring the fourteen religious alluded to because it is in the interest of God and of Your Majesty that religious should go to that conversion as soon as possible because of the great lack of them that exists there.

Second, that the cacique of the Province of Carlos having asked for religious from the bishop of Havana, and this prelate having written to Your Majesty about it, and mentioning to the supplicant that the royal zeal of Your Majesty for the spread of the Holy Gospel would wish that the religious should establish a beachhead in the said Province of Carlos, that [Your Majesty] would take measures so that out of the religious who are to go on this said mission, four or six of them may be assigned [to Carlos] so that they may be transported directly to the said Province of Carlos from the port of Havana.

Third, that in the same vessel in which the governor and royal officials of the said city of Havana transports them, they should provide them with everything necessary for the sustenance of the said religious as well as with the ornaments and the rest that is necessary to celebrate and administer the holy sacraments, and that from this time on the alms that Your Majesty gives them for their sustenance be sent from the said city of Havana, because it is the port closest to the said conversion, subtracting it from the alms that Your Majesty gives for the sustenance of the religious who reside in the conversions of the Province of Florida, for it is my understanding that Your Majesty has ordered that the *situado* for the said Province of Florida that is collected in Mexico should come to Havana, where the governor will be able to separate out the portion assigned to these religious.

Fourth, that the religious for this mission be transported by way of the Canary Islands, because this is the quickest route, in the first ship that sails for Havana from the said islands, putting them on board in the place of the families from the Canary Islands whom Your Majesty orders transported to it, and that the governor and

2. Technically, he was a provincial, not a *custodio*. A *custodia,* or "custody," in the Franciscan organization is the name given to a province that does not have enough convents to constitute a province. Florida achieved provincial status early in the seventeenth century.

captain general of the said Canary Islands be ordered to assist with
what is necessary for the said sailing in which he will receive a
favorable hearing as he expects from the great justice of Your
Majesty.
Fray Feliciano López

The notes written at the Council of the Indies begin on the back of
the folio on which the preceding petition by Fray López ends.

Sire

Fray Feliciano López
Missionary preacher of Florida
Council, October 20, 1695.

To the señor fiscal, so that he may see it and give an answer
concerning this dispatch and the rest like it.

Council
    He states that he has come to these kingdoms on business
pertaining to the growth of the conversion and to the propagation of
the holy Gospel in that province, and that he appealed to the
commissary general of the Indies, Fray Julian Chumillas, that he
might bring back [with him] the fourteen religious for the mission
that were granted for Florida last year and that did not go for lack
of the means. And he asks that the bringing of the said fourteen
religious be approved because of the great need of them that exists.
    That the cacique of the Province of Carlos has requested religious
from the bishop of Cuba, about which the bishop has written, and
the supplicant asks that of the fourteen alluded to, four or six be
assigned to and conducted directly to the Province of Carlos from
Havana, and that on the vessel on which they go the governor and
royal officials of that city should provide them with everything
necessary for their sustenance and with the ornaments and the rest
of the things for celebrating [Mass] and administering the holy
sacraments, and that in times to come, the alms that are given to
them for their sustenance be sent to them from Havana because it
is the port closest to the conversion of Carlos, subtracting it from
what is given to the religious of Florida, because of having
understood that the *situado* that goes to that presidio from Mexico

has been ordered to go by way of Havana, whose governor can separate out from it what is assigned to these religious. That the fourteen religious alluded to should be sent by way of the Canaries, because it is the shortest voyage, in the first ship that leaves for Havana from the islands, ordering the President of the Canaries that he assist them with what is necessary for the embarkation.

From the books and papers of the Secretariat it appears that by a dispatch of November 7 of 1693 [issued] at the instance of Fray Francisco de Ayeta [the departure of] the religious priests and two lay brothers for the *doctrinas* and the conversions of Florida at the expense of the royal treasury was authorized; and by another of the same date, a warrant was issued on the Royal Treasury of Mexico for the expenditures that had to be made with them in Spain and for their embarcation and passage. And up to now there is no evidence that anyone of these religious has crossed over.

A draft of a dispatch is brought, of September 12 of 1693, in which the Franciscan Provincial of Florida was charged with the responsibility of sending religious to the conversions of the provinces of the cacique of Carlos and of that of Ais who are asking for holy baptism. And the letter from the bishop of Cuba that is cited in this dispatch is in the possession of the señor fiscal; that he should meet with Father Chumillas and that both should confer [on this] and inform the council of the religious who are appropriate for going to these new provinces. And this was communicated at the same time to the Father commissary general so that he might confer on it with the señor fiscal. And up to now there is no indication in the secretariat that they have done it.

It is provided for that in the *situado* for Florida that is paid in Mexico 70 billets are assigned for Franciscan religious for the *doctrinas* and missions of Florida, and to each one for their sustenance and clothing there is given the same [allotment] as to a soldier, which is 115 ducats per year.

In the fiscal's [records] in view of this memorandum it says: that as is evident . . . [torn] that is in the secretariat on November 7 of [1]693, at the instance of the Father Procurator General of the order of St. Francis the mission of 30 religious priests and 2 lay persons was authorized for Florida and a warrant of the same date was issued so that the expenditure with their sustenance and passage

might be paid in the royal coffers of Mexico; these were to have
gone under the charge of Fray Christóbal de Molina, commissary
custodio for that province. And it is not established that all of them
or any of them crossed over in the following fleet; with the
exception solely [of what is established] by this memorandum in
which it is stated that they failed to cross over because of the lack
of means, in which they ask for 14 of those already granted so that
a part of them might serve in the new conversions and four or six of
them in the province of the Cacique Carlos, and that those who are
assigned to this new conversion should go [there] directly from the
port of Havana without setting foot in Florida, and that the
governor and royal officials of Havana should give them the
provisions necessary for the passage and for the ornaments and
everything else needed for their ministry. And that for their
maintenance in the future, the stipend that belongs to them should
also be sent from the said port of Havana, deducting it from the
situado which comes from Mexico and is assigned to the Province of
Florida because of the supposition [that] it is ordered that the said
situado come to Havana to be delivered. And he asks that this
mission go in the first vessels that may become available for the
Canary Islands so that they may pass from there to the Indies in
the special-permit vessels.[3] And with respect to its being established
by other dispatches that many of the religious that Fray Rodrigo de
la Barrera brought over in the year of [1]690 departed from that
province [Florida], with the provincial Fray Pedro de Luna and the
council of the new chapter employing them in various posts of the
order in Havana with the pretext of having an alternative in that
province[4] (being wrong), and that some of them are ordered to
return to Spain and they are returned to their province, for this
reason it appears that Florida is short of missionaries; for this
[reason] the 14 that are being asked for now must be granted with
the condition that 8 of them are to go destined to be assigned
specifically to the new conversions of San Salvador de Mayaca, San
Antonio Anacapi, La Concepción, and San Joseph de Jororo, with

3. The Canary Islands were exempted from the trade regulations that required all trade between Spain and the Indies to be conducted by way of the
fleets that were supposed to sail yearly from Seville and Cádiz. Special permits
were given to Canary Island ships to sail to various ports in the New World.
4. *Alternativa* refers to the practice of alternating creole and peninsular
friars in office to reduce conflict within the orders.

reference to which in a letter from the chapter, of December 5, [16]93, it has been reported that there were a great number of heathen tribes in those regions and that they had already reduced 400 people, asking for some tools for the new entries, concerning which the fiscal has responded in the margin of the said letter, which he sends. And the other six of the *fourteen* can be destined for the province of the Cacique Carlos as the supplicant requests; for he [the cacique] has appeared personally in Havana to ask for missionaries as is evident from the letter of July 3 of [16]92, written by the bishop of Cuba and by the other of April 10 of [16]88 from Governor Quiroga, that the son of the said cacique, who not ever having done so before, had come with many others to give obedience when he was engaged in the visitation of Apalachee and Timuqua. With an eye to these and to the propositions[5] made concerning this matter by Father Fray Francisco Romero, who attempted to cross over to the said missions on the persuasion of the bishop, the fiscal gave his reply on October 23 of the past year of [16]93, which is included with this dispatch, to which it is returned. And as to what pertains to this point, it appears by a copy of a decree issued by the secretariat that during June of [16]93 a dispatch was sent to the provincial of that province, charging him anew to send religious to the conversions of Indians of those coasts and especially to the land of the cacique Carlos and of Ais, which was dispatched in duplicate on September 12 of the same year. And with respect to the bishop's saying in his letter that he found himself without clerics that he could send to the said mission, on pondering the matter of conscience involved in not sending missionaries after the cacique's having come personally to ask for them, this obligation becomes more pressing. For this [reason] it will be advisable to give an order to the governor and the royal officials of Havana so that, as is asked, they may give to these six missionaries all the supplies necessary for them to cross over to the said land of the Cacique Carlos, and that afterward from the *situado* that should come from Mexico they may send them the portion of the stipend that has been assigned [to them] in it, giving an account of this to the royal officials of Florida so that they may register it on their books, because the fiscal believed that sending it from there [St. Augustine] is bound to be difficult because of the great distance that there is by land from

5. In the microfilm this word is abbreviated *propos*[es].

there to that of the said cacique and because one can cross to there from Havana in three days or even less time. The punctual supplying of these missionaries is very advisable so that they will remain in that region. The fiscal communicated this necessity of this mission to the Father commissary of the Indies as soon as he was ordered to by the council and he agreed with it, even though he had no detailed reports about that region and although he said it was appropriate to await the coming of some religious from that province in order to obtain more details from him than the fiscal presented verbally to the council. And now, with this religious having arrived and with his asking expressly for missionaries for the said province of the Cacique Carlos, and taking into account the earlier reports that have been mentioned and what was requested in the cited reply of October 23 of [16]93, arguments that are forceful enough so that this mission must be developed; that notice must be given to the governor and the royal officials of Florida so that for their part they may seek to assure its maintenance, giving an account on every occasion of the ministry of the religious both in this and in the rest of the conversions. And in reference to the matter of these 14 religious embarking for the Canaries in the vessels that there might be so that they might pass from there to the Indies on the permit ships, this involves the problem that it is customary for them [the ships] to remain in them [the Indies][6] or for others from the islands to cross over incorporated with them without permission, which has proved to be very bad for the Indies and all this is prohibited in law 9, book 1, title 14[7] and it is credible that before this mission is assembled and everything in readiness to be able to embark an opportunity will occur for a direct sailing to Havana or to Veracruz. The council will decide concerning all this what it considers to be the best solution. Madrid, November 27 of 1695.

6. This reflects the crowns' perennial fear even at this late date, when foreign and enemy powers were conducting an extensive contraband trade with various ports in the Indies, that trade policy would be compromised if all trade were not funneled through Seville and Cádiz via the yearly fleets.

7. This is a citation from the *Recopilación de los Leyes de las Indias,* the codification of the welter of decree laws that had been issued by the crown for the government of the Indies.

11. Reflections and Summation by the Council of the Indies, 1695, Spurred by Fray López' Arrival in Spain

Two documents originating at the Council of the Indies late in 1695 throw light on the role played by authorities in Spain in establishing the Calusa mission in 1697. Although there is much overlapping between the two instruments, both merit reproduction. The second one is more valuable because of its greater breadth and richness of detail, but the conciseness of the first document permits a clearer view of the saga of this mission's gestation between 1688 and 1695. Additionally, it presents details and insights not found in the longer document.

Fray Feliciano López' arrival in Spain and the suggestions he made prompted the council to move decisively to establish the mission. The two pieces review developments related to the projected mission that occurred between 1688 and 1695 and reflect the decisions taken by the council during that time. The documents show in particular moves the council made to assign responsibility for the Calusa mission to the Florida Franciscans and to deal with criticism of the friars' conduct in the existing missions by a church authority in Cuba. The documents show that the council endorsed Fray López' proposals to expedite establishment of the mission by making Havana rather than St. Augustine the source of the new mission's umbilical cord. The council's remarks and summary highlight how much this mission was a crown-initiated operation and considerations that influenced the council's decision making.

First Extract of Dispatches Relating to the Proposed Calusa Mission, 1695

AGI, Seville, Santo Domingo 835. This translation was made from a photostat in the Stetson Collection of the P.K. Yonge Library of Florida History. This bundle no. 3302 bears the following notation: "AI 58-1-22/330 Nov. 19, 1695, Madrid. Abstract of certain expedientes caused by the arrival of Fray Feliciano López: two enclosures."

[Heading]
Extract of the contents of the dispatches occasioned by the fact of Fray Feliciano López of the order of St. Francis having arrived at this court from the Provinces of Florida. How the council reached a

decision on them by an agreement of the 2nd[?] of January of [16]95. With what was replied to them by the señor fiscal.

[Document]

The Field Master don Diego de Quiroga y Losada, while he was governor of Florida, and its royal officials gave an account in letters of March of 1688 about having made the general visitation of the Indian settlements together soon after the governor took possession of the government, inasmuch as it has been 30 years since it has been done.[1] That while they were visiting the province of Apalachee and Timuqua, various caciques and leading men from the heathens (*Gentiles*) of that vicinity assembled to give obedience and also the son of the so-called Prince Carlos, who dominates the province of the Keys, giving obedience in the name of his father, not having done so until then, with all of them asking for peace and for missionaries who might indoctrinate them in our holy faith, as is manifest from two letters in their language[2] translated into Castilian that the governor sent. After the said letters had been seen in the council, it sent them to the señor fiscal, who, in his reply of October 23 of [1]693 said that it should be entrusted to the missionary fathers of St. Francis (which is the order that has responsibility for the conversion of the heathens of this province). They should be entrusted with the responsibility for these new conversions because it is their principal objective and because the obligation is greater to see to it that so great a number of souls should not be lost than for attending to the *doctrinas* of those who have been reduced and converted already since the time of their grandfathers. And that with reference to the obedience given by the Prince Carlos, it is established by more recent letters from the bishop and the governor of Havana that the Cacique Carlos has crossed over to that city to ask for missionaries.

At this time a copy of a letter from the bishop of Cuba of July 3,

1. The council's statement is in error here. Just ten years prior to Governor Quiroga's visitation Domingo de Leturiondo visited the same two provinces in the name of Governor Pablo de Hita Salazar. Conceivably the council meant to say that thirty years had passed since a visit had been made by a governor himself, alluding to the Rebolledo visit of 1657.

2. The letters were written in Apalachee and Timucuan by chiefs of those two linguistic groups and signed by the chiefs, who were literate.

[1]692, was seen in the council (the original of which the señor fiscal has) in which he expressed his grief over not having found a sufficient number of priests in his bishopric who would be able to cross over and to be employed in the said new conversions and especially in those of the province of Cacique Carlos and that of Ais, who are the closest to the coast and city of Havana because of the Cacique Carlos's having come through the door asking him for baptism and ministers so that all of his vassals might receive it, in which there would be no resistance, with the bishop supposing that those who were asking for the faith through the portal of baptism would amount to 14,000 souls.

The council in view of it agreed on October 19 of [1]693 to tell the señor fiscal (as was done by a note from señor Don Juan de Larrea of the 24th of it) that, having become acquainted with the contents of the letter from the bishop of Cuba, he should meet with the Father commissary general, Fray Julian Chumillas, and confer with him about the manner and means that it would be well to avail themselves of for the achievement of the reduction of those souls to our holy faith with the greatest Christian utility and benefit, as the council desires so much [to do]. And the Father commissary general was informed by a note on the same day so that with this news he would reach an agreement with the señor fiscal about the day and the hour in which they might get together for this session and so that they might give a report about what resulted [from it].

As a result of having seen another copy of the same letter from the bishop of Cuba, the Franciscan provincial of the Province of Santa Elena of Florida was charged by a dispatch of September 12 of [16]93 to put every effort and vigilance into providing evangelical ministers for all those new conversions and especially for those of the provinces of the Cacique Carlos and that of Ais, who are seeking baptism with such ardor for himself and for his vassals,[3] for this purpose sending the religious that he considers necessary and adequate [and] who would possess the talents and abilities [for]

3. This is a literal translation of the Spanish here, which seems to be incorrect grammatically. The context seems to call for "who is" rather than "who are," as it is only the Calusa chief who seems to have been pressing for friars from the evidence that has been presented here.

what he was given responsibility for[4] in dispatches of September 8 of [16]90, and the 24th of June of [16]92.

In another letter of the 15th of April of [16]88 Governor don Diego de Quiroga reported the arrival in Florida of don Juan Ferro Machado, nominated visitor by the bishop of Cuba to make a visitation. And after having done so without any problem (*embarazo*), he then manifested a desire to hold some secret inquiries [directed] against the religious of St. Francis on the pretext that he had orders from his Majesty to do so. And after having learned about it, he provided an *auto* so that he might present it to them. That he did not do so; neither did he reply. And the governor did not move to take any other action because of the desire he has to serve his Majesty as best he can and not disturb the republic.

After having seen this letter the señor fiscal says in a reply of January 9 of [16]95, that don Juan Ferro Machado alludes to the bishop having delivered to him a decree of August 13 of [1]685, [stipulating] that he should investigate whether the religious *doctrineros* were punishing the Indians without making exception for the nobles and caciques and that he learned that some were guilty of this excess[5] and that [some religious] were undertaking to administer [the *doctrinas*] without knowing the language. And consequently it was necessary for them to hear confessions with an interpreter, which was the occasion for sacrilegious confessions.[6]

That he should verify also whether the *doctrineros* were compelling the Indians to transport their clothing and [other] commodities from St. Augustine to their *doctrinas*. And whether he knows it to be true that the religious were saying that his Majesty was obligated to deliver the *situados* or stipends[7] to them [the

4. My rendition of the elliptical Spanish here is tentative. The Spanish is: "los religiosos que tubiese por suficientes y necess[os] que fuesen delas prendas y partes quel el(?) estava encargado."

5. The governor in that era, Juan Marquez Cabrera, had made such charges against the friars in Apalachee in the wake of his visit of that province.

6. Presumably the sacrilege would arise from the penitent's concealing some of his sins to avoid revealing them to a third party, the interpreter, who would not have the strict obligation of silence imposed on the priest under the seal of the confessional.

7. The subsidy from Mexico from which the soldiers and friars were paid was usually sent in the form of goods rather than in cash.

doctrinas] and that they were not paying anything at all to the Indians for this work.

That, about whether many religious were employed in *doctrinas* where villages were close to one another and could be staffed with fewer religious, and that ten might suffice for the entire province.

That the church (*Ygl^{a}*)[8] was poorly staffed with priests and that there were no more than four [there] and that by arranging for another three under the title of *Plaças muertas*,[9] that would be assigned to them from those that became vacant, with the precondition that one of them should be an organist, because of their not having one there. [Thus] the church would be greatly benefited.

That in reference to the disputes between the religious and the governor, don Juan Marquez Cabrera, they were all motivated by passion, in denying the administration of the sacraments to him. And that he was a very selfless minister and zealous for the royal service. And that don Juan Ferro Machado was not coming to report on some cases that demanded a remedy because he lacked the means. That if he were to be awarded some travel expenses, he would do it.

After having seen this, the señor fiscal said that he had not placed a copy of the cited decree in this dispatch in order to learn whether the bishop had the authority to subdelegate it. That Machado came to Madrid later, and, after he had made some statements against the religious Fray Ayeta, on becoming aware of them, wrote and published a very lengthy memorial that he presented before the council, charging that the statements by Machado were specious and untrue. The latter [Machado] returned to Havana, of which he is a native and where he lives, without giving any counterreply. For this reason his letter should not be given any credence. And + [*sic*] that[10] the governor, having to allude

8. This refers to the church at St. Augustine. That Ferro Machado would assign seven priests to the St. Augustine parish and only ten for all of the Florida missions indicates where his priorities lay.

9. A *plaza muerta* is the pay of a foot soldier being used to support a widow. In this case the pay authorization would be diverted to a different use.

10. It is possible that a line was drawn through the word "that." The cross indicates an insertion of the words *tyendo a referir*, which appear in the margin opposite this line. Three words are definitely crossed out in the next line.

in his,[11] and more[?] acting secretly against the religious, it appears that these reports are contemptible because they are out of date (*antiquadas*) and because of this character's having been in the court.

A copy of this decree of November 3 of 1685 is brought by the señor fiscal, and the council puts it in order (*ordena el conss⁰*). And in it no authority was given to the bishop of Cuba so that he might subdelegate + to another person[12] the responsibility that the aforementioned [bishop] has to go to visit the provinces of Florida, for [undecipherable word or words] the bishopric, nor to remedy the excesses of the religious in the mistreatment they inflicted on the Indians and [that] don Juan Ferro Machado expresses in his letter.

Fray Feliciano López, a missionary preacher of the order of St. Francis, from Florida, reports in his memorial that he has come to these kingdoms on business pertaining to the expansion of the conversions and to the propagation of the holy Gospel in that province, and that it appears to him that the Father commissary general of the Indies has 14 religious from the mission band, which was granted for it [Florida] last year, but that did not go for lack of means. And on the supposition that it will be approved, he would bring them back [to Florida] because of the great need for them that exists [there].

That the cacique of the Province of Carlos has asked for religious from the bishop of Cuba, *sʳ* [?] that *haeseuto* [?].[13] And this religious [Fray López] requests that from the 14 alluded to, four or six be assigned [to Carlos] and be conducted directly to the Province of Carlos from Havana. And that on the vessel on which they go, the governor and royal officials of that city are to provide them with everything necessary for their sustenance and the ornaments and the rest of the things for celebrating [Mass] and administering the holy sacraments. And that for the future the alms that are given to them for their sustenance are to be sent from Havana because it is the port closest to the conversion of Carlos, withdrawing them from what is given for the religious of Florida, because it is understood that the *situado* for that presidio that comes from Mexico has been

11. These are the words that appear in the margin, see note 10 above.

12. These words also appear in the margin. My rendition of *ordena el conss⁰* is also tentative.

13. The context here seems to call for the words "without having received them," but the last of these words does not lend itself to such an interpretation.

ordered to come by way of Havana whose governor can separate from it what is assigned to those religious.

That the 14 that he asks for should be conducted by way of the Canaries on the first ship from the Islands that leaves for Havana because this is the quickest sailing, ordering the president of the Canaries to assist them with what is necessary for the embarkation.

From the books and papers of the secretariat it appears that by a dispatch of November 7 of [16]93, 20 religious priests and two laymen were granted at the request of Fray Francisco de Ayeta at the expense of the royal treasury for the *doctrinas* and conversions of Florida. And by another of the same date the expenditure that would have to be made for them in Spain and for their embarkation and passage was authorized in the royal coffer of Mexico. And until now there is no evidence that any of those religious have crossed over.

It was provided for that in the *situado* for Florida that is paid in Mexico, 70 places are assigned to the religious of St. Francis for the *doctrinas* and missions of Florida. And to each one the same [amount] is given for their sustenance and clothing as to a soldier, which is 115 ducats per year.

After the memorial of Fray Feliciano López was seen in the council, it was sent to the señor fiscal. And in his reply of the 27th of November of [16]93, he said that, according to what is established by the note placed by the aforesaid[?] a mission band of 20 religious priests and two laymen was granted for Florida on the 7th of November of [16]93 at the instance of the procurator general of the Franciscan order and a dispatch bearing the same date was issued later so that the expenditure for their sustenance and passage might be paid in the coffer of Mexico. Those [friars] were to go in charge of Fray Christóbal de Molina, commissary and *custodio* of that province. And it is not established whether any or all of them crossed over in the fleet of this year of [16]95, except only from the statement by this religious that they failed to cross over because of lack of means. And that he is asking for 14 of those already granted so that a part of them may work in the new conversions and four or six in the province of the cacique Carlos. And that those who may be assigned to this new conversion should go directly from the port of Havana without touching in Florida and that the governor and royal officials of Havana should give the necessary supplies for their passage and the ornaments and everything necessary for their ministry and for their maintenance in the future; the stipend that belongs to them should also be sent from Havana, deducting it from the *situado* that comes from Mexico and that is assigned for the Province of Florida on the supposition that it is ordered that the said *situado* should come to Havana to be handed over. And he asks that this mission band should go in the first vessels for the Canary Islands that there may be, so that they may pass from there to the Indies on the permit vessels. [And in reference to its being established from other dispatches that many of the religious that Fray Rodrigo de la Barrera brought over in the year of [16]90 departed [later] from that province, with the provincial, Fray Pedro de la Luna and the *definitorio* of the new chapter employing them in various posts of their order in Havana under the pretext of there being rotation to that province (with its being erroneous), and that some of them have been ordered to return to Spain and to be restored to their province of origin].[14] For which [reason] the 14 that they are asking for should be granted, with the provision that eight of them should go earmarked, so that they may be employed particularly in the new conversions of San Salbador de Mayaca, San Antonio Anacapi, la Concepción, and San Joseph de Jororo. With reference to this, it has been reported in a letter from the provincial council of the 5th of December of [16]93 that there are a great number of heathen nations in those regions and that 400 people had been reduced already, asking for some iron tools for the new *entradas*. He has replied concerning this, in the margin of the said letter, that it be sent. That the other six out of the 14 religious can be destined for the province of the Cacique Carlos, as is requested, for he has appeared personally in Havana to ask for missionaries, as is established by the letter from the bishop of Cuba of the 3rd of July of [16]92; and by another from Governor Quiroga, of the 1st of April of [16]88, that the son of the said cacique, not having done so ever before, had come with many others to render obedience [to the governor] when he went on the visitation of Apalachee and Timuqua. After having viewed these and the proposals made in this vein by Fray Francisco Romero, who intended to cross over to the said missions, persuaded by the bishop, the señor fiscal replied on the 23rd of October of [16]93 (of which mention has been made). That with respect to what pertains to this point it seems from the

14. This sentence is bracketed in the document for unknown reasons.

[decree][15] placed by the aforesaid[?] that around June of [16]93 the Florida provincial was given the responsibility anew of sending religious for the conversions of the Indians of those coasts and in particular for the land of the Cacique Carlos and to that of Ais, which was dispatched *dap*^{O}[16] on the 12th of September of the same year. With reference to the bishop's saying in his letter that he lacked clerics to send for the said mission, raising the question of his scruples about not sending missionaries after the cacique had come personally to ask for them, this obligation has become very pressing. For this [reason] an order to the governor and royal officials of Havana would be appropriate[17] that they should give all the necessary supplies to these six missionaries (as is requested) so that they may cross over to the land of the Cacique Carlos and that later they should send them the portion of stipend from the *situado* that comes from Mexico that they have assigned [to them] in it, giving an account of this arrangement to the royal officials of Florida so that they may record it in their books, because it is the señor fiscal's understanding that the sending of it from there [St. Augustine] would be bound to be difficult because of the great distance by land that is involved to that of the said cacique and because one may cross over to it from Havana in three days. And they are doing it in less time. And that the punctual supplying of those missionaries would be most appropriate so that they may remain in that spot. The señor fiscal made the said need for this mission known to the Father commissary general for the Indies as soon as the council ordered him to. And he assented to it, even though he had no particularized reports about those regions. And he stated that it was advisable to await the arrival of some religious from Florida in order to take the rest of the individuals back. The señor fiscal gave an account of this to the council verbally. [And now, with this religious [Fray López] having arrived and asked expressly for missionaries for the province of the Cacique Carlos, and taking the antecedent reports into consideration that have been

15. My rendition of this abbreviation is tentative. The abbreviation is not very legible, but what follows suggests that it is a "decree" or *cedula*.

16. I have been unable to decipher this abbreviation.

17. The Spanish here is "Porque combendra mandar orden al Gov^{or} y ofi^{s} Rs de la Hav^{a} de (?) que a estos Seis Misioneros." The word *mandar* was thoroughly crossed out as if it was meant to be eliminated; the *de* is also crossed out or blotted.

mentioned, and what was requested in the cited reply of October 23 of [16]93.[18] It appears that these are sufficient [reasons] to make it necessary that this mission be developed. Directions about this must be given to the governor and royal officials of Florida so that they for their part may strive for its maintenance, giving an account on all occasions of their work there relative both to this [conversion] and to the rest of the conversions.

With reference to these 14 religious embarking on the vessels that may be going to the Canaries so that they may cross over to the Indies from there on the permit ships, the señor fiscal states that this has the drawback that [such ships] are wont to remain in them [the Indies] or to cross over without permission to other islands incorporated[?] with them. This has proved to be a source of evil in the Indies and all of this is provided against in the law 9, book 1, Title 14.[19] And *se deve xeher, quantes dete*[20] this mission band assembled and disposed so as to be able to embark directly for Havana or Veracruz should the occasion arise.

As I passed everything and by the attached papers.

Council   Florida

Extract of what is contained in the dispatches occasioned by the arrival at this court from the provinces of Florida of Fray Feliciano López of the Franciscan Order together with what was replied to them by the señor fiscal, as the council instructed him to by a resolution of the 19th of January of 1695.

Done on the 6th of December of [16]95 because of the señor fiscal's not having finished until now[21] bringing the papers that he has in his possession.

The notes on the two remaining pages of this document, which are

18. This would seem to be a logical place for the closing bracket, but there is no closing bracket. As this is not a complete sentence, a comma seems to be called for here, but there is a period instead.

19. This refers to the *Recopilación de los Leyes de las Indias,* the codification of the various laws and decrees issued over the years for the government of Spain's New World kingdoms.

20. I have been unable to decipher these words fully. The sense would seem to be "steps must be taken at once [to have]."

21. The not very legible Spanish here appears to be *hasta el dia,* which might be rendered also as "yet."

undoubtedly the two enclosures alluded to at the beginning of this piece, are omitted as they add nothing useful.

The first page of the second document contains three separate elements. The first, written across the full width of the top of the page and apparently in the same hand as the body of the document, is a four-line note on the contents of the document. The second element, filling the right-hand half of the page, begins about five lines down from the first note and runs for eighteen pages. The third element, written in a different hand, fills the left-hand margin of this page and four lines in the right-hand column between the note at the top and the beginning of the text that occupies most of the document.

Second Extract of Dispatches Relating to the Proposed Calusa Mission, 1695

AGI, Seville, Santo Domingo 228. This piece from the Stetson Collection bears the identification "AI 54-5-13/70 Spain, December 12, 1695" on the library's cover for the photostats. The cover bears the following note: "Abstract of the expedientes relative to matters brought thither from Florida by Fr. Feliciano López, O.S.F. [*sic*], and answers made to him by the fiscal as ordered by an *acuerdo* of nov. 19, 1695."

First is the note that lies across the top of the first page.

Extract of what the dispatches contain that were generated as a result of Fray Feliciano López of the order of St. Francis having arrived at this court from the provinces of Florida along with what the fiscal replied to them as the council ordered him to by a decision of the 19th of November of [1]695.

The following note is from the left-hand margin of the first page, to the extent that I have been able to decipher it.

+Council 12 of *xgAbgs*[?] December —s^r[?] governor *sien*^{acifs} *solors Oit*^{a} *B*^{e}[?] *Part*^{r}. The permission given for the passage of twenty religious and two lay persons is ratified, and if all of them cannot make the voyage, permission is given so that as long as they are not less than the fourteen asked for they may cross over immediately on the account for the twenty, for which purpose the orders will be ratified and issued again [undecipherable word] anticipating in them what the señor fiscal says and communicating it to the bishop, governor of Havana, he of Florida, royal officials so that they may

carry it out and so that everyone may understand it, let the
governor and royal officials of Florida be charged so that they may
send word if the number of the 70 religious[22] destined for that
province is filled up or not and the [numbers] that are lacking and
whether they fulfill the indispensable obligations of their institute
as they should,[23] saying what occurs to them in this matter. And let
a decree of petition and charge be dispatched to the bishop so that
he may visit his bishopric because of having learned how much
time has passed without having had one[24] and of the justified
concern it has caused. Let a commission be given to Ferro Machado
so that by not admonishing him[?] (undecipherable word] possible,
believing that it will be of very special service and please
[undecipherable word] and that in addition to fulfilling their
obligations they will pay heed to them in honoring him and favoring
him above all.

The following text occupies the greater part of this document.

The Field Master don Diego de Quiroga y Losada, while governor
of Florida, and the royal officials gave an account in a letter of the
15th of March and 1st of April of 1688 about having, together, made
the general visitation of the Indian settlements as soon as the
governor took possession of the government because it was thirty
years that this had not been done. That while they were visiting the
provinces of Apalachee and Timuqua various caciques and leading
men from the heathens of that vicinity came to give obedience and
also the son of the so-called Prince Carlos who dominates the
province of the Keys, giving obedience in the name of his father, not
having done so until then, with all of them asking for peace and
missionaries who might indoctrinate them in our holy faith [the
last line on this page did not reproduce on the photocopy] as is
shown from two letters translated into Castilian from their own

22. This is an allusion to the seventy positions allotted for the friars on the
pay roster for the Florida garrison.
23. The two preceding governors had lodged a number of complaints about
the conduct of some of the friars.
24. The last visitation made by the bishop had been the one made by Bishop
Gabriel Días Vara Calderón in 1675, the last one that was to be made before the
destruction of the Florida missions.

language that the governor sent.[25] After the said letters had been
seen in the council, he sent them to the señor fiscal, who in his
reply of July 23 of [1]693 said that the missionary fathers of St.
Francis, (which is the order that has responsibility for the
conversion of the heathens of this province), should be charged
[with it; that] they should undertake these new conversions because
it is their principal objective and because the obligation is greater to
see to it that so great a number of souls should not be lost, than for
the staffing of the *doctrinas* of those who have been brought under
obedience and converted since the time of their grandfathers. And
that in reference to the obedience given by Prince Carlos, it is
evident from recent letters from the bishop and governor of Havana
that Cacique Carlos has crossed over to that city to ask for
missionaries. At this time a copy of the bishop's letter of July 3 of
[1]693 was seen in the council (the original of which the señor fiscal
has), in which he expressed the distress that he felt because of not
having found a sufficient number of priests in his bishopric so that
they might cross over to be employed in the aforesaid new
conversions and especially in the two provinces of the Cacique
Carlos and [cacique] of Ais, who are the closest to the city and coast
of Havana, because of the Cacique Carlos having come to their doors
asking for baptism and ministers so that all his vassals might
receive them, in which there would be no resistance at all, and with
the bishop supposing that those who asked for the faith through the
door of baptism would amount to 14,000 souls. In view of it the
council decided on the 19th of October [?] of [1]693 that the fiscal
should be told (as was done with a paper from señor don Juan de
Larrea of the 14th of it), that, after acquainting himself with the
contents of the letter from the bishop of Cuba, he should speak with
the Father commissary general Fray Julian Chumillas. And after
conferring with him about the manner and measures that it would
be well to avail himself of for the attainment of the reduction of
these souls to our holy faith with the greater Christian utility and
benefit, as the council so greatly desired. And by a dispatch [sent]
the same day, this very thing was communicated to the Father
commissary general, so that with this report he would reach an

25. These are the letters to the king written by the chiefs of Apalachee and
Timucua in 1688. The Apalachee's letter is the only document in that language
that has been discovered to date (see Smith 1860).

accord with the señor fiscal about the day and hour in which they could confer in order to [word illegible because part is cut off] and that they should give an account of what resulted.

After viewing another copy of the same letter from the bishop of Cuba, the provincial of the Franciscans of the Province of Santa Elena of Florida was charged by a dispatch of the 12th of September of [16]93, that he should exercise full care and vigilance in providing evangelical ministers for all those new conversions and especially for the two provinces of the Cacique Carlos and [cacique] of Ais, who have asked for baptism with such great eagerness for themselves and their vassals, sending for this objective the religious whom he considers to be necessary and adequate. That they were of the business and portion that he was given responsibility for in dispatches of September 8 of [16]90 and June 14 of [16]92.

In another letter of the 15th of April of [16]88, the governor don Diego de Quiroga gave an account of don Juan Ferro Machado, visitor named by the bishop of Cuba, having arrived in Florida to make the visitation and having done it without a problem, he then passed on to wanting to make some secret inquiries against the religious of St. Francis with the pretext of having orders for it from his Majesty. And having agreed to, he provided an *auto* so that he might present it to them, which he did not do, and neither did he reply. And the governor did not pass on to any other action because of the desire that he had for the greater service of his Majesty and for not disturbing the republic.

In view of this letter and of a testimony that came with it and two letters from don Juan Ferro Machado of the 8th of August of [1]688 that were joined to it, the señor fiscal says in a reply of the 9th of November[?] of [16]95 that Don Juan Ferro reports the bishop having delivered a decree of August 13, [1]685, so that he would investigate whether the *doctrinero* religious were punishing the Indians without exempting the nobles and caciques. And that he learned that some were committing this excess and that they were passing on to administer them [i.e., the missions] without knowing the language and when necessary they heard their confessions with an interpreter, which gave rise to sacrilegious confessions.[26]

26. To put this into perspective, it should be noted that Ferro Machado was an advocate of compelling all the Indians to learn Spanish. This occurs in a letter by him that I have seen in the past. And in that letter he criticized the

That he investigated also whether the *doctrineros* compelled the Indians to carry loads of their clothing and provisions from St. Augustine to the *doctrinas*. And he learned it was true and that the religious were saying that his Majesty was obliged to place the *situados* or stipends in them, and that they were not paying the Indians anything at all for this work.

That concerning whether many religious were employed in the *doctrinas* whose villages were at a short distance [from one another]. He said that some are close and could be ministered to with fewer religious, and that ten would suffice for the whole province.

That the church [in St. Augustine] was poorly staffed with priests and that there were no more than four. And providing orders for another three under the guise of *Plaças muertas* that would be set aside from those that became vacant,[27] with the proviso that one of them should be an organist as they did not have one. [With this] the church would be much better served.

That in reference to the discords between the religious and the governor, don Juan Marquez Cabrera, they were all motivated by passion in refusing to administer the sacraments to him and that he was a most disinterested minister and zealous for the royal service. And because don Juan Ferro was lacking in means, he was not coming to report some things that begged for a remedy; that if he were to be given some travel allowance, he would do so.

In view of this the señor fiscal says: that he has not put a copy of the decree cited in this dispatch in order to learn whether the bishop had the authority to subdelegate it. That Machado came to Madrid later and after having made some reports against the religious, when Fray Ayeta was notified of it, he wrote and put a very lengthy memorial into print that he presented in the council, characterizing the arguments of Machado as being facile and untrue. Without giving a reply, the latter [Machado] returned to Havana, of which he is a native and where he lives. For this no notice should be taken of his letters. And in relation to the

---

friars who knew the Indian languages for teaching the catechism to the Indians in their own tongue rather than in Spanish.

27. As plazas became available they would be assigned to three priests for the church at St. Augustine. This recommendation casts an interesting light on Ferro Machado's earlier recommendation that ten friars would suffice for all the Indian missions in Florida, but that St. Augustine needed seven priests.

governor's alluding in his [letter], that he was conducting a secret process against the religious, these reports as outdated and this subject, having been in the court, appear now to be worthless.

He brings a copy of the decree of August 13 of 1685 that the señor fiscal cites and that the council orders. And in it no authority is given to the bishop of Cuba for him to subdelegate to another person the duty that he was given that he should go to visit the provinces of Florida, for they belong to his bishopric; not to remedy the excesses of the religious in the mistreatment they inflicted on the Indians and that don Juan Ferro Machado expressed in his letter.

Fray Feliciano López, missionary preacher of the order of St. Francis of Florida, states in his memorial that he has come to these kingdoms on business pertaining to the expansion of the conversion and propagation of the holy Gospel in that province and that to the Father commissary general for the Indies it appears that he is bringing back 14 religious for the mission that were granted for it last year and that did not go for the lack of means. And he begs that this be approved that he bring them because of the great shortage of them that there is.

That the cacique of the province of Carlos has asked the bishop of Cuba for religious, about which he has written. And this religious asks that of the 14 alluded to, four or six be assigned and conducted directly to the Province of Carlos from Havana. And in the embarkation that may take place, the governor and royal officials of that city are to supply them with everything that is necessary for their sustenance and the ornaments and the rest of the things necessary for celebrating [Mass] and administering the holy sacraments and that from this time forward the alms that are given to them for their sustenance are to be sent from Havana because it is the closest port to the conversion of Carlos, setting them aside from that which belongs to the religious of Florida because it is understood that the *situado* that comes from Mexico for that presidio has been ordered to come by way of Havana, whose governor can separate what is assigned to these religious.

That the 14 that he asks for should be brought by way of the Canaries because it is the quickest route, in the first ship that leaves from the islands for Havana, commanding the president of the Canaries to assist them with what is necessary for the embarkation.

By the books and papers of the secretariat[28] it appears that by a dispatch of the 7th of November of [1]693, at the request of Fray Francisco de Ayeta, 20 religious priests and two lay persons were conceded at the expense of the royal treasury for the *doctrinas* and conversions of Florida and by another [dispatch] of the same date a pay warrant was issued in the royal treasury of Mexico for the expense that was going to have to be incurred in Spain for them and for their embarkation and passage and up to the present there is no evidence that any of these religious have passed over.

Let provision be made so that in the *situado* for Florida that is paid in Mexico 70 slots are assigned for the Franciscan religious for the *doctrinas* and missions of Florida and to each one there is to be given for their sustenance and clothing the same [amount] as to a soldier, which is 115 ducats per year.

The memorial of Fray Feliciano López having been seen in the council, it was sent to the señor fiscal and in his reply of the 27th of November of 1695 he says that according to what appears from the note placed by the secretariat on November 7 of [16]93 at the request of the procurator general of the order of St. Francis, a mission of 20 religious priests and two lay people was granted for Florida and a pay warrant was issued with the same date, so that the expenditures for their sustenance and passage should be paid in the treasury of Mexico. These [religious] were to go in the charge of Fray Christóval de Molina, commissary *custodio* for that province. And there is no evidence whether all or any of them passed over in the fleet of this year of [16]95 except solely the word of this religious that they failed to cross over because of the lack of means and that he asks for 14 of those already granted so that a part of them may staff the new conversions and four or six in the province of the Cacique Carlos and that those who are assigned to a new conversion should leave directly from the port of Havana without stopping in Florida and that the governor and royal officials of Havana should give them the necessary supplies for the passage and the ornaments and everything necessary for their ministry and for their sustenance in advance. The stipend that belongs to them is also to be sent from Havana, deducting it from the *situado* that comes from Mexico and is assigned to the Province of Florida

28. The Spanish here is the abbreviation *s.*^{ta}.

because it is presumed that it is ordered that the said *situado* should come to Havana to be delivered. And he asks that this mission go in the first vessels for the Canary Islands that become available so that they may go to the Indies in the special-permit vessels.

And that in relation to its being evident from other dispatches that many of the religious that Fray Rodrigo de la Barrera brought over in the year [1]690 departed from that province, with the provincial, Fray Pedro de Luna and the definitory of the new chapter employing them in Havana in various posts of their order with the pretext of having an alternative in that province (it being wrong) and because some of them were ordered to return to Spain and to rejoin their provinces there.

For this reason it appears to the señor fiscal that Florida is short of missionaries; because the 14 that they ask for must be granted, with the provision that *eight* [*sic*] of them come destined especially to serve the new conversions of San Salvador de Mayaca, San Antonio Anacapi, la Concepción, and San Joseph de Jororo. With respect to these it has been reported in a letter from the definitory of the 5th of December[?] of [16]93 that there are a great number of heathen nations in that area and that they have already reduced 450 people, asking for some iron tools for the new *entradas*. He has replied concerning this in the margin of the said letter, which he is remitting.

That the other six of the 14 religious can be sent destined for the province of the Cacique Carlos as is asked, for he has come to Havana personally to ask for missionaries, as is evident from a letter from the bishop of Cuba of the 3rd of July of [16]92 and from another from Governor Quiroga of the 1st of April of [16]88, that the son of the said cacique, not having ever done it before, had come to give obedience with many others while he [the governor] was traveling on the visitation of Apalachee and Timuqua. In view of the aforementioned and of the proposals made about this matter by Fray Francisco Romero, who attempted to cross over to the said missions at the request of the bishop, the señor fiscal replied on the 23rd of October of [16]93 (about which mention has been made) that with reference to what pertains to this point it appears by a decree placed by the secretariat that around June of [16]93 the provincial of Florida was charged anew that he should send religious for the conversions of the Indians of those coasts and especially to the land of the Cacique Carlos and that of Ais. A duplicate of this [order] was dispatched on the 12th of September of the same year.

That with respect to the bishop's saying in his letter that he found himself without clerics that he might send to the said mission, expounding on his scruples about not sending missionaries when that cacique had come personally to ask for them, this makes this obligation very pressing. For this reason it is appropriate to order the governor and royal officials of Havana that they are to give all the necessary equipment to these six missionaries (as is asked) in order to cross over to the land of the Cacique Carlos and that later, from the *situado* that will come from Mexico, they are to remit the portion of the stipend that they have assigned[?] to them in it, giving an account about this to the royal officials of Florida so that they may set it down in their books, because it is the señor fiscal's understanding that its remittance from there would be found to be difficult because of the great distance by land that there is to that of the said cacique and because one can cross over to it from Havana in three days and even in less time. And that the punctual assistance of these missionaries is most appropriate so that they may remain in that area. The señor fiscal communicated with the Father commissary general for the Indies about the necessity for this mission as soon as the council ordered him to do so and he attended to it; even though he does not have specific reports for that area and said that it was appropriate to await the coming of some religious from Florida in order to obtain the most specific ones [possible]. The señor fiscal verbally gave an account about this to the council.

Now with this religious having arrived and asking expressly for missionaries for the province of the Cacique Carlos, and taking into account the antecedent reports that have been mentioned and what was requested in the cited reply of the 23rd of October of [16]93, it appears that they are sufficient to require the development of this mission. News about this must be given to the governor and royal officials of Florida so that they for their part may strive for its maintenance, giving an account on every occasion about the service of the religious both in this one and in the rest of the conversions.

In reference to the fact that these 14 religious are to embark in the vessels that happen to be going to the Canaries so that from there they may continue on to the Indies in those of the permit type, the señor fiscal says that this involves the problem that these [types of ships] are wont to remain in them [i.e., the Indies] or to pass to others of these islands incorporated with them without permission [to do so], which has proved to be a great evil in the Indies, and all this is foreseen in law 9, Book 1, title 14 and that it must be believed, that before this mission is assembled and ready to be able to embark an opportunity will present itself for them [to go] directly to Havana or Veracruz. This is how it all appears from the appended papers.

The following note appears on the cover page of the preceding document.

Council
Extract of what the dispatches contain that were generated as a result of Fray Feliciano López of the order of St. Francis having arrived at this court from the provinces of Florida along with what the fiscal replied to them as the council ordered him to, by a decision of the 19th of November of 1695.[29]
Entro el Acordado
Ex⁰

12. The Florida Governor's Report on the Revolt of the Mayaca-Jororo Missions, February 1697

In granting permission for the departure to Florida of the fourteen new friars sought by Fray Feliciano López, the council's fiscal specified that the balance of those friars not needed for Calusa be employed in the new conversions of Mayaca and Jororo and various other heathen nations in central-south Florida and on the southeast coast. Before Fray López and his band of five friars sailed from Havana to Calusa to begin their work in September 1697, Florida's governor reported trouble in the Mayaca-Jororo territory where other friars had been laboring for some time. The documents in this section tell of that trouble. The governor's terse report of the trouble is the cover document. A brief note, which gives the council's reaction to the news, follows it. With his re-

29. Except for 695 being written as 1695, this note is identical to the one that appears on the top of first page of this document.

port the governor sent a much longer account composed by the notary Juan Solana, detailing the trouble and the measures that the governor adopted to deal with it.

Governor Laureano de Torres y Ayala to the King, February 3, 1697

AGI, Seville, Santo Domingo 228. This translation was made from a copy in the Jeannette Thurber Connor Collection, reel 3 of the P.K. Yonge Library of Florida History.

Sire

On the fifth day of the past November I received the news from my deputy-governor [whom] I had placed in the province of Mayaca, where various conversions had been begun among heathen natives who dwell in those lands about how those of a place called Atoyquimi had killed the padre *doctrinero* and two Indians who lived with him and helped him to say Mass, and that both the assailants and the rest of the inhabitants of the said village have retreated to the woods (*Montes*). In view of that report, it appeared to me appropriate for the service of God and of your Majesty to send six soldiers to the lieutenant with an order that he apprehend the assailants and with every gentle means seek to bring all the rest back so that they may settle down in their village and be pacified. And that this should be [done] before their fickleness moves them to some greater excess in the rest of the surrounding villages. And three days after having finished the dispatch, I had another letter from my said lieutenant in which he expressed the opinion that a body of people will be necessary in order to pacify them. And I resolved to send ten more soldiers and an active-service adjutant as squad leader, repeating my order once more that they should go to the said province and seek to calm the said Indians and to quiet them and at the same time apprehend the assailants. And after having departed from this presidio, they arrived at the place of Mayaca, which is ancient,[1] and in which the lieutenant resided. And they did not encounter him there, as he had gone on with the first six soldiers on their trip to visit the rest of the places. On learning

1. A mission was established in Mayaca at the start of the seventeenth century and was still in existence in 1655, but it does not appear on the 1675 lists. It reappeared on the 1680 mission list mentioned as a "new conversion."

of this, the said ten soldiers and their squad leader passed on at once to the point (*punto*)[2] to join forces with the lieutenant and the rest. And they went on visiting the places together, without doing them the least injury or receiving anything at all from them, as I stipulated thus in my orders. But rather many of the natives of some villages offered to go with my Spaniards in pursuit of the aforesaid rebellious ones, as was done, both because they were necessary in order to teach them the trails and in order not to hurt their feelings. And the result that came of this was that they put the Spaniards on a trail and placed them in such unfamiliar places, full of brambles, swampy areas, and ponds, that they found their lives in great risk. And they abandoned them finally and left them in the woods without guides. Consequently they found themselves forced by this new unexpected happening to retreat to a place named Jororo from whence they had departed three days earlier and where they had received them with great pleasure. And they [now] found it deserted and everyone in rebellion and the church desecrated and a Spanish soldier dead, who had remained behind in the said village because [he was] ill, and two Indians [dead as well] who served as sacristans. And even though they sought to learn where these assailants and rebels had retreated to, they did not succeed because of not having anyone with whom to speak who knew about it. From this [incident] resulted the rebellion of another village that was called Atisimi. With this, the places in rebellion are three and they have withdrawn to points unknown where a remedy will be applicable only with time, as I shall achieve with divine help once I have provisions and people so that the plaza [St. Augustine] will not be shorthanded. I held a meeting (*junta*) about this with the royal officials, captains, and *reformados* of this presidio. And they were all of this opinion. Consequently, on seeing what the situation was, I concurred.

The padres *doctrineros* who were there were three. They killed one. The [other] two have withdrawn to this presidio. And it was a pity, because they were off to a great beginning for the extention of our holy faith. But their barbarism is great. I am sending Your Majesty all the testimony that I have taken in relation to this affair, so that Your Majesty, after having seen it, may provide what pleases his royal will. May God our Lord preserve your Catholic

2. It is not clear what the governor had in mind as "the point."

royal person for many years as Christendom needs and as we your
vassals desire. Florida, February 3, 1697.

D. Laureano Torres y Ayala

(A page of the same size follows, and in a different hand, which says)

[This document begins with a cross.]

Florida, to His Majesty on the 9th of February of 1697, received on
the 6th of January in the Galleons' dispatch-boat, no. 1.

The Governor Don Laureano de Torres y Ayala

(The extract of this letter [the preceding one] follows, and is
omitted).

Council 24th of January, [1]698

Reply to him that these reports have caused H.M. great emotion
because of the temple having been desecrated, the missionary killed,
and because of those villages having then revolted, when the
conversion of those natives was advancing so, ordering him to do
whatever may be necessary for the reestablishment of those
revolted villages and that he apply whatever efforts may be
necessary so that the preaching of the holy Gospel may go forward
and so that the conversion of that people to the Catholic faith may
be achieved, charging him that, if he should capture the Indians
who have apostatized, he should have them given the punishment
that corresponds to their crime.

Done.

(The following testimony follows on four folios and in a different
hand.)

[This document begins with a cross.]

Testimony in reference to the *autos* for Jororo.

I the Ensign, Juan Solana, notary for the public and for the government of this city of St. Augustine of Florida and its provinces,
certify and give true testimony in the part where it is appropriate
for the gentlemen who may see the present [document] how, among
the papers that remain in my possession and in my office, it is
evident and apparent that on the fourth of the month of November
of the earlier year of one thousand six hundred ninety-six between
eleven and twelve o'clock of this night His lordship the señor don
Laureano de Thorres y Ayala, Knight of the Order of Santiago,
governor and captain general of this said city and of its provinces by

his Majesty, provided an *auto* before me the present notary because of having received a paper from the adjutant, Bernardo de Medina, his lieutenant for the province of Mayaca and Hororo, at the said hour, written in the aforesaid [village] of Mayaca on the first of the said month of November. In it he gave an account to his lordship that the Indians of the place of Atoquime had killed Father Fray Luis Sánchez, religious *doctrinero*, who ministered to them and said Mass. And that they had torn his habit into pieces, bloodied and killed the sacristan and a young cacique, a native of Aypaja. Ordering the putting of the said paper with the *autos* and that investigation into the case be made so that the assailants would receive the punishment that such an atrocity merited. And that the Captain don Juan de Ayala Escobar, who is such of the infantry and commander in this plaza, name six soldiers so that they may go with the necessary order to those of the said lieutenant, Bernardo de Medina. And the said *auto* having been made known to the said Captain don Juan de Ayala at once and without delay, and the naming of the said soldiers having been done, a reply was given by the said señor governor and captain general to his said lieutenant, Bernardo de Medina, with an order-letter of the fifth of the said month and year, the authentic copy of which remained in the *autos*. By the latter it was ordered that he should set out with the six soldiers and the rest of the people that he should be able to assemble in search of the assailants and send them to this presidio with a secure guard, proceeding in the matter with complete caution because it is of such great importance. And on the eighth of the said month of November his Lordship received another letter of the sixth of the said month from his said lieutenant that he sent with Jazinto de Thejeda, a soldier of this presidio who came accompanying the Reverend Father definitor, Fray Salvador Bueno, religious *doctrinero* who worked in the place of Hororo. And from the aforementioned [pair], his lordship learned the truth about what had taken place in the said province. On the said eighth day an *auto* was provided for this purpose, and he ordered the paper alluded to be placed following it and that a statement be taken from the said Jazinto de Thejeda. This was carried out at once. And it is established by it that, while he was in the place of Mayaca in the company of the said lieutenant, Bernardo de Medina, the aforesaid Reverend Father Fray Salvador Bueno, who served as *doctrinero* in the place of Hororo, arrived at the said place on Monday the past twenty-ninth of October and gave the news to the said lieutenant of how the people of the said place had come to his convent weeping and saying that the people of the said place of Atoquime had killed the Padre Fray Luis Sanchez, and that they had seen the habit reduced to shreds and bloodied. And that they had killed two boys, who went with the said priest to help him at Mass. That the people of the place of Hororo had set out with much spirit in search of the assailants and that the said lieutenant, other soldiers, and people had gone out with the said Reverend Father definitor about three leagues to seek positive news about the said religious name Fray Francisco Camacho, who served as *doctrinero* in the place of Jizime[3] because it was presumed that they had killed him. And that they did not go on forward any further because the Indians and caciques said that they wished to go on alone and not with the Spaniards and that the Indian assailants were assembled. And they said that the bullets (*Balas*) were awaiting them (*las esperauan en las manos*). And that the said lieutenant, on seeing them *Dezimidos*[4] and with bad spirit (*mal animo*), returned to Mayaca. And in light of the *autos,* by one provided on the ninth of the said month and year, his lordship ordered that for the better disposition and remedying of what had occurred and so that the assailants might be apprehended and that the Indian places that were in peace and friendship might be supported and so that they might recover the ornaments and sacred vessels from the churches of the places in rebellion, the royal officials, sergeants-major, captains, and other officers of war, both active and pensioned, be called to meet on that same day at four in the afternoon so that, once assembled, they might confer. And having been summoned and assembled in the royal houses of his lordship's residence, all those mentioned in the said *auto* were of one mind and in common accord that the said Province of Mayaca should be assisted with all speed by a column of soldiers in order to support the natives who remained under obedience and to reduce the rebellious ones. And so that they might seek to apprehend the assailants with determination and recover and put under security the ornaments from the churches and search for the religious, Fray

3. This is probably a variant form of Atisime, mentioned elsewhere. This variant suggests that Atissimi may be the origin of the modern Kissimmee which lies in Jororo territory.

4. Possibly this was meant to be *desanimados* (discouraged) or *disimulados* (dissembling).

Francisco Camacho, who was missing. And after his lordship the said señor governor and captain general had concurred with the result, at once without delay, by his *Auto* he ordered the said Captain D. Juan de Ayala to name ten soldiers and as their squad leader, the Adjutant don Favian de Angulo, who is presently sergeant-major in this plaza. And that the treasurer of the royal exchequer is to provide them with munitions. And after having made this known to them and executed everything immediately, it appears from a copy of the order that was attached to the said *autos,* dated on the same ninth day, that the said señor governor and captain general had ordered the said adjutant, don Favian de Angulo, to go and join forces with his said lieutenant, Bernardo de Medina, so that, with the soldiery that had been sent to him from the start and that which the said adjutant, don Favian de Angulo, carried with him, along with the rest that might be added to them, Spaniards and Indians, they might go to the said Province of Mayaca. And bringing along indications of [their] peaceful intentions, they should enter into the places in it. And with the warm reception and display of affection [that is] possible (*con el agasaxo y cariño Posible*), they should go along viewing and reconnoitering the state of affairs in the places, both the ones in rebellion and those who were at peace. And they should welcome the caciques and the rest of the Indians. And they should go on seeking information about the incident and [try to learn] what occasion the Indians of Atoquime might have for having killed the religious. And that they should seek to capture the assailants. And that before entering into the places they should send peace emissaries ahead of them in order to make them aware of their coming and [let them know] that they were not coming in a warlike spirit; that they should come at their call. And that, if they remained stubborn about coming back after they should have sent two successive summons to them, and, if it became clear that they were not going to achieve the [peaceful] entrance into the rebellious places for the pacification that must take place, in this case he may use force until he subdues them and captures the head assailants of the uprising and reassure and give a warm reception to the rest [of them], look for and recover the ornaments, images, and sacred vessels of the churches and put them all in a safe place and pardon all the rest of the villages once they have again sworn to be loyal to his Majesty in whose royal name he was pardoning them for this occasion. And with the greatest cunning they should seek to bring the head assailants to this presidio and search for Father Fray Francisco Camacho, gathering information from the Indians of Tisime, where he resided as *doctrinero,* about where he could possibly be; and also visit the place of Hororo and see if its natives were under obedience. And in this [settlement] and the rest he is to strive with a totally warm reception so that they may persevere under obedience. And if some should have fled to the woods out of fear, he is to seek to find them and bring them back to their villages, maneuvering in all of this with the greatest skill so that he will do the most [that is possible] for the service of both Majesties, which was the objective of his lordship. And on the twelfth of the said month of November of the said year his lordship received a note from his said lieuten[ant], Bernardo de Medina, posted in Mayaca on the tenth of the said month and year in which he recounts that solely the natives of the place of Atoquime were in rebellion and that there had not been any additional deaths beyond those he had reported [already], because the Father Fray Francisco Camacho was well and the rest of the places at peace and under obedience and that the assailants in the deaths had fled to the coast. And by an *auto* of the said twelfth day his lordship ordered the said letter added to [the others] written in connection with this matter and to take a statement from the soldier who brought it [who is] called Francisco Domínguez. He did this at once. And in everything [his statement] agrees with what the cited paper specifies, that is, that all the places were at peace with the exception of that of Atoquime and that, because of having killed the priest, Fray Luis Sánchez, and the aforementioned two boys, its natives had fled to the woods and carried off their women and children and the ornaments of the church and that there was no one at all in the said village. And that with these reports the said lieutenant, Benardo de Medina, and the Ensign Juan Alonso and other soldiers and some Indians were on the point of setting out in search of the ones alluded to [above] and to capture the assailants. Concerning this the said señor governor and captain general replied to the said [officers], the lieutenant, Bernardo de Medina, and don Favian de Angulo, once again giving orders to them by his letter sent on that same twelfth day of November, a copy of which is to be found in the *autos,* that both together with their forces joined should go to visit the said places and give as warm a reception as possible to the caciques and treat them warmly, without their stay among them or that of the soldiery in their villages putting any burden upon them; for half a day would suffice for greeting them warmly and welcoming them, without obliging them to give any meat, fish, or anything else, passing on in this manner [to each] all the way to the said place of Atoquime to capture the leaders of the assailants, making all the inquiries appropriate for that [purpose]. And that, if it should not be possible to capture them, he is to withdraw at once with the soldiery to the place of Mayaca and the said adjutant, don Favian de Angulo, from there to this presidio; for it would seem that there would be nothing else to do for the present and that anything else would only serve as an irritant to the natives, consuming their provisions, with the said lieutenant, Bernardo de Medina, remaining alert always in order to capture the assailants as soon as it may be possible to have them, guiding themselves in all the rest by the prior order that was dispatched to them on the third of December of the said year of six hundred and ninety-six. His lordship received a letter from the said [officers], the lieutenant, Bernardo de Medina, and adjutant don Favian de Angulo, posted in Mayaca on the twenty-ninth of November of the said year, in which they recounted to his lordship how, after having joined forces and being on the point of leaving for the Village of Yuamajiro, where they had reports the assailants had withdrawn to, they provided for their expedition, equipped with arms, munitions, and provisions. And that in the place of Hororo, because of having found it at peace and because of having been received with a warm reception and great affection, they had left a soldier named Jazinto de Thexeda there because of his having stated that he found himself incapacitated for continuing the journey because of having punctured a foot and that he wished to heal himself there. And as they were going along continuing their march, it happened that their scouts and guides that led them, who were two Indians from the said place of Hororo, were bringing them onto swampy [?] and gravelly trails (*por entre caminos variales y cascales*)[5] that were so difficult that they were able to advance some only at the cost of a

5. Neither *varial* nor *cascal* appear in modern Spanish dictionaries, but *varial* is used elsewhere in Florida Spanish documents where it clearly has the sense of bog or swamp and it may be an old cognate of the Portuguese *varzea*. *Cascal* in Portuguese connotes "gravel, pebbles, rock chips."

great deal of labor and delay until the point where, on arriving at a place where the trail formed two paths (*veredas*) they found it necessary to question the scouts about which of them would be the better trail. And on their telling them that both were bad, they had to stop there and they sent the scouts off with an Indian of the Iguaja Nation[6] to see if they might catch some Indian of those of the said place of Yuamajiro so that he might guide them and lead them with more certainty. And after having prearranged with them that they should not go off too far and that on hearing a shot they should return, it came to pass that the said scouts fled and with these the Indians who carried the provisions, from those who were at peace, [who] were going along leaving the *tacalos*[7] and were scared into fleeing [?] (*Auyentandose*), and that for the one [reason] and the other, they had to turn back. And on entering into the place of Hororo, they found it deserted and that they had killed the aforementioned Jazinto de Texeda and another two Indians, and that they had carried off some articles (*Prendas*) from a box of ornaments from the church, and that, after having collected all the ornaments, images, and the rest that it was possible to, they brought them to Mayaca, which they also found uninhabited, although nothing was missing from the convent and church. From this they recognized that all the places were in rebellion and their natives as having fled to the woods and that it was difficult to mount an expedition in search for them because of the harshness of the trails and because they lived on islands and very large lakes (*lagunas Mui Grandes*) and that canoes were necessary in order to be able to mount an expedition and that they would always be bound to be detected beforehand, as the soldier, Julian Jorxe, the bearer of the said letter, will state better. In view of the latter on the same third day of December by the said *auto,* the original was ordered to be placed with them and that statements should be received in accord with its tenor [the *auto*'s] from the said Julian Jorxe and the rest of the soldiers and squad leaders as they returned, with the necessary questions and counter-questions consonant with the context of the said letter and pertaining to the

6. The Iguaja are the Guale Indians of Georgia's coast from the Altamaha northward.

7. This word appears in other Florida documents in contexts that suggest that it represents a sort of container.

motive that the natives of Atoquime might have for the uprising
and the deaths they had inflicted, and who were said to be its
leaders, and the way and manner in which the squad leaders
conducted themselves and what they were doing to mount an
expedition to the said Indians. In virtue of it [that set of questions],
the statement was received from the said Julian Jorxe and from all
the soldiers who went for the said purpose and from the said
[officers], the lieutenant, Bernardo de Medina, and don Favian de
Angulo, as well as from the said Ensign Juan Alonsso Esquivel, who
is presently of the company of Spanish militiamen of this city, a
person who from its beginning has always taken part in operations
such as these because of being a guide (*vaguiano*)[8] for all those
places because of having his cattle ranch in the vicinity of them.
And they all agreed on one fact, that on their arrival, they found all
the places of Mayaca and Hororo at peace; and that the said Jazinto
de Texeda remained in the latter to recuperate; and that they set
out on their expedition and that the scouts and the Indians who
carried the provisions fled from them; and that on the return they
found that they had killed the said soldier and two Iguaja Indians
who had remained with him; and that the said Adjutant don Favian
de Angulo, in the convent of St. Francis of this city, had handed
over to its Presiding Father all the treasures (*alajas*)[9] and ornaments
that had been collected according to the memorial, and this was
sent to his lordship by the aforesaid presiding father, saying that all
of that which had been signed for by the sacristan had been handed
over and ordered to be placed with the *autos* [the memorial
presumably] by one issued on the fifth of December of the said year.
And that the cause of the uprising and deaths was said publicly to
have flowed from the religious having admonished (*de haverles
correxido*) some things of which [correction] the natives were in
need, and from having given them that punishment for it
(*penitencia*)[10] that is customary. And that the squad leaders had

8. *Baquiano* in modern Spanish of the New World. It is a term found particularly in Gaucho literature.

9. This is the modern *alhajas*, I believe, as I have encountered this form, *alajas*, elsewhere in Florida documents in contexts that indicate such to be the case.

10. This also could be rendered as "penance" such as the priest might give to a penitent in the confessional. The punishment might well have been whipping.

fulfilled their obligation completely without giving the natives any
motive for irritation or done any other thing to the natives, but
rather, receiving them warmly and treating them with complete
affection. And that they consider it to be difficult to mount an
expedition to the Indians, because of their having gone to the woods
and because of these being very impenetrable (*yntratables*) and full
of briers (*Malezas*). And the said Ensign Juan Alonsso said the same
[thing] in everything. And that the one who killed the said religious
and the Cacique of Aipaja was an Indian captain from the said
village of Atoquime. And the said Ensign Juan Alonsso alone adds,
because of having been the last one who made a statement, on the
eleventh of January of this present year, that the natives of the
village of Mayaca had returned to their village already, because of
having spoken with them already. And they told him that they had
fled from fear in going to the woods, as is established by all the said
statements, with a greater expression of sentiment on the matter
alluded to (*con mas expresión lo referido*).[11] To which the said señor
governor and captain general, by his *auto* of the past tenth of
January of this present year, in view of everything [that has
occurred], ordered the summoning of the officials of the royal
treasury, sergeants-major, those who have [earlier] been governors
and captains general in this plaza, active captains of infantry and
others *reformados,* and experienced soldiers, for an assembly (*junta*)
at four in the afternoon of that same day so that with all the subject
matters proposed, as they were in the said *autos,* and the things
that have happened that are evident from the said letters and from
the statements taken [being put on the agenda] they may view them
and confer whether it would be wise for the present or in the future
to mount an expedition to the said Indians and whether, despite the
difficulties of the trails, they should see whether there were other
methods and manners with which they could achieve the expedition
(*entrada*) more easily. And all together they resolved on the same
day that in this matter there was presently nothing else to be done
more than what they had done. And that this presidio was short of
provisions and soldiery. And that from what the soldiers and squad

11. My rendition of this elliptical statement is tentative. In the Connor
transcript there is a period after "Statements" and before "with" or "*con*"
which is lower case in the Spanish. In this admittedly muddy passage, "*con
mas expression*" etc. seems to fit better with what precedes it than with what
follows.

leaders said of the harshness (*Maleza*) of the land, it was not appropriate to have the people wandering about making any sort of expedition, as it was the most difficult season [of the year] because of the rains; that as [it was] winter all those swamps and graveled areas recharged (*que como yvierno recoxian todos aquellos Bariales y Cascales*),[12] that the wisest thing [to do] was to strive to attract them back to their villages with kindness and to seek to capture the said Indian captain of Atoquime, the principal head, and the rest involved in the uprising from which all the rest of the deaths and uprisings that there were originated and to punish them in order to teach a lesson [to the others] and for the security of the religious *doctrineros* in the future. The said señor governor and captain general went along with this outcome and resolution. And by his *Auto* of the twenty-second of the said month of January, presenting an account of what was alluded to and resolved upon in the assembly, he ordered that the necessary messages and dispatches be sent to all the provinces of this jurisdiction so that the lieutenants might publish it, stating how, in the name of his Majesty (may God protect him for many years), he was giving a general pardon to all the Indians of the rebellious places of the said Province of Mayaca-Hororo, Atoquime, Tisime, Aypaja, and the rest, with the exception of the said Indian captain of Atoquime and of the rest of the leaders, offering a reward of twenty-five pesos to the one who should hand him over imprisoned and bring him to this presidio, so that after having been heard in court, what was most appropriate might be decided upon in accord with it [the hearing]. And with respect to what pertains to the said Province of Mayaca, he charged the said Ensign Juan Alonsso with the responsibility for this effort, so that as a person familiar with and known to the natives he might make the said dispatch known to them and so that he might strive with every caution and the gentlest and most efficacious means to make them aware of the pardon and to attract them back to their villages, so that just as before they might have their sown fields, fisheries, and hunting trips in them and come again to give their obedience. That they would be received by his lordship with a very warm reception. And on the same day the dispatches alluded to were

12. This seems to imply that both the *Bariales* and the *Cascales* were subject to seasonal flooding. If my assumption that the *Barial* is the Portuguese *varzea* is correct, it would be a "wet meadow" in contrast to the vegetationless *Cascal*.

drawn up in this tenor, as all the matters alluded to are evident and appear at greater length from the said *autos,* of which mention has been made, which remain in my possession and in my office to which I send [them]. And so that it may be evident, by the order of His lordship the said señor governor and captain general, I give the present [certification] in St. Augustine of Florida on the sixth of February of the year one thousand six hundred and ninety-seven. It is written on six pages of common paper with this my seal because stamped paper does not circulate in this presidio. And in witness of it

I make my seal—In witness of the truth

Juan Solana

Notary for the public and for the government

This document closes with a certification by the officials of the royal treasury that Juan Solana was indeed a notary for the public and for the government, whose powers were valid, dated on August 19, 1697, and signed by Thomás Menéndez Marques and Joachín de Florencia and with the note that follows.

It came with a letter from Don Laureano de Torres y Ayala, governor of Florida, of the 3rd of February of [1]697. No. 1. Received on the 7th of January of [16]98 in the dispatch-boat of the Galleons.

(The extract of this testimony follows and is omitted.)

13. The Florida Governor's Report on the Distribution of Fray López' Mission Band, 1697

In this document the governor informed the crown that the twenty priests and two lay brothers brought by Fray López had been distributed in compliance with the royal orders of December 30, 1695. Nine remained in Havana with Fray López for the staffing of the Calusa mission and eleven (ten priests and a lay brother) had traveled on to St. Augustine, whence they were distributed among the established *doctrinas* and the new missions of Mayaca and Jororo, even though, as the governor noted, the natives of the latter two regions were not yet reduced to their settlements. When the governor wrote, the killing of a friar in the Jororo area had already occurred. In the wake of that trou-

ble many of the natives fled to the woods or to the coast. The governor's statement that the royal orders as to the assignment of these
friars had been fulfilled can be interpreted as signifying that some of
the inhabitants of Mayaca and Jororo were considered to be Ais.

Thomás Menéndez Marques to the King, August 8, 1697

AGI, Seville, Santo Domingo 230. Translation made from a copy in the
Jeannette Thurber Connor Collection, reel 3, of the P.K. Yonge Library
of Florida History.

Sire

Your Majesty (whom may God preserve) by his royal decree of
December 30, 1695, deigns to order that we be notified that Your
Majesty is sending twenty religious priests and two lay brothers to
these provinces under the charge of Fray Feliciano López of the
order of St. Francis and procurator of the religious of these
provinces so that they may be employed in the indoctrination and
teaching of the converted Indians of these provinces and in the new
conversions of Mayaca, Jororo, and the Cacique of Carlos in the
form and manner that Your Majesty ordered by the said royal
decree that was presented in this auditors' [office] together with
eleven religious [who were] priests and one lay brother. That, that
out of the said twenty priests and two laymen that Your Majesty
was pleased to order to send from those kingdoms with the said
Fray Feliciano they came to these provinces, with the
aforementioned and the rest of the religious of his [particular]
mission band remaining in Havana in order that, by way of that
port as closer, they might cross over to the conversion of Carlos, as
Your Majesty has disposed and ordered. And the said eleven priests
who arrived here have already been distributed among the *doctrinas*
of these provinces and the ones who are to go there have passed on
to those of Mayaca and Jororo, despite these natives not having been
reduced to their villages as yet.[1] And up to now the lay brother
remains in this convent [that of St. Augustine]. And with the
arrival of the said religious, there are forty-five religious existent in
these provinces, counting the one who is [stationed] in New Spain

1. Most had abandoned their villages in the wake of the killing of a friar in
Jororo and the arrival of soldiers to search for the guilty persons.

for the collection of the alms that Your Majesty gives them[2] and two
lay brothers and a sick priest who remained in Havana, which
amounts to forty-seven [*sic*] religious in all. Of the arrival of those
whom Your Majesty sends and of those who remain today and who
are in these provinces, we give an accounting to Your Majesty in
fulfillment of what he has ordered us [to do]. And we will give it
also, once it comes to pass that the eleven who remain in Havana in
order to cross over to Carlos do so. May Our Lord preserve the
Catholic royal person of Your Majesty for many years as
Christendom requires and as we your vassals desire. Florida,
August 8 of 1697.

Thomas Menéndez Marques   Joachín de Florencia

[On the cover page]
Florida, to his Majesty, on the 8th of August of 1697.
Received on 6, January, [16]98 in the dispatch-boat of the Galleons:
No. 4.
The Royal Officials
[Jeannette Thurber Connor omitted the council's summary of this
letter.]
Council. 2nd of May, [1]698.
Seen

14. The Friars' Arrival at Calusa, September 1697

Fray Feliciano López, superior of the friars of the Calusa mission, wrote
this brief letter shortly after the friars' arrival among the Calusa before the departure of the ship that brought them from Cuba. Fray López
provided a most valuable description of the Calusa's temple and the
structure within which it and its mound were housed, as well as data
on the population and on relations between the new young cacique and
the "great captain." Fray López indicated that there were portents of
serious trouble even in those first days despite a friendly initial reception.

2. Collecting the *situado* payments could be a long tedious process, but
also a lucrative one for the collector, who received a special travel allowance
over and above his regular stipend or salary.

Fray Feliciano López to Fray Pedro Taybo, 1697

AGI, Seville, Santo Domingo, bundle no. 154, R⁰ 6. On the back of the
first page are the following notes: "Copy of the letter that Fray Feliciano López of the order of St. Francis wrote to Father Fray Pedro Taybo
from the Bay of Carlos from the settlement called San Diego de Compostela"; "Fray Francisco Herrero, secretary general for the Indies of
the order of St. Francis, sent it to señor Don Martín de Sierralta with
a paper of April 24 of 1698 so that he might give an account of it to the
council. Corrected." The translation was made from a microfilm copy
and transcript of this document made by Victoria Stapells-Johnson at
the Archive of the Indies at the behest of the Florida Museum of Natural History.

R. P. N.

The troubles and calamities that have beset this poor mission
from the day that we set sail in Havana. That same afternoon, on
leaving the Morro,[1] the General of Galleons ordered the frigate to be
detained. I went to the admiral's ship and it was God's will for
things to be straightened out and we proceeded on our voyage. In a
day and one-half we reached the Key of Bones [Key West], where we
tarried for almost two days. We departed for this of Carlos [and]
arrived early on day 18. We remained about two leagues at sea, and
another that there is from the keys to the settlement, three, because
Ensign Romero's fear was nothing if it was not great. We sent a
message to the cacique, who soon sent a delegation to me that we
were very welcome and that in the afternoon he would come on
board to see me, as he did come. I received him and welcomed him
as best I could [and] I saw in him the fullness of sincerity and I
disembarked in his company and came to his house at night,
completely soaked from the skies and from the sea. There I found
his father don Phelipe almost on his deathbed. And the first word
that he said to me in greeting me was that he was dying with great
unhappiness because priests were not coming, but now that he saw
them in his place, he would die consoled. On the morning of the
following day he called me and said that he was dying, that he was
mine, that I should baptize him. I did so, believing that he would die
very shortly, [but] thanks be to God, he is still living. This day the

1. The Morro is part of the defenses for Havana and its harbor.

cacique sent two *Cayucos*[2] so that they might go about bringing in our poor baggage, and the ship put out more to sea out of fear of the Indians. Lastly they sent me the salt, wet, the maize, the half of it and everything as God might wish, until I sent a message by a sailor in which I told him that he should bring the ship in closer to port or go with God to Havana; that if what he was carrying was to be of no use to me, that he should go with God. The Indians of the settlement and key where I am, it appears, amount to about 400 men, innumerable children, [and as] the women are at home I have not seen them except for those of the house of the cacique, who would be about 20. They tell me there are many people. In all it appears to me that they amount to about one thousand, all idlers, from what I have seen; I do not know how I shall have to accommodate myself with them. While examining the village because of having heard much celebration on the preceding night, and not seeing anything more than a house (*Casa*) in the area where I heard them, they say [it is] the house of *Mahoma,* and when I was most unprepared for it, all the Indians came running and yelling (*hipando*)[3] so that I reckoned that my hour had arrived, but I took it as a joke, making them think that I had not seen it. And as they saw me in celebration they themselves showed me everything. It is a very tall and wide house with its door and an *abujero,*[4] in the middle a hillock (*cuesta*) or very high flat-topped mound (*mogote*),[5] and on top of it a sort of room (*aposento*)[6] [made] of mats (*esteras*)[7] with seats (*barbacoas*)[8] all closed. One can imagine the purpose it

2. The *cayuco* is a type of small canoe similar to one used for fishing by the Indians of Venezuela.

3. This verb is spelled more commonly *jipar* or *gipar* and is sometimes used to signify the war cry.

4. I have not been able to find such a word. Probably it was meant to be *agujero,* or "hole," and refers to the large roof opening characteristic of Florida aboriginal council houses.

5. *Cuesta* is a hill or mount; on any ground rising with a slope. *Mogote* is an insulated rock or cliff with a flat crown, appearing at sea (mesalike); or a pointed stack of corn.

6. "Apartment" is the primary meaning of *aposento.*

7. *Esteras* connotes mats made of rushes or sedge.

8. The connotation of *barbacoas* is of an open latticework seat. The same term was used for the seats around the inside walls of the council houses and the seat reserved for the chief and was used also for the open framework on which meat and fish were smoked and dried.

serves. They dance around it. The walls are entirely covered with masks, one worse than the other. The cacique [has] given his word to me that we may destroy the house, but by my poor understanding, they are opposing it. May God help me and give me his divine assistance as, at this date, I am much afflicted.

At about ten [o'clock] on the first night that I came ashore I dismissed the people because I was anxious to rest. And when I was about to fall asleep, the cacique came and got into the bed with me, speaking half in Timuqua and half in Apalachee. I kept my thoughts to myself (*el discreto*)[9] as to what would happen to the bolster in effect. Although he dirtied my bedclothes,[10] he consoled me, telling me that I was the one giving orders, but his sons are such, duennas (*dueñas*)[11] as they say. My friars very tired, because the poor fellows have accompanied me and have not eaten, but very consoled,[12] and with such great misery, such great fear, and the rest that they await. My Fray Fernando I gave permission to return because he was ill, but he did not wish to.

I had written up to this point, when two leading Indians called me in great secrecy this night, the vespers of St. Matthew, and told me that I should withdraw inside and remain at home with my friars because their Holy One (*su Santo*) was very irritated. And when I told them that my God was more powerful than their Holy One, they told me not to jest [and] that I should take care how I proceeded. The matter deprived me of my sleep, but we are already in the palisade (*palenque*). And it appears to me that on the first next occasion that we return to the house of their superstitions, they will knock us down. May he [God] guide me as it is thus that

9. My rendition of much of this paragraph is tentative. Because of the writer's elliptical style and obscure phraseology it is difficult to be certain that one has grasped his thought. A reviewer has suggested that what the friar viewed as an intrusion was normal behavior for the cacique, who was used to sitting on his own bed to confer with people.

10. This suggests that he may have been wearing body paint or something, such as bear grease, as a protection from biting insects.

11. *Dueñas* can also be rendered as "owner, mistress of the house, or landlady." Its masculine counterpart, *dueño,* also has meanings such as "one who takes command" or "pretends rights or faculties not possessed by one," which may once have been attached to *dueñas* in colloquial usage.

12. At first glance this statement seems to be in contradiction with what follows, but it is used, probably, in the sense of "consoled despite the misery and fear," or possibly it was meant to be *desconsolados.*

Fray Feliciano finds himself among these lambs that are stronger than lions: the spirit is willing but the flesh is weak *solo caro mea est Ynfirma*).[13] Let the will of the Most High be done in everything and by everything, beloved father, in commending myself to God; that I cannot go forward with my labors.
Fray Feliciano

It is a copy of the letter that Fray Francisco Herrero, secretary general of Indies, sent to the council (that it was because the Most Reverend Father Fray Antonio de Cardona, commissary general of the order of St. Francis in this court was absent from Madrid) with a paper of the 24th of April of 1698 so that [it might be returned?][14] the señor don Martín de Sierralta asking that it be returned, and by agreement of the council of the 30th of the said month and year, it was ordered that it be returned, as is done with a paper of the 5th of June of 1698. Madrid, said day.

15. Testimony about the Calusa Mission's Failure, 1698

Confident assurances that the Calusa were ready for conversion proved to be unfounded. As soon as the natives perceived that acceptance of baptism would not bring a stream of gifts from the crown and that the friars meant to abolish the natives' traditional forms of worship, the natives turned hostile. They eventually stripped the five friars of their possessions and deported them to the custody of the Key's Indians. In the Keys they survived for a month or so on the verge of starvation before being rescued by the same ship's captain who had ferried them to the Calusa center only a few months earlier.

The crown's request to be kept informed of the progress of the mission as well as the intense involvement of the crown and its officials since the conception of the enterprise in 1680 made it imperative to hold a formal inquiry to explain to the crown what had been done and why the mission effort had proved to be so abject a failure. A formal questionnaire was drawn up for the inquiry. The five friars who had sailed to and remained in the Calusa territory were asked to respond

13. A reviewer has suggested this idiomatic rendition of this Latin phrase.

14. Something seems to be needed to complete this elliptically worded sentence, but I am not certain that this is what is called for.

to the questions, and their statements under oath were recorded for the enlightenment of the crown and of the Franciscan authorities. But after three of the friars had made their statements, the friar conducting the inquiry resolved to shorten the process by having the statements of the first three friars read to the other two so that they might state whether they were true and include details that they might see fit to add.

The testimony of the three friars is among the most valuable of these documents from this mission for the light that it sheds on the Calusa and the brief interaction between them and the friars. The testimony is a valuable source of information as well on the inhabitants of the Keys in this era.

The record begins with a brief statement by Fray Francisco de Contreras, who conducted the inquiry, and the questionnaire to which the five friars were to respond. The statements of the three friars who testified follow. The process concluded with the statement of assent by the two friars whose testimony was not required and a formal statement by Fray Contreras. The inquiry was initiated on February 26, 1698, and concluded on March 6, 1698.

Testimony of Friars Relating to the Calusa Mission, February–March 1698

AGI, Seville, Santo Domingo, bundle no. 154, R° 6, N° 114ª.

The cover of this document bears a note stating that the record of the testimony "came with a letter of March 5, 1698 from Fray Francisco de Contreras, vice-commissary general for Florida of the order of St. Francis. N 3. Received on the 20th of June from that in the Galleons." The translation was made from a microfilm copy and a transcript of this document made by Victoria Stapells-Johnson at the Archive of the Indies at the behest of the Florida Museum of Natural History.

Statements of the religious
About Fray Feliciano López and the 4 religious that he brought with him having returned from the conversion of the Cacique Carlos.
Auto. In this convent of our father St. Francis of the city of Havana on the twenty-sixth day of the month of February of this present year of one thousand six hundred and ninety-eight N.M.R.[1] Father

1. "N.M.R." probably stands for *Nuestro Muy Reverendo* "Our Very Reverend." In the microfilm, "Father" is abbreviated as well, *Pᵉ*.

Fray Francisco de Contreras, preacher emeritus, examiner
(*Calificador*) of the Holy Office,[2] ex-definitor and chronicler of the
province of San Pedro and San Pablo of Michoacan, and vice-
commissary general and visitor of this [Province] of Santa Elena of
Florida, stated that in view of the priests Fray Feliciano López, Fray
Fernando Samos, Fray Miguel Carrillo, Fray Francisco de Jesus, and
Fray Francisco de San Diego, a lay brother, having arrived at this
port on the twenty-first day of the said month stripped of even their
habits, who, with orders from his majesty (God save him) and the
permission of our superiors, went to the district of the cacique of
Carlos during the month of September of the former year of ninety-
seven to solicit and to bring about the conversion of the heathen of
that district; that he was judging and judged that he ought to make
a report about the motives that the said religious had for giving up
so holy a work and the reasons that there were for their coming in
that naked state; and for that [purpose] he was ordering and ordered
that the said religious should appear before his Very Reverend
Paternity (*M.R.*) to make statements under oath concerning what he
may ask them about this [matter], and in order to do it in due form
he was deciding and decided that they should be examined in accord
with the following questionnaire.

Questionnaire. First question: Who is the subject testifying; in what
province did he take the habit; how long ago did he come to this one;
and with what purposes? Second question: When did he leave in
order to go to the district of the cacique of Carlos; when did the
religious reach it; how did those heathen receive them; and what is
his opinion of their number? Third question: What efforts did they
make to introduce the Gospel among those peoples; what results
followed; and how did everything end? Fourth and last question:
How did they expel them from the said district; whether they did
them any injury; with what arrangements did they dispatch them;
in how many areas did they stay; and in what area did the
Spaniards who brought them to this port find them? And so that
the said religious may be examined and questioned in accord with
the questionnaire and so that their statements may be written down

2. As such he was an officer of the Inquisition assigned to examine books
and writings coming into the province to see that they were not among banned
works or that they did not expound views considered heretical.

in due form in order to give an account to his majesty the king our lord (God save him) [and] to the prelates of their order, his Very Reverend Paternity (P.M.R.) so provided, ordered, and endorsed in the aforesaid convent of Havana on the said day, month, and year as noted above. Fray Francisco de Contreras, vice-commissary general. Before me, Fray Manuel Cardoso, secretary.

Statement. On the twenty-seventh day of the month of February of this present year of one thousand six hundred and ninety-eight, in conformity with the preceding *auto,* the Reverend Father Fray Feliciano López, having been called before the aforesaid Very Reverend Father N., vice-commissary general, whom his Very Reverend Paternity ordered that he should respond under holy obedience[3] and state the truth concerning what he was questioned about. To this, the said Reverend Father said, prostrated, that he was obeying and that under the obligation of obedience and under his oath as a priest, that he made in due form with his hand placed upon his chest, he was promising and promised to tell the truth about what he was questioned on and that he might know about. And notified of the first question, he said he was named Fray Feliciano López; that he took the habit in the Province of Santiago; and came on mission assignment to this one of Florida during the earlier year of one thousand six hundred and seventy-seven with the purpose of becoming employed in the conversion and administration of the Indians and that in the past year of ninety-five he went to the kingdoms of Castile and in them he was given charge of a mission of twenty-two religious that his majesty (God save him) was pleased to grant to this said province, and that he brought it, coming as commissary of it and with the obligation of passing with another four or six religious, those who appeared appropriate to him, to the district of the cacique of Carlos, who, it was said, was asking for holy baptism for himself and for fourteen thousand souls subject to his dominion. And he gave this by way of reply. To the second question he said that he left from this port on the eleventh day of September of the preceding year of ninety-seven with four religious that he indicated and [who] were those whom he judged to be suitable and who were named Fray Fernando Samos,

3. He was probably invoking the obligation of the vow of obedience he had taken as a religious, possibly foreseeing reluctance on the part of the friars to give testimony that might lead to reprisals against the natives.

Fray Miguel Carrillo, Fray Francisco de Jesus, priests, and Fray
Francisco de San Diego, a lay brother, all sons of the said province
of Santiago and of those who came to the mission under his charge,
and that he arrived at the key where the aforementioned cacique of
Carlos and his leading men reside on the nineteenth day of the same
month, where, having made a call, the young cacique came aboard
with the leading men. And on revealing to him the purpose of his
coming, they brought him to shore, where he spoke with the old
chief, who was ill, and they all then replied to him and received him
with signs of pleasure. And with this assurance he had the other
religious disembark and the supplies that they were carrying and
which the governor and the royal officials of this city of Havana had
given to them as what was necessary for settling in it and for
sustaining themselves for the period of six months, according to the
orders of his majesty. And that relative to the number of souls that
there would be and that he is asked about, he judges from what he
saw and learned from what the Indians told him, there would be
about two thousand more or less between children and adults, men
and women.[4] And this he gave as a reply. To the third question he
said that as soon as they arrived and were received in the said
manner, after having placed all the supplies that they brought in a
house of the cacique, they erected a cross of wood and alongside it
on some poles they placed two bells that they brought and they
began to build a house of palm thatch. And in the meantime they
remained about thirteen days in the house of the cacique. And that
the said house having been finished, the religious moved to it on the
third day of October. And they set up an oratory where they could
say Mass and they said Mass on the following day. And that during
all this time they had gone along disposing their spirits little by
little for the acceptance of the faith, making speeches to them and
explaining its mysteries to them and the need to believe in them and
to acknowledge them in order to be able to be saved and seeking to
convince them of the falsity of the [beliefs] by which they were
living. And that the cacique and the rest of the Indians were present
at all this with reasonable signs [of interest] until the said third day

4. In 1570 the Jesuit Antonio Sedeño made a similar estimate of "no more
than two thousand souls" for thirty Calusa chieftainships. But his thirty chieftainships seem to have included peoples tributary to the Calusa chief because
Sedeño reported that twenty-four languages were represented among those
thirty chieftainships (Zubillaga 1946: 425).

of October, when, on seeing the provisions that they brought carried from the house of the cacique to that of the religious and that a portion had been distributed to the Indians, they began to change, saying: why were they not dividing all of it among them and not giving them clothing, because if they were not going to give them clothes and to eat, what use was it [for them] to become Christians? That during this time an accident happened to the old chief over and above his illnesses, and that while this witness was urging him to be baptized, he agreed to it, and in fact he was baptized in the manner decreed by the church in such cases. That, after his having improved, and while he was going along instructing him and disposing him for the reception of the holy chrism and oils, the accident reoccurred with urgency. And on this witness's warning him to consider that he was a Christian and that he must now go to confession if he had committed any sin since his baptism among those that he had explained to him, and that there was another sacrament, [that] of extreme unction, whose essence and effects he also explained to him and how he should ask for it. To this the said cacique replied that he was not a Christian. And on being confronted with the baptism that he had received, he said that it did not matter a whit; that if he had to be a Christian because of four old rags that they had given him, and that he did not want his body to be lost, but rather that they should bring it to where his ancestors were. And he died within a few days in this obstinacy. And that during this same time the young chief said to this witness and to the rest of the religious who were assisting in converting the said ill chief, that they should not disturb his father because he did not wish to be a Christian and that the leading men were becoming irritated by it. And similarly the aforesaid young chief brought two of his little children during this same time, saying that he should baptize them. And this witness having baptized them and given them as names Antonio and Francisco, the said cacique asked where the clothes were that they were supposed to give him. And that after this witness having given him two little pieces of cloth and other trifles, the said cacique stated that that was not right; that he should give him the clothing that the king had ordered him to, because if he was not going to give clothing and food, it was not good to become a Christian and no one would want to become one. And that from that day on they began to subject the religious to some harassment, mistreating them by words and deeds and stealing from them repeatedly. And that one night, which, it appears to him, was the eighteenth of October, having learned that the Indians were at the place where they had the idols and where they venerate them, three of the said religious, at the order of this witness who was their superior, went to the said place to dissuade them and withdraw them from those idolatries. And on seeing them all the said Indians fled. And on the following day the great captain, who is a brother of the cacique, came to say to this witness that he would not permit that the religious should return to his church when they were in it because the Indians would kill them; that they know that their holy one (*su santo*) was irritated because they had received them and had them there. And that notwithstanding this [warning], on the night of the twenty-sixth of the said month, knowing that they were engaged in their rites in the said place, the religious went to it again. And before they reached it, they [the Indians] came out on to the trail armed to block their coming. And when the religious insisted on going on forward, the Indians seized them and brought them back to the house, carrying them, having mistreated them with some blows. And the religious having retreated and applied themselves to sowing a jug (*botija*) of wheat, the Indians did not cease to bother them, nettling them so that they would leave and telling them on repeated occasions that they would ship them off, as in fact they did on the second day of December. And this was his response.

To the fourth and last question he said that the chief and his Indians told him clearly, as he has stated, that they did not wish to become Christians and that the religious should leave or they would kill them. And that in addition to the injuries and the harm that has been reported already, they did the following to them. In Carlos on the day they shipped them off, they stripped them of the greater part of the provisions and ornaments and on the following day at night, on a key called Teyu, they finished stripping them of their clothing and the provisions that they brought, with the box of the ornaments, and tossing the religious in the water. And finally on the next day on the Key of Muspa, they stripped everyone of their habits, cowls, and underdrawers, leaving them solely the little undershirts. And that they passed from these said keys to others until they reached that of Matacombe where Francisco Romero arrived with another seven companions and they remained with them on the fishing trip that brought them there until the said

twenty-first day of February, when they reached the said port. And he gave this as his reply and that everything that he has said is the truth under the burden of the oath that he has taken and the command of obedience that was imposed on him. And that he was ratifying it and ratified it, omitting alluding to many other grievances that the Indians inflicted on them in order to be brief. And the said witness signed it together with the said our Most Reverend Father vice-commissary general on the said day, month, and year noted earlier.
Fray Feliciano López
Fray Francisco de Contreras, vice-commissary general
Before me, Fray Manuel Cardoso, secretary

Statement. On the said day, month, and said year Father Fray Fernando de Samos appeared, having been called before his Very Reverend Paternity, from whom the oath was received in due form, which he took *in verbo sacerdotis*[5] with his hand placed on his chest, promising to tell the truth about what he knows and about what he is questioned on. And having been [questioned] following the order of the questionnaire, to the first question he said that he was called Fray Fernando de Samos and was a son of the Province of Santiago, from whence he came on mission to this [Province] of Florida the past year of ninety-six with desires of applying himself in it to the conversion of the Gentiles, who were said to be many and to be asking for baptism. To the second he said that he sailed from this port around the eleventh day of September of last year for the district of the cacique of Carlos, where he arrived along with his companions on the nineteenth day of the same month and where they were received with moderate signs [of pleasure] on the part of the caciques and leading men and that in reference to the number of souls that is asked about, he can say only that on the basis of his experience in the village of the said cacique, which consists of sixteen houses, and that from the other little ones [settlements] that he saw on the keys in which he was, it appears to him that it would be about two thousand more or less in all. And this was his reply. To the third question he said that right after their arrival they were lodged in a house of the cacique on a part (*pedazo*) that they pointed

5. *In verbo sacerdotis,* "on the word of a priest," is underlined in the original.

out to them and that on the day following their arrival, they placed
a cross near there and put two bells in place, beginning at once to
give shape to the making of a house for the religious and that it was
made by they themselves [the friars], the Indians having brought
them the lumber and palms for covering it, the father commissary
paying them for it from the supplies that he brought. And when
about thirteen days had passed that they expended in making the
said house, the religious moved over into it and separated a piece [of
it] for an oratory where on the following day, the fourth of October,
they all said Mass. And that during the time that they were
building the said house the religious gave various and repeated
talks (*practicas*) to the Indians, went about learning their language
and teaching them the Castilian [language] and how to make the
sign of the cross and to say the prayers and that thus to this [end],
how to pray the crown of the Virgin our Lady [the Franciscan
Rosary of seven decades commemorating the Seven Joys of Mary],
which they did every night. In the house of the cacique he saw and
experienced that only the boys (*muchachos*)[6] attended. And that he
heard the father commissary say that he had baptized the old chief
who was ill on the point of death and that after having improved for
some days, his illness again worsened, this witness went with the
said father commissary and he saw and he heard that when he
urged him so that he might receive the holy oil[7] as a Christian, and
that when he reminded him of the baptism that he had received and
promised to bury him in the church as a Christian or at the foot of
the cross, he said that it did not matter [to him], and that he did not
want to be a Christian, nor that they should bury him there, where
everybody would step on them, but rather that he wished that his
body should not be lost, but that it should be placed instead where
the [bodies] of his own [people] were. And that the young chief, on
seeing that the religious did not cease to go to exhort him, said to
the father commissary that they should not go to bother his father
because both he and the leading men resented it. And that since the
day that the religious moved to the said house and brought their
clothing and provisions to it from that of the cacique, he noted that

6. This could also be rendered as "children," including girls as well.
7. This is a reference to the sacrament of extreme unction, a part of the
last rites given to one who is seriously ill, along with confession and communion or viaticum when the person is conscious.

the Indians began to change their attitude saying, Why did they not
distribute all of that? And that the aforesaid young chief a few days
after their arrival brought two boys, one of whom he said was his
son and the other his nephew so that he might baptize them. And
that after the said father commissary having baptized them and
after having given each one of them two yards of cloth and some
ribbons, the said cacique said to him: give me the clothing that the
king gives, and that, after his having responded to him that he did
not bring any and that he could make them with that cloth, the said
cacique replied that this was not good, [that] if he does not give
clothes and food, what is the use of becoming Christians? And that
one night when the religious were in their house already and
knowing that the Indians were in their synagogue[8] performing their
idolatries or obscenities (*torpezas*), three religious went to dissuade
them and to draw them away from the said evils, with this witness
remaining in the house with the father commissary. And that the
said religious returned a short time later, saying [that] they had not
encountered any Indian at all because they heard them coming and
they all fled. And that on another night, which he remembers was
that of the octave of San Pedro de Alcantara, this witness with two
other religious, knowing that the Indians were engaged in the same
obscenities and idolatries, decided to go to preach to them. And in
fact they went out from the house, with this witness wearing a
surplice and with a statue of Our Lady in his hands and the others
lanterns (*luzes*)[9] with which they lit the way and that a short
distance from the said house the Indians armed with darts (*dardos*)
and arrows sallied forth to block the passage and that with the
religious insisting on going on and the Indians on resisting, [alerted]
by the uproar the said father commissary, who had remained in the
house, came out, telling them that they should let the said religious
pass. And when he made a lunge in an effort to go forward, an
Indian grabbed him and put his hand over his mouth as if with the
intent of wanting to suffocate him, but that he was able to free
himself from him, and on his going forward another one picked him
up and brought him to where the other religious were, and at this
time they also picked the others up with violence and ill usage and

8. The Spanish word used here is *sinagoga*.
9. This generic term could be rendered variously as "lantern," "candle,"
"torch," or anything else that gives light that might have been available at that
time.

brought them to the house. And that on the following day a brother of the cacique, whom they call the great captain, came with others to reprehend them for what they had tried to do that night and with a message from the cacique in which he said to them that they were not to go back again to his church because his Holy One was very irritated, and that this witness had heard this very thing said, that the Indians had said it on other occasions. And that while this witness was alone in the house on the eighteenth day of November because of the other religious having gone to search for firewood, the same great captain entered the house with another Indian and without saying a word grabbed the one testifying by the throat, throttling him as if he wished to strangle him, and that he freed himself [from his grasp] as best he could and took off fleeing to call his companions. And in the meantime they stole the linen from the bed of the father commissary, but on their complaining to the cacique, he ordered it returned. And that on another day, that he does not remember what [day] it was, while the cacique was in the house of the religious with all the Indians annoying them, the father commissary having said to the cacique that he should order the Indians to leave and let the religious pray, the said cacique became angry and gave the said father commissary a number of blows to the face. And that when he had gone to the old chief to complain, the young one and the Indians went along behind him. This witness and another two religious followed them [in turn and] they saw that the young chief drove away with blows[10] the said father commissary from the bed of the said old chief on which he was sitting, and that after he had gone outside the house he raised a cudgel (*palo*) to hit him, that this witness grabbed him from behind and blocked his intent, and that on this occasion one of the Indians from the crowd came up to the priest Fray Miguel Carrillo and rubbed human excrement on his face, and that on the vespers of St. Andrew an Indian came up to this same religious to try to make him lose his temper while he was praying, and when he did not succeed in this, he urinated on him, saying to him, "man boy, why are you so small?" And lastly he heard the said Indians say many times that they did not want to become Christians, that they should go away. And this was his reply. To the fourth and last question he said that on the second day of December, as has been stated, they decided to

10. The Spanish here, *le dió de empellones,* might also be rendered as "with pushes" or "with shoves."

embark in three canoes that the chief had arranged for them for this [purpose] and that, while bringing to them the clothing, the box belonging to the church, and the provisions that they still had, having given a good portion of them to the Indians beforehand, the Indians who were carrying these [articles] fled with what they were carrying, and only the box belonging to the church reached the said canoes and some portion that the religious themselves carried and brought along and that the cacique disappeared, feigning that he was following the Indians. And that a brother of the old chief offered to bring the said religious, saying to the father commissary, "Did I not tell you, Father, that this cacique was so evil a man? Go quickly, because if you do not, they are going to kill you." And with that they departed in one of the three canoes, the Indians having taken away the other two and carried off a sack of maize and that around the afternoon of the following day they reached the mouth of a river, where the Indians said that they had to sleep, and in effect they remained there that night, although with fear because of the evil intentions that they had perceived in the said Indians. And that at dawn some Indians came swimming and tipped the father commissary out of the canoe, who was in great risk of drowning. And similarly they threw the priest Fray Francisco de Jesus and this witness, who were the ones who remained in the canoe, into the water, because the other two religious were on land, making a fire to warm themselves. And that the said Indians took off with the canoe, carrying off in it the box belonging to the church and the few clothes and provisions that had been left to us, leaving them with solely the clothes that they were wearing. And that during the morning of the following day the young Indians who were rowing returned with the canoe empty, the leading man, brother of the old chief, having remained around there[11] and that they then embarked in the said canoe to go on to Muspa and that during this transit the Indians themselves stripped them of their cloaks (*mantos*) and made breechclouts out of them there at once. And that on reaching the said Key of Maspa [*sic*], where they remained for a day, they left on the following day for another key called Casitua. And on this trail four Indians, whom the cacique of Muspa gave them for rowing, stripped them of their habits, hoods, and underclothes, leaving

11. It is not clear from the Spanish *por allá* whether the "there" being alluded to is back in the village or there with the friars.

them only their little undershirts. And that it was in this fashion
that they reached the said key. And from it they passed to others
with great cold, hunger, and toils until the twenty-ninth day of
December, when Francisco Romero, a resident of this city, found
them on Matacombe Key as he was going about through those keys
fishing with other companions and that they remained with them
until their arrival at this port, which was on the twenty-first day of
the current February. And this he gave as a response. And that
everything that he has alluded to is the truth under the burden of
the oath he has taken and under the command of obedience. And
that he was ratifying and ratified it, having omitted alluding to a
few things for the sake of brevity. And he signed it together with
the said our Very Reverend Father vice-commissary general on the
said day, month, and year as above.
Fray Francisco de Contreras, vice-commissary general
Fray Fernando de Samos
Before me, Fray Manuel Cardoso, Secretary

Statement. On the twenty-eighth day of the said month and year
the priest Fray Miguel Carrillo appeared on being called before the
aforementioned our Very Reverend Father vice-commissary
general, from whom the oath was received in due form which he
made *in verbo sacerdotis* with his hand placed on his chest, and
under the obligation of obedience that was imposed on him,
promising to tell the truth in that which he was questioned about
and that he knew about. And on being [questioned] in accord with
the questionnaire, he said [in reply] to the first question, that his
name was Fray Miguel Carrillo and he had taken the habit of our
father St. Francis and taken his vows in the Province of Santiago,
and that it was a little less than two years ago that he departed
from it on a mission to this one of Florida with the desire of serving
in the instruction and conversion of the Indians. And this he
replied. To the second question he said that on the eleventh day of
last September he set out from this port with his comrades for the
district of the cacique of Carlos in a sloop (*Balandra*) under the
command of Francisco Romero. And that on the nineteenth day of
the same month they reached the place where he lives, which is a
small key of about half a league, and that as soon as they cast
anchor the young chief came out with other Indians in various
cayucos and showing great affability they brought the father

commissary, Fray Feliciano, and the lay brother to shore, and from the next day until the day following they were busy carrying the supplies to the house of the said cacique and they all landed. And as to their number, as is asked about, from what he saw and understood, he reckons that there would be a little more than two thousand souls between men, children, and women. And this he replied. To the third question he said that when he went on shore he heard it said that on the preceding day the old cacique, who was ill, had suffered a seizure and that the said father commissary had baptized him as being near death.[12] And that early on the following day they set up some bells and raised a cross and they marked the spot where they were going to build the convent, and that during the interval, while the Indians were going to bring some logs and palms for covering a house in which the religious would live, they remained in the house of the cacique, where they said the rosary (*la Corona*) every night, and during the day they gave repeated talks and instructed the young men (*muchachos*)[13] in the doctrine and instructed themselves in their language. And that this lasted for twelve or thirteen days during which the said house was built and the religious moved to it. They divided off a part of it that served them as an oratory and church for the time that they were there and that from that day they began to have fears concerning the Indians because they saw their attitude changed and heard them say, Why were they not giving them handouts from what they brought? Why had they not brought them clothes? Why did they go there [i.e., to their own convent]? And from that said day they began to steal things, and to bother them, and to mistreat them almost everyone of the following days and to say to them on repeated occasions that they should leave, that they did not want to become Christians. And when they responded to them by saying to them: "But did not you or your caciques ask the señor bishop to send them ministers so that they might baptize them?" they replied that the old chief had made this request, but that he was no longer in

12. That is, with an abbreviated ceremony consisting only of the core of the ritual, the pouring of water over the forehead while saying "I baptize thee in the name of the Father and of the Son and of the Holy Ghost," without the usual instruction in the basic beliefs of the Catholic faith, and quite possibly in this case without the chief's being in any condition to say yes or no to what he was being subjected to.

13. This could also be rendered as "young people," neutral as to gender.

charge, and that just as the Christians could not cease to be
Christians and live without the rosary, neither could they abandon
their law and become Christians; that at the beginning they told
them that they would baptize the children who should be born, but
it was their experience that maliciously some were born and others
died without their being advised, and that only the young chief
brought two boys one day so that they might be baptized and when
they had been baptized, he asked for the clothing that the king was
wont to send. And although the father commissary had given him a
little bit of cloth for each one, a cap (*montera*),[14] and some ribbons,
the said cacique stated that it was not good, that if they were not
going to give them food and clothing, what was the use of becoming
Christians? And that when this witness was asking some Indians
on one occasion why they had not advised the religious that a girl
was dying, who died without their hearing of it, they replied that [it
was] because they had an order from their cacique not to advise
them. And that he knew that others had given the same response to
other religious. And that the said cacique on repeated occasions told
the commissary and the rest of the religious all together that they
should go, that they did not want to become Christians, neither he,
nor his leading men, that they were all annoyed because their God
was annoyed with them because they had received them [i.e., the
religious] and kept them there. And that he heard it said that when
the old chief's life was once again in danger and when the father
commissary and the rest of the religious on various occasions were
urging him to receive the holy oils as a Christian, he stated that he
was not one. And on confronting him with the baptism that he had
received, he stated that it did not matter, that he was not about to
become a Christian for four rags that he had been given, and that
he did not want his body to be lost. And that after seeing this and
many other matters, together with the persistent requests that the
cacique and leading men were making that the religious should
leave them, and that on the two nights that they had gone to the
place where they have the idol, knowing that they were there
worshiping the idol, [and that] on the one occasion they had fled and
that on the other they had impeded them with arms in hand and
violent treatment, they resolved to leave them and they asked the
cacique to give them the canoes necessary for this [purpose]. He

14. The *montera* is a kind of cloth cap worn by the common people in Spain.

promised to do so. And this is how everything ended. And he gave this as a response. To the fourth and last question he said that they had repulsed them with the aforesaid evil treatment and with the uttering of the words that have been alluded to, and that in addition to the injuries that have been recounted, they inflicted many others on them such as the cacique's having struck the said father commissary, another Indian's having tried to drown Father Samos, and of another's having scratched the face of this witness, after having urinated on him and after having said some derisive words to him. And that on the occasion that the cacique gave the blows to the father commissary, another spread excrement all over the face of this witness. And with reference to the measures with which they sent us off and which are asked about, he said that they consisted solely in providing three canoes and the cacique's giving an order to the Indians that they should load up the clothing and bring it from the house to the landing place, but that the purpose was to flee with everything that they loaded up, without the cacique's appearing there, with the result that they found themselves with no more than what the religious themselves carried and brought; that all [this] fitted in one canoe and that they departed in it accompanied by an uncle of the cacique and by the cacique of Muspa with another two or three Indians. And that on arriving at a mouth of a river near a spot that they call Tello, they carried off the canoe and obliged them to remain there that night. And that while this witness was on shore with another religious making a fire and warming himself, he heard it said that the father commissary was drowning, and the both of them going to his aid, they found him in the middle of the river asking that they should give him absolution. And that the lay religious, who was the one who accompanied this witness, went into the water as far as he could and with a long stick helped the said father commissary to come out of the river. And that when they all went toward where the canoe was, they found the other two religious soaking wet on the bank of the river, saying that the Indians had thrown them into the water sound asleep and taken the canoe with everything it contained. And that after they had remained there at the fire until it was daytime, the aforementioned cacique of Muspa and the Indians who were rowing came back in the same canoe [now] empty and they got in in order to go to his district, and that on the way they stripped them of their cloaks (*Mantos*) and made loincloths out

of them there in their presence. And that after having reached
Muspa in this fashion, they were detained there for a day, and on
the following [day] the said cacique gave them four different Indians
so that they might carry them in the same canoe. And these
[Indians] a short time after they had left that spot, stripped them of
their habits, cowls, and underclothes, leaving them with only their
little shirts. And they brought them thus to a spot that they call
Casitua, where they remained ten days. And during this time the
cacique of the Key of Bones [Key West] arrived there; that with
another two Indians from that spot he brought them to Matacombe
Key, where Francisco Romero, a resident of this city who was
passing through those keys to fish with another seven persons,
found them on the twenty-ninth day of December and they
remained with them until the twenty-first day of February, when
they arrived at this port. And he gave this as his reply. And that
everything that he has spoken of is the truth under the burden of
the oath that he has taken and of the obedience imposed. And that
he could allude to other things that happened to them, but does
not do so for the sake of brevity and because what he has stated
appears sufficient to him. And he was reaffirming it and reaffirmed
it. And he signed it along with the said our Very Reverend Father
vice-commissary general on the said day, month, and year as noted
above.
Fray Francisco de Contreras, vice-commissary general
Fray Miguel Carrillo
Before me, Fray Manuel Cardoso, secretary

Auto. In the aforementioned convent of Havana on the said day,
month, and year as above our Very Reverend Father Fray Francisco
de Contreras, vice-commissary general and judge for this inquiry,
stated that in view of the three statements that the priests Fray
Feliciano López, Fray Fernando Samos, and Fray Miguel Carrillo
have made being sufficient to make it possible to enter into a
knowledge of the truth that there is in the proportion and
enterprise for the conversion of the district of the cacique of Carlos,
his Very Reverend Paternity was ordering and ordered, for the sake
of avoiding prolixity, that the Father Fray Francisco de Jesus,
priest, and the brother, Fray Francisco de San Diego, a layman,
should be called before him together and that they should read the
aforesaid three statements to them word for word and under oath

and with the precept of obedience that they should be ordered to say whether what was stated in them was true and that their responses should be placed following this *auto*. And by it he so provided, order, and signed.

Fray Francisco de Contreras, vice-commissary general
Before me, Fray Manuel Cardoso, secretary

Statement. On the first of March of this said year, in consequence of the above *auto* of our Very Reverend Father Fray Francisco de Contreras, vice-commissary general, the Father Fray Francisco de Jesus, priest, and the Brother Fray Francisco de San Diego appeared on being called. And the oath which they took in due form having been received from them, and ordering them under holy obedience that they should pay attention to the statements that will be read to them, and that from their content they should see and declare whether what the witnesses said in them is true or not. They replied to this that they were obeying and that under the burden of the oath taken, they promised to tell the truth. And [the statements] having been read to them word for word by me the present secretary, they said that they had heard them and understood them and that everything that the said priests stated in them is true and that this is what they experienced and heard and that they could add many other very serious things, such as the Indians one day having wished to kill the said religious, surrounding the house with darts and arrows and that they are aware that the same thing [happened] on another two nights and they learned that the great captain prevented it for then. And that when the father commissary went to complain to the old chief, the Indians prevented him from entering and by means of the said captain he was able to enter and to meet with him and that as he was leaving an Indian raised a hatchet in order to kill the said father commissary and the said captain prevented it, giving some blows to the Indian. And that on learning of this the cacique, his brother, hit the said captain with a cudgel and with his hand because he had prevented them from killing the said father commissary this time and for having blocked everyone from doing it in the other cases alluded to. That they heard and learned from the Indians that their not being killed was at the insistence of the old chief who said that if they killed them, little squadrons would come from Havana and from Apalachee to kill them and that they learned this and heard this on repeated occasions but that they recognized above all that the Indians had no desire to become Christians. And that all of this is the truth under the burden of the oath that they have taken. And they reaffirmed it and they signed it together with the said our Very Reverend Father vice-commissary general on the said day, month, and year as above.

Fray Francisco de Contreras, vice-commissary general
Fray Francisco Antonio de Jesus   Fray Francisco de San Diego
Before me, Fray Manuel Cardoso, secretary

Auto. On the said day, month, and year the aforesaid Very Reverend Father vice-commissary general Fray Francisco de Contreras, judge for this inquiry, after having seen it, stated that he was holding and held it as concluded and that in order to give an account with it to his majesty, the king our lord (may God save him) and to the superiors of the order, he was ordering and ordered that the necessary copies should be made from it to the letter and that they should be brought corrected and authorized in public form for the purposes mentioned. And that this original should be placed in the archive of this convent, making a notation about it in its register. His Very Reverend Paternity so provided, ordered, and endorsed it on the said day, month, and year as above.

Fray Francisco de Contreras, vice-commissary general
Before me, Fray Manuel Cardoso, secretary

It agrees with its original, which remains in the archive of the province in this convent of Havana [under] the title, reports, to which I refer. And at the order of our Very Reverend Father Fray Francisco de Contreras, vice-commissary general and visitor of this Province of Florida, I furnished the present [document] in four copies, which go faithfully and legally copied and corrected, which I certify and I sign it in the aforesaid convent of Havana on the sixth day of the month of March of the year one thousand six hundred and ninety-eight.

In witness of the truth, Fray Manuel Cardoso, secretary

The following document represents the other half of the inquiry into the Calusa mission's failure conducted by Fray Francisco de Contreras. As in the case of the testimony of the friars contained in the preceding document, the statements of laymen involved with the mission were to be forwarded to the crown and to the Franciscan authorities.

The document begins with a request to the governor at Havana by Fray Contreras that the governor order the captain and crew of the ship that rescued the friars to testify under oath about the conditions in which the ship's captain and crew found the friars, what they had learned from the Indians with whom they spoke in the Keys concerning the treatment of the friars at the hands of the Indians, and about the circumstances of their expulsion from Calusa territory. Next appears the Havana governor's formal declaration acceding to the friar's request and stipulating the questions to which Captain Romero and his crew were to respond. The governor ordered that a statement be taken additionally from Ensign Pedro de Ojeda, an expert pilot, about the governor's having sent Ojeda to Carlos with a letter for Fray López and with instructions to inquire about the friars' welfare and whether the friars had any messages to send back.

The testimony from the various lay witnesses was taken on February 25 and 26, 1698. The first to speak was Francisco Romero, master of the ship that brought the friars to Calusa in September of 1697 and that rescued them in the Keys late the following December. Romero's statement is followed by a copy of the governor's order of December 4, 1697, by which Romero was sent on his voyage to contact the friars. Statements by two of the ship's crew follow.

The testimony of Romero and his crew provides additional firsthand information on developments during the first several days of the mission while the ship was still in the Bay of Carlos and valuable secondhand details on the Indians' mistreatment of the friars and on the friars' experiences at the hands of Indians as they were being conveyed from Carlos to the Keys. The laymen's testimony is far more revealing about the hardships and dangers suffered by the friars than is the testimony of the friars themselves, although the friars' tales to the crew were undoubtedly the source of much of the information given by the captain and his crewmen.

The most informative of these statements, perhaps, is the one that follows the testimony of the two crewmen. It was made by Juan Esteva, a young man from Veracruz, Mexico, and a servant for the ship's owner. Having sailed with the friars in September with the intention of returning to Cuba with the ship, Fray López prevailed upon him to stay behind with the friars in Calusa. This young man's testimony is the most graphic of all, adding valuable details to the testimony of the friars about the confrontations between the friars and hostile Calusa, about the natives' mistreatment of the friars, about the natives' temple and other structures, and about the Indians' conduct in general.

A brief statement by the pilot, Pedro de Ojeda, follows the testimony of the young servant who had shared the friars' experiences. Ojeda's testimony is followed in turn by an order from Havana's governor that the governor's order and other documentation connected with Ojeda's mission be appended to Ojeda's statement.

Testimony of Lay Witnesses Relating to the Calusa Mission, February–March 1698

AGI, Seville, Santo Domingo, bundle no. 154, R^0 6. n^0 114a.

The cover page bears the following salutation.

I am prostrate at the feet of Your Highness
Your chaplain[15]
Fray Francisco de Contreras

The back of the cover page bears the following notes made by personnel of the Council of the Indies.

> It came with a letter from Fray Francisco de Contreras, vice-commissary general of Florida for the order of St. Francis, of the 5th of March of 1698, no. 3, received on the 20th of June of it, in the Galleons.
>
> Report by lay witnesses.
> N^0 2^0
>> About Fray Feliciano López and the 4 religious that he brought with him having returned from the conversion of the cacique Carlos.

The following piece is Fray Contreras's request to the governor at Havana to conduct the inquiry.

---

15. This is not meant in the literal present-day sense of chaplain. It was common for the friars in the missions supported by the royal treasury to refer to themselves as chaplains of the king and to avail themselves of that title to offer advice to the king about problems they saw in Florida as if they were members of his personal household.

Fray Francisco de Contreras of the Friars Minor of the Regular
Observance of Our Seraphic Father St. Francis, preacher emeritus,
officer of the Holy Office, ex-definitor, and chronicler of the holy
province of Sts. Peter and Paul of Michoacan, and vice-commissary
general and visitor of this Province of Santa Elena of Florida, etc.,
to the most illustrious señor don Diego de Cordova Laso de la Vega,
governor and captain general by his Majesty of this city of Havana
and island of Cuba, health and everlasting happiness. Inasmuch as
the king our lord (may God save him) has commanded us in
repeated dispatches that we should report about the turn taken by
the conversions that were solicited at the expense of the royal
treasury in the district of the cacique of Carlos to which five
religious were dispatched by your lordship, [who] crossed over
during the month of September of the past year of ninety-seven, and
these have just arrived at this port stripped of even their habits, the
aforementioned cacique and his Indians having expelled them,
mistreated them, and taken away from them the ornaments,
clothing, and provisions. In order to fulfill our obligation and in
order to make his Majesty aware of it [more] completely than by the
present [statements][16] signed by our hand, sealed with the seal of
our ministry, countersigned by our secretary on the part of our
order and in his own name, we beg and ask and request that Your
Lordship deign to order that Francisco Romero and the rest of his
companions who found and brought the said religious back should
appear before you and that you should make them state under oath
the place in which they found us, with what habits and supplies,
and what they learned from the Indians with whom they spoke
about our treatment and expulsions, and that we should be given
four copies of an authenticated deposition made from the
statements that they make thus at your order and, similarly,
another [deposition made] in the same manner and number about
the arrival of the said five religious at this port and about the state
of nudity in which they entered it. In doing so, over and above its
being the just thing to do, you shall gain the favor of our order and
we shall always be mindful of it and [ready to respond in kind]
whenever we may be requested [to do so]. They are dated in this our
convent of St. Francis of Havana on the twenty-second day of the

16. This refers to the statements made by the friars involved on the preceding day.

month of February of the year one thousand six hundred and
ninety-eight.
Fray Francisco de Contreras, vice-commissary general and visitor
By the order of his Very Reverend Paternity, Fray Manuel Cardoso,
secretary

Auto. In the city of Havana on the twenty-fifth of February of the
year one thousand six hundred and ninety-eight, the señor Field
Master don Diego de Cordova Laso de la Vega, governor and captain
general of this said city and of the island of Cuba by his Majesty,
having seen the petition that is contained on the page preceding this
one, dispatched by the Very Reverend Father Fray Francisco de
Contreras of the Friars Minor of the Regular Observance of Our
Seraphic Father St. Francis, priest emeritus, officer of the Holy
Office, ex-definitor, and chronicler of the holy province of San Pedro
and San Pablo of Michoacan and vice-commissary general, and
visitor of Santa Elena of Florida, that his Very Reverend Paternity
sent to his lordship, ordered that Francisco Romero and the rest of
his companions who found and brought back the five religious, who
during the month of September of the past year of ninety-seven
went for the conversion of the Indians of the chiefdom of Carlos in
virtue of the royal orders of his Majesty, that they should declare
under oath, how long ago it was that the said religious went for the
said conversion, the manner in which they were deposited on the
said key, the place in which they currently found them, with what
habits and supplies, and what they learned concerning their
treatment and their expulsion from the Indians with whom they
spoke. And that the said Francisco Romero should declare likewise
the orders that he received from his lordship in writing and orally
for the transport of the said religious, exhibiting those that he has
in his possession so that they may be appended to these *Autos.* And
similarly that a statement be received from the Ensign Pedro de
Ojeda, an expert pilot for these coasts, about the orders that his
lordship gave him so that he might go to the said chiefdom of Carlos
and see the condition in which the said priests of the mission were,
and whether anything occurred to them [to report], and the letter
for the said religious that his lordship gave to him, whether he
delivered it, or if it is still in his possession, that he should show it
so that it may be appended to these *Autos.* And likewise let them
receive the statements that may appear to be appropriate for the

tenor of this *Auto,* and by this he so ordered and signed.

Don Diego de Cordova Laso de la Vega

Before me, Bernardo de Ojeda, head notary for the Government

Statement by the Ensign Francisco Romero. In the city of Havana on the said day month and said year, his lordship the said señor governor and captain general, in virtue of what was ordered by the *Auto* on this page, caused the Ensign Francisco Romero, pilot for these coasts, to appear before him and he received the oath from the aforementioned. And having taken it by God and the cross according to the law, under the burden of it he promised to tell the truth, and questioned according to the tenor of the *Auto* of this page, and it having been read to him word for word, he said that what happened and what he knows is that on the eleventh day of September of this recent past year of one thousand six hundred and ninety-seven, the deponent departed from this port in a sloop that was chartered at the expense of his Majesty in which were embarked five religious of the order of Our Father St. Francis, the one named father commissary Fray Feliciano López, another named Father Jesus, another named Father Carrillo, and the other two religious named Fray Francisco, that he does not remember the surname of these last two, nor the names of the ten[?] prior to them; that they were going for the conversion of the Indians of the chiefdom of Carlos, bringing along on the said sloop provisions and ornaments and others things necessary for the said conversion, with the deponent carrying orders from the señor governor and captain general that he should transport the said five religious to the Keys of Carlos; that, in fact, the said sloop reached the Key of Carlos after seven days of sailing, and that some Indians of Carlos having come to it in canoes as soon as the sloop arrived, the deponent delivered to them a sealed letter for the cacique from his lordship, the señor governor and captain general, and a cane with an ivory head and another gift of tobacco and honey that he was sending to the said cacique. They accepted these, and one of the priests having read the letter to them, they said that those lands belonged to the king and that it was necessary to obey, but that as soon as the said religious, the provisions, and the rests of the things that have been alluded to were on land, he saw their expression change, because they considered that all of that was for them, and that when the said Indians saw some hoes that had been landed,

those who were streetwise (*ladinos*) asked why they had not
brought blacks who might dig with the hoes, because the Indians
did not know how to hoe, and that after having remained there on
the said key for a matter of three or four days, he returned to this
city with the said sloop with the people of his crew with which he
had left this city, who numbered eight men, and he arrived back at
this port. That the voyage out, the stay there, and the return
consumed fourteen days. And that after entering into this port, he
gave an account to his lordship of how the said religious had
remained behind on the said key. And that on the fourth day of
December of the said year of ninety-seven, he departed as pilot of a
sloop that was going to the keys with an order from the señor
governor and captain general that he was to go to the
aforementioned Key of Carlos and deliver a bundle of letters to the
Reverend Father Fray Feliciano López, for which he was to bring
back a reply, and that if he found the said religious short of
provisions, he was to assist them with what he could, as is evident
from the order from his lordship that he has and which he is
exhibiting and that, having gone to the said keys by virtue of it, he
made an effort to look for the Indians to inform himself about the
religious and about what condition they were in, from those of
Matacombe Key. The latter gave them the news that those of Carlos
had thrown the said religious out with two sacks of maize and their
clothing so that if some ship were to pass, they might bring them to
this city from the said Key of Matacombe. And that when he had
anchored on the key alluded to with the said sloop, an Indian from
Carlos came aboard the said sloop and told him that on the
following day he was going to his key. As a result the one testifying
wrote a paper to send to the said father commissary Fray Feliciano
López in which he gave him the news of how he was there and that
he was bringing a bundle of letters for his Reverend Paternity from
the señor governor that he was only supposed to give to him
personally; that he was suffering from an attack of fevers; and that,
notwithstanding this, he would go on approaching the said key to
look for his Paternity in order to speak to him and to give him the
said bundle of letters, and on handing the said paper over sealed to
the said Indian from Carlos so that he might bring it to the said
religious and that on the following day, in effect, the said Indian
from Carlos to whom he had given the said paper left in a canoe for
the return to Carlos with the other Indians [who were] of those

from the mouths[17] and that at the end of fourteen days, when he had recovered from his attack, he resumed his journey, heading for the said key and that at the end of Key Largo he found the said five religious on those beaches, burned from the sun, dead with hunger, without habits or breeches, but solely with their little shirts that had become so tattered that they could see their skin, and the father commissary Fray Feliciano and the other religious among those alluded to, having come on board the said sloop in a canoe that they had; and on seeing them naked and their flesh showing, he offered them his chest of clothing; and as a result they remedied matters as best they could, and he gave him the sealed letter from the señor governor and captain general and he showed them the order that he has exhibited; and he told him that in reference to the food, he would give them a plentiful supply, as much as they needed, because this is what his lordship had ordered; and that he was to make them masters of everything that was his; and the said religious told the deponent that, after his having left them among the said Indians of Carlos, at the time that he transported them to the said key, the fathers prayed the rosary, wearing their cross and rochets,[18] and that on going to the synagogue where they had their idols praying the said rosary, the Indians fled; and that on the following night, they went again in the said manner praying the said rosary while approaching the said synagogue in order to see whether, with these efforts, they could induce them to give up that idolatry and the abominable evils that they committed in it; and that on that night the Indians armed themselves with arrows and spears (*chuzos*)[19] and they surrounded the said religious fathers, giving them many shoves and blows to the face and [other] blows and that the said father commissary, Father Fray Feliciano López, had told him and the rest of the religious fathers that God must not

17. The Spanish here, *de los de las vocas,* is probably an allusion to natives from the area of *Boca de ratones* (Boca Raton) and *las bocas de* Miguel Mora.

18. The rochet is a white linen vestment resembling a surplice with close-fitting sleeves worn especially by bishops and privileged prelates and which it was the custom of the Franciscans to use as well.

19. When the friars described this encounter the Spanish word used was *dardos,* which can mean "dart" or "spear." "Boarding pike" is the primary meaning of *chuzo.* Gary Shapiro suggested that these might be atlatls or spear-throwers in view of atlatls having been found in this area, but for such a close encounter the atlatl would not seem to be necessary.

have wanted us to die as martyrs, for these armed Indians have not killed us with their arms, even though they have given us so many blows and such mistreatment. Let us withdraw to our house. And that on the day that the cacique sent to ask the said religious for a jug of honey or wine [and] on that day the said religious did not give it to him, he gave the order to the Indians that they should not give them fish. And that the said Indians acted accordingly. And that on some occasions the reason for the denial was because the said father commissary found himself unable to give the said Indians what they were asking him for. And the said father commissary also told him how the cacique of Carlos had said to him that they should leave because [otherwise] all the people would leave and leave him alone in the village, and that if they did not, they would kill them, and that, in fact, they had donned their arms one day in order to kill all the said religious; that they did not do so because the old chief defended them so that they might not kill them and that he gave them a canoe with some Indians so that they might carry them to the Keys, where the deponent found them. And while coming from the said Key of Carlos in the said canoe to cast them on those of Matacombe, when they entered into a [river's] mouth, they sent an ambushing party from Carlos so that they might strip them of the clothing and provisions, and they stripped them naked. And that while the father commissary was in the canoe [alone], because the rest of the religious were on land at the fire, having perceived that they were taking the canoe away from land, he got up and, asking who was pulling, the Indian who was doing it gave him a shove and tossed him into the water; and that he went toward it swimming until he was able to touch bottom; that, having found it, he called to the rest of the religious, because he was almost on the point of dying and so that they might throw him absolution. And that one of them, having come down to the river saying, "Our father is drowning," looked for a long pole in order to throw it to the said priest so that holding onto to it they might be able to haul him in, because the current had pushed him to the other side. And, in effect, with the said pole the said religious brought [him] from the other side of the river. The Indians from Carlos having carried off the canoe with all the provisions and the rest of the things that he was bringing, and that later the brother of the cacique had come, who is the one who had brought the said religious, reappearing again and asking the fathers what that was. And the said father commissary grabbed the keys for the boxes and handed them over to the said brother of the cacique so that he might carry them off and that the said Indians accepted them. And that, after having gone with the said keys, he returned later, bringing them the canoe empty, and that the said religious embarked there with the said Indians, who brought them along on an inland route by way of ponds as they did not wish to bring them along the coast so that they might not see any ships belonging to Spaniards because they had had news that the Ensign Pedro de Ojeda had come with an order from the señor governor to talk with the said priests. The said Indians had refused [to say anything] to the said Pedro de Ojeda, even though they were on board his vessel [and] even though the aforementioned asked about them. That later they reached the Key of Muspa and when they had arrived, the Indians of the said key stripped them, taking away their habits, cowls, and underclothes, leaving them solely their little shirts and that from there they had passed to the end of Key Largo, and it was there that the deponent found them. And that these toils and wanderings from the time that they left them on the coast of the said Key of Carlos went on for more than thirty days, that so the said father commissary told him, and how on the second, having reached the said Key Largo, he arrived at it and the one testifying met up with them and that he believes that the misfortunes and toils that the said fathers have suffered are true because he saw them so debilitated, dispirited, and worn out; that when he had given them a little bit of chocolate and fish, they could not hold it down because it came right back up; and that the said Indians of Matacombe told him in [their] presence he declares[20] how the God of the priests had already abandoned the said religious and [left them] naked; and that the deponent said to them that they were dogs, that God had not abandoned the religious, but rather that he had sent the deponent there so that he might bring them to Havana; and that if the life of anyone of them had been at risk, soldiers would have come from Florida and from Havana and would have killed them all. And that although the said father commissary told him of other toils, cases, and incidents that there were with the said Indians, he has not been able to remember them except for the ones he has already

20. A copyist may have omitted something here in passing from one page to the next, as something seems to be missing here to complete the sense of this statement, or else it is a very elliptical one.

mentioned. That he said it was the truth under the burden of his oath and that he is sixty-three years of age. And his lordship initialed it. And the deponent added that he found a boy named Juan with the said religious, whom they had brought with them from here when the said Fathers went, who could give an account of what happened with more specificity, as above.

And likewise the deponent added that the said priests came on board the said sloop and into this port on the twenty-first day of the current [month] as above.

Francisco Romero

Before me, Bernardo de Ojeda, head notary for the Government

Order. The Field Master don Diego de Cordova Laso de la Vega, governor and captain general of this city of San Christóval of Havana and of the Island of Cuba by his Majesty. With reference to the occasion of the Reverend Father preacher Fray Feliciano López having crossed over for the conversion of the Indians, inhabitants of the chiefdom of Carlos, and it being appropriate to the service of both Majesties to learn of the status of so holy an enterprise, I have granted permission as I [grant] it to the Ensign Francisco Romero so that he may go with his launch to the keys of the other coast as the pilot that he is for them, with the condition and obligation that he is to touch at the [key] of Carlos alluded to and deliver my bundle of letters that he carries in his care to the reverend missionary father from whom he will collect a reply for his own security. And similarly I order and command that in case he finds [the friars] short of provisions, he will supply them with what he can and what the hold of his launch will permit because of the degree that the maintenance of the said priest and the rest of the religious is important for the conversion of those souls to our holy Catholic faith. He will carry this out in the manner alluded to without departing from it in any way. Given in Havana on the fourth of December of the year one thousand six hundred and ninety-seven. Cordoba.

By order of his lordship, Don Diego Thenorio

Statement of Alexandro Angel. In the city of Havana on the twenty-sixth of February of the year one thousand six hundred and ninety-eight, the señor Field Master don Diego de Cordova Laso de la Vega, governor and captain general of this said city and of the Island of

Cuba by his Majesty, in virtue of what is decreed by the *Auto* which is on page two of these [pages] caused Alexandro Angel, resident (*residente*) in this said city and who said he was an inhabitant (*vezino*) of the presidio of Florida, to appear before him. And the oath was received from the aforementioned and having taken it by God and the cross in accord with the law, under the burden of it he promised to tell the truth and questioned in accord with the tenor of the said *auto,* and it having been read to him word for word, he said that the deponent departed from this said port embarked on a sloop that left it for the Keys about three and one-half months ago in the company of the Ensign Francisco Romero, pilot of these coasts, who, he knows, carried an order from the señor governor and captain general to go to the keys of Carlos to see the state in which the religious of the señor St. Francis were, whom the said Francisco Romero had carried there earlier and a sealed letter for the father commissary, Fray Feliciano López, and that they spent thirty days in the attempt to go to the said keys of Carlos, at the end of which, on coming toward Matacumbe, from news that the Indians of that area had given to them of how the Indians of Carlos had expelled the priests who went for the conversion of the said Indians, on searching for them, they came upon them on the said Key of Matacumbe, naked, without habits or underclothes except for their little shirts, closer to being dead than to being alive, weakened and enfeebled to such a degree that, even though they gave them some things to eat, they could not hold it and threw it up. And that there the Ensign Francisco Romero and the rest of his companions gave them some clothing to wear so that they might cover their private parts, and that there the said father commissary told them when they questioned him as to what had been the cause of [their] having expelled them, the said religious having asked [for it], he said: that because they had not given them everything that the priests brought for their sustenance and because the father commissary, on seeing himself unable to give them everything that they asked for, gave them part of it; and that notwithstanding this [gesture], they took up arms to kill them, which they would in fact have done if the old chief had not defended them and sent them off in a canoe with Indians so that they might cross over to Muspa. And that on the way the said Indians took away the provisions that the said priests were carrying and that all the ornaments and the rest of the things and provisions that they had brought remained behind with them, the Indians of Carlos. And the few [provisions] that the said Indians gave them for the trip, the neighboring Indians where they were traveling so that they might pass to the outside keys, had taken away all their provisions and went on constraining them until they left them naked, and that the said Father Fray Feliciano López recounted how the said Indians of Carlos made fun of the five religious and that on the occasions that they went out praying the rosary they had mistreated them and given them blows and made them return to their house. And he recounted many other toils, injuries, and hardships that they suffered, both the said religious as well as another who accompanied him in a canoe, and they went to the vessel as soon as they reached the area where they had found them. And that afterwards another three religious went aboard and a boy named Juan, whom the said priests had brought to the conversion of the said Indians of Carlos so that he might serve them, and that the latter and all the rest of the religious told of the many troubles and toils that they had endured with the said Indians and bad treatment and that they brought the said priests along with them in their company in the said sloop for about a month until they brought them to this city and entered into it on the twenty-first day of the current [month]. And he said that what he has stated is the truth under the burden of the oath, and he signed it. And that he is forty-seven years of age. And his Lordship initialed it.

Alexandro Angel

Before me, Bernardo de Ojeda, head notary for the government

Statement of Sevastian Sánchez. In the city of Havana on the said day, month, and said year, his lordship the said señor governor and captain general by virtue of what was ordered by the *auto* of page two, caused a man to appear before him who said he was named Sevastian Sánchez and that he was a native of Cádiz, and he received the oath from the aforementioned, and after he had made it by God and by the cross, according to the law he promised to tell the truth, and questioned in accord with the tenor of the said *autto* and it having been read to him word for word, he said that what he knows and can say [is] that about three months ago the deponent departed from this port in a sloop that was going to the Keys, and that Francisco Romero went in it as pilot and that they spent a month on the Key of Cows and that at the end of the said time they went to Key Largo, and on Matacumbe on the way back they came upon the five priests who had gone on the mission and conversion of the Indians of the Key of Carlos; that the father commissary is named Fray Feliciano López; that of the other four, he no longer remembers the names of two; that they are Father Jesus, Father Carrillo, and Fray Fernando, whom they found on land with the Indians of Matacumbe eating shellfish (*marisco*). And as soon as they saw the sloop, the father commissary, Fray Feliciano López, and Father Jesus went on board it, naked except for their little undershirts, and [those] torn, with their skin showing. And the said priest told about the many extortions, troubles, and thefts that the Indians of Carlos had subjected them to, and that they had thrown them into the water, and that they had also taken away their provisions, and the habits, and their pants. And the said father commissary and his companion, Father Jesus, having returned to land for the rest of the religious, they brought back the other three religious in the canoe in which they had come to the sloop, and a boy. And that the said priests were very weak and so thin that if they had remained with the Indians another three or four days, they all would have died. And that the said religious recounted how the Indians of Matacumbe, where they found them, did not give them anything to eat, but rather the priests looked for shellfish, even though they saw them eat and that they made them carry jugs of water for the said Indians to drink. And the feebleness and the weakness of the said religious were so great that when they had given two sops of biscuit soaked in wine (*dos sopas de vizcocho mojado en vino*) and a little bit of chocolate to the said father commissary, Fray Feliciano López, in the sloop, he threw it up without being able to hold it down. And he also heard the said religious recount that because they had gone out praying the rosary, they [i.e., the Indians] had wanted to kill them and that they pummeled them with their fists on the said Key of Carlos. And that they had choked one of the said religious, who is called Fray Fernando, having grabbed him by the throat. And the deponent, feeling pity on seeing the said religious with their skin showing, in addition to some old clothes that they had given them on the sloop, cut four pairs of white linen pants from a tent (*cortó de un pabellon quatro pares de calzones blancoa de lienzo*) for four of the religious. And that he knows that the said Ensign Francisco Romero was carrying an order from his lordship to acquire news about what state the said religious were in on the said Key of Carlos, and that he was carrying a letter for the said father commissary Fray Feliciano and that the deponent saw him give it to him, when they found them on Matacumbe, and that the said father commissary opened it in the presence of everyone and read it to himself; and that prior to what he has recounted, while they were on the keys of the Mouths, they saw an Indian from Carlos and that when he wished to come to the sloop with others they refused him, telling him that he should come aboard alone, and when he had done so, the said Ensign Francisco Romero wrote a note to the father commissary Fray Feliciano and he sealed it and handed it to the said Indian to say that he was coming to Carlos and that when he asked for news on the state of the said priests, the said Indian from Carlos told how they had expelled them from Carlos. And when the said Ensign Francisco Romero said to him that they should have regard for what they were doing because the señor governor would be bound to send [men] to punish them and that [they would do] the same from Florida, to these arguments the said Indian offered jests and laughter. And that although the said father commissary and the rest of the religious told of the ignominies, troubles, and sorrows that the said Indians of Carlos had inflicted on them, he does not remember anything more now than what he has stated. And that after the said religious had been in the sloop for a month and one half with the deponent and the rest of his comrades, they came to this city, entering into its port on the twenty-first day of the current [month] when the sun had set. And this was his response. And he said that what he has stated is the truth under the burden of the oath. He did not sign because he does not know how, and that he is fifty-two years of age. And his lordship signed it.   Cordova

Before me, Bernardo de Ojeda, head notary for the government

Statement of Juan Esteva. This witness remained with the religious and tells of what happened firsthand. In the City of Havana on the twenty-sixth of February of the year one thousand six hundred and ninety-eight his lordship the said señor governor and captain general, by virtue of what is ordered by the *Auto* that is on page two, summoned a young man to appear before him, who said that his name was Juan Estevan and that he was a native of Veracruz. And the oath was received from the aforementioned. And having taken it according to the law, under the burden of it he promised to tell the truth. And questioned in accord with the tenor of the said *auto,* he said that what happens is that the deponent is a servant of don Carlos de Paralta, owner of the sloop that was chartered on the part of his Majesty to carry the five religious of our father St. Francis to the conversion of the chiefdom of Carlos, on which the Ensign Francisco Romero went as pilot, and that in view of the fact that the said sloop [belonged] to his employer, he embarked on it and went to the keys of Carlos with the intention of coming back. And after having reached them and after the Indians had received them, when the deponent wanted to return in the said sloop, because the Father Fray Feliciano López asked him not to go, [and] that he should accompany them, he remained with the said five priests in effect. One is the said father commissary. Another Fray Francisco de Jesus, and another Fray Miguel Carrillo, and another, Fray Fernando, that he does not know his surname, and another, Fray Francisco de San Diego, a layman. And that when the sloop had arrived and the pilot, Francisco Romero, had delivered a letter from the señor governor to the young cacique of Carlos, it was opened and read by an interpreter; he said that all the lands belonged to the King of Spain and that he was ready to become baptized and to profess the law of the Christians and that all the children below the age of eight would be baptized; and that it would be difficult to withdraw the old people away from what their ancestors had observed. And that he saw that the said pilot gave him a cane, a hat, and other gifts that his lordship the said señor governor and captain general had sent to him and the said father commissary gave to him. With this [done] the said religious and the deponent having gone to the shore, the said young cacique brought them to his house to live, where they lived for some days afflicted by the sun and by the water, when it rained and by the nighttime dews because the said hut (*Bugio*) of palm-thatch (*guano*) had many holes (*agujeros*). And that there the father commissary, Fray Feliciano López, because the Cacique Carlos was very ill, having given him a blanket so that he might cover himself and other little pieces of clothing, and [thinking?] that he would want to be baptized, because he was very ill and about to die, and very happy that the priests had arrived, that they would remain in his place, and that as a result, the said father commissary baptized him, and that when the said old cacique was in the last moments of his life, the said father commissary attended him in order to help him to die well, exhorting him and telling him that he was a Christian and that they would bury him in holy ground. To this the old chief said that he was not a Christian, that he was not about to become one for four old pieces of clothing, and that he wanted to be buried like his ancestors. That during that time he did not die from that illness, [and that he said] that if he were to die then, they should kill the said priests and the deponent in accord with the desires that the young cacique had; because each time that he surrounded the house with bowmen, the old cacique, on his going to complain, ordered them to withdraw. That after [the stay there] alluded to, the priests built a hut (*Bujio*), with the Indians bringing the palms and the logs and with him paying them in maize and tobacco. This said hut was [good] solely for shutting out the sun, because when it rained the water entered from everywhere. And that after the matters alluded to, the said young cacique in order to see whether the priests brought some clothing to give to them had a son baptized and a niece[21] and they were baptized in effect; but on the niece they only poured the water while for the son [it was done] with their full ritual[22] and that the reason for not having done the baptism of the niece [with the full ritual] as with that of the son of the cacique was because in the interim, when he was performing the first one, the Indians stole as much as there was [to steal] with the result that when he had poured the water on the said niece, they said that they would put the oils on her later. And that following what has been alluded to, the said young chief, on seeing that they had baptized his son and niece and that they had not given them any clothing or anything to eat, spoke about it to all the priests. With that they gave him a little bit of blue serge and some curious red riding caps (*monteritas*). And notwithstanding the said religious being there, [and] that they preached to them and exhorted them so that they might embrace the law of God, nevertheless the Indians said that they did not wish to become Christians unless they gave them clothing. And they engaged in their idolatries in a hut apart, where there are many wooden masks, painted in white, red, and black,

21. The Spanish here is clearly *sobrina*, or "niece," but in one or more of the earlier statements this word was *sobrino*, or "nephew."

22. The Spanish here, *con todos sus Sacramentos*, translated literally would be "with all their sacraments." But the allusion is clearly to the other ceremonies that are part of the baptism ritual.

with noses two yards in length and where they go every three
nights and they keep these masks above (*sobre*)[23] a type of altar
with a mat (*estera*)[24] in front of it in the fashion of a frontal.[25] And
the said religious, in order to see whether they could bring them
around, went out at night praying the rosary, one wearing a
surplice and stole, the most holy Virgin in his hands, two with their
lanterns (*linternas*), and the one testifying in front with a cross,
with the other two religious remaining behind to guard the house.
And saying the rosary in this form, they even managed to enter into
the said synagogue and with the novelty of the lanterns the Indians
fled without anyone appearing, and that for five or six days they
left off going to the said synagogue; and at the end of them they
returned. With this the religious went out again that night in the
same way as on the first one, with the deponent saying the rosary.
And all the Indians were inside the synagogue already furnished
with arrows; with the result that, when other Indians had detained
them so that they would not go to the said synagogue because they
would have to kill them. This incident of having encountered the
said Indians and that they had detained them happened because of a
miracle of the most holy Virgin, because when the said priests
continued to head toward the said synagogue, despite the fears that
the others [the Indians who detained them] instilled in them, they
did not find any Indian in it. And the said Indians returned to the
said synagogue the following night, and when the priests set out for
it to continue their rosary, and after going about halfway on the
trail and before they reached the said synagogue, the young chief
and other leading Indians came out to the said priests and sought to
dissuade the said priests from going to the synagogue because they
would have to kill them; and the said Indians, grabbing hold of the
priests, with two or three [holding] each one, the father
commissary, Fray Feliciano López, who had remained behind,
guarding the house, provisions, and ornaments, on hearing the
noise, went to where the religious [and] the deponent were going
along saying the rosary and the Indians who were detaining them.

23. *Sobre* could also possibly be rendered as "on top of."
24. In the sense of a textile woven of sedge or rushes.
25. This is used probably in its sense of the rich cloth hanging that covers
the space under the altar once Mass has been said in the morning, although
the word also has other meanings.

And after incorporating himself with them, he told him that he
should proceed with the rosary. On seeing this resolution, the
young cacique ordered all the Indian bowmen sent for. And in a
short time a great number of them assembled with their arrows and
with the said young cacique ordering them that, if the priests
should step off the trail, they should kill them. And the said Indians
aimed at them with the said arrows, but they never fired them. And
when some of the religious approached them, they pushed them
back to their house with shoves and blows to the throat. And the
deponent brought an Indian along with him, who had grabbed him
by the throat. And they broke off [the engagement] with the priests
in their said house. And that notwithstanding the bad treatment
and the ignominies that they inflicted on them, in order to see if
they could go to the synagogue to withdraw them from their
idolatries, they fell to their knees, each one with a crucifix in hand,
preaching the word of God to them and denouncing their idolatries
and evil practices. When this did not suffice, they again pushed
them back to their house with shoves [and], on seeing that for that
night it was impossible to go to the synagogue, notwithstanding the
fact that they had the will to try to continue. [At this point] the
young cacique sent them a message with the great captain, as the
Indians call him, a brother of the said young chief, telling them that
there was no point to their tiring themselves preaching to them;
that they did not wish to become Christians; that they should go or
they would kill them. On seeing this determination, the priests said
to the Indians that they should send them to Apalachee and they
said that they did not wish to because there were brothers on the
way and notwithstanding the rejections, the recollections, and the
threats from the Indians alluded to, the priests celebrated Mass in
their hut and were continuing to make their efforts as they did
during the four months' time that they remained among the said
Indians of Carlos and [during which] they never found a method of
bringing them around; because on the day of All Saints, while he
was saying Mass, when the said priests ordered the said cacique
and the other leading Indians to fall to their knees for the elevation
of the host in which was the Body of the Lord, they seated
themselves more determinedly and ordered those who were
kneeling to sit. When the priests were preaching the young cacique
was accustomed to enter, making fun of them and letting out
shouts, and that on one occasion, while one of the priests, who was

called Fray Miguel Carrillo, was at the door of the hut preaching to
them with a crucifix in his hand and teaching them to make the
sign of the cross, the Indians came with mud and filth and let him
have it in the face and at other times with soot from the *casuelas*
and [then] fled; and in ridiculing them; and others turned around
and showed them their buttocks. And the said cacique told the
priests on repeated occasions that they would end up going, that he
had a canoe there; that they should go to the Key of Bones [Key
West] in it; that he would give them Indians so that they might
bring them [there]. And from there to this city when some vessel
should pass [headed] for this city, and that the said priests adopted
the expedient of embarking in the said canoe with four Indians and
some bundles and boxes and some provisions and that, having fixed
up two fishing boats (*cayucos*) to build a raft on top of them[26] with a
bushel[27] and a one-half of maize per *cayuco* and a yard of cloth in
which to put all their bundles. The Indians took off and they
carried off the *Cayucos* and the maize that they had given them for
them, stealing everything that was brought to the beach by their
hands; that they did not succeed in keeping anything and nothing
reached it [the beach] except for what the religious brought on their
backs. And that in pursuing their voyage in the said canoe by way
of lagoons (*lagunatos*) that extend between the keys, they slept on a
beach the first night and that on that night the Indians who came
in the canoe opened a jug of wine and made themselves drunk. And
they tarried there until midday of the next day with the thought
that the young cacique[28] would go on ahead and that he would lead
them astray[29] as he did. That having reached the settlement of Teyú
at about three in the afternoon, with the deponent arriving first in a
Cayuco in which he was carrying three jugs of honey, two of wine,

26. They apparently built a catamaran of sorts with the two *cayucos,* which
is a small fishing canoe used in Venezuela. Ponce de León reported seeing a
similar catamaran arrangement in 1513 on Florida's southwest coast (Herrera
1720: 248).

27. *Fanega* is the Spanish term used here, and as a measure of grain and
seed it is equivalent to about a hundredweight or English bushel.

28. It is not clear who this young cacique was, as the ruling young cacique
is supposed to have disappeared while they were loading the canoes and other
accounts say it was the brother of the old chief who accompanied them.

29. The meaning of this is not clear to me. The Spanish here is "con animo
de que el cacique mozo passase delante, y los descaminase, como lo hizo."

and one of sugar, and while a canoe was passing with four Indian men and two Indian women from Muspa [headed] for Carlos, they took a jug of honey away from the deponent through the use of violence. And that the priests arrived that night in the large canoe and they all slept together there because the bundles had arrived wet. And that same evening they put them out to dry. And once they were dry, they put them back in the boxes again; that they were the ornaments, the clothing of the priests, and some provisions. And that during the night at midnight the Indians untied the canoe, and that the father commissary, Fray Feliciano, awoke with the noise, and on [his] asking who was launching the canoe, the Indians continued to proceed and to embark within it without making any response at all. And they came to the priests and they tossed them into the water except for one of the religious who was on land. And had it not been for a fire-lock (*escopeta*) that the said father commissary had in his hand with which he fell into the water and the wind that caught the habits, he would have drowned as it was over his head and a very strong current. That the deponent and the rest of the priests, these were able to touch bottom soon after they tossed them into the water. And the deponent fell in the deep part and came swimming. And the father commissary asking for help, because he was becoming tired, one of the religious, who is the lay priest [*sic*] Fray Francisco de San Diego, threw him a long pole which he grabbed and they went about pulling him to shore with the said pole until he could touch bottom and with the gun. Because it was very long he stuck it in the bottom and was able to support himself until they tossed him the said pole. And the Indians from Carlos and the young chief, having carried off the canoe with all the boxes, and everything that there was in it the canoe and a raft on which there were some things also, while an uncle of the young chief remained with the said priests. That he feigned being asleep and as if he did not know anything, and he said, in recounting to the priests how they had robbed them and how the Indians had carried off the canoe and everything that was within it and what there was on the raft with it. The said Indian stated that he who had done that, that it had been the great chief. With that the priests said to him that since he has carried off the boxes, that he might as well take the keys, with the hope that they would bring them some provisions and not leave them there to perish. And that on the following day, two hours before dawn, the

Indians of the village of Teyú came by land with arrows and
harpoons (*harpones*), and while the priests were drying themselves
at the fire, the said Indians arrived and took away their cloaks
(*mantos*). And when dawn came, while going along from beach to
beach to pass beyond the said village of Teyú even though they
might kill them, as they considered it certain they would, while
they were passing, they saw the canoe come with the cacique of the
Key of Muspa without bringing the boxes or the rest of what they
had carried off, [but] bringing along in a *Cayuco* four or five sacks of
maize and another of biscuit, that they had allotted them in their
divisions, and likewise a little box with the books of the priests.
And when the five religious and the deponent had embarked in the
large canoe, which they had emptied, and departed from that post
about the distance of a musket shot, the said cacique of Muspa
stripped the said priests, taking the habits (*havitos*) and leaving
them solely with the cowl (*capilla*), little undershirt (*tuniquillo*), and
linen breeches (*calzones de lienzo*). And when they had passed to
Muspa, the said cacique said to them that they were not to depart
from there until the cacique of the Key of Bones should come, who
had gone to Carlos, so that he might bring them to the village of
Bones, and that from there they would come to this city. That they
were there for a night and day, and that [then], on their having
succeeded in seeing the sloop in which the Ensign Pedro de Ojeda
was coming, they told them that they should go and he gave them
three Indians so that he might bring them in the canoe to the Key of
Cuchiapa.[30] And that on the way the three Indians who had brought
them out of Muspa stripped the priests of the cowls and breeches,
leaving them with the little undershirts next to their skin and bare
of foot and leg, because those of Muspa had already taken their
stockings and shoes. And they left the deponent naked with some
torn breeches of hemp that the said Indians gave him, because the
said Indians said that the ones that the deponent had [made] of
cloth, that they were good for breechclouts. And that the said
Indians who finished stripping them brought them to the village of
Cuchiaga, where they remained ten days, suffering cold and hunger
and drinking salt water and much sun during the day. That they
had no other recourse except to place themselves in the shade of the
canoe in which they had come. And that at the end of ten days, the

30. It is written thus, but it should be Cuchiaga.

cacique of the Key of Bones came and brought them to the village of Tancha, where they remained eight days, eating a little bit of fish on rare occasions. That he obliged the deponent to embark with the Indians in order to help them so that the priest and the deponent might eat. And that two Indians having come from the mouths (vocas)[31] they made smoke signals so that those who were on Tancha might come to Matacumbe. And the Indians of Tancha having come with their families, they embarked for Matacumbe, leaving the deponent and the priests behind alone. And that two Indians of the Key of Bones, who were there, brought the said priests and the deponent to Matacumbe. And when they had been there for twelve days, at the end of them Indian men and Indian women came from the mouths on some rafts and gave the news that the Ensign Francisco Romero, pilot, was there and that he would come there on the following day. With this report, the said priests were consoled. And that Francisco Romero came on the following day and the priests went on board. That they came very weak. And that the said Romero and his companions gave them and the deponent some clothes to put on such as breeches (*calzones*) that they made from a tent and they gave them to eat. And they remained in the sloop about a month more or less, with the said pilot feeding them. And at the end of the said time the religious came to this city and entered into its port with their little shirts (*tuniquillog*) and breeches, of those which Romero and his companions had given them on the sloop, on Friday the twenty-first day of the current [month]. And that they suffered many other circumstances of toils and troubles in Carlos, that for now he cannot remember all of them impromptu, the risks of life and the bad treatment that they inflicted on the deponent when he went to fetch water for the priests. And this he replies. And he said it is the truth under the burden of the oath. He did not sign because he does not know how and that he is seventeen years of age. And his lordship signed it.

Cordoba

Before me, Bernardo de Ojeda, head notary

Statement of the Ensign Pedro de Ojeda. In the city of Havana on the said day, month, and said year his lordship the said señor

31. The identity of these *vocas* is not indicated. This term was used for underwater rocks.

governor and captain general for greater adherence to and
fulfillment of what was ordered by the said *auto* of page two,
summoned to appear before him the Ensign Pedro de Ojeda, a
resident of this said city and pilot of these coasts. And the oath was
received from the aforementioned, and having made it by God and
the cross according to the law, under the burden of it he promised
to tell the truth, and questioned in accord with the tenor of the said
auto, and it having been read to him word for word, he said that he
who is testifying left for the Keys as captain of a sloop with orders
from the señor governor and captain general so that he might touch
at the Key of Carlos and deliver a bundle of letters to the
missionary father Fray Feliciano López and that, in case he found
him short of provisions, they should assist him with what he could,
as is evident from the order that he exhibits and [that] was given to
him by his lordship, the said señor governor and captain general.
And that by virtue of the said order, having gone to the said Keys of
Carlos and made inquiries in order to see if he could see some
Indians in order to ask about the said religious and that he might
deliver the letter for the priest, Fray Feliciano López and see what
state they were in. On not seeing any Indian on those beaches, he
entered by way of the narrow mouth of a large lagoon to make some
smoke signals to see if some Indians would come. In this effort the
sloop collided with a protruding headland[32] of rock and the rudder
was broken. They repaired it as well as they were able to and they
went out into the open water again at great risk and in going to and
coming from the said keys, he did not see an Indian in those of
Carlos. As a result, having come to this city he returned the sealed
letter that he was carrying to the señor governor and captain
general. And this he replied. And he said that what he had stated is
the truth under the burden of his oath. He did not sign because of
not knowing how to. And that he is sixty years of age. And his
lordship signed it.
Cordova
Before me, Bernardo de Ojeda, head notary for the government

---

32. The Spanish here is *dió la valandra con un cabezón de piedra.* My dictionaries give the meaning of *cabezón* as "tax register," "collar of a shirt," and
other alternatives that do not fit this context. As cabeza or "head" is the root
of this word, I have translated it as "protruding headland."

In the city of Havana on the twenty-eighth day of the month of February of the year one thousand six hundred and ninety-eight, the señor Field Master don Diego de Cordoba Laso de la Vega, governor and captain of this said city and Island of Cuba for his Majesty, having seen these *autos,* commanded that the order exhibited by the Ensign Pedro de Ojeda be appended to it. And in view of the fact that it is established from the statement of the Ensign Francisco Romero that he had delivered the letter to his lordship sent to the said father commissary with the said pilot to the Reverend Father Commissary, Fray Feliciano López, at the time that he found him with the rest of the religious on the Key of Matacumbe, expelled by the Indians of Carlos. And that the one that the said Ensign Pedro de Ojeda has brought back because of not having found the said priests is a duplicate of the one that the said pilot, Ensign Francisco Romero, carried. Let it also be appended to these *autos* and let them give copies of all of them [that is] of all the said *autos* word for word and of the rest that he asked for to the Very Reverend Father Fray Francisco de Contreras, preacher emeritus, an official of the holy office, ex-definitor and chronicler of the holy Province of San Pedro and San Pablo de Michoacan, and vice-commisary general and visitor of Santa Elena of Florida, which he asked for by means of the request of the twenty-second of the current month. And by this I so order and sign.
Cordova
Before me, Bernardo de Ojeda, notary for the Governorment

Order. The Field Master don Diego de Cordoba Laso de la Vega, governor and captain general of this city of San Christóval of Havana and of the Island of Cuba for his Majesty.

Inasmuch as on the occasion of the Reverend Father Preacher Fray Feliciano López having crossed over for the conversion of the Indian inhabitants of the chiefdom of Carlos, and inasmuch as it was appropriate for the service of Both Majesties to learn the present status of that so holy enterprise, I have granted permission, as I am granting it, to the Ensign Pedro de Ojeda so that he may go with his sloop to the keys of the other coast in his capacity as pilot of them with the condition and obligation that he is to touch at the [Key] of Carlos alluded to and to deliver my bundle of letters for the reverend father missionary that he carries in his care. He is to

collect a reply from him, which he is to take care of. And similarly I
order and command that, in case he should find them short of
provisions, he should assist them with what he is able to and with
what the hold of his sloop will permit, because of the degree to
which the maintenance of the said reverend and the rest of the
religious is important for the conversion of those souls to our holy
Catholic faith. He shall execute this [order] in the manner alluded
to without disobeying anything at all in it. Given in Havana on the
fifth of December of the year one thousand six hundred and
ninety-seven.
Cordova
By order of his lordship.   Don Diego Thenorio

Letter. My lord, I am dispatching this sloop to that spot with the
desire of learning of the health of your Reverence and about the
status of your holy and Christian effort at the present time, [as well
as] the conversion of the inhabitants of those dominions. I hope in
Our Lord that this will be achieved very successfully by dint of
your labor and teaching. And to achieve it, let your Reverence
furnish these reports to me. In addition to this launch I am leaving
you prior notice about another that will go out within a very short
time for the same purpose [and] that I must say to your Reverence
that with your report [in hand] and in your succeeding in subjecting
the heathen of these peoples to the Catholic religion as his Majesty
desires, I shall proceed punctually to provide and furnish to your
Reverence what you may need and that would be for your
assistance and pleasing to you and so that your Reverence may
understand it as [my] desire, the captain of this launch carries an
order so that he may assist your Reverence with what he can. And
the one whom I mention is about to leave; he will carry the same.
That this is what occurs to me to say to your Reverence, whose life
may God preserve for many years. Havana, December 5, of one
thousand six hundred and ninety-seven. The servant of your
excellency, who kisses your hand.
Don Diego de Cordova Laso de la Vega.
Rmo. Father Fray Feliciano López

It agrees with its originals, which remain among the papers of my
office from which I send them and at the request of the Most
Reverend Father Fray Francisco de Contreras, preacher emeritus,

official of the holy office, ex-definitor and chronicler of the holy
Province of San Pedro and San Pablo of Michoacan, vice-
commissary general and visitor of Santa Elena of Florida, I give the
present in Havana on common paper, because we do not have the
stamped kind, on the eleventh of March of the year one thousand
six hundred and ninety-eight.
I make my sign in witness of the truth.
Bernardo de Ojeda, head notary for the government

We certify that Bernardo de Ojeda by whom this copy goes sealed
and signed is a notary; that he faithfully and legally exercises and
practices [the function] as he is said to, and all his dispatches have
been given faith and credit in court and outside of it. Havana,
March eleventh of the year one thousand six hundred and
ninety-eight.
Antonio Fernández de Velasco, notary public
Dionissio de Sotto, notary public

Fray Francisco de Contreras to the King, March 5, 1698, Cover Letter for His Inquiry

This letter accompanied the statements made by the friars and lay
witnesses.

Most High and Powerful Lord
Sir
On the advice of Your Highness the king our lord (may God save
him) deigned to order that from the twenty-two religious that Fray
Feliciano López brought on his mission at the expense of the royal
treasury that in this city I should choose the four or six who
appeared most suitable, and after having been provisioned by the
governor and the royal officials of this city, cross over with them to
the district of the cacique of Carlos, who was seeking holy baptism
for himself and fourteen thousand souls of his jurisdiction,[33]
according to what the reverend father doctor in Christ, don Diego
Evelino de Compostela, bishop of this bishopric, reported to your
Majesty. And, having made the crossing during the past month of
September, on the 21st of February of this current year, the

---

33. The Spanish here is *dicion*. I am presuming it was meant to be *juris-
dicion*.

religious arrived at this port in the manner and for the reasons that
are laid out in the *Auttos* and statements, which I send along to
Your Highness with this [letter], so that [having been provided
thus] with the knowledge of the state of this enterprise, he may
deign to order what he judges to be most suitable. May God
preserve Your Highness and favor him for many years. Havana,
March 5 of 1698.
Most High and Powerful Lord

16. The Council's Comments on the Calusa Mission Debacle, 1698

The last document from the Council of the Indies for the ill-fated 1697
Calusa mission of San Diego de Compostela is the council's comments
after receiving the testimony gathered by Fray Francisco de Contreras
detailing the hostility encountered by the friars, which led to their expulsion and despoliation. The council's notes contain a very brief
sketch of the historical background of the mission, together with
comments on recent developments in the Mayaca-Jororo missions, and
a summary of developments at the Calusa mission during the friars'
brief stay in Calusa territory. The council concluded that the Calusa's
request for friars was not sincere but motivated by material self-
interest. The council moved to thank those involved for their efforts
and recommended that, to the degree that the royal treasury's condition permitted, preparations should be made by way of anticipation to
be in a position to move forward should the Calusa have a change of
heart.

Notes by the Council of the Indies, August 8, 1698

AGI, Seville, Santo Domingo, bundle no. 154, R° 6. There is a possibility that this document is not filed under the Audiencia de Santo Domingo. In the microfilm copy of this document the following is the
first notation on the cover: "General Archive of the Indies, Seville.
Lima 154." But only the Audiencia of Santo Domingo citation appears
on Victoria Stapells-Johnson's transcript of this document. While com-
paring her transcript with the microfilm copy of this document, I found
that her transcript of the council's comments contains material that I
was not able to locate on her microfilm copy of this part of the assemblage. The translation was made from the microfilm copy of the doc-

ument and a transcript made by Stapells-Johnson at the Archive of the Indies at the request of the Florida Museum of Natural History.

The following notes and comments begin on the back side of the cover sheet and precede the testimony of the friars and the lay witnesses.

Havana, to his Majesty. On the 5th of March of 1698. Received on the 20th of June of it, in the Galleons. *N⁰ 3*
Fray Francisco de Contreras. Vice-commissary general of Florida for the order of St. Francis.
Council   8th of August 1698
Let the señor fiscal see it and afterward pass it on to the receiver[1]
Villar.

It recounts that of the 22 religious whom Fray Feliciano López brought on mission at the expense of the royal treasury, four or six were chosen, and after the governor and royal officials having outfitted them, they crossed over to the district of the Cacique Carlos, who was asking for holy baptism for himself and for his subjects. And having gone during September of [1]697, the said religious returned to Havana on the 21st of February of [16]98 in the manner and for the reasons that are contained in the statements attached.

They bring another two letters from this religious concerning the same [topic], one of the 30th of November of 1696, n⁰ 5, and the other of the 4th of March of . . . [torn], n⁰ 4. And three letters from don Diego de Cordova Laso de la Vega, governor of Havana, two of them of the second of September of [16]97, numbered 6 and 7, and the other of the 11th of March of [1]698, n⁰ 8, touching on this matter.[2]

They also bring the reports, which they had prior to this, about Fray Feliciano López having gone with four religious of his mission to the conversion of the Cacique Carlos, and what was provided for it by the council.

1. This is used probably in the sense of the secretary or actuary who attends a delegate judge.
2. Although the reference to this last document (n⁰ 8) belongs here logically with the other two, it is not so located in the document itself. Instead it appears in the top right-hand corner of the page just above the paragraph that follows.

The fiscal, having looked at this letter from the vice-commissary general of the missions of Florida of the order of St. Francis and the letters of the governor of Havana along with different statements that accompany them, says that, after the prevailing lack of religious in it for the conversions had been reported to the council on the part of Fray Francisco de Ayeta and Fray Feliciano López, a religious of the province of Florida, and after the letters from the bishop of Cuba and from the governor and royal officials of Florida had been seen in the council at the same time, in which they gave an account of how some caciques and leading men of that province had come to that government to give obedience to his Majesty, and among them a son of the cacique of Carlos, who is the one who has the Province of the Keys, and that there were 14,000 souls in it with a desire of being brought within the pale of the church, in decrees of the 30th of December of 1695, which were dispatched to the governors of Florida and Havana and to the vice-commissary of Florida, various provisions were applied for these conversions and in the decree that is copied authentically on page 14 of Statement no. 1, the governor of Havana was ordered that in this manner he should dispatch from Havana the 20 religious and two lay brothers who were permittd to pass over to the Province of Florida and who went under the charge of Fray Feliciano López, [namely,] 8 of them so that they might work in the new conversions of Mayaca, Jororo, Anacapi, San Anttonio, and San Joseph; six for the province of the cacique of Carlos. They should cross over directly to this mission from Havana with the necessary supplies, arranging for them beforehand and dispatching them and the remainder of the 22 religious, that they should go to the missions of Florida. And this mission having arrived at Havana, the governor gave execution to the decree. And as is evident from the letter of this same vice-commissary, dated the 5th of March of this year, even though in the missions of Mayaca and Jororo around October of the year of [16]96 the Indians of that district killed a missionary religious, by the present [document] it appears that this mission has recovered and that the vice-commissary has hopes of achieving the goal of the conversion of those natives that is desired. And with respect to what pertains to the conversion of the Indians of the Province of Carlos, what has happened is as it is presented in the statements that accompany this letter, [that is], that on the 11th day of September of [16]97 a sloop departed from the Port of Havana under the charge of the Ensign Francisco Romero and which was chartered at the expense of his Majesty, on which Fray Feliciano López and the other 5 religious were embarked along with the provisions and ornaments and other things necessary for maintaining themselves in the conversion. And after 7 days of sailing the sloop reached the Key or Province of Carlos, and some Indians having seen it, they came at once in canoes. And after the religious and the supplies had been disembarked and after the Indians and the religious remained very pleased, the Ensign Francisco Romero returned to Havana with his sloop. And as is evident from the statement of Fray Feliciano López and the other religious, even though in the beginning the principal cacique and his sons manifested great pleasure at the letter that they received from the governor of Havana and gave them permission for disembarking, with the cacique bringing them to his house, where they remained for 13 days while they built a house of palm so that they might withdraw to it and celebrate divine services in it, and even though the old cacique, with the motive of a strong seizure that he suffered, acquiesced to receiving baptism, no success was achieved with his son and with the rest of the Indians, even though the religious sought to persuade them that they should receive it, preaching to them and teaching them the principal mysteries of our sacred religion and even the old cacique, the seizure having become more serious, died without any other sign of interest in religion than what he had professed earlier, letting it be known that his having acquiesced to receiving baptism had been caused by the little ornaments (*alajuelas*), food, and clothing that the missionaries had given to him [and] showing displeasure over their having removed the provisions from his house. And although the religious remained there until the 27th day of October, the Indians did not cease to adore their idols or to frequent the place that they had set aside for this. And finally the son of the cacique warned them that if they did not make preparations for withdrawing they would have to take their life because their Gods were becoming irritated, and if they were not going to give them food and clothing, then they did not need them there. In the wake of this, mistreating them by word and by deed, they carried them off from that key or spot to another key named Teyú and there they completed the work of stripping them of the clothing and provisions and the ornaments that they brought. And on the Key of Muspa, which is another spot, they stripped them of all their clothing, leaving them naked. And they passed from there to Mattacombe Key, where the Ensign Francisco Romero found them; that he had returned with his sloop; that he had sailed from Havana on the 7th day of December with letters from the governor and supplies for these religious. And taking them on board his sloop and trying to provide them with clothing as best he was able to, they entered the Port of Havana on the 21st day of February of this year. And the governor of Havana and the vice-commissary for the missions of Florida forwarded the letters and cited statements that give an account of this. And that what occurs to the fiscal to report is that according to what is noted by the secretariat, the Province of the Keys and the territory of the cacique of Carlos is called by this name because of Carlos Ponze's having discovered these keys in the Mexican Gulf. And they are areas at 50 degrees of longitude and 25 degrees of latitude in which they are islands and a peninsula that is part of the mainland of Florida and a land of sand and ponds. And although it was reported to the council earlier that there were 14,000 Indians in the province of the Cacique of Carlos so that the means for their conversion would be supplied, what is apparent from this dispatch[3] and from the statements of the religious is that there are only up to 2,000 souls in all this province and that what one can conclude and gather from this dispatch is that as long as the religious gave provisions to the Indians and some things of those that they brought from Havana, they showed some inclination or appearance of becoming converts. And from what happened afterward one can certify that they were moved solely by self-interest and that the cacique of Carlos [also was], when he passed to Florida[4] to give obedience and assured the governor that he and the Indians of his province were going to become converts. As a result of which it appears that, after giving thanks to the governor of Havana and to the vice-commissary for what they have done in this matter and by their mediation, the religious, that it will be appropriate that, to the degree that the royal treasury will permit, preparations should be made by way of anticipation that they may apply toward and take measures looking toward the

3. The remainder of this document, which appears on pages 5 and 6 of the Stapells-Johnson transcript was not included on the microfilm.
4. This is obviously a reference to Cacique Carlos's visit with Governor Quiroga in 1688 while he was conducting his visit of Apalachee and Timucua.

conversion of these souls; that it must be done by gentle means and without violence, while looking out at the same time for the life and the security of the religious who may voluntarily wish to apply themselves to the work that is so much in the interest and so much the desire of both majesties. The council will determine what is most suitable. Madrid, <u>August 15, 1698.</u>

Sirs: Your S. Most Illustrious, Sierra, Carnero, Solis, Colen, Bastida. Seen and endorsed (*lo acordado*)[5] by the secretariat. Madrid, September 19 of 1698.
Licienciate Villar
With the señor fiscal
Done

17. Governor of Florida's Reports on the Calusa and Mayaca-Jororo Missions, September 1699

Just prior to the receipt of the news about the failure of the Calusa mission, on June 16, 1698, the crown ordered Florida's governor to report on the status of the new missions in Calusa territory and in Mayaca and Jororo. The following document is the governor's reply to that order with respect to the Calusa mission, with some brief comments on the Mayaca-Jororo missions, even though the governor had dealt separately with the latter missions in a letter to the crown three days before he wrote this letter.

Governor Laureano de Torres y Ayala to the King, September 19, 1699

AGI, Seville, Santo Domingo 228. This translation was made from a copy in the Jeannette Thurber Connor Collection, reel 3, of the P. K. Yonge Library of Florida History.

5. *Lo acordado* is a stock phrase signifying "Decree of a tribunal enforcing the observance of prior proceedings" in the sense that the secretariat of the Council of the Indies is lending its support to this policy recommendation made by Villar and the fiscal of the council. However, this recommendation would become crown policy only after having been recommended by the council itself and then sanctioned by the king, to whom the council would submit their recommendation for approval or disapproval.

Sire

I received a royal decree from Your Majesty, dated the sixteenth of
June of the past year of [16]98, in which Your Majesty deigned to
order me to give an account of the status in which Fray Pheliciano
López finds himself in the conversion of the Cacique Carlos. Soon
after the latter [friar] arrived at the said bay of Carlos, the Indians,
after a few days, mistreated him and the religious [who were] his
companions in such a fashion that they took everything away from
them that they had brought with them, and that they ran the risk
of losing their lives, because the objective of casting them out on
some uninhabited keys does not appear to have been other than
that. However, Divine Providence assisted them in the form of a
vessel from Havana that arrived at the said keys on that occasion.
They were transportd to the said city on it. Later they came to the
Province of Apalachee. And the said Fray Pheliciano López is
staying in Mexico presently as procurator of the holy province for
the collection of the alms that Your Majesty has assigned to them.
And the other religious are in the Province of Apalachee. At the
same time Your Majesty orders me in the said royal decree to give
him an account of the state of affairs in Mayaca and Jororo; Atisme
and Atocuime.[1] And I am doing so on this occasion in a letter of the
sixteenth of the current [month]. Nevertheless, I must tell Your
Majesty that neither the village of San Salbador de Mayaca nor that
of San Antonio [Anacapi] ever rebelled, and that five religious that
went to Mayaca from the mission band of Fray Pheliciano López[2]
were in the said village with the intention of awaiting the coming of
those from Jororo and Atisme. But as they were delayed, three of
the five religious withdrew, and of the other two, one remained in
Mayaca and the other in San Antonio where they remain
(presently), administering to these villages and to the newly arrived
ones that I have told Your Majesty about in the letter mentioned
[above], until they assume the form of a village (*pueblo*) and until
the ministers go there that I have already asked for for them from
the provincial of this province. When Your Majesty has learned of

1. The latter two are the names of individual settlements, Atissimi and
Atoyquime.
2. It is not clear from the context whether the governor means from the
band Fray López took with him to the Bay of Carlos or from the others that
came from Spain with him.

this, may he order me to do whatever is his royal will, whose Catholic and royal person may God preserve for many years for the good of Christendom. St. Augustine of Florida   September 19 of 1699.

D. Laureano de Torres y Ayala

The second document is the Florida governor's report on the Mayaca-Jororo mission written on September 16, 1699. In his report Governor Torres y Ayala detailed the steps that he had taken to restore peace to the Mayaca-Jororo territory and to promote the resettlement of the villagers who had fled after some of the natives of the Jororo village of Atoyquime had killed their friar and after other natives subsequently killed a Spanish soldier left among them because he was injured. The governor informed the king that flight into unknown regions by the relatively few natives involved in the murders had, for the present, thwarted his efforts to bring the guilty parties to justice. The crown's insistence on punishment of those involved in this episode contrasts sharply with its reaction to the Calusa's mistreatment of the friars. In the latter case the crown made no recommendation for punishment but rather instructed its authorities to be ready to resume the mission effort should the Calusa experience a change of heart. The shedding of Spanish blood by the Jororo undoubtedly accounts for the difference.

Governor Laureano de Torres y Ayala to the King, September 16, 1699

Sire

I received a royal decree from Your Majesty, dated the tenth of May of the year one thousand six hundred and ninety-eight, in which Your Majesty deigned to give me orders about what I was to do with the assailants who occasioned and caused the death of the missionary religious who worked in the conversions of Jororo in the village of Atocuime and [the death] of the soldier and other companions (*consortes*)[3] that their barbarism killed. And I must say to Your Majesty that my desire that justice be done as Your Majesty orders has persisted, although the said assailants have fled. As a result, we cannot put our hands on them, except with the passage of time. And presently I am giving an accounting to Your Majesty

3. As the primary meaning of *consortes* is "accomplices," it is possible that it refers to accomplices of the assailants, but the context seems to suggest otherwise. Several loyal Indians were also killed by the assailants.

about how all the Indians of Jororo and of other villages have come back in complete peace. And I have received them in the same [spirit] and given them lands where they asked for them. And they remain in two areas; one, a site that they call Las Cofas. And up to one hundred persons between men, children, and women are there. And the other spot is called the woods (*montes*)[4] of Afafa, and up to sixty persons were there according to what the lieutenant of the said province has reported to me. And at the same time the captain, Joachín de Florencia, treasurer of the royal exchequer, whom I dispatched from this presidio on that occasion so that he might receive them and welcome them and settle them where they requested, as he did. And today they are working at building their settlements, churches, and general house of the village (*Casa Gen[l] del Pueblo*),[5] where they assemble for conducting their business. And as soon as they have it completed, I have prearranged with the provincial of this holy province for him to send two ministers, who will work among them. And in the meantime the minister who is in Mayaca and the one who is in San Antonio are doing so. That all these villages are located two days' journey distant from one another and one day in other regions. And before all these Indians of Jororo, whom I have mentioned to Your Majesty already, had come back, those of the village of Ypaja, who had never risen in rebellion, made it known that they wished to become incorporated in the village of San Antonio, where they remain at present. Out of all this Province of San Salbador de Mayaca only those of the village of Atisme remain [to be resettled]. That these [people also] did not rise in revolt. They merely withdrew to the woods. I have sent various messengers to them [drawn] from the natives themselves, to call them back, offering them a full welcome. And those who have been going and coming assure me that their return will be achieved, as I hope in God [it will]. The other village is that of Atuquime, which is the one that rebelled. There has been no sign of any of these. And they assure me that the sole principal instigator with ten men is the one who is the head and who has retreated to a very unknown region. And that the rest [of the people] from the said village, who would amount up to thirty, have scattered into

4. *Montes* might be rendered also as "hills," but it has been my experience that in Florida documents from this period it most commonly means "woods."

5. This is the first time that I have seen this expression used to designate "council house." Usually the terms used are *bujio* or *bujio principal*.

different areas. And it is possible that some of them are among the very ones who have come back, who because they were not party to the murders would not be fearful. This is [simply] my rumination, as I have no special report about this. I shall give an account to Your Majesty, as he has ordered me to do, about everything that occurs pertaining to this business, as I am giving it also with respect to having given them some iron tools for their farming (*sus cultibos*), as Your Majesty has ordered me to. May God Our Lord preserve Your Majesty for many years as Christendom requires. St. Augustine of Florida, September 16 of 1699.

D. Laureano de Torres y Ayala

The following are the cover notes made at the Council of the Indies.

Florida to his Majesty.   On the 16th of September of 1699.
Received on the 2nd dispatch-boat on the 15th of March of 1699.
No. 9.
The Governor D^n. Laureano de Torres y Ayala.

An extract of this letter follows and is omitted.

Council
On the 28th of May 1700
To the señor fiscal with anterior (*antecedentes*) [documents]
The anterior [documents] came (*Vinieron los antez^{tes}*).

    The fiscal, having seen this letter and having taken the extract of the secretariat into account, states that this governor must be charged with responsibility for pursuing the inquiry into the whereabouts of these delinquents. And if he can put his hands on them, he should punish them in accordance with the law. And if they should have any possessions, he should sell them, arranging the matter in conformity with the laws of those kingdoms. And with respect to the Indians whom he reports as having come to offer their vassalage to his Majesty, the fiscal states that he should be charged with responsibility for supporting and encouraging them in accordance with what his Majesty has resolved [and], above all, with what the council will resolve. Madrid, July 23 of [1]700.
[This document ends with a cross.]

In the Connor microfilm the preceding note by the fiscal is followed by two successive copies of Governor Torres y Ayala's letter to the king of September 16, 1699, each accompanied by a lengthy extract of the governor's letter made by someone at the Council of the Indies, reproducing the letter virtually word for word. On the whole the two additional copies of the governor's letter faithfully reproduce the first copy, which I have translated above. But in several passages these two copies depart in matters that are of significance from the copy that I translated. In the passage in which the governor reported that the returned fugitives from the Mayaca-Jororo missions were being resettled at Las Cofas and at the woods of Afafa, where the first copy has "And today they are working at building their settlements, churches (*Yglesias*), and general house of the village," the second and third copies have "fields" (*glebas*)[6] instead of "Churches" (*Yglesias*). In the two sets of extracts, however, the word "churches" appears at this point. A second discrepancy involves the size of Atoyquime's population. In the first copy, in addition to the head instigator and the ten men with him, the fugitive population of Atoyquime is given as "up to thirty" (*hasta treinta*). The second copy gives that number as "up to three hundred" (*hasta trecientta*). But in the third copy and in one of the extracts it appears as "thirty." In the first extract it appears as the numeral 30. In the third copy the number of resettled villagers at the woods of Afafa is given as "seventy" (*setenta*) rather than as the "sixty" mentioned in the first two copies and in both extracts.

6. The English equivalent of *gleba, glebe,* is land belonging or yielding revenue to a parish church or ecclesiastical benefice, according to Webster's dictionary.

PART II

Calusa

in the Late Sixteenth Century

INTRODUCTION

This section presents some of the documentation (most of it as yet unpublished in translation) that illuminates the Calusa world at contact and during the first years thereafter through the 1560s. Although the first recorded contact of Europeans with the Calusa dates to Ponce de León's 1513 voyage of discovery, neither his two contacts nor subsequent activity along the Calusa coast prior to the 1560s provides much information of ethnohistorical value. What Ponce de León recorded about his experiences in 1513 survives only in filtered form in the history of the royal chronicler Antonio de Herrera (1720). Accounts from the Narváez and de Soto expeditions do not even hint at the existence of the important Calusa chiefdom not very far south of the region where they landed.

French and Spanish activity in Florida in the 1560s provides our first significant ethnographic information about the Calusa. In 1564 René Laudonnière established a short-lived French settlement at the mouth of the St. Johns River. Although the French settlers did not visit Calusa, they met with Indians who were in contact with the Calusa and they recorded testimony from two shipwrecked Spaniards whom they ransomed from Indians living upriver along the St. Johns. The Spaniards had been held as slaves for a time by the Calusa. Pedro Menéndez de Avilés' contacts with the Calusa in the latter half of the 1560s and the Jesuit missions among them and the Tequesta, which Menéndez de Avilés sponsored, produced more extensive information on the peoples of south and southwest Florida in general and on the Calusa in particular.

Early in 1566 Menéndez de Avilés visited the Calusa head chief, Carlos, establishing friendly relations with him and accepting pro forma a sister of Carlos as his wife in order to strengthen those relations. As Menéndez de Avilés entered the inlet on which Carlos' settlement was located, he was met by Escalante Fontaneda, whose *Memoir* is one of the major translated published sources on the Calusa of the period. Fontaneda had spent many years among the natives as a captive. Later that same year Menéndez de Avilés sent a small force under Captain Francisco Reinoso to establish a fort and Spanish colony at the village of the Calusa ruler. When Menéndez de Avilés revisited that Calusa center in March 1567, the surface amity of the preceding year between Chief Carlos and Menéndez de Avilés had largely dissipated. Menéndez de Avilés' insistence during that visit that Carlos make peace with his traditional enemy, the Tocobaga of Tampa Bay, did not improve the temper of Cacique Carlos toward his erstwhile Spanish allies.

At this inauspicious moment, the Jesuit Father Juan Rogel arrived with Menéndez de Avilés to begin formal mission work among the Calusa. Prior to that some soldiers had been teaching Christian prayers and explaining Christian beliefs informally to the natives. Contemporaneously, Pedro Menéndez Marquéz, a nephew of Menéndez de Avilés, left thirty soldiers and a few carpenters along with a Jesuit lay brother, Francisco Villareal, at Tequesta, a non-Calusa settlement at the mouth of the Miami River which was tributary to Chief Carlos, at times at least. The Spaniards were to build a stockade and houses and presumably a chapel as well for the religious instruction Brother Villareal was to impart to the natives (Hann 1990: 427–428; Lyon 1983: 147–150, 177; Parks 1985: 24–25).

The Jesuit missions established at the Calusa center and at Tequesta in 1567 originated from requests by Menéndez de Avilés in 1565 and by Philip II in May 1566 to the future Saint Francis Borja, who was then the Jesuits' superior general, to provide priests for the Florida enterprise. Although the new religious order was only thirty-two years old, Philip II had asked ambitiously for twenty-four Jesuits for Florida. Rogel and Villareal had sailed for Florida in June 1566 along with Father Pedro Martínez, who was killed by Mocama near the mouth of the St. Johns River before he could begin his work in Florida.[1]

1. Kathleen Deagan identifies Mocama as the dialect of Timucua spoken by two subgroups within the Saltwater Timucua, the Saturiwa and the Tacatacuru. As a tribal name Mocama seems to have been identified with the Tacatacuru of Cumberland Island and other places north of the St. Johns River

The first three Jesuits to work in Florida came from Spain to Havana on a Flemish ship. Unable to find a pilot in Havana familiar with Florida waters, the Flemings set out for St. Augustine with the Jesuits with only written instructions on how to recognize the entrance to the port. They missed the entrance to St. Augustine and wandered along the coast for a month, unable to find their destination. Father Martínez was lost along with several of the sailors when they went ashore in a small boat to inquire of the Indians how far they were from St. Augustine. Martínez and his companions were stranded there well to the north of St. Augustine when a sudden storm forced their ship out to sea, and the ship returned to Havana at the insistence of its Flemish crew. The small boat had almost reached the mouth of the St. Johns River when the fatal encounter occurred with Mocama, who were allies of the French and hostile to the Spaniards, who had ousted the French (Alegre 1956: 45–48, 52; Vargas Ugarte 1935: 61).

The Spaniards' situation among the Calusa was scarcely less tense when Rogel attempted to begin his work there in March 1567, except that the Spaniards and the Calusa were still on speaking terms and that there was a Calusa faction opposed to Carlos. It forewarned the Spaniards of dangers from Carlos or even possibly misrepresented Carlos' intentions in order to win Spanish support for his removal. As Rogel himself put it, "While Carlos was alive, I never had the opportunity, nor did he give it for me to be able to teach anyone the things of our holy faith" (Zubillaga 1946: 290). For example, when Menéndez de Avilés, before his return to Havana, decided to move his colony to an island distinct from that on which Chief Carlos lived, the chief offered canoes and men to assist the Spaniards, but allegedly with the intention of drowning the Spaniards en route and throwing their supplies into the water. On learning of the planned treachery, Menéndez de Avilés used his own small boats for the transfer.

Although Menéndez de Avilés increased the size of the garrison in Calusa substantially before his departure in the latter part of March, Cacique Carlos' animosity persisted. Rogel learned that Carlos had instructed certain of his servants to kidnap the priest if they found him outside of the fort. Carlos, Rogel noted, "had a great hate against me especially because I discredited and spoke evil about his idols." Conse-

---

whose ceramics and shell-midden patterns differ from those of the Saturiwa living southward from the mouth of the St. Johns (Deagan 1978: 90–91, 100–101).

quently Rogel went on to observe, "I did not go out more than once each day for a thing that could not be avoided and I did not go farther than a stone's throw from [the fort]" (Lyon 1983: 178; Zubillaga 1946: 290, 306–309). In that atmosphere Rogel had little opportunity to preach to the Indians except for the few who came to the cross at the fort, enticed by handouts of maize. The persistence of Cacique Carlos's animosity and the revelation of additional plans by the cacique to kill the Spaniards led the Spanish commander to propose killing Carlos, which Rogel opposed prior to the fact but later came to rationalize as having been justified.

Only about a month after his arrival in Calusa territory, Rogel took advantage of the arrival of a ship from Havana to return to Cuba to seek provisions for the forts, having heard that the soldiers at Tocobaga were in dire straits. Only three days after Rogel's departure, Captain Reinoso, on learning that Carlos allegedly had new plans for the massacre of the Spaniards, persuaded Carlos to come to the fort to talk. Reinoso seized him and the two Indians who accompanied him and had them killed.

If the Spanish sources are to be believed, there was, initially, a relatively smooth transition in which the Calusa leader Felipe, who held the position of great captain, was installed as head chief. He was leader of a Calusa faction that had kept the Spaniards informed of Carlos's hostile intentions.

According to Rogel's account, the great captain Felipe, a nephew of an earlier head cacique, had been designated by that head cacique as his legitimate successor to the chieftainship, even though the Calusa had a father-son line of succession rather than the matrilineal regime that seems to have prevailed elsewhere in Florida. That cacique, not having a son of his own, had adopted Felipe as his son and as one of the tokens of his position as heir-apparent had betrothed Felipe to his daughter. When that cacique died, Felipe was not yet of age to assume the chieftainship, and a brother of the deceased chief, who was head shaman, insisted on a regency until Felipe should come of age and inserted himself as regent. Once empowered, the head shaman refused to hand over the chieftainship to Felipe when he came of age, determining to install his own son, Carlos, as new head chief when he should come of age. The shaman pressured the old chief's widow to consent to the dissolution of the marriage of her daughter to Felipe and to allow her daughter to be married to Carlos, his son. As a sop to Felipe the head shaman granted the position of great captain, then held by Felipe's father, to Felipe.

However calmly the Calusa may have initially appeared to acquiesce to the killing of Carlos and installation of Felipe, the new head cacique's position soon became tenuous. The chiefs of at least two settlements subject to Felipe transferred their allegiance to Tocobaga with impunity. Rogel himself observed that when he returned from a subsequent trip to Havana in December 1567, Cacique Felipe showed great joy at learning that he had returned and that he would be residing there permanently "because matters in that province have come to such a pass and have been so disposed that the reign and life of that cacique depends on the Christians not withdrawing their support from him because he is so disliked by so many caciques and captains among his vassals that, were it not for the favor and support that he enjoys among the Christians, they would have killed him quite a while ago" (Zubillaga 1946: 337). Despite that support, attempts and plots had been made on Felipe's life, and, Rogel noted, Felipe had killed more than fifteen principal men and heads of villages involved in such activities. Rogel recorded that on his return from Havana the Indians "were holding a celebration and dancing with the heads of four chiefs that he [Felipe] learned were intending to revolt and go with their peoples to others of his enemies and that for that he ordered them killed."

Despite his dependence on Spanish support to maintain his rule, Felipe showed no more inclination to accept the Spaniards' religion than had Carlos, beyond making promises that he would become a Christian when Menéndez de Avilés returned from Spain. Rogel's exchanges with Felipe show that neither Felipe nor his people were disposed to abandon the native gods. And they show also that neither Felipe nor others among the ruling elite were willing to abandon their polygamous practices to become Christians. Felipe told Rogel frankly that the priest might try to train the children in the new ways but that he could not expect adults to adopt them. Felipe claimed persistently that Carlos and he had a pledge from Menéndez de Avilés that they would be allowed to continue the old ways undisturbed until Menéndez de Avilés' return. Thus, after being installed as cacique, Felipe insisted on marrying his sister, as caciques were expected to, ignoring Rogel's vehement protests that such action was incompatible with his pledges that he would shortly become a Christian. That the pledges were specious and merely temporizing maneuvers is suggested by an incident recorded by Rogel in which the natives attempted to bring one of their religious processions into the Spanish compound itself, a move Rogel interpreted as an attempt to force the Spaniards to adore the natives' gods represented by mask-wearing natives. Rogel was permitted to instruct the Calusa willing to hear him and was able to attract an audience as long as he had gifts to distribute to those who attended, but he made no converts.

The people said that they could not abandon the old ways until their cacique did, and the cacique in his turn alleged that for the present the people's expectations required him to maintain the old traditions. In his proselytizing efforts Rogel faced a no-win situation.

Central to Rogel's failure to convince Carlos and Felipe to become Christians was the native leaders' deep involvement in and control over the tribal religious cult and marriage practices enjoined on the ruler by native customs that conflicted sharply with Catholic mores. The head cacique was expected to take one of his siblings as a wife, and his acceptance of wives from the various villages that gave allegiance to him was a bond that testified to and cemented that allegiance. The latter practice commenced as soon as the future cacique was designated heir-apparent by the incumbent. To Rogel's badgering on the matter of his incestuous marriage, Felipe replied that "he had asked permission from us to live in accord with his own rites and heathenism until the Adelantado should come; and that it was a very ancient custom among them for the cacique to have his own sister as a wife; . . . and, accordingly, his vassals had requested of him that, in the meantime until he became a Christian, he take this sister as wife; and that he could not fail to do what his vassals asked him to."

The strength of the two rulers' attachment to their idols suggests (in addition to the probable sincerity of their belief in the rightness of their own view of the cosmos) that the Calusas' religious system was a major bulwark of the ruling elite's claim to the power and privileges that it enjoyed. The head shaman in the era of Carlos's immediate predecessor was a brother of the head cacique. The head cacique himself and the great captain and, doubtless, others among the ruling elite were deeply involved in the religious ritual. Both Carlos's and Felipe's mention of the elite's possession of esoteric religious knowledge that was a badge of the legitimacy of their claim to rule points in the same direction as well. Thus Felipe argued that "because it is expedient for him to show to his vassals and to his neighboring kings that he is the legitimate king of this kingdom, and because, to that end, they taught and instructed him during his childhood in all the things that it is expedient for the king to know about the cult and veneration of the idols, if he were to forsake the idolatry suddenly at the beginning of his reign, the aforementioned kings and vassals would say that he was not a legitimate king, as he did not know what kings are obliged to know; that for this reason he had forsaken the cult of the idols and had received the Christian law" (Zubillaga 1946: 286-287, 289-290). That cult seems to have been no less rooted among the people themselves, not only among the Calusa of the 1560s but also among the Jororo of the 1690s, as was noted in Part I.

Because of this and other factors and despite Felipe's dependence on the Spaniards, his relations with them deteriorated in their turn, and he was eventually removed by the Spaniards and killed along with many other Calusa leaders. That development led the rest of the Calusa to burn their villages in the vicinity of the Spanish fort and withdraw to points beyond the reach of the Spaniards of the fort. Not long thereafter the Spaniards themselves abandoned the site.

The documentation resulting from this mission and the other Jesuit missions of Spanish Florida was the most fruitful result of their effort. No minds or souls were won, and in the wake of the killing of all but one of those who went to Virginia's Ajacán and the sterility of the labors elsewhere, the remaining Florida Jesuits were ordered to Mexico. The missionary episode of the Jesuits in Florida is elsewhere called "the Jesuit Failure" (Lanning 1935: 33). A more balanced assessment, however, might note that from Calusa territory to Guale and Santa Elena the Jesuits dealt with natives whose confidence in their own value systems and *Weltanschauung* had not been sufficiently shaken to make them susceptible to the European Christian message. However much Rogel might have browbeaten the Calusa with his superior training in rhetoric and logic and the advantages of a cult whose divine message was fixed in writing to convince them of the superiority of his message, he could not move them to abandon their own system of beliefs. Rogel expressed this succinctly in his remark "And as they saw that the things that I am telling them make sense and that they cannot do the same for theirs because they are clearly false and evil, they said to me that their forebears had lived under this law from the beginning of time and that they also wanted to live under it, that I should let them be, that they did not want to listen to me" (Zubillaga 1946: 281).

As the documents contained here demonstrate, the Calusa never lost that confidence sufficiently to forsake their own ways, even in the mid-eighteenth century when they and a remnant of several other south Florida tribes were on the verge of extinction. For reasons that we do not understand fully, the Guale and many other groups did eventually find the newcomers' philosophy sufficiently attractive to make that break with the past, however strong a psychological wrench it may have been. Consequently a more just assessment of the Jesuit effort in Florida is that it was made before the time was right and, in the case of the Calusa, to people for whom the time would never be right.

The Calusa world that Fontaneda described and that the Spaniards encountered in the 1560s was a complex chiefdom, headed by the Calusa ruler Carlos. According to Fontaneda, Carlos, and his father before him, was the lord of fifty towns, some of which were as far inland as Lake Okeechobee and two of which were in the Keys. Still others were tributary to the Calusa ruler, at times at least. The power of that chiefdom is reflected, as Henry F. Dobyns (1983: 131–132) observed, in the mid-sixteenth-century Spaniards' perception of its ruler as a king. Dobyns went on to describe the Calusa polity as a "conquest kingdom" and remarked that its pattern of tribute collection "very much resembled that of the Aztecs and the Incas, although Calusa society was smaller in scale." One might view that comparison as stretching a point, but the basis for the remark leaves no doubt as to the Calusa polity's chiefdom status.

The development of so impressive a chiefdom by nonagriculturists has been viewed as an anomaly by anthropologists and archaeologists. Despite Dobyns's recent attempt to eliminate that anomaly by portraying the Calusa as people who engaged in agriculture at contact, there is no firm evidence to support his claim (1983: 126–130). The same year that Dobyns's work appeared, Randolph J. Widmer presented his impressive dissertation entitled *The Evolution of the Calusa: a Non-Agricultural Chiefdom on the Southwest Florida Coast* (1983), which has since been published (1988). In a more recent article Jerald Milanich (1987: 180) refuted Dobyns point by point, although in his conclusion he left the door slightly ajar for Dobyns's thesis if new evidence should appear. But until solid new evidence is found, one must agree with John W. Griffin that "All of the ethnohistorical sources characterize South Florida as non-agricultural at the time of contact" (1988: 146). And they remained so long after contact. In 1697, on seeing hoes the friars brought with them, the Calusa asked what purpose they would serve inasmuch as they had not brought blacks to wield them, implying that in no way could the Indians be induced to use them.

Control of the head chieftainship in the 1560s and later seems to have been monopolized by one family or kin group. The head shaman under Carlos's predecessor was a brother of the head chief, as was the great captain, the other major figure among the leadership elite. Although the position of head chief was the most important one, that of great captain was a powerful one as well. The great captaincy among the Calusa may possibly have represented an institutionalized form of the "great warrior" or *Tustunnuggee thlucco* among the later Creek. The institution of great captain appeared as well among the Tocobaga to the north of the Calusa and among the Ais of the east coast around Cape Canaveral but seems to have been confined to south Florida. The Spanish never used the term in speaking of leadership elements among the Apalachee, Chacato, Guale, or Timucua. For those peoples *inija* was the title for the official mentioned most commonly after the chief. As Marquardt has noted, "The Calusa paramount chief was thought responsible for the productivity of the environment . . . and he regularly retired with his close associates to a temple where special rites were performed" (1988: 170). Part of the enigma posited by Marquardt in his introduction is the Calusa rulers' ability to maintain their people's faith in their powers even in the face of internecine struggles for control among the power elite and even when the Calusas' control over their world was fading quickly or had faded already. This contrasts with the fate of rulers of Mississippian-type societies farther north, some of whom initiated abandonment of their traditional religious practices and destruction of their idols, presumably because they felt that acquisition of new esoterica from the Spanish would be a better bulwark for their power and position. As Marquardt remarked, forty-two years after the trauma of the late 1560s in which the Calusa chief lost some of his tributaries to the hated Tocobaga, "a new chief referred to as Carlos was in power . . . and was said to have 'more than 70 towns of his own, without counting another very great number which . . . pay him tribute. . . .' Obviously a significant reconsolidation of the Calusa domain had occurred," although "no details are known" (1987: 108).

This section on Calusa in the 1560s contains six pieces. Two are translations of documents written by Father Juan Rogel, who served the Calusa mission for most of its brief existence at that time. The third contains excerpts from a letter written by Rogel, the fourth contains two letters by Pedro Menéndez de Avilés, and the fifth is a listing of provisions sent to the forts of Carlos, Tequesta, and Tocobaga. The last piece contains excerpts from Juan López de Velasco's *Geografía y Descripción Universal de las Indias* that describe and name features of the coast from Tampa Bay southward through the Keys and then northward beyond present-day Miami.

The most important and the longest of these documents is the first one, which appears as Document 85 in the Spanish text of the sixteenth-century-Florida Jesuit correspondence published by Felix Zubillaga, in *Monumenta Antiquae Floridae.* Although this document's contents are reflected to a degree in Clifford M. Lewis's chapter on the Calusa in *Tacachale,* edited by Jerald T. Milanich and Samuel Proctor (1978), the document itself still merits publication in translation so that its content and context will be available fully to anthropologists, archaeologists, and historians.

The most valuable aspect, perhaps, of this Rogel letter is his depiction of the interchange of ideas that occurred between him and the two successive Calusa rulers, Carlos and Felipe, as the Jesuit sought to present the rudiments of Christian belief to those native leaders and as those leaders responded, indicating elements that had a parallel in their own ethos and the ones that they found most contrary to their own belief system and even laughable. Of particular interest are the allusions to the nature of the soul and its destiny.

The discussion reveals that the Calusa concept of the nature and destiny of souls was analogous in part to that of other North American groups for which we have such knowledge, but it had some possibly unique features as well. Thus the Calusa believed in multiple manifestations of the soul or types of soul, as did groups such as the Delaware and Ojibwa, and in the transmigration of souls (Müller 1968: 169, 170, 179). But the Calusas' beliefs about the transmigration of souls have a certain analogy also with Far Eastern beliefs such as nirvana. The Calusa believed that when a person was killed, the soul that was the vital element, out of the three souls that they posited, entered an animal or fish on departing from the human body. When that animal or fish was killed in its turn, that soul then moved to a lesser living form in a regression that led ultimately little by little to the soul's being reduced to nothing. So deeply rooted was this belief that Rogel's attempts to explain the Christian concept and its concomitant of reward or punishment in an afterlife were greeted with laughter. This is but one example of the richness of the content of this document especially in matters pertaining to religious belief. There is no parallel for it for any of the other peoples of Spanish Florida.

Rogel's observations in this document on the Calusa political situation and the rival claims of Carlos and Felipe to the chieftainship need to be viewed with skepticism because the major sources of Rogel's information were Felipe himself and his supporters, and because of the self-serving nature of the legitimation of Felipe's claim to the chiefship. On the other hand the anomalousness of Felipe's position as great captain in view of his rivalry with Carlos lends some verisimilitude to his claims. In the other examples that we know of, the great captain was a brother of the head cacique rather than his first cousin.

THE DOCUMENTS

1. Calusa in the 1560s

The following piece is Document 85 from Felix Zubillaga's *Monumenta Antiquae Floridae,* published in Rome in 1946 by Monumenta Historica Societatis Iesu. The document appears on pages 272–311 of that work. Zubillaga published the letters in their original Spanish, but his introduction and notes for this piece as well as his general introduction for the volume are in Latin. Zubillaga's preface and outline obviate a more lengthy introduction.

In sections 1, 2, and 3 of Part II, I have translated Zubillaga's notes along with the documents. The numbered end notes are Zubillaga's; my notes have also been numbered but appear as footnotes on each page, with the numeral set in italics so that the numbering systems are distinguishable.

Father Juan Rogel to Father Jerónimo Ruiz del Portillo, April 25, 1568[1]

From the original in codex Peru 19, folios 7–20 (previously 49–60). Letter in an unknown hand written by Father Rogel, who corrected it not a little in his own hand and introduced it somewhat, has been revised.

Preface. On the last day of February 1567 Menéndez de Avilés, whom the missionaries Father Rogel and Brother Villarreal were accompanying, set sail from the port of Havana as leader of six ships and one hundred and fifty men to visit Florida and at the same time to investigate whether or not the western part of that peninsula was connected with the eastern part by a water channel. After a few days the sailors landed at the province of Calus. The principal ruler of the region, named Carlos, having established friendship with Spanish soldiers of the fort there, had not yet broken it off publicly. At the same time Menéndez, [after] having tarried for a little while, proceeded with his ally-ruler to the province of Tocobaga near the present-day Tampa Bay on the western shore of the Florida peninsula, where he brought the rulers of the two provinces together in a semblance of peace, [who were] great adversaries to one another. Then, however, having established a fort there with thirty soldiers, he returned to the province of Calus. The ruler of this province, angered with Menéndez and his men, intended to kill the governor, [but] he was dissuaded from this plan by his own [people]. With this hostile feeling toward the Spaniards prevailing, Pedro Menéndez, leaving his soldiers behind in the fort at Calus in order to confirm Spanish control in that region as well as to broaden it, returned to Havana. Father Rogel was designated missionary for the region (Zubillaga, *La Florida* 266–72).

Calus, the principal town of the province of that name, seat of the ruler, was one among the islands of Charlotte Bay[1] in the western part of southern Florida ([see] note 77). This island, just like the coastal region of all of Florida, was intensely poor, with not many inhabitants, for it was seen to have scarcely thirty families (o.c. 275s). The natives are believed to have belonged to the great Muskogean family (general introdution Ia 1 part 2). About their religion and customs, Father Rogel in his letters provides not a little [information].

The importance of this letter is great, for it contains, as we have noted above, a great deal about the religion and customs of the Muskogean tribes of the northern Indians that was not known about them. Now accordingly, Father Rogel merits faith in his assertions that he was writing about with this through the year (from the month of March 1567 until July 1568) when he remained among the natives. For on entering the Calusa province in March 1567 he was established [there] as a missionary until leaving in May

1. Modern authorities (Lewis 1978: 19; Widmer 1988: 5) place the seat of the Calusa ruler on Mound Key in Estero Bay.

of the same year, he was brought back to Havana; similarly he spent time there going out toward May; on the first day of July in Calusa he went to the province of Tocobaga and that he sailed for Havana once more on December 10, 1567, where he remained for a month. After Epiphany of the year 1568 he returned again to Calus; on Thursday of Holy Week (April 15) he finally left the mission of that province for Havana. He made a great deal public both about the customs, religious faith, and other matters pertaining to the natives of the province of Calus, [gathered] not only from the Spaniards of the fort but also from the natives and from the ruler himself.

About the history of the letter there is little to be noted. Father Rogel, [in] the month of May 1567 probably [from] Havana, where he tarried for a short time (as we have noted above), sent letters and copies of them to Rome and to Spain with the fleet of New Spain. Also in the month of July of the same year, he sent another letter about the death of Carlos, the principal ruler of that region, again to Spain. All these letters, however, [which] were received, appear to have been lost by those to whom they were sent.

Father Rogel returned to Havana from the province of Calus on the fifteenth day of April with the very letter of Father Portillo, dated Hispali, 28th day of September 1567, and others which he received from the Fathers of Spain. In responding, however, to this [copy] of the letter of Father Portillo he sent duplicate letters by way of Peru [and] a copy to Spain also, from which a copy was sent from Spain to the Father General.[2] All these [letters] are lost, it seems. Father Rogel himself, however, sent one with the letters to the Father General (doc. 89) of July 25, 1568, *datis* another copy of these letters of April 25 to Rome (*doc.* 89 *par.* 1), which same letters in fact are seen to be those that we publish here.

Authors. Sacchini, *Historiae,* part III, book III, 146–147, 200; Pérez de Rivas, *Historia de los triumphos,* 745; Alegre, *Historia,* I, 14–18; Astrain, *Historia,* II, 291; Zubillaga, *La Florida,* 273–302.

---

2. My rendition of parts of this sentence is tentative, and this is true to a lesser degree of my rendition of the phrase that follows as well. The Latin text of this sentence is "Ipse vero P. Rogel una cum litteris 25 iulii 1568 Patri Generali datis (doc. 89) aliam transcriptionem harum litterarum 25 aprilis Romam mittit (doc. 89 par. 1) quae quidem litterae eaedem, quas hic edimus, esse videntur."

Outline (*Textus*)

1. About letters received. 2. About delight from new companions. 3. About letters sent. 4. About travel to the province of Tocobaga and about the catechesis given to the natives. 5-6. Trip to the province of Calus; about the death of the ruler, Carlos; about the letters received from Havana. 7. About Escampaba, new ruler of the province of Calus, who declared himself a retainer (*clientem*) (vassal) [*sic*] of the king of Spain; about catechesis and about the errors of the Indians concerning the soul. 8. Natives' concept of God. 9. Other errors and vices; catechesis. 10. Natives' fear toward Spaniards, ruler to whom (*quibus regulus*), on what foundation the hope of the conversion of the province is based. 11. Faith and errors of the ruler and of the natives; catechesis. 12. The Devil among the natives. 13-15. Deception of the ruler who took his sister in matrimony and that he does not permit the baptism of daughters in danger of death; catechesis concerning the Trinity, incarnation, and immortality of the soul. 16. The Spanish leader (captain) denies the need for Father Rogel to visit neighboring provinces. 17. Catechesis. 18-19. Father Rogel heads for Havana; ministry; baptism of the natives of Florida. 20. Trip to the province of Tocobaga; killing of the Spanish soldiers of the fort by the natives; cause of the disaster. 21. Ruler of the province of Calus wishes to make war against ruler of Tocobaga. 22-23. New ruler and new method for catechizing in Calus province; missionary attracts natives with maize (*maizio*). 24. Francisco Toral begs for maize from the bishop of Popayan. 25-29. Letter of the bishop; about the labors of the missionaries; about the misfortune of Menéndez de Avilés; about the missionaries' compassionate zeal toward the natives; he shows himself prepared to relieve the needs of Florida. 30. Because of the lack of maize the natives do not assemble for catechism. 31. Baptism of the natives in danger of death; he fails healed by faith (*sanatus a fide deficit?*). 32. Inhabitants of Tocobaga assemble at Calus (*Tocobagae incolae Calus conveniunt?*); equivocal disposition of the ruler toward religion of the missionaries also mediator among the natives. 34. Misfortune of the fort of Tequesta where Brother Villareal was stationed. 35. Father Rogel relinquishes the mission of Calus and makes arrangements to go to meet Father Segura and his companions; he asks for prayers. 36. About the letter sent to Spain. 37-39. Ruler Carlos killed by the Spaniards; accessory

circumstances and causes of this deed. 40–41. Oath of the commander of the province for the government (*gubernium*) of that region.

† Jesus. Very Rev. Father in Christ

1. The peace of Christ etc. While I was in the fort of St. Anthony,[2] which is the one they call of Carlos[3] in Florida, I received two letters from your Reverence and one from Father Luis López.[4] Brother Francisco, who came to Havana by chance while the fleet from Nombre de Dios[5] was here, brought them to me. On leaving the residence at Tequesta[6] the Brother went to where I was residing.[7] One of your Reverence's two letters was about the trip, written in Cartagena[8] on the second of January to our Father General; the other one, of January 4, also from Cartagena, written to me. And the one from Father Luis López was written in Nombre de Dios on the 20th of January to Father Bautista Segura, vice-provincial of these regions, and, in his absence, to me. And with them I received two books of letters from the Indies. If your Reverence has written any other letter to me besides these, with the sailor who is named Herrera, who came in the storeship (*hurca*)[3] that came for master Francisco Muñoz, I have not received that one.

2. The consolation that I received was very great on seeing that the Lord has favored me in sending prelates and superiors to these regions so that they may direct me and most charitable Fathers and Brothers so that they may assist me with their most holy sacrifices and prayers and so that, with great fervor, all of us may seek the glory of the Lord and the welfare of so many souls in such great need, as there are throughout all these regions. That I am truly most happy, Father, on seeing that the Lord, in his infinite mercy, has seen fit to send me to regions where there are so many opportunities for the Lord to be glorified through me in bringing the cross and in spreading the true knowledge of their Creator in so many souls so much in need of it. May it please his divine Majesty

3. Cassell's dictionary defines *urca* as "hooker, dogger; storeship." Webster's dictionary defines hooker as "a one-masted fishing vessel used on the English and Irish coasts" or as "an old outmoded or clumsy boat." Hoffman defines it as a "general name for a Flemish ship-type characterized by large carrying capacity" and cheap construction often rendered as "hulk" (1980: 266). I have seen the term used elsewhere where storeship was clearly the meaning.

not to permit that [this work] should falter because of my sins and shortcomings rather than going forward and that the treasure should be lost that can be extracted from such very rich mines as have been entrusted to me and thus my damnation be doubled or quadrupled.

3. And as your Reverence in your [letter] orders me to give him an account of the results and the dispositions of these parts, I shall do so, beginning from the latest letters that I wrote to Spain at the end of the past year of 1567,[9] which I sent in the fleet of New Spain in duplicate. And I have been comforted greatly that you have also received there the one that I wrote in the first days of the following July[10] from the fort of San Antonio[4] of Florida in which I reported the death of Cacique Carlos.[11]

4. When I went to Florida from Havana with Pero Méndez Marqués[12] around the feast of St. John of the year of [15]67, I went on with him to the fort at Tocobaga[13] in order to hear the confessions of the Christians[14] who were there and to see the disposition of that people in order to plant the gospel there. And we were there four days, during which I heard the confessions and gave communion to all the Christians of that fort with the exception of an interpreter who was living in public concubinage with a heathen woman.[15] I found that some of the heathens' children knew the Christian doctrine in Spanish, that is to say, the four prayers. But the king and the adults (*la gente mayor*)[5] were very attached to their idols. On the feast of St. John the Baptist I said mass there and I made the king and his leading men[16] (*cavalleros*)[6] attend until the offertory,[7] and through an interpreter I preached to them about the oneness (*unidad*) of God and about how he is the Creator and universal Lord of all the world to whom all men owe vassalage and reverence and about the immortality of the soul and resurrection of the dead and about the reward and punishment that God has in the next life for those [who are] good and those [who are] evil and about

4. San Antonio was the name of the Spanish fort at Carlos.

5. This might be rendered also as "leading people."

6. This might be rendered also as "noblemen," "gentlemen," or "councillors."

7. This practice dated from Christianity's earliest days and is the so-called Mass of the Catechumens. While still under instruction, neophytes were required to leave the church at the beginning of the offertory and were thus excluded from participation in the heart of this Catholic ritual.

their self-deception in their adorations of their idols. After this I preached to the Spaniards in his presence. What I learned about that King was that he was so attached to his idols that, when his subjects had told him falsely that we were going to destroy his idols, he wrapped himself in a shroud (*el se amortajo*) [and] was determined and prepared so that, if we should burn them, he would throw himself into the fire together with his wife and children so that they might be burned along with them.[17] And it has been shown accordingly by what he has done later[18] how indisposed and averse he was to wanting to receive the law of God and to abandoning his evil sect. And so it seemed that his hour had not come.[19]

5. We returned from Tocobaga to the fort of San Antonio on the first day of July and on the second Pero Marqués departed from there for Havana. And with him I sent (*scrivi*)[8] that letter about the death of cacique Carlos.[20] And although your Reverence will already have learned summarily by the one that I wrote to Spain[21] how the death of Carlos came about, nevertheless, because back here I have come to understand it more in depth, and so that your Reverence may learn about it and know how to explain it to those who question you about it, and so that it may be seen how these Spaniards were compelled to do this, and [that] it was [self]-defense on the part of a blameless guardian.[9] I shall write [about it] again, even though I may have to expatiate on it at some length.

6. After having written the above while I was here in Havana, where I arrived on Holy Thursday,[22] as I shall tell your Reverence later, I received another [letter] from your Reverence, written in Seville on September 28 of the year [15]67 along with others from Father Bautista de Segura and other Fathers from Spain in a ship among those of the Adelantado [Menéndez de Avilés] that came loaded with provisions and clothing. Because of its coming, my going to St. Augustine[23] has been moved up to occur earlier than I had expected. Accordingly, in order to cut this [letter] short, I will abandon for now the telling of this story of the death of Carlos and go on to other matters because I would not have time to be so expansive. And when, the Lord willing, I may be more at my leisure

8. Literally *scrivi*, a variant form of *escribir*, means "I wrote," but in this context the sense is clearly "I sent."

9. In this phrase Rogel lapsed into Latin (*et fuit defensio inculpatae tutellae*).

in St. Augustine and have [other] priests who may help me, I shall write to your Reverence about what I am now leaving out.

7. When, during the past June of [15]67, Pero Menéndez Marqués and I went from Havana to Escampaba,[24] that this is what the kingdom of Carlos is called, the one who is now the cacique[25] determined to become a vassal of the king of Spain on seeing that this was what was appropriate for the security of his kingdom and for living in peace and quiet. And thus, in order to carry out his installation and as a symbol of vassalage, he and his captains and caciques from individual villages that were here brought tribute [consisting] of the things that his vassals give to him, all of which are miserable things that amount to little and consisted of some feathers and mats (*esteras*) and fruits and other things to eat. And as a vassal of the king of Spain, in his name he handed them over publicly there to the captain, Pero Marqués, in the presence of all the Spaniards and of his Indians. Early the next day Pero Marqués left for Havana and I remained behind in that fort and began to discuss with him about his becoming a Christian. And although he was somewhat difficult at the beginning and averse to the idea, he came around to saying that he wished to become one and that they should teach him the law of the Christians. At this [point] I offered myself for the teaching of it, not only to him but also to all of his vassals who might wish to listen to me. And for this [purpose] we marked out a place where we were to come together for [doing] that. We set up a large cross in it. And he came there each day and had all his councillors (*cavalleros*) and leading people (*gente principal*) and women and children come to hear me. I began to catechize them in this fashion. First I recited the Our Father to them in Castilian and the Hail Mary chanted. And then I told them that these words served for speaking with God and for asking him for everything that we might have need of. And each day little by little I went along teaching them through an interpreter, first, about the oneness of God and how he is the creater and universal lord of the entire world; and how he is all-powerful; and how he created the world, and then the first man and woman. And on explaining to them the creation of the soul, I corrected many errors that they have about it, which I shall explain to your Reverence so that you may understand how blind these poor men are. They say that each man has three souls. One is the little pupil (*niñeta*) of the eye; another is the shadow that each one casts;[25a] and the last is the image of oneself that

each one sees in a mirror or in a calm pool of water. And that when a man dies, they say that two of the souls leave the body and that the third one, which is the pupil of the eye, remains in the body always. And thus they go to the burial place (*enteramiento*) to speak with the deceased ones and to ask their advice about the things that they have to do as if they were alive. And I believe that the devil speaks to them there, because from what they [the deceased] say to them there, they learn about many things that happen in other regions or that come to pass later on.[26] They also tell them that they should kill Christians and other evil things. And when someone becomes ill, they say that one of the souls has left him and the shamans go there to search for it in the *alcabucos*[10] and they say that they bring it back, making the same movements as people make who are driving some sheep or goat into a corral that does not want to be shut up. And then they put a great deal of fire at the door of the house and at the windows so that it will not go out again. And they say that they put it back in the man again through the nape of the neck (*cogote*), doing certain ceremonies there.[26a] They have another error also, that when a man dies, his soul enters into some animal or fish. And when they kill such an animal, it enters into another lesser one so that little by little it reaches the point of being reduced into nothing.[27] And they are so fixed in this belief that there is need for special favor and help from God in order to persuade them of the immortality of the soul and the resurrection of the dead and the reward and punishment of the next life. They laugh at me when I tell them in the catechism lessons that all the souls of as many men as there have been in the world are alive in heaven or in hell and that they cannot die. And that they have to return again to be joined with their bodies and to live immortally; and that they are to be rewarded or punished in accord with the works that they have done in this world.

8. The oneness (*unidad*) of God[28] and his being the creator[29] of every good, they admit to. They also believe those who govern the world to be three persons,[30] but in such a manner that they say that the first one, who is greater than the other two, is the one to whom the universal government of the most universal and common things belongs, such as the heavenly movements and the seasons (*tiempos*),

10. I have not found this word in any dictionary. Lewis rendered it as "woods."

etc. And that the second one is greater than the third, that to him belongs the government of the kingdoms, empires, and republics. The third one, who is the least of all and the one who helps in the wars. And to the side to which he attaches himself, they say that that one gains victory.

9. A short time after they had begun to come, when I began to undeceive them of their errors and idolatries and evil customs and wicked laws that they have, such as killing their children or permitting sodomies[31] (*sometias?*),[11] killing innocent persons, etc., they soon began to abandon coming to the catechism lessons. And when I showed them clearly and to their face the falsity and deception of their idols, they threw up to me our adoration of the cross. And in order to make them understand the reasons why we venerated the cross, I explained to them the abhorrence that God has for sin and how he was angered with mankind, and how the Son of God became man in order to be a mediator between God and mankind, and how, while he was teaching men and preaching to them about how they must serve God, because he reproached their sins, some evil men put him to death on the cross and he offered that death to his Father in satisfaction for the sins of men. And with that he made us friends of God and he opened the gate of heaven for us so that we would be able to enter there. And as they saw that the things that I am telling them make sense and that they cannot do the same for theirs because they are clearly false and evil, they said to me, that their forebears had lived under this law from the beginning of time and that they also wanted to live under it, that I should let them be, that they did not want to listen to me. However, by treating them with gentleness and with love and bringing them a little bit of maize at times, while we had it, with that bait they were frequenting the catechism lessons. Although the king had already left off coming because of being so busy with and involved in his idolatry, they [the rest] learned the prayers well while the handouts lasted and they were already beginning to believe the things that I was telling them. But when the handouts ended, they all took off.

11. I have not been able to find *sometias* in any Spanish dictionary. I am following Zubillaga here. In note 31 he equated *sometias* with *sodomias*. It should be noted, however, that the root *someter* suggests "enslavement" as a possible meaning, though enslavement would not evoke the same horror as would sodomy in this context.

10. The troubles have been great that the devil has raised and is raising every day among these Indians in order to make them turn away so that the law of God may not be preached to them, instilling great fears in them, raising charges against us that we wish to ravage them and carry them off as captives. And thus many times they have been determined to leave us and to go to the lakes to live, because, since they killed Carlos, they have conceived a great fear of the Spaniards so that they no longer discuss (*no tratan*) as before; that they would wish to kill us if it were not for how they would flee from us. And for this purpose the Lord has provided this king, who now reigns, [who] is like another king of Bungo in Japan[32] because he encourages his people and gives very good advice to us as to how we should deal with the Indians in order to keep them and to plant the faith in them. And he himself admonishes them and persuades them to it, telling them that he intends to do it also at the coming of the Adelantado and that all should follow him. He said to them also that the best means that they can take to live in their houses with calm and rest and without any fright is to maintain strong friendship with the Spaniards; and that for this reason he has become a vassal of the king of Spain. And he has kept them reassured with this. That as he is a prudent man and one of good judgment, he knows very well how to conduct himself both with his own people and with the Spaniards. Because of his being on such good terms with us, some of his vassals have attempted to kill him, some by treachery and others with witchcraft. These he has punished. And thus, with the support that he has from the Spaniards, he makes himself feared and is served by all his vassals. And because of this he is strongly bound to us and I strive to do everything that I am able to so that all of us may cherish him and avoid giving him any offense, because, if this [man] were to continue his rule peacefully with our support and if he were to be well treated by the Spaniards, it would be a very great incentive for all the other caciques [who are] his neighbors to do the same and voluntarily and of their own accord come to be vassals of the king of Spain, as this one has done, and the faith of our Lord Jesus Christ and his holy Gospel would come to be planted in all these provinces, especially after their having seen that the Spaniards have treated so badly those like Carlos and Saturiba[33] who have been rebellious and wicked toward us.

11. One of the good signs that I see in this cacique that he truly

wishes to become a Christian is that he tells me clearly when he does not believe the things that I tell him about our faith and he listens and ponders the things that are told to him. And thus, when I questioned him one day whether he believed in the immortality of the soul and the resurrection of the dead, he replied to me that he did not. I then questioned him again whether he believed in the oneness of God and in his being the creator of the universe and the one who governed it all, he replied that he did, and that this was one of the secrets that he and his forebears, the kings, held guarded in their breasts and that they did not communicate it to anyone except to their successors. I questioned him again whether he believed that God had power to create the immortal soul and to raise up the dead. He replied to me that he did. I then returned to questioning him whether he considered God to be true and that he told the truth in everything he said and that he never told any lie. He replied to me that he did. I said to him then that he had told it and revealed it to us. He asked me how I knew that which God had said to us. I replied to him that we had it written down so, since very many years ago, ever since the time that he spoke it and revealed it. And with this he was brought up short and replied that the things that we have in our law have a much greater semblance of truth than did theirs even though they appeared more difficult and obscure. Because we have the things of our law in writing, thus they never change; and as they do not have it so, but only by tradition, by the second or third passing down of it, it becomes entirely changed. And thus it appears that he became more inclined (*mas combencido*)[12] to accept this truth about the immortality of the soul and the resurrection of the dead. Even so, I always saw a great resistance in him to believe this article, because I have no doubt but that if this truth were to have an impression on him, he would have more enthusiasm for the desire of his salvation than what he has. Nevertheless I discuss it with him in great detail and I seek almost constantly to instill it in him, constantly bringing up, apropos of this, the reward and punishment of the next life and the great value of the soul; how it is not what they think it to be but rather one of the most esteemed and precious things that there is in all the world,

12. Literally rendered this would be "more convinced," but such a rendering does not make much sense in this context.

and that, in its value, a soul is worth more than all the heavens and the earth and the sea; and that it is so exalted a thing that it is of the lineage of God; and that, accordingly, just as one cannot see God in this world, neither can the soul be seen.

Even so, some challenge me also about this truth that God cannot be seen in this world; and they say that they have heard it said by their forebears that they saw God in their burials (*enterramientos*); and that, in order to see him, they fasted for many days and that, while fasting, they ran much; that this is the method that they have for venerating their idols. To this [end] I sought to convince them by telling them that God does not have a body; and that that which their forebears saw was nothing other than the devil who appeared to them in those forms (*figuras*) that they told of, in order to keep them deceived. But the argument by which they are convinced the most is [that] of giving them to understand that they and all their forebears have been enemies of God and have offended God very greatly, because the honor that is due to Him alone, such as asking for health, long life, victory against their enemies, an abundance of goods and provisions, after all this being given to them by God, they ask for it from their idols and give thanks to their idols for it. In this they do God a great injury. And I make them understand this by posing to them a like situation with their king: if one of his own vassals were to proffer to his enemy the respect and service that he owed to him, that would be a great offense to the king and he would be greatly angered over it. And thus they, in the idols that they have, have always adored the devil, the enemy of God. And therefore, the one who appeared to their forebears was not God but rather the devil, whose vassals they were. Because God is not in the habit of doing such favors for one who is his enemy and intends always to offer him injuries and insults. And this is the method that I am following with them, striving to understand what are the things in the articles of our holy Catholic faith that give them the most difficulty; and with respect to them, putting them through reason on the right road to believing them, as we are obliged to. And even though they raise none of these difficulties with me when I am discussing things with them, nonetheless, I strive to have the interpreters strike up friendship with the Indians and learn what they talk about among themselves when the cacique is seated on his bench or platform (*en su banco o estrado)*[13] with all his people during the mornings before the dawn breaks, because it is then that they discuss these things and reveal what they feel about the things that I talk to them about.[34]

12. Neither do they understand who the devil is or the enmity that he has against God and against us. And to make them understand this, I have discussed with them the creation of the angels and the fall of the bad ones. And as they do not understand what an angel is, I call them persons whom God created in the heaven who do not have a body and are of the same category (*linaje*) as our souls and they cannot die.

13. The cacique has promised me many times that upon the coming of the Adelantado he will abandon all of his idolatry and hand over all of his idols to me so that we may burn them, and that he will cut his hair, which is one of the great sacrifices that they can make. And although he always promises me this by words, I look at his deeds and I find them to be contrary to his words, because I see him very much involved in his idolatries and strongly attached to his witchcrafts and superstitions. And when some things do not seem to me to be right (*bien*), I summon him to tell him of my feelings about it. And what he replies to me is that he has asked permission to live according to his rites until the Adelantado should come; that we should permit him to do so until then and then we shall see how he will abandon it all. On the other hand some Christians and some Indians have told me of how they have seen him some times at night on his knees before a cross that we have in this our fort and his house. And he himself has told me, without my questioning him about it, that he does it each night. And, in his own fashion, he offers himself to God with all his heart, and he offers him a certain sacrifice that he is accustomed to offer to his idols. With these things the soul errs (*Con estas cosas heret animus?*)[14] and I am in great doubt and perplexity because of not

13. *Estrado* may be rendered also as "stage," "drawing-room," "drawing-room furniture," "dais, for a throne," and "baker's table."

14. My rendition of the last two words of this phrase is tentative. *Heret animus* is Latin, but I have not found a Latin verb that would produce the form *heret*. It is conceivable that Rogel was transliterating from the Spanish *herir* (to wound).

knowing whether this man may be persuaded to believe that the
things of our holy Catholic faith are true and become aware of the
lies and deceptions of his sect. And, accordingly, what I have
decided upon is that when, God willing, the Adelantado should
come, I shall ask for his word and take everything that he may give
me:[15] [namely], to burn his idols and cut his hair and dress in the
Spanish manner and be instructed in all the things of the Christian
faith; and to hold him as a catechumen, without baptizing him,
until I am assured that he is asking for holy baptism from his heart
and in reality and I see signs in him that he abhors and detests all
the rites from his heathenism. For in two things that he has done
since he said that he wishes to become Christian and another that I
shall tell about further on in its place, he has made me very
suspicious that he is not proceeding in this [matter] with as much
sincerity as I would like. The first thing was that, since he has said
that he wanted to become Christian, he has married a sister by his
father and mother, not to mention the many other women that he
has.[35] And before this marriage was performed (*se efectuase*), they
advised me about it, that he intended to do it. And I summoned him
and argued with him so that he would not do it. And I made him
aware of how abominable and detestable a thing such a marriage
was in the eyes of God. For even the heathens (*gentiles*) themselves
and those who do not know God perceive this to be evil and
contrary to the Natural Law and consider those who commit such a
crime as evil. And that as, within a few days, God willing, he was to
become a Christian, from now on he should begin to show how he
wished to obey God and that he should not do something that he
abhors so much, because in this we would come to understand that
he wished to become Christian out of a good heart and will, if from
this moment on he showed himself in this [matter] as willing to
submit to the law that God and nature sanctions. He did not reply to
this as I desired, saying that he had asked permission from us to
live in accord with his own rites and heathenism (*gentilidad*) until
the Adelantado should come; and that it was a very ancient custom
among them for the cacique to have his own sister as a wife; and

15. This is a literal rendition of the Spanish text here, which is *pedirle su
palabra y tomar todo lo que me diere*. As this literal rendition does not make too
much sense in this context, I suspect that what Rogel meant to say was "that
he would take him at his word and hold him to everything that he may give me."

that this was permitted for him alone; and, accordingly, his vassals had requested of him that, in the meantime until he became a Christian, he would take this sister as wife; and that he could not fail to do what his vassals asked him to; that he was giving me his word that before he should become a Christian, he would leave her. And as the occasion seemed appropriate then for bringing up the matter of monogamy[36] and how Christians do not consent to polygamy and a multitude of wives (for a long time before this I was looking for the opportunity to ascertain his will in this matter and I had not touched on it because the occasion for speaking to him on it had not come up, nor a favorable opportunity), I did not want to let this one pass that was being offered to me. And I explained the law of God [on this matter] to him, which is that no man can have more than one woman;[37] and, accordingly, when God created the first man in this world, he did not give him more than one sole woman for company. From this man and woman, all we men of the world are descended. And, consequently, that on becoming a Christian[38] he would have to resolve to share his life with that one alone who was his legitimate wife.[39] He did not receive this with such good will as [he did] the rest that we had told him about that he would have to do in order to be a Christian. And, consequently, he replied to me that I already knew that it is a very troublesome and difficult thing for men to change who have been accustomed from their infancy with one manner of living so that, after putting aside that manner [of living] totally, they should undertake another very different one. And, consequently, my wanting to strip old men and men of adult age of all their customs and make them perfect Christians was not possible of achievement; that I might instruct the little children and youths (*niños y muchachos*), who up to now know nothing about their rites, in the things of the Christians as I saw fit; but, as to the big ones, that I could not totally strip them of everything; that I should content myself with his forsaking and burning his idols and all the witchcraft (*hechizerias*) that he has practiced up to now; that he would totally remove the sodomites (*someticos*); that they would not kill children even when his sons or he himself die or something that he likes very much.[40] Neither will he stain himself black (*se tiznará*) on his face or on his body as he has done until now. And he will cut his hair and [do] all the rest that I may tell him to, but to prevent him from having more than one wife, that he will not be able to endure; that we should permit him this, for in all the rest, he wants to do everything that God commands. And thus I see no impediment to the implantation of the faith of our Lord Jesus Christ in this entire heathendom, if his Majesty should deign to illuminate their minds and move their wills so that they would obey his most holy law in this [respect]. And consequently, I have a need that, in requesting this from the Lord, I be assisted by all the holy sacrifices and prayers of your Reverence and of all the fathers and brothers of the province[41] and by the entire company's making prayers, offering sacrifices particularly for this intention. For this cacique is so immovable on this [point], that speaking to me on it on another occasion on his own initiative, he said to me that he would see to it that those who should marry from this time on would not have more than one wife and that he would not have more than two, when he should become a Christian. And the conversion of the entire kingdom depends on that of the head, because all the vassals, when I appeal to them that they should abandon their idolatry and become Christians, reply to me that it is not possible for them to do so until their cacique should become one. And I believe it, because even in the very idolatries that the vassals maintain they know nothing about what they adore or about the cult of the idols beyond that which the king and the head shaman (*hechizero mayor*) tell them. As a result they live in accord with the faith of their betters (*viven in fide maiorum*). Thus, in converting these two head people, all the rest are converted, because if they ask a vassal what it is that they believe about their idols, he says that he does not know, that his king is the one who knows it. And the same if they ask them about the origin of their idols.

14. The second thing in which I have had some doubt in trying to see if this king is telling the truth in saying that he wishes to become a Christian is that a few days ago one of his daughters fell sick, a young girl (*muchacha*) whom he loves supremely. And she was in danger of dying. I went to see her and I sought to persuade her father that she should be made a Christian and that we should baptize her; that I trusted in God that by virtue of the holy baptism the child might be cured; and that, should it be God's will to take her, that her soul, having been baptized, would go to heaven; and that, if she were to die without baptism, she would to go hell; and that, consequently, if he loved his daughter so much, that he should not do her such great harm as to deprive her of so great a benefit. And as much as I tried to convince him, he played deaf and dumb

and never gave me a reply, but rather, cured her with his witchcrafts (*hechizerias*) and inventions of the devil. As I have said, I am very perplexed with all these things and very desirous that the Lord should send us the Adelantado with profit so that it may be seen from the deed whether he fulfills what he has promised to.

15. In the meantime I am striving to instruct them in that which is appropriate for becoming Christians. Many of them know the prayers already. And because, when I tell them of the oneness of God, they reply to me that they had been led to understand that there are three persons in heaven who govern the entire world, I have been compelled to explain to them the mystery of the most holy Trinity earlier than I would have done so, if they had not stumbled onto this. For in order to make them understand the error that they have concerning it, I have been compelled to explain this mystery to them. I also have been explaining to them the most holy mystery of the Incarnation because of what they stumbled across about it in the matter of the adoration of the cross. However, that which I expound most commonly among them is the immense power of God and the immortality of the soul and the resurrection of the dead and about eternal life after this one and the reward and punishment that there will be in it. And so it already appears that they are paying more attention to what I am telling them. And they do not receive the jolt that they received at the beginning, when I revealed the deceptions of their sect to them and the falseness of their idols. No matter how badly I speak about them, it no longer fazes them. But when I try to convince them that they should forsake them, they reply to me that they are awaiting for their king to forsake them, because until then they would not be able to forsake them, even though they understand well that they and their forebears have lived deceived. The cacique says the same thing; that he well recognizes his[16] law to be false and full of errors; but because it is expedient for him to show to his vassals and to his neighboring kings that he is the legitimate king of this kingdom and because to that end during his childhood they taught and instructed him in all the things that it is expedient for the king to know about the cult and veneration of the idols, if he were suddenly to forsake the idolatry at the beginning of his reign, the aforementioned kings and vassals would say that he was not a legitimate king, as he did

16. The Spanish here, *su,* could be rendered also as "their."

not know what kings are obliged to know; that for this reason he
had forsaken the cult of the idols (*que por esso avia dexado el culto de
los idolos*)[17] and had received the Christian law. In order not to
undergo this ignominy he had asked permission to follow his own
rites until the coming of the Adelantado, because during this time
he would hasten to reveal all the discrepancies[18] of the cults of their
idols (*a hazer todas las diferencias de los cultos de sus idolos?*). And
thus they would understand that he was not forsaking them
because of any ignorance of them that he has.

16. While Carlos was alive, I never had the opportunity, nor did
he give it, for me to be able to teach anyone the things of our holy
faith. And thus during the past month of July of the year of [15]67[42]
I began to preach to them and to teach them. And from then until
the eighth of December[43] no boat at all ever went to that fort from
here in Havana. And during this time I tried many times to go to the
Martyrs (the Keys)[44] where, an interpreter told me, the Indians
were well disposed to become Christians and had already thrown
part of their idols into the sea and those that remained to them,
they were holding in order to burn [them]. They permitted those,
however (*pero dexavanlos*), so that they could hold the burning
solemnly when I or someone else should go to preach the faith of
our Lord Jesus Christ to them. When I heard about this favorable
disposition, and [aware] that there was to be no remedy here until
the coming of the Adelantado, with great determination I set myself
to wanting to go there on many occasions, but the captain[45] of that
fort and the soldiers constantly opposed me [on this point]. And as I
would have to go sailing along the coast by sea, they did not wish to
give me the gear for that. And, on seeing this, I asked the cacique of
the Indians to give me a pair of canoes and Indians to man (?)
(*votasen*) [them] so that an interpreter and I might go there. But the
captain was so cunning that he persuaded him not to give them to
me. The reason that he gave for doing so was not very adequate; for
he said that he did not want to send me among the Indians, where I
would have to be alone, without the company of the Spaniards; that
if the Indians should kill me, he would have no acceptable account
to give about me to the Adelantado, even though there was no basis

17. The word *dexado* or "forsaken" could conceivably be rendered also as
"permitted." Either sense would seem to fit the context.

18. My rendition of this idiomatic expression is tentative.

for suspecting such a thing, because the Indians of the Martyrs are great friends of the Spaniards. For this reason I refrained from going there. I also attempted to go to Tequesta[46] to visit Brother Francisco and those Christians and to see the success that is being achieved there in the conversion of those heathens. And neither did they permit me to go there. I also desired to go to Tocobaga[47] to console those Christians who were there, because we were receiving reports that they were in great distress and trouble. But inasmuch as Tocobaga[48] [the ruler] was an enemy of this don Felipe (that this is the name that I have given to this king, successor to Carlos), there was no Indian to be found among these who would dare to take me there. And persuading the Spanish captain that he should give me soldiers so that they might take me [there] was the same as singing fables to a deaf man.[49] And thus I remained in that fort all the time.

17. The modus operandi that I have maintained has been this. Each day I went to the cross[50] two times to catechize the Indians and afterward I would go to my room (*aposento*) in the fort to study that which God was helping me to. And I found that many Indians came to see the books and the images that it[19] had and other little things. And I received them amicably and soon, after entering into their [conversation] I turned it around to my [topic],[20] because I sought to have an interpreter at my side always. And I discussed the things of our holy faith with them in clear language. And this is what I have discovered from this method; that this modus operandi is more productive than my going to the cross with the objective of preaching to them, because they do not go there so voluntarily, nor do they pay as much attention to what I say to them [there] as [they do] here. And thus, for a period of time (*una temporada*) with some coming and others going almost the entire day, they have given me something to think about in this [exercise]. And later, here, when I have used this approach, they show more interest and are more inclined to believe the truths that I tell them about.

18. However, as I did not have anything to offer them so that they would come to my apartment, nor anything to give them, I was somewhat distressed. And in order to go forward with this exercise

19. The Spanish here, *tenia,* might be rendered also as "I had."
20. The Spanish here, *y luego entrando con la dellos salia con la mia,* is either most elliptic or idiomatic.

and in order to be able to have something to give them, and also, and even principally, because we were very fearful about the misfortune (*desgracia*) that had occurred in Tocobaga and because we had learned that it was very certain that they were suffering very great need, because with the abundant rains that occurred, all their provisions had become soaked and rotten and because the provisions that came on the boat on the eighth of December were very scant for both forts, it seemed to the captain and soldiers of that fort that it was expedient that I should go to Havana in that boat in order to let the suppliers (*hazedores*) of the Adelantado know about what was happening in Tocobaga so that they might send supplies as quickly as possible to those of Tocobaga.[51] And, although it was burdensome and difficult for me to go to Havana, because it seemed that my going there so many times gave cause for suspecting that I was fleeing from the hardships (*cruz*) of being in Florida, nevertheless, after entrusting myself to God, it seemed to me that it was more conducive to his service to go in order to provide help for the extreme and very urgent need that we suspected with great probability afflicted those of Tocobaga. And thus I departed from there for here on December 10 and came to this port in two days, in which I encountered Captain Pero Menéndez Marqués,[52] who had arrived then from the forts of St. Augustine and San Matheo and Santa Helena. And I acquainted him and his companions with the [reason] for my coming, putting the responsibility on their conscience so that they might provide the provisions as quickly as possible in order to return shortly and to go to Tocobaga. However, the providing of what was necessary could not be done so quickly, as we were not [less] than a month in providing it.[21] And when I saw that I was detained there, I began to engage (*entender*)[22] in our customary ministries of preaching, hearing confessions, and teaching catechism. I taught the catechism each day to the children of the church of San Juan, first gathering them together and going through the streets singing. In addition to this, as there is great neglect in this village in looking to the salvation of the dark-skinned people (*la gente morena*),[53] I did what I could to persuade their

21. The Spanish here is *que no estubiesemos un mes en proverlo.*
22. The primary meaning of *entender* is "to understand." Rogel, however, has used it a number of times in contexts that demand that it be rendered in some other fashion.

masters (*amos*) so that they would look out for the Christianization of their family in five sermons that I preached at that time, and also in reprimanding other public vices that exist here. I believe that the Lord was served by that coming of mine, for it already seems that some public sinners are trying to abandon them, and especially the blacks (*morenos*) (who, as in most cases, all or the majority were living in concubinage) (*que, ut in plorium [sic] todos o los mas estavan amancebados?*)[23] some were already trying to marry their lovers and others to separate from them. In addition to the catechism that I taught to the children in the afternoons, at sunset, when the laborers abandon their work, each day I went to the fortress that is being built presently in this town,[54] where more than one hundred blacks, slaves belonging to the king, are engaged in this project, and I had all of them assembled as they were coming out from their work and I taught them the catechism and I would give them a short talk concerning it. And [it is] certain, Father, that it is a great pity to see the great ignorance that they have in all matters pertaining to the Christian faith, for, in reality, very many of them do not show signs of having anything other than the outward mark (*caráter*)[24] [of it] only,[55] because in these regions they have no other accounting to give than to bring their daily wage to their masters each day and as for the rest they let them do everything that they wish to and to go wherever they wish and to do anything they want to. I am writing all this to your Reverence at such length so that if it should seem suitable to you in the Lord to write to Spain [about it, you would] so as to strive to see to it that the king and those of his council would be aware of this and so that they would provide some remedy for such a great multitude of souls going to hell because of the lack of concern and negligence of those who have charge of them.

19. Here I also baptized an Indian woman[56] (*una india*)[25] whom the Adelantado brought from that land where I have resided. I taught her catechism when I came to this land for the first time in the supply ship (*hurca*) before I went to Florida, together with the

23. My rendition of *ut in plorium* is tentative. I am presuming that this Latin expression was meant to be *plurium*, the genitive plural of *pluris* as in the familiar *E pluribus unum*.

24. In the sense of having had no other exposure to Christianization than having been baptized.

25. This might also be rendered as "girl."

others who came from there, whom I have mentioned[57] in others [i.e., letters]. And because I did not then have the conviction, which it was appropriate that I should have, that she was seeking holy baptism with all her heart or that she was well enough instructed or catechized as yet, I left her like that here in Havana. And when I came during December they told me that she had asked many times that they might baptize her and out of negligence they had not done so. I summoned her and reassured myself that she was ready for it and I examined her about the motives that she had for becoming a Christian. She replied to me that we said that, after this life there was another one and that in that life God punished those who were not his vassals in this life with great torments and fire, and that he gave great rewards to those who were. And that she believed this more than the lies that her forebears told and that she was saddened when she saw that she still was not a Christian or a vassal of God, because of the great fear that she had of dying before she would be. On seeing so good a motive, I resolved to baptize her before going to the fort and I completed her instruction in what she needed to know in order to become a Christian. And it seemed appropriate to me to hold this baptism with great solemnity so that the Indians with whom I deal would understand how much we esteem their becoming Christians sincerely and with all their hearts. For when they are asking me the reason for our coming to this land, as I tell them that it is for no other [reason] than solely to bring it about that they come to the knowledge of God and become his vassals so that by this means they may come to achieve eternal life, the holding of this baptism with great solemnity would be to confirm in the deed what I am saying in words. And for this [purpose], in one of the sermons I invited everyone in the settlement for this baptism, and I begged the Governor[58] and a leading lady of this town to be her godparents. And thus, on the day of the Kings,[26] before the principal Mass, I baptized her with the entire village present. And many among the leading men of the village went to the godmother's house for her and brought her very well dressed and brought her with great solemnity. And there at the door of the church, with the interpreters that I had there, when I questioned her on the catechism, she replied to all the questions. I left this

26. The feast of the Epiphany celebrated on January 6 in the church calendar commemorates the coming of the Magi.

Christian woman in the house of some residents of the settlement, well-to-do people and very virtuous, so that they would take her in hand to guide her in the observance of God's commandments and see to it that she was a good Christian, with the thought in mind that, if she were seen to persevere in goodness and virtue, and if with the passage of time she maintained firm signs of Christianity, such as those I have seen at the beginning, when, God willing, the Adelantado should come, he may take her with his people and see to it that they marry her to a Spaniard so that she may assist me in the conversion of the Indians.

20. Soon after this was over, we made ready to go with the provisions and supplies for our fort and that of Tocobaga. And the captain, Pero Marqués, set out with three boats (*barcos*). And on arriving at our fort, we left what had come for there and went on to Tocobaga. And I went there also in order to console the Christians spiritually who were there, by hearing their confessions and saying Mass for them and preaching to them during the days that we remained there; and in order to persuade Tocobaga that he should make amends to don Felipe for certain wrongs that he had done to him in carrying off some of his towns and breaking the peace established with the Adelantado.[59] When we reached there, as no one came out to receive us [and] as we saw no Indian at all walking about through the settlement, we suspected that there had been some great wrong or some betrayal. And thus the Captain Pero Menéndez Marqués held a consultation as to whether it would be appropriate to land at once or to wait until the morning of the next day to see if perchance some Christian might come to the boats or if we would be able to obtain some news about this turn of events. And at dusk they fired some shots so that, if there should be some Christian hidden in the woods, he would learn that we were there and would come. And as no one appeared, on the following day fifteen or sixteen soldiers, well armed and ready for war, went ashore and they found no one in the settlement except for two dead Christians, whom they had killed on the day before when they saw us coming. Because as it [the inlet] is eighteen leagues in length and, as they saw us coming long before we arrived, they then killed those two Christians and another whom they threw into the river. As we learned later, these they had kept alive in order to use them as slaves, having killed all the rest, as they were caught off-guard and unawares, and scattered about, some in one area and others in

another. And when they saw us come they killed these three, either
so that we should not learn the reason why they had done this evil
or for other reasons. And, on seeing this, the soldiers set fire to the
entire village and to the house of the idols. And with this they
returned to their boats, bringing the bodies of the deceased with
them and we read the service for the dead over them and we threw
them [into the water] at the bar (*los hechamos en la barra*) and we
were there all that day and we [then] returned to our fort of Santo
Antonio.

The reason why they killed these Christians, according to what
the Indians told us, who deserted Carlos for Tocobaga, who have
now returned to obedience to their king, except for one out of the
four who were involved, who remained on that side, was, he said
[*sic*], because the Spaniards who were there were very mean-spirited
(*de muy chico corazon,* literally of very small heart). And they say
that they put their hands on everyone except for the king and his
captain general. And also, as their food rotted on them, it ran out
earlier than those who were to resupply them expected it to. I
believe that with the hunger they began to be more of a burden (*mas
pessados*) and more bothersome to the Indians than they would have
preferred to [have been]. And I do not know whether the captain of
Tocobaga, who is the one who killed them while Tocobaga himself
was absent in his own village at the mouth of the bar, was fearful
lest those soldiers should do to him what those in the fort of Santo
Antonio did to Carlos. And thus he wanted to get the jump on them.
In sum, the Indians differ considerably in stating the cause, because
some say that Tocobaga was not to blame and others say that it was
arranged for between him and his captain, who carried it out.

21. This king, don Felipe, has not been grieved by Tocobaga's
having treated the Spaniards so badly because, as they got along
with one another so poorly and always waged war with one another,
consequently he now has what he desired so much, Spanish support
against his enemy. And so now he intends to make war and ruin
Tocobaga completely and make himself king of all his kingdom in
retribution and punishment for the vassals that he has subverted
and the friendship that he has broken with him and with the
Spaniards. And for this purpose, in all of his kingdom, he has
ordered that they should make an abundance of weapons, and he
has sent spies in order to learn where Tocobaga is, and from the
captain, Pero Menéndez Marqués, he has asked for more people for

the fort of Santo Antonio, so that, if some opportunity or occasion should occur for launching an attack on Tocobaga before the coming of the Adelantado, there would be soldiers who might go with him and soldiers who might remain to protect the fort. And consequently Pero Marqués left ten soldiers more there than he was to have left and came to Havana.

22. When I went to Havana this last time, I brought a certain quantity of maize back with me, although not all that I would have wished to, and some trade goods in the form of fishhooks (*anzuelos*), and knives, sickles (*fiegas?*),[27] hatchets (*achas*) and adzes (*azuelas*), nails, and other pieces of iron, all of which individual residents of this town gave to me to give to the Indians and attract them with this bait so that they might come to hear me. On account of this, while the bounty lasts, there is a very notable result in the way of their coming willingly at the smell of the lure that is given to them to hear matters pertaining to their salvation. And they listen with great attention to everything that I wish to say to them. And the word of God makes an impression on many of them and they awake, as if from a dream, from the blindness in which they have lived until now. And they confess clearly and manifest that they and their forebears have lived deceived and they seek to know what they are obliged to [learn] in order to become Christians and vassals of God. And, consequently, while this bounty lasted, for some time more than on the other [occasion], they kept me busy all day, and I even had need for a boy, who I had with me, to help me to teach them the prayers. And I have always sought to send them away satisfied by my giving them something. In addition to this, more people attended the catechism lesson than was the case when I spoke at the cross. And on completing the catechism lesson, I brought out a little bit of maize that I distributed to those who came to it. And in addition to this, every 15 days I have awarded prizes to the one who knows more of the catechism the best and who answers my questions. And because of this they have such enthusiasm in learning it that they are in their houses at night, saying it and questioning one another. And consequently these little trifles that I brought along offer a great opportunity for them to come to a knowledge of the truth of the Gospel, in listening to it

27. I am presuming that Zubillaga miscopied an 's' as an 'f,' and that Rogel wrote *siegas* rather than *fiegas,* as there is no such word.

with attention and willingly; and, in addition to this, for learning what they are obliged to know in order to become Christians. In addition to this I go each day to the king's women to recite the catechism to them and to preach to them. And they also listen to me attentively now, which they did not do earlier when I began to teach them the catechism. And because of their slight desire to listen to me that I saw in them [then] and because of the many excuses they raised for not listening to me, I had given up the pursuit. And now, because of sending them some trifles of this sort once in a while, they have come around to listening to me willingly and they receive and learn what I teach them. The result that I have seen, since I went [there] this last time in the dissemination of the Christian doctrine is this: they are no longer engaged with their idolatries to so great a degree as they were customarily or with such fervor as they were wont to [show]. *Immo*[28] already many of them clearly and openly confess that all this is a fraud and a lie, which, if they had said it earlier, would have cost them their lives.

23. I have not made any sallies out from the fort to the other little neighboring settlements to teach the catechism to this heathendom because of two considerations: the one, because the conversion that would be achieved among the people where the fort is, which is the court of this king, will be a very great preparation for that of the entire kingdom; for it is certain that on the conversion of the king and his councillors and the captains that are with him, the vassals and common people will be converted easily; the second reason is that, in order to be able to go out to other areas to teach, I do not have the tools in the way of maize and trade goods that are expedient for one to have in order to achieve results. For to think that these natives are going to come at the beginning on their own initiative without some interest [to draw them] is a pipedream, unless the Lord should assist them with a very special help [i.e., grace] for that [purpose]. Thus, by bringing along a bait in order to entice them to come to listen to me, great results will be achieved; and without it, I do not think that very much will be achieved, because these Indians are very simple and humble and not at all curious or open to hearing new things.

24. And because of this consideration, in order to have sufficient

---

28. There is no such word in Spanish that I am aware of. *Immo* is possibly a copyist's error.

maize to give them, before I set out from here this past January, an occasion and need arose to appeal (*describir*) to the bishop of Yucatan[60] about a certain case with which I was involved (*sobre cierto casso que vino a mis manos*).[29] And because I had learned that he is very much a servant of God and desirous for the conversion of the heathens, [and] especially that he has a particular concern for helping those of us who are working in Florida, and that with great care he has assisted these forts with a quantity of maize in their time of need, I made bold to beg and ask him as an alms that he might send me some amount of maize for the aforementioned [purpose]. And when the letter had reached his hands, he answered me, sending me much more than I had asked for; for he was not content just to send me the maize; but in addition to it, he sent me such [good] and such sound advice, enlightening me as to how I should proceed in the conversion of these natives, as a man of great experience and one full of the spirit of God, that it seemed to me that it would be the thing to do to send a copy to your Reverence so that all of us who are involved in this enterprise would enjoy the benefit of these saintly counsels. And, accordingly, I am enclosing a copy of the letter here.

25. Copy of a letter that the bishop of Yucatan wrote to a priest of the Company of Jesus:

Very Reverend Father. May the name of the lord be blessed.[30]

I read yours, written in Havana on the seventh of January,[61] in this city of Merida on the 25 of February, but I do not know who held it up. I received the fullness of joy from it and I praise our Lord that he brought you to where there is such great need for his holy service. What I ask of you at the present above all else is that you should commend me to our Lord as the most needy one of all.[31] That I, although unworthy, will do the same [for you]. You will experience no lack of troubles and afflictions of soul and body

29. My free rendition of this rather obscurely worded passage is tentative. On the whole Rogel's prose is straightforward, but infrequently, as in the above sentence, his syntax becomes tortuous and his choice of words is less than felicitous.

30. This sentence is written in Latin *Sit nomen domine beneditum*. It might also be rendered as "Let the name of the Lord be blessed," or "Blessed be the name of the Lord."

31. In the sense of needing their prayers and the help of the Lord.

because all the three capital enemies are bound to appear with new
snares to hinder that holy, heroic, and apostolic work, as you will
see by experience each day. It will be necessary to keep in mind
what the holy reading has taught you and what our Lord has given
you a taste of in your meditation for consolation and encouragement
in those labors. The royal prophet David did just that when he said:
Except that your law is my meditation, then I would perish
perchance in my lowly state[32] (*Nisi que* [sic] *les tua meditacio mea est,
tunc fortte periissen in umilitate mea*);[62] you will find help, support,
and consolation only in the Lord. So that all these labors may be a
pleasure for him and a rest taken by his divine Majesty and as a
spiritual remedy for those neighbors.[33] Although there would be no
need for this for one who has such good spirit; but as I have seen in
the conversion of these natives, who have given me such great
difficulties that I have been tempted to abandon the work. I say this
to one for whom I desire full perseverance, lest another snatch your
crown[34] (*ne alius arripiat coranan tuan*).[63]

26. In that which pertains to the business of the woman, I wrote
to Pero Menéndez Marqués what that man said to me, and not
because I believed that the Adelantado had done him an injury,
because I have known him for many years and I have always
considered him and I consider him as a good Christian. And since
that woman said that this one is not her husband, let him provide
the remedy that is appropriate for the salvation of both and he has
the matter under control (*entre manos*).[35]

27. The matters (*cosas*) of the Indians will have shown well what
talent we shall require for them, because, for this reason not only do
they become greatly disgusted (*se desgracian mucho*)[36] with them

32. Either the bishop's Latin was rather rusty or some copyist miscopied
him. *Que* should be *quod* and *les* should be *lex*, as Zubillaga noted in his note.
A modern version of this passage is "Unless your law had been my delight, I
would then have perished in my affliction."

33. The bishop's style here is somewhat elliptic and confusing in this
passage.

34. In the latter part of this sentence the bishop again lapsed into a rather
distorted Latin. In the note Zubillaga presents a variant version of this quota-
tion from the Apocalypse.

35. My rendition here is tentative.

36. This might be rendered also as "fail," "quarrel," or "lose one's former
perfection."

but they even come to loathe them, and our Lord does not require of anyone more than [is possible] from the talents that he gave him. They are rational animals well prepared for saving themselves. Keeping them in hand, they are a harvest so ripe that one can swing the sickle on whatever side one chooses, as they see in the minister one who is looking out for their salvation and their spiritual and temporal welfare and who preaches life and doctrine to them. The ministers of God who deal with them must not grow weary or become angry because of the things that they do or the needs (*miserias*)[37] that they have, [but must do] as does the mother with the child that she rears. She may clean it a thousand times a day and does not become disgusted by this. It is necessary that the minister have love and fear. And they will do this easily on learning that he truly loves them. And if the true understanding is lacking in them, the love and zeal for our Lord, whose ministers we are and whose doctrine we preach, must not be found wanting in us; that it is beyond comparison,[38] for our Lord suffers more for us than we are capable of suffering for them for their many careless acts and the many failings that they have.

28. As to the rest that you spoke of concerning Florida's needs, we must all assist in meeting them. And as to the matter of the altar stones (*haras*)[39] and corporals that the priest Fray Alonso Agustino spoke to him about, as Christianity begins to spread and as priests arrive, you will not want for them with the divine assistance. I have sent some corporals. I have not learned whether they have given them. When you have a reliable person who is coming with the intention of returning, you should let me know, and I shall furnish these things. The maize that you requested, the master (*arráez*) or pilot of the boat will bring if he is able to with the one who may bring it; that if it is wanting, it will be lacking because of him. That if he is bothered greatly by having to carry

37. This might be rendered also as "misery," "wretchedness," "meanness," "stinginess," or "hardness."

38. My rendition of this passage is tentative. The bishop has a talent for obscure prose. The Spanish here is "que sin comparacion mas nos sufre nuestro Señor, que nosotros les podemos sufrir, por muchos descuidos y defectos que tengan."

39. *Haras* might be rendered also as "altar." The corporal is the stiffly starched square of linen cloth on which the consecrated bread and wine are placed during Mass.

such things to be delivered, when some known person comes, charge him to be made responsible for bringing at least twenty *anegas*[64] [40] for those children who attend the catechism lessons; that we will gladly send it to those soldiers in each boat.

Encourage and strive greatly for every virtue, so that by having them in hand and [having] gained them,[41] the conversion of the natives may be achieved more easily. That experience has taught me that the bad example of some Christians does a great deal to prevent the ministers of God from converting the natives with their example and teaching.[65] [42] And if these heathens see that the Spaniards observe what is being preached to them, they believe and receive the Christian teaching very easily. And it is necessary, consequently, not to leave out or forget the Spaniards because of the Indians. I have gone on at great length in these matters, but [I did so] out of the zeal that I have for the honor of God and for the salvation of everyone and so that they may succeed in this holy enterprise and your lordship will put everything right. I beg our Lord to give you his holy grace for his glory. From Mérida de Yucatan on the 27th of February of 1568.

Franciscus, bishop

29. This letter has encouraged me greatly and I believe that it will do so for all those who read it and for this [reason] I am sending it to your Reverence.

30. As they did not bring me this maize and as from that which I had brought from here for the Indians, I had given half to the soldiers because they promised me that they would not eat meat during Lent, which they have kept very well, my maize ran out at the end of two months. And as this is the time when the Indians suffer much from hunger, they no longer frequented the catechism

---

40. Anegas is meant to be *fanegas*. Zubillaga explains its significance in his note. My rendition of this sentence is tentative. The Spanish here is "que si a él haze muy de mal llevar cosas de encomienda, quando biniere alguna persona conocida, encargalle se encargue de llebar siquiera veinte anegas[64] para essos niños que acuden a la doctrina."

41. My rendition here is tentative as well. The Spanish is "para que teniendolos de la mano y ganados ellos."

42. My rendition is tentative here also. The Spanish is "que mas perbierten los malos exemplos de algunos cristianos, que conbierten de los naturales los ministros de Dios con."

lessons as much. For with the hunger that hounded them, they gave little importance to the other trade goods.

31. It occurred to me at the beginning of this past March that, with the great desire that I had that some of these natives should go to heaven, I gave the responsibility to the interpreters [to inform me] and I made a special effort to learn when someone became ill and was very close to death so as to urge them to become Christian so that I might baptize them on their asking for it and so that they would go to heaven accordingly. It happened that a councillor (*cavallero*) of this don Felipe came down ill with a pain in the side and it brought him to such a point that we thought that he was in his final agony already. They called me at night so that I might go to visit him and begin to persuade him that he might become a Christian and look favorably on becoming a vassal of God and abandon all idol worship. And he showed good indications, saying that he believed in God and in Jesus Christ his son, who became man in order to make men friends of God, and he died on the cross for them and on the third day he arose from the dead. And that he believed everything that Catholic Christians believe and that he regretted the blindness in which he had lived all his life, and that he intended, if God should give him life, to never adore the idols again and to be a good Christian and a vassal of God. And with this I waited a little while to see whether he would get worse or get better. And as I saw that the illness was tightening its grip on him, and as all we Spaniards who were there judged that he would die before the dawning of the next day, with this I decided to baptize him and I baptized him. And from that point on he began to get better at once and he went on improving continually until he was completely well and healthy. And from the time that I baptized him, I took him under my charge at once and gave him to eat from those provisions (*proveza*) that were to be had in the fort, regaling him as much as I was able to and giving him other little things to attach him to us so that he would come to be with us. And, consequently, for some days after he became healthy, he came to the fort constantly and was given [something] to eat. And I promised him that it would be given to him always as long as he did not return to worshiping idols; and if he wished to be clothed and to adopt the clothing of a Christian, I would clothe him also. And he persevered thus for some days, coming to me often to avoid all occasions for a relapse on his part. I spoke to the cacique, don Felipe, so that he

might free him from all the duties that he had in the house of the idols and so that he would not order him to be involved in anything pertaining to those rites, for he was now a Christian and he promised me that he would do so. And later that same day the shamans (*hechizeros*) were to perform certain sorceries (*hechizerias*) and idolatry. And as this Christian was one of them, he adorned himself after their fashion in order to go there, and as they informed me of it, I sent word to him that he should not do it. Despite this and despite my request to the king, that same day he went to participate in the idol worship. And this is the third bad sign that I have seen in this king to justify my presumption that he does not intend really to become a Christian.

32. At the time that this occurred, as those three towns of the Tocobaga out of the four that threw off their obedience [to the Calusa chief] came to ask pardon from their king and to return to their obedience and vassalage [to him], we Christians were fearful, as the chief himself was, lest they should have come with some cunning or treachery in mind, sent by Tocobaga under this pretense in order to kill us or their cacique. And for this reason all the soldiers were put on alert and strengthened the fort more than it was, and the captain and the soldiers notified me that I should not go down to the huts (*buios*) of the Indians to teach the Christian doctrine to the queens (*reinas*)[66] nor to the cross. It seemed to me that it was proper to agree to what they asked of me and to leave off what had been begun until we felt more secure and understood the purpose of the coming of those peoples. And what we believed was that, as the Spaniards were killed in Tocobaga and as they [the Spaniards] are great friends of don Felipe, they wished to return to the good graces of their king before the Spaniards should go out against Tocobaga, so that they might live in peace and quiet. But even with all this we remained ill at ease all the time that they remained there [and] during that time I ceased to teach the catechism. And the cacique, believing that I had ceased to do so because of the grief that he caused me when the other [leader] apostatized, came to the fort each day so that I might speak to him about the things of God and saying that he would carry out what he had promised and that I would see it when the Adelantado should come how he was abandoning it all. I did not cease to show a sad countenance, showing my feelings about it, although on the other hand, I showed him much love and gave him [gifts] from the things

that I had, and we ate together on many occasions in my lodging. I spoke to him clearly, telling him with great gentleness that in everything he was showing himself to be our friend and that we always found that he discussed matters truthfully with us, but that he was far from wishing to become a Christian. And with this grief that I pretended, I would tell him what I desired that he do in order to become a good Christian.

33. When I came to Havana around the month of December, I proposed to these señores stewards of the Adelantado whether it seemed appropriate to them to carry me to St. Augustine during this Lent in order to preach and to help with the confessions there. They replied to me that it would be better to remain where I was in order to preserve the peace between the Spaniards and the Indians and in order to move ahead with what had been begun among the Indians. And it certainly has been very necessary that there should be someone who would be on hand for those who would inflict injuries, because, as they are soldiers and as they are in the Indies, which is free country [in the sense that the usual restraints do not apply], it seems to them that everything is owed to them. And, consequently, I have had some problem with them in restraining them and preventing them from mistreating the Indians. And if the captain of the Spaniards had not helped me in this himself, as he has helped me, [my effort] would not have sufficed.

34. On the 4th of the present [month], Passion Sunday, a vessel came to our fort in which Brother Francisco[67] traveled with 18 soldiers from those who were in the fort of Tequesta.[68] He is writing to your Reverence about the misfortune that occurred in that fort;[69] how the Indians killed four soldiers and how the captain, Pero Marqués, withdrew the rest from there and sent them to our fort. Then the Brother came here to Havana and found the letters here that your Reverence wrote to me from Cartagena and Nonbre [*sic*] de Dios and he brought them to me there.

35. I very much wanted to remain in that fort, even though it is not very necessary and Brother Francisco can substitute very well for me. But it seemed best to the soldiers that I should come in order to arrange with those señores so that they would well provide that fort with provisions; for out of the three that he had left[70] [in South Florida], only that one that was still in existence had survived. And as I am now so annoyed with carrying these messages so out of character with my profession, I proposed to

come with the resolve of not returning there any more until the Adelantado should come, unless holy obedience orders otherwise. And, consequently, I am now about to depart for St. Augustine, where I expect, with God's help, to run into the priests[71] because this ship that entered this port on yesterday and the ships on which the fathers are coming left Spain at the same time. And, consequently, we consider it as certain that they will have arrived at St. Augustine. If I do meet the fathers there, I believe that we will return here to put everything in order. My going to St. Augustine now is for no other [purpose] than to give a report to the Father vice-provincial[72] about things in Florida and about the state in which they are. For, as he is bringing six or eight companions with him, he should not begin to make the assignment of them there without having a true report about the state of affairs in Florida, and because he orders me that I should go to the port where it seems best to me for us to get together. May your Reverence for the love of our Lord, commend me to his divine Majesty so that I may succeed in serving him truly, in everything seeking only his divine glory. And may your Reverence visit us, for the sake of his divine love, as quickly as you may be able to.[73] To all my dearest fathers and brothers of those parts may your Reverence send my intimate respects in the Lord [and] especially to my most dear Father Albarez, Father Fuentes, and Brother Francisco[74] and tell Father Albarez not to forget his Rogel.

36. Because it has been almost a year[75] since I have written to Spain, I will send a copy of this in this fleet that they are expecting here from New Spain, so that they may send it to our Father General,[76] and the duplicate of this will go by another channel. May God our Lord be with your Reverence and may he fill you with his holy spirit so that you may succeed in fulfilling his divine will in everything. From Havana, on the 25th of April of the year 1568.

From the useless son of your Reverence and servant in the Lord
    †Juan Rogel

37. Because, after this was written, the journey has been delayed for two days, I shall write now what I omitted telling about above on the first page of the letter.

38. As the Cacique Carlos had come back from the journey that he made to Tocobaga with the Adelantado very discontented and annoyed against the Christians, he always sought to avenge himself on us for the offenses that he said that the Adelantado had

committed against him, as I wrote about to Spain to your
Reverence. And he tried to kill the Adelantado as he was
disembarking in his land, but his [people] did not support him,
saying that he could not bring it off and that he himself would be
lost instead. And as he could not then carry out his evil intention,
he arranged to do it on the following day, it seeming to him that he
would have the opportunity, because we were to move to another
island[77] on which the Adelantado was to have left us before
departing from here. And accordingly he sent to ask him to give us
a dozen canoes in order to move our supplies (*ato*). And he arranged
with the Indians who were to man them that, while they were in a
deep channel, that we had to cross over, they should sink the canoes
with everything that was in them and that if there were any
Christians in them they should drown them. But it pleased the Lord
to free us from this danger, because we crossed over with
everything that we had in the Adelantado's vessels and canoes were
not needed. And once we had crossed over to the place where we
were to remain, the Adelantado left for Havana and took Brother
Francisco with him in order to leave him in Tequesta[78] and we were
left, as they say, [facing] the horns of the bull, if the Lord in his
mercy had not protected us. He soon began to arrange to kill us and
to dance with our heads,[79] and then to seek refuge with all his
people by living on some ponds (*lagunas*) to which the Spaniards
would not be able to go. We lived with a great deal of caution and
vigilance, even though, as we saw, he was wont to come to where
we were and eat with us and treated us so familiarly and sent us
fish and whatever he had, and Indians for the things of which we
were in need, [And although] we thought that his anger had passed,
nonetheless, we never lowered our guard because of this. And while
we were on that island, he arranged that one of his villages should
come armed early in the morning as the dawn was breaking, and
that if we had happened to let our guard down, they were to enter
and kill us; and that he would seek to be there also. And so it was
done. But as it was the habit of the soldiers to maintain their
sentinels and to arm themselves whenever they saw a multitude of
Indians, and as he [Carlos] saw that there was no opportunity [for
surprise], he went out to tell them before they should disembark,
that they should pass by at a distance. And thus that plan came
undone then. After this he made many other arrangements and
agreements with his vassals in order to seek a way of killing us

without danger to himself. And thus he ordered that all his vassals should make bows and arrows and that all of them should be well provided with weapons for the time when he should send to call them. In this [interval] the time arrived in which we were to return to the post where we were before, having built a wooden house there. And it was then that he began to reveal his evil intention. Having offered to assist us in bringing our supplies across, and while he was coming in person with three canoes for that [purpose], throwing the greater part of the ammunition and the food that the soldiers had into the water and trying to drown some soldiers who fell into the sea, all of this was made known to us later by his captain general, who is now the cacique, as a matter planned ahead of time. Because this captain and some Indians, because they were at odds with Carlos, were on good terms with us and kept us informed of all the things that the other one did. And when the captain of the Christians learned of this, he spoke to me, asking for my opinion whether he should kill Carlos for that treachery that he had practiced. And I opposed him [on it], which irritated him so much that he said to me that he would do it and that I would not know about it until it was done.

39. Carlos did not content himself nor was he satisfied with that harm that he did to the Christians but, rather, constantly sought to move forward on his wicked intentions to have us killed. And he had a great hate against me especially because I discredited and spoke evil about his idols. And he arranged with certain of his servants to kidnap me when I should go outside of the fort, [but did not succeed] as I did not go out more than once each day for a thing that could not be avoided and I did not go farther than a stone's throw from it. What he was saying was that, as I carried no weapons, they would be able to catch me and cover my mouth and carry me off to wherever they might wish to. And this was told to me by one of his servants with whom he discussed it, who is one now for this cacique. During this time a vessel that came from Campeche arrived loaded with maize for our fort. After it was unloaded, I came to Havana in it. And during this same time Carlos withdrew his women and treasures from there and carried them to another village. And it was, as we learned later, so that he would be more unencumbered and prepared to achieve this feat. And during this said time Carlos' captain kept us informed about everything that was going on, as a consequence of which, when I came from

there, the matter was festering badly. And consequently I came with a very great concern for returning quickly with provisions, because the Christians remained at very great risk and already a sister of Carlos, who was Christian,[80] whom the Adelantado had left with us, no longer was [with us] but with her brother instead. And they say that he ordered the assembling of certain of his villages there, with the pretext of holding certain celebrations (*fiestas*), as they are accustomed to do at various times, and that they should bring gold and silver so that they might trade with it among the Christians and that while they were occupied in that, other Indians would come who would be in ambush and they were to kill them. But the captain of the Christians got the jump on him and found ways to make him come to our fort and there they killed him with another two Indians who came with him. And they sent to call his captain, who was not there then so that he might come to be king. There is information here about all of this [obtained] by taking the statements of the very Indians with whom Carlos discussed all these matters. And this happened three days after my departure for here.[81] And when Pero Marqués and I went [there], we found the captain of Carlos made cacique and that he was in peaceful possession of his kingdom.

40. During the lifetime of Carlos, although I saw the enmity that existed between him and his captain and that the captain wanted to be king with a strong desire, I never set myself to inquire whether that pretention was just or unjust. But after I saw him in possession of the kingdom and that the Spaniards had been the means to it, I wanted to know what claim (*ación*) the captain had to the kingdom. And for this [purpose] I gathered information from the Christians who had been here for a long time about what they knew. I sent the report about this to Spain last year.[82] And later here, to reassure myself further I begged the cacique himself, who is so at present, to give me an account of how the entire case came to pass. What he told me goes like this.

41. A king or cacique of this kingdom, uncle of this don Felipe and of Carlos, had a sister and a brother. This brother was the great shaman (*hechizero mayor*) or high priest of the idols. And his sister married and had this don Felipe as a son. And while this don Felipe was a child, as his uncle the king did not have sons, he adopted him as a son and named him as his successor in the kingdom and he made the father of don Felipe his captain general.

And when the child was a little older, about seven or eight years of age, his uncle placed the royal insignia on him, which are a gold *chaguala*,[83] [43] on the forehead and some strings of beads on the legs. And after all of this the king had a daughter, whom, when she was four years of age, he married with this his nephew and successor, who would be ten or twelve years of age. And with this wedding he confirmed the succession in the kingdom and he said that when don Felipe was of an age to govern, that he would give him possession of the kingdom, removing himself from the royal bench or seat and putting don Felipe on it and that he would be captain general and head shaman, which were the two offices that his brother-in-law and his brother held. And his brother-in-law, he would make his second captain. And that he would order his brother to live without any responsibility (*cargo*) or office (*oficio*). And for greater confirmation of the succession in the kingdom, the villages (*pueblos*) began to give women to don Felipe, which is the method that they have in this land for swearing allegiance (*jurar a*) to someone as king. For when they receive one as king, in recognition of vassalage, each village gives him a woman. And thus two villages gave women to this don Felipe then. And when he was already a youth and his father-in-law wanting to hand his daughter, who was still a child, over to him, and that the marriage be published, and that the celebrations be held (*se hiziesen las fiestas*) etc., the King, father-in-law of don Felipe, died. And the father of don Felipe, his brother-in-law, and the next[44] brother of the deceased, who was the head shaman, came together and agreed among themselves that until don Felipe should reach the age for governing, one of them should be viceroy and govern the kingdom. And the brother of the deceased suborned two villages so that they would request that he be it. And the father of don Felipe consented to it with the condition that, two years from then, when don Felipe would already be able to govern, that they deliver possession of the kingdom to him. And with this the brother of the deceased took possession. And while he remained in possession of it, he had a son who was Carlos and he took possession of the kingdom in such a manner that he did not fulfill

43. This word does not appear in most modern dictionaries. Here it refers to a small ornament. Spaniards used the word also to designate the gold nose-rings worn by the Cuna of Panama.

44. The Spanish here, *otro*, might be rendered also as "other."

what he had agreed to with his brother-in-law and with his nephew. And when five or six years had passed, this king called his widowed sister-in-law, wife of the deceased king, and told her to unmarry her daughter from don Felipe and that they should marry her with his son, Carlos, and that Carlos would be king after his days and her daughter would be the principal queen. The widow, as she was alone and helpless, did not dare to contradict him and thus the young girl was unmarried from don Felipe and they married her with Carlos. And, as his brother-in-law, father of don Felipe, who was always captain, was greatly offended by this and showed himself to be greatly disgusted, the king, in order to placate him, gave one of his daughters[84] as a wife for don Felipe and named him as captain general of the king after his father. And from then on there always were enmities between don Felipe and his father and Carlos and his father. And as don Felipe turned out to be a more sensible and valorous man than Carlos, don Felipe always had Carlos under vassalage, although he was king and the villages leaned more to the side of this don Felipe, who was captain than to that of Carlos, even though he was king. And don Felipe even attempted to kill Carlos (*Y aun pretendió matar a Carlos el don Felipe*) when the Spaniards came, but they prevented it, as I wrote last year. But the wretch did not know how to preserve the friendship that he had with them and for this he was made to pay. This is, Father, the confession of this king (*la confesión deste rey*) concerning the claim and the right that he has to this kingdom and it seems that it agrees with what the interpreters told me and [that] I wrote to Spain last year. And as I have drawn this out to such great length I say no more except to ask you again to remember me again as above in your Reverence's holy sacrifices[45] and prayers.

Useless son of your Reverence and servant in the Lord

†Juan Rogel

7 Title in the hand of Father Rogel. †Jesus. Copy of one that Father Rogel of the Company of Jesus wrote from Florida to Father Portillo, provincial of the same Company of Jesus in Spain's West Indies at the city of Lima in Peru. To Rome and all Europe etc. It is from June of 1567 to April of 1568.

45. This is intended probably in the sense of "Holy Sacrifice of the Mass," one of the expressions Catholics use to designate the ritual of the Eucharist.

Second hand. 1567 and 1568
Third hand. 1588.
A trace of the seal.

Zubillaga's Notes

1. Father Portillo, provincial of the West Indies, also superior of the missionaries of Florida.

2. Governor Menéndez de Avilés in the year 1565 discovered the harbor in present-day Charlotte Bay on the west [coast] of Florida to which he gave the name of Saint Anthony "because of the devotion which the Adelantado had developed for the señor St. Anthony so that he might find those Christian men and women he was searching for" (Ruidíaz, *La Florida* I, 166). [In the Spanish text this is note 3 because word order is often different than it is in the equivalent English sentence. To avoid the incongruity of having notes 3 and 4 precede note 2 in the English translation, I have changed the numbering whenever that situation arises and stated the change in the note involved. As has been observed elsewhere, modern authorities believe that the head Calusa village in the 1560s was on Mound Key in Estero Bay rather than at Charlotte Harbor, as Zubillaga maintained].

3. Generally, in Spanish documents, the province and principal town, Calus, are referred to by the name of Carlos, their ruler. [This is note 4 in the Spanish text.]

4. Father Luis López of the Castilian Province, who proceeded to Peru in the first missionary band. Father Rogel became acquainted with him in the Toledan college (Tolet. 12 f. 20; see Lopetegui, S.J., *El Padre José de Acosta y las misiones* 110 adnot. 64). More is said about it in *Monumentis Peruvianis*. [This is note 2 in the Spanish text.]

5. A Panamanian port on the Caribbean coast.

6. Brother Francisco Villarreal began his missionary labors in the province of Tequesta in the month of March of 1567 (see doc. 74).

7. Calusa Province.

8. This letter pertains to *Monumenta Peruviana*.

9. A lost letter (see Preface, doc. 50a).

10. A lost letter (see Preface, doc. 57a).

11. From the letters of Father Avellaneda of December 31, 1567, Granada, written to the Father General (see doc. 70), we know of this letter of Father Rogel received in Spain, from whence it was sent to Rome. See below where Father Rogel speaks of the death of the ruler Carlos.

12. Nephew of Governor Menéndez. [In modern texts he is referred to as Pedro Menéndez Marques. Pero is a form found commonly among the Portuguese of this era, as in Pero Vaz de Caminha].

13. Tocobaga, town and province that extends along the northern part of Tampa Bay (Florida).

14. In the year 1567 Menéndez de Avilés established a fort of thirty soldiers under the command of Garciá de Cos so that they might teach Christian doctrine to the natives and so that they might explore the region further.

15. When Menéndez and his soldiers first landed in the province of Tocobaga, the natives fled to the hills (*montes*), leaving the ruler behind. [The Latin *montes* may be used here by Zubillaga in the sense of its Spanish equivalent, which in Florida contexts usually means "woods" rather than "hills" or "mountains."]

16. Generally those whom Father Rogel characterizes as leading men (or councillors) (*equites*) were called *principales* (leading men) by contemporary chroniclers, who might be viewed as councillors of the ruler.

17. This ruler also showed his love toward his idols at the first coming of Menéndez into his province, for he himself made it known through a messenger "that his people had fled and that he had remained in his house of prayer and house of his gods; that he preferred to die rather than to forsake them" (Ruidíaz, *La Florida* I 286).

18. See further on where the priest speaks about the natives' killing of the Spaniards of the fort.

19. John VII 20.

20. Lost letter (see Preface, doc. 57a).

21. He seems to refer to the letter of the preceding note (see note 11).

22. April 15.

23. As the father himself claimed below after the journey of the Father viceprovincial Segura had been carried out, [that] he intended to render an account about the status of the Florida mission, inasmuch as he would do it better [when] he had explored the region of Guale and Santa Elena in northern Florida (see doc. 89).

24. López de Velasco asserted this, "The bay of Carlos, which they call Excampaba in the language of the Indians for a cacique of this name who later called himself Carlos out of devotion to the Emperor" (*Geografía* 164). In our work *La Florida* (passim) we wrote the modern transcription, that in the archive of the Monumenta the following, Tocampaba, was to be found. [My rendition of his sentence is tentative. The Latin is "In nostro opere *La Florida* (passim) transcriptionem modernam, quae in archivo Monumentorum inveniebatur sequentes, Tocampaba scripsimus."] On examining the original of this letter carefully, we saw Escampaba or Escampaha to be written.

25. Philip, concerning whom [see] below.

25a. Not infrequently natives of the northern Indies supposed the soul or souls of men (which they often believed to be many) to be a shadow or shadows (*umbram*) (Schmidt, *Der Ursprung der Gottesidee V*, 455ff., 642ff., 648ff.). No other tribe of that region however, we know of asserts the soul [to be] the pupil.

26. Indians of the eastern and southern region of the northern Indies believed in the existence of these spirits called demon (*daemon*) by the missionaries whenever they were called up after death (Schmidt, *Der Ursprung der Gottesidee* V 417). About this demon, as we shall see, there is frequent mention in the letters of the missionaries. On the other hand, in these superstitious ceremonies the shaman (*magos*) is believed to have had a very great part. Thus the chronicler Lemoyne as a witness (*Sic, teste chronista Lemoyne*) that the ruler living near the St. Johns River (in Florida) consulted a shaman (*magum*) about the outcome of a battle to be fought with an enemy. The same Lemoyne asserted that what the shaman predicted came to pass (*Brevis narratio* XIII; see doc. 93, note 37).

26a. These details about the three souls among the Calusan natives, which Father Rogel brings up, are of great importance. Indeed, concerning this and similar beliefs pertaining to the soul among tribes of the southern and eastern region of the northern Indies we know almost nothing (see Schmidt, *Der Ursprung der Gottesidee* V 455ff.).

27. Natives of the northern Indies, whether from the eastern or western part, designate some place either in the heavens or in the nether regions for souls after earthly life (Schmidt, *op. cit.* V 457-459). This statement of our missionary about the opinion of the natives of Calus concerning the destruction of the soul is therefore worthy of note.

28. Monotheism flourished among some tribes of the northern provinces of the Indies (Schmidt, *op. cit.* V 395-397, 403, 419, 465); which indeed often lacked a concept more often even imperfect of a spiritual nature. [My rendition of the latter part of this footnote is tentative. The Latin is "qui quidem conceptus saepe saepius valde imperfectus indole spirituali carebat."]

29. All tribes of the northern Indies generally admit a creator god (Schmidt, *op. cit.* V 178, 222-230, 310, 409, 485ff.). Although none also acknowledge creation from nothing (*l. c.* 64, 270, 524), some, not a few, attempt to explain the existence of all things and the reciprocal flux of the same by magical forces (Hodge, *Handbook* "Religion").

30. Not uncommonly natives of the provinces of the northern Indies devised various divinities. Thus some tribes of the great Algonquian family fashioned three: a father, whose name was Atahokan, his son, and also Mesu, in such a fashion that they assign control of the earth to the father and of the sea to the son (Schmidt, *Der Ursprung der Gottesidee* V 532ff.). Also some tribes of the same Algonquian family acknowledge two (*l. c.* 542); infrequently[?] (*non semel*) four divinities are enumerated (*l. c.* 601). These in fact are distributed among the divine forces (*inter numina*) in control of the world.

31. *Sometías* or sodomies.

32. King Bungi, not yet a Christian, supported Christianity to a great extent. Baptized on the 28th day of August 1587, he is known by the name Francis (Frois, *Segunda parte da Historia de Japam,* see I 1–24).

33. As we know, ruler of the region that extended along the St. Johns River whose subjects killed Father Martínez and his companions (see doc. 41).

34. In those early morning assemblies of the natives, it is known that they deliberated on the more serious matters. Thus the chronicler Lemoyne told of the Timucuan natives living near the St. Johns River; *"By What Proceedings Floridians Deliberate About Serious Matters.* In the morning the king is accustomed to meet daily on the days of the year with certain nobles[46] in a public place destined for that, in which large benches (*in quo magna scamna*)[47] are constructed almost in a semicircle of seats (*quasi in hemicyclum*)[48] between which there is another one in the hollow at the beginning (*aliud antrorsum*)[49] projecting out a little (*paululum prominens*), consisting of nine round lopped-off trunks lined up (*novem truncis lineis rotundis constans*) for the king's seat (*pro Regis sede*)[50] on which he alone sits[51] so that he may be able to be distinguished from the others. And there, one at a time in order, they come to offer the greeting to him, with the older ones beginning the salutation with both hands raised twice to the height of the head and pronouncing (*proferentibus*) ha, he, ya, ha, ha, and then with the rest responding, ha, ha. As each one completes the salutation, he withdraws to his sitting-place on the bench (*in scamnis sessum concedit*).[52] If there is anything of a serious nature to be taken up, the king summons *Iaiias,*[53] that is, his priests, and elders (*seniores*), from each of whom he

---

46. The Latin here is *Rex cum nobilibus certis anni diebus quotidie mane convenire solet.* The standard translations such as those of Bennett and Lorant link "certain" to "days" rather than to "nobles" to which it is closer in the Latin text. As some potentially significant details are lost in the existing free translations of this passage, I shall make mine a very literal one.

47. Although *magna scamna* is clearly plural, Bennett rendered this as "a long bench."

48. "Almost in a semicircle of seats" is omitted by Bennett.

49. Bennett reduced this clause to "having at the middle of it."

50. Bennett changed "King's" to "chief's."

51. In the Latin *in qua solus residet, solus* might be rendered also as "by himself," as Bennett has presented it.

52. From the beginning of Lemoyne's Latin text down to this point is one sentence.

53. Bennett presented this as *laüas.*

seeks [their] opinion one at a time. Indeed they reach a determination about nothing whatsoever without first convoking several councils, and they deliberate thoroughly before they reach a decision"[54] (*Brevis narratio* XXIX).

35. From these things that the father asserts about Muskogeans, to which the Calusa tribe is seen to belong (see the general introduction Ia 1 paragraph 2), multiple wives were permitted for the ruler. This is seen to have been the custom similarly in the Timucuan family. For instance, the chronicler Lemoyne describes the solemnity in which the wife chosen by the king was received. In this solemnity, in fact, the king revealed the reasons why he accepted her as his *primary wife* (*Brevis narratio XXXVIII*). The chronicler himself (*op. cit.* 4) asserted clearly [that] among the individual natives other than the king there were single wives.

36. The general idea of monogamy was prevalent among many natives of the northern Indies (Schmidt, *Der Ursprung der Gottesidee* V 447; Hodge, *Handbook* "Marriage"). In the province of Calus, in fact, and the Muskogean family, not only the ruler (see the note above) but also the rest (which even Father Rogel indicates below) plural wives were permitted.

37. Simultaneous plurality of wives or polygamy goes against the law of nature, not only as to the primary [goal in that] he relinquished possible procreation and education of the offspring, but also the secondary one, in good faith of course, which is mutual obedience of the spouses(?) (*coniugum*) in those [matters] that pertain to domestic life and conjugal duties and the relief of concupiscence. This dispensation, it is to be admitted, was granted in general to the patriarchs of the Old Testament without its being possible to determine easily its time and manner. [My rendition of this tortuously worded note is tentative.]

38. The law of monogamy, as a precept of the natural law (see the earlier note), as is evident, also obliges heathens [?] (*gentes*).[55] Father Rogel chose not to insist on the law until after baptism.

39. Paul III in the apostolic letters, "Height of the divine Council" (*Altitudo divini Consilii*), of the 1st of June of 1537 decreed this concerning the marriages of the Indians: "as to those who before conversion had multiple wives according to their custom and does not recall which of them he took first, on being converted to the faith, they may choose the one whom they wish and contract matrimony with her in accord with the statement of the present [pronouncement] as is the custom. The one who did indeed remember which one he took first, was to retain her, dismissing the others" (Hernáez, *Colección de Bulas* I

---

54. In his caption or notes for Lemoyne's illustration number 38, Lorant omitted much of the original text found in de Bry's work and in Bennett's translation of the same.

55. The usual meanings of *gens* are "clan," "offspring or descendents," "people," "tribe," "nation," and in the plural, *gentes,* "foreigners."

66). And in particular Pius V in the apostolic letters "Romani Pontificis" of August 2, 1571, permitted as to Indians "who are baptized and who are to be baptized in the future have to remain with the wife with which he was baptized or will be baptized, as his legitimate wife, dismissing the others" (*l. c.* 76). As is clearly evident, if indeed Pius V had not yet issued his apostolic document, the law of Paul III would have been in order for fulfillment. Concerning the Order of Pius V see Rayanna, S.J., *De Constitutione S. Pii Papae V "Romani Pontificis"* Rome, 1938; Lopetegui, S.J., *La Constitución "Romani Pontificis"* in the periodical, *Estudios Eclesiásticos* 16 (1942) 487-511.

40. Lemoyne (*Brevis Narratio* XL), in describing the ceremonies for the funeral for a king and priest, makes no mention of victims that were sacrificed at that time. However, he asserts that among the Timucuan natives of the region of the St. Johns River (Florida) it was the custom to offer the firstborn male to the king as a victim, and he described the reasoning for which this bloody immolation was carried out (*op. cit.* XXXIII). Similar sacrifices were seen to be carried out in the province of Calus, of which Rogel speaks, and Tequesta (see doc. 74 paragraph 5).

41. Of the West Indies with the exception of Brazil.

42. When the missionary, after the killing of the ruler, Carlos, returned from Havana to the province of Calus (see preface).

43. The day on which the father headed for Havana.

44. Fontaneda, a Spaniard who lived in the province of Calus for many years, in the year 1591 asserted that the islands of the Martyrs stretched from the west to the east part of Florida and ended "close to a settlement of Indians that are named Tequesta" (*C.D.I.Am.* V 543). López de Velasco (*Geografía* 165) described them thus: "From the farthest point of the mainland, which is at 25 degrees, it heads toward the sea on a northeast southeast orientation until at 24½ degrees it becomes a chain of shoals, full of little islands that are called the *Martyrs,* and they are countless, with the greater part of them inhabited by Indians subject to the cacique Carlos, great archers and spear throwers. One may sail among them with light-draft vessels and canoes. All the islands are covered with trees, although many of them are inundated frequently" (see doc. 41 note 54).

45. Francisco de Reinoso.

46. A province in the eastern region of southern Florida.

47. A province that extended along the northern part of Tampa Bay (Florida).

48. Ruler of the province of the same name [?] (*homonymae*).

49. A proverb taken from this verse of Terence: "Nae ille haud scit, quam mihi nunc surdo narret fabulam" (Heaut. 2. 1. 10).

50. When Governor Menéndez first landed in the Calusan province in the month of February 1566, he persuaded the ruler that he should erect a cross near his own house (Zubillaga, *La Florida* 258ff). In the month of October of the same year, Spanish soldiers under the captain, Francisco de Reinoso, after

building a fort, erected another cross near camp (*l. c.* 260ff). Rogel seems to be speaking of the first cross.

51. See paragraph 20 below.

52. This difficulty of providing a supply of provisions for the garrisons of soldiers was a principal reason why the plans of Pedro Menéndez for establishing settlements and missions in Florida failed (see general introduction IIa. 2 paragraph 3).

53. See doc. 41 paragraph 51-53.

54. In the islands of the Antilles, the second plan of Pedro Menéndez was to leave these fortresses constructed [?] (*extruebantur*) or those established strengthened against attacks of the enemies in the Indies that were feared (see doc. 41, notes 84, 85).

55. The baptismal character, of course, which they received on coming to the island (see doc. 41 paragraph 51).

56. By going over to the Province of Calus in the month of October of the year 1566, a garrison of soldiers was established. The Spaniards, bowing [?] (*anauentes*) to the desires of Governor Menéndez, sent some natives to Havana as hostages, leading people among [them] (among these were to be found Antonia, sister of the ruler) (Zubillaga, *La Florida* 260ff). Similarly, six other Tequesta natives, the first of whom was related to the ruler, were spending their time in that city. Father Rogel and his companion, who, on coming out in 1566, landed in that city, threw themselves with great zeal into their instruction (*op. cit.* 260ff.). All of these natives seem to have been carried back to Florida by Pedro Menéndez in going back in March of the year 1567 (*op. cit.* 266-272). Later, however, other natives were carried to Havana to be instructed in the rudiments of the faith and to be baptized.

57. See doc. 41 paragraph 48-50.

58. Garcia Osorio.

59. Pedro Menéndez, in association with the ruler of the province of Calus, going to the province of the Tocobaga in March of the year 1567, after landing established peace between the two rulers (Ruidíaz, *La Florida* I 290ff; Zubillaga, *La Florida* 269-271).

60. Fray Francisco de Toral O.F.M., born in the town of Ubedae (Jaén), entered the Franciscan order in the province of Baetica. The missionary landed in Mexico in the year 1542. The following year as guardian he attended the general chapter held at Salamanca. In the years 1557-1560 in Mexico he occupied the post of provincial of the Province of the Holy Gospel of which the Custodies of Michoacan and Jalisco were a part. On the 15th day of August 1562, however much he objected to the nomination, he was consecrated as a bishop in Spain. In the year 1565 he took part in the Mexican council held under Archbishop Montuffar. On the 20th day of April 1571, in that same city to which he had come on affairs of his diocese, he was laid to rest in a holy fashion in the great

cemetery (*coenobio*) of St. Francis (Ricard, *Etudes et Documents* 55[30]; *Cartas de Indias* 847ff.).

61. A lost letter (see doc. 71a).

62. Ps. 118 verse 92: *Nisi quod lex tua meditatio mea est, tunc forte periissem in humilitate mea.* [The numbering of the Psalms has been changed since Zubillaga made this observation. It is now Psalm 119.]

63. Apocalypse III, 1: *Tene quod habes, ut nemo accipiat coronam tuam.*

64. A measure of capacity almost equivalent to 55 and a half liters. The volume varies in accord with the diverse regions of Spain.

65. See for example, letters of the 20th day of February of the year 1559 of the bishop in New Spain *degentis* sent to Phillip II, in which he exposes the evil effects that result for the Indians of the region of Jalisco that arise from the abuses of the procurators (audiencia judges) (*Cartas de Indias* 139).

66. Namely, the wives of the ruler who have been spoken of above.

67. Brother Francisco Villarreal.

68. See doc. 74.

69. Lost letter (see doc. 84a).

70. Forts of Tequesta, Tocobaga, and Calus.

71. The expedition of Father Segura and his companions.

72. Father Juan Baptista de Segura.

73. Father Portillo, provincial in the Spanish Indies, never visited Florida.

74. Fathers Antonio Alvarez and Miguel de Fuentes and Brother Francisco de Medina about whom more is said in *Monumentis Peruvianis* (see doc. 33 note 2).

75. He wrote to Spain in the month of May 1567 (see preface).

76. He himself thereupon sent another copy to the Father General (see preface).

77. López de Velasco described thus the bay that he himself called Carlos: "Its entrance is very narrow and full of shoals, as a consequence of which only boats are able to enter. Within it is spacious, about four or five leagues in circumference, although all subject to flooding. There is a little island in the middle that has a circumference of about half a league, with other little islets around it. On this island cacique Carlos had his headquarters and his successors presently have it there [as well]" (*Geografía* 164). The Spaniards seem to have occupied some among these islands that surrounded the ruler's town.

78. See preface doc. 74.

79. The manner by which the natives of the province of Calus celebrated victory over the enemy can be learned from the similar customs of the natives of the region of the St. Johns River (Florida). These, indeed, with the enemy vanquished, Lemoyne said, collected as trophies "bloody arms, scalps removed from the head, and with solemn pomp they place them on long poles driven into the ground, set in a row as it were. Then, with the men and women sitting

in a circle before these body parts, the shaman, holding a small image (*imagun-culam*) with a customary style of low murmured curses . . . [*sic*]. From the side of the open space across from him three men sit on bended knee . . . making a clatter like that of a bell, singing in the native fashion (*patrio ritu canentes*), accompanying the murmurings of the shaman. They are accustomed to celebrate these feast days (*dies festos*) as often as they capture some enemies" (*Brevis narratio* XVI).

80. Antonia.

81. About the 13th day of December. For the Father had set out for Havana on the 10th day of the same month.

82. It seems to allude to the letters about the death of the ruler Carlos that he sent to Spain and of which Father Avellaneda makes mention in his letter to the Father General of December 31, 1567 (see doc. 70).

83. Although Rogel speaks of an ornament placed on the forehead, this name generally designates an ornament that the natives wore hanging from their nostrils.

84. As it appears, this daughter was a sister of Carlos.

2. Rogel's First Contact with Florida's Natives, 1566-1567

The following piece records Father Rogel's activity in Cuba from November 1566 to the end of January 1567, not long after his arrival there from Spain. Only a small portion of this lengthy letter that deals with Calusa and Tequesta is reproduced here. Much of its information about those two provinces is secondhand, as Rogel had not yet been in Florida when he wrote it. But he had already begun the catechization of eighteen Calusans and Tequestans who had come to Cuba not long after Rogel's own arrival there, and he had talked with some of the Spaniards held captive by the Calusa whose freedom Menéndez de Avilés had secured during his first visit to Calus. Rogel included an interesting explanation of the evolution of the native name Caalus (his spelling) to the Hispanicized Carlos. In addition to Rogel's comments on Calusa and Tequesta, much of the material in these excerpts deals with his contacts with the visiting Florida natives and his reasons for delaying the start of his projected work in Calus. Because of its intrinsic interest for the nomenclature of Florida, I have included a comment by Rogel dealing with a feature of the underwater landscape of Florida and northern Cuba, the *ratones* (as in *boca de ratones*).

The following excerpts are from Document 41 from Zubillaga's *Mon-*

umenta Antiquae Floridae. The document occupies pages 101–140 of this work. Zubillaga's notes, appearing here as endnotes, are numbered 117–152. My notes, appearing as footnotes, are numbered in italics beginning at 1.

Father Juan Rogel to Father Didacus Avellaneda, November 1566 to January 1567

From the original in *cod. Hisp.* 105 ff. 72–77 (formerly 593–598 back). . . .

40. We set out from Monte Christi on St. Catherine's Day, the 25th of November, while we were still ill; and some people from the town, with great charity, on seeing that we were going in that state, provided us with some gifts for the sea, especially some birds (*aves*), without our knowing of it, sending them to the ship with the pilot.

41. On this trip, until we reached Havana, the Lord visited us with gifts very much greater than the past ones, because after we left port with very fine weather and traveled with it for three or four days, we were becalmed and after that [came] a north crosswind that cast us among some islets that are called keys (*cayos*)[117] where we came close to having the ship run aground on one of them. In order to avoid that problem, they threw out an anchor with a new and stout rope of hemp (*cable . . . de cañamo*) and at once some rocks (*piedras*) that are on the sea floor, which are called *ratones,*[1] tore it to pieces. With this anchor lost they threw out another one, which was broken as well in a very short space of time. And then we dropped another one after them, in which they had full confidence because it was the best one that the supply ship (*urca*) carried. This one lasted up to 12 or 14 hours and finally gave way as well. . . .

46. Soon after our arrival here [Havana] the brother[2] and I suffered attacks of tertian fever [a form of malaria] that lasted the entire month of December. Here they also bled me and purged me and they purged the brother also. Now, blessed be the Lord, we both have our health. . . .

---

1. O'Scanlan (1974) in his maritime dictionary gives the origin of this word as due to the abrasive and cutting action of these sharp chunks of coral being like that of gnawing mice. There is a verb *ratonar* as well with the same meaning of chafe or abrade.

2. Brother Francisco Villarreal.

47. Soon after we arrived here the treasurer showed me a letter from the Adelantado in which he said to him that when I should arrive here, if I should wish to go to Florida, that I could go to a province of a king, who lives near here; that they go there from Havana in two days; who is called Caalus [*sic*], which the Spaniards mispronouncing the word called him Carlos[123] and he is the greatest of the caciques that there is in all this coast of Florida, where there are 14 or 15 Spaniards[124] whom the Adelantado has stationed there. And he [Menéndez] also has been there and has had a meeting with him and they are both great friends. And they tell me even that he has given his word to the Adelantado that he will become a Christian.[125] I, because we were then so ill and lacking in strength for working and also because I wrote to the Adelantado himself in that letter that, if it seemed best to me, I would wait for him here so that he might carry me there.[126] I decided to wait for him so that, if he should come within a short space of time, it would be better for me to go in his company so that the word of God and what I should teach them might have more authority among the heathens. And for this [reason] I have stayed on here until now, which is the time in which we are expecting the Adelantado momentarily because all his armada and people have come to this port already. And he went to Santiago de Cuba and to Bayamo, which are two villages of this island, to place people there on garrison duty. And that he was coming here then.[127] And thus I believe that we will be going to Carlos around the beginning of Lent.[128]

48. Also I did the right thing in remaining here, because, since we have been here, eighteen Indians have come from the provinces of Florida, twelve of them from Carlos,[129] and six from the other cacique, who is called Tequesta, who also is near here.[130] They come here because of the reputation for the good treatment that the Adelantado gives them there and here, the people of this town. And it is certain that they do so, that they treat them very well and keep them entertained and they give them trinkets (*dijes*) that they are very pleased with. They all very willingly wish to become Christians. And thus they come every day to the church where I am, so that I may teach the Christian doctrine to them. I do it accordingly, and also by means of some interpreters (*lenguas*)[131] that they brought with them, people who know how to speak the Spanish language. I go along explaining the fundamentals of the Christian faith and what they are obliged to believe. They take it

well with a strong will. Nevertheless, despite all this, I shall not dare to baptize them so soon,[132] unless some emergency or danger of death should occur, until I shall be satisfied that they will not return to the vomit of their idolatries and until they know very well everything that the Christian is obliged to know. And some time will pass before this may be accomplished because of their being simple folk and of scant understanding.

49. Among those who have come from the Province of Carlos, one of his sisters[133] has come, whom they say he loves very much (*quiere mucho*) and another of his relatives,[134] to whom they say that the kingdom that Carlos has belonged by right.[135] And among those from Tequesta, a second son of the cacique[136] has come. There is another good sign that Carlos wants to become a Christian in that he sent to ask for some Spanish people to defend himself from another cacique[137] who makes war on him. May it please the Lord that those who are here will be the first fruits of the great conversion which is to follow in all of this Florida.

50. For this [purpose] let our dearest fathers and brothers ready themselves to come to labor in this vineyard of the Lord, drilling themselves now in many virtues and striving to acquire great readiness to suffer much for the love of the Lord because there are many opportunities for it here. I have taught them the prayers in Castilian, because I do not dare to translate them into their language because I do not put much trust in these who are the tongues or interpreters on account of their knowing little of the Castilian language because of their having been among the Indians since they were children,[138] and on account of their being not very intelligent, for they are a brown-skinned woman (*una morena*) and a mulatto. I have begun to formulate a vocabulary of the language of Carlos. I am planning to continue it there by means of a Spaniard, who they tell me is there, who knows both languages very well and is a capable man. . . . [139]

57. These soldiers who have been in Florida have told me some things that they say have taken place there, because of which the Indians have been moved to have reverence for the things of the Christian religion. I shall tell about two of them. The first one was that, while the Adelantado was going to visit a cacique[149] during a time when his maize fields were on the point of being lost for want of rain, the cacique said to him that, inasmuch as the God of the Christians was so powerful, would the Adelantado ask his God to

make it rain so that he would not lose his crops of maize. The Adelantado replied in a very Christian fashion that he was a great sinner; that he had offended his God, for the which [reason] he did not merit that he should hear him or grant him what he might ask for. But, despite all this, [he said] that he would ask for it and that if it did not rain it would be on account of his unworthiness. And so he knelt down there before a cross, he and all the people that he brought and they offered up a prayer and shortly thereafter, about half an hour, the Lord sent a very copious rain so that the land was thoroughly wetted and matters were remedied for the crops. The cacique was so edified by this that he had a cross placed there at once and he and all his people go there to venerate it.[150]

58. The other one was that a son of a cacique, who was called Guale, swore at and beat a young little Spaniard whom the Adelantado[151] had placed there so that he might learn the language. And to cause him greater grief, he said to him that he was going to remove a cross that was placed in a certain area,[152] and he did so and removed it. And the Spaniard said to him that he would beg the cacique of heaven to punish him for it. And it happened that within three days of his having said this to him, that son of the cacique died who had shown this disrespect for the cross. On seeing this, his father and his vassals restored the cross to where it was with great veneration and they maintain it there with great reverence. And they fear the Spaniards and they do not dare to make them angry. . . .

From Havana on the thirtieth of January of the year 1567.

By the hand of Rogel.[3] From the unworthy son of your Reverence and servant in the Lord.

†Juan Rogel

Zubillaga's Notes

117. Little islands that extend along the northern part of the island of Cuba.

123. In our *Monumenta* we speak more at length about this province and fort.

124. In the month of October of 1566 Pedro Menéndez sent Captain Francisco de Reinoso to the province of Calus with thirty soldiers and they built (*efforarent?*) a fort there, taught catechism to the natives, and investigated whether

---

3. These two words, *Manu Rogel,* are in Latin.

the Caloosahatchee River of that province flowed out of Lake Okeechobee (Zubillaga, *La Florida,* 260ff.).

125. Pedro Menéndez went twice to the province and town of Carlos, in the middle of February in 1566 and the month of June of the same year. The ruler, partly out of fear, partly out of a desire for Spanish help against the ruler of the Province of Tocobaga, gave tokens of friendship to the Spanish leader and made a promise of conversion (Zubillaga, *La Florida,* 251–261).

126. In the month of October 1566 Florida's leader sent Captain Reinoso to Calusa Province (note 124). And he promised likewise that he would go back there after three or four months (Zubillaga, *La Florida,* 261). Without doubt, he had thought of carrying the missionaries with him on such a journey as in fact happened (*op. cit.* 266).

127. Menéndez designated Captain Baltasar de Barreda so that with two hundred soldiers he might establish a strong fort for that port and town against French attacks. Soldiers arriving at the port of Havana in the month of January 1567, the Adelantado announced his proximate departure for Florida. He came to here finally from the port of Bayamo, journeying by land, going out to that place in the month of January and coming back in February (Ruidíaz, *La Florida,* I, 272–275).

128. The missionaries of the Society of Jesus departed from the port of Havana on the last day of February, with Fray Rogel being stationed in the Province of Calus and Brother Villarreal in Tequesta (Zubillaga, *La Florida,* 266–272, 296–302).

129. Captain Reinoso had scarcely arrived in Calusa Province with his [men] and at the very moment that they established themselves (note 124) they received some natives, as had Menéndez. They decided to send them to Havana. For why Menéndez wanted these natives for Havana or to know who they were, see doc. 39, note 32.

130. Concerning the arrival of these natives in Havana, see Zubillaga, *La Florida,* 294–296.

131. Some soldiers who stayed for a longer time in the village of Tequesta (see Zubillaga, *loc. cit.*) understood the language of the natives suitably, it is to be believed, which in fact was a language similar to or the same as Calusan (General Introduction Ia. 1 par. 2). Likewise, as Fray Rogel indicates below (paragraph 50, note 138), among the Spaniards who accompanied the natives one was *alterve* who had lived among the Indians still longer, had almost forgotten his own tongue.

132. Among the Calusa natives, Antonia, sister of the ruler, is known to have received baptism. Likewise according to [*iuxta?*] contemporary testimony she is believed to have been baptized twice (see Zubillaga, *La Florida,* 257ff.). Perhaps it was not done the first time with the solemn ceremonies for baptism.

133. Antonia (see Zubillaga, *La Florida, loc. cit.*).

134. He was called Philip [Felipe] by the Spaniards and distinguished by the

title of captain. Joined in matrimony to a sister of the ruler who in turn was married to a sister of Philip himself. He enjoyed such great authority among the Indians that he was considered to be a rival by the ruler, Carlos, who feared him (Ruidíaz, *La Florida,* I, 167, 278). Perhaps he came to Havana about the month of November 1566 with the natives who accompanied Antonia (note 29).

135. Concerning the right of Philip [Felipe] to the throne of Calus, see doc. 85, par. 40, 41).

136. Solís de Merás (Ruidíaz, *La Florida,* I, 281) claims that the Tequestan ruler sent a certain brother of his to Havana along with other natives (note 130). Perhaps both the brother and the son of the ruler were to be found among them. But it is more probable that both Rogel and Solís are talking about one and the same native. By then certainly, the missionary, who was communicating for a long time with these natives, *corundem* would be able to have more accurate reports.

137. The ruler of the Province of Tocobaga. As Menéndez reconciled these two rulers with one another, he established himself as a mediator (Zubillaga, *La Florida,* 265–271). Carlos sought aid from the Spanish soldiers so that he might vanquish his adversary. For this reason it should be evident to anyone that Carlos's desire to embrace the Catholic religion was not really sincere. The Spaniards were slowly made more certain of this matter afterward.

138. It was reported among the Spaniards that the ruler of the Province of Calus held many Christians captive among them, many of whom this cruel ruler offered to his gods each year in sacrifice. The principal objective of Menéndez' first journey to the Calusa Province in the month of February 1566 was to liberate these Christians. The Spaniards who accompanied Governor Menéndez, as they were approaching close to the coast of that province, found a certain Christian who had been living among the natives probably from the times when Hernando de Soto visited that province (1540). When Pedro Menéndez was returning to Havana after a few days, he brought seven Christians with him whom the ruler was detaining in addition to the sister of the ruler, Antonia, and other natives. (Ruidíaz, *La Florida,* I 149–168; Zubillaga, *La Florida,* 252–258). The interpreters whom Father Rogel mentioned could be from these former captives.

139. Perhaps he was also one of those who are mentioned as captive among the natives for many years (see the note above).

149. The ruler of the Province of Guale.

150. Solís de Merás tells of this exploit a little differently (see Ruidíaz, *La Florida,* I 211ff.). The Spaniards who made the exploration of the Rio San Mateo with Menéndez around July (1566) were also witnesses of similar exploits (see *op. cit.,* I 248ff.).

151. When Menéndez first visited the Province of Guale in the month of April (1566), he left fifteen young Spaniards there so that they might teach

Christian doctrine to the natives. After a short time one of them, Alonso Menéndez Marqués, nephew of the commander, was laid to rest dead. Returning again as the month of August (1566) was ending or September was beginning to the aforementioned province, he established a fort here with thirty soldiers (Zubillaga, *La Florida,* 358-360).

152. Menéndez erected a cross in the Province of Guale when he first visited it in the month of April (1566) (Zubillaga, *La Florida,* 254).

3. The Florida Missions, 1607-1611

The following is a translation of a piece which appears as Document 139 on pages 604-616 of Felix Zubillaga's *Monumenta Antiquae Floridae.* It is a summary history of the Jesuit experience in Spanish Florida from the time of the arrival of the first three members of the Society in 1566 to the definitive departure of the last of the Florida Jesuits for Mexico from Havana, where they had contemplated remaining for a brief period in the early 1570s.

In view of the outline of its contents provided by Zubillaga, an introduction per se is not needed for this document. Pertinent to the Calusa it presents an interesting account of the Calusa religious leaders' attempt to carry a procession of their mask-idols up onto the hill on which the Spanish fort was located. Rogel interpreted this move as an attempt by the natives to force them to acknowledge the natives' gods. The account presents a clear image of the arrangement of the hill on which the Spaniards built their fort vis-à-vis the little hill on which the natives had their houses and the intervening valley or plaza between the two elevated points, which the natives used for their ceremonies and processions.

As most of the details in Zubillaga's Latin preface to this piece are not pertinent for our topic, the preface is not presented here in translation. The following few notes contain its pertinent remarks. Rogel's report survived in a transcription of it made by Father Juan Sánchez in his *Historia Novae Hispaniae ab anno 1571 ad 1580.* Sánchez was a contemporary of the Florida Jesuits, having entered the Society in 1568 and having been ordained in Mexico in 1573. Rogel's report was not dated, but internal evidence points to the years 1607-1611 as the time of its composition. Rogel mentions clearly that he is writing during one of the two terms of Viceroy Luis de Velasco the younger. A statement by Alegre, in quoting from Rogel's report, indicates that the report was written over forty years after the killing of the Jesuits in Ajacán.

The system of endnotes (Zubillaga's notes) and footnotes (my notes) is the same as in the preceding two sections.

Report on the Florida Missions by Father Juan Rogel, Written Between the Years 1607 and 1611

Outline

1. First expedition of the missionaries to Florida; death of Father Martínez; Father Rogel and Brother Villarreal exercise the ministry at Havana. 2. Father Rogel, missionary to the province of Calus and Brother Villarreal to the Province of Tequesta; ministry of Father Rogel in the Province of Calus; house of the idols; idolatry; natives seek to kill Father Rogel. 3. Second expedition of missionaries to Florida; all the missionaries assemble in Havana. 4. Distribution of the missionaries between Havana and Florida. 5. The ruler of the Province of Calus; Governor Menéndez and the daughter (*filia*) (*sic*)[1] of the ruler of that province. 6. Marriage of the ruler with his sister; killing of the ruler. 7. Father Rogel, missionary to the Province of Santa Elena. 8. Luis, son of the ruler of Florida in Spain; expeditions of the missionaries to the Province of Ajacán with Luis; the missionaries abandoned by Luis; killing of the missionaries; Alphonso escapes unharmed; interment of the corpses. 9. Spaniards' expedition to the Province of Ajacán as the fate of the missionaries became more certain; two captured natives refuse to state the truth. 10. A new Spanish expedition in order to investigate the fate of the missionaries and punish the guilty ones; natives killed. Portent of the Crucified One (*Prodigium Crucifixi?*); the missionaries return to Havana. 11. Father Sedeño, at the order of Father Sánchez, provincial, comes to New Spain; brought back to Havana, he decided to leave that city with the missionaries.[2] 12. The missionaries also abandon Havana. 13. Fruit of the ministries of the missionaries with blacks in the city of Havana.

1. The first persons belonging to the Company of Jesus, who came to these West Indies, who went in the fleet of the year of 1566,

1. He seems to be talking of Carlos' sister whom Menéndez married.
2. My rendition of this clause is tentative. The Latin here is *Habanam redux illam urbem cum missionariis relinquere decernit.*

were three who came to Florida at the request of the *Adelantado,* Pedro Meléndez: the Fathers Pedro Martínez and Juan Rogel and Brother Francisco de Villarreal. And because of not having pilots that had been to it [Florida], they brought the directions that they were to follow in writing. Those [directions] were unreliable. Because of this, when they reached Florida in a Fleming supply ship, they spent the space of a month sailing along that coast in search of the port of St. Augustine[1] (where the adelantado Pedro Meléndez was) without being able to find it. And for this reason it seemed proper to Father Pedro Martínez to go on shore to search for it and to learn where it was from some Indians. And during this landing they killed him, because those Indians were then at war against the Spaniards. And the pilot of the supply ship, because of the threats that the Flemings made against him, was forced to head for Havana. There Father Juan Rogel and Brother Francisco engaged in our ministries until the Adelantado of Florida came, who was also Governor of Havana.[2]

2. And there they arranged for his departure for the Province of Carlos with him, where the Father remained in a fort of the Spaniards,[3] because Carlos and his principal vassals lived there. And he brought Brother Francisco de Villarreal to Tequesta to another Spanish fort.[4] At Carlos Father Juan Rogel busied himself in preaching, hearing the confessions of the Spaniards, and teaching the Indians through interpreters (that they were good ones, [drawn] from some Spaniards, who were stranded from a shipwreck that occurred in the Martyrs[5] and whom Carlos held as slaves).[6] While the said father was there, a notable thing happened. And it was that [there] was a temple of idols[7] there, which were some very ugly masks, which some Indians donned, delegated by it. And they went out into the village with them. And the wretches performed their worship and adored them, with the women singing certain canticles (*canticos*). And in order to lead them out of such great blindness, the father preached the truth to them about what was involved in that fraud. For this reason its authors conceived a great hate against him because he had revealed their secrets and profaned their religion. As a result, according to what was learned later, they sought to capture him outside of the fort and bring him to their temple and to sacrifice him there, giving his people to understand that, however much it might disturb us, they would make us adore their idols. And they even attempted to climb

up to our fort to hold a procession (*a dar el paseo*) with their masks, coming from a little hill (*zerrillo*), where they had their houses, to the hill (*zerro*) on which our fort was located. Between these hills there was a little valley (*vallecillo*) where they were accustomed to promenade in view of the people with the ceremony and abuses alluded to. And the women adored them and sang their praises, in the sight of whom they put their plan into execution one day. And thus these masked idols climbed up from the valley to the Spanish fort at a time when Father Juan Rogel was at its gate. The latter shouted at them, ordering them not to come up. But they, without paying any attention to him, persisted in climbing up. And then the father called to Captain Francisco de Reinoso so that he might block their attempt. And on going out with a half lance, he hit one of the ones out in front on the head with the butt end and knocked him down. The Indians, when they saw their idol injured in this fashion, became angry and rushed out of their houses with their clubs (*macanas*) and atlatls (*botadores*). But they did not dare to climb up to the fort because now the soldiers were at the ready, and thus the coming up of the idols ceased and there was no more mystery than this in that war. And one thing that is certain is that not fifty Indians came out to fight.[8]

3. When the death of Father Pedro Martínez in Florida was known in Spain, Father Portillo, who was in Seville, having been named as provincial of Peru (under whose obedience our Father General had placed those of Florida) sent Father Baptista de Segura as vice-provincial.[9] And with him came Father Antonio Sedeño, Father Alamo, Brother Domingo Augustín and Domingo Váez,[10] Brother Juan de la Carrera, Brother Pedro de Linares, and other young men who intended to join the Company so as to be received there. Among these were Brother Juan de Salcedo and Brother Pedro Ruiz de Salvatierra, and others whom I do not remember.[11] And in Florida a relative of the Adelantado joined them, who was called Gabriel de Solís.[11a] He, with the rest who had not yet been accepted, were received there. These disembarked in the port of St. Augustine. During that period Father Rogel was in Havana and went to St. Augustine and, picking up en route Brother Francisco de Villareal, who was in Tequesta, they were all housed in the church of San Juan, where there was lodging, although rather crowded.[12]

4. There an assembly and council was held to make the

assignments. And Havana fell to Father Juan Rogel and to accompany him they appointed Brother Villarreal and Brother Carrera, Juan de Salcedo and Pedro Ruiz in order to become masters of a school that the father vice-provincial established at the request of the Adelantado, in which the young sons of the caciques of Florida and the others of the Spaniards would be instructed and taught the faith and Christian customs. And Father Alamo was assigned to the Province of Carlos with a companion. And Father Sedeño was chosen as his companion so that he might go with him. And they came to make their residence in Guale[13] (after the rest had been assigned to other regions in order to learn the language). It assigned Brother Domingo Augustine to St. Augustine and later moved him to Guale. And he learned the language so well that the father vice-provincial decided to send him to preach to the Indians. And Our Lord took him to himself in Guale.[14]

5. In the meantime the Adelantado went to Spain[15] and before his departure don Phelipe, successor of the Cacique Carlos (whom the Spaniards of the fort killed at the urging of this don Phelipe), gave his word that on his return from Spain he would become a Christian;[16] that it seems that it was a punishment for what Carlos had done, which was to marry a sister of his with the Adelantado. Saying that he was married in Spain[17] did not suffice for him to be able to excuse himself. And he pressed him in such a way that the Adelantado, after consulting with his captains, made a pretense of marrying her, with one of them baptizing her and giving her the name doña Antonia. This one had been wife of her brother Carlos and was repudiated by him. The Adelantado did this because it seemed to his people that it was advisable to condescend to and to please that Indian at whose insistence his captains influenced him to receive doña Antonia, who always remained in the Spanish fort dressed in the Spanish manner. And later after the passage of some years, she died in Havana, Father Juan Rogel having heard her confession during that illness, which greatly consoled her, although he was not present at her death because of having left for Florida prior to it.[3] And later the Adelantado assured this priest that he

3. To some degree this seems to contradict document 85, in which Rogel noted that prior to the killing of Carlos, when he and his people had withdrawn from the village near the fort, Antonia also had left the fort to be with her people. The Spanish text that I rendered as "greatly consoled her" could as easily be rendered as "greatly consoled him."

never knew her, not even on the very night of the nuptials.

6. While the Adelantado was in Spain, Father Rogel had an encounter with the cacique, don Phelipe, alluded to already over his wanting to marry a sister of his, as he did marry her.[18] For then it seemed that he had a hold on him, because, as the father had him as a catachumen, he sent word to him that he should consider carefully what he was doing, for, when the Adelantado should come, whom he was expecting shortly, he was to be baptized, [and] it was a thing very much prohibited in the law of God to marry one's sister. And, consequently, on his part, he urged him strongly not to do it. He replied to him that it was a custom of the caciques to marry their sisters; that when he became a Christian, he would leave her. Later, with the passage of time, while Father Alamo was residing there, this cacique tried to kill the Spaniards who were in the fort. And when the Adelantado had learned of this, he sent his nephew Pedro Meléndez Marqués to the province of Carlos with an order to kill don Phelipe; and he did so.[19]

7. The father vice-provincial ordered Father Rogel, who was then in Havana, to go to the fort of Santa Elena and that he should reside in a village of Indians that was four leagues from there that was called Orista in order to learn that language and that on the Sundays and feast days he should go to Santa Elena to preach to and hear the confessions of those at the fort and of the settlers whom the Adelantado had brought; that they established a settlement and he brought his wife and all his household there.[20]

8. And he returned to Spain,[21] where he ran into a Christian Indian native to Florida,[22] [4] whom some Dominican friars,[23] while they were passing by it, carried with them to Mexico, and there he received baptism, with don Luis de Velasco, father of the one who is viceroy now,[24] serving as his godfather. And consequently the Indian was named don Luis, son of a little cacique (*caciquillo*) from Florida. The Adelantado brought him from Spain and he (don Luis) was very cunning (*muy ladino*)[5] and he handed him over to Father Baptista in Havana as he was proclaiming that he was the son of a great cacique, and as such, our king in Spain ordered that he be given an allowance and he clothed him. And he knew so much that

4. In the wide sense of sixteenth-century Spanish Florida, as don Luis was from Virginia.

5. This could be rendered also as "very hispanicized," but "cunning" or "crafty" seems to be called for here.

he went to confession and received communion.[6] And thus it seemed appropriate that the father vice-provincial should carry him with him as interpreter. And he believed that [in him] he was carrying along a helper such as St. Paul had in Timothy,[25] and taking the matter so much to heart that he would not hear of anything else. And when the matter was discussed in Santa Elena, where Father Rogel was and where Father Sedeño[26] found himself, he never wished to submit to discussion, who was to go with don Luis. And even though both offered themselves for it, as persons experienced in that land, he would not accept either one of them even as a companion, but rather decided to bring along with him Father Quirós and Brother Gabriel Gómez, recently arrived from Spain, and Brother Sancho de Çavallos, who also was inexperienced, and Brothers Juan Baptista, Pedro de Linares, Christóval Redondo, Gabriel de Solís, and other young men who were seeking admittance to the Company.[27] All these went with don Luis for the conversion of that land of Florida and on entering into the Province of Ajacán, don Luis soon went astray and abandoned the priests, devoting himself to women, with the fathers and brothers remaining alone; because on the very day that they reached the port the father vice-provincial gave orders to the pilot[28] that, as soon as they had unloaded what they brought, he should depart from the port and return to Havana. And consequently he did so, which was the cause of their death; because if they had tarried there with the boat for some days, from the experience that they gained in the first days from the poor disposition that they encountered and the scant fruit that was promised, they would have returned to Santa Elena to wait for a better opportunity. But on seeing themselves with no other recourse and cut off thus, they built a little house in which to shelter themselves and to say Mass, remaining alone, without any help, suffering very great hunger and discomforts. As a result, in order to sustain themselves, they went some leagues to the woods (*montes*) in search of persimmons (*nísperos*) and they sustained themselves in this fashion for six or seven months. When don Luis withdrew from them, he went to a little settlement which was [that] of a relative of his, about ten leagues from where the fathers made their residence. And Father Baptista, as he desired to begin to treat of the conversion, and don

6. Full participation in Catholic rites was sometimes withheld for some time for such recent converts to test the sincerity and depth of their conversion.

Luis did not come, and as they had no other guide or means for doing so, sent Father Quirós to where he was to beg him to come. And as the miserable fellow had become completely depraved, he replied to Father Quirós to go, that he would soon come after him. And at night he kept his word, because, bringing people with him, he killed him before he reached the spot where Father Baptista was. And from there the Indian went to where ours were and he found the vice-provincial in bed, indisposed and in prayer; that it seems that Our Lord was preparing them for that critical moment, because on the vespers of the Purification of Our Lady[7] they all made a general confession and received communion with great feeling; that this was learned from a boy, son of one of the residents of Santa Elena whom the father vice-provincial had brought with him so that he might help at Mass, who was named Alonso. And the Indians did not kill him because of his tender age or because God ordered it so. This one gave a report about the incident and said that upon the arrival of don Luis with his people armed with war clubs (*macanas*) and atlatls (*botadores*) (which are some long sticks [*palos largos*] fashioned like the haft of a spear [*a manera de hastas de lança*]), he greeted Father Baptista, who was [ill] as we have noted, and that his raising of the war club and his greeting of him was all one gesture, in such a fashion that in giving him greetings, he took his life. And they killed all the rest. And, going out in search of Brother Sancho de Çavallos, who at that period had gone to the wood (*monte*) for firewood, they killed him in it. And consequently only little Alonso (Alonsico) escaped. It should be noted about him that he had a strong desire to die together with the Fathers. And a brother of don Luis prevented it, who concealed and hid him in a house, coming out to seek protection for him when they had killed the fathers. And later, when they had calmed down, don Luis called Alonsico over and told him to teach the Indians how they were to bury the bodies of the fathers as Christians were accustomed to. And thus they dug a grave in the chapel where they said Mass and they buried them in it.

9. The manner by which the death of the father vice-provincial and his companions was learned with certainty was because of his having left Father Juan Rogel, who remained in Santa Elena, charged with the responsibility, before his departure, of coming to

7. This feast is celebrated on February 2.

Havana after some days to ask the governor and officials to send them some provisions.[29] And the father set out [from Santa Elena] for that [purpose] and did what it was possible for [him to do], but because of there not being more than one pilot who knew that port of Ajacán where the fathers were and because they had this fellow employed in other matters, this provisioning could not be carried out until a year and a half had passed. And then Brother Salcedo was dispatched with this pilot (named Vicente Gonçález), who carried as many provisions as Father Juan Rogel was able to assemble.[30] On arriving to anchor in the port, fearful of some disaster, they did not want to go on shore until someone from the company should come or they should have news of them. Don Luisillo, according to what they learned afterwards, desired strongly for them to disembark so that he might capture them and kill them. And on seeing how they were delaying and waiting until they should see some of the fathers, the Indians used this trick, which was to take the clothing from the deceased and dress themselves with it and walk along the beach. And the rest shouted that the fathers were there; that they should come on. But with their suspicion growing stronger, they refused to go on shore. With matters at this [impasse], they came to the ship's boat. These they captured and weighing anchor, they set sail and turned back toward Havana with them, but as they were entering the Bahama Channel, as they saw the land very close, one of them threw himself into the water and nothing more was heard of him. And they brought the other one to Havana imprisoned and they held him in order to return later with him to find out for certain what happened (that they did not confess to it when they were captured in the ship) nor did the one who was left wish to reveal the truth.

10. Having seen that the fate of the fathers was not known for certain and as the Adelantado was making a voyage to Spain then, it seemed appropriate to him to pass through Florida and to bring in his company Father Rogel and Brother Carrera and Brother Francisco de Villarreal. On arriving at the port, the Adelantado went ashore with an accompaniment of soldiers with a strong desire of learning of their fate and punishing the guilty ones. And after having captured some Indians from those who had helped don Luis and made himself aware of the case, he sought to impose punishment on eight or ten. These were catechized and baptized by Father Rogel by means of Alonsico, who served as interpreter, and

they hung them on the vessel on which the Adelantado was traveling, hanging them from the lateen yards (*las entenas*). With this justice done, Father Rogel begged the Adelantado to give him a guard of soldiers so that he might go in to where the burial of the fathers was in order to bring back their bodies and recover their vestments. However, as the Adelantado was on the point of departure and winter was beginning, they were not able to tarry and this desire was not followed through on, but he promised that he would return within a year and that he would go for them.[31] And on this occasion they learned of a miracle that happened with the ornaments belonging to the fathers when they killed them. And it was that an Indian, with greed for the booty, went to a box in which the fathers kept the ornaments for saying Mass and within the box there was an image of Christ (*un Christo de bulto*); and wishing to open it or break it in order to pull out what was within, the Indian fell dead there. And at once another one sought to force it open and the same thing happened to him. And another one, who, without taking any notice of those two unfortunate ones, sought to try the same thing as they had, accompanied them in death. After that they no longer dared approach the box, but rather it is maintained until the present with great veneration. Alonsico recounted this incident and later some old soldiers who came from Florida and who had been in Ajacán told Father Rogel that the Indians had maintained the box under guard without daring to touch it until now.[32] On seeing that there was nothing else to be done, Father Juan Rogel and Brothers Villareal and Carrera returned to Havana, where they met Father Sedeño.

11. With the arrival of the Adelantado from Spain[33] the death of the fathers, of which there was now news through letters, was learned with certainty. And after considering the scant fruit that was expected from that land, Father Pedro Sánchez, elected provincial of New Spain, wrote to Father Sedeño, who was in Havana, that he should come to Mexico to take a house for himself and his companions.[34] The latter soon made his voyage and he lodged them in the Hospital of Our Lady. Within a few days Father Pedro Sánchez sent Father Sedeño back to Havana not only so that he might visit those belonging to the company who had remained there but also in order to see whether it would be possible to establish some house. However, as the assignments from the company that had been made in Havana were principally for

assembling Indians from Florida, and as this came to an end, it did not seem appropriate to Father Sedeño to found an establishment of the company there.[35]

12. During this time, as those of Havana realized the great benefit that they had in having the company there, they wrote to His Majesty so that he might order that Father Sedeño not depart from there.[36] The latter wrote that, if His Majesty were to order that the company should remain there to exercise its ministries, he should be aware that that land was very short of resources for them to live from alms and, consequently, that they would not be able to support themselves if His Majesty did not order that it be assisted with the ordinary support from the royal coffer.[37] His Majesty did not reply to this at that time and, consequently, Father Sedeño sent Father Rogel and Brother Estevan Gómez[38] and another one[39] to Mexico to give the father provincial an account of what was happening. And in the meantime Father Sedeño received letters from His Majesty in which he ordered that the company should not abandon its work in Havana.[40] On account of this he wrote to Mexico again so that Father Rogel might come in order to fulfill that which His Majesty was ordering. The father provincial complied with this and, consequently, he returned.[41] However, on seeing that they did not respond on the matter of support and that they were not assisting in it and that instead the needs and the problems were growing day by day, with an order from the said father provincial, Father Sedeño decided to come to Mexico with all his people. And a house which they left behind was handed over to one of the residents with the responsibility that he would have to give rooms and lodging to those belonging to the company who should pass through there.

13. The special [ministry] to which they dedicated themselves in Havana was the ceaseless teaching of the gospel, sermons, and discussions [that produced] many results. However, what was most particularly edifying was the work that they did with more than fifty newly imported blacks that his Majesty bought there.[42] Because of doubting whether they were Christians,[8] after

8. That is, in the minimal sense of having been baptized before being shipped from Africa. Among the Portuguese, who were the major suppliers at this time, it was common practice to baptize such slaves without any instruction before shipping them out in view of the high death toll among such slaves during the passage to the New World.

consulting with the bishop, the doctor don Joan de Castilla,[43] they were baptized conditionally after having been very well instructed. And they were such good Christians that, while going about working on the project of the fortress, they went along saying their rosaries. And as they had been so unacculturated (*tan boçales*) some friars made fun of them, thinking that it was a ceremony of the blacks, not knowing of their strong devotion and Christianity. And those who examined them out of curiosity found them to be so well instructed that they were astonished and edified. And some who married conducted themselves with great edification and Christian spirit, with Father Sedeño employing as an artifice with the king's female black slaves during the time that the project lasted that at night he would shut them up in a separate house in order to avoid problems. And the black males and them [the women] bore it with great contentment because, as he preached to them each afternoon after work and instructed them in the catechism, they dealt with and developed a taste for matters of virtue. That this was the fruit that Our Lord drew from that difficult mission in addition to the many labors and deprivations with which he prepared our [men] for so fortunate a death.[9] We have hope in the divine goodness that that land with such great and highly populated provinces will produce fruit some day from so precious a watering.[10]

Zubillaga's Notes

1. According to the testimony of Father Rogel himself, the mariners wanted to find the port of Santa Helena (document 41, paragraph 15).

2. Those which are told about in passing in this paragraph, you will find fully described in document 41.

3. See document 85.

4. See document 74.

5. The subject of conversation is about the islands of the Martyrs.

6. See document 41, note 138; document 85, note 3.

7. This temple of idols was similar, as is evident, to the house of prayer and of the gods about which there is a discussion in Solís de Merás (Ruidíaz, *La Florida* I 286; see document 85, note 17). As we know nothing about the tem-

---

9. In the sense of achieving the crown of martyrdom.

10. A reference to the belief that the blood of martyrs often causes the flowering of the seed sown by those who follow them in that work.

ples of the idols of the province of Calus, this description by Father Rogel is of great worth.

8. This deed described by the Father was the cause, at least in part, of the hostile feeling between the Spaniards and the natives of Calus and led likewise to the termination of the Spanish fort and mission. The killing of the ruler Carlos and of Philip [Felipe], which followed from this exploit (see document 85, 107) is seen to have been the result of this hostile spirit.

9. The missionaries for Florida were not designated by Father Portillo but by the Father General.

10. Brother Domingo and Augustín Váez are actually one and the same.

11. All seven or eight were youths (document 93, paragraph 2, note 7). To these whom the father enumerates are to be added Juan Baptista Menéndez and Christóforo Redondo, who were killed by the natives in the province of Ajacán (see document 125, note 28).

11a. This one was killed also by the natives in the province of Ajacán.

12. See all of this fully described in documents 91, 93.

13. Concerning all of these, see *ibid.*

14. See document 108.

15. At the beginning of the year 1569.

16. See document 99.

17. Concerning this union of Pedro Menéndez with Antonia, sister of the ruler, see Solís de Merás (Ruidíaz, *La Florida,* I, 165ff; Zubillaga, *La Florida,* 257).

18. See document 85 where the father speaks fully about all this.

19. See document 107.

20. The discussion of all of these things is in documents 104, 125.

21. When Menéndez left Florida almost into the month of June of the year 1570, he reached Spain in the month of August (document 21, note 2).

22. Luis then was living at Havana, whence he accompanied the missionaries to the Province of Santa Helena, thence indeed to the Province of Ajacán (see Zubillaga, *La Florida,* 394-396; document 138, note 53).

23. See Zubillaga, *op. cit.* 394.

24. The father was viceroy of New Spain in the years 1550-1564; the son, who was called by the same name, [held] the post twice, in the years 1590-1595 [and] 1605-1611. Father Rogel seems to allude to the second period (see the preface).

25. Timothy was called "my helper" and "my dearest son" by St. Paul (Romans XVI, 21; 1 Cor. IV, 17).

26. See document 125, note 30.

27. The principal documents that treat about the mission of Ajacán province are 125, 135, 137, 138 (see preface).

28. Vicente González (see document 138, paragraph 27).

29. This pressing order applied more to Father Rogel so that the yearly pro-

vision ship might be sent to the Province of Ajacán. [My rendition of this note is tentative.] (See document 130.)

30. See document 137, paragraph 49–50.

31. This journey to carry this out was not ordered.

32. See the preface.

33. Pedro Menéndez came to Spain from the punishment inflicted on the natives of the Province of Ajacán (document 135).

34. A letter not found as yet (see document 128i).

35. See appendix 1.

36. This is seen to be signaled in the letter of Francisco Briceño of December 12, 1572, given to Philip II (see appendix 1).

37. A letter not found as yet, which does not pertain to the Florida mission.

38. Born on the Island of Tenerife in the Canaries, about the year 1564, entered the Society in Mexico on the 19th day of February of the year 1578, took simple vows in the year 1580 and perpetual ones in the month of June of the year 1592 (*Mex.* 4ff., 14, 36, 45 back, 67 back, 73 back, 121, 158, 174 back, 200 back, 244, 270). Much is said about him in *Monumentis Mexicanis*.

39. Brother Francisco Villarreal as is evident.

40. A letter not found as yet.

41. See appendix 1.

42. See document 129.

43. Juan del Castillo (document 137, note 55).

4. Two Letters of Pedro Menéndez de Avilés, October 20, 1566

The following two pieces contain excerpts from letters to the king written by Pedro Menéndez de Avilés on October 20, 1566. Menéndez de Avilés began the first of these letters noting that he last wrote to the king on September 19, 1566, and that he intended to cover developments that he had learned of since that date. A major purpose of the letter is his report of mutinies among his soldiers at Santa Elena and San Mateo. The excerpt of this letter presented here begins with Menéndez de Avilés' account of an aftermath of the San Mateo mutiny, which involved over 100 soldiers. After the mutiny the soldiers set out for Havana on a galliot that had been taken from the French. When the mutineers stopped at Tequesta for water, some of the men were stranded there. The excerpt details their experience and presents comments by Menéndez de Avilés on his securing the release of Hernando de Escalante Fontaneda and other Spaniards held captive by the Calusa. The excerpts from the second letter present details on Menéndez de Avilés' exploratory voyage up the St. Johns River and his comments on the Tequesta and Calusa.

Transcription of the script presented some difficulties because the letters are written in a very small hand and the ink has faded in places. A more serious problem is the clipping off of a small portion of the right-hand side of the pages in the process of photoreproduction. Where such excisions created problems is indicated in the text and accompanying notes.

Pedro Menéndez de Avilés to the King, October 20, 1566
AGI, Seville, Santo Domingo 115. Stetson Collection of the P.K. Yonge Library of Florida History.

In the vicinity of the Martyrs the land [clipped off] of this Florida, the frigate stopped in a port to take on water and many Indians came on board [word clipped off] and twenty soldiers went on shore without any arms in order not to irritate the Indians. And [word clipped off] that in the meantime the frigate was forced to make sail and the twenty soldiers remained there.[1] [word clipped off] believed that the Indians killed them soon thereafter. And it was because the people of the place are very warlike and they have [killed?][2] many Christians).[3] While one of my brigs was going to Havana, it entered that port and found twelve of [those soldiers][4] and picked them up and brought them to Havana. They say that the Indians showed them great friendship and [good?][5] treatment and that the other soldiers are all well; that no one died because, although [word clipped off] Carlos that chief my friend and one hundred leagues[6]

1. The last letter of what I presume is *allá* was clipped off, along with the initial letters of the word following it.

2. Only the *mu* of *muerto* appears here.

3. At this point there is a closing parentheses sign. Presumably the opening one disappeared in one of the excisions.

4. The clipping here removed the underlined letters from the words *destos soldados*.

5. This word was clipped off. I presume that it was "good."

6. The interruption of the flow of thought makes it difficult to ascertain what he meant to say here. The sense is possibly "although Carlos, the chief, who is my friend, is one hundred leagues away." Elsewhere the distance between Calus and Tequesta was given as forty leagues.

these Indians are his friends and they know of the cross [that]⁷ I
gave them and that he adores it. And all these Indians have a red
one at their throat. And they wanted and [word clipped off: have?
there?]⁸ a big one on which they have adored and that they have
been abandoning their idolatries. I dispatched [word clipped off]⁹
there with a letter for the said soldiers who remained there that if
[undecipherable word]¹⁰ and played [the role of?] religious in seeking
to teach the Christian doctrine to the Indians with care and to learn
the language well and two [word or words clipped off]¹¹ the land and
the trails well. And that they should seek diligently to maintain
friendship with those Indians and that within [word clipped off]
years I would take them out of there and intercede for them that
Your Majesty might pardon them for their treason that they
committed in mutinying¹² at San Mateo and in leaving the fort
deserted. And he sent a present to the chief and I ordered¹³ that
[this?]¹⁴ brig should go to Carlos from there with a letter to him
from me. And I sent twelve soldiers there, [six?]¹⁵ of them farmers¹⁶
and the other six nobles, the best people that I have found and chief
among them Francisco de Reynoso, who has been a man of arms,¹⁷
so that they might seek [word clipped off] to preserve the friendship
of this chief and teach them the catechism until [word clipped off,

7. The word was clipped off here. "That" fits the context.
8. The word that I have surmised was "there" is difficult to decipher. The
clipped-off word preceding it is possibly "they have." The Spanish here is "y
todos estos yndios Hayan una colorada al pescuezo y queria y que ti _____ al-
lá(?) grande." The script of *allá* is difficult to decipher and could well be *otra* or
"other" rather than *allá*.
9. The Spanish here is "Yo despacho dias unbero _____ alli."
10. The Spanish here seems to be "que se es tenguedos y hagan el _____ de
religiosos." The undecipherable word is possibly "if they stayed on."
11. The missing word or words are possibly "reconnoiter" in view of the
context.
12. The last letters of this word were excised thus, "amotin__."
13. The Spanish here was abbreviated *mᵈᵉ*.
14. The word was clipped off here but the context seems to call for "this."
15. The word was clipped off here, but the context calls for "six."
16. The Spanish here is *labrador*. Most commonly it means "farmer," "plough-
man," "industrious," etc, but in this context it might well be rendered as
"commoner" or "peon" as contrasted with "gentleman."
17. As the script was not very clear here, my rendition of this word as
"arms" is tentative.

followed by two undecipherable words] to cultivate the land. And he
sent the heir of Carlos himself, whom I am bringing along with me
[word clipped off] a very good Indian because on the death[18] of an
Indian that he brought as a servant and he took [it] not without
[word clipped off][19] [and] said that he would strive very hard so that
the caciques of that land would all be my friends. And he sent two
Christians along with him, whom Carlos gave to me, so that he
might do it better, whom it appears [word clipped off][20] they have
had for [almost] twenty years [and] who, in order to thank me for
what I have done for them in bringing them out [word clipped off][21]
a strong desire to help in this. One of them [was very good
looking][22] of noble parents, the son of the late Garcia Descalante, a
Conquistador of Cartagena and he is called Hernando Descalante,
one of two brothers, boys of 10 years of age: they were being sent to
Salamanca when their ship was lost. The people aboard escaped,
but over the years the father of this [chief] Carlos had killed 42 of
the captives already, among whom was the elder brother [of this
Escalante].[23] Among them there was a [two undecipherable words]
five and five women, all of them mestizas [word clipped off][24] and
one black female.[25] Among those Carlos [gave?][26] me, two men chose
not to come and remained there.[27]

18. Because of the difficulty of the script my rendition of this word is tentative.

19. The initial letters of the word were *emis.*

20. The word clipped off here was, I believe, the word "almost," which I
have inserted further on in this sentence.

21. The letters *ban* survived from this mutilated word. I suspect the word
was *mostraban* or "they showed."

22. At this point much of the script that I used became difficult to decipher
because of the combination of the clipping of words combined with the right-
hand side of the photoreproduction being out of focus. As this passage is reproduced by Lyon (1983: 148), I have filled in the gaps of the portion in brackets by
using the part of the passage quoted by Lyon. The words "very good looking"
are taken from Lyon. I had rendered them tentatively as "of very good character."

23. "Of this Escalante" is rendered by Lyon as "his."

24. The first three letters of the word clipped off were *des.*

25. My rendition of these last two words is tentative.

26. The word was clipped off here, but the context suggests that the missing word probably was "gave."

27. The letter continues on beyond this point, but the rest of its contents

Pedro Menéndez de Avilés to the King, October 20, 1566

AGI, Seville, Santo Domingo 115. Stetson Collection of the P.K. Yonge Library of Florida History.

With the pilot Domingo Fernándes, whom I dispatched to Your Majesty with the report of the arrival of the assistance that Your Majesty sent to these provinces. . . . And the Indians from these regions came out. I strengthened my friendship with them and reconfirmed it and had some Christians spread among them in pairs by the chiefs so that they might learn the language and acquaint them with the catechism so that all of them might forsake their idols. . . .[28]

I ascended fifty leagues by this river [the St. Johns], more rather than less. . . . And this river has two fathoms of water at its shallowest point and is very navigable. And on arriving at a [village?][29] that is called Mayacuya,[30] I found the river narrow, but with very good depth and blocked by huge logs to prevent my going on ahead. And from there I sent[31] guides ahead along the river. And we received news that there was a lake about which I had great reports that it has a circumference of more than thirty leagues; that it is very deep, and that the water that falls from the land is collected there. And as it is flat land, it is like a sea. And this River of San Mateo [the St. Johns] flows from it and another River descends to Carlos, the Sa[32] to which my friend [went?], who was within twenty leagues of there. And that this lake empties out into the sea by way of two other ports, which means that one of them is Tequesta, that good port, that I wrote to Your Majesty about; that it was close to the Martyrs and that it was suspected that there were Frenchmen there, newly come and settled. And I had a very strong

---

are not pertinent to the Indians of south Florida. The death of Father Martínez at the hands of the Mocama is one of the items that he discusses.

28. It is not clear what Indians Menéndez de Avilés is talking about in the above passage. Further on in this letter he tells about his trip up the St. Johns River.

29. I did not decipher the word here, but the context suggests "village."

30. This could be a corruption of the Mayaca, the Mayajuaca of Escalante Fontaneda, the Mayarca, or the Mathiaqua of the French.

31. My rendition here is tentative.

32. My rendition of both "descends" and "the Sa" are tentative.

desire to reach this lake and to learn thereby whether the French were in Tequesta. But I was discouraged from this. And even though it was no more than twenty leagues to this lake, because they told me[33] that the river was narrow though deep and that the people were many and very warlike and all friends of Saturiva and enemies [of][34] Carlos and [with the prospect] of leaving enemies in my rear, I did not dare go forward, because the two sloops did not carry more than fifty soldiers and all harquebusiers. . . . I regret very much that I did not complete the exploration of this river [all the way to the sea of New Spain][35] where it comes out at the land of Carlos at twenty-seven degrees and to learn the secret of Tequesta, as I had a great desire to establish friendship with the cacique of Tequesta. I [carried][36] one of his daughters with me, a girl of about nine or ten years of age and whom the [Indians][37] of Carlos intended to kill as they are his enemies. I ransomed her and now I am sending this little girl to the Countess of Ni____[38] so that she may live there for three or four years and then I shall bring her back to her land so that she may tell them and her parents about it and that they [the Indians] live like animals and by here [undecipherable word] more [word clipped off] to be Christians and to the obedience of [Your Majesty].

The upper right-hand side of the next page is unreadable because of the photoreproduction seemingly being out of focus. And from the point where the text becomes readable again there is nothing else pertinent to the Calusa.

5. Flour, Biscuit, Wine, and Meat, 1566-1567

The following translation of a list of provisions sent to south Florida in 1566 and 1567 was made in 1978 for the Granada Project from a less-than-perfect photocopy of the document furnished to me when I

33. My rendition of this is tentative.

34. From this point on in this manuscript a small part of the right side of the page has been cut off in the process of photoreproduction.

35. My rendition of all the words within these brackets is tentative.

36. About one-half of the letters of this word were excised.

37. About one-half of the word was excised.

38. About one-half of the name was excised.

undertook that work. The photocopy was made from a document in the Archive of the Indies, Contaduria 1, 174. For the present Southwest Florida Project, Victoria Stapells-Johnson provided Dr. Marquardt with a microfilm copy of a document that was also from Contaduria 1, 174, which contains the same information as does the translation below relative to the provisions delivered but in a somewhat different format than that of the 1978 photocopy. I no longer have the 1978 photocopy of the Spanish text to compare the two copies directly, but my 1978 translation and the notes it bears indicate that the Stapells-Johnson microfilm copy of this document omitted the initial pages that I translated in 1978.

In the microfilm copy the first listing of provisions sent to Carlos appears on page 34 of the document. The first few pages consist of introductory documents and the remainder down through the first few lines at the top of page 34 list provisions sent to St. Augustine, San Mateo, and Santa Elena. The first and subsequent listings for Carlos follow without any break or special heading and are interspersed with several more listings of provisions sent to St. Augustine and Santa Elena. In the microfilm copy the words *por(?) cargo del contador J^{u} menendez marques* follow immediately the opening phrase in which the date of the delivery is given. The signature of Juan Menéndez Marqués appears at the end of all these listings. My 1978 translations give no indication that Menéndez Marqués' name appeared anywhere in the copy from which they were made.

In the 1978 photocopy of this Contaduria document the following heading note appeared in the margin on the top left-hand side of the page and the first several letters of the first word of this heading were clipped off in the process of copying the page. Consequently, I was unable to decipher this first incompletely reproduced word. The following is that heading: "_____acta of the provinces [of] Florida in the [ports] of Carlos and Tequesta and Tocobaga of flour, wine, biscuit, and meat [in][1] the year of 1566 to 7." At the top of the right-hand side of the page the photocopy also bore the heading note: "Flour, biscuit, wine, meat." Neither of those heading notes appears in the Stapells-Johnson microfilm version of this document. The name "Carlos" appears in the left-hand margin where the entry begins and the words "flour, biscuit, wine, meat" appear below one another respectively in the left-hand

---

1. The words "of" and "in" were clipped off by the copier. *Puertos* lost its first two letters.

margin, and this was done in the margins of every page containing such a listing.

The photocopied pages contained a second series of listings of provisions delivered that began on page 116 of the copied pages. This second listing represents the obverse of the first one in the sense that it repeats the same statistics as presented from the receiving end in contrast to the first set, which emanated from the sender. The listings presented on the Stapells-Johnson microfilm appear to correspond to this second series in the photocopied pages.

A Listing of Provisions Sent to the Forts at Carlos, Tequesta, and Tocobaga, 1566–1567

AGI, Seville, Contaduria 1, 174.

On the tenth of December of the year fifteen hundred and sixty-six Alonso de Candamo, master of the ship named *Nuestra Señora del Rosario,* delivered to Blas Alvarez, keeper of provisions of the said fort of Carlos and houses of Tequesta and Tocobaga, seventeen barrels of flour and ten barrels of wine and one hundred arrobas of meat and eighty quintales of biscuit as is evident from the letters of receipt from the said keeper of provisions.

At the end of April of the year fifteen hundred and sixty-seven Vicente, Master of the advice-boat named *Santa Cruz,* delivered in the said fort of Carlos to Blas Alvarez, keeper of provisions of the said fort, eleven barrels of wine and one hundred and fifty bottles, *peruleras,* of wine and two hundred *fanegas* of maize and one hundred quintales of biscuit and twenty-five arrobas[2] of oil and one barrel of vinegar, as is evident from the letter of receipt of the said keeper of provisions.

At the end of February of the said year of fifteen hundred and sixty-seven Nuño Barbudo, Master of the advice-boat named *El Espiritu Santo,* delivered at the said fort of Carlos to Blas Alvarez, keeper of provisions of the said fort, one hundred bottles of wine and three hundred *fanegas* of maize and fifty arrobas of oil and seventy-five quintales of biscuit, as appears in the letter of receipt signed by the said Blas Alvares.

On the fifteenth day of the month of August of the said year of

---

2. A *fanega* is about 1.5 bushels, an arroba about twenty-five pounds, and a quintal is a hundred-weight. A *perulera* is an earthenware jug.

sixty-seven Alonso de Candamo, Master of the ship named *Nuestra Señora del Rosario,* delivered to the said Blas Albarez, keeper of provisions of the said fort of Carlos, two hundred *colginatas,*[3] three hundred arrobas of meat and six barrels of wine and one barrel of vinegar and twenty-five arrobas of oil according as it appears from the letter of receipt signed by the said Blas Alvarez.

On the first day of the month of January of the year fifteen hundred and sixty-eight Nuño Barbudo, Master of the frigate named *El Espiritu Santo,* delivered in the said fort of Carlos to the said Blas Albarez, keeper of the provisions of the said fort, two hundred *fanegas* of maize and six barrels of wine and three hundred arrobas of meat and ten barrels of flour and one hundred quintales of biscuit and one barrel of vinegar as is evident from the letter of receipt signed by the said keeper of provisions.

On the fifteenth day of the month of June of the year fifteen hundred and sixty-eight Albaro Pérez, Master of the sloop named *Santa Ysabel,* delivered to the said Blas Alvarez, keeper of provisions of the said fort of Carlos, two hundred boxes of manioc-cake and one hundred quintales of biscuit and three hundred arrobas of meat and ten barrels of wine and twenty arrobas of oil as is evident from the letter of receipt signed by the said keeper of provisions.

On the third day of the month of November of the said year of sixty-eight Alonso de Candamo, Master of the advice-boat named *N^a Señora del Rosario,* delivered to the said Blas Alvarez, keeper of provisions of the said fort of Carlos, two hundred *fanegas* of maize and one hundred hens, thirty goats, two arrobas of wax and six bottles of honey as is evident from the letter of receipt signed by the said keeper of provisions.

On the thirtieth day of the month of September of the year fifteen hundred and sixty-nine Pedro de la Cerra, Master of the frigate named *San Felipe,* delivered to the said Blas Albarez, keeper of provisions of the said fort of Carlos, one hundred and forty-five quintales of biscuit and three barrels of flour and two hundred arrobas of meat and eight barrels of wine and thirty arrobas of oil and one hundred *colginatas,* two barrels of vinegar according as appears from the letter of receipt from the said keeper of provisions signed with his name.

3. I have not found this word in modern Spanish, but its root of *colgar* (to hang) suggests that they are ropes of onions or garlic.

On the first of the month of April of the year fifteen hundred and seventy Nuño Barbudo, Master of the boat named *Santa Cruz,* delivered to the said Blas Alvarez, keeper of provisions of the said fort of Carlos, fifty *fanegas* of maize, three hundred arrobas of meat and six barrels of wine, fifty perunleras bie＿＿ of wine as is evident and as appears from the letters of receipt of the said keeper of provisions signed with his name.

On the first day of the month of June of the said year of seventy Alonso de Candamo, Master of the boat named *El Espiritu Santo,* delivered to the said Blas Alvarez, keeper of provisions of the said fort of Carlos, fifty loads (*cargas*) of manioc-cake and fifty *fanegas* of maize, according as appears from the letter of receipt signed by the keeper of provisions.

On the fifth day of the month of August of the said year of seventy Pedro de Soto, Captain and Master of the frigate named *El Espiritu Santo,* delivered to Alonso Menéndez, keeper of provisions of the fort of Santa Elena in the provinces of Florida, three hundred *fanegas,* rather [*sic*], three hundred and sixty *fanegas* of maize and sixty-one barrels of flour and thirty quintales(?) (*gintalenos*) casks of biscuit for distribution to the soldiers of the said fort, as is all evident from a draft of the Captain Juan Menéndez Marqués and letter of receipt for it that the said keeper of provisions gave me signed with his name . . . which remains in my possession.

[The paragraph that follows included the total for each of the items mentioned above that were dispatched to the forts of Carlos, Tequesta, and Tocobaga between 1566 and 1567. It closed on the following page after giving the unit price for each of those items. The document was signed by Baltasar Barreda and Francisco de Avalos.][4]

The following are the first several entries from the second series of pages from the photocopy of this document from 1978, which represent the obverse of what was presented in the preceding pages.

On the tenth of December of the year fifteen hundred and sixty-six, I, Juan Menéndez Marqués, assumed the responsibility as auditor for Blas Albarez, keeper of provisions and supplies for his

---

4. My rendition of this last name is tentative because of the difficulty of the script.

Majesty of the forts of Carlos, Tequesta, and Tocobaga, for seventeen barrels of flour, and one hundred arrobas of meat, and eighty quintales of biscuit and ten barrels of wine for distribution to the soldiers of the said forts. These he received from Alonso de Candamo, Master, who brought them as cargo on the ship named *Nuestra Señora del Rosario*

J^u Menéndez Marques   Blas Albarez

At the end of April of this year of fifteen hundred and sixty-seven I, Juan Menéndez Marqués, assumed responsibility as auditor for Blas Alvarez, keeper of provisions for the said forts of Carlos, Tequesta, and Tocobaga, for eleven barrels of wine and one hundred and fifty *peruleras* bottles of wine and two hundred manegas [*sic*] of maize and one hundred quintales of biscuit and twenty-five arrobas of oil and one barrel of vinegar. . . .

At the end of February of this year of fifteen hundred and sixty-seven I, J^u Menéndez Marqués, assumed responsibility as auditor for Blas Alvarez, keeper of provisions and munitions for his Majesty of the forts of Carlos, Tequesta, and Tocobaga, for one hundred bottles of wine and three hundred *fanegas* of maize and fifty arrobas of oil and seventy-five quintales of biscuit. . . .

The remainder of the entries from this series presented no data not contained in the earlier series. However, as the script here was easier to read than it was for the earlier series, perusal of these entries enabled me to resolve some uncertainties about the proper rendition of a number of words that were difficult to decipher in the entries of the first series.

6. Juan López de Velasco on the Geography and Customs of Florida, 1575

Part 1. Excerpt from *Geografía y Descripción Universal de las Indias*

The following excerpts present López de Velasco's references to the Indians of south Florida and his description of the features of the coast from Tampa Bay southward around the Keys and on up the east coast to Cape Canaveral.

Juan López de Velasco, *Geografía y Descripción Universal de las*

Indias. Edition of Don Marcos Jiménez de la Espada, vol. 248 of the *Biblioteca de Autores Españoles desde la Formación del Lenguaje hasta Nuestros Días.* Madrid: Ediciones Atlas, 1971.

The said Juan Ponce [de León] went as governor of it [Florida] the year of [15]15,[1] and after having landed on the bay that was called, of Juan Ponce, in his name, and now [is renamed Bay] of Carlos, for a cacique who was so named, the Indians routed him and inflicted a wound on him from which he died. . . .

Abandoned Settlements and Forts

The year of [15]66 the *adelantado* Pedro Menéndez put a settlement in the Bay of Carlos on an islet that is in the middle [of it], with thirty-six houses encircled with brushwood faggots and lumber (*rodeadas de fagina y madera*). This settlement lasted until the year of [15]71. That, the Indians having rebelled against the Spaniards and having created problems for them, Pedro Menéndez Marqués, by order of the *adelantado,* beheaded the cacique along with twenty-two other leading Indians and abandoned the said fort.

The year of [15]67 the *adelantado* Pedro Menéndez put a settlement in Tocobaga with twenty-four houses and its fort of brushwood faggot and lumber. The Indians killed the Spaniards and thus it was abandoned.

The year of [15]67 the aforementioned Pedro Menéndez Marques, in the name of the *adelantado,* put a settlement on the point of Tecuesta with twenty-eight houses surrounded by its fort of brushwood faggots (*rodeadas de su fuerte de fagina*). He himself abandoned it in the year of [15]70 because the Indians had put the Christians under great pressure. . . .

Orography and Description of the Coast of Florida

The sea of all this coast is generally good in the summer. . . .

Bay of the Holy Spirit where the district (*gobernación*)[2] of Florida begins, at twenty-nine degrees of latitude, twenty or thirty leagues from Tocobaga Bay, to the west.

1. López de Velasco is in error on the date of Ponce de León's return to Florida, which did not occur until the beginning of the 1520s.

2. Gobernación is used here in the sense of the territory then under the jurisdiction of Florida's governor. In view of the distance given, it is not clear what López de Velasco means here by Bay of the Holy Spirit. The Mississippi was one of the bodies of water to which the name was applied at this era.

The Bay of Tocobaga, [known] by the other names of [Bay] of the Holy Spirit or of Miruelo, is at 29½ degrees of latitude. The entrance has its passage to the west (*la entrada tiene por travesia el oeste*).[3] It would have three leagues at the mouth and three little islets in it on which there is nothing at all except sand and birds. On the northern side, within it the coast runs about two leagues from west to east and then an arm of the sea three leagues wide turns directly to the north, [penetrating] into the land for eighteen leagues up to the village of Tocobaga itself, a settlement of Indians where it terminates. In order to sail in it, one must stay close to the eastern shore continually because the other one is all shoal. In crossing the said arm, another arm, wider than the above-mentioned one, turns off [from it].[4] No one has sailed to the east northeast. For this [reason] it is not known where it leads to.

The three islands of the entrance of the bay form four entryways. And all the said islands thrust shoals out from themselves that stick out about one-quarter of a league into the sea. Although the biggest one of all is that of the island on the southern side which forms two entry passes along the length of the coast (*á luengo de la costa*), it has no more than a fathom of water at high tide for frigates. And the next one would have about a fathom and one-half. And the other two entry passes belonging to the northern island are good ones because at full low tide they have three fathoms of water, and because of the tides being strong there, the water will rise up to a fathom and one-half [above that]. Once one enters within the bay, it is all clear and there is plenty of water in which the ships can remain securely.

From Tocobaga to Tampa is thirty-three leagues. The coast runs north-south, quadrant of the northwest-southeast. As one passes from the bay to two leagues of shrubless land (*tierra pelada*), which serves as a distinguishing mark for recognizing the entrance from the south (*al sur*),[5] there is a little creek that penetrates about half a league into the land. And it leads soon into an arm of the sea that runs from there along the length of the coast down to the very port of Tampa, all frequently inundated [land] (*todo añegadizo*) and full of

3. My rendition here is free and tentative. A literal rendition would be "the entrance has the west for passage."

4. The Spanish here is *en pasando el dicho brazo vuelve otro brazo mas ancho que el sobredicho*. The verb *vuelve* could possibly be rendered differently.

5. This might be rendered also as "to the south" or "on the south."

islets and keys, making the entire coast an island about half a league wide more or less, covered with trees and with some huts (*cabañas*).

The Bay of Tampa, which could be *bahia honda,*[6] has shoal water (*va con bajo*)[7] that is described on the old charts. It is a large bay and would have a width of three leagues at the entrance, all full of shoals and within, all frequently inundated (*toda añegadiza*) and filled with islands.

The entrance of the south side has a little entrance (*entradilla*) for frigates. There is a great mullet fishery in it, which they fish for with nets as in Spain.

From the above-mentioned bay [Tampa] the coast runs twelve leagues down to Carlos. There is a port at four leagues, the entrance of which would be of fifty or sixty paces (*pasos*). Ships can remain within it securely. The sea goes running out toward the south until one is close to Carlos, making an island of all the coast like the [one] farther up, except that it is not so cluttered (*sucio?*), although it has its islands within [it]. On the outside the greater [part] is clear (*limpia*)[8] until the entrance of a creek (*riachuelo*) that is two leagues from the Bay of Carlos. From that point forward everything is shoals (*bajos*). That creek communicates with the aforementioned arm of the sea.

Alongside (*Junto*) and on the island that forms the coast there are trees and some huts.

The Bay of Carlos, which is called Escampaba in the language of the Indians, for a cacique of that name, who later called himself Carlos out of a devotion for the Emperor, appears to be the same one that is called, of Juan Ponce, because he landed in it during the year of [15]15, where he lost his people and where the Indians gave him wounds from which he died. It is at 26½ plus degrees (*esta en 26 grados y ½ largos?*).[9] Its entrance is very narrow and full of shoals as a consequence of which only boats (*barcos*) are able to enter. Within it is spacious, about four or five leagues in circumference, although all subject to flooding. There is a little island in the middle that has

6. I have left this in Spanish because I believe that it was used here as a place name. Literally it means "deep bay."

7. Literally rendered, this would be "goes with shallow water."

8. This might be rendered also as "clean."

9. Literally this should be rendered as "long degrees." As far as I am aware there was only one standard length for the degree of latitude.

a circumference of about half a league, with other little islets around it. On this [island] Cacique Carlos had his headquarters and presently his successors have it there [as well]. From there one may go by canoes to the arm of the sea that goes toward Tampa by way of some channels (*caños*) that there are between one sea and another.

From Carlos to the point of Muspa, which would be at 25¾ degrees and would be about twelve or thirteen leagues, the coast runs north-south and there are five creeks scattered along the coast that are outlets as it were (*como desaguaderos*) of the ponds (*lagunas*) and swamps (*pantanos*) that are inland. As in all the rest of the coasts, one may travel in canoes without going out to sea.

From the Bay of Tocobaga to the Martyrs the aforesaid point of Muspa projects a shoal of a league toward the sea (*echa un bajo una legua a la mar?*),[10] between which and the mainland there is passage for the frigates. As distinguishing marks it has three little groves on top of it that are about half a league distant from one another. Once past the point of Muspa, the coast turns, forming a bay (*ensenada*) of about two leagues toward the east, from which point the coast turns at once to a north-south orientation down to the Martyrs, forming some coves (*ensenadas*) and shoals (*bajios*) and some creeks and frequently inundated marshes (*pantanos añegadizos*). All of it is a wretched coast (*es ruin costa*) because for a distance of four or five leagues to seaward there is no more than a fathom and one-half of water, in which many fish die.

From the farthest point of the mainland, which is at 25 degrees, it runs toward the sea on a northeast-southwest orientation until at 24½ degrees it becomes a chain of shoals (*cordillera de bajos*), full of little islands that they call the Martyrs. And they are countless, with the greater part of them inhabited by Indians subject to the cacique, Carlos, great archers and spear throwers. One may sail among them with light-draft vessels (*chalupas*) and canoes. All the islands are covered with trees, although many of them are frequently inundated.

From the aforesaid point along the entire length of the Martyrs, to the east, a league and one-half to the seaward, there is a rock reef

10. This might also be rendered conceivably as "From the Bay of Tocobaga to the Martyrs the said point of Muspa has a deep spot of a league to the seaward."

that has openings at intervals (*que va haciendo bocas*) through which any ship whatsoever may pass and anchor within freely, because there is plenty of deep water, more than fourteen or fifteen fathoms, so that many ships can remain inside them safely, if they hit the mark in entering through the channels (*bocas*) in which there are many protruding keys of sand (*muchos cayos de arena descubiertos*) to enable one to keep one's distance from them.

The chain of the aforesaid shoals (*bajos*) of the Martyrs from their point [of origin] follows an east-west line of about sixteen leagues and then turns to the east-northeast until it takes on some more height, which would be for about eight leagues or less. Then the coast turns from the northeast quadrant to the east (*luego vuelve la costa al nordeste cuarta al leste*) until it reaches a point a little short of 25 degrees (*25 grados escasos*),[11] which would be about twelve leagues, and then it turns to the north another six. In these [six leagues] there are only two little keys and all sea within, although shallow (*bajio*). And on the entire coast and edge (*orilla*) of the aforesaid Martyrs, there are many islands, as has been stated. And at a distance from the edge, which turns toward the northeast for eighteen leagues, there is a long tree-covered island [extending] for all that eighteen leagues, and about half a league in width and with a low spot (*quebrada*)[12] in the middle at which it gives the appearance that it is going to break in two. The islands of the coast are distant from one another a league, and a league and one-half, and [at times] by two and three leagues and more.

The long and big island, which is at the end of the Martyrs, is also inhabited by Indians, like the others, whose cacique is called Matecumbe. There is a shoal of rock (*bajo de piedra*) along the length of the island a league and one-half to seaward, which runs the length of the island, at the foot of which there is so much water that there is no bottom in many areas. But for the one who has to go from Florida to Havana, he should go in close to the shoal (*bajo*) for the sake of the current that is so strong that if they do not catch much wind, it will push them back. And if the ship should be a frigate, it will be able to go inside of the reef, sailing by day and anchoring by night.

11. As in the case of the earlier "long degrees," this expression, rendered literally, would be "scant" or "short degrees," but such a rendition does not make sense according to a nautical expert.

12. *Quebrada* could be rendered also as "indentation."

At the very point of Tequesta there enters into the sea a freshwater river, which comes from the interior, and to all appearances runs from west to east. There are many fish and eels in it. Alongside it on the north side is the Indian settlement that is called Tequesta, from which the point takes its name. A settlement of Spaniards was established here in the year of [15]67, which was abandoned later, in the year of [15]70. They say it would be advantageous to build a fort there for the security of the ships that might have to come out of the [Bahama] Channel [there] and because the land is good for settlement.

From Tequesta the coast runs to the north, falling off to the north-northwest until it reaches 27 degrees. From the aforesaid point to the Sweet River (*Rio Dulce*), which would be six leagues, there are three islands [running] north-south along the length of the coast; that all three would have the said six leagues of length (*que tendran todas tres de largo las dichas seis leguas*).[13] And they are so close together that there is a narrow entrance between one and the other only for boats (*barcos*), because there is no water at a distance from them (*á lo largo dellas*).[14] A league from the sea there is a sandbank (*placel*) of nine fathoms of water, all clear sand, where any vessel (*nao*) whatsoever may anchor that comes out [of the channel], because beyond it is where the Bahama Channel runs the most. The whales come to this pool (*placel*) in winter, where the Indians take some of them. Four leagues farther to the north of the Sweet River and along the length of the coast there is a small shoal area (*un bajo pequeno*) that would have a fathom and one-half above it, of three leagues in length, and within it, between it and the coast, four fathoms of clear sand. All the rest of the coast is clear up to 26½ degrees, where another little river enters into the sea, which could be the one that is called the Rio Dulce in some descriptions, which opens and closes when there is a storm, and, accordingly, casts up some shoals in its vicinity.

The River Asis is at 27 degrees. It is a small one that only boats (*barcos*) can enter. And from it up to Cape Canaveral the coast runs north-south until the cove (*ensenada*) of the same cape, which takes

13. My rendition here is tentative, as this expression may have some idio-matic meaning that escapes me.

14. This might also be rendered, with equal justice, as "along the length of them."

a turn to the northeast [there]. The coast is clear and anchorable, although there is no port along its length.

Part 2. Brief Memorials and Notes, 1569(?)

The following pieces are portions of brief memorials and notes by Juan López de Velasco. My translations are made from copies found in reel 1, volume 2, of the Florida State University Library copy of the Woodbury Lowery Collection. Stapells-Johnson provided a transcript and microfilm of the first of the Lowery memorials, obviously taken from a different source as her version differs in places from the copy provided by Lowery. The divergences are indicated in notes. The Stapells-Johnson microfilm copy of the first of the memorials bears a handwritten note in the frame preceding the document: "Indiferente 1529. Memorial concerning the customs of the Indians of Florida. 7F."

The last page of the Lowery copy of these memorials bears the following note: "Endorsed. Caciques y costumbres de los yndios de la florida." The original is undated, but bears a label recently attached by the archives (i.e., on fresh paper) with a date of 1569. It is enclosed in a cover with a document relating to Menéndez Marques date Feb. 29, 1576, which does not belong to the file.

Below it in what appears to be a different hand is the following comment: "Looks like signature of Fontenada (MR)."

Swanton (1922: 374, 389; 1946: 722) viewed these pieces in the Lowery collection and published translations of them. Unfortunately, he used translations made by Brooks that left much to be desired and deleted important details as well. For example my literal translation of the following two passages concerning the Calusa runs thus: "That they say that their idol eats human men's eyes. And they dance *with* his head *each year. They have this as a custom.*" "And the fourth *sacrifice* is that *after* the summer some shamans *come* in the guise of the devil." (My italics call attention to the divergences.) Brooks rendered these passages thus: "And they say that *it* has to eat *every year* the eyes of a man, and then they *all* dance *around* the *dead man's* head." "Fourth. *Every year* after the summer *begins they make witches,* in the shape of devils." For this last passage Lowery's Spanish is clearly "Y el quarto çacrificio es que despues del verano bienen unos hichizeros en figura del demonio." Brooks obviously read this carelessly as "after the summer comes," ignoring the fact that "summer" is singular and the verb *bienen,* which she paired it with, is plural, and then blithely inserted her own verb "they make," completely changing the meaning of the original Spanish text. In her rendition of the description of the Tequesta's burial custom, Brooks omitted the detail that after the natives had removed the larger bones from the chief's body, "they bury the little bones with the body." I will not belabor the point further as others have already pointed out the deficiencies of both her transcriptions and her translations. These are but a sample of the words omitted and added by Brooks in these few short passages, not to mention her mistranslations, such as rendering *ballena* or "whale" as "sea cow."

Florida
Two short memorials about the customs of the Indians of Florida
They bear notes and annotations of the cosmographer López de Velasco. (Without a date.)
Archive of the Indies, Seville. Stand 135, Box 7, Bundle 8.

Memorial
About what happens in Florida concerning the Indians of the same land. Those of Carlos firstly have as a custom each time a son of the cacique dies each inhabitant sacrifices his sons or daughters, who go in company of the death of the cacique's son; the second sacrifice is that when the chief himself or the chieftainness dies, they kill his or her own servants, and this is the second sacrifice.

The third sacrifice is that each year they kill a Christian captive so that they may feed their idol, which they adore in [doing] it. That they say their idol eats human men's eyes. And they dance with his head each year. They have this as a custom.

And the fourth sacrifice is that after the summer some shamans (*hichizeros*) come in the guise (*figura*) of the devil with some horns on their head. And they come howling like wolves and many other different idols, which make noises like animals from the woods (*del monte*). And these idols are four months that they never rest neither day nor night that they go running about with great fury. That the great bestiality that they do is a thing to tell about.

Caciques
Guarugumbe on the point of the Martyrs. His subjects are Cuchiaga[1]
Farther on 40 on the very head. _____

1. It is not clear whether the line following Cuchiaga is meant to pertain to it or not, as the first word is capitalized.

Tatesta farther on 80. ————————————————

From the Martyrs to St. Augustine, Tequesta/Gega/Ays./ ———

Satureba, St. Augustine, and to San Mateo by the coast. ————

By the land to the interior Utina/Potano/Mayaca/Mayguiya/
Moloa ——————————————————————

Orista, Santa Elena.² ——————————————————

Carlos 20 U. [20,000]³ ——————————————————

Tocobaa 6. U. [6,000] ——————————————————

Mococo ——————————————————————

Abalachiso ——————————————————————

Olagabe toward (*hacia*) the Chichimecas. ————————————

In that of the Carlos the Captain Reynoso with 40.⁴ ——————

In St. Augustine Estevino de las Alas and Bartolomé Meléndez
with 300 ——————————————————————

San Mateo is abandoned, closed (*cegado*). They moved on to
Catacoru, to which the artillery was moved. Vaseo Canala is there
with 200 men.⁵ —————————————————————

In Sancta Elena Pero Meléndez Marqués with 500, with 48
married couples (casados). ——————————————————

Pero Menéndez ——————————————————————

Captain Reynoso governor of the provinces of Carlos and fort of
Sant Anton, which is moved (*se pasa*) fifty leagues farther on from
San Mateo *celes, atuba*⁶ ———————————————————

Captain Aguirre. ——————————————————————

Florencia de Esquivel. ——————————————————

Captain Juan Pardo. ——————————————————

Hernando de Miranda. ——————————————————

Salzedo native of Madrid ——————————————————

Don Antonio who was page to the Archbishop. ————————

2. Orista and Santa Elena do not appear in the Stapells-Johnson version
because the bottom of the page had rotted away.

3. The Stapells-Johnson version has "10 U" for Carlos, the symbol "U"
without a number for Mococo, and a "U" without a number for ".Balachi,"
spelled thus. "Olagabe" does not appear in the Stapells-Johnson version, again
due to the crumbling away of the bottom of the page.

4. None of the rest of this document, beginning with this sentence, appears in the Stappells-Johnson version.

5. The "o" in Vaseo could conceivably be a "d." Canala is rendered subsequently as Canal. *Catacoru* is undoubtedly Tacatacuru (Cumberland Island).

6. This is possibly a place name, but it is not one that I am familiar with.

Captain Antonio del Prado Escalante. _____

_____

There are there: _____
  Esteban de las Alas lieutenant general _____
  Captain Pedro Menéndez Marqués explorer of the coast and
governor and warden (*alcayde*) of Sancta Elena _____
  Bartolomé Menéndez Warden and governor of St. Augustine _____
  Vaseo Canal captain and governor of Catacoru _____
  Diego García de Sierra governor of Guale. _____
The selectmen and magistrates (*alcaldes y regidores*) in all five gov-
ernments, rather, in the two, which are Sancta Elena and Sanct
Augustine. _____

(in the memorials)[7] _____

Memorial of the Indians and ceremonies of the Indians of Tocobaga
  When a cacique from the leading ones dies, they break him into
pieces (*hazenlo pedazos*) and *quesenlos*[8] in some large jars (*ollas*) and
they *quesenlo* two days until the flesh separates from the bones
(*guesos*) and they take the bones and they join (*encajan*) one bone
with another until they mount the man (*armar al ombre*) as he was
and they place him in a house that they have as a temple while they
finish putting them together (*que los acaban de componer*).[9] They
fast four days. At the end of the four days they assemble all the
people of the village and go out with him to the procession and they
lock it up (*encienrralo*),[10] making many reverences to him

7. This phrase begins at the extreme left-hand margin of the page. It is
possible that something was cropped off when I photocopied this page from the
microfilm.

8. Conceivably this could be *guesen*. In either form there is no such word
in modern Spanish. From the context the sense of this verb seems to be "to de-
bone by cooking."

9. *Componer* could be rendered also as "arrange," "repair," "decorate." The
period could be placed after "temple," and "while they finish . . ." could be
joined to "they fast four days."

10. There is no such word as *encienrrar*. It is probably meant to be *encier-
rar,* which appears again correctly written only a few lines away from this example. However, it could conceivably be a misspelling of *enterrar* which has the
form *entierran* in the third person plural of the present tense. It would fit the
context as well as it means "to bury or inter."

(*hazyendole muchas reberencias*), and then they say that all those who go to the procession gain indulgences _____

The Indians of Tegesta, which is another province from the Martyrs up to the *cañaveral.* [11] _____

When a cacique or leading man dies, they take him apart (*deseayuntalo*) and remove the larger bones from the body and they bury (*entierran*) the little bones (*guesos menudos*) with the body. And in the cacique's house they place a large box (*caxa*) and they enclose (*encierran*) the large bones in this box and the whole village comes there to adore and they hold these bones as their gods.

And in the winter all the canoes go out to the sea. Among all these Indians one Indian sent (*enbixado?*) [12] goes out, who carries three stakes in his belt and he throws the lasso around its neck (*y echale el laço al pesquezo*) and while the whale is proceeding to disappear, he shoves a stake through one of its nostrils (*por una ventana de las narizes*) and thus [as it] is tied up (*como se cabulle*) [13] he does not lose it because he goes on top of it. And in killing it as he is killing it (*y en matandola que la mata*) they pull it in until it runs aground on the sand. And the first thing that they do to it [is that] they open the head and extract two bones that it has in the skull and they throw these two bones in this chest (*caja*) in which they place the deceased and in this they adore.

7. Rumor of Enemy Settlement on the Gulf Coast, 1604

In 1604 the governor at Havana received word from Florida's governor that Indians of Florida had told the governor that a European enemy of Spain was establishing a settlement somewhere on Florida's Gulf Coast north of the Bay of Carlos. At once Cuba's governor dispatched his son

11. This is obviously a reference to Cape Canaveral.

12. There is no such word and in this case I am unsure whether my rendition captures what the author was trying to say in his less-than-perfect spelling. "Sent" would be *enviado*. What appears to be the word *veinte* or "twenty" is written above *enbixado* in a different and smaller hand.

13. The verb *cabullir* does not appear in modern Spanish dictionaries, but I believe that I have seen the verb used in Spanish-American literature. It does exist in the forms *encabullar* and *encabuyar* in New World Spanish meaning "to tie with sisal" or "to wrap." It comes from *cabuya,* the name for the common American agave and sisal-hemp.

and a small force on a frigate to search every bay and inlet and river estuary from the Bay of Carlos to Apalachee Cape. The following excerpt from a letter by Cuba's governor represents the governor's report to the king about this episode.

Pedro de Valdés to the King, July 11, 1604

AGI, Seville, Santo Domingo 129 (54–2–7/14). Pedro de Valdés, letter to the king, Havana, July 11, 1604. Stetson Collection of the P.K. Yonge Library of Florida History.

On the 19th of May a dispatch-boat left here, which I dispatched with the news that the governor of Florida had given, to the effect that the enemy were making a settlement beyond the Bay (*ensenada*) of Carlos in the Bay (*baya*) of Tocopaua, the duplicate of which I am now sending. And on the very day after the sending of the report, a dispatch arrived from the said governor of Florida in which he said that the second report that he had concerning this [matter] he had sent to Your Majesty in haste with an advice-boat (*pataje*), without letting me know what it contained (as he had offered to by his letter). Because of this, on seeing how appropriate it was to know with certainty what there was to this, so as to give an account of it to Your Majesty. I made an agreement with the royal officials to ready a little frigate (*fragatilla*), the lightest one that there was in this port, and to put eighteen selected men on it, soldiers and sailors, with a very experienced pilot. And so that they might make the search that the matter required with greater security and caution, I sent my son, Don Fernando de Valdés, on the said frigate, so that he might assume the responsibility and survey and explore all the bays, ports, rivers, keys, and coves (*caletas*)[1] that there may be from the said Bay (*Vaya*) of Carlos, which is at 27½ degrees, to the Cape of Apalachee, which is at more than 30, close to the river of the Holy Spirit, which is in the region where the enemy are likely to be, if they have taken a port in order to settle. And after having been engaged in this search for about fifty days with the full caution that the matter required, he did not encounter any trace of anything at all of a fort. This implies that the report that the

1. *Caletas* could be rendered also as "creeks" or "inlets."

governor of Florida had and gave to me was false and that the
Indians have deceived him as one [who is] new to the land and with
little experience in it and of things pertaining to it. That it gave me
a great deal of anxiety, considering how much [trouble] it could
give, if it had proved to be correct. And so it seems to me that there
will be no cause for alarm in relation to what touches on this
[report].

Calusa

in the Early Eighteenth Century

Introduction

This section presents documentation that traces the fate of the Calusa and other natives of south Florida during the first half of the eighteenth century, when most of the remaining aboriginal population disappeared. In the documents the virtual extinction of these peoples is attributed to the inroads of disease, frequent raids by Indians allied to the British such as the Yamasee and Uchise, internecine strife among south Florida's natives, and a number of migrations to Cuba to escape Yamasee and Uchise raids. The documentation in this part concludes this book with the report from an abortive mission attempt made by two Jesuits in 1743.

The attrition of the population from migration and from attacks by natives allied with the British began as early as 1704, the year of the destruction of most of the remaining north Florida missions. Until then those missions had been a barrier to incursions deep into Florida by natives allied with the English. A sizable migration of 270 occurred in 1711 and another smaller one in the latter 1750s. Between those years there were several other migrations about which little is known, not to mention the frequent trips to Cuba taken by small groups of native leaders drawn particularly from the Calusa and the natives of the Keys.

Disease exacted a very heavy toll among those who migrated to Cuba. Of the 270 migrants of 1711, up to two hundred of the ordinary Indians soon died from epidemics, as did the hereditary cacique of Carlos, his great captain, the caciques of Jove, Maimi, Cancha, Muspa, and Rioseco, three unnamed caciques, and one identified as "the principal cacique, who took the glorious name of Your Majesty at his baptism"

(Guëmes y Horcasitas 1743). Cuba's governor in 1743 reported that the fate of the 1704 migrants and of those who came on other occasions had been similar. So great was the mistrust engendered by this heavy death toll that, after asking for transport to Cuba in 1732, when two vessels arrived from Cuba that year the natives declined to board them. Nonetheless, visits to Cuba by the leaders appear to have been relatively frequent as late as the 1740s.

Disease brought to Florida by Spaniards who frequented south Florida's waters for their fisheries was doubtless another major source of attrition. So frequent was such contact that Father Alaña noted in 1743 that "For the most part the adult men understand and speak Castilian moderately because of the frequent commerce with the boatmen from Havana." Much of the work of catching and curing the fish was done by the natives. So regular was this commerce that the natives came to depend on the fishermen for transportation for one leg of their seasonal migration, that part which took them from the Keys to the fishing grounds of Florida's southwest coast. Such intermeshing interests created a strong bond of trust in the Spaniards, as indicated in the Indians' confidence in seeking refuge in Cuba in 1704 and 1711 so soon after their mistreatment of the friars in 1697.

In his report Alaña attributed some of the decline in population to the dissolution and excesses linked to the natives' access to alcohol from the frequent shipwrecks and from their work for the Spanish fishermen. The Jesuit gave dramatic testimony to what he termed their "incredible passion" for rum, noting that the Indian would give the equivalent of 100 pesos for a flask of rum, that he and his party were chided constantly for not having brought any, and that the Indians told them flatly that "without the rum, they neither can be nor wish to be Christians." Alaña went on to comment that the natives had already traded away most of the firearms given to them by Cuba's governor to defend themselves against the Uchise, having bartered the guns for rum. When the natives became drunk, he observed, they lost all sense of moderation and took on an extraordinary brutality so that "There is no longer a son for the father, nor wife for the husband," and that flight to the woods was the family's only security.

Alaña also signaled internecine strife among other causes as a reason for a steady shrinking of the population. "These dimunitive nations," he noted, "fight among themselves at every opportunity and they are shrinking as is indicated by the memory of the much greater number that there were just twenty years ago, so that, if they continue in their barbarous style, they will have disappeared within a few years either because of the skirmishes, or because of the rum that they drink until they burst, or because of the children whom they kill, or because of those whom the smallpox carries off in the absence of remedies, or because of those who perish at the hands of the Uchises."

The war with intruders from the north was probably a major source of population loss, whether directly from battle casualties and captives enslaved or indirectly from the migrations to Cuba those attacks inspired. The initial raids until the year 1715 have been attributed to the Yamasee. The Yamasee's leading role in the native uprising in South Carolina, which has been called the Yamasee War, made them anathema to the English, and most of the Yamasee thereafter became prey of the other Indians allied to the English rather than the predators that they had been. Later raids into south Florida were always attributed to the Hitchiti-speaking Uchise, although other components of the Creek and emerging Seminole were doubtless involved in some of those raids, just as the Yamasee were not solely responsible for the earlier ones.

Contemporaneous documents discovered to date make no mention of the 1704 attack that must have been behind the migration of the Indians of Key West to Cuba. If the attackers were Yamasee, they may well have come from the community known to have existed in Mayaca territory at that time. Yamasee are mentioned as involved in the hostilities that led to the 1711 migration to Cuba.

In addition to successive waves of migration to Cuba, others among the natives of central and south Florida moved northward to seek shelter in the vicinity of St. Augustine. A group identified as Costa are generally believed to have come from central or south Florida. The name Costa was used by a Spaniard in 1764 to refer to Indians of the Keys. A certain cacique Antonio Pojoy in 1734 identified himself as head of the "Alafaia Costas nation." Costa near St. Augustine maintained a separate village as late as 1739. In 1759 Nombre de Dios had one Costa household containing nine individuals. Swanton identified the Costa with the Ais and "the other tribes formerly living near them" (1946: 85). Diego Peña placed Costas Alafayes among the non-Creek living in the Creek country in 1716: "In this province abound greatly the Apalachee nation, Costas Alafayes and some Timucuans and from the Mocama" (1716). It is conceivable that the people Peña identified as Costas Alafayes were from the Tocobaga community in Apalachee that migrated northward during the attacks of 1704. Mayaca-speaking Jororo also occupied a couple of settlements near St. Augustine during this period. Pojoy from the Tampa Bay area, including the above-mentioned Alafay, also lived near St. Augustine until the mid-1720s and reappeared for several years in the early 1730s. In the early years of this period at least, some of the Tocobaga who had migrated to Apalachee during the second half of the seventeenth century were still in that former mission territory. But their greatly shrunken numbers were decimated further during a 1718 attack by erstwhile allies, the Pojoy.

Throughout this period south Florida's natives continued to cling to their own religious traditions, although in times of stress they spoke of being willing to become Christians in order to obtain what they wanted from Spanish authorities. For most such statements seem to have been no more than a ploy. In 1743 Alaña remarked that although the "idolatrous errors and superstitions of this people are of the crudest sort . . . what is surprising is the very tenacious attachment with which they maintain toward all this and the ridicule they make of beliefs contrary [to theirs]."

Alaña noted that he and Father Monaco had received a very rude reception, observing that once the natives had taken from them "with intolerable importunity" the provisions they knew were destined for them, "they openly declared their displeasure over our coming, to the point of denying on repeated occasions, with evident falsity, that while in Havana they had asked for priests who would make Christians of them." "According to their way of thinking," he added, "this matter of becoming Christians has no other significance than the receiving of the sacramental water with these conditions [for doing so]." The natives' conditions involved the king's supplying them with food, clothing, and rum, allowing their own religion to remain in place, and respecting their tradition that punishment not be used in the teaching of their children. Alaña concluded that, as had been the case among other Indian groups, if south Florida's natives were to be truly Christianized the priests would need to be backed by military force so that "the necessary rigor can be employed in order to root out even the relics of their superstition, as this is necessary so that their little children may not learn it."

We are indebted to Alaña for some additional descriptions that add to our knowledge of the south Florida natives' iconography, religious rituals, and religious leaders. Of the two idols Alaña had seen, the principal one he described as "a board sheathed in deerskin with its poorly formed image of a fish that looks like the barracuda and other figures like tongues." The second idol, Alaña noted, representing the god of the cemetery, was a bird's head sculptured in pine, "which in the matter of hideousness well represented its original," which was probably a vulture. The priests were able to smash and burn the latter idol along with the hut that served as the natives' temple, but the natives hid the other idol before the priests could do anything more disrespectful to it than stepping on it. Alaña noted also that the natives had a large log that, on certain days, they adorned with flowers and feathers and celebrated. At one point silver had been buried at the foot of this log. By 1743 their head shaman had acquired the Spanish title of bishop. The shaman who functioned as medicine man and seer was called "*tirupo* or like God." While curing, this shaman made "great howls and gestures . . . over the one who is ill, adorning himself with feathers and painting himself horribly." The cacique and his sons were venerated with incensings performed by the so-called bishop. Upon the death of the cacique and other leading men, children were killed, supposedly that they might serve the deceased in the other life as long as it lasted. For Alaña remarked, as had Rogel in the 1560s, that the natives "obstinately affirm that human souls do not survive their bodies, swallowing the absurdity of their not being any better than the beasts, laughing at the strongest of arguments and turning their backs when they were confounded." Alaña noted as well that the natives almost daily application of body paint was done for the honor of the principal idol. While the deceased spirits survived, the natives remained in great fear of their dead, at whose graves offerings of food, tobacco, and other goods were made daily. Their fear of the dead led them to avoid the naming of them and to keep the cemeteries at some distance from the village.

Throughout this period, despite their frequent visits to Cuba, where they would have become acquainted with agriculture, the south Florida natives remained fisher-hunter-gatherers. In speaking of their rootlessness, Cuba's governor in 1743 spoke of them as being "accustomed to migrate as do the birds." Alaña provided more details on their migrations, noting that in the course of a year they had three principal living places. These were the mouth of the Miami River, where they remained until the end of September, Perchel Key and the southwest coast of Florida, to which the Havana fishermen carried them, and finally, Cow Key. Alaña attributed their persistence in this way of life to their "supreme indolence," observing that "lacking the desire to cultivate the land, they content themselves with the fish and the small amount of wild fruit that the aforesaid places successively supply them with of themselves." Although he felt that if they were to be Christianized sooner or later they would have to be taught to cultivate the land, he advised that "compassion does not permit that we press them at once [on this point], for, at the very least, this would keep them aloof from our religion." At times, however, these Indians had access to a source of maize. Just four years later a black from New England, who was the sole survivor of a grounded logwood sloop captured by about sixty Indians in about twenty canoes, recounted that during the five weeks that he spent as their captive he was fed on "boiled corn, which is what they often eat themselves" (Hammon 1760).

A curious aspect of these south Florida natives' migratory habits not mentioned elsewhere is recorded in documentation from a 1732 episode arising when native leaders expressed an interest in migrating to Cuba with their people to become Christians. Two ships were dispatched to the Keys with the native leaders who had made the request. But after three days during which the natives frequented the ships for food and rum, all of them disappeared to the mainland, taking both their houses (*casas*) and storage buildings (*barracas*) with them. Unfortunately there is no indication of the nature of those structures.

In none of the documentation of the south Florida natives' frequent trips to Cuba included here is there mention of the natives' having made the trip to or from Cuba in their own canoes. When the conveyance is mentioned, it is a Spanish vessel. And for the actual or planned migrations (except for that of 1704, for which the means of travel is not mentioned), the natives asked for passage on Spanish vessels. That those natives relied on Spanish fishermen for their annual migratory voyage to the west coast fishing grounds might suggest that the natives would hardly have braved the more perilous overseas passage to Cuba in their own canoes. But, as they were going also to assist the Spaniards with their fishing, their utilization of Spanish vessels may only have been a matter of convenience. However, in the incident mentioned above involving the New England black, some of his captors seem to have gone to Cuba in their own vessels. When a Spanish ship captain carried the black off to Cuba, some of the Indians followed, reaching Cuba only four days later than did the black. Even in this case there is no mention of the conveyance they used, but the rapidity with which they arrived to protest to the governor suggests that they probably used their own vessels (Hammon 1760). An account of Uchise's having killed a group of Costa or Keys Indians on February 28, 1762, on Key West while the Costa were on their way to Havana might also be interpreted as indicating that the natives were traveling in their own canoes (Elijio de la Puente 1764).

On the occasion of the capture of the black from New England, the Keys natives passed up the opportunity to acquire the grounded New England sloop, which might have been refloated by throwing its cargo overboard. The sloop's captain had resisted his crew's presure for him to jettison all but twenty tons of the logwood. The Indians simply killed the crew and set the vessel afire, watching it burn to the water's edge before heading for shore (Hammon 1760).

There appears to be little Spanish documentation attesting to the fate of the remnants of south Florida's peoples after 1743. During the latter half of the 1750s more of those natives migrated to Cuba in some fashion. We know of that migration only because the crown requested information about it on learning of it. In a 1764 report to Havana's governor, the Floridian Juan José Elijio de la Puente noted that the Costa (the name he used for the Indians of the Keys) had always inhabited the Keys and been faithful vassals of Spain's monarch since the discovery of them. But, he continued, "At the end of the year 1761, because the said Costas were being persecuted by the Uchise Indians and because they had destroyed their villages in such a fashion that they were forced to live on the above-mentioned Key of Bones, they decided to abandon it and to withdraw to this city [Havana], where most of them have perished from the rigors of hunger and misery; and at the moment the few who have survived are to be found scattered about at various spots on this island [Cuba] and those Keys are without any of their former natives and, in a word, inhabited from then until now only by the English from Providence [Bahamas], . . . cutting wood and fishing for turtles" (Elijio de la Puente 1764). It was doubtless some of that same band, who had not departed as yet, who were killed or captured by a band of forty-eight Uchise at the end of February 1762 (Elijio de la Puente 1764). A few appear to have remained in the Keys until Florida passed under British control. Parks noted that Bernard Romans, an English surveyor, wrote that Key West and Cow Key were the Calusa's last refuge in Florida and that "in 1763 the remnant of these people consisting of about eighty families, left this last possession of their native lands and went to Havannah" (1985: 69).

Part III contains documentation on the Calusa and other natives of south and central Florida as their numbers began to be reduced severely in the eighteenth century or as they began to scatter from their original homelands. Eight items are included.

The first item is a letter written by Cuba's bishop in 1711 and other pieces associated with it written in Spain that bear dates as late as 1716. These pieces tell of the migration to Cuba of 270 south Florida natives—who included Calusa, Jove, Maimi, Tancha, Muspa, and Rio Seco—drawn from the Atlantic and the gulf coasts, the interior around Lake Okeechobee, and the peninsula's southern tip at Cape Sable. In 1711 thousands more were allegedly ready to do the same had shipping been made available by Cuba's political officials as requested by the bishop.

The second item contains excerpts from two letters written in 1718 by the commander of the Spanish garrison at San Marcos de Apalachee, telling of the presence of remnants of the Tocobaga, who had migrated into Apalachee about half a century earlier. Those excerpts are followed by several pieces documenting the Tocobaga's presence in Apalachee in 1677 and 1694 and shedding light on the role those Tocobaga played in the mission economy.

The third item is a 1723 report by Florida's Governor Benavides describing the native villages around St. Augustine and detailing the natives whom friars had baptized between 1718 and early 1723. Among the tribes represented from central and south Florida were the Pojoy of Tampa Bay, Jororo, Alafay, possibly from Tampa Bay as well, and Costa, about whose identity there is some dispute but who seem to have been Keys Indians.

The fourth item is the same governor's record from his visit to the native villages around St. Augustine in 1726, giving the population of each. The inhabitants of one settlement not mentioned in 1723 are referred to as "Indians of the *rinconada* of Carlos of the Piaxa Nation."

The fifth item is a 1728 report on the status of the Florida mission settlements in the vicinities of St. Augustine and San Marcos in Apalachee Province. The report is particularly useful for its brief sketches of the migrations of the inhabitants of the native settlements during the preceding years as their inhabitants reeled from the impact of epidemics and attacks by natives allied to the British. Also noted is the disappearance of many of the settlements mentioned in 1726.

The sixth item is a 1732 letter by Cuba's governor and other pieces associated with his letter that tell of renewed efforts to bring south Florida natives to Cuba, who purportedly wished to become Christian as well as to escape attack by the Uchise. These documents shed light on the fate of the 270 immigrants of 1711, on the foot-dragging by Cuba's governors and treasury officials between 1711 and 1732 in not informing the crown of the south Florida natives' various appeals for assistance, and on those officials' adamant refusal to release any royal funds for the response to those appeals espoused by church authorities and sanctioned by the king since 1716.

The seventh item contains two letters written by Cuba's governor in July and September 1743 and various documents enclosed in them. The letters and enclosures provide substantial background information for the 1743 mission by two Jesuits to the Indians living in the Keys and at the present site of Miami. The first of the letters also contains a review of the Cuban authorities' relations with south Florida's natives since 1704.

The eighth item is a version of the 1743 mission's report issued in 1760 in a form that differs slightly from the one written in 1743. The 1760 version was prepared in response to the crown's request for information on a group of south Florida Indians who had gone to Cuba several years earlier to escape attacks by the Uchise.

The Documents

1. South Florida Natives' Flight to Cuba, 1711

The central piece of this collection of documents is a letter to the king written by Bishop Gerónimo Valdés on December 9, 1711. In it he reported an appeal from Cacique Carlos and other south Florida native leaders for assistance to bring many natives from south Florida to Cuba so that they might become Christians and escape frequent attacks by Yamasee, who were implementing the English design of stripping Florida of its aboriginal population aligned with the Spaniards. The bishop reported the action that he had taken in response to that appeal in cooperation with the governor and royal officials of Cuba as well as those political officials' opposition to any further action or the expenditure of royal funds, once an initial contingent of 270 natives had been brought to Cuba from the Keys.

The bishop's letter was accompanied by a testimonial, drawn up by the bishop, recording his meeting with the governor, treasury officials, and other interested parties in which the decision was reached to bring no additional Indians to Cuba from Florida until the king's intentions were known.

The collection also contains additional pieces, most (if not all) dating from 1716, when action was finally taken in Spain in response to this letter after the authorities had waited in vain for four years for a promised report on the matter by the governor. The first of these pieces includes several notes written by people at the Council of the Indies summarizing the bishop's letter and its enclosure and making recommendations as to the response to be made to the authorities in Cuba. The collection concludes with several letters on this matter addressed by the king to the bishop and to the governor and royal officials at Havana.

This document is rather badly faded in places and consequently somewhat difficult to decipher in those sections, but it is legible for the most part. The copies of the king's letters are rough drafts, containing portions that are crossed out. The revisions to replace them appear in the wide left-hand margin of the original.

Bishop Gerónimo Valdés to the King, December 9, 1711

AGI, Seville, Santo Domingo 860. Transcription of this document was made from a xerographic copy taken from the microfilm copy of the Stetson Collection photostat. For passages in which the xerographic copy was illegible, the Stetson photostat was used. The page order followed in my translation is that of the photostats, which differs from that of the microfilm copy at one point. The Stetson Collection identification for the document is: AGI 58-2-10/1, Bishop Gerónimo Valdés of Cuba to the king, December 9, 1711. The bishop's letter occupies the right-hand side of the first six pages of this collection of documents. Notes made at the Council of the Indies fill the left-hand side of those pages. The first piece reproduced here is a brief note made at the council, probably at the time of the arrival in Spain of the bishop's letter.

Havana to H.M. on the 9th of Dec. of 1711, the bishop of that Diocese. He gives an account, with a testimonial, of having made arrangements for the passage to that city of the heathen Indians Carlos, Coleto, and others, in order to receive the holy sacrament of baptism to which they *alananen* and that some desisted from going because of measures not having been taken by the governor and royal officials for their transport. He asks that a decision be taken concerning this.

The following is the bishop's letter to the king.

In the past month of February of this year a ship entered this port that came from the keys that border on the mouth of the Bahama Channel and the mainland of Florida. In those keys live the heathen Indians of the chiefs Carlos, Coleto, and others. And some of the above-mentioned Indians, having come in the said ship, told me of the very serious persecutions and hostilities, which they are experiencing and have experienced in other keys that the Indians who are called Yamases have destroyed. That they have killed some of the above-mentioned Keys Indians, have made others flee, and that they have captured the greater part of them, whom, it is said, they carry off and sell, placing them into slavery in the port of San Jorge [Charleston, South Carolina] of the English nation and our enemies. And as a remedy for these injuries they gave an account to me of their very strong desire that I should assist in transporting them to this city with their families, wives, and children (*hijos*) to receive the holy sacrament of baptism and to follow Christianity, thereby assuring their reduction and the welfare of their souls and security for their lives. For this [purpose] they have begged me with total submission that I assist in the best fashion that I am able to in their being transported and brought over here and that it be carried out as soon as may be possible. With this in view, being desirous that it should come to pass, taking into consideration that all [these happenings] alluded to may be an intervention from on high and that his Divine Majesty may have seized on this development as an instrument for the conversion of so great a number of souls to our holy Catholic faith, having before me Your Majesty's decree of July 20, 1709, in which you were pleased to order that we should be attentive to the needs of the said Indians with full concern and vigilance, and having in mind, similarly, the obligation from my responsibility, along with the strong desire to gain so many souls and converting them to our holy faith and to obedience to Your Majesty, I issued an *auto* on the fifth of May of this said year, composing a report about everything spoken of above, ordering that the governors of the political and the military spheres be invited to take part, while exhorting and begging them to deign to order the provision of the most appropriate means so that the matter alluded to above might come to pass. I immediately offered one hundred pesos in ready money as help for the costs of the vessels necessary for their transport, begging and urging all the people presently in this city as well as its inhabitants so that, out of their fervent zeal and Christian piety, they might voluntarily wish to help with some monies. I ordered the publication of an edict with serious penalties, so that no one might impede it, but rather, protect and support this cause as one that is of such great service to both Majesties. And when this had been communicated to the said governors, in their replies they promised to provide the assistance that should be necessary concerning this matter and that they would contribute the resources for it that they could. Other residents of this city did likewise. And when those which seemed to be necessary had been assembled, two vessels were dispatched under the charge of Captain Luis Perdomo, an experienced person and one of sufficient intelligence and worth for the transport of the said Indians, carrying a letter from the said governors and me for the said cacique, assuring him in Your Majesty's name that he would be assisted and protected and supported in whatever might occur. And having arrived at the said Keys, after not having encountered the aforesaid [cacique] because of his being far away in a savage war with his enemies, the Yamasee, a message was sent to him. And the said Captain Perdomo decided to come back with a brother of the aforesaid cacique and other Indians of the first rank, for the purpose of conferring in this city and discussing the most appropriate method for their preservation and transportation because of all those of that province being of a mind to be converted to our holy Catholic faith. And, as a result, the said captain brought up to two hundred and seventy to this said city. And he stated that he would have brought more than two thousand had he had the vessels. And that those who are asking for the water of baptism surpass six thousand. In relation to this he ordered that the said governor, royal officials, my vicar-general, and the rest of the people who were thought should be involved be convoked for a meeting to give their opinion about so important a matter. And as a result my auxilary bishop, the aforesaid governors, royal officials, the vicar-general, and the aforementioned Luis Perdomo, as an experienced and intelligent person, assembled in my palace on the assigned day. And when they were assembled, I acquainted them with the aforementioned royal decree of July 20, 1709, along with others that speak to this particular matter. And I touched on the matter so necessary and urgent mentioned earlier, so that they would express their opinion and determine the most opportune manner for the transportation and maintenance of the said Indians. In virtue of this, after having conferred on it, they proceeded to give their opinion and views. I discovered that the said governors and royal officials and my auxiliary bishop decided that we should not provide transportation for any more of the [Indians] alluded to without an explicit order from Your Majesty and that no monies could be provided from the royal coffers in the absence of such an order, as has been laid down by various Royal Laws, with the aforesaid military governor and royal officials expressing themselves more at length on this [matter]. And despite this, I pressed the matter again with the said decree [of 1709], pledging[1] to give five hundred pesos in reales from my funds, despite my finding myself burdened with the building of the home for foundling children that Your Majesty had given me responsibility for, and offering to provide surety lay, unencumbered, and creditable (*fiança Lega, llana, y abonada*)[2] for the amount that they should provide from the said royal coffers and to make satisfaction for them in the eventuality that Your Majesty does not approve it, solely with the purpose of achieving what he desired so strongly. But by means of dispatches that the aforementioned sent to me, they maintained their position in their pronouncements alluded to, alleging various arguments in opposition to my proposals and alleging finally that they could not hand down any determination whatsoever in this business that involved expenditures. All this is evident from the *autos,* the copy of which I am sending to Your Majesty enclosed in this. With this [outcome], on seeing that I, for my part, could not undertake this [enterprise] alone and see it through, I put it on hold with great sorrow and disappointment, inasmuch as the present opportunity would be lost and inasmuch as it could happen that it would not come again in the future.[3] From the said *autos* Your Majesty will recognize the great anxiety and distress that this importuning to see my claim succeed has cost me and that if I could have remedied matters with the blood from my veins, I would have done so because the Indians have become greatly disappointed and disgusted because of the contrary outcome. And as a result of this, many of those whom Perdomo brought over have gone back, on seeing that we did not carry out what had been promised them and [live up to] the

1. In the Spanish text "pledging" is repeated thus, *obligando-me obligando-me.*

2. This is a stock phrase used when bond is being posted and may be rendered somewhat differently than the way I have phrased it. The need for the surety to be lay may be an allusion to the clerical exemption or *fuero* that removed them from the jurisdiction of the ordinary courts.

3. This might be rendered more literally as "in the future it could happen that it would not be achieved."

assurances that they had been given in the letter mentioned above that was written to them. And from this there followed the untimely result that they encountered. And although I raised these very considerations before the said governor and royal officials, they were not enough to bring them around so that they would condescend to my proposals and so that they would carry out that which Your Majesty has charged them so much with doing by the said royal decrees. In respect to this I beseech Your Majesty submissively to deign to order the provision of the most prompt and efficacious measures that you find to be necessary and that you determine what should be done in this situation, remaining ready, as I do, to make a special effort in this matter to the extent that it is within my power and to spend everything that I am able to so that it will succeed, carrying out what Your Majesty orders, which will be what is most proper. May God preserve your Catholic royal person for the many years that Christendom needs.
Havana   December 9 of 1711.

> Gerónimo Bishop of Cuba
> J.M.J.[4]

Testimonial from the *Autos* made in relation to the transportation to the city of Havana of the heathen Indians of the caciques Carlos, Coleto, and others from the keys that border on the Bahama Channel and mainland of the provinces of Florida.

In the city of Havana on the fifth of March of this year one thousand seven hundred and eleven the Reverend señor *Mŕo* [Master?] don Gerónimo Valdés, bishop of this island of Santiago de Cuba, Xamaica and Florida, of the council of H.M., our lord, stated that, inasmuch as a vessel had entered into this city a few days ago from the keys that border on the mouth of the Bahama Channel and the mainland of the provinces of St. Augustine of Florida, in the which said keys the heathen Indians of the caciques Carlos, Coleto, and others live, [and] some of the Indians alluded to came from these in the said vessel and have communicated to his Excellency the most serious oppression and hostilities that they are experiencing and have experienced on other keys, which the Indians whom they call Yamasees have destroyed. The latter have killed some of them from the said keys, have made others flee, and imprisoned the majority. That he said that they carry them off and

4. These initials probably stand for Jesus, Mary, and Joseph.

sell them, placing them into slavery in the Port of San Jorge of the English nation and our enemies. And as a remedy for these injuries, they have made a report to his Excellency about the very strong desire that they have of coming to this city with their families, women, and children, so that all of them may be given the holy sacrament of baptism and follow Christianity, securing their reduction in this manner, the welfare of their souls, and the security of their lives. For this they have begged with total submission that he assist them in the best manner that he is able to for their passage and transport and that everything alluded to be done as quickly as may be possible, for the service of both Majesties. His Excellency orders the making of this *auto* of communication that he is issuing, directed toward the señores governors of matters political and military in this said city. That on the part of our holy mother church, he exhorts them and asks them, and on his own part, he begs that he deign to order that the measures be taken that seem most appropriate for achieving the result alluded to above. That as a help with the expense, his Excellency offers to give one hundred pesos in reales immediately and he begs and charges all the people presently in this city along with its inhabitants that they might voluntarily wish to help with some monies out of their fervent zeal and Christian piety in order to provide a remedy for such great injuries. Let them do it by taking part in so holy and pious a work, in which it is recognized that his divine majesty is served in the conversion of these poor Indians[5] to the body of our holy mother church, assuring thereby [the security of] their lives. . . . [Due to the fading of the script the few remaining lines of this testimonial are illegible except for the closing signature and notarization, which are as follows.]

Gerónimo, bishop of Cuba

Before me, Thomas[?] Núñes, notary public, in Havana on the sixth[?] of March of this year

Next are the notes made at the Council of the Indies that appear on the left-hand side of pages 1 through 5 of the preceding document.

The fiscal, having seen the content of this letter from the

5. All of this page is badly faded. The word here might well be *infieles* rather than *Indios. Infieles* is "heathens."

reverend bishop of Cuba of December 9 of [1]711 [says] that it
amounts to his recounting that with the motive of some Indians
from the Keys of Florida having told him of the hostilities that the
Yamasee Indians waged against them, killing some, making others
flee, and capturing the greater part, whom they sold in the port of
San Jorge of the English nation and of their desire to be transported
to Havana with their families in order to receive baptism, he made
this known to the governors of the political and military spheres, so
that they might adopt the appropriate measures for their transport,
with the reverend bishop offering 100 pesos and urging the
residents of that city to contribute alms. And that, after having
provisioned and dispatched two vessels under the charge of Captain
Luis Perdomo with the means that had been assembled, with letters
from the reverend bishop and governors to Cacique Carlos, offering
to him in H.M.'s name that they would look out for him. They
returned with 270 Indians, some of them leading men (*principales*),
and a brother of the cacique mentioned above in order to confer over
the preservation and bringing over of all the [Indians] of that
province who were of a mind to be converted to the holy Catholic
faith, with the said captain saying that he would have brought
more than two thousand Indians if he had had the vessels, and that
those who were asking for the water of baptism surpassed 6,000.

And from the testimonial that the reverend bishop sends it is
evident that in virtue of the urgings of the prelate, a formal meeting
(*Junta*) was held at which were present his auxiliary bishop, his
vicar-general, the two governors of the political and military
spheres, the royal officials, and the said captain, Luis Perdomo, in
which they conferred concerning this matter and were of the
opinion (except for the reverend bishop and his vicar-general) that
no more Indians should be brought, nor any monies furnished from
the royal coffers without explicit orders from H.M., because it was
against the laws. And despite the reverend bishop's having repeated
his suggestion that what was necessary for the transportation of all
the Indians who wished to cross over to Havana to receive baptism
be furnished from the royal treasury, with the bishop offering 500
pesos from his own funds and surety, lay, unencumbered, and
creditable, to restore to the royal coffers what was withdrawn from
them for the said purpose in case H.M. did not approve of it. The
military governor and royal officials persisted in their opinion, with
the governor telling the bishop that he should give an account [of

the matter] to H.M.; that he also would do so, but according to a note from the secretariat, he has not done so. And the bishop concluded his letter asking for provision to be made as to what they are to do.

Keeping in mind what is mentioned above and in the supposition of the governor and royal officials having fulfilled what is ordered by laws 13 and 17, title 1°, book 4 and 19 and 2ª, title 28, book 8° in not having given any amount from the royal coffer for the transport of the said Indians because of not having power for it, despite the surety that the reverend bishop offered. What is worthy of note [is] that in the course of four years they have not given any account about a matter of such great importance, the omission of which, even though it may have been because of the cacique and the Indians not having persevered in their desire to cross over to Havana to receive baptism, as one is led to believe from the reverend bishop's not having repeated his request. This is something for which they are deserving of reprehension. And it being possible that these Indians are among the many who have come under the dominion of H.M. (as the council is aware), it seems that there is no reason to make any provision ahead of time with respect to the orders that it has given, except for the case that some of them and others should cross over to Havana voluntarily to receive baptism, [then] the governor and royal officials are to favor and support them and defend them, as is ordered by the laws, especially the first one, title 1° and the 3rd, title 5[?], book 6. And the reverend bishop is to be charged with responsibility for this, telling him that the council is aware of his zeal and devotion to the service of both Majesties, along with whatever else may seem appropriate to the council. Madrid, January 18 of 1716.

The council, 19th of February 1716.

With the señor fiscal. And let him charge the governor and royal officials with the responsibility of informing them about this, expressing dismay over their not having done so up to now. And let it go by way of letters uniformly agreed on (*por cartas acordadas*) on this occasion.

The council, 20th of Feb[ruary] of 1716

Having once again discussed this dispatch because of its gravity and its scruples, [the council] has agreed with this [position]. Then, that H.M. should approve that along with the present royal notes[?], that measures be taken so that the necessary expenditures may be made with the participation of the bishop. And that he be thanked for his efforts, and that the governor and royal officials be made aware of our surprise over their not having given us an account about matters of such seriousness.

The bishop's letter to the king is followed by a brief note made at the council confirming that the bishop was thanked and so forth.

RO[?] On February 23 of 1716.
Done. To the bishop of Cuba, giving him thanks for what he did with respect to the crossing over to the city of Havana of the Indians from the keys who received holy baptism and concerning[?] the measures[?] that are to be taken for the transport of as many of them as ask for it.

This note is followed by three letters written by the king. The first letter is addressed to the bishop and the other two to the governor at Havana, with the first of the latter two addressed to the treasury officials as well. Most of the king's letter to the bishop is omitted from this translation, because the omitted sections recapitulate the content of the bishop's letter to the king and of the testimonial.

Reverend in Christ, Father Bishop
of the cathedral church of the city
of Santiago and resident in that of Havana.
                    I the King
In a letter of December 9 of 1711 with *autos* from the efforts that you made in order to bring over various Indians from the Keys of Florida. . . . And you concluded asking me to deign to order what should be done. It was seen in my Council of the Indies with what[?] my fiscal said. Nonetheless, until now, the reports that the governor and royal officials should have made in a matter of such gravity have not arrived. I have resolved concerning the *conss*^{ta} [*consulta* ?] of the 21st of the current month that a strict order be given (as by a dispatch of the date of this one is being done) to the governor and royal officials of that city to the effect that from whatsoever resources [there are] from the royal treasury, with your participation, they are to make from them all the expenditures

necessary for the transport of the Indians who may wish to receive holy baptism, and that, in accord as they proceed to arrive, they are to assign villages for them where they may live a civilized existence and Christianly under my vassalage and protection. While expressing my displeasure to the governor and royal officials over their not having rendered an account over so long a time concerning a matter of such grave importance, about the resolution of which it has seemed appropriate to me to advise them, so that they may have this report. To you, I give special thanks (as I am doing) for the charitable and Catholic zeal with which you have managed this affair and I remain completely confident that you will pay heed equally to its importance in the future, assisting on your part in the most effective fulfillment of this my decision in such a way that through the medium of your prudent, correct conduct success can be achieved in a matter so pertinent to the service of God and me, giving me an account of what develops, at the first opportunity. That this is my will. Done.

The next page in the photostats is a cover page for the king's three letters, indicating that the three letters were written on February 23, 1716. It also bears the following notes written apparently at the Council of the Indies:

On the 23 of February of 1716
    To the governor and royal officials of Havana, expressing dismay over their not having rendered an account about the Indians who crossed over to solicit reception of holy baptism and what they are going to do with the rest who are desirous of the same benefit.

This is accompanied by the following marginal note: "On 21 of December of 1720 a duplicate and a triplicate of this dispatch were sent." The second and third letters by the king follow.

The King
    To the governor and captain general of the Island of Cuba and city of San Christóbal of Havana and officials of my royal treasury of this [city]; the bishop of their island in a letter of December 9 of 1711 gives an account with *autos* of the efforts that he made so that various Indians of the Keys of Florida, who desired to receive holy baptism, might be brought to this city and that to this end he

contributed 100 pesos with which and along with the alms that it was possible to assemble and other measures that were supplied on your part, it was possible to achieve the provisioning of a vessel in which 270 Indians came along with a brother of their cacique, who went on to confer about the bringing over and preservation of the rest who desired the same benefit. These he having manifested would amount to more than six thousand (*6d*) who intended to embrace the holy Catholic faith, a meeting was convoked in which you participated along with the bishop of this island, his auxiliary, and his vicar-general, and the captain of the vessel that had brought them, in order to discuss the coming over of those who remained behind. And in it, it was decided that no more Indians should be brought over and that no monies at all should be furnished from my royal coffers without my express order, with the exception of the bishop and his vicar-general, who were of the opposite opinion. And when they insisted that the money necessary be provided from my royal treasury for the bringing over of all the Indians who might wish to cross over to this city, with the bishop offering 500 pesos from his funds and surety for the restitution to the royal coffers of what was furnished from them in the case that I should not approve of these expenditures, they did not change their opinion, because it was contrary to what was provided for by the laws, telling the bishop that he should give me an account of it, inasmuch as you would do the same for your part at the first opportunity. And the bishop concluded by asking me to deign to resolve on what should be done. And after this [letter's] having been seen in my Council of the Indies, together with what my fiscal had to say, I have resolved concerning the Consulta (*Conss*^{ta}[?]) of the 21st of the current month to manifest to you how great my displeasure has been that in the course of the more than four years that have passed they have given no account about a matter of such great importance, and burdensome to the conscience, the omission of which has been most remarkable and deserving of the most severe reprehension, which I am giving you. And without passing on for now to any other manifestation of it, I order you and command you (as I am doing) that from any resources whatsoever of my royal treasury that there may be in the coffers of that city, without fail, the necessary expenditures are to be made for the bringing over of the Indians who may wish to receive holy baptism and that this is to be done with the participation of the bishop of that island (who is being made aware of this resolution by a dispatch of this same date). And you will arrange that in accord as the Indians proceed to arrive at that city you will indicate villages where they may live Christianly and in a civilized manner under my vassalage and protection, giving me an account at the first opportunity by way of the dispatch boats about every development that occurs in this business so important for the service of God and me. You will dedicate yourselves to its effective achievement with the greatest attention, zeal, and vigilance, without leaving room for even the slightest oversight nor for the culpable omission that has prevailed until now. That this is what is my will. Done in Madrid on the 23rd of February of 1716.

I the King

By order of the king our lord, Don Diego de Morales y Velasco

The King

To my governor and captain general of the Island of Cuba and city of San Christóbal of Havana. By a separate dispatch bearing this date, issued with the insertion of another of the 23rd of February, it has seemed appropriate to me to express my displeasure and to reprehend you for the culpable omission that has occurred, as I also [have done] to the officials of my royal treasury of that city, in [not] giving me an account about the efforts made for the transport of 270 Indians from the Keys of Florida who desired to receive holy baptism and about the rest who wished to achieve the same benefit. I am repeating to you the orders that I have given on that subject so that from whatsoever funds of my royal treasury, which there may be in that city, the portions that are needed are to be furnished for so important an objective in the interim until, with a fuller knowledge of this matter, it may be possible to decide and indicate all the money that would be appropriate annually for its attainment. It is my decision to order and command you separately (as I am doing) that as soon as you receive this dispatch you are to inform me with full detail and at the first opportunity that arises about everything that has occurred pertaining to this matter from the year of 1711, when it began, to the status that it may have at present, with details on the progress that has been experienced with these conversions, the progress that can be hoped for in the future, in accord with the number of the above-mentioned Indians and the disposition that you recognize in them; and the measures that you consider should be applied for its achievement, the amount of money more or less that you will need in each year for the expenditures alluded to, and the branch of the royal treasury that could be utilized for this objective in addition to the alms that may be collected, with everything else that may occur to you in so important a subject and a notice of the whereabouts of the aforementioned 270 Indians whom the bishop of that island spoke about in his letter of December 9, 1711, as having converted to our holy faith, explaining whether those who have persevered in it are many or few and whether they are staying in that city or island or in other places to which they may have passed; that this is what is appropriate for the service of God and my [service]. Done in . . . . [This copy ends in this fashion, reflecting the fact that the texts of the three notes written by the king that appear here are rough drafts of those letters.]

2. Tocobaga in Apalachee, 1677-1718

One of the least mentioned of the aboriginal peoples of Florida is the Tocobaga, whose leader bearing the same name seems to have dominated much of the region around Tampa Bay in the 1560s and to have been a major rival to Cacique Carlos. But after the 1560s Tocobaga and his people appear in the records rarely and in the briefest of passing remarks. An exception to some degree is a group of Tocobaga who lived in Apalachee in the last quarter of the seventeenth century. They are the last of their people to have been mentioned by that name.

The Apalachee Tocobaga, or Tocopaca as Spaniards then preferred to call them, were first mentioned in 1677, but they seem to have been living in that province for a considerable time before then. These Tocobaga settled at a place named Wacissa on the river of that name. Their village contained other unidentified peoples as well. The documentation does not indicate the circumstances of their arrival. They are only one of a number of non-Apalachee people (Tama, Yamasee, Chacato, Chine, Amacano, Pacara) who appear in the records of the 1670s and thereafter as living in Apalachee. In contrast to those other outlanders' settlements, the Tocobaga's village never became a mission site, although it survived until the general destruction of the missions in 1704. However, we know that the Tocobaga had contact with friars or devout natives from Ivitachuco because a number of them were baptized on their deathbed and buried at the church of Ivitachuco. The

1677 visitor's chiding of the Tocobaga for not having become Christians, despite having lived among Christians for many years, suggests that the Tocobaga may have been keeping the friars at arms' length.

The Tocobaga provided a valuable service to the Spanish. By river and by sea the Tocobaga moved commodities needed in St. Augustine from Apalachee and westernmost Timucua to points on the Suwannee and Santa Fe rivers, from which they went on to St. Augustine by packhorse or mule, or in earlier days they were possibly packed by Indians.

Nothing is known specifically about the fate of these Apalachee Tocobaga during the destruction of the missions. They are not mentioned by name in any of the accounts of that cataclysm. But when a Spanish force returned to Apalachee in 1718 to establish a fort at St. Marks, the fort's commander reported that a cacique of Oconi had brought him news that a few Tocobaga were settled at Wacissa. Fearful for the safety of the Tocobaga at so isolated a spot, the commander announced his intention of having those Tocobaga moved to the Rio Guacara near the fort he was building. Subsequently the commander noted that about one-half of the group under one of their two chiefs had moved from a settlement on Cacina Point (near the fort) to the mouth of the Wacissa and that, around midnight of July 29, 1718, they were attacked by Pojoy. The Pojoy killed eight of the Tocobaga and carried off three. In the wake of the attack the commander placed the survivors from both communities on an island close to the fort.

During the mission period the only mention of the Tocobaga's presence in Apalachee occurs in visitation records for 1677–1678 and 1694–1695. The 1670s record is the more informative one, of value particularly for shedding light on the Tocobaga's economic role in Apalachee.

The Tocobaga appear in two portions of that visitation record, that for Apalachee and that for western Timucua. The record for Apalachee reflects the visitor's formal visitation of the Tocobaga settlement at Wacissa. For Timucua, Tocobaga are mentioned in connection with the visitor's efforts to recruit Yustagan settlers as a nucleus for a projected new village named Santa Rosa de Ivitanayo, which Spanish authorities wished to establish as a way station between the St. Johns River crossing at Salamototo and the Potano mission of Santa Fé. Tocobaga were to be contracted to transport the migrating Yustaga's provisions and household goods down the Wacissa to the sea by canoe, then along the coast to the Suwannee, and up that river to a landing place known as Pulihica. From there Santa Fé's chief would move the baggage on to Ivitanayo by packhorse.

In contrast to the 1677 visitor, the 1694 visitor did not go to Wacissa to hold his visitation for that settlement. Instead he required the Tocobaga to come to Ivitachuco, where he held a separate formal visitation for the Tocobaga after he had completed his visitation of Ivitachuco itself.

Excerpts from Domingo de Leturiondo's Inspection of the Provinces of Apalachee and Timucua, January 9 and 16, 1678

AGI, Seville, Escribanía de Cámara, leg. 156B, folios 519-615. Stetson Collection of the P.K. Yonge Library of Florida History. The visitation record for Tocobaga appears on folios 561v-563 and the mention of Tocobaga during the visitation of Timucua on folios 598v-599.

Auto. In the place of the Tocopacas, of a heathen nation on the ninth day of the month of January of the year one thousand and six hundred and seventy and eight the señor Sergeant-major Domingo de Leturiondo, lieutenant of the governor and captain general and visitor of these Provinces of Apalachee and Timuqua, having visited them and made them aware of the general *auto* of the visitation through the medium of Diego Salvador, interpreter, and of Martín Ruiz, of their same tongue, his Excellency proposed to them jointly (*juntamente*) telling them how the señor governor and captain general was ordering and commanding them to close the Channel of Bazisa [Wacissa], where the said Tocopacas live mixed up (*rebueltos?*) with other tribes because of the concerns with the enemy English that are to be feared and with other pirates of the sea. And after having conferred about this matter at length, they said that they had no complaint at all except some concern that they wished to expel them from that spot, even though they caused no harm to anybody but rather were of great assistance to the neighboring places. For in their canoes and with their pirogues[?][1] they carried the maize and the rest of the things that were shipped to the presidio when the occasion arose for this, as they were doing

1. The Spanish here is p^{as}. Conceivably there is an additional letter before the "*a.*" I presume that this is an abbreviation for *piraguas.*

at the moment. That for this purpose they went out by an arm of
the channel which they had concealed so that they could enter and
leave by it because of the principal [channel's] being closed off with
trees. And in relation to the [danger] from the enemy, they will be
more at risk whenever (*todas las vezes*) they leave the spot where
they are for forcibly they would have to live spread out along the
entire coast with the result that it would be very easy to capture
them and to use them as spies. And that while they remain where
they are, they are more secure, because they do not go out to the sea
except once in a while, and that when they do go out, they go with
care lest they should capture them because they are concerned
about their lives and the injuries that they know they would do to
all of them. And should the case arise that they should capture one
of them to use them as spies, it would be more certain that this
would serve more as a warning than as a source of harm, for it
would not be possible for them to catch everyone that would be in
that place; that even though no more than one escaped, he would
give the alarm to the neighboring places of Apalachee. And the
opposite would happen in the case that they should come without
there being anyone in the said spot of Basisa [Wacissa] as they have,
who might detect them. After having seen this and taken it into
account, his Excellency ordered that they should remain alert (*en
quietos?*) and live where they have been until now, charging them
with the responsibility of being careful in this matter. His
Excellency passed then to speak to them about their having been
among Christians for so many years, [asking] why they had not
sought to become so. To this they replied that they were not
refusing to become so, but that there had not been anyone, either
ecclesiastics or lay people, who might teach them and tell them
what the law of God contained. They know only confusedly [that] it
is good (y^{da})[2] and that there have been more than eighteen or
twenty who have died in this faith and who were buried as
Christians in the church of Hivitachuco; that they have requested
baptism at the hour of death. And his Excellency urged them with
many arguments that they should embrace the law of the Gospel,
explaining to them how much they were losing in not being
Christians; that he would strive to give them someone who might
instruct them in the law of God. And his Excellency ordered the

2. I have not deciphered this not very clearly written abbreviation.

counting of the number of people that there were and he found 348
persons between men, women, and children without [counting]
some whom they said were away traveling. And they asked his
Excellency to install and give possession to one of their caciques
and that he should confirm him in the name of His Majesty. This
was done with the solemnity that is customary. And they received
him as such, offering him obedience. With this the visitation of this
said village was concluded. His Excellency signed it jointly with the
said *atequi*. This I certify.

Domingo de Leturiondo   Diego Salvador
Before me, Martín Lorenzo de Labora, notary for the visitation

Having completed the visitation of Apalachee with his visitation of
the Tocopaca settlement, the visitor Domingo de Leturiondo returned
to Ivitachuco, where he issued a number of orders and regulations to
be observed by the inhabitants of the province of Apalachee and particularly by its deputy-governor or lieutenant. Among those orders was
the following one pertaining to the Tocobaga.

Likewise his Excellency ordered that he should not disturb the
Tocopaca nation and those of the other [nations] who live with
them or expel them from where they are, because of their great
importance in the service of His Majesty, not to mention the hopes
that they will become Christians, as some of them have died so. And
his Excellency orders that a copy of this his *auto* be sent to him [the
lieutenant] so that he may carry out everything that has been
alluded to [above], as this is appropriate for the royal service.

The passages that follow are excerpts from the 1678 visitation of
western Timucua in which reference is made to the Tocobaga. The
visitor had issued his call for volunteers to found the new settlement
of Santa Rosa de Ivitanayo while he was conducting the general session for the entire province of Yustaga at San Pedro de Potohiriba on
January 15, 1678. At that session the visitor's request elicited no response from the Yustaga. But on the following day a cacique of San
Matheo de Tolapatafi approached the visitor with the tentative offer
of volunteers, as recorded in the following excerpt.

San Pedro. I the Captain Martín Lorenzo de Labora, notary for the
visitation, certify and give true testimony how, on the sixteenth day

of January after the conclusion of the visitation in the principal
council house of San Pedro de Potohirive, Antonio, cacique of those
of the place of San Matheo, appeared before his Excellency the
señor visitor, stating that during the assembly that was held in the
said place it had been discussed and conferred upon whether there
might be some cacique who might have some vassals who might be
willing to go with them to settle the region of Hivitanayo at the
midway point between San Francisco [de Potano] and Salamototo
because of its being a very appropriate spot for the traffic of the
royal road. And despite there being some drawbacks [in the project],
he would go with some of his relatives and with the eight families it
had been proposed to take from the villages of San Pedro, Machava,
and San Matheo, and he would make a start on the said settlement
and would develop it with the condition and the provision that they
be assisted on the part of His Majesty both in the transporting of
their maize and the rest of their goods as well as of their persons
and in his giving him some axes in order to begin the opening of the
royal road and of their fields because they do not have them at
present because of their being poor, as all of them were. His
Excellency replied to this that he would do everything that he asked
because of his having recognized it to be very important that he
should be helped. And at once, without delay, his Excellency having
reached an agreement with him about the matter alluded to, he
wrote to the lieutenants, Captain Juan Fernández de Florencia and
Captain Andrés Pérez, the one so that he might arrange for some
canoes from the Tocopacas so that they might transport the maize
and the rest of the goods that he spoke of through Basisa to the
River of St. Martin [the Suwannee] as far as Pulihica and from
there the cacique of Santa Fée obligated himself to transport them
on horseback to the said region of Hivitanayo, and to the Captain
Andrés Pérez so that two soldiers might come escorting them to it
and with his Excellency promising to the families alluded to that he
would petition the governor and the royal officials about the need
for the axes and that he considered it certain that their excellencies,
after recognizing its development to be so appropriate, would give
the assistance that they were able to. And he promised it likewise in
the name of His Majesty, making a gift to them of those lands of
Hivitanayo for the said purpose and that, until the village should be
well established and have plenty of people, digging Indians (*yndios
de Caua*) would not be taken from it for some years. And likewise

they asked his Excellency [to see to it] that they might have a religious so that he would administer the holy sacraments to them and similarly that he would develop the said place on his part. And his Excellency said to them in reply that, although they [the religious] were in short supply at the present, they were awaiting the [arrival] of a mission shortly and that, once he had them, the reverend father provincial of this holy province doubtless would assist in their spiritual consolation as one so zealous for the service of God our Lord and as the responsibility for what he was petitioning for would fall on his reverend paternity. With this the matter was considered concluded and settled so that it would be put into execution at once. And at the request of his Excellency I give the present testimonial on the said sixteenth day of January of the year one thousand and six hundred and seventy and eight so that it may be evident in these *autos* of the visitation. This I certify.

Martín Lorenzo de Labora, notary for the visitation

The last of these excerpts from the 1677-1678 visitation record appears among the orders that the visitor issued at San Francisco Potano for the provinces of western Timucua as he was about to leave the region for Salamototo.

Likewise in the general assembly the founding of a settlement in the region of Hivitanayo was dealt with and it was agreed upon with the cacique of San Matheo, named Antonio, that he should come to the said region to settle with some of his relatives (*parientes*) and eight families that are ordered to be drawn from the villages of San Pedro, Machava, and San Matheo. And they were offered complete support so that they would be able to bring the said families with security and to see to the embarking of their maize and the rest of their possessions (*demas trastes*) on the river of Basisa so that they might bring them as far as Pulilica [*sic*]. The aforesaid lieutenant, Andrés Pérez, ordered that all of this should be carried out. And he supplied two soldiers for it so that, after having brought their maize and the rest of their possessions to that spot, they might convoy these families as far as Hivitanayo for their greater security.

The following is the brief record from the 1694-1695 visitation of the Tocobaga living in Apalachee.

Excerpt from Joaquín de Florencia's Inspection of the Provinces of Apalachee and Timucua, December 3, 1694

AGI, Seville, Escribanía de Cámara, leg. 157A, cuaderno I, folios 44–205. Stetson Collection of the P.K. Yonge Library of Florida History, on folios 65v–66. Joaquín de Florencia was the visitor and his visitation record bears the title "General Visitation that the Captain Joaquín de Florencia Made of the Provinces of Apalachee and Timucua, Interim Treasurer of the Presidio of St. Augustine of Florida, Judge Commissary and Inspector-General of Them by Title and Nomination of don Laureano de Torres y Ayala, Knight of the Order of Santiago, Governor and Captain General of the Said Presidio and Provinces by His Majesty."

> In the said village of Ivitachuco on the third day of December of the year one thousand six hundred and ninety-four, his Excellency the señor visitor had the Tocopaca Indians called who reside in Wacissa and he had the general *auto* of the visitation explained to them. And when they were asked whether they had anything to petition for, to relate, or to report to his Excellency, they said that nothing occurred to them in relation to what was included in it and that they were content and pleased; and his Excellency exhorted, begged, and charged them that they should seek to learn the Christian doctrine and to teach it to their children and that they should try to educate them in it. And they said that they would do so and that they would seek to take care of it. With that his Excellency considered the visitation of the aforesaid Tocopacas as concluded, leaving them their claim and suit secure for everything that might occur to them. And so that it might be evident his Excellency signed it together with the assisting witnesses, who were Francisco Domíngues, Antonio Entonado, and Joachín de Florencia, and I who certify it.

> Joachín de Florencia
> Antonio Denttonado
> Fran^co Domíngues
> Juachín de Florencia
> Before me, D^n Antt^o Ponse de León, notary for the visitation.
> Without costs I certify.

There is no indication that a mission was established among the Tocobaga during the remaining nine years or so before the dissolution of the missions in Apalachee in 1704. The Tocobaga are not mentioned on a 1697 listing of the missions or during the hastily conducted extraordinary visitation held by Juan de Ayala Escobar in 1698. Neither the Spanish authorities nor Colonel James Moore mention the Tocobaga in their accounts of Moore's attack on Apalachee early in 1704 or of the subsequent Creek attack of June–July 1704, which led the surviving Spaniards, Apalachee, and Chacato to abandon the region.

Only after Spaniards returned to Apalachee in 1718 were there a few passing references to a renewed or continued presence of a few Tocobaga in the province. The following excerpts contain those references. The first excerpt is from a running letter to the governor written between April 28, 1718, and August 3, 1718, by the commandant of the Spanish forces at St. Marks.

Joseph Primo de Rivera to Governor Juan de Ayala y Escobar, April 28 to August 3, 1718

AGI, Seville, Santo Domingo 843. The transcription was made from a microfilm copy of the Stetson Collection photostat of the document. In the Stetson Collection the document bears the source identification of AGI 58-1-30.

Señor, Governor and Captain General

Sire, I am giving your lordship an account of having achieved my arrival in this province and at the *chiquassa*[3] of Tomole on the 15th day of March with complete success and no damage. . . .

I received the [letter] from your lordship, dated March 30 with the cacique of Oconi. . . . The said cacique of Oconi brought me news that some ten Tocopacas are settled in Basisa with five or six women. That these promised obedience to the cacique of Caveta with a *capuche*,[4] which he received in this post and presented (*me lo press^{to}*[?]) to me as chief head (*caveca maior*) of the province. That,

3. The Apalachee name for "abandoned village," it is usually spelled *chicasa*.

4. There is no such word in modern Spanish. *Capucha* means a friar's cowl, hood of a woman's cloak, or circumflex accent. A more plausible alternative is *capote*, among the many meanings of which is a sleeved raincloak or military greatcoat.

accordingly, they gave[?] me to understand where I considered it more correct (*q assi me lo dieron[?] a entender donde tube por mas asertado*) to command them in his Majesty's name that they should order all the peoples that. . . . [The next several lines are illegible in the microfilm due to the fading of the ink.] Nonetheless, at the departure of the Lieutenant Peña for that presidio, the corporal, Francisco Domingos, with two soldiers goes along with him as far as Aiubale and from there to Bacisa and he is to bring them here, inasmuch as one cannot trust in the words of these ones. That they could be carried off or be killed there, without our knowing that it has been done. I will collect and unite them here at this River of Guacara or Tosquache. That even though these [people] have their small plots of maize already [planted], they will go to see them every week and in this fashion the opportunity [for such mischance] will be removed. And they will be of great comfort to us.

Joseph Primo de Rivera to Governor Juan de Ayala y Escobar, August 3, 1718

AGI, Seville, Santo Domingo 843. The second excerpt is from a letter to the governor by the commandant at St. Marks written on August 3, 1718. The transcription was made from the Florida State University Strozier Library's microfilm copy of the North Carolina Collection of copies of Spanish documents, reel 14.

I have gathered the Tocopacas within the range of the cannon for the reason that the half who were on Casina Point [one of the headlands at the mouth of the St. Marks River, see Leonard 1939: 283, 304], as they were two caciques, one crossed over to the mouth of the Bacisa to make his settlement. And on the 29th day about midnight the enemy Pojoy entered among them and killed eight persons and carried off three. These, according to what they say, came by sea to make this assault against them. And they have obliged the poor souls, the one and the other [group], to seek refuge on a key that is in this river, close to this fort. I have given this news to Chaliquisliche,[5] and it is to be supposed that people will come down to this garrison and from here they will be supplied with canoes so that they may go out in search of those rogues (*picaros*) to see whether it is possible to capture them, because it is

5. This is Cherokeeleechee or Cherokee-Killer of English sources.

certain, they say, that they do not want friendship with anyone. Also because they are few, all of them about 25 or 30 men, I do not doubt that it [can be] done. That if they decide on the aforesaid, bringing along some archers from those, the enterprise will succeed. . . . San Marcos, August 3, 1718.

3. Governor Benavides' Report on Natives Baptized Between 1718 and Early 1723

In this letter to the king the governor of Florida reported the progress that had been made toward the conversion of Florida's natives since his assumption of the governorship on the third of August 1718. English defeat of the general native uprising in South Carolina in 1715, which is known as the Yamasee War, had brought an influx of non-Christian natives to the vicinity of St. Augustine. The governor reported the total of the natives baptized during that period as 465 adults and 193 children. All the converts were drawn from settlements in the vicinity of St. Augustine or of the fort at San Marcos de Apalachee. The governor's letter was dated March 8, 1723. His letter is followed by a lengthy summary of its contents made at the Council of the Indies. The final piece within this section is a register of the natives baptized between August 1718 and the beginning of 1723, composed at the governor's request by the friars who served those natives. The register lists each settlement by name or by the name of the natives who lived in it, identifies the tribal affiliation of the newly baptized, and details the number of adults and children among the newly baptized in each of those settlements. The name of the friar who served them is included.

The governor's letter is not reproduced here as its contents are summarized adequately in the notes on it made at the Council of the Indies. The first piece reproduced here represents those notes. It is followed by the register of the newly baptized composed by the friars.

Several groups among the natives mentioned in this listing originated in south Florida or had an association with natives from south Florida. Those mentioned in the register as belonging to the Costa nation Guasacara definitely originated somewhere in south Florida. Juan José Elijio de la Puente applied the name Costas to the Indians of the Keys, remarking that the "Keys were always inhabited by the Costas Indians" (Elijio de la Puente 1764). Swanton identified the Costa as probably the Ais or "tribes formerly living near them" (1946: 85), but he did not specify the evidence on which his opinion was based. In 1735 the name Costas was applied by an Alafay chief to his own nation thus, "Don Antonio Pojoy, head as I am of the Alafaia Costas Nation" (Aguilar, Jesus y Casas, and Rossa 1735). To my knowledge the name Guasacara appears nowhere else, unlike the name Costas, which appears repeatedly from 1723 into the 1760s. In 1723 the Alafay were living in a settlement identified simply as "Village of Timucua." Undoubtedly it is the village of Santa Fé, "a settlement of the Timucuan and Pojois nation," of the 1726 census. This and the name of the Alafay chief, Antonio Pojoy, establish clearly that the Alafay of 1723 and thereafter were part of the Pojoy. Their name attached to the Alafia River probably indicates where they lived originally. The Hororo are the Jororo mentioned earlier in this book, who formerly lived south or southwest of Mayaca in the portion of south-central Florida identified vaguely as the *rinconada* or the *rinconada de Carlos*.

The identity of other groups on this 1723 list presents problems, particularly the Casipuia and Chiluque. The Amapira probably were Yamasee. Other sources (see Hann 1988: 291–292) indicate that the natives who settled near San Marcos during this era were Yamasee, Apalachee, and Tocobaga. As the number of Yamasee in the area was far greater than either the Apalachee or the Tocobaga, the ninety-one Amapira listed as having been baptized seems to eliminate the other two. The seventy-nine adults baptized would rule out their being the already Christianized Apalachee. The total of ninety-one baptisms seems to eliminate the Tocobaga, as only a few Tocobaga are known to have been present in the San Marcos region at this time. Swanton suggested that the Casipuia may have been Cusabo (1946: 129), based on the resemblance of Cosapuya (the spelling of the 1726 census) to Coçapoy, but Swanton was not certain that such was the case. If such were the case, that would seem to undermine the position of those who include the Escamacu and Orista among the Guale, as the Casipuia were identified in a 1717 census as of the Casipuya language (Ayala y Escobar 1717).

Establishing the identity of the Chiluque presents the greatest problem. It is most probable that the Chiluque of 1723 and thereafter were the Mocama of the 1717 census's village of San Buena Bentura de Palica. Swanton's identification of the Chiluque as Cherokee (1922: 90) seems to be ruled out by the absence of adults among the newly baptized reported on this 1723 list. That assumption is confirmed by the 1726 list's identification of the Chiluca inhabitants of San Buena Bentura as seventy "old Christians." Swanton himself changed his mind, acknowledging in 1946 that the Chiluca were probably Mocama on the basis of the Mocama's earlier association with the name Buena Ventura and on the characterization of the 1726 Chiluca as old Christians (1946: 119). But raising doubts about the correctness of the identification of the Chiluque of 1723 and thereafter with the Mocama is a 1738 statement by Fray Joseph de Hita, who was *doctrinero* at Palica in 1723. He characterized himself as *atequi* or interpreter for the Timucuan and Chiluque languages (Montiano 1738). Of course, he may have used the term *language* in the sense of *dialect*. And there are other complications as well. In 1680 Chiluque along with Chichumeco (Westo) and Uchise attacked the Georgia missions of San Buenaventura de Guadalquini and Santa Catalina de Guale. If the Chiluque of 1680 were Mocama, it would mean Mocama attacking Mocama, as Guadalquini's inhabitants in that era were Mocama (Hann 1987: 8; Serrano y Sanz 1912: 216-217). Verner Crane identified the 1680 Chiluque as Cherokee without giving a source for that identification (1956: 17). There is no completely satisfactory explanation of the identity of either of these groups of Chiluque or any explanation of why Spaniards from 1723 on always seemingly referred to Mocama as Chiluque. On the 1726 census the inhabitants of Nombre de Dios also were identified as of the Chiluca nation.

Palica was the name of the 1723 village where the Chiluque lived. In 1567 Palica or Palican was designated by Menéndez de Avilés as a site for a blockhouse to be built on an elevation on an island near the Matanzas River five leagues south of St. Augustine. At the start of the seventeenth century there was a mission village named Palica about five leagues from St. Augustine and two from Capoaca (Hann 1990: 431-432). In 1728 Palica was spoken of as having been four leagues from the city.

The name Amacarisa attached to Nombre de Dios appears to be a place name. In 1728 the settlement was introduced as Macariz alias Nombre de Dios. In 1738 the name was given as Nombre de Dios de Macariz (Montiano 1738).

Notes by the Council of the Indies, September 17, 1723

AGI, Seville, Santo Domingo 865 (58-2-16/81). Antonio de Benavides, letter to the king, March 8, 1723. Stetson Collection of the P.K. Yonge Library of Florida History.

Florida   To His Majesty March 8 of 1723

Received on the 17th of September of 1723 with the paper from the Sr. Marques de Grimaldo of the 15th of the said month so that it may be viewed in the council and given the course that befits it, after consulting with His Majesty about what may be necessary.

He reports that since he took possession of that governorship, which was in August of the year 1718, he has been most strongly interested in the conversion of the Indians of all those provinces, as is evident from the registers from the religious of the *doctrinas,* which he sends, which exist in the vicinity of that presidio, who have been reduced to our holy Catholic faith, 465 adult Indians and 193 children, expecting that the conversions will show more progress, if orders are given in the course of time for the settling of the Province of Apalachee with families from the Canary Islands. Concerning this he requests that measures be taken so that the French and the English do not achieve their intentions of seizing control of that territory. And likewise, that he see to it also so that the poor families of that district, who are many widows and orphans who do not enjoy a salary, may cross over to the island of Cuba where they would be free from the risks from the heathen Indians who threaten ruin and from the need that they suffer because of there not being any workers who might cultivate the soil and so that the population may be reduced to the small number of the garrison of the fort.

The council's summary is followed by a copy of the Franciscan provincial's order to his friars in the various *doctrinas* under their vow of obedience to comply with the governor's order as vice-patron[1] to provide a report of the number of natives who were baptized in each of the *doctrinas* since August 1718 when Benavides assumed the governorship. This order by Fray Blas Pulido was dated in St. Augustine on February 17, 1723, and written by the provincial secretary, Fray Joseph del Castillo, who also composed the register of the Indians baptized since August 1718 from the reports submitted by the various friars. Fray Pulido's order is not reproduced here as it contains nothing pertaining

1. This is an allusion to the Royal *Patronato* or Patronage. As perceived by the Castilian monarchs, it involved the subordination of the Spanish church to the crown in all spheres except the definition of dogma and the maintenance of religious discipline. This power was extended over the church in the New World in particular under the Bulls of Donation, which gave the monarch sole responsibility for the evangelization of the Indies (McAlister 1984: 194).

to the missions or the natives of south Florida. The following is the register composed by Fray Castillo, dated February 25, 1723. The register begins with a note on the natives baptized at the friary in St. Augustine whose tribal affiliation is not indicated.

Nations of
Indians

Children = Adults

Quantities 7 = 23	By certification from the Reverend Father Fray Domingo Garza, guardian of the convent, it is established that seven children and twenty-three adults have been baptized in it from the year one thousand seven hundred and eighteen up to the present.
Yamasees 7 = 18	By another certification from the aforesaid father guardian it is established that seven children and eighteen adults were baptized at the garrison of St. Marks of Apalachee during the time that he was there.
Guasacaras 15 = 39	By certification from the father definitor, Fray Joseph López de Toledo, *doctrinero* of the village of the Costa nation Guasacara, it is established that fifteen children and thirty-nine adults have been baptized.
Yamasees 21 = 26	By certification from the father guardian, Fray Juan Martínez de San Joseph, *doctrinero* of the village of Nombre de Dios Chiquito, it is established that twenty-one children and twenty-six adults have been baptized in the said time.
Casipuias 7 = 8	By certification from the father preacher, Fray Pedro Morales, *doctrinero* of the village of the Casipuyas, it is established that seven children and eight adults have been baptized.
Chiluques 15 =	By certification from Father Fray Joseph de Hita, *doctrinero* of the village of Palica, it is established that fifteen children have been baptized.
Alafaes 28 = 134	By certification from the father guardian, Fray Pedro Bogado, *doctrinero* of the village of Timuqua, it is established[2] that twenty-eight children and one hundred and thirty-four adults have been baptized.
Yamasees 4 = 13	By certification of the father guardian, Fray Joseph de Flores, *doctrinero* of the village of Poco Talaqua, it is established that four children and thirteen adults have been baptized.

2. The Spanish word here, *Costa*, is probably a copyist error and meant to be *Consta*, or "it is established."

Hororos 4 = 26	By certification from the Father Fray Francisco Gil de Reyna, *doctrinero* of the village of Hororo, it is established that four children and twenty-six adults have been baptized.
Yamasees 23 = 82	By certification from the Father Fray Antonio de Hita, *doctrinero* of the village of la Tama, it is established that twenty-three children and eighty-two adults have been baptized.
Timucuans 18 = 4	By certification of the Reverend Father Claudio de Florencia, *doctrinero* of the village of Nombre de Dios Amacarisa it is established that eighteen children and four adults have been baptized.
Apalachee 6 =	By certification of the father guardian, Fray Pedro de Riera, *doctrinero* of the village of Moze, it is established that six children have been baptized.
Ibaja 26 = 13	By certification from the Reverend Father Fray Antonio Romero, *doctrinero* of the village of Tolomato, it is established that twenty-six children and thirteen adults were baptized during that time.
Ama piras 12 = 79	By another certification from the said Father Fray Joseph de Hita, who served in San Marcos de Apalachee, it is established that twelve children and seventy-nine adults were baptized during that time.
193 = 465	Thus the six hundred and fifty-eight people, who, it is established by the said certifications as having been baptized from the year of one thousand seven hundred and eighteen up to the present from the nations that have been mentioned in the margin, with one hundred and ninety-three of them being children and four hundred and sixty-five adults, after having first christened the most important caciques of the nations that have been cited. And so that it may be evident from the request of the señor don Antonio de Benavides Basan y Molina, colonel, cavalry of the royal armies of His Majesty and subaltern officer (*exempto*) of his royal guards, governor and captain general of this city and of its provinces by the king our lord, I issue the present in this our convent of St. Augustine of Florida on the twenty-fifth of February of one thousand seven hundred and twenty three.

Fr. Blas Pulido, provincial minister by order of S.P.M.R.[3]

Fr. Joseph del Castillo def[initor] and secretary

3. This abbreviation possibly stands for *Su Paternidad Muy Reverendo,* or "His Most Reverend Paternity."

4. Governor Benavides' Visitation of 1726

The governor's record of his 1726 visitation of the native settlements in the vicinity of St. Augustine and San Marcos de Apalachee complements the 1723 listing, giving the total population for each settlement, broken down into categories of men, women, and children, boys and girls, old Christians, new converts, and heathens. It notes the material of which churches were built in settlements that possessed one. This listing of sixteen settlements includes two more than were mentioned in 1723. Even so not all the settlements mentioned in 1723 can be matched with counterparts on the 1726 list. For some the match is obvious. This includes the Costa, Casapuya, Chiluque, Apalachee San Luis, Tolomato, and the two San Antonios and San Diego inhabited by Yamasee. As was noted in the general introductory essay to Part III, the Piaxa (Aypaja) of the *rinconada* de Carlos are probably the Hororo of 1723. The Timucua and Pojoy of Santa Fé are the Village of Timucua and Alafay of 1723. Santa Catarina has no equivalent on the 1723 list, but does appear on a 1717 census. The Iguaja settlement of San Joseph has no counterpart on either the 1723 or 1717 lists. The Indians of the *rinconada* of the Macapiros nation represent a new group, which came, probably, from somewhere in or close to the Jororo territory.

Governor Antonio de Benavides' Visitation of Settlements near St. Augustine and San Marcos de Apalachee, December 1-11, 1726

AGI, Seville, Santo Domingo 866. This translation was made from a microfilm copy supplied to Dr. Marquardt by Victoria Stapells-Johnson.

Florida———Year———of 1726
Report
of the inquiries made during the visitation of the settlements of the Indians, which his lordship made in virtue of the order from His Majesty, which are located in the vicinity of this presidio. And in it one finds the settlements that there are and what men, women, and children each place has.

Autos
In the city of St. Augustine of Florida on the first day of the month of December of this year of one thousand seven hundred and twenty-six his lordship, the señor Don Antonio de Benavides Vazan

y Molina, colonel of cavalry of the armies of H.M. and disengaged
from his royal guards, governor and captain general of this said city
and its provinces, stated that because of finding himself with an
order from His Majesty that he should visit the settlements of the
Christian Indians, which are located in the vicinity of this presidio,
and because of its being appropriate for the better production of the
documents, the present notary is participating in the aforesaid
visitation so that, as it progresses, he can set down by way of
certification and investigation what he may see and what is evident
to him that exists in the said places. He is to do this starting
tomorrow, the second of this month, indicated already,
accompanying him [the governor]. And for what pertains to the two
Indian settlements, which are located in the Province of Apalachee,
established in the said province in the vicinity of the fort of St.
Marks, his lordship has true knowledge of them. And concerning
everything that may be done in virtue of this *auto,* he will compose
the necessary report or reports in order to give an account to His
Majesty. And by it I so provide, order, and sign.

Don Antonio de Benavides

Before me, Juan Solana, notary for the public and for the
government

Visitation which has begun to be made in the settlements of the
Indians of all the nations, the second day of December of this year
one thousand seven hundred and twenty-six, in which there is
declared with authentication the state of the *doctrinas* which exist
in the vicinity of this presidio and of the fort of St. Marks
established in the Province of Apalachee, the number of people of
which each one is composed, the Christian and heathen Indians
which there are in them, and the manner of church that they have
and its fabrication.

1st *doctrina,* San Anttonio, church and convent of palm-thatch
(*palma*). Settlement of the Yamasa nation (Yamasee), recently
converted Christians

Men, twenty-two	*U*o22
Women, sixteen	*U*o16
Children, eleven	*U*o11

2d, San Anttonio, church and convent of palm-thatch. Settlement of the Yamasa nation, recently converted Christians and four heathen.

Men, twenty-one	*U*o21
Women, twelve	*U*o12
Children, sixteen	*U*o16
Heathen, four	*U*ooo (*sic*)

3d, San Diego, church and convent of palm-thatch. Settlement of the Yamasa nation, recently converted Christians.

Men, twenty-six	*U*o26
Women, twenty-seven	*U*o27
Children, twelve	*U*o12

4th, Santta Cathalina, church and convent of palm-thatch. Settlement of the Iguaja nation (Guale), old Christians and recently converted new ones, attached.

Men, thirty-five	*U*o35
Women, forty-seven	*U*o47
Children, twenty-two	*U*o22

5th, Our Lady of Guadalupe, church of boards (*tablas*) and convent of straw (*paja*), settlement of the Yguaja nation, old Christians and six recent converts attached.

Men, eleven	*U*o11
Women, sixteen	*U*o16
Children, eighteen	*U*o18
recently converted, six	

6th, San Joseph, settlement of the Iguaja nation. Ten old Christians, five recent converts, and two women attached.

Men, fifteen	*U*o15
Women, eighteen	*U*o18
Children, five	*U*oo5

This settlement is attached to the fifth one of Our Lady of Guadalupe.

7th, San Buena Bentura, church and convent of palm-thatch. Settlement of the Chiluca nation. Seventy old Christians.

Men, nineteen	*U*o19
Women, twenty-four	*U*o24
Children, twenty-seven	*U*o27

8th, Nombre de Dios, settlement of the Chiluca nation. Church of stone and convent. Fifty-five old Christians and seven recent converts.

Men, nineteen	*U*o19

Women, twenty-three   *Uo*23
Children, twenty   *Uo*20

9th, Santa Fée, settlement of the Timucua and Pojoi nation, attached to the eighth church, Nombre de Dios. Twenty-five old Christians and twenty recent converts.

Men, twenty   *Uo*20
Women, seventeen   *Uo*17
Children, eight   *Uo*o8

10th, San Luis, church and convent of palm-thatch. Settlement of the Apalachee nation. Seventy-eight old Christians and nine recent converts.

Men, thirty-six   *Uo*36
Women, twenty-seven   *Uo*27
Children, twenty-four   *Uo*24

11th, San Anttonio, church and convent of palm-thatch. Settlement of the Cosapuya nation and other nations. Forty-three recently converted Christians, twelve heathens.

Men, twenty-four   *Uo*24
Women, thirteen   *Uo*13
Children, eighteen   *Uo*18

12th, San Anttonio, church and convent of palm-thatch. Settlement of the Costas nation. Thirty-eight recently converted Christians and fifty heathens.

Men, fifty-five   *Uo*55
Women, thirteen   *Uo*13
Children, twenty   *Uo*20

13th, San Anttonio, church and convent of palm-thatch. Settlement of the Yamaza nation established in the province of Apalachee. Forty-eight recently converted Christians, ninety-eight heathens.

Men, sixty-six   *Uo*66
Women, fifty-one   *Uo*51
Children, twenty-nine   *Uo*29

14th, Indians of the *rinconada* of the Macapiras nation, attached to the seventh place of San Buenaventura. Eighteen recently converted Christians, six heathens.

Men, seventeen   *Uo*17
Women, six   *Uo*o6
Child, one   *Uo*o1

15th, Indians of the *rinconada* of Carlos of the Piaja nation— without a church, thirty-eight heathens.

Men, nineteen	Uo19
Women, eleven	Uo11
Children, eight	Uoo8

16th, San Juan, settlement of the Apalachee and Yamasee nation established in the Province of Apalachee, attached to the church of St. Marks. Forty-five Christians, one heathen.

Men, sixteen	Uo16
Women, seventeen	Uo17
Children, thirteen	Uo13
	1Uo11 Total

Certification

I the ensign, Juan Solana, notary for the public and for the government of this city and presidio of St. Augustine of Florida, certify and give witness in the best manner that I can and in the part where it is appropriate to the señores who may see the present [document] how from the second day of this present month of December of this year of one thousand seven hundred and twenty-six until today, the eleventh of the said month and year I have been present in the company of his lordship the señor don Anttonio de Benavides Vazan y Molina, colonel of cavalry of the armies of H.M. and disengaged (*exempto*) from his royal guards *Etre* governor and captain general of this said city and its provinces for His Majesty, at the visitation that his lordship has made in the settlements of the Indians of all nations that are evident and are laid out in the two sheets; with this the places that are [and] the men, women, and children that each settlement has and those there are in them [who are] heathens and Christians. It is evident to me that in each there is a church and convent made of straw (*paja*) and the framework (*ligason*) of wood, capable of housing the religious *doctrinero* with great decency and the churches with their altars and the necessary accoutrements (*Ornamentos*) for the celebration of the divine services; how everything mentioned from hereon forward is evident and appears in the catalogue (*Nomina*) cited; that there are in the sixteen places, both heathen Indians and Christians, women and children; four hundred and twenty-one men; three hundred and thirty-eight women, and two hundred and fifty-two children, which amount to the figure of one thousand and eleven people, barring a slip of the pen or of addition. And so that it may be evident in accord with what was ordered by his lordship through his *auto* furnished on the first of this present month, I give the present [certification] on the said eleventh day of December of the said year of one thousand seven hundred and twenty-six.

Juan Solana, notary for the public and for the government

It agrees with the original visitation of which mention has been made and which remains for now in my possession and office and to which I refer and so that it may be evident in accord with what was ordered by his lordship the said señor governor and captain general, I give the present [certification] in Florida on the thirteenth of December of this year of 1726, written on five sheets along with this one for my signature and on common paper because the stamped [variety] does not circulate in this presidio. And in witness of it

I make my sign   before a notary
duplicated

Juan Solana notary [for] [the] public [and] [for] [the] government

5. Fray Bullones' 1728 Report on the Missions

The 1728 report on the missions by Florida's Franciscan provincial Fray Bullones was a product of the collation controversy, which was a move by the crown and Cuba's bishop to end the Florida native settlements' long enjoyment of their status as mission territory and to convert the *doctrinas* to regular parishes whose pastors would be appointed by the bishop rather than by the Franciscan provincial and receive a salary from ecclesiastical revenues generated in the territory under the pastor's jurisdiction as holders of a benefice. In Canon Law (according to the *New Catholic Dictionary,* III: 999), collation is "the second and most essential of three stages in the provision of an ecclesiastical office or benefice, the first and third of which are presentation and institution [i.e., installation]. In this sense a collation is the act of conferring an ecclestiastical benefice or office on a designated person or presentee."

As the provincial was arguing that Florida's native *doctrinas* were in no way prepared to adjust to and support such an elevation in their status, this factor should be kept in mind in evaluating the evidence that the provincial presented. The provincial definitely poor-mouthed Nombre de Dios as never having had more than ten men and ten women, in obvious contradiction to the 1717 and 1726 censuses. But with that exception and caution, there is no evidence to suggest that the provincial painted a dramatically darker picture of the state of the native settlements than was justified.

The provincial made a very interesting allusion to the undeveloped status of the Florida missions even in the days before the general destruction of the 1702–1704 period. He noted that even then it was not the practice to install standing baptismal fonts or tabernacles for housing the Eucharist in the mission churches because of the danger of revolt from within or attack from without by neighboring heathen tribes. The provincial observed that when communion needed to be brought to natives who were ill, the needed hosts were consecrated at the daily Mass because of the absence of tabernacles.

The provincial's observations are borne out in two inventories of the sacred vessels and other such equipment held by the Florida missions (see Hann 1986: 147–164). I have noted in that context that "One of the puzzling omissions in those inventories is the lack of the mention of any ciboriums, the vessel used to hold the hosts for distribution" to the faithful at communion time, for Viaticum, or for regular visits to the sick (p. 153). One would expect to find at least one ciborium per mission and a secure tabernacle in which to store the host-containing ciborium. For the thirty-four Florida missions, the 1681 inventory listed forty-seven silver chalices with their patens, but only five *sagrarios,* which might be translated either as tabernacles or ciboriums. Similarly, only five holy-water basins were listed in 1681. This reality suggests that many of Florida's mission churches may have been far less elaborate and more primitive structures than has been suspected.

The provincial's interesting comment that the church at Nombre de Dios Chiquito "was not the worst because of having some boards along the sides that kept out the rains and winds" points in the same direction. That remark might be interpreted as indicating that it was not uncommon to have churches that were open at the sides. Such a supposition provides an explanation for the inadequate size of some of the mission churches (among those studied archaeologically) for housing the mission's known population (Hann 1988: 39). Questions have been raised of late about the reliability of some earlier archaeological identifications of structures as churches, especially in Apalachee, where structures identified as churches may be friaries instead (see McEwan 1991, in press; Marrinan 1991; Saunders 1990: 532). Those not able to fit into the enclosed space covered by the roof could assist Mass as easily standing outside.

The provincial's report is possibly the most useful of the three listings of the native settlements reproduced in Part III in that it gives a thumbnail sketch of the migrations of their inhabitants and the location of their settlements over the few preceding years and recounts the destruction of most of those still in existence when Nombre de Dios in Macariz was attacked by an Anglo-Creek force in 1727. The fourteen settlements around St. Augustine of the 1726 listing shrink to nine on the provincial's list even before the destruction of 1727.

The provincial indicated that most of the south Florida natives living near St. Augustine had disappeared by 1728, except for the Costa. All but a few of the Pojoy, Amacapira, and Jororo are revealed as having perished in a 1727 epidemic. The few survivors returned to their former homes in south Florida. The provincial made no mention of the fate of the *rinconada* de Carlos of 1726. Among the settlements inhabited by south Florida natives, only that of the Costa seems to have enjoyed any permanence. It was mentioned in 1738 and 1739 under the name San Antonio de la Costa. In 1738 the village had a population of nineteen, consisting of eight men, four married women, one widow, two boys, and four girls. Only two were Christians. Many had been killed at the hands of their enemies (Montiano 1738). By 1759 nine surviving Costa were living in Nombre de Dios in the last house listed in the census of that year (Ruiz 1759). Throughout most if not all of this period all the south Florida natives living in the vicinity of St. Augustine continued to live as fisher-hunter-gatherers. In his report the provincial noted that when the Costa "feel like it, they leave their camp and go off to eat palm fruit and alligators."

Others among the south Florida natives returned to the vicinity of St. Augustine in the early 1730s. Alafay were mentioned as again living in a village near St. Augustine in 1734 in association with Pojoy and Amacapira at a site only a rifle-shot's distance from a Jororo village. They may have been there as early as 1731. After being redistributed to other sites by a new governor in 1734, who did not keep promises that he made to them or compensate them for work he required of them, they all withdrew furtively to the southern coast (Montiano 1738). For more details on the vicissitudes of these natives, see Hann 1989: 180-200.

Fray Joseph de Bullones to the King, October 5, 1728

AGI, Seville, Santo Domingo 865 (58-2-16/8). Stetson Collection of the P.K. Yonge Library of Florida History.

The first page of this nineteen-page document contains two pieces. The first piece, on the right half of the page, is a brief introductory note written by Fray Joseph de Bullones, explaining the reason for this letter. The left-hand half of the page is filled from top to bottom with a summary of the documents' contents made at the Council of the Indies. The council's notes extend the full width of the page below Bullones' note and fill most of the upper half of the back of the page as well.

Because of the reverend bishop of this island having issued an order, with two royal decrees enclosed, asking for information about the *doctrinas* of the Province of Florida (of which I am presently the provincial) administered by the missionary religious of the seraphic order [that] they be reduced and converted to collated benefices (*beneficios colados*) and that it be carried out in the same manner as is provided for by royal laws of the royal patronage. He went on to give an account to Your Majesty about the reply that I issued concerning the aforesaid requisition and it is that which is evident from the attached *autos* so that once Your Majesty has been informed of everything that the said missions are and have been, he may determine what is most pleasing to him and to his royal will, to which we will submissively give prompt obedience. May God preserve the Catholic royal person of Your Majesty as is needed by Christendom.[1] Havana, October 5 of the year 1728.

In the light of this letter and testimonial from Fray Joseph de Bullones, provincial of the *doctrinas* of the Province of Florida, which (señor don Joseph de Panno sends to the council at the order of His Highness so that the fiscal may report what strikes him

---

1. I am uncertain of my rendition of the first letter in this series of abbreviations that appear to be *L. C. R^l P. de V. M.*

concerning its content.[2] That it consists of giving an account of the
reply that he gave to the reverend bishop of that island concerning
the requisition that he issued to him, with the enclosure of two
royal decrees, in order that the *doctrinas* of Florida (and the
religious of St. Francis administer [them]) may be converted to
beneficed curacies (*beneficios curados*) and so that they may receive
the collation (*collaz^{on}*) from him in accordance with the royal
patronato. And despite the secretariat's having noted that this letter
is a duplicate of another concerning this subject, which has been
seen in the council, the fiscal must make a reflection (in view of the
antecedents of the matter), that, after having asked for reports
concerning the status of the missions of Florida and concerning the
number of people of which they are composed, for which the
governors of Havana, Florida, and the reverend bishop supplied
information that gave rise to His Majesty's having issued the royal
decree on the 13th of May of [1]723 to the reverend bishop so that
the missionary religious might receive the canonical collation from
him in accordance with the royal *patronato* in order to administer
the holy sacraments to the Indians. The missionaries opposed this
because of their being missions and austere (*rigoroses*)
administrations, not *fasnas*,[3] of having been practiced, and other
reasons that they expounded; and nonetheless, other more specific
reports were requested so as to [obtain] a full understanding of the
missions; concerning this, the reverend bishop, and the governor of
Florida, and this provincial sent reports. And after having looked at
them and the antecedents, the lack of formal organization that
characterized the status of those villages was recognized [and that]
they did not have *doctrineros* in due form, as those Indians found
themselves as refugees, living in the vicinity and shelter of the
presidio [i.e., St. Augustine] and as having abandoned their former
settlements because of the enemy invasions. For this [reason] it was
not possible to install the collation of the religious *doctrineros* and to
have to receive them from the reverend bishop, for which reasons
and those the señor fiscal set forth, the council resolved (in a decree

2. There is no end parenthesis symbol to balance the first one. My rendition of this elliptic and convoluted sentence is tentative. In Spanish "El fiscal"
are the opening words of the sentence.

3. A manuscript reviewer suggested that this was possibly meant to be
faenas. As such it could have the sense of "business affair" or even possibly of
"sinecure."

of February 16 of this year) that dispatches be sent out, suspending the execution of the decree concerning the collation of those *doctrinas* [issued] in the year [1]723, taking into account the fact that for now there were no formed villages in that province and that they should be considered only conversions. These dispatches, the secretariat notes, are written and ready to be sent.

In respect to this, he said, there is nothing to be done on the subject, taking into account its being a duplicate of the letter of this religious and the resolution alluded to has been taken by the council and that it does not contain anything new to be resolved. *In^d* on 21st of November of 1729.

Council 24 of November of 1729

Seen

The following page contains additional repetitious notes made at the Council of the Indies, which are not reproduced here. The letter by Fray Bullones, or *auto* as it is entitled, is also omitted here as it contains only an arid discussion of the collation issue, which is not pertinent here. It runs for almost eight pages. At the bottom of page 11 of the document it is followed without a break by the testimonial by Fray Bullones, the translation of which follows, providing information on the current status of the missions and a brief review of the factors that brought them to their sad state at that time.

In this convent of the city of Havana of Our Holy Father Francis on the thirteenth day of the month of August of the year one thousand seven hundred and twenty-eight our Very Reverend Father Fray Joseph Bullones, retired reader, ex-definitor and provincial minister of this Province of Santa Elena of Florida, in view of the requisition issued by *YH$^{mg^{or}}$*4 Master don Gerónimo Valdés, the most worthy bishop of this bishopric of Santiago de Cuba on the ninth of July of the said year [1728], which appears at the beginning of these inquiries, so that the royal decrees, which were issued by the Royal and Supreme Council of the Indies, witnessed to and inserted in it, may be carried out in order that the religious of this said province, who administer the *doctrinas* of Florida, will not be able to do so without first being presented and

4. I have been unable to determine what these abbreviations stand for. The *g^{or}* usually stands for "governor," but that title does not seem pertinent here.

collated in accord with the laws of the royal *patronato* cited in the
said royal decrees and also so that his Most Illustrious lordship may
exercise full vigilance over the fulfillment of the obligation of
doctrineros that are installed thus in accord with what is
established more at length and more extensively in its context. His
most reverend paternity said that he must order and is ordering the
issuance of a supplicatory dispatch to his lordship of Havana so
that, in attention to the fact that the intentions of the king cannot
presently be carried out because no settlement has survived as a
consequence of the demolition, desolation, and total destruction that
characterizes those provinces from the repeated invasions of the
enemy. Let his Most Illustrious lordship deign to hold back and
suspend any whatsoever inquiry until such time as His Majesty
(may God save him), informed formally and truthfully about those
events and about the status of the ones that there are, which are
called *doctrinas,* and about the status of their development, may
thereby arrange his royal will as he sees best. For being most
certain, as it is, that, even in the times when that country enjoyed
some quiet, it was not possible to maintain churches in any of the
so-called *doctrinas* that were other than of straw (*paja*), nor a
tabernacle (*sagrario*)[5] or standing baptismal font (*Pila Baptismal de
pie*) because in [the time] of the greatest calm and while they were
most free of worry, the Indians of the reduction were in the habit of
rising up and rebelling, killing the *doctrineros,* subjecting them to
notable and harsh extortions and torments, [even] the very servants
and help (*siruientes y famulos*) who worked for the service of the
church. And when the ones reduced were not wont to become
angry, they were attacked by the heathens, with the latter always
coming out winners and ours desolated. And if in one or another
case this took some time to happen, those nations are so fickle and
unstable that for any whatsoever slight motive that they arrive at
from their divination (*que deduzen de su Agorismo*), they change
their sites and camps (*sus reales y sitios*) to the region or territory
that their omen (*aguero*) indicates, thinking that the *doctrinero* is
bound to follow them and cherish them anew. For those reasons and
acts experienced repeatedly, they decided ultimately not to have, nor
that they should have the most holy sacrament on hand in a
tabernacle (*sagrario*) in any of the *doctrinas,* which decision has

5. This term could be rendered also as "ciborium."

been observed until the present with the forethought that for the sick Indian it was administered to him at the time Mass was celebrated because of not being able to do so any other time.

After the invasion that the English made, accompanied by the Indians during the year of seven hundred and three[6] in which the Provinces of Abalache, Timuqua, and Guale, of which that country was composed, were depopulated and demolished, many others have followed undertaken both by the English and by the heathen Indians, in which they have annihilated four parts out of the five that comprised the number of the reduced and converted. And the few that remain out of those are camped (*se rancharon*) on various sites with the title of villages, whose names and locations are the following: Nombre de Dios Chiquito—Timuqua—Thama—Jororo—Costa—Tholomato the new—Nombre de Dios en Macariz. And in the year of twenty-two they were increased by the conversion of another two who are called Casapuyas and Pocotalaca.

The village of Nombre de Dios Chiquito was the biggest one because of having two villages united in it, with the two caciques ruling, although they were administered by only one minister. The adult male Indians would reach up to thirty, the women nineteen, and some children (*parbulos*). Their houses are composed of four poles covered with palm. The church was not the worst because of having some boards along the sides that kept out the rains and winds, but the roof was of palm. This village, being two leagues distant from the presidio, retreated to a point close to the city, a rifle-shot away (*distante un tiro de escopeta*)[7] harassed by the

---

6. The attacks occurred in 1702 and 1704. Guale and several Timucua missions on the coast fell in 1702, while most of the Apalachee and Timucua missions were destroyed in 1704. Santa Fé in Timucua and Ocuya in Apalachee did come under attack in 1703, and as Moore's march toward Apalachee began at the end of 1703 it might be spoken of as having occurred then.

7. *Escopeta* could also be rendered as "shot-gun" or "fowling piece." Albert Manucy, in *The Houses of St. Augustine* (1962: 23), identified the distance of a musket-shot as 750 feet. He noted that "during the 1702 siege the Spanish destroyed all their own houses within musket shot of the fort." For that reason, probably all the post-1702 settlements were required to be at least a musket-shot's distance from the castillo, as English snipers had been able to use Spanish structures closer than that to kill soldiers in the fort.

Chickasaw (*Chicazaes*) Indians along with other nations who made war on them.

After the invasion the village of Timuqua had its seat in an area that is called *los Varaderos* (the shipyards),[8] twelve leagues distant from the presidio. And a short while ago it moved and, fearful of the enemy, passed over to [a place] six leagues distant. It had very few Indians because, in being loyal to the Spaniards, they died in their defense and thus came to remain with no more than fifteen men, eight women, and some children. From there they made another withdrawal, approaching to about a cannon's shot of the presidio, camping (*rranchandose*) in a place they call Abosaya and after having suffered a plague, no one was left except for a cacique and two Indians.

Thama was a village of heathen Indians who came from San Jorge, after being with the English. It had up to forty men and through the mediation of the will of God and the zeal of the ministers they reduced and converted the cacique, and many others were baptized following his example. They made their church of palm with the greatest decency, where Mass was said for them and where the Christian doctrine was taught. They were of the Uamas nation[9] hated by the rest of the nations. And they made war on them so much that they were being exterminated little by little.[10] And in the year of twenty-five on All Saints Day[11] the Uchise Indians launched an assault on them in which they killed many of them, both men and women, and they carried some off as prisoners; and they would have exterminated them, if they had not been detected, for even the missionary priest, who was saying Mass at the time of the assault took off clothed with the vestments, fleeing with the chalice in his hand and took a fishing boat (*cayuco*) that was at the edge of the sea close to the said village. And despite their firing some shots at him, he escaped from them miraculously. From there they moved close to the presidio and the governor gave them land in old Tholomato. And a few months later out of fear of the threats

8. This reference is probably to San Juan del Puerto.

9. Obviously Yamasee is what is meant. The first letter could be either a "U" or two "ls" joined together.

10. Because of the Yamasee's role in the 1715 revolt that bears their name, the English conceived an undying hatred for them. When Yamasee killed one of the Caveta chief's sons around 1724, the Creek also turned against them.

11. November 1.

they withdrew and moved to the village of Moze with the Abalachee, abandoning their territory.

Jororo was a village of a nation united with the Pojoyes and Amacapiras. They were all idolaters and heathens except two or three. For a short time these situated themselves about nine leagues from the presidio toward the south. They maintained themselves with their minister, although with great labor because neither did they have a secure territory, nor did they sow, nor did they work. And they wander about (*andan*) all year, women as well as men, searching for the marine life (*marina*) with which they sustain themselves, killing alligators and other unclean animals, which is delectable sustenance to them. And later in an epidemic that occurred during the year of twenty-seven, the most of them having died, the few who remained withdrew to their former lands and to their idolatries.

The Costas Indians were situated a pistol-shot from the *castillo* of the presidio. They are vile by nature. The most [of them] heathens and Charives.[12] Their number would be up to twenty men and eighteen women and about fourteen[?] children. These, when they feel like it, leave their camp and go off to eat palm berries (*Ubas de palma*) and alligators. They have their *doctrinero,* although with great toils because of the uselessness of the nation.

New Tholomato was first situated in an area that they call Old Tholomato, toward the north three leagues distant from the presidio.[13] And out of fear of the Uchise Indians, who were harassing them, they withdrew to an area that they call Ayachin, half a league from the presidio. And a short time later the enemy entered there and killed many Indians. And filled with fear, they retreated and put themselves under the *castillo* a distance of a rifle-shot away. They were governed by two chiefs and each government would have eight men and a like number of women.

Macariz, alias Nombre de Dios, was about two rifle-shots distant from the presidio. It never surpassed ten Indians and a like number of women. The church was always the best one for the reason that

12. The letters *es* are obscured by a blot, and *v* could be interpreted as *u*. Charives is probably a misspelling of Caribes or Caribs, a classification to which Spaniards assigned Indians they did not like.

13. This is doubtless the site of the earlier mission of Nuestra Señora de Guadalupe de Tolomato destroyed in 1702. It is believed to be the Wright's Landing site (Deagan 1978: 106; Hann 1990: 501).

the statue of Our Lady de la Leche was placed in it and with the alms from the devout its walls were made of stone and montar (*cal e canto*). Although the roof was of palm, it was decorated with every decency and the convent also was of lime and stone and roofed with palm.

Palica had its location in an area that was called Palica, four leagues distant. Afterward they withdrew close to the presidio at a distance of a rifle-shot. They had their *doctrinero* who ministered to them. And their number would be up to five men and a like number of women and about three or four children.

Moze was about three-quarters of a league distant from the presidio and was composed of twenty Indians with the ones joined to it, heathens, fifteen women and about seven children. And in a plague that occurred during the past year of twenty-seven no more than three Indians survived and a like number of women.

Casapuyas was a newly assembled village. They were located on the channel of San Julian, two and one-half leagues from Florida (i.e., the presidio). There would be up to fifteen women and a like number of men, the most of them heathens and up to five children.

Pocotalaca had its location in an area called las Rosas about six leagues from the presidio. It would have up to fourteen men and a like number of women in which are included some heathen added (*agregadas*) to them and about five or six children. Afterward they withdrew close to the presidio at the distance of a rifle-shot, where they live during the day. And at night they withdraw within the presidio for fear of the enemy.

Those settlements that are called (*se llaban*)[14] doctrinas existed in this state until, during this present year on the twentieth of March, on the enemy's entering (whose army was composed of two hundred Englishmen and a like number of Indians) into the village of Nombre de Dios in Macariz and into this place alone, after setting fire to it, he robbed the church and the little convent and did some nasty damage to the statues and they killed the docile Indians (*Indios mansos*) who were fleeing and carried off others as prisoners. And two religious who lived there escaped miraculously from the many shots that they fired at them as they took off, fleeing. After the enemy had withdrawn, the governor of the presidio ordered the blowing up of the church and convent, of which nothing more is left

14. This undoubtedly a scribe's error and should be *llaman*.

than the ruins. The said governor also ordered the depopulation and destruction of the villages of Tholomato and la Costa that were close to the *castillo,* knocking down the huts (*chozas*) and even burning the sown fields. The rest of the *doctrinas* remained totally depopulated because all the Indians, because of the great fear, have withdrawn to live within the place of Florida [i.e., St. Augustine], except for some who have set up their huts in the village of Pocotalaca in order to live there during the day. That it is the sole church of straw that has survived. The padres *doctrineros* continue living in the convent of the presidio, with each one ministering to the Indians from their jurisdiction who have survived.

A concomitant to this great misery is the fact that they never have had nor can have any way of acquiring the means for paying for their weddings, wakes, or burials. Instead it happens constantly that the *doctrinero* spends from that which the king our lord gives him [to provide] everything that they need especially for burials, supplying the candles and shroud and saying the Mass for them without any stipend, because such fees have never been known, nor would they have been able to pay them, just as tithes have not been the style in those provinces, neither do they have products on which to levy them.[15] From this one may infer that that [region] is and always will be actual mission territory without the basis of settlements that would permit collated curacies, for one may see that from the scant number of Indians that have survived the majority are not tied down (*leventes*) and transients who, in passing over to some village among the aforementioned ones, would set up residence in it, and on coming to the attention of the *doctrinero,* the latter would seek to attract them with refreshments and gifts of rum, tobacco, and maize and they would remain until they felt like going,[16] with there being so great a variety of tongues that up to the present it has not been possible to calculate what the correct number of them is, for one encounters new languages every day, so that it is physically and morally impossible to understand them.

15. In 1716-1717 and probably later these Indians were living on the royal dole at times. In a year's time 6,870 pesos and six reales were spent by the crown on provisions and goods distributed to these Indians and to visiting Creek. The provisions included 100,245 pounds of maize, 15,699 pounds of flour, 1,525 pounds of beans, 93 pounds of white biscuit, and 872 pounds of brown biscuit (Ayala y Escobar 1717).

16. My rendition of this word is tentative.

Consequently, it seems that there is no room for the collation of beneficed curacies because the most essential prerequisites for them are lacking and similarly, taking into account that at the time of the decision that was taken in the kingdoms of Castile that in order that the religious of the seraphic family should cross over to these and other missions of the Indies some special pacts and promises were in operation between the Catholic kings, our lords and the reverend father commissary general of the Indies that presently have been ratified and extended by many bulls from various pontiffs, our most holy P. P^{es}.[17] Let an account be given to our aforesaid reverend father commissary general of the Indies along with the testimonial about everything associated with this novelty that has taken place so that, with it in view, he may dispose and make a determination concerning our obligation[18] *obb^a* by that which pertains to his reverence. And accordingly by this I so provide, order and sign

Fray Joseph Bullones, provincial minister

Before me, Fray Miguel Garavito, secretary for the province

This is followed by a brief statement testifying to the authenticity of the above copy, dated September 5, 1728, and signed by Garavito.

6. Cuba's Governor on the Fate of the 270 Indians Brought to Havana in 1711 and on Renewed Efforts in 1732 to Bring Natives to Havana

This 1732 letter to the king and the documentation that accompanies it record the first attempt by the crown's political authorities in Cuba to carry out the orders issued by the king on February 23, 1716, in response to Bishop Valdés' appeal of 1711. This collection of documents reveals that as of 1730 no funds had yet been made available from the royal coffers in Cuba for bringing Indians to Cuba from the Keys, despite repeated orders from the king that the financial needs of that mission were to be given a priority claim on the royal treasury's re-

17. This abbreviation could conceivably stand for "Padres" *Pescadores,* or "Father Fishermen," an allusion to the trade of the first pope, the apostle Peter.

18. The context seems possibly to call for "obligation," but *obb^a* does not seem to be a likely abbreviation for *obligation.* A manuscript reviewer suggested it possibly stands for *obligatoria.*

sources. The documents reveal as well that neither had any report been sent to Spain by those crown officials, as they had been ordered to do in 1716, in order to provide the crown with a detailed account of everything that had been done in this matter since the bishop broached the subject in 1711.

Because church authorities continued to press the issue, the king renewed his 1716 order in 1720 and again in 1730. Documents included with the governor's letter of 1732 finally provided the information that the king and council vainly sought in their orders of February 23, 1716. In the wake of the failure of the 1732 mission to the Keys, the governor dismissed the clerical authorities' ideas, advising the king that the use of armed force was the only method that would succeed in making Christians of the Indians of south Florida.

These 1732 documents have a significance that transcends this recording of the attempts to Christianize the natives of south Florida. They provide a prime illustration of problems and weaknesses in the functioning of the Spanish imperial system, illuminating the contrasting outlooks of the policymakers in Spain and the New World officials who implemented their directives, and illustrating the contrasting views of these local officials and their clerical counterparts. This documentation suggests that, in this case at least, the foot-dragging of the local political officials to avoid the waste of crown resources on ill-conceived efforts to convert natives who had no genuine interest in the Europeans' religion seems to have been amply justified. The documents also show the crown's persistence in its idealistic policy and readiness to devote financial resources to its implementation.

This collection of documents begins with the Cuban governor's letter of July 7, 1732. It is followed by lengthy notes made at the Council of the Indies summarizing the governor's letter and the content of some of the enclosures. The council's notes contain some information derived from other sources. The first of the governor's enclosures is a copy of the king's order to the governor and treasury officials of February 23, 1716, sent for the third time in December 1730 along with another order by the king to the same officials that bears the date of December 13, 1730. That order is followed in turn by a copy of the 1730 reissue of the third of the king's orders of February 23, 1716, the one addressed solely to the governor. Those copies are followed by a series of *autos* that document the efforts of the governor and treasury officials to carry out the king's orders of December 1730. The most useful of these is the record of a junta or meeting held by the civil and clerical authorities and attended for part of the time by the Calusa Cacique Don Diego to negotiate and plan measures for bringing south Florida natives to Cuba for Christianization. The *autos* are followed by sworn statements by a number of Spaniards who took part in the trip of two vessels to the Keys to bring back the natives of that region who wished to migrate to Cuba. This collection of documents closes with a copy of an order to Cuba's governor by the king issued in April 1733 after the governor's 1732 letter had reached Spain and had been seen by the Council of the Indies.

Governor Dionisio Martínes de la Vega to the King, July 7, 1732

AGI, Seville, Santo Domingo 860. Transcription of this document was made from a xerographic copy taken from the microfilm copy of the Stetson photostat and, where those copies were illegible, directly from the photostat. The Stetson Collection identification for the document is AGI 58-2-10/4.

Sire

In obedience to two royal dispatches from Your Majesty dated in Seville on December thirteenth of the past year of one thousand seven hundred and thirty, issued so that Your Majesty might be informed about the status of the conversion of the Keys Indians of Florida and about the measures that should be employed for the achievement of the holy baptism that they asked for, in the manner and with the circumstances that are set forth in the royal dispatches cited. I must make known to Your Majesty that I have carried out the measures that are evidenced in the testimony that is enclosed with this [letter] and that few have persevered out of the two hundred and seventy Indians whom the reverend bishop, Dr. Gerónimo Valdés, spoke of, who was [bishop] of this island, whom he had obtained for the achievement of so holy an objective, because the aforementioned [Indians], in being inclined by their nature to negotiate in bad faith,[1] any whatsoever kindly actions that are

1. This governor has a talent for complicated muddy prose. To make this long sentence comprehensible in English, I have had to take liberties with the structure of the sentence. My rendition of the clause that precedes the comma is tentative. The Spanish for that clause and the one that follows it down to "as[?]" is *por que siendo propens[es] al genio de los sobredichos, el que los trat[e]n](?) mal, son infructuosas qualesquiera acciones cariñosas que en ellos se executen*

expended on them are wasted as[?] Your Majesty will understand
from the ones practiced lately, without the report made by don
Christóval de Sayas Bazan, priest, director general of the keys of
Florida, being able to withstand the disintegration of this.[2] For all
those of this type are directed toward pretending feigned desires for
conversion of the Indians, while the experience that I have had has
made me aware of the special purposes for which they make them,
concerning which Your Majesty will not find anything contrary to
this truism, nor a suitable mission that would suffice for reducing
them than that of arms, which is the ultimate among the measures
that will be necessary for their conversion, in relation to which any
other efforts will be illusory. The inveterate vice of the evil way of
life of all those who are adults and even of the younger ones
[assures this?],[3] for there has been no lack of examples of ones who,
after having been brought up here and after having spent thirty
years in the Christian school (*en la escuela xptiana*)[4] have returned
to the keys to follow their evil nature. May our Lord preserve the
Catholic royal person of Your Majesty and grant him as many years
as he can and as Christendom has need of. Havana, 7th of July of
1732.

Dionisio Marz[t] de la Vega[5]

The above letter occupies the right-hand half of the first three pages
of this document. The left-hand half of those pages is crammed with
more than twice as many lines of a smaller script written by someone
at the Council of the Indies, the translation of which follows.

That the deceased gave an account of wanting to reduce various
heathen Indians of the keys of Florida to our holy faith, of whom

---

com[o]*(?).* The letters enclosed in brackets signal another problem that com-
pounds the difficulties of interpreting this script. The crumbling away of the
right-hand margin of this page has taken one or more letters with it at the end
of some lines. My reconstructions are tentative.

2. The Spanish text here is even muddier. It is *sin que obste a desvanezen
esto, la representazion hech*[a] *por D[n] xptobal de Sayas Bazan.*

3. The elliptic Spanish text lacks a verb to make this a complete statement.

4. *Escuela xptiana* is obviously used here in the sense of "school of life."

5. Subsequent exemplars reveal this name to be Martinez.

272[6] were reduced, for which objective he contributed 100 pesos and
other alms, getting together with the governor and royal officials
for the measures for transporting them to that city. And with those
who longed for holy baptism amounting to more than 6,000 (6d),
they did not reach an agreement on the bringing over of the rest of
the Indians, because of the Governor and Royal Officials' not having
an order from Your Majesty for the expenditures that would be
required from those coffers. And for the purpose to which this was
directed, the governor and royal officials were commanded by a
royal decree of February 23 of [1]716 that, from any whatsoever
contents of the royal treasury that there might be in those coffers,
they were to make the expenditures necessary for bringing the
Indians over who might wish to be baptized. And it was to be with
the intervention of the bishop. And the governor and royal officials
were instructed[7] that in accord as the Indians should arrive in that
city, villages should be indicated where they might live under the
protection (*patrocinio*)[8] and vassalage of His Highness and that they
were to give an accounting punctually about the progress that
might be made in the matter. The bishop also was informed about
this.

These dispatches were reissued (*se sobrecartaron*) in the year of
[1]720 because the governor and royal officials claimed not to have
known about them, replying that they had not received them. And
that when demands were made on them on the basis of what was
sent to the bishop, they replied that there were no resources in
those coffers for the purpose expressed. This moved don Christóval
de Zayas (named protector and interpreter for those Indians by the
bishop) to complain to the council, requesting that the dispatches
alluded to be repeated and that a branch of the royal treasury be
indicated for the payment of the expenses alluded to.

And as a result they were repeated on the 13th of December of
[1]730, with [the council] expressing its displeasure with them over
their omission in this matter, and that they had not applied some

6. What appears to be a "2" in the second instance is not as clearly written
as the first one, but is definitely distinct from the "0" in "100 pesos" below.
Everywhere else the number is given as 270.

7. My rendition here is tentative as the script here was not very clear. The
Spanish appears to be *se ecrivino*.

8. *Patrocinio* might be rendered also as "sponsorship," "patronage," or
"favor."

resources for so pious a work and one so dear to H.M., who had resolved[9] that from any whatsoever funds that might enter into those coffers they were to furnish whatever is available, when the occasion arises, for the transport of the Indians to that island for baptism. In the meantime, that with better knowledge H.M. will be able to decide and assign all the money that is needed annually for this expense. And by a separate dispatch of the same date, the governor was ordered to send information to him with all the details about what had taken place in relation to this matter from the year [1]711 to the present. And what one could expect in the future with reference to [their] number and the disposition that they discovered in the said Indians and the measures that they considered should be employed for its achievement; the amount of money more or less that would be needed annually for the expenses alluded to; and the branch that could be used for this purpose, in addition to the alms that are collected, and the places where the 270 Indians alluded to might be staying, who, the dead bishop advised, had been reduced to the holy faith, and those that are persevering in it and are in that city or on that island or in other regions to which they may have passed. And let them repeat these circumstances to the bishop-elect of that city so that he may continue to promote this good work.

And the result from the inquiries that he sent is that, after having received the dispatches, he sought to make efforts to bring the Indians over from the keys, sending a person who (with six among those who were to be found in that city), would cross over to advise them of the royal will; and bringing the principal cacique back with him and another 13 of the most important ones (*de los primeros*)[10] for the aforesaid purpose and so that they might bring all [of them] over. He proposed the decision of His Highness to them and to reassure them more about it, he formed a junta in which the aforesaid governor, the vicar-general of the vacant see, the rector of the University of Santo Domingo, the royal officials, and the protector of the Indians, Bazan, participated. In that [meeting] he proposed what was carried out. And for what remained to be done the cacique alluded to also took part. What Your Majesty desired

9. My rendition of this word is tentative because the script for this word was not very clear.
10. Literally translated this would be "of the first ones."

was proposed to him and the Catholic reasoning leading to the holy
faith and for baptism and about giving them what H.M. was
ordering them to give them. They found all of this [to be]
acceptable.[11] And in that supposition, the junta decided that two
vessels should cross over to the keys (prepared [*dispuestos*] with
people and the said Indians and caciques) for the bringing back of
the rest. The expenses for these [vessels] (for the present) would be
covered from the funds of the vacant see, to be reimbursed from the
first resources from the royal treasury. And those going on board,
dispatched to the keys in this manner, were three days going and
coming from them.[12] The cacique and the others showed up
(*concurrieron*) to eat and to drink and on the fourth day every one of
them that there was in that region (*paraje*) disappeared to the
mainland by way of those lagoons (*lagunas*)[13] carrying with them
huts (*barracas*)[14] and houses (*casas*). And although they waited for
them for the next three days and made some efforts to search for
them, they did not appear. Concerning this [development], the
governor sends a report [drawn] from the very people who crossed
over on this business. On the basis of it, he says, that in the state in
which this matter stands, there is nothing more to be done. And it
appears to him the only thing [to be done] is that we could
acknowledge to the governor receipt of his report and testimony,
advising him beforehand (nonetheless), that he should be on the
lookout in case some of those Indians should happen to return, so
that he may carry out what H.M. ordered and what has been
recommended by his royal decrees as so pious a cause, after
consulting with the reverend bishop over any decision and giving
him an account of what is going on. Concerning all of this, the
council will decide what is most appropriate. Madrid, 8th of

11. My rendition of this last phrase is tentative. The Spanish is *a todo lo
qual sehallan yazepto*.

12. This refers only to the time at sea, not the length of time they were
away.

13. *Lagunas* might be rendered also as "lake" or "pond." In the Spanish
text there is a semicolon after "mainland," but the context suggests that there
should be no break.

14. *Barracas* has the special meaning in New World Spanish of "shed,"
"stall," "warehouse," or "storage building" and this may well be the sense in
which it was used here in view of the use of *casas* or "houses" as well. But it
should be kept in mind that tautology was very much in vogue.

February of 1733.

Council, 13th of February of 1733

As the señor fiscal stated it

The fourth page of this document contains additional summary notes made at the Council of the Indies on what appears to have been the cover page for this document.

Havana (To His Highness) July 7 of 1732

Received with the Quicksilver Ships on 17th of September N⁰ 13

My Governor

He gives an account, with testimony, about the efforts that have been made in fulfillment of what was ordered by the Dispatches of December 13th of 1730 concerning the status of the conversion of the Indians of the Keys of Florida and about the measures that should be employed for their achievement. And he makes it known that of the 270 whom the bishop obtained (*consiguio*) in the year of 1711, there are only a few who have persevered[15] and that don Christóval de Zayas Bazan, in his petition and the rest of that sort, with feigned desires, procede for their own particular purposes. In reference to [this matter], no other means than the use of force will suffice to reduce them

Note

The antecedents remain in the secretariat.

The next page in this document, which marks the beginning of the enclosures, is blank except for the following heading:

"Year   J.M.J.N.[16]   of 1732."

The first of the enclosed documents is a copy of the king's order of February 23, 1716, to the governor and treasury officials of Havana. As this document has been reproduced above, it is omitted from this translation. Appended to this 1730 copy of the 1716 royal decree is the following order from the king to the same officials, dated December 13, 1730.

And afterward, with the motive of Don Christóval de Zayas

15. The Spanish here, *han permanecido,* might be rendered also as "have remained."

16. The last of these abbreviations is not written very clearly.

Basan, priest and resident of that city, having reported to me that by nomination from the bishop of that diocese he was director general of the keys of Florida and of their districts, which desired to receive holy baptism, he had been employed in this work. And that when he had requisitioned you to furnish the expenditures necessary for this purpose, you had excused yourselves, saying that you had not received any order to that effect from me. I deigned to reissue to you (*sobrecartaros*) the dispatch inserted just prior to this one [the one of February 23, 1716] in another copy [dated] the twenty-first of December of seventeen hundred and twenty. And now it has been reported to me again on the part of the aforementioned Don Christóbal that, after he had made various efforts looking toward the fulfillment of the cited orders and requested of you in the year of seventeen hundred and twenty-two, with the abovementioned reissued decree (*sobrecarta*), you responded that there were no funds at all in the coffers under your responsibility, as was established by the testimony of the *autos* that he presented, begging me that, after receiving this intelligence, I should deign to repeat what was ordered by the dispatches alluded to, so that with his intervention you might contribute everything that might be necessary, indicating the branch of the royal treasury that would have the responsibility for meeting the expenses for so holy an objective and the farming (*cultibo*) of that island. And after this had been seen in my Council of the Indies along with the antecedents for this matter and what was set forth by my fiscal and after having comprehended the culpable omission that you have persisted in, in not having given me any account of what you had agreed upon concerning this business with the deceased bishop of that island, nor the receipt of the orders cited, which has been sent to you and that could not have failed to reach your hands because the ones that were directed to the aforementioned bishop touching on the same subject reached his hands. The circumstances surrounding this, it is to be feared, have also involved a serious omission, the fact that you have not employed any funds in fulfillment of the express orders for so pious a work and one pertaining to my own obligation and that of my ministers[17] as this

17. This is an allusion to one of the obligations assumed by the Castilian monarchs of being responsible for the Christianization of the natives of the New World in the agreement with the papacy.

one is, and that must be attended to with preference over other disbursements. It has seemed appropriate to express my displeasure again and to reprehend an omission and to repeat to you (as I do) what is provided for by the dispatch inserted above [the decree of February 23, 1716] ordering you anew that from whatsoever funds that are to be found and that may enter into the coffers of my royal treasury of that city you are to furnish the portions that may be needed in accord as the occasions may arise for transporting some of the aforementioned Indians to this island in order to receive holy baptism until such time that, with a fuller understanding of this matter, I shall be able to decide and assign all the money that will be needed annually for this so privileged expenditure. As to its punctual fulfillment, you will proceed with the care, zeal, and activity that it requires lest by the continuation of your culpable omission you give rise to the carrying out of the corresponding remonstration or punishment on your persons that will be an example for others, notifying me at every opportunity that may arise of the receipt of this dispatch and about what action you have taken in virtue of it and about what resulted, because this is what is appropriate both for the service of God and for my service. Done in Seville on the thirteenth of December of one thousand seven hundred and thirty. I the King. By order of the King our Lord. Don Gerónimo de Uztaris. And at the foot of the said royal decree there are three initials. The royal decree inserted above agrees with the original. That the original to which I refer is in my possession for now. And in virtue of the *Auto* provided on this day by the señores governor and captain general and officials of the royal treasury of this city and of the island of Cuba by H.M., I give the present on common paper because of the lack of the official variety. Written in Havana on three sheets with this on the seventh of June of the year one thousand seven hundred and thirty-two. I make my sign in witness of the truth.

Miguel de Ayala, head notary for the government

The next document among those enclosed here in the governor's letter of July 7, 1732, is a copy of the third letter written by the king on February 23, 1716, the one addressed to the governor alone. As that letter has been reproduced already above, it is omitted here. The reissued copy of the 1716 decree was dated in Seville on December 13, 1730, as was the appended decree of that same date, which has been presented in translation above. The omitted 1730 copy of the third 1716 decree is followed by an authentication by Miguel de Ayala that is identical to the one reproduced above. Consequently it is omitted here.

The next document among those enclosed in the governor's letter is the first of the *autos* detailing the actions taken by the governor and treasury officials at Havana on receiving the orders from the king of December 13, 1730, repeating those first issued almost a generation earlier, which those officials had studiously ignored, providing a fine illustration of the colonial officials' practice enshrined in the phrase *Obedezco pero no cumplo.* The first of these *autos* runs as follows.

Auto of the governor and royal officials for convoking the junta.

In the city of Havana on the seventh of June of the year one thousand seven hundred and thirty-two the señores don Dionisio Martínez de la Vega, brigadier of the armies of H.M., his governor and captain general of this said city and of the island of Cuba, don Juan Thomás de la Barrera Sotomaior accountant, and Don Diego de Peñalber Angulo Uses, officials of its royal treasury, stated that they have received two royal decrees, both dated in Seville on the thirteenth of December of the past year of seven hundred and thirty in which H.M. (May God save him) deigned to express displeasure over the omission that has occurred in giving an account about the Indians of the Keys of Florida who requested holy baptism and that he be informed of the status of their conversion and about other matters. And in order to give punctual execution to so sovereign a mandate with the attention it deserves, they were ordering and ordered that, after having put the copies of the aforesaid two royal decrees at the head of this *auto,* they are convoking a junta to be held on the ninth day of the current month in the fortress (*el castillo de la R^l fuerza*) My señor B^{rgn} Gonsalo Menéndez Valdéz, beneficed pastor of the parishes of this city, beneficed vicar-general and procurator in it and its district (*Partido*) vacant see, M.M.R.P.M. Fray Melchor de Sotolongo of the Order of Preachers, present rector of the Pontifical and Royal University of San Gerónimo, this in the friary of the said order, and Don Christóbal de Sayas y Bazán, cleric, priest, protector of the said Indians, so that after having carefully considered all the appropriate points pertaining to the matter, they may decide what should be done and in virtue of their [decision] provide the measures for its achievement. And for this [purpose] they provided, ordered, and signed it.

Mrns^t de la Vega Barrera Angulo
Before me,
Mig^l de Ayala, head notary for the government

The above piece is followed by three short pieces written by the notary, Miguel de Ayala, recording his notification of Fathers Gonzalo Menéndez Valdés, Melchor de Sotolongo, and Christóbal de Zayas Bazán to attend the junta convoked by the governor and royal officials. These pieces are omitted in this translation. The following piece is the record of that junta.

Junta, 9th of June of 1732.

In the city of Havana, the ninth of June of the year one thousand seven hundred thirty-two in one of the rooms of the fortress the señores don Dionisio Martínes de la Vega, brigadier of the armies of H.M., his governor and captain general of this said city and of the island of Cuba, B^r don Gonzalo Menéndez Valdés, beneficed pastor of the parishes, procurator and vicar-general in it and its district vacant see; the M.[?] R.P.M. Fray Melchor Sotolongo of the Order of Preachers [Order of St. Dominic], present rector of the Pontifical and Royal University of San Gerónimo, established in its friary; don Juan Thomás de la Barrera Sotomaior; and don Diego de Peñalber Angulo, treasury official of the royal treasury; and don Cristóval de Sayas Bazán, cleric, priest, protector of the Indians of the keys of the coast of Florida, [met]. And when they had met and assembled thus, his lordship ordered me, the present head notary for the government, to read to them the two royal decrees issued in Seville on the thirteenth of December of the past year of seven hundred and thirty. And having concluded its reading word by word, the said señor governor and captain general proceeded, stating that, as soon as he received the aforementioned royal decrees, he summoned the Ensign Lucas Gómes, of brown color (*pardo*) in order to discuss the gentlest ways for bringing over the Indians and for achieving the holy objective that H.M. desires. And inasmuch as there were up to the number of six of them to be found in this city, he considered it appropriate to send them to the keys so that they might serve to call the rest of them together and explain the royal decision and intention to them and four of them having been clothed by his lordship's arrangement, without losing a moment they purchased the provisions that appeared to them to be appropriate for the distance and time of the trip. And by virtue of an order that was given to the said ensign he crossed over in a vessel to the keys alluded to and he succeeded in bringing back the person of don Diego, principal cacique, and another thirteen of the first rank, so that with an understanding of what H.M. ordered, all of them might be brought over and so that the rest of what he made him responsible for might be discussed. And his lordship desires that what is most appropriate for the service of God and for that of the king our lord may be resolved now. And when the gentlemen of this junta had been acquainted with what has been set forth up to here, by the decision of the señor governor and captain general, he had the same Cacique don Diego come to this room and he was given a seat next to his lordship and by means of the said ensign and through an interpreter he was told of the promises that had been made in the keys in H.M.'s name for their transfer to this island. These were repeated by his lordship and the rest of the gentlemen, giving him to understand with soft words the love with which H.M. looks out for him and for his people and his desire for their salvation and other Catholic arguments. That the cacique listened to him with attention and with an understanding of all of them, he embraced the will of H.M. and promised to cross over to his villages in person and to transport all the Indians to this plaza, so that, having been instructed in the articles of the faith, they might receive holy baptism and live as Catholics under the protection and vassalage of H.M. And in view of his obedient consent, the señor governor promised to give to him and to his [people] lands on the shores of this island where they might carry out their fisheries and plantings (*labranzas*) and that he would place a minister with them so that he might labor in the vineyard of the Lord, so that by this means H.M.'s desires would be served and carried out. The aforementioned Cacique don Diego accepted this promise with supreme joy. And in this same session, in order not to lose any time, steps were taken so that Marcos de Torres and Juaquín Guerrero, owners of vessels, would appear before them. And after having negotiated about the fee for each voyage and after various propositions had been made by the aforementioned, it was agreed upon to give each one of them one hundred and fifty pesos for their vessel for each trip, whether for those [to be made] presently or for those that might be made in the future. And that the expenditures for the chartering of the vessels as well as for all the rest that might arise over the transport of the said Indians (for now would be paid for from the funds of the vacant see) to be paid back to it from the first funds that [come into] the royal treasury in conformity with the accounting that the señores royal officials may make, to whom this is entrusted. With this the junta adjourned and they signed it.

Don Dionisio Mrn. de la Vega

B^r don Gonsalo Menéndez Valdés

Fray Melchor de Sotolongo, Mr̃. Rector

Juan Thomás de la Barrera Soto Mayor

Diego Peñalbez Angulo

Dn Xpstóbal de Sayas Bazán.

Before me, Miguel de Ayala, head notary of the government of this city of Havana on the seventeenth of June of the year one thousand seven hundred and thirty-two.

To the Señor don Dionisio Martínes de la Vega, brigadier of the armies of H.M., his governor and captain general of this said city and of the island of Cuba. I say that yesterday, the sixteenth, the two vessels that were decided upon in junta of the ninth of the current month departed from this port for the keys and coasts of Florida, commanded by Captin Lucas Gómes, *pardo,* to bring back the Indians who reside there. And in consideration of the fact that the quicksilver ships under the charge of the señor squadron chief, don Gabriel de Alderete, are anchored in the bay and with the intent (*con reserba?*) of taking all the measures that would contribute to the fulfillment of the royal orders, he was commanding and commanded that I the present head notary for the government should make a copy (*testim^o*) of everything that has been done and put it into the hands of his lordship in order to give an accounting to H.M. (may God save him) in his Royal and Supreme Council of the Indies and for this [purpose] I so provide, order, and sign.

Mrns de la Vega

Before me, Miguel de Ayala, head notary for the government

Auto

In the city of Havana on the fifth of July of the year one thousand and seven hundred and thirty-two the señor don Dionisio Martínes de la Vega, brigadier of the armies of H.M., his governor and captain general of this said city and of the island of Cuba, stated that on this day at about eight in the morning, the two vessels, *San Joseph* [and] *Santa Gertrudis y Las Ánimas,* under the charge of

Marcos de Torres and Joaquín Guerrero, which Captain Lucas
Gómes was commanding, have entered into this port from the keys
of the other coast. And the said commandant has made it known
that soon after he arrived at the keys alluded to with the cacique
don Diego and the rest, they disappeared, as well as those who were
living in the aforementioned keys. And although he waited for three
days, while making some investigations, they did not return. And so
that what has been alluded to may be substantiated, he was
ordering and ordered the aforementioned and the rest who seem appropriate to appear before him to make a statement under oath
about everything that they know, addressing the necessary
questions and counterquestions to them. And by this *auto* I [so]
provide, order, and sign.
    Martínez de la Vega
    Before me, Miguel de Ayala, head notary for the government

The next pieces in this item are the formal statements made under
oath by a number of the more important participants in the unsuccessful trip to the Keys to bring back the natives living in that region.

Statement of the Capt. Lucas Gómes
    In the city of Havana on the fifth of July of the year one thousand
seven hundred and thirty-two, his lordship the señor governor and
captain general summoned to his presence the Capt. Lucas Gómes,
pardo, a native and resident (*vecino*) of this city. And the oath was
received from the aforementioned, which he made by God and the
cross in accord with the law. Under the responsibility of it, he
promised to tell the truth. And on being questioned in accord with
the *auto* of this page, he said that on the sixteenth day of June last
he set out from this port in virtue of the commission from his
lordship with two vessels belonging to Marcos de Torres and
Joaquín Guerrero and on them the Cacique don Diego and other
leading Indians (*yndios principales*) of the other coast and the
necessary provisions. And soon after they arrived, the Indians
mentioned went to stay with those whom they encountered in the
land. They remained there for four days during which they were
coming to and going from the said vessels to drink rum and to eat
the provisions. And when the fourth day dawned, they did not see
them, neither did they run into them on the land. And after seeing
that three days had passed and that they were not returning and

that they had set off for the mainland, a certain sign that they did not want to come back, it was decided to return to this port, which they entered on this day. And this was his response. And that what he has stated is truth and under the burden of the oath. That he is fifty-four years of age. And he signed it and his lordship initialed it.

The Captn Lucas Gómes

Before me, Miguel de Ayala, head notary for the government

Statement of Marcos de Torres

Immediately thereafter his lordship summoned into his presence Marcos de Torres, a resident of this city. And the oath was received from the aforementioned, which he made by God and the cross in accord with the law. Under the burden of it he promised to tell the truth and on being questioned in accord with the said *auto,* he said that on the sixteenth day of June he set out from this port as skipper (*Patrón*) of his vessel, *Santa Jetrudis y Las Ánimas,* in the company of another one belonging to Joaquín Guerrero under the command of Capt. Lucas Gomes, [headed] for the keys of the other coast to transport the Indians who resided there. And after having reached them with the Cacique don Diego and others, four days after their arrival they disappeared, without anyone remaining, and they traveled to the mainland, evidence, which time has certified, that they do not wish to come to this city. And despite their having made this flight, the said Capt. Lucas Gómes waited for three days. And on seeing that there was no chance, they decided to come back. And this was his response. And that what he has stated is truth under the burden of his oath. That he is thirty-five years of age. And he signed it and his lordship initialed it.

Marcos de Torres

Before me, Miguel de Ayala, head notary for the government

Statement of Juan Bauptista Marin

Immediately thereafter his lordship summoned to his presence Juan Bautista Marin, a native of Toscana [Tuscany], a resident of this city. And the oath was received from the aforementioned, which he made by God and the cross in accord with the law. Under the burden of it he promised to tell the truth. And, on being questioned according to the tenor of the said *auto,* he stated that on the sixteenth day of June he sailed from this port as mate (*compañero?*) on the vessel belonging to Marcos de Torres, which went with another one belonging to Joaquín Guerrero, commanded by the Capt. Lucas Gómes, to bring back the Indians of the keys of the other coast. And after having reached them with the Cacique Don Diego and others, they disappeared after four days and headed for the mainland, without leaving behind storehouses (*barracas*) and houses (*casas*) that were not carried off. And, nevertheless, the said Captain Lucas Gómes waited three days for them and made other efforts. And after seeing that that was impossible, they withdrew and came back to this port. And this was his response. And that what he has stated is truth under the burden of the oath. That he is forty-four years of age and he signed it and his lordship initialed it.

Juan Bau^ta Marin

Before me, Miguel de Ayala, head notary for the government

Statement of Joaquín Guerrero

Immediately thereafter his lordship summoned to appear before him Joaquín Guerrero, a native of this city. And he received the oath from the aforementioned, which he made by God and the cross according to the law. Under the burden of it, he promised to tell the truth and on being questioned in accord with the said *auto,* he stated that on the sixteenth day of June he set out from this port as skipper (*Patrón*) on his vessel named *San Joseph,* in the company of the one belonging to Marcos de Torres, commanded by Capt. Lucas Gómes, with the Cacique don Diego and others to look for the Indians who live in the keys of the other coast. And after having reached them, they remained there four days, coming on board and going; and [when] the four days were passed, they disappeared, traveling by way of those lagoons and sandbanks (*restingas*)[18] to the mainland without leaving a thing on the said keys. And the said Capt. Lucas Gómes, on seeing that three days had passed since their flight and that there were no indications of their appearing, it was decided to return to this plaza, as was done. And this was his response. And what he has stated is truth under the burden of the oath. That he is twenty-three years of age. And he signed it and his lordship initialed it.

Joaquín Guerrero

Before me, Miguel de Ayala, head notary for the government

18. *Restinga* could be rendered also as "ridge of rocks in the sea."

Statement of Jorge Rico

Immediately thereafter his Lordship summoned to his presence
Jorge Rico, a resident of this city. And he received the oath from the
aforementioned by God and the cross in accord with the law. Under
the burden of it he promised to tell the truth. And on being
questioned in accord with the said *auto,* he stated that on the
sixteenth day of June he set out from this port for the keys of the
other coast as mate on the vessel named *San Joseph* belonging to
Joachín Guerrero, in the company of the one belonging to Marcos de
Torres, both commanded by the Captain, Lucas Gómes, carrying
the cacique don Diego and other Indians on them. And when they
had reached the said keys and communicated with the said Indians
who lived there, at the end of four days they all disappeared and
traveled to the mainland by way of those lagoons and sandbanks,
carrying with them all those storage buildings (*Barracas*) and
houses (*casas*) that were there. And the said Capt. Lucas Gómes,
after seeing that three days had passed since their flight and that
there was no hope that they would return, but rather a certain
signal of their not wanting to come, it was decided to return to this
plaza with the aforementioned vessels entering today after eight in
the morning. And this was his response. That what he has stated is
truth under the burden of the oath. That he is fifty years of age. He
did not sign because he said that he did not know how. His lordship
signed it.

Martínes de la Vega

Before me, Miguel de Ayala, head notary for the government

The above statements are followed by a decree issued by Governor
de la Vega stating that he was sending all the preceding documentation
to Spain at once on the quicksilver ships. The governor's decree is not
reproduced here. The notary's statement (which follows the decree) attesting to the faithfulness of the copies of the witnesses' statements,
which he compared with the originals, is also omitted from this translation. The last piece that forms part of this document is a letter to the
governor of Cuba written by the king on April 29, 1733, after he had
received the above bundle of documents.

The King

My governor and captain general of the Island of Cuba and city of
San Cristóval de la Havana, in a letter of the 7th of July of the past

year in response to dispatches of the 13th of December of 1730 concerning the status of the conversion of the Keys Indians of Florida and the measures that it would be possible to employ for the achievement of it. You brought it to our attention that out of the 270 of the year 1711, whom the bishop achieved for this island, there were few who had persevered, and that don Christóval de Zayas Bazán in his report and the rest of that ilk, with simulated desires, were pursuing particular goals.[19] With respect to the recourse to arms being the ultimate[20] measure that would suffice for reducing them, because these other efforts would be illusory because of the inveterate viciousness of their evil way of life, the letter cited and its copies (*testim⁰*) having been considered in my Council of the Indies together with the antecedent documents concerning this subject and what was set forth by my fiscal, it has seemed fit to us to notify you of its receipt and to order and command you (as I do) that, despite what you have reported to me concerning this matter, you are to remain on the lookout for what may develop, seeing to it, in the case that some of those aforementioned Indians should return, that what I have resolved and ordered by way of the above-mentioned dispatches of the 13th of December of 1730 are fulfilled and carried out, settling on any whatsoever measures that may seem appropriate for its achievement, only in agreement with the bishop of the cathedral church of the city of Santiago de Cuba, and keeping me informed about what may be happening, so that I may be kept aware of it, because this is what is appropriate for the service of God and my [service]. Done in Seville on the 29th of April of 1733.

The following note appears on the cover page for the above letter, which is the last page in the microfilm copy of this document made from the Stetson Collection photostat.

To the governor of Havana informing him of the receipt of his letter and testimony concerning the status of the conversion of the Indians of the Keys of Florida and order to him to remain watchful of what develops in order to execute the orders expressed [herein].

19. The Spanish word *particular* might be rendered also as "private."
20. He seems to be using this term in the sense of "only."

Seen
Island of Española, officially on folio 176
Settled (*Acor^{do}*)

7. Background of the 1743 Alaña-Monaco Report

In early February 1743 a petition addressed to the governor of Cuba, purportedly inspired by several of the principal Calusa leaders, set events in motion that led to a last abortive mission to the Calusa and other remnants of south Florida's aboriginal peoples. The protestations of the native leaders who visited Cuba that they and their people were ready to become Christians proved to be one more chimera.

It is difficult to assess how much the mission's origins stem from the governor's wishful thinking, spawned by a wartime hope for a reliable native base of power in south Florida, and how much it resulted from the native leaders' manipulation of the Spaniards to obtain goods the Spaniards could supply. As Sturtevant has noted, this letter written "in good Spanish" by someone with "an accurate knowledge of the bureaucratic practices of the colonial government and the church" evidently was composed "by someone other than the three Indians" (1978: 142). But those qualities of the letter do not rule out the letter's having been inspired by the native leaders or that portions of it reflect their input, even though when the Jesuits arrived in Florida the natives denied having asked them to come. The native leaders' requests for missionaries that led to the Fray López mission of 1697 and the native leaders' remarks to the two Jesuits in 1743 show the natives to have been what we would describe as remarkably streetwise and keen observers of Spanish ways and weaknesses, and that they were not above asking for missionaries in order to obtain the material goods that came with them and then denying that their presence had been requested once the missionaries arrived.

The documents that I have included here are drawn from two separate packets in the Stetson Collection, which are headed by letters to the king written by Governor Juan Francisco Güemes y Horcasitas on July 26 and September 28, 1743. I have included the two packets together because both treat of the 1743 Jesuit mission and even more because the second of these letters contains enclosures that were inserted originally in the July 26 letter.

The first of the governor's letters is particularly valuable for its review of Spanish relations with south Florida's natives between 1704 and 1743. In 1704 occurred the first of several migrations of south Florida natives to Cuba to escape attacks by natives friendly to the English. The letter notes the subsequent migrations and details the fate of the migrants. The first letter is accompanied by substantial notes made at the Council of the Indies, which reflect the crown's reaction to both reports concerning this mission.

The second letter's most valuable features are its numerous enclosures that trace the origins of the 1743 mission, the steps taken by the governor in collaboration with the bishop to launch the mission, and the governor's contacts with the Jesuit authority in Cuba. The enclosures culminate with a report on the mission written by one of the Jesuit participants, Father Joseph Xavier Alaña, which contains valuable ethnographic information.

Governor Juan Francisco de Güemes y Horcasitas to the King, July 26, 1743

AGI, Seville, Santo Domingo 860. Transcription of this document was made from a xerographic copy taken from the microfilm copy of the Stetson photostat and, where those copies were illegible, directly from the photostat. The Stetson identification for this document is AGI 58-2-10/13, bundle 6084.

Sire

On the eighth of February of this year a petition was made to me by some of the leading Indians of the Keys that the inhabitants on them desired constantly [?] (*conestan temente*) to be instructed in our sacred religion by sending the missionaries to their land. And having seen this petition together with a copy of a royal decree addressed to the Bishop of Durango on the tenth of October of seventeen hundred and twenty-eight, which they presented to me, and those that have been issued individually concerning this subject, two of the thirteenth of December of seventeen hundred and thirty, another of the twenty-second of February of thirty-four, and another of the thirty-first of August of thirty-five, I went immediately to discuss it with the bishop of this diocese. And (after a prolonged conference) in agreement [with him] I continued to calculate the means by which I might be able to approach so important [and] glorious a goal, without failing to observe the laws and what was ordered specifically by Your Majesty in your special orders.

It was recognized at once that in them the royal intention of Your Majesty had contemplated that the Indians who might wish to come over to this island in search of the evangelical law should be transported, settled, and taken care of (*acomodados*) in it in order to pursue a rational and Christianly manner of living; and as this approach of sending [someone] to indoctrinate them in the Keys is different, a new decision from Your Majesty became necessary. While sovereign respect for you was holding me back under this consideration, on the other hand I was stimulated by the efficacy of the successive orders in which Your Majesty has revealed his royal will, so full of piety and religion, which leaves no margin for inferring that there is any effort that contemplates the expansion of the faith and the benefiting of the Indians that would displease him.

And on finding in the compendium of the laws that for occurrences such as this, it is ordered to consult Your Majesty without losing any time [in providing for?] the spiritual welfare of the natives (having communicated with the lector of the Company of Jesus of this college and by way of the obstacle-removing ministers) in a junta with the bishop and with the royal official, don Lorenzo Montalvo, the voyage of two missionaries was decided upon, paid for by the royal treasury in the matter of subsistence for their persons, a servant, and a pilot and of the supplies necessary for celebrating [Mass], going for now as explorers so that (while advancing the conversion of those souls to the degree that they can) they may examine the congeniality of all the Indians, their number, the nature of their places and lands, and all the rest that is necessary so that Your Majesty, well informed, may decide what is most suitable concerning the new system of putting the Keys in order (*de formalizar los Cayos*).

I have communicated this intelligence anew to the dean of the company so that he might pass it on to the religious whom he was nominating. And having been delayed in this for some time, because of one of the requisite ones in this college having been absent until he could be replaced with another from New Spain, the priests, Francisco Xavier de Alaña and Joseph María Monaco, religious of respectable achievements in doctrine, science, and experience, prepared for and well disposed for this holy mission, and with the indispensable provisioning having been made of late, departed from here on the twenty-fourth day of the past month, assisted by the Captain Lucas Gómes, whom the Indians love and respect like a father because of the good offices they have always encountered in him.

The fact of having solicited religious for this mission from the Company of Jesus has resulted from the stated preference of the Indians, who in great part have experienced the first stirrings of their conversion from the love and good example of these religious. Consequently they have come from the Keys expressly to seek them and they have clamored with insistence for their transport [to their land], believing that with their presence and teaching, which is well known throughout the Christian world, they will receive a great benefit in their lands. That they could not have done better in the choice available.[1]

On the principal point of [whether] to bring the said Indians to this island or to settle them down (*o formalizarlos*) in the best places (*puestos*) of their country (*País*), I believe that Your Majesty should decide in favor of the latter system.

First, because the [idea] of bringing them over and settling them is almost hopeless, no less because of the health risks of the island than because of their spirits filled with fears over the less than favorable results that they have experienced since the year four [1704] in which the basic causes for this business began to manifest themselves,[2] for, of the two hundred and eighty[3] that came during the year of ten, and among them the hereditary cacique of Carlos, the great captain, the cacique of Jove, the one from Maimi, the one from Cancha, the one from Muspa, the one from Rioseco, and the principal cacique, who took the glorious name of Your Majesty at his baptism, this one and another three caciques having died and up to two hundred of the Indians from the violent illnesses that their poorly suited constitution left them open to, the rest were split up, with some seeking refuge in private houses and sixteen or eighteen[4]

1. My rendition of this last clause is tentative. The Spanish is *que no dejo que hazer en la eleccion a el arbitrio.*

2. This refers to the destruction of the chain of missions across north Florida that had served as a barrier to the raiding Creek, Yamasee, and English.

3. The figure given usually is 270 and the year 1711.

4. Sturtevant (1978: 143) read this as the years 1716 or 1718. The Spanish

of them returning to the keys according to the reports that have been dug up with careful inquiry, which differs little from what happened in the year of four in which the cacique of the Key of Bones came here with a number of other Indians, and from what has happened on the other occasions following that in which the migrations of these Indians have come to naught, with the result of making them mistrustful, as was manifested in the year of thirty-two, when they made another request [to be brought over]. And when the Captain Lucas Gómes went to get them, they took off as fugitives, saying that, once over here, they were to be sent to the Bay of Jagua[5] once their children had been taken away from them, concerning which I informed Your Majesty on another occasion in fulfillment of your royal mandate.

And the other [reason is] that by keeping them in the keys and promoting their development there, in addition to facilitating the principal goal of their conversion and the harvest of souls [to be had] in the copious number of children who die, it will build a colony of friends in a place of great importance where, even while remaining savages, they have contributed many times to the saving of shipwrecked Spaniards and as a scourge for the enemy. In this war[6] there are examples of this of ample importance, as in the loss of the English ship named *The Tiger* in the keys of the Tortugas, their surprise of a launch (*lancha*) and a sloop (*valandra*) belonging to the same nation, which they attacked and took, killing twelve Englishmen and the assistance they have given us, to the extent that they have been able to furnish it, as they did when the armament of the year of thirty-eight was being readied and in the year just passed of forty-two, on the seventeenth day of May, in defending an advice boat, which I was sending to Florida, which, pursued by an English pirate, landed on the coast, where it found armed protection among the Indians to resist the enemy. And finally they have proved their friendship and good faith with the

---

is *quedando algunos recogidos en casas particulares, y bolviendo a los Cayos diez y seis o diez y ocho segun.*

5. The implication here and from the governor's letter of 1732 is that none of the Indians came to Cuba in 1732. Sturtevant, however, interpreted this passage thus: "In 1732, some others fled from the keys, sending their children ahead, and went to Jagua Bay (Bahia de Cienfuegos), Cuba" (1978: 143–144).

6. This alludes to the War of Jenkins Ear, which provided a pretext for James Oglethorpe's attack on St. Augustine.

fact that for all the boats (*barcas*) that go out to that coast from here for the fishery, they are the ones who do it.

In addition to this, it is known that these Indians have friendship and alliance with the Maimies, ones with whom they share a border and who are neighbors of the warlike Indians farther north, and facilitating at one stroke the conversion and pacification of one and the other, it would be possible from both nations to form a bulwark against the savages, on behalf of whom they may be able perhaps to propagate the seed of the Gospel in accord as the inscrutable providence of the almighty goes along disposing them [for this] and achieve the advantages that could be able to be hoped for from the peaceful possession of all this southern part of Florida with ample penetration of the mainland.

I hope that what has been done up to the present will merit the royal approval of Your Majesty. And with the first news of the arrival, beginning, and progress of the mission, with these and all the rest that occurs thereafter, I will keep Your Majesty informed continually, whose Catholic royal person may God preserve for the many years that Christendom requires. Havana, twenty-sixth of July of 1743.

Don Juan Fran^{co} de Güemes y Horcasitas

The last page of the photographic copy of this document, which is the cover page, bears the following notation made at the Council of the Indies.

Havana 26th of July of 1743
The governor and captain general

Council, 12 of Nov. of 1743.	It gives an account of the efforts that have been made in accord with the bishop of that diocese concerning the request that the Indians of the keys have made
Let the señor Fiscal see it	that missionaries be sent to them so that they may instruct them in our holy Catholic law, a copy of which accompanies this.[7]

As in many of these letters, the governor's letter here occupies only

---

7. That copy no longer accompanies this letter, but is to be found with the second letter to be presented here, which is a distinct document in the Stetson Collection.

the right-hand half of the pages. For the first seven pages of this letter, the left-hand half of the page is filled with the following notes on this letter made at the Council of the Indies.

The governor who confers on everything with this prelate. He says that the conversion and settlement of the Keys Indians has been a subject treated of in the council on repeated occasions and concerning which successive orders and measures have been given from the year of 1711 to the present, addressed to the reverend bishops of that diocese and its governors as also to its royal officials for the furnishing of funds for the achievement of so important and desired a goal, with the one issued most recently on this matter, [the one] in which reports were requested from the reverend bishop concerning the methods and means that should be employed so that their conversion would be effective; what ministers [to use]; and from whence they could be sent for it; and the soldiers that would be necessary for their protection. This resolution was motivated by a letter from this prelate bearing the date of July 20 of 1738 in which he communicated what was happening with respect to this reduction and the great degree to which the Indians themselves desired it. Of the latter, up to the number of eleven had come from their land to the city of Havana, whom he was maintaining [and] whom he had clothed, because they all were naked, concerning which detail thanks were given to this prelate in a decree of November [?] 9th of 1738, which, it appears, was sent to him, although not the one that corresponded[8] and the governor was cited for a certain doubt (*reparo*)[9] that occurred to the honorable señor Count of El Montijo at the time for initialing it; that, although it was corrected later, the said dispatches were not issued, which at the request of[?] the secretariat were returned from it (*della*) on the 16th of January of 1711 without the initial of his excellency, as can be seen from them themselves, and they accompany this dispatch (*expediente*) with the corresponding observations (*esquelas*) and notes made. But even though this has happened, even though the

8. The Spanish here is *sobre cuyo particular se le dieron gracia á este Prelado en cedula de 9 de Nob^re(?) de 1738 la que parece se le remitio aunque no la que correspondia.* My rendition of this convoluted and elliptical passage is tentative.

9. *Reparo* might be rendered also as "remark," "notice," "warning," "reflection," "difficulty," "objection," and by other such variant meanings.

reverend bishop does not acknowledge receipt of his decree, there is no need to repeat it, and less that it be sent and that the suspended one for the governor be circulated, because, if one or the other has received them and has them before them, this will be taken care of by means of the one notified (*por medio de lo actuado*)[10] and with respect to what is reported today concerning this matter pertaining (*a?*) to the same [subject] that was asked and inquired about through the aforementioned decrees, as what this governor sets forth in relation to the course (*curso?*)[11] of the Indians is certain and the juntas that preceded, for the measure that emerged of sending the two religious of the company to the islands of the keys as explorers with the necessary protection and assistance. From these inquiries, without a doubt, will emerge precisely the utility or disutility that would follow from establishing settlements in their own country or that it be on the Island of Havana, because, although all the decrees that the governor cites envision this last [alternative], the prudent reflections and reasons that he proposes have both notable force[?] and so much weight for varying the remedy[?] or at least for suspending its implementation until there are more reliable reports and indications, such as those which could arise from the reports that the two Jesuit religious would make, with an accurate view and experience of that land and of the Indians themselves. From what seems appropriate to the fiscal, that, in approving for now what the reverend bishop and the governor have done up to this point, we can wait for the reports and news that are generated by what results from this expedition. In the light of those it would be possible to deliberate with some greater fullness and knowledge as to what is appropriate with reference to the conversion, development, and settlement that is solicited from this reaction. And above all the council will decide what seems best to it. Madrid, January 29 of 1744.

After this decision had been dispatched and filed in the secretariat, a copy (*un testimonio*) of the *autos* by way of a duplicate of it, that is cited in the prior reply was delivered to the ~~fiscal~~ [*sic*] chaqal, in which the report and news is included that was being

10. My rendition of this convoluted and elliptical passage is tentative.
11. As this and the following two question-marked words were somewhat difficult to decipher, my rendition of them is more or less tentative.

awaited from one of the Jesuit religious, which [arose] by reason of this expedition. This governor has sent this very report in the recent register-ship, which has arrived from Havana accompanied by a letter of the 28th of September of last year. And in the light of it he says that from what emerges from the said report (which it would be possible to present), what seems most appropriate to the fiscal is that we desist for now from the conquest and reduction of those Indians; that to go forward with this enterprise, in addition to the substantial expenditures from the royal treasury that it would give rise to, we can contemplate its success as unattainable in view of the refusal and resistance of the very Indians to admitting the evangelical law. And even when this difficulty perhaps might be diminished with time, its duration is very much at risk and contingent because of the Indians having to remain in their own country. In such a situation there would always be reason to fear a constant flight and fickleness, making the holding of them there very difficult, as the governor himself feels thus, considering this reduction to be unfeasable. As a result, on taking these circumstances into account, one can make the judgment that for now this reduction is not the will of God. And consequently there are many other regions in which these [religious] can exercise their apostolic ministry and with more hope of results than those which could be expected from this conquest. For now, there is no reason to discuss this and it will be possible to approve of the governor's decision concerning the withdrawal of the said mission. Accordingly this will be communicated as well as to the reverend bishop, in which, in the name of H. M., it would seem to be appropriate to manifest to him and also to the rector of the company the gratitude that we feel for the fine desires, zeal, and dedication that they have had in this business. Madrid, February 14 of 1744.

Council, on the 5th of March of 1744.

Let it be done as the señor fiscal states; adding in the decrees to the governor and to the bishop that, despite the small and remote hope that there is of achieving the reduction and conversion of those Indians, let them pay particular attention to the good treatment and the welcoming of those among them who may go to that island, not only so that they may go on being tamed and attracted to our holy faith but also so that they may be kept devoted to us and

subordinate to us in some degree without leaning toward the
enemy.
Done.

Governor Juan Francisco de Güemes y Horcasitas to the King, September 28, 1743

AGI, Seville, Santo Domingo 860. Transcription of this document was
made from the Stetson photostat. The Stetson Collection identification
for this document is AGI 58-2-10/15, bundle 6090.

The first of the pieces in this forty-one-page bundle is the governor's letter, which runs as follows.

Sire

On the twenty-sixth of July last I gave an account to Your
Majesty along with the request [from the Indians] and the *autos*
that I enclose[?] (*duphco*) concerning the petition made by some
Indians from the Keys with reference to the sending of some
missionaries to them in order to instruct them in our sacred
religion and concerning the consultation which he held with the
bishop of this diocese, the decision that was taken in junta and the
voyage that, as a consequence, the Fathers Joseph Xavier de Alaña
and Joseph María Monaco of the Company of Jesus made in the
character of explorers. [And] while propounding what I felt about
preferring the alternative of instructing and settling these Indians
in their country as more achievable and more important than
bringing them and the children to this island and that with the first
reports I would give Your Majesty an accounting.

In consequence of this, and of Father Joseph de Alaña, who
reached the keys, having returned from Florida on Your Majesty's
galley named *Santa Isabel* and delivered the report that *be en Prego*[12]
attached to the copy (*testimonio*) of the *autos*. With great regret I am
able to tell Your Majesty about the little hope offered by our great
effort to heal those souls with the preaching [of the Gospel] in their
lands because of their rootlessness and unalloyed fickleness. For, in
addition to taking into consideration that the means proposed by
the explorer (perhaps the only ones suitable for achieving the
objective in some fashion) are very costly and difficult to

12. I have not deciphered these words. A manuscript reviewer suggested *bá
en pliego,* which means that it is going in a bundle of letters under one cover.

implement, I do not prudently believe that they would suffice, inasmuch as those Indians are accustomed to migrate as do the birds, and that, if force should be able to tie them down, that will be achieved under the burden of maintaining them and of having to establish a fort, adding new obligations to the so difficult and vexing ones that exist already of obtaining[?] and of paying out such swollen sums as those that would be caused, with waste. It would be necessary to fortify not only against them, but also against other invasions to which the ordinary call (*cognato?*) and stimulus of attacking ones enemies can give rise, and the interest of any other objective that its placement on the Bahama Channel could give rise to equally, and because of its having been necessary so that Father Joseph María Monaco could remain in the Keys to ask[?] that the said galley of Your Majesty should give aid[?] with twelve soldiers (for which I reprehended the commanding officer; that he should have brought both religious back, as he has brought him now[?], in the case of not being able to get by without this novelty). In a new meeting with the bishop and the minister of the royal treasury of this[?] city[?], after reflection on all the considerations expressed [above], the complete withdrawal of the mission was decided upon until such time as Your Majesty, with the full report concerning the matter that he has today may decide what pleases him most. May God protect his Catholic royal person many years, as Christendom requires. Havana, September twenty-eight of seventeen hundred and forty-three.

Juan Fran^{co} de Güemes y Horcasitas

The following is the note on the cover page for this document.

Havana	28 of September of 1743
	The Governor and Captain General
Council, 23rd of	Gives an account of what one of the priests has re-
December of	ported, who crossed over to explore the state in which
1743. Let the	the Indians of the Keys were to be found and it accom-
señor fiscal see	panies a duplicate of a report that he had made earlier
it.	and which is in the possession of the said fiscal.

Note

There are prior ones that are in the possession of the señor fiscal.

The above cover page is followed by the *autos* below, which are mentioned earlier as being part of the enclosures with the governor's letter of July 26, 1743.

Year   J. M. J. N.[?]   of 1743
Testimony
from the *Autos* concerning the principal Indian natives from the Keys of Florida having begged for holy baptism and from the rest that they set forth, *Posen*[?] to the corresponding ministers and what measures VS[13] has provided on this subject.

Governor of Havana
Memorial
Honorable señor. We, don Pablo Chichi, cacique of Carlos, don Domingo, great captain, and Sandino, sergeant-major, appear before your Excellency and in the best form that there is place for, and we state that, desiring the clear knowledge of the Creator, that which leads us to seek directly the ultimate purpose for which we were created, we find ourselves through the medium of our great communication with the Christians sufficiently informed that the truth is to be found only in the law of our lord Jesus Christ. And this conviction obliges us to solicit it truly.

And although our forebears desired and sought the same thing effectively and for that purpose in the past years of seven hundred and four, fourteen, and thirty-two they achieved the implementation of some means[14] directed toward this objective, they were of so little efficacy that, without any fault on our part and at the cost of many lives, everything happened very much the opposite of our hope. The events are well known and their memory finds[?] (*jsgra*)[15] us very bitter. We will say only it is not common among the gentiles to solicit its remedy for so many years perseveringly and while being in the vicinity of the Christians, not obtain the waters of holy baptism.

On repeated occasions in the year we appeared in this city and, while it is so populous we found only one person[?] who, sympathetic toward our sad fate, showed himself merciful toward

13. This may stand for *Vuestra Senoria* or "Your Lordship," a reference to the governor.

14. The Spanish here, *medicos* rather than *medios,* is obviously a copyist's error.

15. A manuscript reviewer suggested that *jsgra* was meant to be *juzgara.*

us. It being notorious that both the fishermen and other Christians who arrive at our keys, on being received there by us as brother Christians so that (Honorable señor) we do not encounter any other cause for our unhappy fate than being some poor Indians, for we are knocking at the merciful doors of the church so many times, without finding anyone who will open it to us. God is justly angered because of our faults, but always ready to receive us, if we seek him. Consequently, the fact of so many souls having been lost during the past years and being lost at the present time arises solely from the neglect in placing ministers who would teach us the path to heaven. And this comes from the fact that in making no appraisement of us, they have kept our king and lord ignorant about us and our unhappiness, because on H. M.'s learning about it, he will eliminate the great dismay that is produced in those who, in passing through this port or in arriving at the Keys, encounter regions with so many souls who have been at the gates of Christendom for more than two hundred years without being able to enter into it.

For that [reason] we are taking advantage of the present opportunity in which God has brought us in the person of your Excellency the desired harbinger[?] (*Preciasor*)[16] of our enlightenment (*Luz*), for your fervent zeal, your correct conduct, your skill in making decisions, your activity in undertaking ventures, [and] your constancy in pushing on with what, after mature consultation, you judge to be appropriate to the service of both majesties are so notoriously evident. For that [reason] we became convinced that the time of our good fortune has arrived and that your Excellency will have the glory, that you will have the reknown of having planted the Christian religion in the keys of the north.

Consequently, we ask your Excellency in the name of God and of the king our lord that you provide us with missionaries at once that they may go to our lands to teach us the holy Catholic faith. Your Excellency knows very well that we are subjects in this polity (*civil*), desirous for such a holy ministry; as also that H. M. also has a very special desire that his royal treasury should spend money in converting the heathens (*Gentiles*), with the result that it must not

16. Although this appears rather clearly to be the way in which this word is written, I have presumed that it was meant to be *Precursor*. There is no such word as *Preciasor*.

be viewed as an obstacle that the support and decent upkeep of the missionaries and churches should come from the royal treasury because this has been the practice since they conquered the Indies without any objection ever having been raised. And even if that was not the case, on taking our poverty into account, H. M. would feel very strong regret that so many souls would be condemned in order to avoid a few expenditures.

Waiting for a decision from the court could be judged to be necessary, but this is prudence (*juicio*) and extremely harmful to our souls because of the delay, and truly it has no force at all: first, because the will of the king our lord is clear enough that, in recognizing the delay from that recourse and contingencies of the seas, he has, on the point of conversion of heathens, approved such decisions as have been taken with the intention of giving an accounting about it; this can be understood clearly in the royal decree, the printed transcription of which we are presenting to your Excellency, in which H. M. does not approve the delay that the viceroy of New Spain and the provincial of the company interposed in furnishing the missionaries whom the señor Bishop of Durango asked for. We do not add to what has been said already (because it is notorious) what has happened anew with the Indians from the Dariel[17] at whose first word the president of Panama responded as compassionately as prudently, giving them the missionaries and treating them as he would some lords; we say only that the merits of those [Indians] are in no way superior to those of ours.

Second, what weakens the said argument is that, even though the recourse to the court may be necessary for stable missionaries, it is not [necessary] for sending two priests as explorers so that they may examine the situation and the rest of our circumstances. In the meantime, while these priests are waiting for the order from H. M. to come, they will take the measures necessary for the establishment of Christianity. With this [move] (Most Excellent señor), without blocking the path so that we may come out of so miserable a state felicitously and in a short time, consequently we ask and beseech your Excellency (by the blood of Jesus Christ) that you deign to provide us with the remedy that we have asked for and that his Divine Majesty left us, which is the justice that we wait to receive from the compassionate mercifulness of your Excellency.

17. This is, conceivably, a copyist's error and possibly should be Darien.

Decree. Havana, eighth of February of the year seventeen hundred
and forty-three, taking into consideration what is set forth by these
pleas and what is ordered by the copy of the royal decree that
accompanies it, and his Excellency, having before him the original
orders from H. M. (may God save him) in the *cump*^*to* (fulfillment?),
their dates, two of December thirteenth of seven hundred and
thirty-four and the twenty-first of August of 1735. Without delay on
the day of yesterday, the seventh, he went in person to the episcopal
residences to confer over and discuss the request, which the native
Indians of the Keys of Florida proposed to his most illustrious and
most reverend señor bishop of this diocese, don Fray Juan Lazo de
la Vega y Cansino. And in the lengthy session that his Excellency
had with the aforesaid illustrious señor, after having first
acquainted themselves with the aforesaid royal orders and the
desire that the aforementioned native Indians from the Keys
petition for in the memorial, and after deliberating on the important
point of the apostolic ministers to whom to entrust the progress of a
result so great and useful for the service of both Majesties, it
seemed appropriate to his Excellency and to his Illustrious
[lordship], that for so recomendable a subject the fathers of the
Company of Jesus should be chosen. For it was well known that in
the college that they had established in this city, there were many
men who, because of their learning, religious character, and other
valuable attributes, would offer themselves happily and cross over
to the keys alluded to with the accord and the blessing of their
superior in order to reconnoiter them and to learn the number of
Indians and to begin work on their conversion as their devout and
Christian zeal has done on an infinity of occasions with the gain of
so many souls that they have won to the holy Roman Catholic
Church. And that for this purpose it will be communicated to the
very reverend father rector of the said college of the Company of
Jesus so that with his reply, a start may be made on the orders and
measures that would be suitable for the achievment of everything.

Güemes. Before me, Miguel de Ayala, head notary for the
government and *Grra* (War?)

Copy of the decree.
Royal decree that our Catholic monarch, the señor don Phelipe
the Fifth (God save him) sent to the Illustrious and Reverend señor
Dr. Juan Bemto Crespo, of the Order of Santiago, of the council of

S. M. Uᵃ, being bishop of the holy cathedral church of the city of
Durango in the Province of Nueva Viscaya, of my council, in a letter
of the twenty-second of August of the past year of 1727 you
informed me that, while you were engaged in the general visitation
of your bishopric, more than seventy heathen Indians came out on
the road in the Province of the Pimeria Alta (*Pimas altas*) to meet
you, explaining that they desired to become Catholic Christians and
that, because of not having ministers who might instruct them for
that [purpose], that, after having petitioned the viceroy of New
Spain about the above-mentioned [need] immediately after you had
concluded the said visitation, so that he might provide for three
ministers going there (who would be sufficient for then for that
purpose), he had done nothing at all about it in the year and one-
half that had passed, as neither had the provincial of the Company
of Jesus of Mexico, saying that he did not have any order [to do so].
This despite your having suggested to him *no sede Ubiese*[18] to send
the said ministers because of the lack of means, for you would
assume the obligation of that for their transport and annual
maintenance. And after this had been seen in my Council of the
Indies together with what my fiscal said, whereas by dispatch of
the date of this one, I am ordering the aforementioned viceroy of
New Spain to take measures most promptly to see to it that
missionary ministers go to the above-mentioned province of the
Pimas Altas, putting the responsibility for this under the care of the
religious of the Company of Jesus. The procurator general of this
order, who resides in this court, is being informed similarly so that
the appropriate steps may be taken from all sides. It has seemed appropriate to me to let you know and to thank you for your
dedication to the fulfillment of your pastoral obligation. From that
zeal I expect that you will contribute (as I am charging you to) to
the development of the aforementioned mission and to the greater
succcss of this enterprise, which is of such great importance for the
service of God and for my [service]. Done in Madrid on the tenth of
October of 1728. I the King. By order of the king our lord. Andrés
del Elcorrobarrutia and his petition (*y su pide?*).

The next several pieces record the formalities that preceded the dispatch of the Jesuit mission to the Keys in June 1743, such as the gov-

18. The context seems to call for *no se dejase* (that he should not fail).

ernor's notification of the Jesuit rector of the Indians' request for missionaries and of the hope entertained by the governor and the bishop that Jesuits based in the college in Havana would undertake the exploratory mission until the king could be heard from.

The first of these pieces, dated in Havana on February 11, 1743, is a decree by the governor, Güemes y Horcasitas, addressed to the Jesuit rector, Gerónimo de Varona, forwarding the Indians' memorial, expressing the governor's desire that Jesuits undertake this work, and asking the rector for his ideas as to what "is most in conformity with the service of both Majesties."

The second piece bears the heading "Note." It indicates that the Jesuits were willing to undertake the mission, but that the mission's departure would have to be delayed to permit the arrival from New Spain of one of the candidates, Father Monaco. It is clear from a later piece that someone other than Monaco had been chosen initially to accompany Father Alaña on this mission, but had been excused because of the need for his talents elsewhere.

The third piece, bearing the heading *"Auto"* and dated in Havana on February 12, 1743, records the Jesuit rector's reply. The rector stated that when he submitted the plans proposed by the governor and the bishop, all of the fathers had agreed to the Jesuits' accepting the mission, but he spoke of sending "a minister" (*Ministro*) rather than the two who ultimately went.

The fourth of these pieces dealing with the formalities that preceded the dispatching of the mission in June 1743 is a piece signed by Governor Güemes, dated in Havana on March 16, 1743, and bearing the heading *"Auto."* In it the governor states that, after having seen the above *autos,*

and that the dispositions have advanced to the point where a further decision [needs to be taken] with respect to the petition from the Indians in the interim while his Majesty decides on those more ample ones that need to be adopted concerning the preaching and conversion, concerning the erection of a church, and the rest appropriate for their education in Christian customs and way of life (*política*), his Excellency stated that, inasmuch as he has proceeded in everything in accord with the Illustrious and Reverend señor don Fray Juan Lazo[?] de la Vega y Cansino, of the council of H.M. . . . It is time for them to meet in a junta that his Excellency has decided on for today as an appropriate means of arriving at a mature and efficacious decision. . . . . Güemes.

The next piece, which is fifth in this series, is a partial copy of the record of the junta announced in the preceding piece.

Junta

In the city of Havana, March 16, 1743, in conformity with the *auto* provided this day by Güemes, . . . the aforesaid Güemes, Fray Juan Lazo de la Vega Cansino, the señor don Lorenzo Monlatuo[?], a military officer, met together in one of the rooms of the royal fortress. They considered the request from the Indians from the Keys, the reply of the Jesuit rector, and the royal decrees of December 2, 1730, February 22, 1734, and August 21, 1735. And these gentlemen, after having gone over them [and] conferred about them, he observed that the royal orders are directed toward bringing the Indians who are seeking baptism to this island to live, to progress, and to settle. This request to send missionaries to the Keys is a different matter and requires measures of another *peyo* (stripe?)[19] than those permitted up to now for their employments. These can and must wait. However, to take advantage of the favorable opportunity that the divine compassion offers for the merit of H.M. and to the assidiousness of the supervisory gentlemen, it suffices, in accord with the status that the matter has reached, to send two Jesuit religious with Captain Lucas Gómes, one universally loved and respected by the Indians, and a servant so that, while making as much progress as they can on the conversion, they may investigate the attitude of the rest of the Indians, the number of those who are ready for the evangelical harvest, the quality of the places and lands and the rest necessary for a perfect understanding and faultless decision[?] for the setting up of the new system for establishing the status of the Keys. Beyond the royal objectives[?] (*fuera? de los reales*)[20] the achievement of this holy

19. I have not found any word in Spanish or Portuguese resembling *peyo* that makes sense in this context. But the context suggests that "stripe" or "type" is what is intended here.

20. My rendition of this phrase, suggested by a manuscript reviewer, is tentative. What I interpreted to be *fuera* is not clearly written.

objective is considered (*se reputa?*)[21] impossible and the advantages would be lost that arise from having them settled there for the benefit of this island and of the Spanish sailors along with the scourging of the enemy, the importance of which has been demonstrated sufficiently in this war. They concluded with an accord that an account should be given to H.M. at the first opportunity and that, in the interim, the two religious of the company should go with the fellow mentioned above [Gómes] and the supplies necessary for celebrating Mass and for their subsistence at the expense of the royal treasury so that in accord with the instructions with which they will be equipped and their intelligence, they may acquire and provide information concerning all the items of significance that need to be taken into consideration in this matter in order to pass them on to H.M., and that in accord with the advancements that this exploration may give rise to, his royal magniminity can give the orders that he considers to be appropriate for the greatest [results] from this business.

The last of these preliminary pieces is the following response by the Jesuit rector to a dispatch that he apparently received from Governor Güemes in the wake of the above junta held on March 16, 1743.

Auto
    In the city of Havana on June 2, 1743, Father Gerónimo Varona . . . in view of the dispatch of March 16 of this year from Güemes asking him to say who the religious are whom he has named for the mission. They are Joseph Xavier Alaña and Joseph María Monaco, whom he has considered fitted for the ministry and as the only ones that there are in this college who are not tied down. As a result the departure of one [of those chosen originally] has given rise to the delay of this mission until the arrival of Fr. Monaco from the Kingdon of New Spain (which has been pending [*immediato*]) because of there not being anyone who could be indicated after the promotion of Father Francisco de Oliver to the rectorship of the College of Campeche, for whose indispensable tasks it was necessary in this college that Father Francisco Serrano

21. Here again my rendition is tentative because the script was not very clear.

de Olivera assume responsibility, with the said Father Oliver being the one who, when he would have completed his philosophy course, he had destined to accompany Fr. Alaña, about all of which I have given an account to your Excellency as things were happening. . . .
    Gerónimo Varona
    Before me, Joaquín María de Munabe, secretary

From the introductory letter by Governor Güemes, in which all the rest of these pieces are enclosures, the one that is the raison d'être for all the others is the last piece among the enclosures. That piece is the report on the exploratory mission to the Keys. Although the report bears the names of both Fathers Alaña and Monaco, it appears to have been solely the work of Alaña. Because the Spanish version of this report has been published and commented on by Sturtevant (1978: 146-161), because my 1978 translation of the document has been published (in Parks [1985]: 56–65), and because the 1743 copy of the report has some defects, my translation of it will not be reproduced here, but is substituted by my later translation of another version of the report composed by Alaña in 1760, which follows.

8. The 1760 Version of the Alaña-Monaco Report

Two versions at least of the report on the 1743 Jesuit expedition exist and there is possibly a third as yet undiscovered. The first version is the report submitted to the governor by Father Alaña in July 1743 upon his return from the expedition to the vicinity of present Miami. It is to be found in AGI, Seville, Santo Domingo 860. The P.K. Yonge Library of Florida History has a microfilm copy of the entire *legajo*. A photostatic copy of the 1743 version of the report is contained as an enclosure in the Stetson Collection copy of Governor Güemes y Horcasitas' letter to the king of September 28, 1743. In 1760 Father Alaña made a revised copy of the 1743 report in response to the crown's request to Cuba's governor for information on Indians who several years prior to 1760 had come to Cuba from the Keys to escape harassment by Uchise.

At the end of that 1760 version Father Alaña noted that, although his 1760 version of the document was substantially the same as the one sent to the Council of the Indies in 1743, it was not a literal copy. On the whole the 1760 document follows the earlier one almost word for word, but there are instances where the two documents differ. In places the 1760 report omits phrases found in the 1743 version. At other places in 1760 Alaña added material not found in the 1743 version. These discrepancies together with the close resemblance between the two suggest that Alaña had a somewhat more extensive third version or notes from which the other two were extracted. That third version might well be the source of the details not found in the 1743 version that Francisco Javier Alegre included in his account of the 1743 mission in his history of the Mexican province of the Jesuits. However, Sturtevant's suggestion (1978: 143 n. 2) that Alegre was personally acquainted with Alaña from 1755 to 1762, when Alegre was in Cuba, is an equally plausible explanation.

The 1760 version felicitously resolves some of the problems of the 1743 version, the extant copy of which is in far from perfect shape. One of the more striking puzzles presented by the 1743 version is its apparent description of the native village at the mouth of the Miami River as a "settlement 'without huts'" (Sturtevant 1978: 147). The Spanish text is "*Hallamos a la boca de dho Rio vn Pueblo esto sin chosas en q Vivian* . . ." (Sturtevant 1978: 154). In my 1978 translation it was rendered similarly as "we found a village [of] these [Indians] without huts in which there lived . . . ," although the solution "or five huts" was suggested in brackets on the basis of a guess that the Spanish might originally have been "*sinco chosas.*" In the 1760 version this passage appeared clearly as "*sinco chosas.*" In the 1743 version the letters "*co*" had disappeared into a sinkhole on the page. (Parks 1985: 56).

In my present translation of the 1760 version of this document the material from the 1743 version that was omitted from the 1760 version is presented in footnotes. Material added in the 1760 version is underlined. Other discrepancies between the two versions that are historically or ethnographically significant are indicated in footnotes except in those cases where my 1978 rendition of the 1743 version was of a very tentative nature because of the difficulty of deciphering the script.

Report on the Indians of Southern Florida and Its Keys by Joseph María Monaco and Joseph Javier Alaña[1] Presented to Governor Juan Francisco de Güemes y Horcasitas, 1760

AGI, Santo Domingo 1210. My transcription of this version of the document was made from a microfilm copy furnished by Eugene Lyon.

1. The first name of both of these individuals is abbreviated as "Jph." Ab-

Most Excellent Lord

Having left Havana on the 24th day of June of this present year of 1743, both because of the unfavorable winds and because of being forced off our course by a brig that chased us and that we learned later was Spanish, we were not able to anchor in the mouth of the river that lies about two leagues southwest of Bocarraton until the 13th of July, where we learned on the way that the Keys Indians were to be found.

At the mouth of the said river we found a village, that is, five huts (*chozas*) in which up to one hundred and eighty people were living crowded together between men, women, and children, the [latter of] which made up about half of this number. For the most part the adult men understand and speak Castilian moderately well because of the frequent commerce with the boatmen from Havana. And they all are the remnant of three nations, Keys, Carlos, and Bocarraton. We learned that from another three tribes in addition to these, the Maymies, the Santaluzos, and the Mayacas, which have united [and are] four days' journey away on the mainland, it will be possible to add another hundred souls or a few more.

The Indians of the Keys, as they are commonly called, or of the village of Santa María de Loreto, as we wish them to be called from now on, have three principal living places (*Mansiones*) between which they divide the year: that of the aforesaid river, where they remain until the end of September; that of Perchel[2] Key and the coast of the North West, to which the fishermen from Havana carry them; and last, that of Cow Key. The most potent reason for this rootlessness is their supreme indolence. For, lacking the desire to cultivate the land, they content themselves with the fish and the small amount of wild fruit that the aforesaid places successively supply them with of themselves.

The reception that they gave us was very rude. And once they had taken from us with intolerable[3] importunity the provisions destined for them (that there was no lack of someone to enlighten

---

breviations are very common in this document. They are not noted unless I am in doubt as to their proper rendition.

2. This name might possibly be "Penchel" because Father Alaña's "r" and "n" are often indistinguishable.

3. The Spanish here appears to be *intorenables,* but it was probably meant to be *intolerables.*

them for this),[4] they openly declared their displeasure over our coming, to the point of denying on repeated occasions, with evident falsity, that while in Havana they had asked for priests who would make Christians of them. Nevertheless, out of fear that your Excellency might punish them, they said that they wished to be [Christians]. But, according to their way of thinking, this matter of becoming Christians has no other significance than the receiving of the sacramental water with these conditions [for doing so]: that, without their doing any work, the king our lord is to support and clothe them, and not with burlap (*cañamaso*), which they detest as identified with blacks;[5] and that he is to furnish them with rum, alleging the precedent of Florida;[6] the superstitions that they are full of are to be allowed to remain in place; and last, in the teaching of the children, no punishment at all is to be used. [This was] the first condition that the chief proposed to us in the name of all. Nor is it something to be surprised over. This passion that they have for their sons (*hijos*) reaches the extremity of suffering blows from them; of actually burning themselves or cutting themselves to show their grief over the same thing having happened by accident to the son, without the father ever enjoying any sign of reverence from them.

Their bold proposal of these conditions is born of their being convinced that in admitting our religion in any manner, they are doing us a great favor. They went so far as to say to us that if they were to have to build a church in their village, we would have to pay a daily wage[7] to the Indians, and that if Spaniards were to have to come to settle they would have to pay tribute to the cacique of the

4. This parenthetical remark is not found in the 1743 version of this document. Hereinafter these additions will simply be underlined without a footnote comment.

5. At this point the 1743 version added the comment "despite the fact that both the men and the women walk about naked except for covering what is necessary."

6. In this document the Keys and the Miami area are spoken of as though they were an entity distinct from mainland Florida, and after 1763 Spain was to claim that the Keys were not included in the cession of Florida. The precedent the natives alluded to was the alcoholism that plagued natives living near St. Augustine in the eighteenth century (see Hann 1989: 200).

7. Here the 1743 version said "If we wished to build a church in their village we would have to pay a tax to the Indians."

lands, which belong to him, he said, and not to the King of Spain, words derived from perverse collateral relatives, because from other sides we have recognized good inclinations in the cacique.

The idolatrous errors and superstitions of this people are of the crudest sort. But what is surprising is the very tenacious attachment with which they maintain all this and the ridicule they make of beliefs contrary [to theirs] and of the arguments they [are based on]. We saw two idols. The principal one is a board sheathed in deerskin (*âforrada en gamusa*) with its poorly formed image of a fish that looks like the barracuda (*q^e parese se la Picuda*) and other figures like tongues.[8] They have [now] hidden this one, because one day one of us stepped on it with the purpose of freeing them experiencially of the fear of the disasters that they thought would follow such disrespect for it. And we have but slight hope of taking it from them without violence. The other idol, which is the God of the cemetery, the theater of their most visible superstitions, was a head of a bird, sculptured in pine, which in the matter of hideousness well represented its original, and which we burned after it had been smashed, along with the hut (*choza*) that they had for a church, when it appeared to us that it could be done without a tumult on the part of the Indians,[9] as proved to be the case, although not without many signs of grief and even lamentations and tears from their women. In the said church they had the most ugly mask destined for the festivals of the principal idol, which was placed there on top of a table (mesa) or altar. And they call it *sipi* or *sipil*.[10] We also saw a large log (*palo largo*) which, on certain days, they adorn with flowers and with feathers and celebrate, at the foot of which some silver had been buried that the Indians removed. They have an Indian whom they call bishop, consecrated with three days of races. He drinks many times until he passes out. And they think that such a one dies and returns sanctified. There is another Indian whom they call *tirupo*[11] or like God, terms that are

8. The Spanish here is clearly *leguas* or "leagues," which does not make sense. It must have been meant to be *lenguas* or *ligulas,* both of which suggest a tonguelike or raylike adornment such as the corolla on a flower.

9. At this point the 1743 version added "as we had an armed galley hovering over them, which was there in passing, coming from Florida;."

10. *Sipi* and *sipil* are underlined. *Sipi* appeared to be *sapi* in the 1743 version, which has no variant form equivalent to *sipil.*

11. I am not entirely sure that the first letter is a "t" and the "p" also

synonymous for them, whom they consult concerning the future and the distant. He is considered to be the doctor for the place. His remedies are great howls (*aullidos*) and gestures (*ademanes*)[12] that he makes over the one who is ill, adorning himself with feathers and painting himself horribly. And he is indeed a man who has in his appearance (*aspecto*) I do not know just what traces of [being] an instrument of the Devil.

They venerate the cacique and his sons with incensings (*sahumerios*)[13] in which the bishop takes part. At his death and that of the other leading men they kill children so that they may serve them in the other life, a cruel ceremony that they practice in the [celebration of] peaces [as well], which we prevented even before we arrived in them[14] by sending a Spaniard in a fishing boat (*cayuco*) with a letter for the cacique, that on *Cablo franses*[15] we learned they were to celebrate with the Santaluzes.[16]

They have a great fear of the dead and its effect appears [in] their not suffering their being named; their daily offering to them of foodstuffs, tobacco [and] plants[?] (*llebas*);[17] the covering of the graves with reed mats (*esteras*) and the bestowing of gifts (*regalar*) on the graves. They maintain a guard in the cemetery, which they frequent with pilgrimages (*romerias*), and they keep it somewhat

---

looked very much like an "x" and the "r" could have been an "n." The 1743 version here has *Bruxo* (see Sturtevant 1978: 156). I rendered this passage in 1978 as "whom they affirm to be a sorcerer and like God. . . ."

12. I believe that I have seen *ademanes* used to indicate facial contortions as well.

13. *Sahumerios* can mean variously "smoke, vapor, steam, fumigation," "the medical application of fumes to parts of the body," or "aromatics burnt for perfumes."

14. The Spanish is *de llegar en los que en Cablo franses supimos*.

15. The word *cablo* does not exist. It was probably meant to be *cabo,* which would mean "French Cape." In the 1743 version this was apparently "French Key," although this might be open to question as *cablo* might have been misread as *cayo* in a text as faded as was the 1743 one in places. Sturtevant has "Cayo" (1978: 156).

16. In the 1743 version the Indians were not identified. It read simply "with other Indians." Sturtevant has "cond[ic]has Ynydios" or with said Indians (1978: 156).

17. This word seemed very clearly to begin with the double "ll," but it could conceivably be an "h" as Alaña made it somewhat similarly. In the 1743 version I deciphered this word as *hierbas* or "plants."

distant from the village, fearing lest the dead should do them harm. It was not possible [to get] them to hand over to us the corpse of a little girl whom we baptized because of the risk of her dying, but they buried her instead with their ceremony with the rest of the Gentile Indians. And in order to bury another one, a little boy, with the other Christians, some violence was necessary.[18] In the midst of this they obstinately affirm that human souls do not survive their bodies, swallowing the absurdity of their not being any better than the beasts, laughing at the strongest of arguments, and turning their backs [to us] when they were confounded by having their own erroneous practices thrown up to them.

The men paint themselves variously <u>almost</u> every day, a custom they practice, we have learned, for the honor of the principal idol that they venerate, while they ridicule the God of the Christians, denying his role in the creation of things and stating that they came to be by themselves and denying him as well the power to prevent men from carrying out what they wish to and other <u>blasphemies of this nature</u>.[19]

In summary, Excellent Sire, in order to shorten [this litany] by omitting <u>many other individual cases by which they have shown us their bad faith</u> and other numerous superstitions to which we found them blindly[20] devoted like all the American Indians, in view of the special duplicity, audacity, and obstinacy that these [people] carry to an extreme, we consider it necessary that the conquest of their souls be supported on the same means as it has been over <u>almost</u>[21] all of America, that is, that this mission be secured for some years escorted by <u>20 or</u>[22] 25 soldiers of excellent customs, with whose protection the necessary rigor can be employed in order to root out even the relics of their superstition, as this is necessary so that

18. The 1743 version did not imply the prior existence of a Christian burial place in the Miami area. In it this passage read "and, in order to bury another baptized child with the Christian ritual, some force was necessary." For "Christian ritual" Sturtevant has "Los Vistos Christianos" or "the seen Christians" (1978: 156).

19. In the place of this phrase about blasphemies the 1743 version has "at other moments oddly multiplying the Divinity."

20. In the 1743 version the adverb "blindly" was replaced by "equally."

21. In this 1760 version Alaña added this qualifying "almost" on a number of occasions to statements that were not so hedged in the 1743 version.

22. The number twenty does not appear in the 1743 version.

their little children may not learn it and without the danger either of glorious ends for the missionaries, but very harmful for the Indians themselves, as the repeated events of the past years have shown in which various Jesuits have died on two occasions at the hands of the Florida savages or of a sudden flight, as they have done on one occasion, and which they have given us to understand they intend to, which cannot be prevented without sentinels at night, in which a nomadic people and one that lives on the sea more than on the land, even the little girls and women, may disappear very easily.

A redoubt or stockade could be built at the mouth of the river with very little cost because what is necessary is to be found at hand, without its being able to be beaten from the sea, because the cove has no more than a fathom of depth.[23] These Indians have few firearms because they have traded almost all those that your Excellency gave them for rum, in addition to which, they greatly fear the Spanish soldier. And the Uchises[24] of Florida have encountered resistance [from them only] if, with extraordinary effort, they made an attempt on the village because of the said site's being the most distant from the mainland and its provinces.

Another reason that moves us, Excellent Sire, to consider the military aid necessary is the incredible passion these men have for rum. There have been daily [complaints] over our not having brought them any. They have advanced a thousand arguments [for having it] that the Devil suggests to them. They have gone so far as to throw up to us the matter of the wine for the holy Mass. And, to sum it up, they have told us clearly that, without the rum, they neither can be or wish to be Christians. On the other hand, on their becoming drunk, there is no hope for moderation from them.[25] They lose the little light of reason that they have and take on an extraordinary brutality. There is no longer a son for the father, nor

23. Here the 1743 version added "and the mouth of the river four palms, although it deepens there within to up to ten and twelve palms." A fathom is about six feet. There appears to be a difference of opinion about the length of a palm. One source gives three inches, another, 8.25 inches. The latter seems closer to Velazquez' definition, "length from the thumb to the end of the little finger extended."

24. Here the 1743 version added, "or savage Indians."

25. Here the 1743 version added the following clause in parentheses: "(and it always happens when they have the wherewithal, with the result that it is imprudence to expect moderation from them in this matter)."

wife for the husband, on laying hands on all the arms [available],
according to the report of those who have seen them many times in
their own lands, where they seem like a different species than those
who come to Havana. <u>And God even saw to it</u> that we would be
eyewitnesses of this truth on one day, <u>with plenty of fright</u>,[26] <u>in
that, on the occasion of some boats that were bringing troops to
Havana from Florida, anchoring at Key Biscayne, a number of them</u>
[the Indians] <u>having become drunk</u>, we heard them utter atrocious
calumnies[27] about us. The women of the drunken ones fled to the
woods.[28] An Indian ran after another Negro[29] with a hatchet
without the slightest pretext for killing him. The cacique (one of the
drunken ones) spoke out against Lucas Gómes[30] <u>whatever the rum
suggested to him</u>,[31] even to threatening him with the musket
(*escopeta*), and they revealed their desire to kill him together with

26. From this point on, for the next page or so, there is considerable diversity between the 1743 and the 1760 version of this report. Each contains a number of details omitted by the other. Taking up from the word "Havana" the 1743 account ran thus: "and even from what we gathered by our own eyes one day, in which the chief, *Capitan grande*, and another two or three, on getting drunk, these effects followed. One of them uttered atrocious calumnies about us, and within earshot of us; the wives of the drunkards etc."

27. The Spanish word here appears to be *canulnias*.

28. Here the 1743 version added "where they spent the night for fear that they might kill them or beat them as the husbands are wont to do. The *Capitan Grande* ran after our black with a hatchet etc."

29. This black was identified in the 1743 version as the priests' slave.

30. Lucas Gómez, a free mulatto, was the captain of the ship that brought the two Jesuits to the Miami River in 1743. The Indians apparently blamed Gómez for the coming of this mission in 1743.

31. The phrase "whatever the rum suggested to him" appeared in the 1743 version as "And, to sum it up, as in wine is to be found the truth, as they say," and was followed immediately by the following passage that does not appear in the 1760 version: "The drunken ones bared their chests, and even those who were not, saying that they had the intention of killing the said Lucas and Manuel Hernandez. On many other occasions they showed a genuine hatred against these two. They look on Lucas Gómez as the principal cause of our coming, and that, while being a Mulatto, he should dare they say to give orders, clear signs that all the fondness and subordination that they showed him in Havana was superficial and directed toward the despicable aim of taking him in as much as they could. They view Manual as a guide [who knows] all their lands and one who would be capable of finding them wherever they might flee to."

Manuel Hernandez, because they had so much knowledge of their lands and had been of such service to his mission.

To avoid these disorders,[32] they could announce serious punishment for the boatmen from Havana and Florida. But, over and above the rum that the Indians may acquire from the vessels that perish annually in the Keys and on the coast of Florida, it will be difficult to contain the avarice of a poor fisherman who knows that without rum the Indian is not going to help him with the fishing and the [greed] of anyone else at all, to whom the Indian is accustomed to give the equivalent of a hundred pesos for a flask of rum, at the sight of which he [the boatman] would fear nothing, as is clear to us from many individual cases.

Accordingly, it is necessary [to have the soldiers], because, despite the efforts of the superiors and the missionaries, there are bound to be drunks in the village. A consequence of this is the necessity for punishment to prevent its most pernicious effects and so that vice does not triumph with impunity. This implies the necessity of military assistance, without which the punishment is not feasable without worse problems and [especially] as [punishment] is a word never heard among them, or something that is never practiced, even by the chief.

Last, this aid is necessary for the preservation of the Indians. These diminutive nations fight among themselves at every opportunity and they are shrinking as is indicated by the memory of the much greater number that there were just twenty years ago, so that, if they continue on in their barbarous style, they will have disappeared within a few years either because of the skirmishes, or because of the rum that they drink until they burst, or because of the children whom they kill, or because of those whom the smallpox carries off in the absence of remedies, or because of those who perish at the hands of the Uchises. In such a scenario we would find ourselves without the useful service that these Indians render to our nation, not only because of the aversion that they have toward the English, but also because of their inclination toward us, even though it is based solely on interests.

Another means, Excellent Sire, that we find equally necessary for the permanent settling-down of this people is that some Spanish

32. In the 1743 version this was "Returning now to the rum, something prevented them from hinting serious trouble against the boatmen in Havana and etc."

families be transported there to settle the land (and already a certain number, having seen the country, have asked Father Alaña to achieve this from your Excellency) and also that a dozen forced laborers should go there for a year to clear it. For the pine groves spread [from] the river banks up to a mile inland from there. They are all thick woods and [have] much [undecipherable word][33] lumber.[34]

Among the Indians there will be twenty who are accustomed to the light work of fishing. The rest, either because [they are] leading men or because [they are] soldiers (as they call it), have been exempt from work until now according to their laws. There is no doubt that we must teach the cultivation of the land to all,[35] but compassion does not permit that we press them at once [on this point], for, at the very least, this would make them keep aloof from our religion. But, if we content ourselves with the little that can be achieved with them from a moderate rigor, the time that would be necessary to support them from the royal coffers until the land supplies the [necessary] foodstuffs will be notably prolonged. The Spanish families are requested because the Indians are totally unacquainted with agriculture and they will learn it by associating with ours.

The Spanish settlement at this said point is recognized [as being] useful because it is in the midst of the Keys and the coast of Florida, which are among the most dangerous, and where our ships and those of other nations are lost continually. The land is full of pine trees and pitch trees (*teas*) useful for pitch and pine-tar, and, who knows, but that with time woods useful for ships will be discovered. All of which could be carried easily by the River that crosses the pine groves. According to common report, there is land suitable also for crops and for the raising of hogs and cattle. On a

33. In the 1743 version this undecipherable word was "stout."

34. At this point the two versions diverge completely for a time as the 1743 version proceeded thus: "and, consequently, from this and from the laying-out of the settlement of the aforesaid to the point where the land furnishes food, it will be necessary to maintain not only the Spaniards but also the Indians, at least for all of one year, because, if food is wanting in the said settlement, they will go wandering through the keys. The convicts are requested because among the Indians there are twenty who are accustomed to the light work of fishing. Etc."

35. Here the 1743 version was more explicit, replacing "all" by "to the latter and the former."

piece of beach we saw a little bit of sickly (*annojado*) maize grow to the height of a man in a month without any cultivation. In summary, it appears capable of a settlement that, with one or two years[36] of settlement, will draw the families that remain in St. Augustine of Florida with so many frights and expenses, where the fort can always be left with its garrison.[37]

Of the Indians, excepting those who, like the bad leaven, corrupt the rest, and who went so far one afternoon as to attempt to seize control of our boat, according to the signs [they give], the rest show some docility. The children crowd around us to learn the catechism in the Castilian tongue. And as those of this age are not corrupted by the lewdness and the drunkenness, in the end it is they who are to be the seed of the new Christian settlement, [though] it is true that lately, at the instigation of their fathers [undecipherable word], they all fled.

In view of all this that has been alluded to, so diverse from what had been imaged in Havana [to be the situation], because of reports [that were] not at all sound,[38] and in view of how dangerous the mission would be, were the priests to remain there without an escort, either the two of us should return, because of the consideration that we owed to your Excellency, whose action had [undecipherable word] that which it should be carried forward or, that the other [having been] begun, it should be suspended, it being necessary that one of us should come to Havana to report to your Excellency,[39] we decided to ask aid from the captain who was coming commanding the troops who were returning from Florida.

36. Here the 1743 version seemed to say "ten or twelve years" instead of "one or two." Sturtevant has ten or twelve years (1978: 159).

37. In the 1743 version the sentence closed thus: "Leaving there only the fort with its garrison." At this point the 1743 version and that of 1760 part company for a paragraph. In place of the paragraph that follows here, which is underlined, the 1743 version had the following paragraph: "But for now it will be necessary that his Majesty maintain two boats at the mission: one for the trips to Havana, the other, so that the priest may respond to the ministrations to which he may be called. For, even though the creation of a settlement on the mainland is projected, there will regularly be Indians scattered over the Keys for the fishing as well as for other purposes."

38. In the 1743 version "not at all sound" was replaced by "secondhand."

39. In the 1743 version this clause, beginning with "it being necessary," was placed in parentheses and it lacked the two underlined phrases.

These, I have said, were detained[40] on Key Biscayne. At the mouth of the river we have constructed a regular triangular stockade with a circumference of 108 yards with its middle[?][41] bastions (*medios baluartes sacadas*) protruding and its three wall guns (*pedreros*)[42] with twelve men, a number that appeared sufficient to us,[43] taking into account that Father Alaña, with cunning and cajolery, had brought to Havana the leading Indians who could stir up trouble in the village.[44]

The pines were so close at hand that for the number that allowed themselves to be influenced[?] (*q^e se deja entender*) with the good effort of the people who had come along convoying the troops and some little assistance from the Indians the stockade was built in three days and the terreplein partly [finished].

In summary, Excellent Sire, that is justification for the restraining of some of the Indians for their own good, who with manifest deceit make a mockery of our holy religion, maintaining the adoration of some crude [idols] almost in plain view. The time has passed for permitting some naked creatures to frustrate everything with a stubborn "We do not want it," after their having occupied the time of your Excellency and the rest of the ministers of His Majesty, and after their having caused expenses for the royal coffers.[45] With the measures proposed, or those that your

40. Here the 1743 version had "Galley and troops, which coming from Florida, because of various delays, had to wait some days on Key Biscayne."

41. This might also possibly be rendered as "half-bastions."

42. The 1743 version did not have all these underlined details about the size, shape, and equipment of the stockade, but did present some details not found here in the 1760 version. Taking up from the words "Key Biscayne" at the end of note 40, the 1743 version here ran: "With this help, and with the Indians themselves cooperating out of fear and from a tactful approach [to them], without violence, a stockade of sorts was built in three days at the mouth of the river near (*sobro*) the settlement, with some wall guns (*pedreros*) and twelve men from the garrison."

43. Here the 1743 version added "until we could inform your Excellency."

44. In place of this passage at the end of the paragraph concerning Father Alaña's cunning strategy the 1743 version ran thus: "giving attention at the same time to handling the majority of the rebellious Indians with cunning. During those same days, without a tumult, we managed to burn the church and the idol that we were able to lay our hands on."

45. Most of the essence of this paragraph is to be found in the final paragraph of the 1743 version, but the latter is sufficiently distinct to merit repro-

Excellency may find more appropriate, their idolatry will be abolished and the true religion will be established among this people, and in spite of the obstinate ones, who, with punishments, will come to understand what they were not able to grasp with reasonings.

Though it is not a literal [copy], it is a substantial copy of the report that was sent to the council between the end of May of 1743 and the beginning of [1]744.

Jph Xair Alaña[46]

---

duction here. It runs thus: "This is, Excellent Sire, the status in which the mission remains, which gives us hope it can be carried to success with the measures proposed, or with those your Excellency may consider more appropriate. As far as the Indians are concerned, except for those who, like bad leaven, corrupt the rest, to whom the charges mentioned principally apply, the rest show some degree of docility. The children gathered around us in droves to learn the catechism in the Spanish language, even though they withdrew from us at various times at the instigation of the adults. This will be justification for restraining those who impede the promulgation of the Gospel [and] those, who, with manifest hoaxes, make a laughing-stock of the Spanish Nation and its most holy religion, maintaining the sacriligious adoration of some brute beasts almost within our sight. It is no longer time to permit that some naked ones after having taken up the time of your Excellency, and the rest of His Majesty's ministers [and] after having caused great expense for the royal treasury, frustrate everything with a 'We do not want it.' With the measures proposed, if they should meet with your Excellency's approval, in imitation of almost all the missions of America, idolatry will be stamped out, and the true religion will be established in spite of the obstinate ones who through punishments will come to understand what they refused [to acknowledge] through arguments. Joseph Xavier Alaña of the Company of Jesus."

46. The map that accompanied the 1743 version is not found in the 1760 version, which is followed immediately on this microfilm by the record of the debriefing of some Cuban fishermen who had been captured in the Key Biscayne area and carried north to serve as the slaves of their Uchise captors at a farmstead three months' journey distant.

Bibliography from Zubillaga (1946)

Index Operum Impressorum (Index of Published Works), pp. XXI-XXXIII

Acosta, Josephus de, S.I. *De natura novi Orbis libri duo et de promulgatione evangelii apud barbaras, sive de procuranda Indorum salute libri sex.* Coloniae Agrippinae, 1596.

Alegre, Francisco Javier, S.I. *Historia de la Compañia de Jesús en Nueva España, que estaba escribiendo el P. Fr. J. Alegre al tiempo de su expulsión.* Publicala . . . Carlos María de Bustamante. 3 vols. Mexico, 1841-42.

Astráin, Antonio, S.I. *Historia de la compañia de Jesús en la Asistencia de España.* 7 vols. Madrid, 1902-25.

Colección de documentos inéditos relativos al descubrimiento, conquista y organización de las antiguas posesiones españolas de America y Oceania, sacadas de los archivos del Reino y muy especialmente del de Indias. 42 vols. Madrid, 1864-1884. [C.D.I. Am.]

Frois, Luis, S.I. *Segunda parte da Historia de Japam que trata das couzas, que socederão nesta V. Provincia da hera de 1578 por diante, começando pela conversão del Rey de Bungo. (1578-1582).* Capitulos I a XLIII da Segunda parte da Historia de Japam Editados e anotados por João de Amara Abranches Pinto e Yashitomo Okamoto. Toquio, 1938.

Hernáez, Francisco Javier, S.I. *Colección de Bulas, Breves y otros Documentos relativos a la Iglesia de America y Filapinas.* 2 vols. Bruselos, 1879.

Hodge, Frederick W. *Handbook of American Indians. North of Mexico.* Smithsonian Institution. Bureau of American Ethnology. Bulletin 30. 2 vols. Washington, 1907-1910.

Lemoyne de Morgues, Jacques *Brevis narratio eorum quae in Florida, Americae provincia, Gallis acciderunt, secunda in illa navigatione, duce Renato de Laudonnière, closses praefecto, anno 1564 quae est secunda pars Americae . . .* auctore Iacobo Le Moyne, cui cognomen de Morgues . . . nunc primum gallico sermone a Theodoro de Bry . . . in lucem edita latio vero donata a C.C.A. [Carolo Cluseo Atrebatense.] Francoforte, 1591.

Lopetegui, Leon, S.I. *La Constitución <<Romani Pontificis>> de San Pio V, del 2 de agosto de 1571.* In *Estudios Eclesiasticos* 16 (1942): 487–511.

Lopez de Velasco, Juan. *Geografia y descripción universal de las Indias, recopilado por el cosmógrafo-cronista . . . desde el año 1570 al de 1574.* Publicada por primera vez en el Boletín de la Sociedad Geográfica de Madrid, con adiciones e ilustraciones, por don Justo Zaragoza. Madrid, 1894.

Perez de Ribas, Andrés, S.I. *Historia de los triumphos de nuestra santa fee entre gentes las mas bárbaras y fieras del nuevo Orbe, consequidos por los soldados de la milicia de la Compañia de Jesús en las misiones de la Provincia de Nueva España.* Madrid, 1645.

Rayanna, Petrus Puthota, S.I. *De Constitutione S. Pii Papae V <<Romani Pontificis>>* (2 Augusti 1571). (*Canonis 1125*). Dissertatio ad Lauream in Facultate Iuris Canonici Pontificiae Universitatis Gregorianae. Romae, 1938.

Ricard, Robert *Etudes et documents pour l'histoire missionaire de l' Espagne et du Portugal.* Collection de la section scientifique l' Aucam, n. 1. Louvain, 1926.

Ruidíaz y Caravia, E. *La Florida. Su conquista y colonización por Pedro Menéndez de Avilés.* 2 vols. Madrid, 1893.

Sacchinus, Franciscus, S.I. *Historiae Societatis Iesu pars tertia, sive Borgia.* Romae, 1649.

Schmidt, W., S.V.D. *Der Ursprung der Gottesidee. Eine historisch-kritische und positive Studie.* Vols. 2–7. Munster i. W., 1929–1940.

Zubillaga, Felix, S.I. *La Florida, la misión jesuítica (1566–1572) y la colonización española.* Bibliotheca Instituti Historici S.I. Vol. I. Roma, 1941.

Opera Manuscripta, pp. XXXIII-XXXIV (manuscript works).

Sanchez Vaquero, Juan, S.I. *Historia de las cosas mas dignas de memoria que han acontecido en la fundación, principios y progreso de la Compañia de Jesús en esta provincia y reinos de Nueva España.* 83*.

References

Abbreviations

AGI   Archivo General de Indias
SD   Santo Domingo
SC   Stetson Collection, P.K. Yonge Library of Florida History
WLC Woodbury Lowery Collection
JTCC Jeannette Thurber Connor Collection, P.K. Yonge Library of Florida
     History

Aguilar, Fray Thomás de, Fray Joseph de Jesus y Casas, and Fray Juan de la
Rosa
   1735 Letter to the King, March 15, 1735, St. Augustine. AGI SD 844 JTCC,
        reel 5.
        The letter was actually addressed to the king by three chiefs, Don
        Juan Miguel of the Timucua nation, Don Antonio Pojoy of the Alafaia
        Costas nation, and Don Antonio Joseph of the Yamasee nation, but it
        bears the names of the friars who served as their interpreters.
Alaña, Joseph Xavier, and Joseph María Monaco
   1743 Report that Fathers Joseph María Monaco and Joseph Xavier Alaña of
        the Company of Jesus Present to the Illustrious Sr. D^n Juan Francisco
        Güemes de Horcasitas, Lt. General of the Royal Armies, Governor and
        Captain General of the City of Havana and of the Island of Cuba,
        about the State in which They have Found the Indians of Southern
        Florida and its Keys, Along with what they Considered Necessary for
        its Permanent Reduction. Havana, 1743. AGI SD 860 SC.
        Although the title bears the names of Fathers Monaco and Alaña,
        it was signed only by Alaña and apparently was written by him alone.
   1760 [Same title as above.] AGI SD 1210.

This version, made by Father Alaña in 1760, as Alaña himself noted, is not a literal copy of the 1743 document, although it is substantially the same as the document sent to the Council of the Indies sixteen years earlier. The 1760 copy was made in response to the crown's request to the governor of Cuba for information on Indians from the Keys who had come to Cuba in the later 1750s to escape harassment by the Uchise. The 1760 version omits material found in the 1743 version and adds material as well that is not in the 1743 version. The additions suggest that Alaña had a lengthier version than the one that he sent to the Council in 1743. William C. Sturtevant based his "The Last of the South Florida Aborigines" (1978) largely on this document and published the Spanish text of its 1743 version as an appendix to his essay. My translation of the 1743 version, prepared early in 1978 for the Granada site project, appeared in Arva Moore Parks, *Where the River Found the Bay* (1985). In 1987 I prepared a translation of the 1760 version from a microfilm copy furnished by Eugene Lyon.

Alas, Alonso de
  1600 Letter to the King, January 12, 1600, St. Augustine. AGI SD 229.
Alegre, S.J., Francisco Javier
  1956 *Historia de la Provincia de la Compañia de Jesus de Nueva España.*
        New edition by Ernest J. Burrus, S.J., and Felix Zubillaga, S.J., Vol. 1.
        Rome: Institutum Historicum S.J.
Arrazola, Juan de, and Joseph de Olivera
  1613 Letter to the King, January 6, 1613, St. Augustine. AGI SD 229 SC.
Ayala y Escobar, Juan de
  1717 Letter to the King, April 18, 1717, St. Augustine. AGI SD 843 SC.
Benavides, Antonio de
  1723 Letter to the King, March 8, 1723, St. Augustine. AGI SD 865 SC.
Charles II
  1680 Order to the Bishop of Cuba, December 26, 1680, Madrid. AGI SD 151
        SC.
  1690 Order to the Provincial of the Florida Franciscans, September 8, Madrid. AGI Lima 151.
Chumillas, Fray Julian
  1688 Letter to Antonio Ortiz de Otalore, September 12, 1688, Madrid. AGI
        SD 856 SC.
Connor, Jeannette Thurber (translator and editor)
  1925 *Colonial Records of Spanish Florida.* 2 vols. Deland: Florida State Historical Society.
Council of the Indies
  1680 Notes, December, 1680, AGI SD 226.
  1695 Notes, November 27, 1695, Madrid. AGI SD

Crane, Verner W.
1956 *The Southern Frontier, 1670-1732.* Ann Arbor: University of Michigan Press.

Cruz, Juan Bautista de la
1680 Statement, February 20, 1680, St. Augustine. AGI SD 226 WLC, reel 3, of the Florida State University Library copy.

Deagan, Kathleen A.
1978 Cultures in Transition: Fusion and Assimilation among the Eastern Timucua. In *Tacachale: Essays on the Indians of Florida and Southeastern Georgia During the Historic Period,* ed. Jerald T. Milanich and Samuel Proctor, pp. 89-119. Gainesville: University Presses of Florida.

Días Vara Calderón, Bishop Gabriel
1675 Letter to the Queen, 1675, Havana. AGI SD 151. (Microfilm copy furnished to W.H. Marquardt by Victoria Stapells-Johnson.)

Dickinson, Jonathan
1981 *Jonathan Dickinson's Journal, or God's Protecting Providence, Being the Narrative of a Journey from Port Royal in Jamaica to Philadelphia, August 23, 1696 to April 1st, 1697.* Stuart, Florida: printed for Florida Classics Library, Southeastern Printing Co., Inc.
1985 *Jonathan Dickinson's Journal, or God's Protecting Providence, Being the Narrative of a Journey from Port Royal in Jamaica to Philadelphia, August 23, 1696 to April 1st, 1697.* Port Salerno, Florida: Florida Classics Library.

Dobyns, Henry F.
1983 *Their Number Become Thinned: Native American Population Dynamics in Eastern North America.* Knoxville: University of Tennessee Press.

Ebelino de Compostela, Bishop Diego de
1690 Appeal to the Clergy of his Diocese, January 2, 1690, Havana. AGI Quito 90. (Microfilm copy furnished to W.H. Marquardt by Victoria Stapells-Johnson.)
1692 Letter to the King, July 3, 1692, Havana. AGI Quito 90. (Microfilm copy and typed transcript furnished to W.H. Marquardt by Victoria Stapells-Johnson.)

Elijio de la Puente, Juan José
1764 Letter to the Governor, September 12, 1764, Havana. AGI SD 2595.

Fernández de Olivera, Juan
1612 Letter to the King, October 13, 1612, St. Augustine. AGI SD 229 WLC, reel 3, of the Florida State University Library copy.

Fontaneda, Do. d'Escalante
1944 *Memoir of Do. d'Escalante Fontaneda Respecting Florida, Written in Spain, About the Year 1575.* Translated by Buckingham Smith. Annotated by David O. True. Coral Gables, Fla.: Glades House.

438 References

Gailey, Christine W., and Thomas C. Patterson
1988 State Formation and Uneven Development. In *State and Society: The Emergence and Development of Social Hierarchy and Political Centralization,* ed. Barbara Bender, John Gledhill, and Mogens Trolle Larsen, pp. 77–90. London: George Allen and Unwin.

García, Andrés
1695 *Autos* made Officially by the Adjutant, Andrés García, Lieutenant of the Province of Timucua, against Santiago, Native to the Village of San Pedro. Year of 1695. AGI Escribanía de Cámara, leg. 157A, quaderno I, folios 172ff, SC.
This document is appended to the Joaquín de Florencia visitation record for 1694–1695.

Garcia de Palacios, Bishop Juan
1682 Letter to the King, January 20, 1682, Havana. AGI SD 151 SC.

Gilliland, Marion Spjut
1975 *The Material Culture of Key Marco, Florida.* Gainesville: University Presses of Florida.

Goggin, John M., and William T. Sturtevant
1964 The Calusa: A Stratified Non-Agricultural Society (with Notes on Sibling Marriage). In *Explorations in Cultural Anthropology: Essays in Honor of George Peter Murdock,* ed. Ward Goodenough, 179–219. New York: McGraw-Hill.

Granberry, Julian
1987 *A Grammar and Dictionary of the Timucua Language.* Anthropological Notes no. 1. Island Archaeological Museum. Horseshoe Beach, Florida.

Griffin, John W.
1988 *The Archeology of Everglades National Park: A Synthesis.* Tallahassee: National Park Service, Southeast Archeological Center.

Griffin, John W., Sue B. Richardson, Mary Pohl, Carl D. McMurray, C. Margaret Scarry, Suzanne K. Fish, Elizabeth S. Wing, L. Jill Loucks, and Marcia K. Welch
1985 *Excavations at the Granada Site,* vol. 1 of *Archaeology and History of the Granada Site.* Tallahassee: Florida Division of Archives, History and Records Management.

Güemes y Horcasitas, Juan de
1743 Letter to the King, July 26, 1743, Havana. AGI SD 860 SC.

Guerra y de la Vega, Francisco de la
1668 Letter to the king, July 7, 1668. AGI SD 233 WLC, reel 4.

Guttiérrez de Miranda
1578 Letter to the King, February 13, 1578, Havana. AGI SD 125 SC.

Hammon, Briton
1760 *A Narrative of the Uncommon Sufferings, and Surprizing Deliverance*

of Briton Hammon, a Negro Man, Servant to General Winslow, of Marsh-field in New-England; Who Returned to Boston, after Having Been Absent Almost Thirteen Years. Boston: Green and Russell.

Hann, John H.
1986 Church Furnishings, Sacred Vessels and Vestments Held by the Missions of Florida: Translation of Two Inventories. *Florida Archaeology* 2: 147-164.
1987 Twilight of the Mocamo and Guale Aborigines as Portrayed in the 1695 Spanish Visitation. *Florida Historical Quarterly* 66: 1-24.
1988 *Apalachee: The Land Between the Rivers.* Gainesville: University Presses of Florida.
1989 St. Augustine's Fallout from the Yamasee War. *Florida Historical Quarterly* 68: 180-200.
1990 Summary Guide to Spanish Florida Missions and *Visitas* with Churches in the Sixteenth and Seventeenth Centuries. *The Americas* (April 1990): 417-513.

Herrera [y Tordesillas], Antonio de
1720 *Historia General de los Hechos de los Castillanos en las Islas i Tierra Firme del Mar Oceano.* Madrid: Imprenta Real de Nicolás Rodigas Franco.

Hita Salazar, Pablo de
1675 Letter to the Queen, August 24, 1675. AGI SD 839 SC.
1680 Letter to the King, February 20, 1680, St. Augustine. AGI SD 226 WLC, reel 4, of the Florida State University Library copy.

Ibarra, Pedro de
1608 Letter to the King, August 22, 1608, St. Augustine. AGI SD 224 WLC, reel 3, of the Florida State University Library copy.

Jesus, Fray Alonso de
[1634] Letter to the King, n.d. AGI SD 225 JTCC.

Jones, B. Calvin, John Hann, and John F. Scarry
1991 San Pedro y San Pablo de Patale: A Seventeenth-Century Spanish Mission in Leon County, Florida. *Florida Archaeology* 5.

Knight, Vernon James, Jr.
1986 The Institutional Organization of Mississippian Religion. *American Antiquity* 51: 675-687.

Lanning, John Tate
1935 *The Spanish Missions of Georgia.* Chapel Hill: University of North Carolina Press.

Leonard, Irving (translator)
1939 *Spanish Approach to Pensacola, 1689-1693.* Albuquerque: The Quivira Society.

Leturiondo, Alonso de
[1700] Memorial to the King Our Lord in His Royal and Supreme Council of

the Indies. . . . (Published about 1700.) Translated by John H. Hann. *Florida Archaeology* 2: 165–225.

Leturiondo, Domingo de

1678 Visitation of Apalachee and Timucua, 1677–1678. AGI Escribanía de Cámara, leg. 156B, folios 519–616, SC. Translated by John H. Hann. *Florida Archaeology* 7: in press.

Lewis, Clifford M.

1978 The Calusa. In *Tacachale: Essays on the Indians of Florida and Southeastern Georgia During the Historic Period,* ed. Jerald T. Milanich and Samuel Proctor, pp. 19–49. Gainesville: University Presses of Florida.

López, Fray Feliciano

1695 Letter to the King, October 20, 1695. AGI SD 235. (Microfilm copy furnished to W.H. Marquardt by Victoria Stapells-Johnson.)

1697 Letter to Fray Taybo, September, 1697, San Diego de Compostela, Bay of Carlos. AGI SD 154. (Microfilm copy and typed transcript furnished to W.H. Marquardt by Victoria Stapells-Johnson)

Lyon, Eugene

1983 *The Enterprise of Florida: Pedro Menéndez de Avilés and the Spanish Conquest of 1565–1568.* Gainesville: University Presses of Florida. Originally published 1976.

McAlister, Lyle N.

1984 *Spain and Portugal in the New World, 1492–1700,* vol. 3 of *Europe and the World in The Age of Expansion.* Minneapolis: University of Minnesota Press.

McEwan, Bonnie

1991 San Luis de Talimali: The Archaeology of Spanish-Indian Relations at a Florida Mission. *Historical Archaeology* 25: in press.

Manucy, Albert

1962 *The Houses of St. Augustine.* St. Augustine: The St. Augustine Historical Society; reprint, University of North Florida Press and the St. Augustine Historical Society, 1991.

Marquardt, William H.

1987 The Calusa Social Formation in Protohistoric South Florida. In *Power Relations and State Formation,* ed. Thomas C. Patterson and Christine W. Gailey, 98–116. Washington, D.C.: Archeology Section, American Anthropological Association.

1988 Politics and Production among the Calusa of South Florida. In *Hunters and Gatherers,* vol. 1: *History, Environment, and Social Change among Hunting and Gathering Societies,* ed. David Riches, Tim Ingold, and James Woodburn, 161–188. Department of Anthropology, University College. London: Berg Publishers.

Marquardt, William H. (editor)

1991 *Culture and Environment in the Domain of the Calusa.* University of Florida, Institute of Archaeology and Paleoenvironmental Studies, Monograph no. 1. Gainesville.

Marques Cabrera, Juan

1681 Letter to the King, January 14, 1681, St. Augustine. AGI SD 226 JTCC.

Marrinan, Rochelle A.

1991 The Florida Franciscan Mission Settlement: Questioning the Model. Paper given at the Conference on Historical and Underwater Archaeology, Richmond, Virginia, January 10, 1991.

Milanich, Jerald T.

1987 Corn and Calusa: DeSoto and Demography. In *Coasts, Plain, and Deserts: Essays in Honor of Reynold J. Ruppé,* ed. Sylvia W. Gaines, pp. 173–184. Arizona State University Anthropological Research Papers no. 38.

Milanich, Jerald T., and Samuel Proctor (editors)

1978 *Tacachale: Essays on the Indians of Florida and Southeastern Georgia during the Historic Period.* Gainesville: University Presses of Florida.

Montes, Fray Blas de

1602 Letter to the King, September 16, 1602, St. Augustine. AGI SD 235 WLC, reel 2, of the copy of the Florida State University Library.

Montiano, Manuel de

1738 Letter to the King, June 4, 1738, St. Augustine. AGI SD 865 SC.
      The governor's letter contains various friars' reports on the settlements in which they served.

1739 Report of the Number of Missionaries that there are in this Province of Santa Elena. . . , June 23, 1739, St. Augustine. AGI SD 865 SC.

Müller, Werner

1968 North America. In *Pre-Columbian American Religions,* ed. Walter Krickeberg, pp. 147–229. New York: Holt, Rinehart and Winston.

New Catholic Encyclopedia

1967 *New Catholic Encyclopedia.* New York: McGraw-Hill.

O'Scanlon, Timoteo

1974 *Diccionario Maritimo Espanol.* Madrid: Museo Naval.

Pareja, Fray Francisco, Fray Lorenço Martínez, Fray Pedro Ruiz, Fray Alonso Desquera, Fray Juan de la Cruz, Fray Francisco Moreno de Jesús, Fray Bartolomé Romero

1617 Letter to the King, January 17, 1617, St. Augustine. AGI SD 235 WLC, reel 3, of the Florida State University Library copy.

Parks, Arva Moore

1985 *Where the River Found the Bay: Historical Study of The Granada Site, Miami, Florida,* vol. 2 of *Archaeology and History of the Granada Site.* Tallahassee: Florida Division of Archives, History, and Records Management.

Peña, Diego
1716 Journal, April 6, 1716. AGI SD 843 SC (filed under 1717 in the collection).
Provincial Chapter of the Province of Santa Elena of Florida
1693 Letter to the King, December 5, 1693, St. Augustine. AGI SD 235. (Microfilm copy furnished to W.H. Marquardt by Victoria Stappells-Johnson.)
Purdy, Barbara A.
1988 American Indians after A.D. 1492: A Case Study of Forced Culture Change. *American Anthropologist* 90: 640–655.
Quinn, David B.
1979 *New American World: a Documentary History of North America to 1612.* New York: Arno Press.
Quiroga y Losada, Diego de
1688 Letter to the King, April 1, 1688, St. Augustine. AGI SD 839 SC.
1690 Letter to the King, August 31, 1690, St. Augustine. AGI SD 228 SC.
Rebolledo, Diego de
1657 Testimony from the Visitation that was Made in the Provinces of Apalachee and Timucua and Ustaca. . . . AGI Escribania de Cámara, leg. 155B, no. 18, SC. Translated by John H. Hann. *Florida Archaeology* 2: 81–145.
Rojas y Borja, Luis
1628 Letter to the King, June 30, 1628, St. Augustine. AGI SD 225 WLC, reel 3, of the Florida State University Library copy.
Royal Officials of Havana
1689 Letter to the King, February 15, 1689, Havana. AGI, SD 151, SC.
Ruiz, Fray Alonso
1759 Census of the Indian Village of Nra. Senora de la Leche of the Jurisdiction of this Presidio of St. Augustine of Florida for this Year of One Thousand Seven Hundred and Fifty-nine on the Fourth of February of (illegible word). AGI SD 2604. (Copy furnished by Jane Landers.)
Salinas, Juan de
1623 Letter to the King, January 30, 1623, St. Augustine. AGI SD 225 JTCC, reel 3.
Saunders, Rebecca
1990 Ideal and Innovation: Spanish Mission Architecture in the Southeast, in David Hurst Thomas, ed., *Columbian Consequences,* volume 2, *Archaeological and Historical Perspectives on the Spanish Borderlands East.* Washington, D.C.: Smithsonian Institution Press, pp. 527–542.
Serrano y Sanz, Manuel
1912 *Documentos Históricos de la Florida y al Luisiana, Siglos XVI al XVIII.* Madrid: Librería General de Victoriano Suárez.

Smith, Buckingham
  1860 *Dos Cartas en Lengua Apalachina y Timuguana.* New York: Privately
        printed.
Solana, Juan
  1697 Testimony, February 6, 1697, St. Áugustine. In Laureano de Torres y
        Ayala, Letter to the King, February 3, 1697, St. Augustine. AGI SD
        228 JTCC, reel 3.
Solís de Merás, Gonzalo
  1964 *Pedro Menéndez de Avilés, Adelantado, Governor, and Captain-General
        of Florida: Memorial.* Facsimile reproduction of 1570 edition. Gaines-
        ville: University Presses of Florida.
Steward, Julian (editor)
  1946 *Handbook of South American Indians,* vol. 2. Smithsonian Institution,
        Bureau of American Ethnology, Bulletin no. 143. Washington, D.C.
Sturtevant, William C.
  1960 *The Significance of Ethnological Similarities Between Southeastern North
        America and the Antilles.* New Haven: Yale University Publications in
        Anthropology no. 64.
  1978 The Last of the South Florida Aborigines. In *Tacachale: Essays on the
        Indians of Florida and Southeastern Georgia During the Historic Pe-
        riod,* ed. Jerald T. Milanich and Samuel Proctor, pp. 141–162. Gaines-
        ville: University Presses of Florida.
Swanton, John R.
  1922 *Early History of the Creek Indians and Their Neighbors.* Bureau of
        American Ethnology, Bulletin no. 73. Washington, D.C.: Government
        Printing Office.
  1946 *The Indians of the Southeastern United States.* Bureau of American
        Ethnology Bulletin no. 137. Reprint. New York: Green Press, 1969.
Torres y Ayala, Laureano de, et al.
  1697 Letter to the King, April 20, 1697, St. Augustine. AGI SD 230 JTCC,
        reel 4.
Turner, Victor
  1969 *The Ritual Process: Structure and Anti-Structure.* Chicago: Aldine.
Valdés, Bishop Gerónimo
  1711 Letter to the King, December 9, 1711, Havana. AGI SD 860 SC.
Vargas Ugarte, Rubén
  1935 The First Jesuit Mission in Florida. *The United States Catholic Histor-
        ical Society, Historical Records and Studies* 25: 59–148.
Weddle, Robert S.
  1985 *Spanish Sea: The Gulf of Mexico in North American Discovery, 1500–
        1685.* College Station: Texas A & M University Press.
Widmer, Randolph J.
  1983 The Evolution of the Calusa: A Non-Agricultural Chiefdom on the

Southwest Florida Coast. Ph.D. dissertation, Pennsylvania State University.

1988 *The Evolution of the Calusa: A Nonagricultural Chiefdom on the Southwest Florida Coast.* Tuscaloosa and London: University of Alabama Press.

Zubillaga, Felix (editor)

1946 Monumenta Antiquae Floridae (1566–1572). *Monumenta Missionum Societatis Iesu* no. 3. Rome.

Zúñiga y Zerda, Joseph de

1701 Order to Joachín de Florencia, March 10, 1701, St. Augustine. AGI SD 840 JTCC, reel 5.

1702 Letter to the King, St. Augustine, March 25, 1702. AGI SD 840 JTCC, reel 5.

Index

Abadalquini, 84, 84n.2
Abbacy for Florida, 96
Abosaya, 376
Afafa, woods of: population, 214, 216
Agna River, 21. *See also* Ochlockonee
Aipaja, cacique of. *See* Atoquimi;
  Atoyquimi; Aypaja; Hororo;
  Ypaja
Ais, cacique of: mission to, 95, 96; pop-
  ulation of, 87; request for baptism by,
  82–83. *See also* Aipaja; Aypaja; Ho-
  roro; Jororo; Maiaca; Mayaca;
  Mayaca-Jororo; Ypaja
Alafaes, 361. *See also* Alafaia Costas
  nation; Alafay; Costas Alafayes; Ela-
  fay; Pohoy; Pojoi; Pojoy; Pojoy, don
  Antonio; Pooy
Alafaia Costas nation, 327, 358. *See also*
  Alafaes; Alafay; Costas Alafayes; Ela-
  fay; Pohoy; Pojoi; Pojoy; Pojoy, don
  Antonio; Pooy
Alafay: near St. Augustine, 332, 370;
  part of Pojoy, 358, 363; mentioned,
  328. *See also* Alafaes; Alafaia Costas
  nation; Costas Alafayes; Elafay; Pohoy; Pojoi; Pojoy; Pojoy, don Antonio;
  Pooy

Alafia River, 22
Alamo, Gundisalvo del, 288, 289, 290
Alaña, Francisco Xavier de, 401. *See
  also* Alaña, Joseph Javier
Alaña, Joseph Javier: brings Indian
  troublemakers to Havana, 430; description of fort at Tequesta by (1743),
  430; Indians' abuse of alcohol,
  425–427; Indians' idea of conversion,
  328, 421; and Indian religion,
  328–329, 422–424; mentioned, 326,
  400, 408, 415, 417, 418. *See also*
  Alaña, Francisco Xavier de
Alaña-Monaco report, 1743 version of,
  418–419
Alas, Fray Pedro de las, Augustinian
  prior, Havana, 99, 103, 104, 105
Alcohol: Indians' passion for, 326, 425;
  ritualistic use of, 422
Alcola, population of (1679), 25
Alegre, Francisco Javier, 419
Algonquin deities, 272n.30
Alligators, as food, 370, 377
Alonsico, 292, 293, 294
Alonso, Ensign Juan, 149
Amacapira: and epidemic of 1727, 370;
  near St. Augustine in 1734, 370;

Amacapira (*continued*)
  origin of, 370; in village of Jororo,
  377. *See also* Macapiras; Rinconada
  de Macapiras; Rinconada of the
  Macapiras
Amacarisa, 359. *See also* Chiluca mis-
  sion of Nombre de Dios; Macariz;
  Nombre de Dios de Macariz
Amajuro River, identity of, 22. *See also*
  Majuro; Withlacoochee
Amapiras: baptisms of (1718–1723),
  362; identity of, 358. *See also*
  Yamasee
Amber, trade in, 12, 13, 14, 22, 23
Anacapi, location of, 30n.31. *See also*
  San Antonio de Anacapi
Angel, Alexandro, state of, 189–191
Angulo, Favian de, 148, 149, 150, 152
Antillean contact, 5–6
Antonia, sister of Chief Carlos: bap-
  tism of, 283n.132, 289; death of, 289;
  in Havana, 276n.56, 281, 289; mar-
  riage of, to Carlos, 289; marriage of,
  to Menéndez de Avilés, 289
Apalachee (people): baptisms at Moze
  (1718–1723), 362; baptisms at San
  Juan, 367; in Creek country, 327; at
  mission of San Luis (1726), 366
Apalachee (province): Calusa refusal to
  let friars go to, 197; destiny for some
  of 1695 mission band, 212; point of,
  21; revisionism of identification of
  church remains in, 370; visit by Calusa leaders, 80; mentioned, 13
Apalachocoli River, 22
Apojola Negra, population of (1679), 26
Asis River, 314
Atisimi, flight of, 144. *See also* Atisme;
  Atissimi; Jizime
Atisme, 212, 214. *See also* Atisimi; Atis-
  simi; Jizime
Atissimi: location of, 29–30; variant of
  Kissimmee, 147n.3. *See also* Atisimi;
  Atisme; Jizime
Atocuime, 213. *See also* Atoquimi;
  Atoyquimi
Atoquimi: cause of revolt in, 152;
  church ornaments of, carried off,
  149; friar's killer from, 153; killing of
  friar in, 146, 147, 148, 149; leader of
  revolt in, 154; population of, 214; re-

volt in, 214; remain fugitive, 214;
  mentioned, 150. *See also* Atocuime;
  Atoyquimi
Atoyquimi: killing of friar and Indians
  at, 143; location of, 29–30; population
  of, 216; revolt in, 6, 143. *See also* Atocuime; Atoquimi
Augustinian prior, opposition of, to
  Fray Romero, 95
Augustinians, proposed for south Florida missions, 101, 107, 108–109. *See
  also* Romero, Fray Francisco
Ayala Escobar, Captain don Juan de,
  146, 148
Ayeta, Fray Francisco: reply to Ferro
  Machado by, 127, 137; mentioned,
  129, 139
Aypaja: killing of chief of, 6, 146; move
  to San Antonio Anacapi by, 6. *See
  also* Aipaja; Atoquimi; Atoyquimi;
  Ypaja

Baptismal fonts, lack of, 369, 374
Baptisms in Calusa (1697), 166, 170,
  175, 195
Baptisms near St. Augustine,
  (1718–1723), 360–362
Baquiano, 152n.8
Barrera, Fray Rodrigo de la: head of
  1690 mission band, 130, 140; and
  mission band (1690), 120
Basisa: residence of Tocopaca, 355;
  mentioned, 352. *See also* Vasisa;
  Wacissa
Bazisa, channel of, 349
Bejarano, Francisco, 34, 36, 58. *See also*
  Vexarano, Francisco
Benavides Basan y Molina, Antonia de,
  reports by, 360–367
Bennett, Charles E., 273nn.46–51, 53
Birdhead idol, 422
Bishop of Cuba, mission appeal by, 34,
  36, 37, 85–91
Bishop of Durango, 412
Bishop of Yucatan, letter by, 257–260
Blockhouse at San Luis de Talimali, 81
Boca de Ratones, 186n.17. *See also*
  Ratones
Bocarraton, 420
Bocas, Indians of, 201
Bocas de Miguel Mora, 186n.17

Body-painting as religious ritual, 424
Bones, Key of: Costa on, 331. *See also*
Cayo de Huesos; Key West
Bones, village of (1697), 200
Bueno, Fray Salvador: at Hororo, 146;
on revolt at Atoquimi, 146-147
Bullones, Fray Joseph de, 368, 371-380
Bungo, King of, 241

Caalus, cacique, 280. *See also* Carlos,
cacique; Carlos, chief
Cacina Point, 348, 356
Cadereita, Marquis of: and salvage, 21.
See also Cadereyta, Marquis de
Cadereyta, Marquis de: and report of
shipwreck, 19. *See also* Cadereita,
Marquis of
Calus (village): described, 231, 288;
Spanish enclave at, 309. *See also*
Carlos
Calus, Key of: in 1560s, 277n.77,
311-312; in 1697, 173. *See also* Carlos, Key of; Key of Calusa
Calusa (people): agriculture, aversion
to, 43, 184-185, 428; Apalachee, visit
to, 36; assemblies of, 242-243,
273n.34; and blacks, 184-185, 421,
426, 426n.31; body-painting by, 245;
burials of, 166, 169, 175, 196, 242,
423-424; canoes of, 4-5, 10; and curing, 238, 247, 423; dancing with
heads by, 223, 265; and the dead, 238,
423-424; deception in request for
mission by, 206, 420-421; early contact with Europeans by, 4; economy
of, xv; enigma of, xv; expulsion of
friars by, 167; factionalism among,
221, 222, 266, 269; fear of Spaniards
by, 178-179, 240, 425; gifts expected
by, for conversion, 166, 170, 175, 195,
421; gold and silver among, 267;
great captain of, 167, 171, 178, 187,
197; hair length of, 243, 245; hostility
of, 8-9, 29, 44, 161-201 passim; and
hunger, 260-261; indolence of, 159,
420; knowledge of, xvi, 224-225, 246,
247-248; lack of contact with St.
Augustine by, 4; ladino qualities of,
43, 184-185, 421; last refuge of, 331;
leaders of, killed by Spaniards, 8,
222, 236, 267, 290, 309; and marriage

as political bond, 224; marriage of,
to sibling, 223, 224; meeting with
governor by (1688), 80; mistreatment
of friars by, 44-45, 164-201 passim,
212; migration to Cuba by, 325-326,
327, 331, 332, 335-347 passim,
380-398 passim, 402-403; obedience
of, to Spanish crown, 36-37, 80, 208,
237; patilineality among, 222; and
peace with Spaniards (1612), 9, 10,
11; persecution of, by Yamasee, 336,
339; and polygamy, 223, 245,
274nn.35, 36; population of (1690s),
42, 99, 99n.9, 125, 135, 159, 164, 165,
168, 174, 205, 208, 210; request for
missions by, 43, 206, 210, 421; ridicule of friars' preaching by, 197-198;
and sodomy, 239, 239n.11; trade by
(1690s), 169, 195; warning to friars
by, 209; weapons of, 170, 171, 178,
186, 186n.19, 197, 288. *See also* Carlos Indians
—children of: baptized (1697), 166, 170,
179, 195; baptized (1743), 424; fondness for, 421; killing of, 239, 245, 316,
329, 423, 427; punishment of, forbidden, 328, 421
Calusa cacique: bench of, 237n.34,
242-243; speaks Apalachee and
Timuqua (1690s), 160. *See also* Carlos, Cacique
Calusa chief: called "great chief," 28,
86, 96; enmity of, toward Rogel, 287;
gifts to (1697), 184, 194; head village
of (1689), 86; house of, 42, 194; insignia of, 268; request for baptism by,
89, 135, 164, 174, 194, 207; tribute
paid to, 11, 237, 268; visit to Havana
by (1689), 38, 88-90. *See also* Caalus,
cacique; Calusa cacique; Carlos,
Cacique
—, old (1697): baptism of, 166, 169, 174,
194, 209; death of, 166; denial of
Christianization by, 166, 169, 175,
195; friars' lives saved by, 178, 187,
190, 195. *See also* Phelipe, don (Calusa chief, 1697)
—, young (1697): assault on friar by,
171; forbids hectoring of his father,
165, 169; greets friars, 165, 173, 194;
orders killing of friars, 197; presents

Calusa chief, young (*continued*)
children for baptism, 166, 170, 175, 195; readiness of, for baptism, 194; mentioned, 158, 160, 172, 187, 199, 208. *See also* Carlos, Cacique, son of (1688)

Calusa government: change, postcontact, xvi, xvii; diverse views on complexity of, xvi–xvii; as polity, resemblance to Aztec and Inca, 226, 227; shaman as regent, 268; shaman's role in, 222–223, 227; shaman's usurpation of chieftainship, 268–269; succession in, 222, 223, 267; and tribute, xv, 23, 237; tribute-based state type, xvii

Calusa head village: neighboring settlements, 256; number of houses in, 41, 42, 168

Calusa hostages, in Cuba, 276n.56, 280, 281

Calusa language, interpreters for, 280, 281, 284n.138

Calusa military force, xv

Calusa mission (1697): failure of, 161, 163–164; first steps of, 40–41; genesis of, 51; given to Franciscans, 92; initial reception of, 158, 159, 160, 161, 165–166, 168, 169–170; orders for, reissued, 74–75; review of history of, 124–125, 128–132; secular volunteers for, 34. *See also* Missions to Calusa

Calusa mission band (1695), support for requested, 117–118, 119

Calusa mission compound (1697), description of, 165, 169

Calusa mission of 1697: well documented, 3; role of crown in, 122, 123

Calusa missions, Cuban connection of, 6

Calusa province: client chiefs of, 262; domain, expansion and limits of, 26n.21, 86, 87; languages, diversity of, 115n.13; migrants to, from Cuba (early postcontact), 5. *See also* Carlos, province of

—villages, number of: 16th century, 226; 17th century, 11, 217

Calusa religion: on afterlife, xv, 238, 241, 424; and ancestors, offerings to, xv, 423; belief system of, xv; change

in, xvi, xvii, 241; and curing, 238, 423; and fasting, 242; gods of, irritated over friars' presence, 160, 167, 175, 209; and monotheism, 238, 241; as political bulwark, xvi, 224; resistance of, to missionization, 4, 160, 166, 167, 169, 171, 175, 221, 225, 243, 421; seeing God, 242; singing by women in, xv, 287, 288; soul and illness in, 228, 237–238; temple of, 42–43, 44, 159–160, 167, 170, 171, 195–196, 287, 422; traditionalism in, 43, 44, 174–175, 223, 225–226, 239, 243, 246, 247, 285, 287–288; triuneness of deity in, 238–239, 272n.30

—masks of, xv, 42, 160, 422; described, 195–196; representing gods, 224, 287, 288; wearing of, 224, 287

Calusa social structure, xv, xvi, xvii

Camacho, Fray Francisco, doctrinero at Jizime, 147, 148, 149

Campeche, College of, 417

Cancha, chief of: death of, 325, 402; migration to Cuba by, 47, 325, 402. *See also* Tancha, chief of

Capitán Grande, 426nn.26, 28. *See also* Great Captain

Carlos, Bay of: called Escampaba, 311; described, 277n.77, 311; search for salvage in, 19; mentioned, 158, 212

Carlos, Cacique (1560s): death of, 236, 267; enmity to Spaniards of, 221, 222, 231, 264–265, 266, 267, 287; enmity of, to Tocobaga, 220; origin of name of, 280; sibling marriage of, 289; usurpation of chieftainship by, 268–269. *See also* Caalus, cacique; Calusa cacique; Calusa chief

Carlos, Cacique (1680s–1690s): land of, 52; request for baptism by, 82, 83, 98, 207; visit to Havana by, 98, 121, 124, 125, 130, 135, 140. *See also* Calusa cacique; Calusa chief

Carlos, Cacique (1711): request for transportation to Cuba by, 335–336; mentioned, 46, 334, 341

Carlos, cacique of (1612), 9, 11, 26

Carlos, cacique of (1690s), 156, 163, 164, 187, 205. *See also* Calusa cacique; Calusa chief

Calusa, cacique of (1711): death of, 3, 5, 402

Carlos, Cacique, son of (1688): meeting of, with governor, 121, 124, 130, 134, 140. *See also* Calusa chief, young

Carlos, chiefdom of, 189

Carlos, Key of, 185, 187, 188, 192, 193, 202, 203, 209. *See also* Calus, Key of; Key of Calusa

Carlos, province of: not visited by friars (1617), 14-15; source of name of, 210; mentioned, 98, 100. *See also* Calusa province

Carlos, village of: black at (1612), 11

Carlos Indians (1743), 420. *See also* Calusa (people)

Carrillo, Fray Miguel: friar at Calusa, 163, 165, 184, 192, 194, 198; testimony of, 173-177

Carrera, Brother Juan de la, 288, 289, 293, 294

Casipuia, migrants to St. Augustine (1717), 358. *See also* Casipuya

Casipuya: language of, 358; number of (1726), 366; baptisms of (1718-1723), 361; mentioned, 363, 375. *See also* Casipuia

Casitua (spot), 177

Casitua, Key of, 172

Castillo, Fray Joseph del, 360, 361, 362

Catamaran, 198, 198n.26

Çavallos, Brother Sancho de, 291, 292

Caveta, cacique of: hostility to friars by, 29; mentioned, 355

Cayo de Huesos, 41. *See also* Key of Bones; Key West

Chagualas, 11, 11n.6, 268

Chaliquisliche, 356. *See also* Cherokeeleechee

Cherokeeleechee, 356n.5. *See also* Chaliquisliche

Chichi, don Pablo, cacique of Carlos (1743), 410

Chichimeco, 359

Chickasaw, 375-376

Children, Indian: killing of, 239, 245, 316, 329, 423, 427; not punished, 328, 421

Chiluca mission of Nombre de Dios (1726), 365

Chiluca mission of San Buenaventura (1726), 365

Chiluque: identity of, 358, 359; language of, 359; mentioned, 363

Chiluque at Palica, baptisms of (1718-1723), 361

Christians, number of (1617), 13

Chumillas, Fray Julian, 118, 119, 135

Church at Nombre de Dios Chiquito, 369

Church furnishings, Hororo: removed to St. Augustine, 152

Cisneros, Canon don Juan de: absence from benefice justified, 65, 68; departure opposed, 34, 35, 36, 60-61; vetoed, 71, 73; insincerity of, 92; retention of canonry by, 61-62; mentioned, 58-59, 93, 98

Claraquachine River, 22n.18. *See also* Agna River; Ochlockonee River

Clergy, distinction between secular and regular, 69nn.5, 6

Coasts, features of, 21-22

Cofas, Las, population of, 214, 216

Coleto, Chief (1711): in Keys, 46, 335, 339; persecuted by Yamasee, 336, 339; requests transport to Cuba, 336

Collation, 380; controversy over, 368-369, 371, 372-374

Concepción (Atoyquime): new conversion at, 110; mentioned, 120, 130, 140. *See also* Atoquimi; Atoyquimi

Contreras, Fray Francisco de, 162, 163, 178, 179, 180, 181, 182, 183, 203, 206

Cordova Laso de la Vega, don Diego de, governor of Cuba, 182, 183, 189, 203

Costa: identified as Ais, 357-358; identity of, disputed, 327, 332; as Keys Indians, 327, 331, 332, 357; killed, 370; migration to Cuba by, 331; nomadism of, 370, 377

Costa Nation Guasacara: baptisms of (1718-1723), 361; mentioned, 357, 358, 363, 370, 375

Costas: heathen, 377; on Key of Bones, 331; persecution of, by Uchise, 331; population of, 377

Costas Alafayes, 327. *See also* Alafaes; Alafaia Costas; Alafay; Elafay; Pohoy; Pojoi; Pojoy; Pojoy, don Antonio; Pooy

Costa village of San Anttonio (1726), 366, 379

Cow Key, 329, 331. *See also* Key of Cows

Crespo, Juan Bento, bishop of Durango, 413-414

Crown, Spanish: orders continued search for Jororo rebels, 215; persistent support of mission to Calusa, 206, 210-211; role in 1697 mission, 39-40
Cuban clergy, desire of, to missionize Florida Indians, 28
Cuban expedition to Keys (1732), 386, 394, 395, 396, 397
Cuban fishermen, captured by Uchise, 431n.46
Cuchiaga: subject to Guarugumbe, 316; village of, 200. *See also* Key of Cuchiapa
Cuna, 11n.6
Cusabo, 358

Días Vara Calderón, Bishop Gabriel, description of coasts by, 21
Dickinson, Jonathan, xviii, 30, 44
Diego, don, Calusa cacique (1732), 382, 392, 394, 395, 396, 397
Dobyns, Henry F., 5, 226
Domingo, don, great captain, 410
Domínguez, Francisco, soldier from Mayaca, 149
Dominican mission, 36, 66, 69, 71-73

Ebelino de Compostela, Bishop Diego: suggests Fray Romero for south Florida missions, 95, 99, 100, 103, 105, 108; on soldiers needed at missions, 76-77; on unavailability of seculars, 75-76. *See also* Oratorians; Romero, Fray Francisco; St. Philip Neri
Elafay, 26, 26n.23. *See also* Alafaes; Alafaia Costas Nation; Alafay; Costas Alafayes; Pohoy; Pojoi; Pojoy; Pojoy, don Antonio; Pooy
Elijio de la Puente, Juan José: on identity of Costas, 357; on Keys Indians, 331
Encomienda, 33, 33n.35
Entradas by friars, 14
Epidemics, 13, 325, 370
Escalante Fontaneda, Hernando, 220, 301
Escampaha: name of Bay of Carlos and chief of Carlos, 271n.24, 311; name of kingdom of Carlos, 237, 271n.24. *See also* Tocampaha
Esquivel, Ensign Juan Alonso, 152, 153, 154

Esteva, Juan: statement of, 193-201; mentioned, 180

Felipe (Calusa, 1560s): betrothal of, to old chief's daughter, 222; claim to chieftainship by, 222, 267-269, 281; denial of chieftainship to, 222, 268-269; dependence on Spaniards by, 223; desire of, to be chief, 267; enmity of, with Carlos, 267, 269, 289; execution of dissidents by, 223; in Cuba, 281, 283-284n.134; killed, 225, 309; leader of pro-Spanish faction, 309; as great captain, 222-223, 269; marriage to and divorce from old chief's daughter, 268-269; monogamy, attitude to, 245-246; opposition to, 223, 240; pleased by Tocobaga's break with Spaniards, 254; rivalry of, with Carlos, 222; sibling marriage of, 223, 244, 290; as successor to Carlos, 222, 267
Felipe (Calusa councillor, 1560s), 261-262
Fernández Cordova Ponce de León, Governor don Joseph, 59
Fernández de Olivera, Governor Juan, 9, 12
Ferro Machado, don Juan: investigation of friars by, 126, 127-128, 136, 137-138; in Spain, 127, 137; on teaching of Spanish, 136n.26
Fishermen from Cuba, 4, 173, 326, 404, 411, 420, 423, 427
Fishkills (1575), 312
Florencia, Joachín de, 214, 354
Fonseca y Haze, don Thomás de, 34, 36, 57-58, 88, 93
Fort, Tequesta (1560s), 309
Fort, Tocobaga, 309
Fort in Keys, suggestion for, 8, 9
Fort on Miami River, 430
Fort of St. Anthony, 234. *See also* Fort of San Antonio
Fort of San Antonio: described, 309; garrison of, enlarged, 255; supplies for, 305-308; mentioned, 235, 235n.4, 236. *See also* Fort of St. Anthony
Franciscans: Crown's choice of, for south Florida missions, 36, 37, 39, 121, 124, 125, 130-131, 135, 136, 140-141; ethnocentrism of, 44; ex-

pulsion of, from Calusa, 41, 161–210 passim; neglect of royal orders about south Florida missions by, 36, 37, 39

Friar at Mayaca-Jororo mission, 143, 144, 145, 146–152 passim, 208, 213

Friars: arrival of, at Calusa, 41, 157, 164, 165, 168, 173; billets of, authorized, 114, 119, 129, 134, 139; friction of, with governor, 12, 13–14, 16, 17; house of, at Calusa, 174, 195; ignorance of native languages, 126, 136; invasion of native temple by, 167, 170, 186, 196; and mission band (1693), 119; number for Carlos, 117, 128, 129, 130, 138, 139, 140; number for Mayaca-Jororo, 120, 130, 140; number in Florida (1697), 156–157; possessions of, taken by natives, 161, 163, 167, 171, 172, 176, 182, 187, 188, 190–191, 192, 195, 198, 199–200; punishment of Indians by, 15, 16, 126, 128, 136; requested by cacique of Carlos, 117, 118, 121, 128; return to Cuba of, 201, 205–206; sent and supplied from Havana, 117, 118, 120, 121–122, 123, 128, 129, 131, 138, 139, 141; shortage of, in Florida, 117, 118, 120, 128, 138, 140, 208; supplies for, Indians forced to transport, 126–127, 137; transferred from Florida, 120, 130, 140

García de Palacios, Bishop Juan: appeal for volunteers by, 49–57; death of, 36, 74; insincerity of, 35; questioned, 78; support of mission by, 34, 35

Gentiles, 111n.3

Gomes, Captain Lucas, 391, 392, 393, 394, 395, 396, 397, 402, 403, 416, 426nn.30, 31

Gomez, Brother Estevan, 295

Gomez, Brother Gabriel, 291

Gonçalez, Vicente, 293

Granberry, Julian, 5

Great cacique of the Keys of Carlos, 80

Great captain, 222, 227. *See also* Capitan Grande

"Great Chief," title of Calusa chief, 86, 96

Griffin, John W., 4, 226

Guacara, repopulation of, 81

Guarugumbe, Chief, location of, 316

Güemes y Horcasitas, Governor Juan Francisco de, 415, 416, 417, 418

Guerra y de la Vega, Governor don Francisco de, 34, 35, 64–65, 67

Guerrero, Juaquín, shipowner, 392, 394, 396, 397

Hammon, Briton, 330, 331

Havana: as base for 1697 mission, 40; distance to Carlos, 184

Heathens beyond the missions, unchanged since contact, 113

Heras, Vicente de las, 58

Hernández, Manuel, 427

Herrera, Antonio de, and Ponce de León, 219

Hibinieza, point of, 21

Hita Salazar, Governor Pablo de: and 1697 mission, 6, 28–29, 51; and expedition to Gulf coast, 23

Hivitinayo, region of, 352, 353

Holy Spirit, bay of, 21; limit of Florida jurisdiction (1575), 309

Honey, 184, 187

Hororo: church furnishings withdrawn from, 152; killing of Indians serving friar at, 151; mission, 149, 150, 151; mentioned, 146–152 passim

Hororo (people of): assistance of, to soldiers, 147; as migrants to St. Augustine, 358, 362, 363; rebels flee to Yuamajiro, 150; report revolt, 147

Hororo (village of near St. Augustine), baptisms of (1718–1723), 362

Hunger, seasonal, among Calusa, 260–261

Ibaja at Tolomato, baptisms of (1718–1723), 362

Idols, 315, 316

Iguaja, 151, 151n.6, 152

Iguaja mission: of San Joseph (1726), 365; of Santta Cathalina (1726), 365; at village of San Joseph (1720s), 363. *See also* Yguaja mission

Indians: conversion of, 17; flight from missions, 16; gifts used to attract, 249–250, 255–256, 257, 379; of Keys, 312; living near St. Augustine (1720s), 379; of Martyrs, 249; poverty of, 379; raids by those allied to British, 327, 370, 375, 378; requests for

Indians (*continued*)
missionaries by, 400, 402, 404, 405, 408, 410–413, 416; of rinconada of Carlos (1726), 366; of rinconada of Macapiras Nation (1726), 366; of Santa Lucia (1623), 19; of Upper St. Johns River, 303
—, migrations of: from Antilles, 5; to Cuba, funded by crown, 384–385, 388–389, 398, 401, 405, 411–412; to Cuba opposed, 341–342, 345, 382–383, 384, 388, 402, 403, 407
Indians of south Florida: and absence of agriculture, 329–330, 428; and alcohol, 425, 426, 426nn.28, 30, 31, 427; alliance with Spain by, 403, 407–408, 417; attacks on English (1740s) by, 403; barracuda, idol of, 328, 422; blacks disdained by, 426, 426nn.28, 30; cemetery of, 423–424; contact with Cuban fishermen by, 326, 404, 411, 420, 423, 427; curing ritual of, 329, 423; daily offerings to the dead, 423, dead, fear of, 329, 423, 424; extinction of, 325, 427; and firearms, 425; indolence of, 329, 420; internecine strife by, 326, 427; and knowledge of Spanish, 326, 420; migration of (1711), 336, 337, 341; migrations to Cuba of, 327–340 passim, 357, 358, 380, 382, 384, 391, 392–393, 402; moving of houses of, 330, 386, 396, 397; near St. Augustine (1720s–1730s), 370, 371; nomadism of, 329, 374, 409, 420, 425; and peace with Spaniards (1620s), 20, (1740s), 403, 411; population of (1711), 341, (1743), 420; seasonal migrations of, 329, 420; sold as slaves, 339–340, 341; streetwise, 399, 420–421; travel to Cuba by, 330–331; use of maize, 330; work for Cuban fishermen, 326, 404, 427
—religion of: afterlife, 329, 424; bodypainting as ritual, 329, 424; idols, 328–329, 422; mask called sipi, 422; traditionalism of, xix, 328, 422, 425
Ivitachuco, 354
Ivitanayo, 23, 81, 81n.5

Jeaga, 19–20
Jesuits: arrival in Ajacán, 291; arrival in Florida, 220; burning of temple and idol by, 422, 422n.9; deaths in Ajacán described, 291–292; expedition of (1743), 408, 409, 420–431; reputed failure of questioned (1560s), 225, 226; suggested for Calusa mission (1680s–1690s), 36, 66, 69; withdrawal from Florida (1572), 225, 294–295; work with black slaves in Havana, 295–296
—missions: of 1560s, origin of, 220; of 1743, 400–418 passim; rejected (1680s–1690s), 71, 73
Jesús, Fray Francisco de, friar at Calusa, 163, 165, 172, 177, 184, 192, 194
Jizime, friar at, 147
Jobe, chief of: migration to Cuba by (1711), 47. *See also* Jove
Jororo: as "Cape Indians," 30; identity of inhabitants (1720s), 377; killing of Indians serving friar, 147; lack of docility, 30; language of, 327; location of, 29, 30; living near St. Augustine, 327, 332, 358, 370, 375; and 1727 epidemic, 370; united with Pojoy (1720s), 377; village, desecration of church in, 144; mentioned, 45, 142, 156, 212. *See also* Hororo
Jororo, Pojoy, Amacapira, 377
Jororo province: number of friars in, 144; revolt in, 143, 144, 146, 147, 148, 149–150; return of fugitives to, 213–214; fugitives resettled at Las Cofras and Afafa, 216
Jorxe, Julian, 151, 152
Jove: death of cacique of, 325, 402; migration to Cuba by (1711), 332. *See also* Jobe
Jurisdictional disputes between religious orders, Crown's fear of, 38–39, 54–55

Key Largo, 186, 188, 192
Key of Bones: cacique of, 177, 200, 201, 403; Indians of, 200, 201; mentioned, 158, 198. *See also* Bones, Key of; Cayo de Huesos; Key West
Key of Calusa, 173
Key of Cows, 191. *See also* Cow Key
Key of Cuchiapa, 200. *See also* Cuchiaga
Key of Matacombe, 167, 173, 177, 185,

187, 190. *See also* Key of Matecumbe; Matacumbe; Mattacombe Key

Key of Matacumbe, 203. *See also* Key of Matacombe; Matacumbe; Mattacombe Key

Key of Muspa: cacique of, 200; Indians of, 188, 200. *See also* Musepa; Muspa; Muspa, Key of

Keys, fishing in by Spaniards, 173, 177

Keys Indians: alliance of, with Maimies, 404; economy of, lack of agriculture in, 428; killed by Uchise, 336; killed by Yamasee, 46; killing of, 339, 341; most exempt from labor, 428; Spanish alliance of, 403, 417, 427; visits to Cuba by, 4; mentioned, 161, 382, 408, 409, 420

Keys of Carlos: location of, 210; mentioned, 190, 194, 202. *See also* Carlos, Key of

Keys of the Mouths, 193

Keys province, dominated by Prince Carlos, 124

Key West, origin of name of, 41n.37. *See also* Cayo de Huesos

Key West Indians, migration to Cuba by, 45

Knight, James Vernon, xvii

Laudonnière, René, 219

Lazo de la Vega y Cansino, Fray Juan, bishop of Cuba, 413, 415, 416

Leturiondo, Domingo de, and Tocobaga, 349, 351

Lewis, Clifford M., 228

Linares, Brother Pedro de, 288, 291

López, Fray Feliciano: almost drowned, 187, 199; and Andrés Ransom affair, 40, 83–84; background of, 164; as director of Calusa mission, 40; and mission band, destiny of, 142; return of, from Calusa, 163, 174, 193; in Spain, 116, 118, 122, 123, 128, 130, 131, 132, 133, 138, 141; testimony of, 164–168; mentioned, 55, 156, 157, 180, 181, 184, 186, 190, 191, 192, 194, 196, 202, 203, 205, 207, 208, 209. *See also* López, Fray Pheliciano

López, Fray Pheliciano: sent to Mexico, 212. *See also* López, Fray Feliciano

López de Velasco, Juan: Bay of Carlos described by, 277n.77

Luis, don, Indian from Ajacán, 290–292

Luna, Fray Pedro de la, and transferral of friars to Havana, 120, 130, 140

Lyon, Eugene, salvors' contact with Indians, 18

Macapiras, 30, 366. *See also* Amacapira; Rinconada de Macapiras; Rinconada of the Macapiras

Macariz: alias for Nombre de Dios, 377; name for Nombre de Dios, 359; church of stone, 377–378. *See also* Amacarisa

Mahoma, house of, 44, 159. *See also* Mohammed, house of

Maimi, cacique of: death of, 325, 402; migration to Cuba by (1711), 47, 332

Majuro, 20. *See also* Amajuro River; Withlacoochee River

Manatee River, 22

Marin, Juan Bauptista, 395–396

Marquardt, William H.: on Calusa government, postcontact changes, xvii; on Calusa polity's persistence, 227; on religious role of Calusa chief, 227

Marquez Cabrera, Governor don Juan, and conflict with clergy, 127, 137

Martínez, Pedro, killing of, 220, 221, 287

Martínez de la Vega, Dionisio, Governor of Cuba, 390, 391, 393

Martyrs, head of: fort proposed for, 8, 9; location of, 8, 11

Martyrs, the: description and location of, 312, 313; identity of, 8, 312

Matacojo, Bay of, 21

Matacombe, Indians of, 188, 192. *See also* Key of Matacombe; Key of Matacumbe; Matacumbe; Matecumbe; Mattacombe Key

Matacumbe, 190, 192, 193, 201; keys of, searched for salvage (1623), 19. *See also* Key of Matacombe; Key of Matacumbe; Matacombe; Matecumbe; Mattacombe Key

Matecumbe: chief, 313; island, description of, 313. *See also* Key of Matacombe; Key of Matacumbe; Matacombe; Matacumbe; Mattacombe Key

Mattacombe Key, 210. *See also* Key of

Mattacombe Key (*continued*)
  Matacombe; Key of Matacumbe;
  Matacombe; Matacumbe; Matecumbe
Mayaca: ancient place, 143; flight of
  inhabitants of, 151; friars at (1699),
  212, 214; return of inhabitants of,
  153; site of older mission, 143n.1;
  mentioned, 142, 146, 147, 148, 149,
  150, 152, 156
Mayaca and Jororo provinces, as part of
  Ais, 155–156
Mayaca Province: agriculture in (1696),
  154; deputy-governor of, 143, 144,
  147; incudes Jororo, 148
Mayacas, 420
Mayaca-Jororo: conversions, number of,
  110–111, 115, 121, 130, 140; as
  hunter-gatherers, 110, 111, 115; iron
  tools for, 100, 111, 115, 140, 215; and
  neighbors, nonagricultural, 111;
  neighbors' diversity of languages,
  111, 115; peace restored to, 213, 214;
  revolt in, 6, 153–154; surrounding
  territory of, 111
—missions: establishment of, 29–30;
  new friars for, 208; mentioned,
  37–38, 40
Mayacuya, visit by Menéndez de Avilés
  to, 302, 302n.30
Maymi, Lake of, 21
Maymies Indians, 420
Medina, Bernardo de, deputy-governor,
  Mayaca-Jororo, 146, 148, 149, 150, 152
Medina, don Thomás de (cacique of
  Santa Fé): contact with Tocobaga by,
  23; deserts Gulf coast expedition, 26;
  reports Spanish slaves at Carlos, 23,
  24
Meléndez Marques, Pedro, 290. *See also*
  Menéndez Marques, Pedro; Menéndez
  Marquez, Pero
Menéndez de Avilés, Pedro: ascent of
  St. Johns River by, 302, 303; and Car-
  los's peace with Tocobaga, 220; dete-
  rioration of relations with Carlos,
  220; finds soldier-mutineers at Te-
  questa, 299–300; marriage of, to Car-
  los's sister, 220, 289; meets Escalante
  Fontaneda, 220; places garrison in
  Calusa, 220; ransoms Tequesta's
  daughter, 303; requests Jesuits for
  Florida, 220; rescues enslaved Span-

iards, 301; retaliation by, in Ajacán,
  293–294; visits to Calus by, 220,
  230–231; visits to Tocobaga by, 220,
  231, 276n.59; mentioned, 219
Menéndez Marques, Juan, praised by
  friars, 18
Menéndez Marques, Pedro, 220, 309.
  See also Meléndez Marques, Pedro;
  Menéndez Marquez, Pero
Menéndez Marquez, Pero, 237. *See also*
  Meléndez Marques, Pedro; Menéndez
  Marques, Pedro
Miami River, village on (1743), 420
Migrants to Cuba: death of, in epidem-
  ics, 325, 402–403; funds for autho-
  rized by king, 343–344, 345; return
  of, to Keys, 402–403
Migrations: of 1704, 402, 403; of 1711,
  402; demand by king for information
  on and reprimand for, 346–347
Migrations to Cuba, 45, 46–47, 327–340
  passim
Migration to Florida from South Amer-
  ica, 5
Milanich, Jerald, 226
Missionaries for south Florida, qualifi-
  cations for, 94
Mission band of 1693–1694, 119, 128,
  129, 138, 139
Mission band of 1695: departure of,
  133; disposition of, 155, 156–157, 208;
  size of, 207, 208
Mission in south Florida (1679), 27
Missions: number (1690), 26; staffing
  reduction suggested, 127, 137
Missions (1728), 374
Missions to Calusa and Ais, 121, 125,
  135, 136, 140–141
Missions to south Florida: assigned to
  Franciscans (1692), 82–83; and Cu-
  ban connection, 31–34
Mission to Calusa: first assigned to
  Franciscans, 73; genesis of, 31–33, 34;
  initiation of, 208–209; result of
  Crown initiative, 52–53; to be sup-
  ported by Crown, 32, 33, 53–54. *See
  also* Calusa mission (1697)
Mission to Keys, 424–425, 427
Mocama: alliance of, with French, 221;
  in Creek country, 327; identity of,
  220n.1; kill Jesuit, 220; referred to as
  Chiluque, 358, 359

Mohammed, House of, 44. *See also* Mahoma, House of

Molina, Fray Christóbal de, head of 1693-1694 mission band, 120, 129, 139

Monaco, Joseph María, 401, 408, 409, 415, 417, 418

Monlatuo, Lorenzo, 416

Mortality among mission Indians (1614-1617), 13

Mosquitos, Bar of, 22. *See also* Surruque

Mouths (bocas): definition of, 201n.31; Indians of, 185-186; women of, 201

Moze: and epidemic of 1727, 378; inhabited by Apalachee, 377; location of, 378; population of, 378

Musepa, chief of: migration to Cuba by (1711), 47. *See also* Muspa

Muspa: point of, location and description, 312; theft by Indian from, 199; village of, 177

Muspa, chief of: allotted spoils from friars' possessions, 200; death of, 325, 402; theft by, 172, 176, 199, 200. *See also* Musepa, chief of

Muspa, Key of: searched for salvage (1623), 19; mentioned, 167, 172, 177, 188, 190, 209

Muspa, migration to Cuba by (1711), 332

Nombre de Dios (1726): number and identity of inhabitants of, 365-366; poor-mouthed, 369. *See also* Amacarisa; Chiluca mission of Nombre de Dios; Macariz; Nombre de Dios de Macariz

Nombre de Dios Chiquito: baptisms at (1718-1723), 361; church described, 375; identity of inhabitants of, 361; population of, 375

Nombre de Dios de Macariz: attacked (1720s), 370, 378; destroyed, 378-379. *See also* Amacarisa; Chiluca mission of Nombre de Dios; Macariz; Nombre de Dios; Nombre de Dios de Macariz

Obedezco pero no cumplo, 390

Ochlockonee River, 21, 22. *See also* Agna River; Claraquachine

Ocita, 9n.4

Oconi, cacique of, 348, 355

Ojeda, Pedro de: statement of, 201-202; mentioned, 180, 181, 183, 188, 200, 203

Oliver, Francisco de, 417-418

Orange wares, 5

Oratorians, 95n.1, 98, 100

Our Lady of Guadalupe (1726): number and identity of inhabitants of, 365. *See also* Tholomato; Tholomato, New

Palica: baptisms at (1718-1723), 361; identity of inhabitants, 358, 361, 365; location of, 359, 378; population of, 365, 378. *See also* San Buena Bentura; San Buena Bentura de Palica

Palm fruit, 370, 377

Paralta, Carlos de, 194

Parks, Arva Moore, 4

Perchel Key, 329

Perdomo, Luis, 337, 338, 341

Pérez de la Cerda, Sebastian: and Cuban clergy for Florida missions, 28; mentioned, 31, 34, 52

Permit ship: request for passage on for 1695 mission band, 116, 117-118, 119, 120, 129, 130, 138, 140; use of, criticized, 122, 132, 141-142

Phelipe (Calusa chief, 1560s), enmity of, toward Spaniards, 290

Phelipe, don (Calusa chief, 1697): baptized, 158; mentioned, 165, 166, 169, 171, 174, 178, 187, 194, 195, 208, 209

Phelipe V, letter to Bishop of Durango by, 413-414

Philip II, requests Jesuits for Florida, 220

Piaja Nation (1726): origin and population of, 366-367; mentioned, 6. *See also* Aypaja; Atoquimi, Atoyquimi; Piaxa Nation; Ypaja

Piaxa Nation: linked to Hororo, 363; origin of, 332. *See also* Aypaja; Atoquimi; Atoyquimi; Piaja Nation; Ypaja

Pimeria Alta, 414

Pocotalaca: location of, 378; population of, 378; mentioned, 375. *See also* Poco Talaqua

Poco Talaqua: baptisms at (1718-1723), 361; identity of inhabitants of, 361

Pohoy, 30. *See also* Pojoi; Pojoy; Pooy

Pojoi: at Santa Fée (1726), 366; popula-

Pojoi (*continued*)
tion of (1679), 26. *See also* Pohoy; Pojoy; Pooy
Pojoy: attack on Tocobaga by (1718),
328, 348, 356; hostility of, 29; identity of, 26n.23; location of, 10; nomadism of, 377; River of, 21, 22; and 1727
epidemic, 370, 377; and Tocobaga,
Spanish attack on, 9; united with
Jororo (1720s), 377; mentioned,
26nn.21-23, 332, 358, 363. *See also*
Pohoy; Pojoi; Pooy
Pojoy, don Antonio, cacique: head of the
Alafaia Costas nation, 327, 358. *See
also* Alafaes; Alafaia Costas nation;
Alafay; Costas Alafayes; Elafay; Po-
hoy; Pojoi; Pojoy; Pooy
Ponce de León, Juan: contact of, with
Calusa, 4, 219; meets Spanish-
speaking native, 5
Ponze, Carlos, discoverer of Keys, 210
Pooy: cacique of, 10; district of, 11; loca-
tion of, 10, 10n.4; variant of Pojoy,
9n.3. *See also* Pohoy; Pojoi; Pojoy
Pooy, Bay of: capacity of, 12; as de So-
to's landing place, 12; identity of,
10n.4, 22. *See also* Pohoy; Pojoi; Pojoy
Popaian, province of, 101, 107. *See also*
Popayan, province of
Popayan, province of: identity of,
100n.10; mentioned, 100, 102. *See
also* Popaian, province of
Population: of Calusa, 42, 164, 165, 168,
174, 205, 208, 210, 317, 317n.3; of Ca-
lusa head village (1697), 159; of mis-
sions (1726), 364-367; of south
Florida, 384; of Tocobaa, 317 (*see also*
Tocobaga; Tocopaca)
Prince Carlos, visit to Havana by, 82
Pulihica, 348-349, 352, 353
Purdy, Barbara, 5-6
Pusâle, beach of, 21

Quiroga y Losada, Governor don Diego
de: and Ferro Machado, 126, 134,
136, 140; obedience of Calusa to, 121,
124, 130, 140; visitation of Apalachee
and Timuqua by, 79-81. *See also*
Ferro Machado, don Juan
Quiros, Father, 291, 292

Ransom, Andrés, 83, 84
Ratones, definition of, 279, 279n.1. *See
also* Boca de Ratones
Rebolledo, Governor Diego de, and
amber trade, 22. *See also* Amber,
trade in
Redondo, Brother Christóval de, 291
Reinoso, Captain Francisco: arrival of,
in Calus, 275-276n.50, 276n.56,
282n.124; commander at Calus, 220;
kills Chief Carlos, 222; sent to Car-
los, 300
Rico, Jorge, 397
Rincón, definition of, 6-7
Rinconada, 6-7
Rinconada, La, name for peninsular
Florida, 7
Rinconada de Carlos: location of, 6, 7;
mentioned, 332, 363, 366. *See also*
Piaxa Nation
Rinconada de Macapiras, 6. *See also*
Amacapiras; Macapiras; Rinconada
of the Macapiras
Rinconada of the Macapiras, 363, 366.
See also Amacapiras; Macapiras; Rinconada de Macapiras
Rioseco, chief of: death of, 325, 402; mi-
gration to Cuba by, 47, 332
Rodríguez de Cortaya, Juan: expedition
of, to Calusa, 9-12; meeting of, with
chief of Carlos, 10-11
Rogel, Juan: arrival of, in Calus, 235;
assignment of, to Havana, 289; at
Orista and Santa Elena, 290; attempt
to go to Tequesta by, 249; baptism of
Calusa woman by, 251-252; blacks,
work with, 249-250; catechetical
techniques of, 237, 238-239, 242, 245,
247, 249, 250, 255, 256; defense of killing of Carlos, 236; departure for St.
Augustine by, 264, 288; ethnocentrism of, 244; first arrival in Cuba of,
278, 279; and gifts for Indians, 222,
224, 239, 255, 256; learns of deaths in
Ajacán, 293; length of stay at Calus,
231-232; letter to bishop of Yucatan
by, 257; obstacles to work of, 221,
222; opposes killing of Carlos, 266;
sails for Calus, 230; teaches women
of chief, 256; work at Calus begun
by, 220, 221

Rojas y Borja, Governor Luis, friendship of, with Indians of south Florida, 20

Romans, Bernard, 331

Romero, Ensign Francisco: return of, 167, 177; statement by, 184–189; mentioned, 158, 173, 180, 182, 183, 190, 191, 192, 193, 194, 201, 203, 208, 209, 210

Romero, Fray Francisco: bid for Calusa mission by, 121, 130, 140; proposed for Calusa mission, 95; recruitment of priests by, 38; as revivalist, 97–98; as volunteer for Calusa mission, 102, 103; mentioned, 39, 95–108 passim. *See also* Augustinian prior; Augustinians

Royal officials (Cuba), and responsibility of, for south Florida missions, 32, 34, 53–54, 63, 64, 65, 78, 87, 128, 184, 343, 344, 345, 346, 380, 381, 388, 389

Royal officials (Florida), praised by friars, 17–18

Ruiz, Martín, 349

Ruiz de Salvatierra, Brother Pedro, 288, 289

Sacrifice: of chief's servants, 35; of Christian captives, 315

St. Augustine parish, staffing increase suggested, 129, 137

St. Marks (Apalachee): baptisms at (1718–1723), 361; fort of, 364; mentioned, 21

St. Martin: Port of, 21; River of, 25, 352

St. Philip Neri, oratories of, 28n.28, 95

Salaries: of friar, 33; of friars and soldiers, 114, 119, 129

Salcedo, Brother Juan de, 288, 289, 293

Salvador, Diego (Indian), interpreter, 349

Samos, Fray Fernando: friar at Calusa, 163, 164, 176, 177; testimony by, 168–173

San Antonio [Anacapi]: friar at (1699), 212, 214; no rebellion at (1696), 212. *See also* San Antonio Anacapi; San Antonio de Anacapi

San Antonio Anacapi, 120, 130, 140. *See also* San Antonio [Anacapi]; San Antonio de Anacapi

San Antonio de Anacapi, new conversion at, 110. *See also* San Antonio [Anacapi]: San Antonio Anacapi

San Antonio de la Costa, population of (1738), 370. *See also* Costa; Costa Nation Guasacara; Costa village of San Anttonio

San Anttonio (Cosapuya and others, 1726), population of, 366. *See also* Casapuia; Casapuya

San Anttonio (Costas, 1726), population of, 366. *See also* Costa; Costa Nation Guasacara; Costa village of San Anttonio; San Antonio de la Costa

San Anttonio (Yamasa, near St. Augustine, 1726), population of, 364–365. *See also* Yamasee missions

San Anttonio (Yamaza in Apalachee, 1726), population of, 366. *See also* Yamasee missions

San Buena Bentura (Chiluca, 1726), population of, 365. *See also* Chiluque at Palica; Palica; San Buena Bentura de Palica

San Buena Bentura de Palica, 358–359. *See also* Chiluque at Palica; Palica; San Buena Bentura

Sánchez, Fray Luis, doctrinero at Atoquimi, 6, 146, 147, 149

Sánchez, Pedro, 294

Sánchez, Sevastian, statement by, 191–193

San Diego, Fray Francisco de, friar at Calusa, 163, 164, 165, 177, 178, 194, 199

San Diego (Yamasa, 1726), population of, 365. *See also* Yamasee missions

San Diego de Compostela (Calusa, 1697), 158, 206

San Diego de Salamototo, 23

Sandino (native), 410

San Joseph (Iguaja, 1726), population of, 365. *See also* Iguaja

San Joseph de Jororo: new conversion, 110; mentioned, 120, 130, 140

San Juan (Apalachee and Yamasee in Apalachee, 1726), population of, 367

San Juan del Puerto, 84

San Luis (Apalachee, near St. Augustine, 1726), population of, 366

San Marcos (in Apalachee), 358

San Marcos de Apalachee, 357
San Matheo de Tolapatafi, chief of: and Ivitanayo, 351–352; mentioned, 84
San Pedro de Potohiriba, 351, 352
San Salvador de Maiaca, new conversion at, 110. *See also* Mayaca; San Salvador de Mayaca
San Salvador de Mayaca: flight from, 7, 151; location of, 30n.31; no rebellion at, 153, 212; mentioned, 29–30, 120, 130, 140. *See also* Mayaca; San Salvador de Maiaca
Santa Catarina, 363
Santa Fé, cacique of, 23. *See also* Medina, don Thomás de; Santa Fée, chief of
Santa Fée (Timucua and Pojoi, 1726), population of, 366
Santa Fée, chief of: and Ivitanayo, 352. *See also* Medina, don Thomás de; Santa Fé, cacique of
Santa Helena, 13
Santa Lucia: Indians kill shipwreck survivors, 19–20. *See also* Santaluzos Indians
Santaluzos Indians, 420. *See also* Santa Lucia
Santa María de Loreto (1743), 420
Santa Rosa de Ivitanayo, 24, 348, 351. *See also* Ivitanayo
Santiago de Cuba, Bishop of, and responsibility for south Florida missions, 31–32, 33–34, 52–53, 74, 87
Santta Cathalina (Iguaja, 1726), population of, 365. *See also* Santa Catarina
Saturiva, 303
Savacola, missions among, 29
Sayas Bazan, don Christóbal, de, director-general of the Keys, 383–388 passim, 390, 391, 398
School for Florida caciques' sons, 289
Secular clergy, unavailable for Calusa mission, 92, 93, 96, 98–99, 121, 125, 131, 135, 141
Sedeño, Antonio: assigned to Carlos, 289; mentioned, 291, 294, 295
Segura, Juan Baptista de, 288, 292
Senquene (Calusa), 5
Shaman: called bishop, 329; howl like wolves, 316; importance of, among Calusa, 222; running as ritual, 316; wear horns, 316

Shipwrecks: report of (1622), 18–19; salvage of, 18, 19, 20–21; survivors killed, 19–20
Sibling marriage among Calusa, 223, 224, 244, 289, 290
Situado: defined, 33n.35; mentioned, 33, 53, 54, 64, 65, 128, 130, 131, 137, 138, 139, 141
Slaves (Spaniards) at Carlos, 23, 24, 284n.138, 298, 301
Smoke signals, 201
Sodomites, sodomy, 239, 239n.11, 245
Solana, Juan (notary), report on Jororo revolt, 145–155
Soldiers: mistreatment of Indians by, 263; need for, at missions, 76
Solís, Gabriel de, 288, 291
Soto, Hernando de: landing place of, 12; mentioned, 21, 219
Sotolongo, Fray Melchor de, 390, 391
Souls: mortal, 238, 424; multiplicity of, 237–238; transmigration of, 238
South Florida Indians: cannibalism by, alleged, 8; diet of, 8; knowledge of Spanish by, 86, 420; nonagricultural, 8; population of, 76; visits to Havana by, 86. *See also* Indians of south Florida
South Florida mission (1679), 27
South Florida missions, volunteers for, 57–58
South Florida natives of interior: docility of, 27–28; tribute to Calusa chief paid by, 28
Spaniards enslaved by Calusa; ransomed by French, 219; rescued, 301; sacrificed, 301
Spanish commanders (1560s), 317, 318
Spanish garrisons (1560s), size of, 317
Stallings Island wares, 5
Steward, Julian, 100n.10
Sturtevant, William C.: migrations to Florida, 5–6; mentioned, 4, 399, 418
Surruque, Bar of, 22, *See also* Mosquitos, Bar of
Sweet River (Rio Dulce), 314

Tabernacles and ciboria, lack of, 369, 374
Tacatacuru, identity of, 220n.1

Tachista, Key of, seached for salvage (1623), 19

Tama, 13

Tama, La, village of, 362. *See also* Thama; Yamasee

Tames Indians: identified as Tunebo, 100n.10; mentioned, 100, 101, 102, 107, 109

Tampa, Bay of, 311

Tampa, Key of, searched for salvage (1623), 19

Tampa, Port of: identity of, 22; location of, 21, 310

Tampa River: identity of, 22; location of, 10, 10n.5; settlements on, subject to Carlos, 10

Tancha: Indians of, 201; migration to Cuba by (1711), 332; village of, and friars, 201

Taxaquachile, Bay of, 21–22

Tecuesta, Spanish enclave at, 309. *See also* Tegesta; Tequesta

Tegesta: burial customs, 319. *See also* Tecuesta; Tequesta

Tello, 176. *See also* Teyú

Tequesta: chief's daughter captive at Carlos, 303; as hostages in Cuba, 276n.56, 280, 281; killing of Spaniards by (1574), 8; location of, 220, 314; name of cacique of, 280; people of, 4; Spanish at, 220, 263, 298, 299, 314; tributary to Calusa, 8, 220; village of, 7; mentioned, 265, 283n.131, 288, 302. *See also* Tecuesta; Tegesta

Texeda, Jazinto: killing of, 151, 152; mentioned, 146. *See also* Thexeda, Jazinto

Teyú: Key of, 167, 209; village of, 198, 200; weapons at, 199–200. *See also* Tello

Thama: people of, move to Moze, 376; population of, 376; village of, 375, 376. *See also* Tama; Yamasee

Thexeda, Jazinto de: left at Hororo, 150, 152; soldier at Mayaca, 146. *See also* Texeda, Jazinto

Tholomato, destroyed, 379

Tholomato, New: location and population of, 377. *See also* Our Lady of Guadalupe

Timucua: baptisms at Nombre de Dios

Amacarisa (1718–1723), 362; celebration of defeat of enemy by, 277–278n.79; council house described, 273n.34; in Creek country, 327; human sacrifice by, 274n.40; language of, 5; polygamy of, 274n.35; Saltwater, 220n.1. *See also* Timuqua

Timuqua, village of (18th century), 375, 376. *See also* Timucua

Tiquijagua, population of (1679), 26. *See also* Yagua

Tirupo, meaning of, 329

Tisime, residence of Fray Camacho, 149. *See also* Atisimi; Atissimi; Jizime

Tobacco, 184, 195

Tocampaha, 271n.24. *See also* Escampaha

Tocobaa, 317

Tocobaga: ally of Pojoy, 26nn.22, 23; Bay of, described, 310; burial customs of, 318–319; burial of, at Ivitachuco, 347; chief's attachment to his idols, 235, 236, 271n.17; description of, 253; distance of bay from Carlos, 8; fort at, 235, 271n.14; gains allegiance of Calusa clients, 223; garrison at, 250, 253–254, 262; Spanish enclave at, 309; village of, 310; visit by Menéndez de Avilés, 231; mentioned, 137, 249, 262, 284n.137. *See also* Tocobaa; Tocopacas; Tocopaua

—in Apalachee: economic role in, 23, 348, 349; location of, 9, 9n.3; in 1678–1694, 347–348; in 1718, 328, 332, 355–357

Tocopacas: place of, 349; population of, 351; remain non-Christian, 350, 354; River of, 21, 22; variant for Tocobaga, 9n.3, 347. *See also* Tocobaa; Tocobaga; Tocopaua

—in Apalachee: attacked, 356; burial at Hivitachuco, 350; moved, 356; in 1718, 355–356; visitation (1678), 349–351; visitation (1694), 354

Tocopaua, Bay of, 320. *See also* Tocobaa; Tocobaga; Tocopacas

Tools, iron, 111, 112–113, 114, 115

Torres, Marcos de, 392, 394, 395, 397

Torres y Ayala, Governor Laureano de: and Jororo revolt, 143–145

Tortugas, 4–5, 403

Troncoso, Juan, 58

460   *Index*

Uchise: attack Georgia mission (1680),
359; attacks on south Florida, 4, 325,
327, 330–331, 333, 377, 425, 427; attack Thama (1720s), 376
Urca, definition of, 234n.3

Váez, Brother Augustine, 288, 297n.10
Valdés, Bishop Gerónimo, 334, 335–339,
340, 382
Varona, Gerónimo de, 415, 416, 417
Vasisa, Tocobaga at, 80, 80n.4. *See also*
Basisa; Wacissa
Vexarano, Francisco, 88. *See also* Bexa-
rano, Francisco
Villareal, Brother Francisco: assigned
to Havana, 289; brought to Tequesta,
287; replaces Rogel at Calus, 263;
sails for Florida, 230; at Tequesta,
220; withdraws from Tequesta, 263;
mentioned, 265, 288, 293
Volunteers (secular): departure of,
blocked by lack of funds, 64–65, 67
Vulture idol, 329

Wacissa, Tocobaga settlement at, 347,
348, 354. *See also* Basisa; Vasisa

West Indies, contact of, with Florida,
5–6
Whales, hunting of, 314, 319
Wheat, sown at Calusa, 167
Widmer, Randolph J., xvi, 226
Withlacoochee River, 22. *See also* Ama-
juro River; Majuro
Women, used for political bonding, 268

Yagua, Calusa town, 26n.24. *See also*
Tiquijagua
Yamasee: attacks by, 46, 325, 327, 334,
336, 339, 341; baptisms of
(1718–1723), 361, 362; at Mayaca, 7;
in missions of 1726, 364–365, 366,
367; raiders, mistaken for Chisca, 46;
at San Juan in Apalachee (1726), 367;
mentioned, 358, 363, 376n.9. *See also*
Tama; Thama
Yamasee War, 327, 357
Yguaja mission (1726), 365. *See also*
Ibaja; Iguaja
Yndios cimarrones, 45–46
Ypaja, village of (Jororo), 214. *See also*
Aipaja; Aypaja
Yuamajiro, as refuge of Hororo rebels,
30, 150, 151
Yustaga, 23, 351